ACTIVE LITERATURE

Christopher Burke

Active literature

Jan Tschichold and New Typography

HYPHEN PRESS . LONDON

Published by Hyphen Press, London, in 2007

Text copyright © Christopher Burke, 2007

The book was designed, typeset and made into
pages by Christopher Burke, Devizes; its illustrations were also prepared by him for reproduction.
The text was output in the typefaces FF Celeste
and FF Celeste Sans, designed by Christopher
Burke, and in his digital version of Jan Tschichold's
'quick and easy method of lettering'. The index
was made by Christine Shuttleworth, London.
Proofs of the pages in progress were read by
Robin Kinross, London. The book was printed
in Belgium by Die Keure, Bruges, and bound in
the Netherlands by Boekbinderij Van Waarden,
Zaandam

ISBN 978-0-907259-32-9

www.hyphenpress.co.uk

We are grateful to Pro Helvetia, Swiss Arts
Council, for financial support in making
this edition

swiss arts council
prohelvetia

Contents

Acknowledgments

This book builds on the contributions of several writers who have studied Tschichold over the years – Ruari McLean, Gerd Fleischmann, Gerrit Willem Ovink, Georg Kurt Schauer – and in particular on the recent, outstanding scholarship of Robin Kinross and Josep M. Pujol in their respective introductions to the English and Spanish editions of *Die neue Typographie*.

The principal research for this book was enabled by the generous award of a Library Research Grant by the Getty Research Institute, Los Angeles.

The author would like to thank the following people for their assistance:
Paul Barnes, Felix Wiedler, Norbert Löderbusch, Michael Twyman, Susan Walker, Mathieu Lommen, Hans Reichardt, Roland Reuß & Peter Staengle, Richard Hollis, Philipp Luidl, Ole Lund, Ann Pillar, Eric Kindel, Hans Dieter Reichert, Petra Černe Oven, Gerry Leonidas, Jost Hochuli, Fred Smeijers & Corina Cotorobai, Toshiaki Koga & Kiyonori Muroga (*Idea* magazine), Markus Rathgeb, Dr Frieder Schmidt & Gabriele Netsch (DNB Leipzig), Virginia Mokslaveskas (& staff at the Getty), Merrill C. Berman & Jim Frank, Stephanie Ehret-Pohl (Klingspor-Museum), Dr Rolf Thalmann (Basler Plakatsammlung), Alexander Bieri & Thomas Casutt (Roche), Gabriele Mierzwa & Gerlinde Simon (MAN), Nigel Roche (& staff at St Bride Library), Candace Banks (MOMA), N. Macurová (Museum of Decorative Arts, Prague), Josep M. Pujol, Juan Jesús Arrausi, Graham Twemlow, Michael Richardson & Hannah Lowery (Bristol University Library), Kathryn James (Yale University Library), András Furész, Rudolf Barmettler, James Mosley, Robert Harling, Jasia Reichardt, Harry Blacker, Ernst Georg Kühle, Tom Grace, Veronika Burian, Jeremy Aynsley, Jean François Porchez, Günter-Karl Bose, Wolfgang Homola, Martin & Verity Andrews, Richard Southall, Kurt Weidemann.

Finally, many thanks to Lilo Tschichold-Link and Cornelia & Oliver Tschichold for their cooperation and advice, and without whose permission to reproduce Jan Tschichold's work this book would not have been possible.

Note on translations, references and captions

This book draws on two principal archive sources: the Jan & Edith Tschichold papers at the Getty Research Institute (Los Angeles) and the collection of Jan Tschichold's working material at the Deutsche Nationalbibliothek (Leipzig).

When no other archive reference is given in footnotes for correspondence, it can be assumed to have been quoted from the Getty papers. References to other archives are explained in the note on sources (p.326). Unless otherwise noted, all correspondence quoted has been translated by the author from German (except for Ben Nicholson's letters, which were originally in English); similarly, all citations from published works in German have been translated by the author unless otherwise credited. In making translations, an attempt has been made to remain as faithful as possible to the original. This may occasionally result in less than elegant English, for which the reader's tolerance is requested. For citations from *Die neue Typographie*, references are given to the English edition when the translation is taken from it; when an alternative translation is offered, reference to the original German edition is given. Where citations are made from correspondence or writings, in which no capital letters were used, that style is retained. In referring to titles of books, articles, films, exhibitions, etc., the following consistent style has been adopted: conventional German orthography for German titles; for English- and other-language titles, capitals are used only for the first letter of the first word and for the first letter of proper names. 'New Typography' is capitalized throughout in order to distinguish it as an historical genre.

Where no author is given for writings cited in footnotes, the author is Tschichold, and full details are given in the select bibliography of his writings included here on p.321. Full details of writings by other authors, which are cited in footnotes, can be found in the general bibliography.

Where no designer is credited in captions for examples of typographic design work, they can be assumed to have been designed by Tschichold. Many items are illustrated with kind permission of the Deutsche Nationalbibliothek (Leipzig).

Foreword   **Towards a critical understanding of Tschichold's work**

Robin Kinross

When Jan Tschichold died in August 1974, a number of key documents about his life and work had either recently been published or were in the process of publication. The first of these had appeared in 1972, on his seventieth birthday, when the *Typographische Monatsblätter* published a special number on him, with an essay appraising his life and work, which was signed with the name 'Reminiscor'.[1] As was almost obvious – though several passages of strong praise for the subject must have given its early readers some doubt about this – the piece had been written by Tschichold himself. This essay was accompanied by an extensive showing of his work in reproduction, and a full bibliography.

The book *Leben und Werk des Typographen Jan Tschichold*, published in 1977 in Dresden, was essentially an amplification of the *TM* special issue: the same essay by 'Reminiscor', a conspectus of work in reproduction (now much expanded), and a bibliography. To this was added five of Tschichold's most substantial essays in reprint. The project of this *Leben und Werk* had been started during the subject's lifetime, and he had evidently contributed to the plan of it. In effect it was Tschichold's monument to himself. Such a monograph, issued in the fullness of a subject's life, is quite usual in art and design publishing, and this example of the genre was and still is a useful and touching work. In its design and production, the *Leben und Werk* was especially touching. It seemed to represent a return for Tschichold to the time and place of his youth: though in 1977, Dresden was then in the East Germany of the 'Democratic Republic'. Tschichold seemed to be going out of his way to avoid both his adopted country of Switzerland and what was then West Germany. Printed letterpress, at a time when that technic was all but finished, the *Leben und Werk* possesses the gravity and dignity that one might expect from its subject, and yet – this was also typical of him – it is modest and self-denying in its design.

Another book, planned in Tschichold's lifetime, and designed by him, was issued posthumously. This was the *Ausgewählte Aufsätze über Fragen der Gestalt des Buches*

und der Typographie, published in 1975 by Birkhäuser in Basel. The book collected some of Tschichold's most pregnant thoughts on book design, and, as usual with him, worked as much through its own design – wonderfully modest and unassuming (and it was also printed letterpress) – as in its explicit utterances.[2]

In Switzerland and Britain, two countries with which Tschichold had special relationships, accounts of his life and work soon appeared. In 1976, an exhibition of the work was shown at the Kunstgewerbemuseum in Zurich, and this was accompanied by a small book with useful documentation: essays by colleagues, descriptions of the work, a bibliography (essentially the bibliography of 1972). In 1975, the book by Ruari McLean, *Jan Tschichold: typographer*, was published in London. This was essentially a piece of book-making from existing materials. As would become common in publications on Tschichold, this book managed to contradict most of his principles of design. McLean relied on the 'Reminiscor' account, though could supplement this with personal knowledge, as a friend of Jan Tschichold. So McLean's book provided a concise account that followed contours laid down by the subject himself. It was reprinted in paperback (1990), then issued again in a reduced edition as *Jan Tschichold: a life in typography* (1997), and has until recently provided the only available single account of Tschichold.

All of these works bore the mark of Jan Tschichold himself. Influence of a dead subject beyond the grave is quite usual; in this case, it is easy enough to see how it happened. One might reprehend Tschichold for being disingenuous in his 'Reminiscor' essay, and McLean for being less than scrupulous in not acknowledging 'Reminiscor' as his main source. But now (2007) Tschichold has been dead for more than thirty years, and Ruari McLean died in 2006. It is time to look freshly at Tschichold, without fear of the Master's gaze on us.

In fact a second wave of Tschichold reception got under way already in the mid-1980s. In 1986, Tschichold's *Elementare Typographie* of 1925 was issued in facsimile by the Verlag H. Schmidt in Mainz, at the initiative of the German committee of the Type Directors Club of New York. Not only did this bring the young Tschichold back into print, uncensored by the older Tschichold, but the publication had introductory essays that established some historical context.

In 1987 Tschichold's *Die neue Typographie* was reissued by the small firm of Brinkmann & Bose in Berlin. Although

1. This was one of a series of very useful retrospective special numbers of *TM*; among other subjects were El Lissitzky (December 1970), Emil Ruder (March 1971), Karl Gerstner (February 1972).
2. An English-language edition, which included most but not all of these texts, was issued

in 1991 as *The form of the book* (Vancouver: Hartley & Marks / London: Lund Humphries). This edition suffered from a too-precious translation and a design that, while evidently hoping to follow in the Master's steps, managed to look reverent and oversized, especially when seen next to the small, self-

effacing original work. In 1994 a French-language edition, *Livre et typographie: essais choisis*, was issued by Allia in Paris. An Italian-language edition, *La forma del libro* (Milan: Edizioni Sylvestre Bonnard, 2003) derives clearly from the Canadian edition, including its introduction by Robert Bringhurst.

the title page of their edition describes it as a second edition, and the imprint page ascribes copyright in the text to the new publishers, in fact the pages that follow are facsimile reprints of the book of 1928. The paper and binding of the book follow the original book quite closely and the facsimile reproduction is good, so the book works very well as a substitute for the rare and fragile original edition. Readers could at last have easy access to a fabled object, which the author himself would not have allowed back into print without substantial changes. Brinkmann & Bose did well to separate out their commentary and supplementary material to a 48-page booklet that accompanied the facsimile.

Brinkmann & Bose followed this with a fairly complete collection of Tschichold's essays and articles: the *Schriften 1925–1974*, published in two volumes, the first in 1990 and the second in 1991. The edition made Tschichold's texts easily available, and secured copyright in these texts for their new publisher, Brinkmann & Bose. A further work, *Jan Tschichold: Typograph*, 'a collection of his typographic work, reproduced in a large-format book' was announced at the end of each of the *Schriften* volumes, but it was not published.

The two works published by Brinkmann & Bose, *Die neue Typographie* and the *Schriften*, pointed to one of the major dilemmas in publishing Tschichold after his death. Tschichold designed all of his own books, and the design-production qualities of his books were an integral part of their content. If the design is changed, then the content changes. A facsimile edition is the only way around this dilemma, and it is hard to achieve, especially within printing and publishing scenes that are so different from those in which Tschichold worked. With *Die neue Typographie*, Brinkmann & Bose had a single book to imitate, and thus a clear path to follow. With the *Schriften*, they had no model, and – more difficult still – their subject had changed the style of his work radically in the middle of his life. They met the problem of designing the *Schriften* by following in page size and typographic style an edition of an earlier book that Tschichold himself had supervised in a later edition. Their model was the English-language edition of *Typographische Gestaltung* (1935), which appeared in 1967 under the title *Asymmetric typography*. The compromises and confusions of that book are echoed in the design of the *Schriften*.[3]

These German-language publications of Tschichold's writing began to stimulate translations. For the English-language world, a major event came in 1995 when the University of California Press issued *The New Typography*, in an edition that followed the design of the original book, but with less finesse than Brinkmann & Bose had achieved. The very fact of an English-language text, however well the typesetting of the original German pages was copied, ensured that the book would belong to a different visual sphere; though the success of this imitation was prejudiced

by incorporating fresh introductory material into the book, and typesetting that in the same way as the main text. (The added material included an introduction by the present writer, and a foreword by the translator, Ruari McLean, with indications of how Tschichold had wanted the book changed for a second edition and English translation.)

In 2003, Campgràfic in Valencia issued their *La nueva tipogafía*, following the pattern of the University of California Press edition, though now usefully setting their long introduction (by Josep M. Pujol) in a visibly different way from the main text of the book. In 2007, a Brazilian-Portuguese edition of this work is due from Altamira in São Paolo, and the same publishers are also working on an edition of *Elementare Typographie*.

With these publications, it is clear that the author Tschichold is now beginning to travel beyond the Germano-Anglo spheres (with certain European outposts, mainly to the north), which had been his main constituency during his lifetime and in the first twenty or so years after his death. One can speculate that this spread of publication is being encouraged by the ways in which the typographic culture has enlarged so greatly, with the phenomenon of desktop publishing and the opening up of typesetting and also typeface design to so many more people. The advent of the internet is another factor here, hastening the spread of knowledge.

One can understand the production of the Sabon Next family of fonts, issued by the Linotype company in 2002, in this light. The new typeface, designed in Paris by Jean François Porchez, develops Tschichold's typeface of 1967 in ways that Tschichold himself would surely have disapproved of (the extra bold and black fonts, the swash characters). The enterprise rests on the now almost mythical status of Tschichold, known to young designers around the world, whose work is assumed to be worth reviving regardless of any intrinsic merits it might have possessed. In the case of the typeface Sabon, it is not clear why we need yet another Garamond revival, and especially now that the initial constraints of the design (it had to cater for three different composition systems) have disappeared.

The world-wide discovery of Tschichold is now clearly in development. East Asian interest was signalled in 1991 by a Korean edition of *Asymmetric typography* (the English-language *Typographische Gestaltung*), translated by the designer Ahn Sang-Soo and published by his own Ahn Graphics company. In 1998, a Japanese edition of the *Meisterbuch der Schrift* (1952) was published by Robundo in Tokyo. A special issue on Tschichold of *Idea*, the principal Japanese graphic-design magazine, has appeared in 2007. One might have expected Japanese publication of his

---

3. The sharpest published comments on this book may be in the four reviews that Anthony Froshaug wrote, published in Kinross, *Anthony Froshaug: Typography & texts*, pp.191–5.

work to have started earlier, given his own attention to Far
Eastern graphic culture, and – though this risks too easy
stereotyping – given Tschichold's 'eastern' sense of repose.
Certainly some examination of Tschichold's work on Japanese and Chinese printing is due, and by people who really
know about these topics.

Evaluation of Tschichold's work is not yet much developed. Designers have let themselves be overawed by the
mastery of his design work. Gerrit Noordzij's dissection of
the weakness of Tschichold's claim to authority in his writings has been a rare instance of the application of genuinely
critical thought – and it came from a designer who appreciated the quality of Tschichold's design work.[4] Art and design
historians are still scarcely able to discuss Tschichold's work
in any interesting way, lumping the work of the 1920s and
1930s together with Bauhaus typography, under the catch-
all term of 'modernism'. The character and qualities of typographic design are usually beyond these commentators;
they have no language with which to discuss these things.

Now that so much of Jan Tschichold's work, with many
of his surviving papers, is in publicly accessible archives,
there can be no excuse for the unquestioning recycling of
the stories that surrounded him during his lifetime and in
the years after his death. Serious discussion needs to begin
with the primary material: the artefacts themselves rather
than reproductions of them, typescripts and proof copies,
letters and postcards to and from the subject, magazines
and pamphlets that may not have been opened for many
years. Tschichold also needs to be seen in his contexts, in
discussion with colleagues, and engaged in the production
of the 'active literature' that he preferred. The present book
represents a notable start along this road.

4. Gerrit Noordzij, 'Rule
or law', in Barnes (ed.), *Jan
Tschichold: reflections and
reappraisals*, pp.25–31.

Prologue

The Tschichold family at Christmas (c.1917).
From the left: Maria, Werner, Erich, Franz and
Jan (or rather Johannes, as he was then).

Tschichold with his parents. c.1918.
(The photograph on the previous page seems
to have been taken at the same session.)

The elusive nature of Jan Tschichold's historical persona begins with the name, that string of eight consonants with merely two vowels, which only native German speakers are entirely sure of how to pronounce. The repeated 'ch' in particular gives false clues to speakers of Romance languages. It is a Germanized spelling of a Slavic name, which is rendered simpler in the writing systems of Slavic languages: Czychold in Polish, Čichold in Czech, and Чихольд in Russian.[1] Both of Tschichold's parents, Maria (née Zapff) and Franz, were of Slavic extraction: his mother had Russian ancestry;[2] his father's parents originated from Pförten in lower Lusatia, which was then part of Prussia, but is currently in Poland, where the town is now known as Brody. Lusatia is the homeland of the Wends or Sorbs, a Slavic people that never managed to form itself into a nation state, largely due to centuries of German domination. In Tschichold's earliest appearances in print, the spelling of the family name was even more complex: Tzschichhold. Dropping the z and the third h was a simplification adopted by the family in the 1920s, and Tschichold was using the shorter form by 1925.[3]

Then there is the matter of his Christian name, which was given to him at birth in 1902 as Johannes. Before settling on Jan in 1926, there had been an interlude of about two years in which he had rechristened himself Ivan, due to a passionate sympathy with Russian revolutionary culture. Such an adaptability in the principal sign of one's public identity does not indicate uncertainty of character, but perhaps the opposite: Tschichold was certainly sure of himself, and there is a strong sense of continuity underlying the famous changes of standpoint towards typography that marked his career. Certain figures of the European avant-garde whom he came to admire in his early twenties had also reinvented themselves, perhaps providing some inspiration: Le Corbusier (Charles-Edouard Jeanneret); Tristan Tzara, the Rumanian Dadaist (given name Sami Rosenstock); Lazar Lissitzky, who took only the initial of his first name (El); John Heartfield, Dadaist and photomonteur (born Helmut Held, later Herzfelde), who changed his German name by deed poll in protest at anti-English propaganda during the First World War; and then there was the founder of De Stijl, Theo van Doesburg, who had several pseudonyms, having been christened C.E.M. Küppers.[4]

Tschichold proclaimed that he felt himself to be 'ethnically a Slav' in the autobiographical essay written on the occasion of his seventieth birthday and entitled 'Jan Tschichold: praeceptor typographiae' (typographical instructor).[5] This text is invaluable to the Tschichold scholar but must be treated with circumspection. It was written in the third person with an omniscient tone and Tschichold's own authorship of it was lightly cloaked again in Latin: it is simply credited to 'Reminiscor' – 'he who remembers'.[6] The essay was reprinted in the posthumous volume on Tschichold's 'life and work' that he had helped to prepare before his death. In reviewing that book, the printing scholar Georg Kurt Schauer described this text as 'a curious mixture' incorporating elements of confession, autobiography, history, polemic and swansong. Schauer was pained by Tschichold's unashamed use of superlative in writing about himself and it prompted him to wonder 'why nobody told the author that one should not write like that – above all about oneself'. He was particularly disturbed by Tschichold's description of German printing culture in the first two decades of the twentieth century as a decadent and arid environment, from which he was nevertheless able to emerge as a kind of self-taught virtuoso. Schauer countered that, contrary to the 'degenerate' typography around 1925 that Tschichold claimed to have remedied with his first publication, this was instead a period of brilliant accomplishments by the German private presses. Schauer feared that Tschichold, in his old age, was retrospectively pushing aside 'a rich and varied tradition to make room for his own fame'.[7]

A slightly more balanced view was given by Tschichold in an essay that he wrote two years before his 'Reminiscor' article, called 'Flöhe ins Ohr' (Planting ideas in the head). Here there was a clearer demarcation of his personal intervention (described in the first person) from a general, historical account. Among typographic achievements since the 1890s he praised above all the English private presses (in particular the Doves Press). While he was mostly non-specific about German typography of note from the beginning of the twentieth century, he probably had in mind the Bremer Presse (which surpassed the Doves Press in a similar vein) when he grudgingly admitted: 'There were also a few private presses [in Germany], which produced books carefully typeset in proprietary typefaces and printed on fine paper.'[8]

1. A phonetic transcription is tʃɪçɔlt.

2. Weidemann, 'Jan Tschichold: Anmerkungen zu einer tragischen Interpretation', p.A115.

3. In two of Tschichold's early Ex Libris his surname is spelled with a final t; one typeset in fraktur (with ch ligatures) is letterspaced to emphasize structure: Tʒſchichhold.

4. Lesser known is the fact that Dziga Vertov, the pioneer of Russian cinema, was born Boris Kaufman in Bialystok (now in Poland but at that time part of Russia). His chosen pseudonym means 'spinning top'. Tschichold may initially not have been aware that the poster artist he described in Die neue Typographie (p.190) as the 'Frenchman A.M. Cassandre' was born in Russia as Adolphe Jean-Marie Mouron.

5. One of Tschichold's mentors, Carl Ernst Poeschel, had been described as 'Praeceptor Germaniae typographicus' by Julius Zeitler on the occasion of his sixtieth birthday in 1934. See Schmidt-Kunsemüller, William Morris und die neuere Buchkunst, p.143.

6. An account of Tschichold's early years must rely heavily on this essay, as Ruari McLean noted in his book Jan Tschichold: typographer (p.17). McLean's second chapter indeed contains much that is almost literally translated from Tschichold's text. An example serves to illustrate the care needed in interpreting Tschichold's autobiographical essay: a lengthy citation in praise of Tschichold – 'Tschichold the typographical moralist, is a man of reason, a thinker and logician. ...' – is credited to Kurt Weidemann. Yet this paragraph was written by Tschichold himself as an addition to the text for an exhibition catalogue, which he revised before its publication in 1963 (he even rewrote this first sentence for citation by 'Reminscor'). It was included in the English translation of the original essay: Weidemann, 'Designer's profile: Jan Tschichold'. I am grateful to Prof. Weidemann for confirming this to me (letter to the author, 31 October 2006).

7. Schauer, 'Wer war Jan Tschichold', p.A190.

8. 'Flöhe ins Ohr', p.360. The Bremer Presse even fulfilled his desired criteria of not exclusively producing luxury editions: it printed trade editions of some books and even collaborated with the socialist book club Büchergilde Gutenberg in 1925, at the time that Tschichold was connected with it. On the Bremer Presse see Burke, 'Luxury and austerity', Typography papers, 2 (1997), pp.105–28.

Looking back, Tschichold also reserved praise for book design work by one of his early teachers in Leipzig, Walter Tiemann. Tschichold was distinguished from other leading exponents of New Typography by having had a formal education in the crafts of calligraphy and printing, not coming from a background in art or architecture. Perhaps the only other contemporary modernist typographer with a similar background was Georg Trump. Tschichold shared the visions and ideas of contemporary artists-turned-designers and maintained an interest in modern art for the whole of his life. Yet, while he drew parallels between non-objective art and typography, he always affirmed the differences between them. His attention to the details of typographic practice in his writings shows that he was working from within printing tradition outwards, not from the outside in, as were László Moholy-Nagy, El Lissitzky and Theo van Doesburg.

He further distinguished himself from his contemporaries by the profusion of his writings about typography from the very beginning of his career. 'I am always lecturing', he once wrote of himself.[9] He was a precise and prolific writer, taking initial cues from short theoretical texts by Moholy-Nagy and Lissitzky, but seeking to harness a workable typography to the Utopian ideas that he shared with them – to establish New Typography on a theoretical and historical basis for the printing trade. However, Tschichold did not pursue a traditional apprenticeship in any aspect of printing and never held a full-time position in a printing firm, and in this respect he was also an outsider in his chosen field. The readership that he addressed consisted of printers, type compositors and apprentices & students of printing, although it now seems implicit in Tschichold's writings that he was reaching towards the modern roles of typographer or graphic designer. These had not yet been fully formed in the 1920s; perhaps Tschichold was one of the first. Indeed he claimed later that, in 1923, he began to practise the 'hitherto unknown profession of typographic designer' for the Leipzig printing house of Fischer & Wittig.[10] Certainly others, both in Germany (Paul Renner) and elsewhere (Bruce Rogers), could have claimed to precede him in this respect. Yet no other figure in typography combined eloquent practice with such a wealth of reflective and informative writing on the subject; Schauer described him as having created a 'theoretical system, which stands there in the landscape of the field of graphic design like a monolith'.[11]

In *Pioneers of modern typography*, Herbert Spencer recognized the role of Tschichold's published writings in explaining 'asymmetrical typography in terms which printers and compositors could readily grasp and could immediately apply in their everyday work.' Yet Spencer, whose own work was fundamentally influenced by Tschichold, simultaneously criticized him for this, claiming that such a codification was 'neither necessary nor relevant' and indeed contradicted

Door label giving Tschichold's office hours (and home address) for his post as typographer at Fischer & Wittig printing house. c.1923. 5.4 × 13 cm.

'the spirit of modern typography'.[12] Hints towards such a criticism were made personally to Tschichold by his contemporaries, Piet Zwart and Herbert Bayer, who felt that his written exposition of New Typography was too narrow. But it is precisely his double role as practitioner and theorist that enriches his legacy and ensures his continuing relevance.

The evolution of Tschichold's activity and writings will be largely reflected here through the prism of friendships, meetings and correspondence with his contemporaries. Mapping contacts is not only about charting influence but also a way of examining how, in creating his illustrated canon of New Typography, Tschichold relied on acquaintances to a large extent for information and original material. This, along with his own interests and biases as a figure in the movement, inevitably affected his version of its historical development.

This book deals with Tschichold principally as a chronicler and practitioner of New Typography, up to the point where its last traces disappear from his work: in other words, the first half of his career is the main subject here. His work for Penguin Books in the late 1940s provides a cut-off point, as it effectively put a seal on Tschichold's reversion to a traditionalist approach. That episode will not be dealt with here in any detail. After Penguin he increasingly dedicated himself to writing about printing and typography. Although this book is not strictly biographical, it is a kind of a professional biography: in this sense, while Tschichold's book design work and writings from the settled Swiss years of his born-again classicist period are admirable and undoubtedly important, an account of that later period would – in this author's opinion – make for less interesting reading (and writing) than the years of revolutionary zeal and conflict in Weimar Germany and the period of his adaptation to exile. The tension that energized Tschichold's work and writings reflected the broader struggle within Weimar culture between traditional and modern tendencies, which were frequently carried to extremes and contributed to this short period in Germany becoming a crucible of the modern world.

9. From a letter cited by Bertold Hack in 'Jan Tschichold: zu Person und Werk', p.B104. According to Paul Renner, Tschichold was a 'confessor'. (Burke, *Paul Renner*, p.176n.)

10. 'Jan Tschichold: praeceptor typographiae', p.16.

11. Schauer, 'Jan Tschichold', p.A421.

12. **Spencer,** *Pioneers of modern typography*, pp.51 & 147.

Spencer's complaint was prefigured by an early commentator in English, Frederic Ehrlich, in *The new typography and modern layouts* (London: Chapman & Hall, 1934), p.31.

1　From Johannes
　　to Ivan

(Above) This photograph was taken in Meissen in July 1919, probably on an outing from the Leipzig academy. Tschichold is in pride of place in the centre.

(Right) Tschichold with other students on the steps of the Dresden Akademie für Kunstgewerbe, 9 July 1920. The older man on the left is possibly Heinrich Wieynck.

Johannes Tzschichhold was born in Leipzig on 2 April 1902. His father was a sign painter with business premises located in the heart of the city. Leipzig was an important centre of the German printing industry, home to many notable publishers, printing houses, binderies and type-foundries. Already before the First World War the city's Buchgewerbehaus (Book trade house) contained a printing museum, open free to the public, in which there was a bust of Gutenberg and portraits of Senefelder (inventor of litho-graphy) and König (inventor of the machine press). In 1914, the adolescent Tschichold had the opportunity to visit the Weltausstellung für Buchgewerbe und Graphik (World exhi-bition for book production and graphic arts) that took place in his hometown. Looking back from the age of seventy, Tschichold described the effect this exhibition had on him (referring to himself in the third person):

> In August 1914 the World War broke out. Bugra – that was the abbreviation of the name of the Leipzig exhibition – closed its doors in autumn 1914 but there remained open its 'Hall of Culture', a domed building with a magnificent display of cultural development. Equipped with a season ticket, Tschi-chold, then a twelve-year old youth, spent hundreds of his free hours acquainting himself with the cultural history of all periods and peoples, and with the history of books and script. For this could not have been revealed to him in school. Here, on the other hand, there was everything, accompanied by an excellent descriptive catalogue. The 'Hall of Culture' and this catalogue laid the foundation for Tschichold's education.[1]

The desire of young Johannes to be an artist was bargained down by his parents to training as an art teacher, and so he began his teacher training in 1916 at the college in Grimma, near Leipzig. Here he received a good grounding in Latin and French. But his interest in script and typography persisted: in his spare time at college he studied 'with great enthusiasm' the calligraphy manuals of both Rudolf von Larisch and Edward Johnston.[2] Aged 17 he tried his hand at designing the letterhead for his father's business, and became aware that he had much to learn.[3] He had often assisted his father in painting letters and commented later that he was 'pressed by background and inclination' towards an early decision to become a 'lettering artist' (Schriftzeichner).[4] His parents agreed to let him change direction in his education and so, at Easter 1919, he entered Leipzig's Staatliche Akademie für graphische Künste und Buchgewerbe (State academy for the graphic arts and book production).

In later recalling this turbulent period in German history Tschichold borrowed the title of a book by Theodor Plievier: 'The Kaiser went, the generals stayed.'[5] After the November Revolution of 1918, many parts of Germany were racked by a bloody counter-revolution; one of Tschichold's student contemporaries in Leipzig recalled that there was armed unrest in the streets, with shots being fired, but that inside the academy, peace prevailed.[6] Tschichold enrolled in the 'script class' of Hermann Delitsch, which he recalled in some autobiographical notes written in 1944:

> Delitsch was more a historian of the medieval art of script than an actual calligrapher; he had an almost unparalleled mastery of the history of calligraphy and the development of letterforms. In fact he 'wrote' only occasionally, but he had a thorough knowledge of writing technique. His manner of teaching was a synthesis of the writing methods of the Englishman Edward Johnston and the Austrian Rudolf von Larisch, and consequently his instruction hardly addressed the knowledge of form and development in printing types.[7]

Tschichold took additional classes in printmaking tech-niques and bookbinding but, towards the end of his life, he claimed that typographic design was taught nowhere at that time, not even at the Leipzig academy:

> … neither he [Delitsch] nor my other teachers made me aware of the history of style in typefaces, nor with the aesthetic val-ues of old books. The art history classes at the academy did not address these issues either. I knew little, then, of old book culture and its traditions and made my judgements based on what I saw around me. And much of that was dire enough.

In 1944 Tschichold seemed thankful to Delitsch, whose stimulating teaching found in him a student eager to learn. Yet, by 1970, he considered his teachers at the Leipzig acad-emy to have been unapproachable 'demi-gods' from whom he did not learn much.[8] Among the teachers of Buchkunst (book art) there were Walter Tiemann, Hugo Steiner-Prag, Georg Alexander Mathéy (a former pupil of Emil Rudolf Weiß) and Georg Belwe. They may not have been rigor-ous designers according to Tschichold's later criteria, yet it seems unlikely that he would not have picked up something useful in the fields of composition and printing during his five years there.[9]

In his first year at the Leipzig academy Tschichold exe-cuted at least two of the 'Palatino' series of poetry books published by Karl Schnabel in Berlin, which were printed lithographically from texts written out by calligraphers. It was a remarkable feat for a 17-year-old. This series was

1. 'Jan Tschichold: praeceptor typographiae', pp.12–13.
2. Larisch, Unterricht in orna-mentaler Schrift (1905); John-ston, Writing & illuminating, & lettering (1906; translated into German by Anna Simons, 1910).

3. Letter to Alfred Fairbank, appendix to McLean, Jan Tschi-chold: typographer, p.148.
4. 'Jan Tschichold 1924–1944: zwanzig Jahre typographischer Wandlungen und persönlicher Geschichte' (unpublished type-script; DNB Leipzig), p.1.

5. 'Jan Tschichold: praeceptor typographiae', p.14.
6. Heinrich Hussmann, 'Johannes Tzschichhold' in Luidl, J.T., p.9.
7. 'Jan Tschichold 1924–1944', pp.1–2. Johnston was in fact a Scotsman, born in Uruguay.

8. 'Flöhe ins Ohr', pp.361–2.
9. In The art of the book (London/Paris/New York: The Studio, 1914) L. Deubner remarked of German book art: 'But many who at first occupied themselves with this kind of work in a more or less dilet-tante spirit, have by quiet seri-

ous labour and steady develop-ment mastered its problems and have come to devote them-selves almost exclusively to the graphic arts and the industry of book production' (p.131). In this connection he named Tiemann, J.V. Cissarz, F.H. Ehmcke, the Kleukens brothers, Rudolf

Koch, Paul Renner, Steiner-Prag and Heinrich Wieynck. The sug-gestion that Tschichold under-valued the professors in Leipzig was first made by Schauer and examined at length by Pujol in 'Jan Tschichold y la tipografía moderna'.

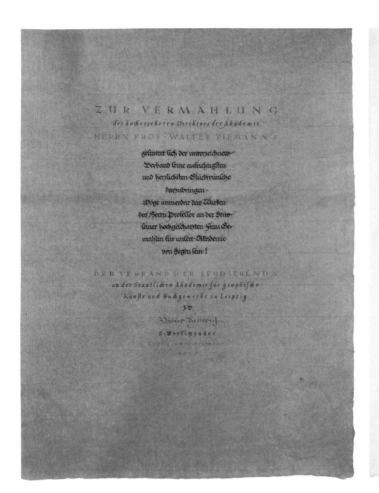

Early calligraphic work by Tschichold. *c.*1920–2. All greatly reduced. (Top left) Wedding congratulation to Leipzig academy director, Walter Tiemann.

Title-page from Hölderlin, *Hymne an die Freiheit*.
1919. 33.2 × 26.4 cm.

Detail of colophon (55% of actual size) from
the book shown on the left. It was seventh in
the series of 'Palatino' books. The credit reads:
'Designed and written by Johannes Tzfchichhold'.
Printed lithographically. Initials were added by
hand, as some copies feature gold instead of red.

directed by Heinrich Wieynck, an established typeface
designer and professor at the Dresden Akademie für Kunstgewerbe (Academy of applied art). Tschichold had already
established contact with Wieynck before beginning his
formal studies in the graphic arts; indeed Wieynck remembered that, when they first met around 1918, Tschichold
was wearing his secondary school cap. He went to Dresden
at Easter 1920 to study for half a year with Wieynck, who
described the attitude of the nineteen-year-old Tschichold
thus: 'he perceived his ideal in the elite artistic enterprise
of a cloistered scriptorium and showed an exceptional gift
for the art of script'.[10] Tschichold himself explained later
the importance of his sustained calligraphic work in writing lengthy texts: 'This silent work, which demands great
concentration, is the real foundation for all my later work.'[11]
On his return to Leipzig Tschichold became a master student (*Meisterschüler*) of Walter Tiemann, the director of the
academy and a noted *Schriftkünstler* (type artist). Tiemann
now invited him to assist Delitsch in teaching the evening
class in formal writing, which obviously signals the young
Tschichold's prodigious expertise in calligraphy.

In 1922 an exhibition was held in Leipzig of work by master
calligrapher Rudolf Koch and his students. Tschichold had
admired Koch since seeing one of his handwritten books

at the Bugra exhibition in 1914 and was now again deeply
impressed by his work. He travelled twice to Offenbach
am Main, near Frankfurt, to visit Koch but decided that he
could not become his 'spiritual follower' (*geistiger Schüler*)
due to differences of outlook. Tschichold felt later that
Koch, who was so strongly attached to the idea of a German
tradition in letterforms, could not understand the 'complex
philosophy of the cultivated person in the present day'.[12]
This perhaps says more about Tschichold than Koch; as
Tschichold himself admitted, Koch's calligraphy shared an
exuberance with modern, expressionist art. One thread of
Koch's work, in which the spaces created between delicate
letter strokes are filled with solid washes of colour (evoking
Mondrian), was emulated by the young Tschichold.

From 1921, while still a student, Tschichold took on
numerous commissions to make calligraphic advertisements for the Leipzig trade fairs. This allowed him to make
a relatively good living during the following few years of

10. Wieynck, 'Die Wand-
lungen des Johannes', p.77.
Tschichold gives a date of
Easter 1920 for beginning his
studies with Wieynck in 'Jan
Tschichold 1924–1944' (p.1) but
in 'Jan Tschichold: praeceptor
typographiae' (p.14) he stated
that he went to Dresden after
two years in Leipzig, so at
Easter 1921. The dated photograph reproduced here on p.16
confirms the earlier date.

11. 'Jan Tschichold 1924–
1944', p.2.
12. 'Jan Tschichold 1924–
1944', p.3.

„Wehe nun! mein Paradies erbebte!
Fluch verhieß der Elemente Wut!
Und der Nächte schwarzem Schoß entschwebte
mit des Geiers Blick der Übermut;
wehe! weinend floh ich mit der Liebe,
mit der Unschuld in den Himmel hin –
welke, Blume! rief ich ernst und trübe,
welke, nimmer, nimmer aufzublühn!

„Keck erhub sich des Gesetzes Rute,
nachzubilden, was die Liebe schuf;
ach! gegeißelt von dem Übermute,
fühlte keiner göttlichen Beruf;
vor dem Geist in schwarzen Ungewittern,
vor dem Racheschwerte des Gerichts
lernte so der blinde Sklave zittern,
frönt und starb im Schrecken seines Nichts.

Spread from Hölderlin, *Hymne an die Freiheit*.
1919. 33.2 × 26.4 cm.

Dense gothic calligraphy (29.2 × 16.2 cm) and hand coloured, linocut lettering (22 × 15.2 cm), both echoing Rudolf Koch's work of the early 1920s. c.1922/3.

Sketch for journal cover. c.1923. 20.8 × 16 cm.

Artwork for Leipzig trade fair advertisement. 1922. 25.7 × 18.5 cm. Pasted up from photo-graphic reductions but a couple of lines are written in actual size.

Printed examples of calligraphic advertisements for the Leipzig trade fairs. 1922. (Above) 14.4 × 23.6 cm; (below) 19.2 × 39 cm.

astronomic inflation in Germany. He began to build up a personal library on the history of letterforms and the book, which he described as comparable with the best private libraries of its kind.[13] His financial solvency also allowed him to move from his parents' house into an apartment in the Gohlis area of Leipzig, which he later shared with his fellow student Walter Cyliax.

During his years at the Leipzig academy Tschichold began to acquaint himself with the best in classical typography: firstly, by regular visits to the library of the main German printing trade organization, the Börsenverein der Deutschen Buchhändler, which housed an outstanding collection of historical examples; and secondly, by volunteer work at the printing house of Poeschel & Trepte, where he gained practical experience in typesetting.[14] This firm was well known for the quality of its work, in which it pioneered the revival of certain classic typefaces. Its proprietor, Carl Ernst Poeschel, was acquainted with William Morris's principles for reform in printing, and, as one of the directors of the Insel publishing house, he secured the collaboration of Morris's colleague, Emery Walker, in designing its series of classics from 1905. So, by the end of his studies, Tschichold had availed himself of all that the considerable printing culture of Leipzig could offer him.

He made his first steps into the field of *Buchkunst*, beginning with the customary starting point for 'book artists' – bindings and title-pages, most of which he executed by drawing or calligraphy. It was also around this time that Tschichold made his first typeface design drawings, for both a roman and a gothic typeface.[15]

However, in 1923 Tschichold had an experience that shook his belief in the traditions in which he had been schooled and had begun to work. Sometime between July and September he visited the first exhibition of work at the Bauhaus in Weimar, a short train ride away from his home in Leipzig. He had heard talk of the new '-isms' in art, which the art historian at the Leipzig academy, Julius Zeitler, could not explain to him, and so he decided to go and find out about

13. Letter Tschichold to Kner, 19 June 1925 (Békés Archive). Here Tschichold claimed to have got rid of most of his library, which by then corresponded to his 'earlier field of activity'. Of his 'luxury editions' he kept only those that he considered to be 'defining achievements', including the Marées-Gesellschaft edition of Sappho's poetry (1921), printed from copper plates containing both the original Greek text engraved by E.R. Weiß and drawings engraved by his wife, the artist Renée Sintenis.

14. Tschichold's contact with Poeschel is likely to have arisen through Tiemann, who had been a friend of his since childhood. In Poeschel's own programmatic essay of 1904, 'Zeitgemäße Buchdruckkunst', he was one of the first to criticize 'block setting', the tendency to always square up a typographic composition, instead advocating division of elements into smaller groups. This was an idea that resurfaced often in Tschichold's typographical writings; indeed Poeschel's text set a pattern for Tschichold's

later traditionalist work. It was reprinted in Sichowsky & Tiemann (ed.) *Typographie und Bibliophilie*, a compilation of texts for which Tschichold advised in the selection.

15. 'Jan Tschichold: praeceptor typographiae', pp.14–16. In a letter to Imre Kner of 4 November 1924, Tschichold stated that a gothic typeface of his design would be released from Switzerland half a year later, but no such type appeared.

Tschichold's first drawings for typefaces, which remained unproduced. 1923. 21.8 × 29.5 cm.

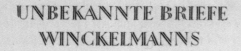

Title-page produced by copper-engraving.
Publisher: Poeschel & Trepte, 1921.

Book jacket, 1922. 26 × 20.2 cm.

Two designs for lettering on title-pages of Insel
Verlag editions. 1923 & 1925. The lower example
is signed 'Tzschichholt'.

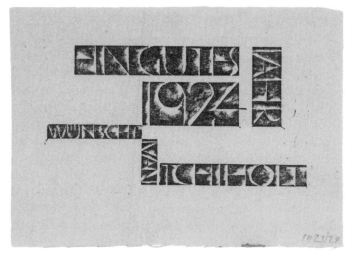

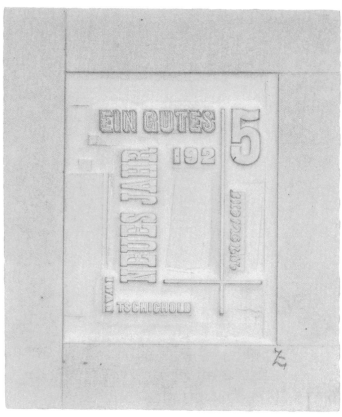

Two new year's cards for 1924 and 1925.
75% of actual size. Here the change from a
somewhat expressionst linocut (with a further
alternative spelling 'Tchiholt') to a more constructivist, typeset design signals Tschichold's
transformation at this time. The later example
was probably never printed, hence Tschichold
keeping record of it as a flong.

the new tendencies for himself. He later stated that he came
back from the exhibition 'in turmoil' (*aufgewühlt*), and it
was not long before he established contact with László
Moholy-Nagy, the Hungarian Constructivist in charge of the
preliminary course at the Bauhaus. It was most probably
through Moholy-Nagy that Tschichold began to learn about
contemporary Russian art and design, which excited him
so much that, around the turn of 1924, he adopted the name
Ivan instead of Johannes (although he was inconsistent in
spelling it; sometimes he was Iwan). Wieynck commented
a few years later that 'he threw his good German forename
Johannes overboard, named himself *Iwan* and campaigned
for elemental typography and photomontage'.[16]

His transformation into a modernist did not occur overnight, nor was it ever absolute: throughout the 1920s he
designed title-pages and bindings for the Insel Verlag in a
suitably classical style. Yet from 1924 he began to find work
that allowed him to move away from historical scripts and
calligraphy towards experimental, geometric lettering, and
away from centred arrangement to more dynamic compositions using sanserif type. At the end of 1924, in correspondence with the Hungarian printer Imre Kner, Tschichold
commented of his calligraphic work:

> Nowadays I have given up these things more than ever, and
> I work now only in typography, at least where it does not
> concern things which, due to their very nature, should be
> drawn by hand (book spines, posters).[17]

TAMBOUR

Masthead for a magazine, as shown in Fritz
Ehmcke's book, *Schrift* (1925), where it was
dated 1924. Actual size. Tschichold signed it
with cyrillic initials. It is not clear whether the
magazine was ever published.

16. Wieynck, 'Die Wandlungen
des Johannes', p.77.
17. Letter Tschichold to Kner,
4 November 1924 (Békés Archive).

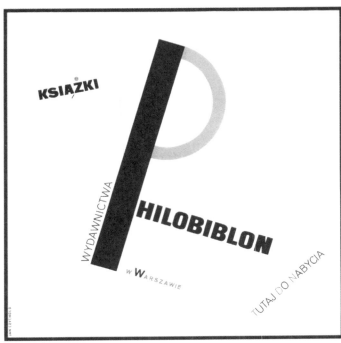

Original sketch (13.9 × 13.7 cm) and printed reproduction of poster for Warsaw publisher Philobiblon. 1924. The printed version bears its designer's signature in Polish orthography: Jan Czychold. This must have been his first use of the forename Jan, two years before he settled on it. The printed signature was expunged from the version shown in Tschichold's *Leben und Werk*.

Tschichold himself later cited his 1924 design of a poster for the Polish publisher Philobiblon as decisive for his change of direction: it exemplified 'formation instead of the art of script'.[18]

On 8 December 1924 Tschichold emerged as a public speaker with a lecture organized by the Typographische Vereinigung (Typographical association) of Leipzig and entitled 'On Constructivism'. The invitation for the event announced that the lecture would be 'supported by numerous slides' and proposed that it would 'bring to our colleagues something new in the field of printing design'.[19]

18. *Anordnung statt Schrift-kunst.* 'Jan Tschichold: praeceptor typographiae' p.17.
19. Invitation reproduced in Doede, 'Jan Tschichold', p.13.

Sketch showing Tschichold's developing interest in geometrically constructed letterforms around 1924/5. 34.7 × 25.5 cm.

2   Making history

DIE NEUE TYPOGRAPHIE

IWAN TSCHICHOLD:

1 TYPOGRAPHIE ist die exakte graphische Form der **Mitteilung** auf dem Wege des Hochdruckverfahrens. *aller graphischen Verfahren.*

2 Diese Mitteilung kann sein **1)** werbend,
2) abhandelnd.

3 **Werbende TYPOGRAPHIE: Plakate,** Inserate, Prospekte, Umschläge.
Abhandelnde TYPOGRAPHIE: Artikel, Abhandlungen, „Literatur".

4 Eine Mitteilung soll die **1) KÜRZESTE**
2) EINFACHSTE
3) EINDRINGLICHSTE Form haben.

5 Kürze, Einfachheit, Eindringlichkeit werden umso zwingendere Notwendigkeiten, je mehr sich die Mitteilung von der Form der „LITERATUR" entfernt und sich dem Wesen des **PLAKATS** nähert.

6 Die neue Typographie ist **zweckbetont** —: siehe **4** und **5.**

7 **Typographie IM SINNE NEUER GESTALTUNG** ist konstruktiver Aufbau zweckmäßigsten Materials
1) einfachster FORM
2) sparsamster MENGE
gemäß den Funktionen der zu schaffenden Mitteilungsform.

8 Die **MITTEL** der neuen Typographie sind **ausschließlich die DURCH DIE AUFGABE gegebenen:** die **BUCHSTABEN** und **MESSINGLINIEN** des Setzkastens. Ornament auch einfachster Form (fettfeine Linien!) ist, da überflüssig, unzulässig.

9 Die einfachste, darum allein überzeugende **Form** der europäischen **SCHRIFT** ist die **Block-**(Grotesk)-**Schrift.**

10 Durch Anwendung **fetter** und MAGERER Charaktere und verschiedener Schriftgrade können stärkste Gegensätze gestaltet werden.

11 Im fortlaufenden Textsatz ist die heutige Form der **GROTESK** schwerer lesbar als die bis jetzt meist angewandte MEDIÄVAL-ANTIQUA. Lesetechnische Gründe, vertieft durch ökonomische Erwägungen zwingen also zur vorläufigen Beibehaltung des Textsatzes aus ANTIQUA.

12 Alle wichtigen Teile (Überschriften, Zahlen, wichtige Satzteile) werden aus **GROTESK** verschiedenster Grauwerte gesetzt.

13 **Nationale** Schriften (𝔉𝔯𝔞𝔨𝔱𝔲𝔯, 𝔊𝔬𝔱𝔦𝔰𝔠𝔥, Altslawisch) werden als nicht allgemein verständlich und der Geschichte angehörend von der Verwendung **ausgeschlossen.** Ökonomische Erwägungen vertiefen diese Notwendigkeit.

14 Um das **Sensationelle** Neuer Typographie zu steigern und zugleich um den statischen Ausgleich zu schaffen, sind neben horizontalen auch vertikale und schräge Zeilen**richtungen,** auch die **SCHRÄGSTELLUNG GANZER GRUPPEN,** möglich.

9

Tschichold's first manifesto on typography in *Kulturschau*, Heft 4, [spring]1925. Actual size. As well as adopting the title of Moholy-Nagy's Bauhaus essay of 1923, Tschichold emulated its design by running his name vertically in the left margin. He also takes to heart Moholy-Nagy's recommendation to use contrast between different typefaces in 'surprising formation'.

Elemental typography

Tschichold soon began to formulate his ideas for writing something about the significance of new movements in art and design for typography. Perhaps his scholarly approach to writing the history of New Typography as it happened shows the zeal of the converted. His infamous retreat from modernism in the 1930s was in fact a kind of reversion; his first conversion was here in 1923–5 from an established and expert classicism, fuelled no doubt by his youthful enthusiasm for such a departure from tradition. 'There are people here who try to breathe new life into the old, but here the past is already dead,' he declared in summer 1925.[1] Like other figures of the Central European avant-garde at this time, Tschichold was energized by an optimism for a purifying new movement suited to a new epoch that had begun with the end of the First World War, the fall of the old order, and, for many, with the Russian Revolution.

From the beginning of 1925 Tschichold was compiling material about Constructivism in typography for a special issue of *Typographische Mitteilungen* (Typographic news), the journal of the Bildungsverband der Deutschen Buchdrucker (Educational association of the German printing trade union), which was based in Leipzig. The project inevitably took longer to prepare than Tschichold had planned: by Easter 1925 he lamented that it was already delayed and hoped that it would appear in July,[2] but it was finally published under the title *Elementare Typographie* (Elemental typography) in the issue of *Typographische Mitteilungen* for October 1925. In the meantime, Tschichold worked on another, shorter text about New Typography, a manifesto which predates the one he published in *Elementare Typographie*. This earlier manifesto has not previously been mentioned in literature about Tschichold (not even by Tschichold himself). It was published in a small, cultural review called *Kulturschau*, subtitled 'Allgemeiner Anzeiger für die linksgerichtete Literatur' (General advertiser for left-oriented literature). Along with his connection to the Bildungsverband, Tschichold's association with this magazine confirms his affinity with the socialist movement in Leipzig at that time. *Kulturschau* was edited by Arthur Wolf, a member of the Communist Party and director of the important socialist publishing house in Leipzig called Die Wölfe.*

Tschichold's sixteen-point manifesto here was entitled 'Die neue Typographie' (New Typography, following the first published use of the term by Moholy-Nagy in the Bauhaus exhibition catalogue of 1923). Although it overlaps to some extent with 'Elementare Typographie', it is worth quoting here in full as the first, concise statement of his modernist position (Tschichold's pencil correction opposite has been taken into the translation):

1 TYPOGRAPHY is the precise graphic form of **communication** in the realm of graphic processes.
2 This communication can be
    1) advertising
    2) editorial.
3 **Advertising** TYPOGRAPHY: **posters**, advertisements, prospectuses, book jackets.
  Editorial TYPOGRAPHY: **articles**, essays, 'literature'.
4 A communication should have the
    1) BRIEFEST
    2) SIMPLEST
    3) MOST URGENT form.
5 The more a communication distances itself from 'LITERATURE' and approaches the nature of a POSTER, the more compelling becomes the necessity for brevity, simplicity and urgency.
6 New Typography is **oriented towards purpose** –: see **4** and **5**.
7 **Typography**, IN THE SENSE OF NEW DESIGN, is construction with the most suitable materials
    1) in the **simplest** FORM
    2) with the **minimum** MEANS
  according to the function of the kind of communication to be achieved.
8 The **exclusive** MATERIALS of New Typography are those **given** BY THE TASK: the LETTERS and RULES in the typecase. Ornament of even the simplest form (shaded rules!) is superfluous, impermissible.
9 The simplest and therefore only persuasive **form** of European SCRIPT is the **Block**-(sanserif)-**type**.
10 The strongest differentiations can be formed through the use of **bold** and LIGHT weights and different type-sizes.
11 In continuous text setting the current form of SANSERIF is less legible than the OLD STYLE ROMAN type mostly used until now. Technical reasons of reading, compounded by economic considerations, compel us to retain temporarily text typesetting in ROMAN.
12 All important elements (headings, numbering, important parts of the text) will be typeset in SANSERIF of the most contrasting grey-value.
13 **National** typefaces (Fraktur, Textura, Old Slavonic) are **excluded** as generally incomprehensible and as leftovers from history. Economic considerations compound this necessity.
14 In order to heighten the **sensational** effect of New Typography and at the same time to compensate for static, horizontal and vertical elements, diagonal line **directions** are also possible, even DIAGONAL PLACEMENT OF WHOLE LINE GROUPINGS.
15 **Photography** is more persuasive than drawing. With increasing usage and the corresponding reduction in cost of the new reproduction technologies, there is no further obstruction to the exclusive and expanded application of photography as a means of illustration, which we fundamentally aspire to.
16 The realization of these principles, with increasing technological development, will result in a **completely new form for the book**.

1. Letter Tschichold to Kner, 19 June 1925 (Békés Archive).   **2**. Letter Tschichold to Kner, 'Pfingsten' 1925 (Békés Archive).   * For more about this publisher see Schütte, *Die Wölfe*.

Cover of *Kulturschau*, Heft 4, 1925 (presumably not designed by Tschichold) and second spread from his manifesto contained within. Tschichold's comments on the illustrations are as follows: 'El Lissitzky, Russian, one of the early members of the Russian artists' group

UNOWIS (=champions of new art), strives in his typographic design for a representation of the rhythmic and textual stresses of the spoken word with typographical means. The Suprematists are united in UNOWIS. Suprematism is one of the newest Russian forms of art. The illustrated

example of Lissitzky's typography is influenced by the Suprematist method of design. He has now gone over to the Constructivists. ... Ladislaus Moholy-Nagy, Hungarian, is one of the masters at the now dissolved Weimar Bauhaus, and we wish him success in continuing his activity in Dessau.'

With its references to 'economic considerations' and 'minimum means', this is certainly a document of its time and place: of Germany emerging from catastrophic inflation into an economic recovery funded by American loans and accompanying theories of industrial 'rationalization'. The influence of Constructivism is also clear, though not yet explicit. While Tschichold was working towards *Elementare Typographie*, he equated 'elemental typography' with 'Constructivism'.[3] The two illustrations that he included in his piece for *Kulturschau* show work by El Lissitzky and Moholy-Nagy, the two key figures in bringing Constructivism to Germany from Russia and Hungary respectively. He did not regard examples of New Typography from Hungary that he he had seen as very good, as he explained to the Hungarian printer Imre Kner, with whom he corresponded actively at this time:

> But in general it is not much better here. Only a select few individuals work in a rigorous manner, above all also Moholy-Nagy. The most important representative of New Typography, as well as of New 'Art' (for me this expression is unpleasant) is the Russian El Lissitzky ...[4]

The Soviet/Constructivist influence is betrayed by this disdain for 'art', and the similar suspicion of 'literature' indicated by his placing it in quotation marks in his manifesto.

The impact of Lissitzky's work on Tschichold is evident from experiments he made for personal stationery when re-inventing himself as Ivan – compositions from intersecting coloured bars and sanserif type, which resulted in his elegant printed letterhead. His inclination towards Eastern Europe around 1925 is indicated by his designing stationery, publicity and title-pages for the publisher Philobiblon in Warsaw, and letterheads for some clients in Moscow. The same inclination marks his initial attempt to define the new approaches to typography in writing. 'New Typography,' he asserted, 'is founded on the knowledge imparted by the logically consistent work of Russian Suprematism, Dutch Neo-plasticism and especially Constructivism.' So began his exposition of 'Die neue Gestaltung' (New design) in the *Sonderheft* (special issue) *elementare Typographie*, published by the Bildungsverband.[5] 'Bildung' was the revered German, humanist tradition of cultured self-improvement and, in the context of the trade union movement, it was natural for the Bildungsverband's journal to have a left-wing orientation. Its readership consisted mainly of type compositors and apprentices in the field of letterpress printing. In some ways it set itself against the *Zeitschrift für Deutschlands Buchdrucker*, the journal for printing

3. Letter Tschichold to Kner, 'Pfingsten' 1925 (Békés Archive).
4. Letter Tschichold to Kner, 12 June 1925 (Békés Archive). He had seen some examples of modernist typography in the Hungarian journal *Magyar Grafika*.
5. 'Die neue Gestaltung', p.193.

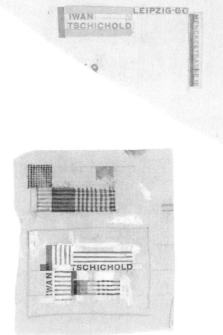

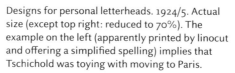

Designs for personal letterheads. 1924/5. Actual size (except top right: reduced to 70%). The example on the left (apparently printed by linocut and offering a simplified spelling) implies that Tschichold was toying with moving to Paris.

house proprietors, which accordingly tended towards the political right in its editorial stance. *Typographische Mitteilungen* provided a friendly environment for Tschichold's communist-tinged exposition.

Here some clarification of the term Constructivism is perhaps in order, given the temptation to use it as a catch-all term. The difficulty of defining it properly stems from its meaning having been far from clear even in its heyday. The term was coined with the founding of the Working Group of Constructivists in March 1921, which arose from vigorous debate on the purpose of art at the Moscow design school, Vkhutemas. Among its members were the artists Alexander Rodchenko, Varvara Stepanova, the Stenberg brothers, Georgii and Vladimir, and the writer & critic Aleksei Gan. The group's written programme countered the Realist manifesto by Naum Gabo and his brother Antoine Pevsner of 1920, which held out for an autonomous value for art.[6] Lissitzky was briefly affiliated with Vkhutemas in 1921, but he was not a member of the Constructivist group; instead he was more closely associated with Suprematism and the Unovis group around Kasimir Malevich at the artistic-technical institute in Vitebsk (Belarus). Lissitzky directed

the workshops of architecture and printing & the graphic arts there between 1919 and 1921. On several occasions after moving to Germany Lissitzky expressed his dislike for the Constructivists' emphasis on utilitarianism, particularly in the trilingual journal *Veshch/Gegenstand/Objet* that he created in Berlin with Ilya Ehrenburg.[7] While taking the part of 'constructive art', this journal sought alignment with other European tendencies, publishing essays by Van Doesburg and Le Corbusier.[8] To confuse matters, Lissitzky was one of the named co-founders, along with Van Doesburg and Hans Richter, of the International Faction of Constructivists that emerged from the International Congress of Progressive Artists held at Düsseldorf in May 1922. Lissitzky once again distanced himself from Constructivism in the book that he co-wrote with Hans Arp covering all of the '-isms of art', *Die Kunstismen* (1925), commenting of it (in the peculiar English of the tri-lingual text): 'The shortsighteds see therein only the machine.'

El Lissitzky and Moholy-Nagy moved in overlapping circles around Berlin, Hanover and Weimar during the early 1920s; in the same constellation were Theo van Doesburg, founder of the Dutch De Stijl movement that espoused

6. The Constructivist manifesto (as reprinted from *Elementare Typographie*) is mistakenly credited to Natan Altman in Gerd Fleischmann's essential sourcebook, *Bauhaus*.
7. See also his lecture 'New Russian art' (1922) in Lissitzky-

Küppers, *El Lissitzky* (p.338), where he accuses 'Tatlin and his colleagues' of 'material-fetishism'. Some scholars believe that *Veshch* was financed by the Soviet state, given that its participants were paid in rubles, although

Peter Nisbet suggests this may simply have been due to the instability of the Reichsmark at that time. (Nisbet, *El Lissitzky 1890–1941*, p.49 n.46.) The Berlin publishers of *Veshch* were the Scythians, a group of Russian emigrés in favour of

revolutionary change in Russia but unsympathetic to Bolshevism. They were evidently unhappy with how the journal developed and so discontinued it after only three issues. For some work by Lissitzky from his Berlin years that escaped

Tschichold's notice see Nisbet's catalogue in *El Lissitzky 1890–1941*, and Victor Margolin's essay in Railing (ed.), *Voices of revolution*.
8. In *The Russian experiment in art* (p.275) Camilla Gray called *Veshch* 'the first post-war, multi-

lingual, international magazine of the visual arts to unite the ideas and personalities which created the international functionalist school of design'.

zeitschrift des bildungsverbandes der deutschen buchdrucker leipzig ● oktoberheft 1925

mitteilungen

typographische

sonderheft

elementare
typographie

natan altman
otto baumberger
herbert bayer
max burchartz
el lissitzky
ladislaus moholy-nagy
molnár f. farkas
johannes molzahn
kurt schwitters
mart stam
ivan tschichold

(Opposite) Cover of *Elementare Typographie*. 1925. 31 × 23.5 cm.

Tschichold's compilation did not occupy the whole of the October 1925 issue of *Typographische Mitteilungen*. The inside cover and first page (above left) show the customary typographic style of the magazine.

The title page for *Elementare Typographie* occurs some pages into the publication, signalling the beginning of Tschichold's own typographic design.

As one of the first extensive jobs of text design done by Tschichold, his typography here was a little raw. For example, the way that the column width of the main text changes arbitrarily was a feature never to reappear in his later work. (Compare the book illustrated on pp.220–1 below.)

Neo-plasticism, and Kurt Schwitters, who moved from Dada via De Stijl to Constructivism. Teachers at the Bauhaus generally kept their distance from the play of sometimes mutually attracting and then repelling '-isms' in the art world. They were absent from the seemingly contradictory 'Constructivist and Dadaist Congress' held in the home town of the Bauhaus, Weimar, and organized by Van Doesburg, who had installed himself there in 1921 in the vain hope of getting a job on the Bauhaus staff. Along with Lissitzky, Moholy-Nagy did attend this conference but he had not yet been appointed as director of the preliminary course at the Bauhaus, a position he took up in spring of 1923.

Moholy-Nagy was a former law student who, on returning from service in the First World War, became associated with the avant-garde magazine *Ma* (Today), created by Lajos Kassak and published in Budapest from 1916. *Ma* supported the brief Hungarian Soviet Republic of 1919, and so Kassak and Moholy-Nagy had to flee Hungary when that regime was suppressed. Kassak settled in Vienna, where *Ma* continued to be published, taking on an increasingly Constructivist outlook. Moholy-Nagy set out for Germany, working as a sign painter to pay his way from Vienna to Berlin. There he was able to exhibit his paintings at Herwarth Walden's Sturm gallery in early 1922, and he also designed covers for Walden's publication of the same name. *Der Sturm* had close links with *Ma* in Vienna, and Moholy-Nagy functioned as the latter's correspondent in Berlin, co-editing with Kassak the *Buch neuer Künstler* (Book of new artists; 1922), an important compilation of contemporary artistic trends. There was a large, artistic community of Russian and Hungarian exiles in Berlin; El Lissitzky arrived there in late 1921 and visited Moholy-Nagy in his studio.

Spreads from *Elementare Typographie*, including Bauhaus work by Moholy-Nagy and his article 'Typo-photo'. The illustration of the Bauhaus prospectus was not photographically reproduced but recomposed in the typefaces used for the special issue.

(Below right) Illustration of Lissitzky's cover to *For the voice* (the original was printed on buff card). Tschichold gave the date of 1922/3 for Lissitzky's design of the book.

Moholy-Nagy was the most important figure at the Bauhaus in the new approach to typography, bringing demands for machine-age dynamism and directness, along with theories of rationalization. Despite a certain lack of finesse in the handling of type, his typographic design of the catalogue for the Bauhaus exhibition of 1923 was an incunable of New Typography. With a cover by Moholy-Nagy's best pupil in typography, Herbert Bayer, it made a bold statement: titles in large sanserif capitals, with author's names running vertically up the left-hand margin; bold sanserif types used, along with heavy structural rules, to organize the contents list. The catalogue contained Moholy-Nagy's seminal essay, 'Die neue Typographie', in which he stressed the possibilities in New Typography for effects of contrast and, above all, the need for clarity – both points that Tschichold would soon elaborate in greater detail.[9]

Tschichold's contact with Moholy-Nagy flourished into a close and lasting friendship. Both the journal *Ma* and the *Buch neuer Künstler* are included in the useful list of relevant works given in *Elementare Typographie*.[10] It also contained Moholy-Nagy's text 'Typo-photo', an excerpt from his Bauhaus book, *Malerei, Fotografie, Film* (1925). Tschichold explained in the notes at the back of his publication that it was first envisioned as a Bauhaus book, but that 'the Bauhaus is however only one base in the front-line of new

9. True to his enduring interests in film and photography, the main theme of Moholy-Nagy's essay is that photography should be the illustrative technique of the future. Essay reprinted in Fleischmann, *Bauhaus*, and translated in Kostelanetz (ed.), *Moholy-Nagy*.

10. Another Hungarian, Farkas Molnár, whose cover design for *Ma* is illustrated in *Elementare Typographie*, was a student at the Bauhaus between 1921 and 1925. Tschichold is likely to have seen some of his work in the crucial Weimar exhibition of 1923. Inspired by

Van Doesburg's Weimar classes, Molnár led a rationalist group among Bauhaus students to counter the mysticism of Johannes Itten, who directed the preliminary course. On returning to Budapest Molnár became an important, modernist architect.

Spread from *Elementare Typographie* illustrating a personal postcard for Tschichold (left) and Herbert Bayer's million mark banknote (right). Variations were printed of Bayer's banknotes with different colours: one million mark notes survive in at least two variants with yellow and turquoise used respectively as second colours; there may also have been a red variant of it, but its reproduction in red here was also determined by that being the only colour available.

culture'. It probably became clear to him through contact with Moholy-Nagy that typography had no real firm footing yet at the Bauhaus; this, combined with the administrative and economic difficulties that delayed the appearance of the first Bauhaus books, may have encouraged him to look elsewhere for a publisher.

Although Tschichold made it clear in *Elementare Typographie* that the Bauhaus was not the only place in which New Typography was practised, he naturally realized the importance of the institution: not only did he cultivate strong links with several of its staff members active in typography, but he also personally ordered a matching table and chair (with horsehair upholstery) directly from the Bauhaus, and requested details of a bench designed by Marcel Breuer and a rug based on a design by Paul Klee.[11] Presumably through Moholy-Nagy Tschichold began to correspond with Herbert Bayer from early in 1925. The Austrian Bayer, of a similar age to Tschichold, began his working life with apprenticeships in architectural studios, followed by two years' study at the Weimar Bauhaus (1921–3). After a year travelling in Italy he took up the position as 'master' of the Bauhaus printing workshop, which was only established properly as the Reklameabteilung (publicity department) at Dessau in spring 1927.[12] It was during his student years at the Bauhaus, during the period of astronomical inflation, that Bayer designed the remarkable, emergency banknotes for the Thuringian state bank. It seems somewhat incongruous that these uniquely modernist contributions to banknote design were made for

a dying currency, the Reichsmark soon to be replaced by the Rentenmark. Tschichold included Bayer's million mark note in *Elementare Typographie*, having been able to acquire examples of his typography directly from him during preparation of the publication.

Although it had already been decided at the beginning of 1925 that *Elementare Typographie* would be published in *Typographische Mitteilungen*, and not as a Bauhaus book, Tschichold continued to discuss collaboration with Bayer on a possible Bauhaus publication about 'advertising and typography'. The project was postponed and then never realized; in any case Bayer informed Tschichold that a book exclusively about Bauhaus advertising should appear first, and that he himself was planning to put together a book about typography and type (*Schrift*), although no such books by him were ever projected under the Bauhaus books imprint.[13] Bayer's difficulty in achieving these scholarly ambitions led him to appreciate Tschichold in the role of contemporary, typographical historian, and so it was not long before he suggested that Tschichold write an article on the theme of designing standardized letterheads. This was an issue that they discussed with some enthusiasm, indicating the excitement felt by some modernists for standardization in the area of printing. Bayer gave Tschichold the details of a firm in Dessau which manufactured inexpensive window envelopes for use with letters that accorded with DIN standards. This seems trivial now, but it must be remembered that these standards were quite new in the 1920s. Bayer told Tschichold that he had hoped to write a

11. Tschichold's initial order was confirmed in a letter of 17 August 1925 signed by Gropius. Bauhaus Gmbh informed Tschichold that the Klee rug did not unfortunately cost 80 marks, as originally quoted, but that, due to the complexity of the design, it would cost between 280 and 300 marks. Letters Bauhaus Gmbh to Tschichold, November 1925.

12. Letter Bayer to Tschichold, 21 March 1927. At the Weimar Bauhaus there were only manual presses for printmaking, as the printing machinery had been seized in 1914 from its precursor, the Großherzogliche Kunstschule, as personal property of its Belgian director, Henry van de Velde, who became an enemy alien at the outbreak of the First World War. See Nonne-Schmidt & Loew, *Joost Schmidt: Lehre und Arbeit am Bauhaus 1919–32*, p.19.

13. Letter Bayer to Tschichold, 30 October 1925. Something of Bayer's project may have been realized in the special Bauhaus issue of *Offset*. Among the Bauhaus books that were initially listed but never appeared was one by Lissitzky entitled 'Reklame und Typographie'.

short article about the new kind of 'commercial letter', but had not managed to complete it:

> due to standardization a new type [of letter] is developing (or will develop) which is encapsulated by the designed concept of the 'letterhead'.
>
> as you can handle a pen well, are you not interested in writing something? if so, i can put my illustrative material at your disposal. ... i believe that we two are the first to deal with this. it would be a shame to miss the opportunity to publish something.[14]

Bayer realized the value of having an article published about an approach in this area that he felt was new and original, and naturally perceived the potential for good publicity in being featured in Tschichold's writings about New Typography. He keenly kept Tschichold supplied with examples of his own design work in an exchange of material that lasted until 1933 (and possibly beyond).[15] Consequently Bayer's design work is represented in equal measure (although lesser quantity) to that of Lissitzky in the publication.

More decisive for the content of *Elementare Typographie* than his Bauhaus connection was Tschichold's interest in Russian Constructivism and his contact with El Lissitzky, whom he described as the leading figure (*Führer*) of New Typography. In his endnotes to *Elementare Typographie*, Tschichold explained:

> Therefore it was necessary that the projected issue did not restrict itself to the typographic work already carried out at the BAUHAUS, but instead took into account the work from ALL lands where representatives in this field are to be found. Foremost among these is Russia, represented by Lissitzky, the archetype of the new designer, who counts among the best practitioners of New Typography.[16]

He realized that Lissitzky was a key to his understanding of how contemporary typography related to non-objective painting, and it was through Moholy-Nagy that he contacted Lissitzky in January 1925. Tschichold may well have seen typographic work done by other Russian revolutionary artists, most probably acquiring some issues of the Constructivist journal *Lef* with its striking design by Alexander Rodchenko, but personal contact with them would have been rendered difficult by the geographical, political and language barriers.[17] Although it was his passion for Soviet art and design that had inspired him to change his name from Johannes to Ivan, Tschichold never travelled to the USSR, and, despite his Slavic ancestry, he had not inherited any significant Slavic language skills.[18] Lissitzky, on the other hand, had a more than adequate, if not quite perfect, mastery of German, having trained in Darmstadt as an architect before the First World War and worked in Berlin between 1921 and 1924. Tschichold was therefore able to correspond easily with him.

After the Rapallo and Locarno treaties had normalized relations between the USSR and Germany, and especially in the more liberal climate created by the Soviet New Economic Policy, many more Russians travelled freely to Germany: there grew up a kind of 'special relationship' between the two countries, with the Comintern still actively hoping that Germany was next on the roster of World Revolution.[19] It has been suggested that Lissitzky went to Germany after the revolution in a semi-official capacity to help in 'launching a modified concept of Constructivism in the West as part of an overall strategy intended to promote a radical, international art movement in Europe'.[20] Certainly his boundless energy for travelling throughout Europe adds weight to this idea, although there is no supporting evidence in his letters to Tschichold or the copious correspondence with his German wife, Sophie, which all deal with personal and artistic matters.[21] Yet, if it was partly Lissitzky's intention to spread the influence of communist culture, then Tschichold certainly helped him by his bias towards Eastern Europe and Constructivism. By the time of compiling *Elementare Typographie*, Tschichold knew of the Dutch De Stijl group and its eponymous journal but he included no illustration of De Stijl typography in comparison to five items of Lissitzky's work.

Opposite: (Above) The programme of the Constructivists as published in Tschichold's German adaptation, accompanied by examples of Lissitzky's work. The cover of *Broom* is entirely reconfigured based on a sketch sent to Tschichold. (Below) Thumbnails of *A tale of two squares*.

14. Letter Bayer to Tschichold, 7 April 1926.

15. In an article about the use of gothic type for display with roman type ('Gebrochene Schriften als Auszeichnung zur Antiqua' [1939]) Tschichold illustrates a book designed by Bayer showing the opposite usage.

16. *Elementare Typographie*, p.212. Tschichold apparently planned a second publication soon after his first that was to be dedicated entirely to Russian typography, with 16 pages of colour illustrations reserved for Lissitzky, but nothing came of this. See Lissitzky-Küppers, *El Lissitzky*, p.68.

17. Moholy-Nagy was in contact with Rodchenko already by 1923, and it is likely that Tschichold would have become aware of his work through this connection, although he did not establish personal contact with Rodchenko until later (see p.112). Moholy-Nagy wrote to Rodchenko in December 1923 asking him to write about Constructivism for a projected Bauhaus publication: 'We are quite lacking the collaboration of our Russian comrades (those living in Russia) and we are not entirely certain that the statements and positions of the here well-known Lissitzky and Gabo are valid for all Russian artists.' Cited in *Rodtschenko: Aufsätze, autobiographische Notizen, Briefe, Erinnerungen*, p.172. *Lef* was also referred to by Trotsky in his book *Literature and revolution*, which was published in German in 1924 and which Tschichold had read, quoting from it in 'Die neue Gestaltung'.

18. It seems that he applied himself to learning some Russian. A letter of 19 June 1925, in which he explained to Kner the relationship of Lissitzky's typography in *A tale of two squares* to the phonetics of the Russian language, shows that he was able to extract a great deal of sense from that text, seemingly without Lissitzky having explained it to him in any detail. (Békés Archive.)

19. Willett, *The new sobriety*, p.72.

20. Lodder, 'El Lissitzky and the export of Constructivism' in Perloff & Reed (ed.), *Situating El Lissitzky*, p.36. Willett suggested that Lissitzky's principal reason for going to Berlin was to help organize the First Russian Art exhibition that opened in October 1922 (*The new sobriety*, p.76). Nisbet cites a draft autobiographical statement of 1941 in asserting that Lissitzky was working for the publishing division of the Comintern in 1921 (*El Lissitzky 1890–1941*, p.48).

21. See Lissitzky-Küppers, *El Lissitzky*. In *El Lissitzky: beyond the abstract cabinet*, Margarita Tupitsyn publishes some other letters from the 1930s that do reflect close links with influential Soviet leaders, which was inevitable considering his (and his wife's) involvment in designing official propaganda at that time.

PROGRAMM DER KONSTRUKTIVISTEN

Die Konstruktivisten stellen sich die Gestaltung des Stoffes zur Aufgabe. Grundlage ihrer Arbeit sind wissenschaftliche Erkenntnisse. Um die Voraussetzung dafür herbeizuführen, dass diese Erkenntnisse in praktischer Arbeit verwertet werden, erstreben die Konstruktivisten die Schaffung des sinnvollen Zusammenhangs (die Synthese) aller Wissens- und Schaffensgebiete.
Alleinige und grundlegende Voraussetzung des Konstruktivismus sind die Erkenntnisse des historischen Materialismus. Das Experiment der Sowjets liess die Konstruktivisten die Notwendigkeit erkennen, dass ihre bisherige, ausserhalb des Lebens stehende, durch wissenschaftliche Versuche ausgefüllte Tätigkeit auf das Gebiet des Wirklichen zu verlegen ist und in der Lösung praktischer Aufgaben ihre Berechtigung erweisen muss.

DIE ARBEITSMITTEL DER KONSTRUKTIVISTEN SIND:

1. Faktur, **2.** Tektonik, **3.** Konstruktion.
Die *Faktur* ist das mit technischer Notwendigkeit ausgewählte und bearbeitete Material.
Die *Tektonik* erwächst aus der, dem Zweck des zu schaffenden Gegenstands entsprechenden, Ausnützung des Materials.

El Lissitzky 1922: Verkleinertes Titelblatt einer amerikanischen Zeitschrift

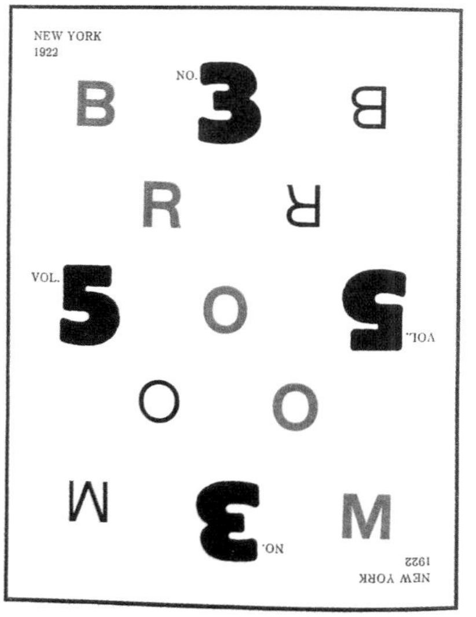
NEW YORK
1922
NO.
VOL.

196

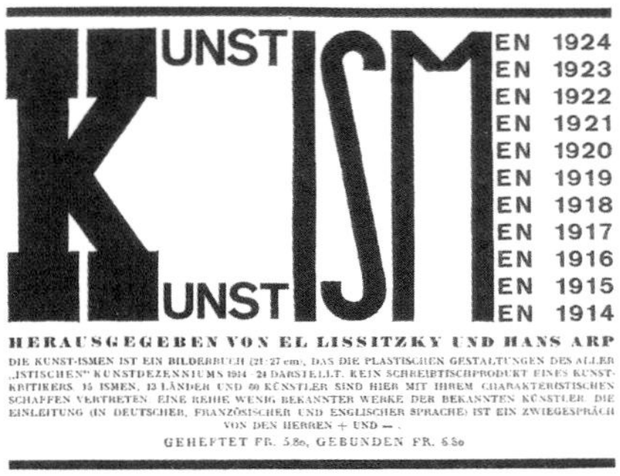
KUNSTISMEN 1924
EN 1923
EN 1922
EN 1921
EN 1920
EN 1919
EN 1918
EN 1917
EN 1916
EN 1915
EN 1914
HERAUSGEGEBEN VON EL LISSITZKY UND HANS ARP
DIE KUNST-ISMEN IST EIN BILDERBUCH (21·27 cm), DAS DIE PLASTISCHEN GESTALTUNGEN DES ALLER „ISTISCHEN" KUNSTDEZENNIUMS 1914–24 DARSTELLT. KEIN SCHREIBTISCHPRODUKT EINES KUNSTKRITIKERS. 15 ISMEN, 13 LÄNDER UND 60 KÜNSTLER SIND HIER MIT IHREM CHARAKTERISTISCHEN SCHAFFEN VERTRETEN. EINE REIHE WENIG BEKANNTER WERKE DER BEKANNTEN KÜNSTLER. DIE EINLEITUNG (IN DEUTSCHER, FRANZÖSISCHER UND ENGLISCHER SPRACHE) IST EIN ZWIEGESPRÄCH VON DEN HERREN + UND –.
GEHEFTET FR. 5.80, GEBUNDEN FR. 6.80

El Lissitzky 1924: Inserat

Die *Konstruktion* (die Gestaltung) ist eine bis zum Äussersten gehende, formende Tätigkeit: die Organisation des Materials. Nur jeweilige wissenschaftliche Erkenntnisse vermögen der Tektonik oder der Konstruktion Grenzen zu ziehen.

DIE STOFFLICHEN MITTEL SIND:

1. Stoff überhaupt. Die Kenntnis seiner Entstehung und der Veränderungen, die er in der Rohproduktion und in der Verarbeitung erfährt. Seine Eigentümlichkeiten, seine Bedeutung für die Wirtschaft, seine Beziehung zu andern Stoffen.
2. Die Erscheinungsformen des Stoffes in Raum und Licht: Volumen (die räumliche Ausdehnung), Oberfläche, Farbe. Der Stoff an sich und seine Erscheinungsform können nicht getrennt betrachtet werden, darum stehen die Konstruktivisten im gleichen Verhältnis zu beiden von ihnen.

DIE AUFGABEN DER KONSTRUKTIVISTEN SIND:

1. Herstellung einer Verbindung mit allen Produktionszentren und Haupteinrichtungen des Landes; **2.** Konstruktion von Plänen; **3.** Organisation von Ausstellungen; **4.** Agitation in der Presse:
a) Die Gruppe erklärt rücksichtslosen Krieg gegen alle Kunst.
b) Sie erweist die Unmöglichkeit eines allmählichen Übergangs der vergangenen künstlerischen Kultur in die konstruktiven Formen der neuen Gesellschaft.
c) Sie strebt an, dass die intellektuelle Produktion gleichberechtigt neben der realen Produktion am Aufbau der neuen Kultur teilnimmt. (NACH DEM RUSSISCHEN. Deutsche Bearbeitung von I. T.)

Unser einziger Fehler war, uns mit der sogenannten Kunst überhaupt ernsthaft beschäftigt zu haben. GEORGE GROSZ

197

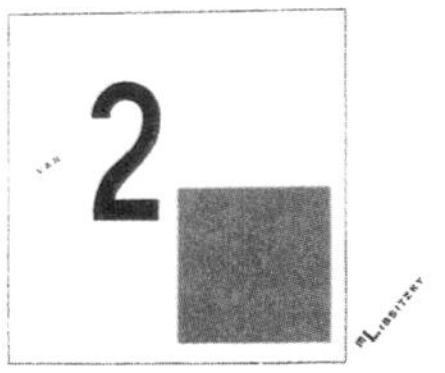
2

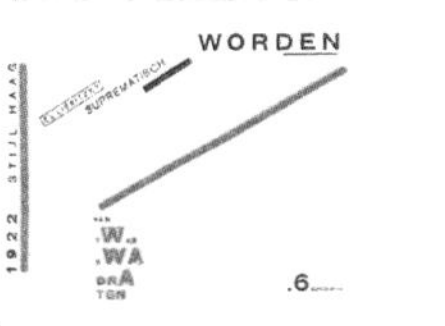
WORDEN
SUPREMATISCH
1922 STIJL HAAG
.6

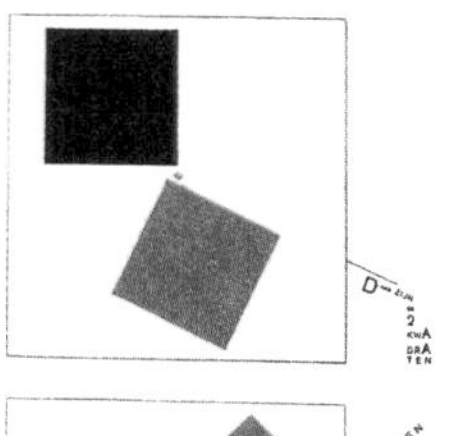

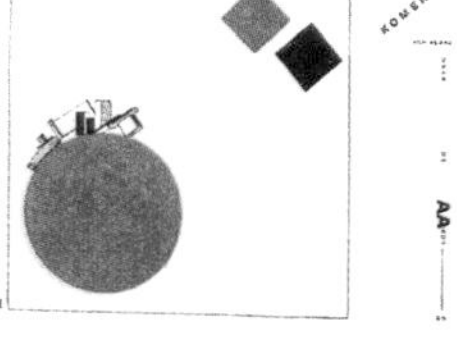

← Dies sind die verkleinerten Bilder eines Kinderbuchs, der MÄR VON ZWEI QUADRATEN von EL LISSITZKY (konstruiert in Witebsk [Russland] 1920) ● Die Übersetzung lautet: **1** Von 2 ■ El Lissitzky **2** El Lissitzky: Suprematische Mär von zwei Quadraten in 6 Konstruktionen **3** das sind die 2 Quadrate **4** kommen von ferne auf die Erde — und **5** und sehen eine schwarze Wüste **6** ein Stoss — alles stürzt **7** und auf schwarzem Gebild klar — wahr **8** hier Ende — und vorwärts ● Die wirkliche Grösse verhält sich zu diesen Abbildungen fast genau wie 3 : 1. Abgebildet ist die holländische Ausgabe, die im Verlag der Zeitschrift »De Stijl«, Clamart (Seine), Frankreich, 64 avenue Schneider, erschien (fast vergriffen). Die ursprüngliche Ausgabe in russischer Sprache erschien im Skythen-Verlag, Berlin-Grunewald, Karlsbader Strasse 16. Der typographische Satz neben den Bildern ist ein Beispiel für die Forderung Lissitzkys, dass Typographie den Zug- und Druckspannungen des Inhalts entsprechen müsse. (Lissitzky: Die Wörter des gedruckten Bogens werden abgesehen, nicht abgehört.)

Der erste Maler, der (schon vor dem Kriege) versucht hatte, mit elementaren Mitteln elementare, gesetzmässige Beziehungen von Farbe, Form, Licht, Zeit zu gestalten, war der Führer des russischen SUPREMATISMUS: Kasimir *Malewitsch*. Seine Werke: elementare Beziehungen abstrakter farbiger und unbunter Flächen im unendlichen weissen Raum. Die konsequente Arbeit dieses Malers führt das Bild als Flächengestaltung auf den Nullpunkt. 1919 hört der Suprematismus auf. Eins der Bilder Malewitschs ist das schwarze Quadrat (auf weisser quadratischer Grundfläche). Die westliche Parallelerscheinung ist der holländische NEOPLASTIZISMUS *(Mondrian, van Doesburg)*, der räumlich-dynamischen (bewegten) Gestaltung des Suprematismus entgegengesetzt durch flächig-statische Form.
Der Russe *El Lissitzky* (el) ist der Erfinder des von ihm so benannten PROUN. Das ist eine Bildform. Lissitzky fasst die Splitterteile der Gestaltungen des Suprematismus zusammen und schafft Werke, die inspiriert sind von der Phantasie eines von der Schönheit und den ausserordentlichen Möglichkeiten der modernen Technik restlos begeisterten Künstlers. Seine Prounen sind Illusionen von Spannungen plastisch-gesehener Körper in unendlichen Räumen. Der Schritt von dieser Arbeit, die, mit Ausnahme des Proun, noch immer Illusionen, wenn auch abstrakte (gegenstandslose), gab, zu einer realen (wirklichen) Gestaltung war klein. Das Ende des Krieges, in allen Ländern gleich niederschlagend, zwang diesen Schritt geradezu herbei. Was die Kubisten, unter ihnen besonders Picasso, schon vor dem Kriege versucht hatten, die Einbeziehung dem Bilde bisher fremder Materialien (Metall, Papier, Holz), führten die Russen konsequent weiter — an die Stelle der durch die Farbe gegebenen Illusionen trat die ausschliessliche Verwendung *wirklicher* Stoffe: Blech, Draht, Glas, Holz usw., anfänglich charakterisiert durch das sogenannte Konterrelief *Tatlins* (KONSTRUKTIVISMUS). Die Bedeutung dieser Arbeit liegt weniger in ihrem zwar neuen, doch immerhin ästhetischen Moment, als darin, dass sich die Künstler nunmehr mit wirklichen Materialien beschäftigten und die Beziehungen der neuen Stoffe zueinander studierten. Es ist unwesentlich, dass diese Bewegung im Anfang einem Romantismus: der Liebe zu den Maschinen, Apparaten, den *neuen* Dingen, entsprang; denn fast zu gleicher Zeit setzte, in ihr gegründet, die *reale Gestaltung von Gegenständen* ein.
Diese Bewegung beginnt mit Entwurf und Modell des Turms der Dritten Internationale von Tatlin (Moskau 1918). Hier war ein »Gegenstand«, ein Bauwerk von ungeheurem Ausmass, eine Spirale aus Glas und Eisen, 200 m höher als der Eiffelturm, ein grosser Ausdruck der Bewegung, die in der russischen Revolution den ersten weltpolitischen Erfolg errang. Aber kein blosses Denkmal: ein Zweckbau, mit Räumen für das EKKI (Exekutiv-Komitee der Kommunistischen Internationale), die Museen der Revolution, eine wissenschaftliche Versuchs- und Funkstation. Trotzki hat in 194

195 seinem Buche »Literatur und Revolution« an diesem Bauwerk eine berechtigte Kritik geübt. Er setzt an ihm aus, dass für Tatlin der Zweck doch immerhin im Hintergrund gestanden habe, dass er noch zu sehr von frei-künstlerischen Gesichtspunkten ausgegangen sei. Das ist sicher richtig, mindert aber nicht die grundsätzliche Bedeutung dieser Schöpfung, die den Anfang der Bewegung darstellt, die sich die Gestaltung der Gegenstände des wirklichen Lebens zur Aufgabe gestellt hat und die früher den Namen »Konstruktivismus« trug.* Die deutsche, übrigens unabhängige Parallelbewegung findet in der Gründung des WEIMARER BAUHAUSES durch *Walter Gropius* ihren Ausdruck. Auch in Russland gibt es ein »Bauhaus«, die 1918 in Moskau gegründete Schule WCHUTEMAS (Abkürzung des russischen Ausdrucks für »Höhere Staatliche Kunstwerkstätten«). Beide, unabhängig und ohne Wissen voneinander zu fast gleicher Zeit gegründet, führte ihre konsequente Arbeit auf denselben Weg: Die Einordnung des gesamten künstlerischen Schaffens in den Bau, in dem es ja erst Sinn erhält. Darum ist auch die erste grosse Leistung des Bauhauses nicht die Schaffung neuer »schönerer« Bilder, sondern der Bau des Musterhauses, des »Hauses am Horn« in Weimar, das man zur Bauhaus-Ausstellung im September 1923 dort sah. An dieser Stelle mag ein Auszug aus dem oben genannten ausgezeichneten Buche von *Trotzki* Platz finden:

»Die Scheidewand zwischen Kunst und Industrie wird fallen. Der künftige grosse Stil wird nicht verzierend, sondern formierend sein. Es wäre irrig, wollte man dies deuten als Liquidierung der Kunst, als deren Selbstausschaltung vor der Technik. Für die Schaffung eines »idealen« Gegenstandes bedarf es, abgesehen von der Beherrschung des Materials und der Bearbeitungsmethoden, auch noch der Phantasie und des Geschmackes. Ganz im Einklang mit der ganzen Tendenz der Industriekultur glauben wir, dass die künstlerische Phantasie auf dem Gebiete der Produktion der materiellen Güter sich mit der Aufstellung der idealen Form des Gegenstandes als solchem befassen wird und nicht mit der Verzierung als künstlerischer Gratisbeilage zu dem Gegenstande selbst. Das bedeutet keineswegs eine Liquidierung der Werkkunst, nicht einmal in entfernter Zukunft. In den Vordergrund wird wahrscheinlich die unmittelbare Zusammenarbeit mit allen übrigen Zweigen der Technik rücken.«

Die Kunst der Zukunft wird die Grenzen der bisherigen sogenannten Kunst überschreiten und sich wahrscheinlich mehr und mehr der PHOTOGRAPHIE und des FILMS bedienen. Auf diesen Gebieten haben schon gearbeitet: der in Paris lebende Amerikaner *Man Ray* (abstrakte Photographie), der leider kürzlich verstorbene schwedische Maler *Viking Eggeling*, die Deutschen *Hans Richter* und *L. Hirschfeld-Mack* (abstrakter Film, reflektorische Lichtspiele), *Moholy-Nagy, Fernand Léger* (mechanischer Film).
Wann unsre, von einer neuen Ethik erfüllten Bestrebungen allgemein anerkannt sein werden, wann sie sich völlig durchsetzen können, das hängt von Umständen ab, die wir einzelnen nicht beherrschen oder gar bestimmen können. Aber dass sie sich durchsetzen werden, ist sicher, und unsre objektive, unpersönliche, für Alle bestimmte kollektive Arbeit bildet die bestimmte Gewähr dafür.

* Das Wort »Konstruktivismus« wurde in Russland aufgebracht. Es bezeichnete eine Kunst, die an Stelle des konventionellen Materials modernes Konstruktionsmaterial verwendet. Auf dem Internationalen Kongress in Düsseldorf, Mai 1922, wurde der Name Konstruktivismus (allerdings in verändertem Sinn, s. Stijl Nr. 8, Jahrgang V) von der Opposition aufgenommen.
Da ich zusammen mit meinen Freunden Doesburg und Lissitzky an dieser Proklamation des Konstruktivismus »schuld« bin, so will ich auch seine Beerdigung beginnen: Das, was heute unter diesem Namen geht, hat nichts mehr mit elementarer Gestaltung, unsrer Forderung auf dem Kongress, zu tun. Der Name wurde damals aufgenommen als Losungswort derjenigen, die sich sowohl um eine Gesetzmässigkeit des künstlerischen Ausdrucks als auch um sinnvoll zeitgemässe Aufgabe bemühen gegenüber einer Majorität des Kongresses der Individualisten. (Kongressbericht siehe: Stijl Nr. 4, Jahrg. V.) Inzwischen hat die Kunsthandel-Ölbildmalerei sich den Namen zugelegt und unter Konstruktivismus marschieren die Individualisten, Arrangeure, Ölmaler, Dekorativisten, die gesamte Spekulation. *Hans Richter* (in »Pasmo«).

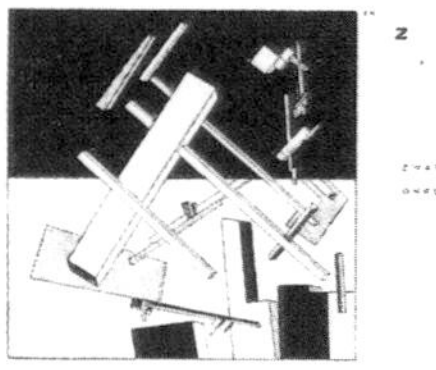

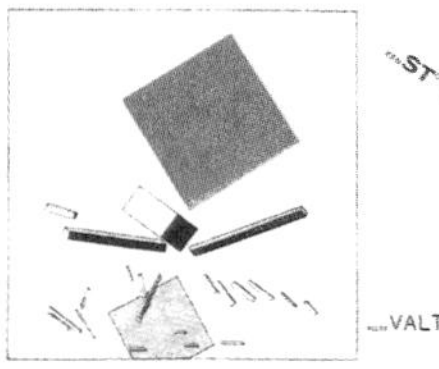

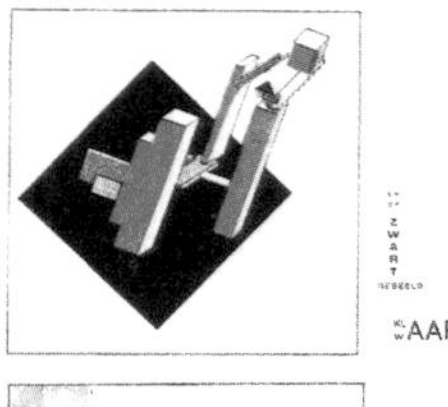

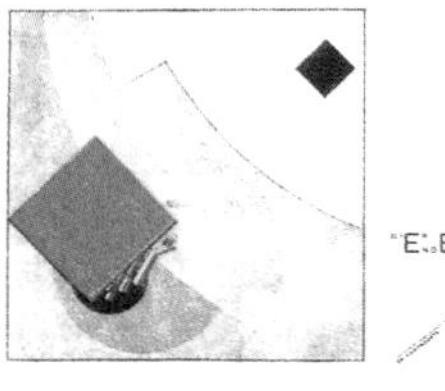

Tschichold's manifesto within *Elementare Typographie*. 1925.

In his introductory essay to *Elementare Typographie*, 'Die neue Gestaltung', Tschichold's approach to the very recent history of Constructivism was scholarly and clear. He had obviously absorbed Lissitzky's views but he was reluctant to jettison its origins in his own advocacy of it. He stated:

> It is not important that this movement derived originally from a romanticism: the love of machines, gadgets and *new* things; for almost simultaneously, as a central part of it, the *real design of objects* established itself. [22]

Tschichold's compilation contains the Constructivists' Programme in an edited and abridged – one might even say adulterated – German version adapted by Tschichold himself. The Marxist-Leninist rhetoric of the original is significantly toned down: for example, the proclamation in the original that reads 'Our sole ideology is scientific communism based on the theory of historical materialism' loses the reference to scientific communism in Tschichold's version.[23] He was obviously tailoring the text for his readership in

Germany, where the November Revolution immediately after the First World War had been ruthlessly suppressed. The German Communist Party leaders, Karl Liebknecht and Rosa Luxemburg, were murdered in cold blood on 15 January 1919 by right-wing, counter-revolutionary troops with the tacit acceptance of the Social Democrat government of the Weimar Republic itself.

Tschichold himself called for an 'objective, impersonal, collective work destined for all', espousing a vaguely leftwing but not overtly communist point of view common to many statements from this period of International Constructivism in Germany. Despite quoting Trotsky in *Elementare Typographie*, Tschichold did not belong to the German Communist Party, nor was he associated with any particular '-ism' or group, apart from the Ring 'neue Werbegestalter' later in the 1920s and early 1930s, which had no political dimension.[24]

22. 'Die neue Gestaltung', p.194. Italic in original.
23. Quotation from Christina Lodder's translation of the Russian original in Harrison & Wood (ed.) *Art in theory 1900–2000*, p.342. Tschichold commented mysteriously in his notes at the end of the publication that the structure of the Constructivists' programme needed alteration. The original Russian text was published in the journal *Ermitazh* (no.13, 1922) and in the Constructivists' organ, *Lef* (no.1, 1923). The Hungarian journal *Egység* (Unity; based in Vienna, later in Berlin) published an English translation (no.2, June 1922), which is reprinted in [Naum] *Gabo: constructions, sculpture, paintings, drawings, engravings* (London: Lund Humphries, 1957), where he entitles the it the 'The program of the Productivist group' and dates it 1921. This version is reprinted with an erroneous date of 1920 in Benton & Sharp (ed.), *Form and function*, pp.91–2. Tschichold's version seems to be the first appearance of the text in German and has hitherto not been taken into account in the bibliography of Constructivism.
24. *Elementare Typographie* does display a quotation from Georg Grosz, a member of the KPD and leading light in the association of communist artists, Rote Gruppe.

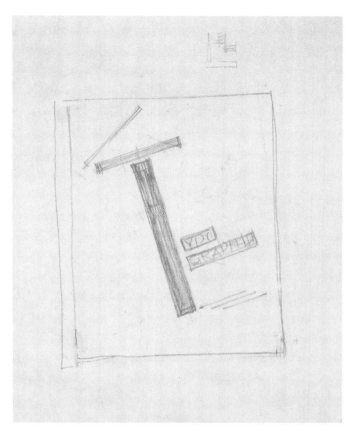

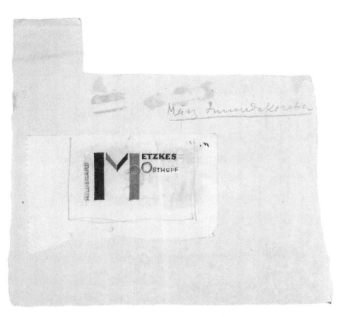

Sketches by Tschichold. c.1925. 56% of actual size. These show the strong influence of Lissitzky: note the similarity of the 'elementally' constructed 'M' on the right to that in the spread from *For the voice*, illustrated opposite (turned 90°) in *Elementare Typographie*.

One of the texts chosen by Tschichold for reprinting in his special issue of *Typographische Mitteilungen* is Natan Altman's manifesto 'Elementare Gesichtspunkte' (Elemental points of view), which first appeared in the German Constructivist journal *G* (*Gestaltung* – the title was Lissitzky's idea). Although none of Altman's graphic work is illustrated, Tschichold refers to him as among 'the best representatives of new Russian art', being not only a painter and sculptor, but designing stage settings and 'the decorative architectonic for Meetings in Moscow'.[25] Altman had in fact been appointed head of the Petrograd section of the fine arts department within Narkompros (People's commissariat for enlightenment) in 1918 and was responsible for decorating the Winter Palace square for the celebrations of the first anniversary of the Revolution.[26] He also designed several commemorative postage stamps, including a striking modernist design of 1922. Altman's manifesto is in the spirit of the original Constructivist Programme, criticizing art for its own sake as self-indulgent and instead calling for: 'Designing with forms that are dependent on the precise laws determined by the natural qualities of the material, and created with the intention of serving society.' Tschichold's own manifesto text applies similar principles to the practice of typography (see appendix A). In this way, the editorial direction of the publication as a whole calls on the original hard line of Constructivism, while softening it with the views and work of Lissitzky, who was partly responsible for spreading a less politically charged idea of Constructivism in Germany, and was criticized from within the Soviet Union for it. The 'Prouns' that he began in 1920 are a synthesis of Suprematism and Constructivism.

Although Tschichold respectfully placed the 'Programme of the Constructivists', with its declared 'retrospective war on all art', before his own manifesto for typography, he deliberately did not brand his own text, or the publication as a whole, as 'Constructivist'. Instead he chose the more neutral term 'elemental typography', which he felt better fitted the 'sense of our work'. As he explained in his scrupulous endnotes: 'In the end the misleading name of "Constructivism", which has been brought into disrepute by fellow travellers, should be avoided.'[27] Additionally he may have seen the pitfalls of adopting the Soviet-tinged term in a publication to be distributed in the generally conservative German printing trade: in not doing so he would usefully have avoided alienating certain segments of his potential readership any more than he was already bound to do.

25. Tschichold's notes in *Elementare Typographie*, p.212: English word 'Meetings' in original.

26. See Gray, *The Russian experiment in art*, pp.230–2. Altman was also a professor at the Petrograd Free Studios, and came to Berlin in connection with the 1922 Russian art exhibition, in which his work was shown.

27. Tschichold must have taken seriously the opinion of Hans Richter, one of the founders of International Constructivism, that 'what goes under this name today has nothing more to do with elemental design'. (Richter quoted from the Czech Devětsil journal *Pásmo* in 'Die neue Gestaltung', p.195.) The title of Altman's manifesto and the full title of the journal *G – Zeitschrift für elementare Gestaltung* (Journal for elemental design; co-edited by Richter) are likely to have inspired Tschichold's choice of title. In October 1921 *De Stijl* had also published a manifesto, 'Aufruf zur Elementaren Kunst' (Appeal for an elemental art) by Moholy-Nagy, Ivan Puni, Raoul Hausmann and Hans Arp.

1925 JANUAR 19.

HERRN EL.LISSITZKI, AMBRI-SOTTO, TESSIN, SCHWEIZ.

SEHR GEEHRTER HERR LISSITZKI,

ICH VEROEFFENTLICHE GERADE EINE ARBEIT UEBER KONSTRUKTIVI-
STISCHE TYPOGRAPHIE. TROTZ GROSSER ANSTRENGUNGEN IST ES MIR
NICHT GELUNGEN, VON IHREN MIR BEKANNT GEWORDENEN ARBEITEN
(MAJAKOWSKIJ: DLJA GOLSSA UND DIE ZEITSCHRIFT L' OBJET)
UEBERHAUPT ETWAS ZU BESCHAFFEN. NUN MUESSEN SIE ABER UNBE-
DINGT IN DIESEM AUFSATZ, DER IN DEN "TYPOGRAPHISCHEN MIT-
TEILUNGEN", LEIPZIG (AUFLAGE: 20.000) ERSCHEINT UND DER UM-
FASSEND SEIN SOLL,VERTRETEN SEIN. ICH BITTE SIE DAHER, UM
DIE FREUNDLICHKEIT, MIR ALLE ZUR VERFUEGUNG STEHENDEN ARBEI-
TEN TYPOGRAPHISCHER ART IN EINEM EXEMPLAR SENDEN ZU WOLLEN.
DIEJENIGEN ARBEITEN, DIE NICHT IN MEHR ALS EINEM EXEMPLARE
MEHR VORHANDEN SIND UND DIEJENIGEN, DIE SIE AUS ANDEREN GRUN-
DEN ZURUECKHABEN WOLLEN; VERSPRECHE ICH IHNEN SOFORT NACH DER
FOTOGRAPHISCHEN AUFNAHME ZURUECKZUSENDEN.
HERR MOHOLY-NAGY KENNT MICH SEHR GUT UND HAT MIR IHRE ADRES-
SE GEGEBEN. ICH PERSOENLICH BIN DER EINZIGE TYPOGRAPHISCHE KON-
STRUKTIVISTISCHEIN LEIPZIG. SEHR ERGEBEN

Iwan Tschichold

Tschichold's first letter to Lissitzky. 1925. 28.1 ×
19.4 cm. Of this letterhead design he commented
soon after: 'I still find my current letterhead very
"pretty" but I am no longer fully in favour of it.
I used too many colours and additional forms.'
(Letter to Kner, 19 June 1925; Békés Archive.)

Tschichold's adoption of utilitarian principles made sense for typography, which is a technical craft, more often than not 'oriented towards purpose', as Tschichold expressed it. Here there is no need of such a radical redefinition as Constructivism brought to art; indeed this was the view taken by several critics of Tschichold's special issue of *Typographische Mitteilungen* – that he was not offering anything essentially new.[28] Constructivism's emphasis on appropriate use of materials found natural resonance in Tschichold's elemental typography, with its restriction to content-carrying elements ('letters, figures, signs, rules') and combination with 'the precise image' of photography. What he was mainly aiming for was a clearing away, in visual terms, of the gratuitous decoration endemic in the majority of German commercial printing. Towards the end of his life he recalled (with a perhaps not entirely undue lack of modesty):

In this area the situation could not have been worse than it was. Even the typography of 1895 was much better than the advertisements around 1925. These all made me so sick that I decided on a radical change. I even succeeded, as a 23-year-old![29]

Tschichold relied on Lissitzky to provide him with certain key materials for his publication, reflecting the difficulties of acquiring objects of avant-garde design, or first hand knowledge of them, when the initial editions were usually small, and had not yet perhaps come to settle in library or museum collections. In his first letter to Lissitzky of 19 January 1925, Tschichold explained: 'Despite great efforts, I have not succeeded at all in acquiring some of your works that have come to my attention (Mayakovsy: Dlja Golossa and the journal L'Objet).' The first of these items is the edition of Vladimir Mayakovsky's poetry, *For the voice* (1923), in which Lissitzky is credited as 'book constructor'. It was issued by the Soviet state publishing house but printed in Berlin and intended mainly for the large community of Russian emigrés there at that time. Tschichold asked Lissitzky to send copies of all his available typographical work, and promised to send back those items he only had one copy of. He signed off with words surely intended to signal kinship: 'Mr Moholy-Nagy knows me very well and he gave me your address. I am the only typographic Constructivist in Leipzig.'[30]

Lissitzky's initial reply to Tschichold was short, expressing his willingness to supply examples of his work, but requesting that Tschichold wait until some friends of his could come and help him pack things for posting: 'I am laid up at the moment (am ill).' Lissitzky was replying from Minusio in Switzerland, where he had retired to convalesce

in February 1924 after being diagnosed with tuberculosis. In late January 1925 Lissitzky sent Tschichold several items: a copy of Mayakovsky's *For the voice*; number 8/9 of Kurt Schwitters's *Merz* periodical, which had been co-edited and designed by Lissitzky; the Dutch edition of his *Tale of two squares*, a Suprematist fable, and some photographic reproductions of the original Russian edition.[31] He regretted not being able to send more, but explained that he himself did not have copies of many items. Of his work in Russia before 1921, he had nothing to hand. He had no copy of the original edition of the *Tale of two squares*, and had to ask Tschichold to send back the Dutch edition and the Mayakovksy book in March when he was preparing to return to the Soviet Union.[32] Tschichold described the *Tale of two squares* in *Elementare Typographie* as belonging to 'the best and most interesting achievements of New Typography', and his admiration was expressed by his emulating its title page in a book cover that he himself designed in 1925 (below).

Book cover design. As reproduced in *Archiv für Buchgewerbe und Gebrauchsgraphik*, 1925. Tschichold signed with Cyrillic initials. It is unclear whether the book was published.

28. See Friedrich Friedl, 'Echo und Reaktionen auf das Sonderheft »elementare Typographie«'.
29. 'Flöhe ins Ohr', p.360.
30. Letter Tschichold to Lissitzky, 19 January 1925. See opposite for original.

31. The book was published in 1922 by the Scythians in Berlin, but Lissitzky claimed to have designed it two years earlier in 'Our book' (1926), reprinted in Lissitzky-Küppers, *El Lissitzky*. So it originates from Lissitzky's time with

Malevich (see also p.126, n.222). The Dutch edition of *Tale of two squares* (published as an issue of *De Stijl*) arose from connections to Van Doesburg.
32. Lissitzky informed Tschichold of a Russian bookshop in Berlin where the *Veschch* jour-

nal might be obtained, and it was from here that Tschichold evidently acquired copies of the original Russian *Tale of two squares* that he sent to Lissitzky in March. Tschichold made some trial reproductions of this item and also sent these

to Lissitzky, who was inspired by them to suggest that Tschichold should find a publisher for a German-language edition, something that never materialized. Thumbnail, monochrome reproductions of all pages in the Russian version, along with

illustrations of *For the voice*, also appeared uncomfortably within the traditionalist confines of the *Gutenberg Festschrift* (1925) in Lissitzky's manifesto, 'Typographische Tatsachen' (Typographical facts).

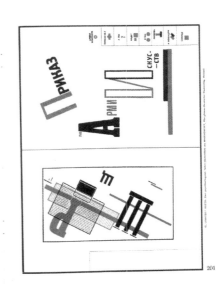

Spread from *Elementare Typographie* showing the last half of Tschichold's manifesto, an advertisement by Burchartz and pages from *For the voice* (turned 90°).

Lissitzky had to leave Switzerland in May 1925 due to problems with the authorities, and he returned to the Soviet Union via Germany.[33] From Russia he was able to provide Tschichold with more material:

> I was suffering from travel nerves, the journey was a lengthy one, and I reached home in a fever. Now I have done my best to satisfy the wishes expressed in your letter of 15th inst. as far as possible. I live, you see, in a village outside Moscow and very seldom go into the city – only to see the doctor. My old works are scattered to the wind. It was all done for the daily needs of the Revolution, and I did not collect it. I am sending you as printed matter by registered mail:
> 1. POSTER from the period of the war with Poland. It was issued by the Staff on the Western Front. I found at home a completely battered and decayed copy, which I would like to keep for myself, so I am sending you a tracing done in the original colours. The type means: WITH THE WEDGE WITH THE RED STRIKE THE WHITE, but you can see that it cannot be translated. It grows from four to nine words and nothing remains of the sound: KLINOM KRASSNYM BYEI BELIKH. The whole thing is mine, words and design.[34]

The poster better known in English as 'Beat the whites with the red wedge' (1920) was not reproduced by Tschichold in *Elementare Typographie*, nor later in *Die neue Typographie*, perhaps due to its nature as Soviet propaganda.[35] A photograph supplied by Lissitzky of *For the voice*, intended to show the book's famous index tabs, was also not included in Tschichold's first compilation, which instead contains several schematized and flattened page openings. The photograph surfaced later in *Die neue Typographie*, but still gives little sense of the book's object qualities. The tab index marking each poem with a symbolic representation inspired Tschichold to compare it with an alphabetical file for correspondence, but the source for Lissitzky's use of this feature may have been even more quotidian: two of his surviving personal address books, crammed with names of avant-garde contemporaries, have well-thumbed alphabetic index tabs, some of which Lissitzky coloured manually in red.[36]

Lissitzky also sent Tschichold a sketch of a cover design he had made for an American literary journal, *Broom* (edited by Peggy Guggenheim's cousin, Harold Loeb). He had no printed example to hand but he insisted that the design should be included in *Elementare Typographie* because he felt it was 'characteristic' of his work.[37] Tschichold probably made his own copy drawing as a guide for typesetting the design anew, as Lissitzky had suggested. Indeed, several of the illustrations of work featured in Tschichold's compilation were made this way, including a full-size reconstruction of Moholy-Nagy's prospectus for Bauhaus books and some of Herbert Bayer's work. These items could have been reproduced photographically, but instead all of the text was recomposed in the same typefaces used for the issue of *Typographische Mitteilungen*. No doubt it was less expensive to do it that way but it also marks a flexible, and not always entirely faithful, view of reproducing graphic material that Tschichold maintained throughout his life.

There is a sense in which Tschichold was promoting the approach of artists such as Moholy-Nagy and Lissitzky to

33. Lissitzky's return home was also spurred by the suicide of his beloved sister. Lissitzky-Küppers, *El Lissitzky*, p.58.
34. Letter Lissitzky to Tschichold, 22 July 1925. Translated

in Perloff & Reed, *Situating El Lissitzky*, p.243.
35. Lissitzky's copy drawing (duly returned to him by Tschichold) probably served as the basis for subsequent reproduc-

tions. See Nisbet, *El Lissitzky 1890–1941*, p.182.
36. Held in the Getty Research Institute.
37. Letter Lissitzky to Tschichold, 25 January 1925. He dated

his cover in 1922 but, as Peter Nisbet points out, this does not accord with *Broom*'s publication history. It must have dated from 1923, although the design was not used for vol.5, no.3, as

Lissitzky stated, but for the next issue. It was also repeated for the magazine's last number, which was suppressed by the US Post Office for obscenity, explaining Lissitzky's remark

that his copies had been seized at customs. Nisbet, *El Lissitzky 1890–1941*, pp.187–8. A different version of the design appears as illustration 68 in Lissitzky-Küppers, *El Lissitzky*.

Spread from *Elementare Typographie*. Lissitzky's letterhead on the right has been reconstituted for printing here from typographic rules (hence the visible gaps in the red and black bars), sanserif type and a typewriter typeface. The only element photographically reproduced must have been his signature.

typography as a purifying agent, a breath of fresh air to blow away the cobwebs from unthinking traditionalism in printing, but which then needed to be consolidated for everyday practice in that trade. Moholy-Nagy predicted that whole editions of books would soon be produced by exposing a master image through a stack of light sensitive paper by means of x-rays, and Lissitzky prophesied the 'electro-library', which is now almost upon us with the internet.[38] They were impatient with the physical restrictions of typography, hoping that it would soon break free from its paper substrate. Writing forty years after his first contact with Lissitzky, Tschichold summed up the Russian's approach:

> Not even the new was enough for him. All his works, fables of the coming technological age, visionary anticipations of future forms, apotheoses of engineering, cast the unrepeatable spell of revolutionary experiment.

In this appreciative but sternly critical assessment of his old friend's work, Tschichold continued:

> In 1922 Lissitzky the typographer had of course to work with Gutenberg's lead type, which was nearly five hundred years old, quite unsuited to his formal concepts and much too clumsy. The technical inadequacies and failings of his diagonal setting are obvious to anyone who knows the subject. Lissitzky did not develop his characteristic forms from normal typesetting techniques; he was probably not concerned about how the compositor was to set up his sketches. Very often drawing was the only course open to him, because type was incapable of producing what he wanted. The technical perfection of his personal letterhead is a shining exception,

still beautiful today. Everything else, original and powerful though it might be, betrays the struggle of the amateur typographer with the ancient, intractable mysteries of printing. The tone blocks and metal type, which cannot have been nearly flexible enough to express the forms he had envisaged must have weighed him down like leaden feet.[39]

Tschichold remarked that Lissitzky had anticipated the freedom of photographic typesetting, which would only become viable forty years later and in which everything was possible.

From his mature traditionalist position, Tschichold perhaps overstated the case: Lissitzky expressed how important he felt it was to go and 'stand by the machines' when his book projects were being realized. In this way he was able to persuade compositors and printers to go beyond their normal practice and produce some remarkable innovations. His insistence on using typecase material to make the illustrative constructions in *For the voice* was met with initial incomprehension by the compositor at the small Berlin printer, Lutze & Vogt.[40] Compared with Lissitzky's visionary approach to typography, Tschichold's was more pragmatic and expository. As would be more fully demonstrated in his instructional writings, allied to his sustained period of teaching, Tschichold was concerned with mastering the precise measures and vocabulary used in communicating with printing technicians: hence his decision to have his first two major publications issued by a printing trade body, the Bildungsverband.

38. Moholy-Nagy, 'Elementare Buchtechnik', p.62; Lissitzky, 'Topographie der Typographie' (translated in Kinross, *Modern typography*, p.105).
39. Tschichold, 'El Lissitzky (1890–1941)' in Lissitzky-Küppers, *El Lissitzky*, p.389. The date given here for this essay is 1965, although it was not published in *Typographische Mitteilungen*, as stated, because that journal had long ceased to exist. What was perhaps referred to was its intended publication in *Typographische Monatsblätter*, in which it eventually appeared (no.12, 1970). The essay began life as Tschichold's speech on the occasion of the first major retrospective exhibition of Lissitzky's work outside the USSR at Basel Kunsthalle in January 1966, and was published in the Basel *National Zeitung* (Nr 86).
40. Related by Lissitzky in an interview partially reprinted in Railing, *Voices of revolution*, pp.35–6. Tschichold later called the tab index in *For the voice* 'an artistic conceit, aimed at achieving a "new" form, not in any sense a piece of engineering.' 'El Lissitzky (1890–1941)', p.389.

The editor of *Typographische Mitteilungen* was Bruno Dressler, who was also the initiator of the socialist book club affiliated to the Bildungsverband, the Büchergilde Gutenberg. This was founded at the meeting of the Verband der deutschen Buchdrucker in Leipzig on 29 August 1924 and the Büchergilde's main office was initially located there. Tschichold designed its fifth book, Colin Ross's *Das Fahrten- und Abenteuerbuch*, published in 1925. The Büchergilde's eponymous magazine, distributed to its members (of whom Tschichold may well have been one) was listed among the recommended journals in *Elementare Typographie*.

By making his first publication an issue of *Typographische Mitteilungen*, Tschichold reached a readership of over 20,000 instead of circulation among the few hundred readers typical of avant-garde art journals such as *De Stijl* or *G*.[41] His publication therefore made a significant impression on the German, Swiss and Austrian printing trades, fulfilling the declared Constructivist aim of 'agitation in the press'.[42] He asserted later that it had 'an enormous effect' – every type compositor knew Tschichold's name.[43] Allowing for his later tendency to mythologize himself, there may well be some truth in this. Responses to the special issue were collected and reprinted in a series of editorial features during the following year in *Typographische Mitteilungen*, the first of which stated: 'Probably no other issue of "Typographische Mitteilungen" has received such critical attention as last year's October issue.'[44]

There were some sympathetic voices among the responses to *Elementare Typographie*. Heinrich Bachmair wrote in *Typographische Jahrbücher* (Typographic yearbook, another Leipzig periodical):

> It is a curious yet on the other hand quite understandable fact ... that the supporters of the struggle for new artistic forms of expression are, for the most part, also close to the endeavours aimed at changing the existing forms of society – in other words 'left-oriented'.[45]

But for many the Constructivist bias in Tschichold's publication was like a red rag to a bull. A particularly hostile review was printed simultaneously in the *Zeitschrift für Deutschlands Buchdruckers* and the Swiss printing trade journal, *Schweizer graphische Mitteilungen*. Accusations of 'communist style' and 'bolshevism' were levelled at the work it contained, and the reviewer Hermann Hoffmann went so far as to assert: 'The movement stems from Moscow, on orders from which the otherwise capable graphic designer Tschichold aligned himself with Constructivism and then

held lectures about it in several German cities, which were however very critically received.'[46] Even if we accept that Lissitzky was somehow representing the Soviet government as a cultural missionary, there is no evidence that Tschichold had any connections with the Comintern.

One of the lectures referred to here was given by Tschichold on 16 September 1925, just before the publication of *Elementare Typographie*, at the Typographische Gesellschaft (Typographical society) of Leipzig. A lengthy and somewhat hostile report of the event was written by Albert Giesecke and published in the Leipzig printing journal *Offset: Buch- und Werbekunst* under the heading 'Ein Verfechter des Konstruktivismus' (A fighter for Constructivism). Giesecke described the substance of the lecture as 'the theory of elemental design', which, in his view, offered nothing really new and was marred by unclear ideas; nevertheless he felt duty bound to address the issues raised by Tschichold 'in order to warn the impressionable among us of such fantasies'. He gave an intriguing portrait of the 23-year-old 'Johannes-Iwan', as he called him:

> It is necessary to mention in advance that one got the impression from the lecture that the speaker did not himself quite believe in what he was saying, despite having remarked initially that it was an expression of his world-view; otherwise he would not have presented it with a half embarrassed, half winsome smile, which would lead a psychologist to conclude that one was dealing with the seething delusions of a youth just emerging from puberty. Yet as a representative type of a large part of the German people, who have allowed themselves to be captivated by Russian ideas, he was quite interesting, and it is probably necessary to get to know such types.

Tschichold evidently judged the work of Kurt Schwitters in his lecture as too romantic, instead stressing the derivation of Constructivism from 'historical materialism', which led Giesecke to mock 'the prophet Johannes' with some erudition. The potential for Tschichold's proposals to become a communist-style, closed system was perceived by Giesecke in 'the baffling quickness with which he simply "denied" everything which did not fit his doctrine'. Giesecke alleged that:

> With commendable frankness he then declared himself also to be a convinced supporter of Russian Communism; indeed he believes that a breakthrough of the ideas of elemental design can only really be enabled by a full revolution and the eradication of the bourgeoisie.[47]

41. Tschichold gave the edition of the journal as 20,000 in his first letter to Lissitzky. In *Archiv für Buchgewerbe und Gebrauchsgraphik* (Jg.56, H.11/12, 1919, pp.201–5) Dressler claimed that the number of subscribers to *Typographische Mitteilungen* increased from

10,000 at the beginning of 1919 to 23,000 in October of the same year. A circulation figure of 22,000 for the journal in 1925 was given by Bertram Evans in 'Modern typography on the continent', p.30. Tschichold himself, in *Eine Stunde Druckgestaltung*, stated that

28,000 copies were printed of his special issue, and that it was no longer available (*Schriften*, 1, p.89).
42. *Elementare Typographie*, p.197.
43. 'Jan Tschichold: praeceptor typographiae', p.19. Some confirmation is given by Paul

Renner: 'overnight his name became better known in the printing trade than that of any other graphic designer'. (Draft of 'Über moderne Typographie', 1948 [p.1]; Haushofer Archive).
44. *Typographische Mitteilungen* published the responses in four parts between August

and December 1926 under the heading 'Über die Kritik der neuen Satzgestaltung' (On the critique of the new text composition).
45. 'Über die Kritik der neuen Satzgestaltung', *Typographische Mitteilungen*, Jg.23, H.12, 1926, p.333.

46. Cited by Friedl, 'Echo und Reaktion auf das Sonderheft »elementare Typographie«', p.9.
47. Giesecke, 'Ein Verfechter des Konstruktivismus', pp.735–6, 738–9.

Tschichold's first book for the Büchergilde Gutenberg. 1925. Actual size.

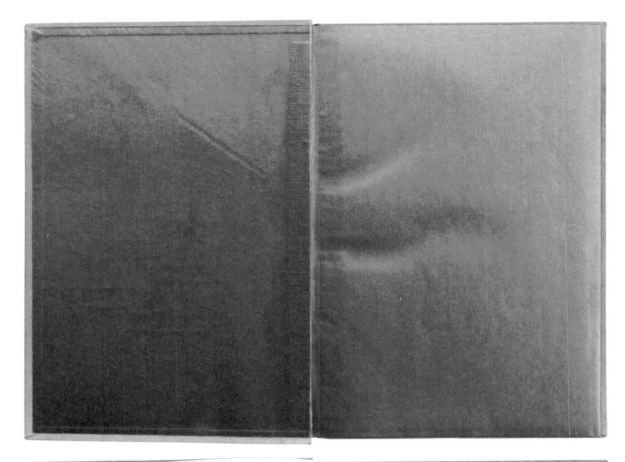

COLIN ROSS

FAHRTEN-
UND
ABENTEUERBUCH

1925
VERLAG DER BÜCHERGILDE GUTENBERG LEIPZIG

Front endpapers and title-page spread from
Ross, *Das Fahrten- und Abenteuerbuch*. 1925.
24 × 17 cm.

Colin Ross (1885–1945) was a German of Scottish
descent and this book documents his exploits as
a travelling adventurer.

Whatever Tschichold's exact words were, his admission provoked Giesecke to call him a 'Kunstbolschewist' (Art-bolshevist): this accusation would return to plague him after the Nazis came to power, with Giesecke's report serving as evidence (see p.138).

More constructive criticism came from Tschichold's former teacher, Heinrich Wieynck. Writing in the pages of *Archiv für Buchgewerbe und Gebrauchsgraphik*, he admitted that 'die neue Sachlichkeit' had provided 'valuable stimuli' to typography and recognized the revolutionary desires of 'a few prophets from Soviet Russia together with their German followers, among whom the Leipziger Johannes (now Iwan) Tzschichold [sic] is a noteworthy personality'. Yet Wieynck could not resist parodying Tschichold's numbered principles of elemental typography and declared:

> The manifestos of the Constructivists operate all too often with unclear concepts and hollow words; the predicates elemental, constructive and functional are used without meaningful justification for matters in which, until now, we have been able to make ourselves quite understood without such phrases.

Tschichold's own later view of his work at this point were, in some respects, uncannily anticipated by Wieynck's reflective criticisms: 'Every reforming idea contains by definition an exaggeration, and New Typography also cannot avoid this danger.' On Tschichold's purging of ornament, Wieynck commented: 'A form can however not simply be pronounced good because it carries *no* decoration, and ornament in itself is neither good nor bad.'[48]

By contrast, *Elementare Typographie* was received warmly at the Bauhaus. Moholy-Nagy wrote to Tschichold:

> the typographische mitteilungen is a great achievement. in general i share your view completely and in all respects; i find only a few particulars still ripe for discussion.

He looked forward to Tschichold visiting him again so that they could discuss it. Gropius, too, sent Tschichold his congratulations:

> i have received your typographical booklet and find it very beautiful. it has also been of great use to me in the struggle for the exclusive use of small letters [*kleinschrift*] here in dessau.[49]

(Tschichold advocated *Kleinschreibung* – literally translated: writing small, i.e. without capital letters – in 'Elementare Typographie' but it was not typeset in this manner.)

Lissitzky was full of praise for *Elementare Typographie* and especially conscious of its potentially wide readership. On receiving a copy of the journal he wrote:

> DEAR TSCHICHOLD,
>
> BRAVO,
>
> BRAVO,
>
> I most warmly congratulate you on the beautiful piece of printing that is Elementare Typographie. It is a physical pleasure for me to hold a work of such quality in my hands, my fingers, my eyes. My nerve antennae stretch, and the whole motor increases its speed. And that is ultimately what it is all about – overcoming inertia.
>
> It is good and gives the work its value that the literary half is so coherently presented and, without contrived populism, is understandable to everyone. This is all your doing. It is an achievement that this is a special issue of a professional journal /not an art journal/ and so I hope it will reach the working printer and he will gain self-confidence, and this will stimulate him to inventive uses of his typecase.

Yet he now felt that his own work in typography was a thing of the past:

> The issue pleased me personally because it sums up a period that is already behind me and that I can now view from a distance. I am now heavily pregnant with architecture. But typographic issues busy me constantly, only the local technical resources are so pitiful that it is impossible to achieve anything in practice /except laboratory work/.[50]

Lissitzky's architectural ambitions were frustrated by the hard economic realities of Soviet life, and so he returned frequently to graphic design, more in the role of art director for printed propaganda and in his pioneering exhibition work, both of which proved him to be a master of photomontage. His Soviet section at the Pressa exhibition of 1928 in Cologne possessed a cinematic energy that set a standard for modernist work in this field. Yet, during his initial contact with Tschichold, he seemed to view typography and advertising work more as a temporary means of earning a living. Indeed a stipend from the Hanover firm Günther Wagner was arranged for him to design advertisements for their Pelikan brand of writing materials during his recovery from illness in Switzerland, giving much needed help with his medical expenses.[51] Such work was sought by a number of painters and architects in Germany from around 1923 due to the disastrous state of the economy. Inflation had made the German mark almost worthless and there was little money in selling art or designing buildings; the relatively small-scale commercial activity of printing, requiring less investment in material and labour than architecture, provided opportunities. Kurt Schwitters set up his one-man agency, Merz Werbezentrale, after the high-point of inflation in 1924 and made graphic design his main occupation for the next decade.

A short article co-written by Lissitzky and the Dutch architect Mart Stam about 'Typoreklame' (Typo-advertising)

48. Wieynck, 'Neueste Wege der Typographie', pp.374–6. See also p.150, n.9 below for Wieynck's comments on sanserif. Ironically, Wieynck made a more radical suggestion than Tschichold ever did concerning unjustified typesetting, which he felt could be of use in typography if well ordered with indents.

49. Letters Moholy-Nagy and Gropius to Tschichold, 27 October 1925 and 9 November 1925 respectively (DNB Leipzig).

50. Letter Lissitzky to Tschichold, 22 October 1925. Translated in Perloff & Reed, *Situating El Lissitzky*, p.247.

51. This was probably arranged through Schwitters, who also also designed publicity for Pelikan, and for whom Lissitzky continued to work on issue 8/9 of *Merz* while in Switzerland. Tschichold featured Schwitters's 'Typosignet' for Pelikan in *Elementare Typographie*. *Merz* 11 featured mainly Pelikan advertisements.

was reprinted in Tschichold's special issue of *Typograph-ische Mitteilungen*, having first been published in the Swiss magazine *ABC*.[52] It is unclear whether Tschichold knew of Lissitzky's important manifesto text of 1923, 'Topographie der Typographie' (Topography of typography) before contacting him, but he certainly did soon afterwards. The issue of *Merz* that Lissitzky sent him spurred Tschichold to subscribe to this irregular journal edited in Hanover by Kurt Schwitters, and to request all of its previous issues, number 4 of which had contained Lissitzky's text.[53] Around 1923, perhaps encouraged by his friendships with both Lissitzky and Van Doesburg, Schwitters moved away from his Dada beginnings towards a more rationalist approach. Schwitters and Van Doesburg visited each other during a regular collaboration that culminated in the fable book, *Die Scheuche* (The scarecrow, 1925), which was composed entirely from type-case material, following the example of *For the voice* designed by Lissitzky. Käthe Steinitz, who was patron & partner to Schwitters in this publishing venture, commented that they met with little resistance to the fanciful use of type material from their friendly printer, in contrast to Lissitzky's difficult experience in having *For the voice* typeset.[54] Following the bizarre Dada–Constructivist summit organized by Van Doesburg in Weimar (September 1922) Lissitzky had visited Schwitters in his home town of Hanover and was introduced to its art community, includ-ing Lissitzky's future wife Sophie Küppers, a curator at the progressive Kestner-Gesellschaft.[55]

Tschichold would have known Schwitters's manifesto 'Thesen über Typographie' (Theses on typography; pub-lished in *Merz* no.11) during the preparation of *Elementare Typographie*. He may not have sympathized with it as much as he did with writings by Lissitzky or Moholy-Nagy, given its Dada-spirited beginning: 'Innumerable rules get written about typography. The most important is: never do it as someone has done it before you.' Yet Schwitters goes on to list some tenets of New Typography that Tschichold would adopt, including the assertion that 'The textually negative elements, the unprinted parts of the printed paper, are also of positive typographic value'.[56] Also buried in Schwitters's clumsily designed manifesto is a reference to a pamphlet by Max Burchartz, 'Gestaltung der Reklame' (Advertising design), which Tschichold lost no time in pursuing. He wrote to Burchartz at the end of February 1925 and soon received from him some examples of his typographic work, which went on to be featured in *Elementare Typographie*.

Burchartz had trained in his father's furniture-making firm as a salesman and then at the Düsseldorf Kunstakad-emie before the First World War. After serving in the war, he began painting in an expressionist style, contributing to one of the first Bauhaus print collections. He lived in Weimar from 1919, and attended Van Doesburg's alternative course there in 1922; indeed some of the seminars were held at Burchartz's home. He became a member of De Stijl and attended the Dada–Constructivist congress, thereby entering a circle that included Lissitzky and Schwitters. Burchartz was never closely associated with the Bauhaus, but he acted as translator for the Bauhaus books by Van Doesburg and Piet Mondrian. Despite his close connection with Van Doesburg he supported the choice of Moholy-Nagy for the position at the Bauhaus vacated by Johannes Itten in 1923.[57] In 1924, finding it difficult to make a living from painting, he moved from Weimar to Bochum in the industrial Ruhr region, where along with Johannes Canis he formed Werbe-bau, a prototype of the modern advertising agency. One of their first clients was the furniture firm of Wilhelm Engst-feld (Wehag), for which they not only designed strikingly modern publicity material but Burchartz also designed furniture and fittings such as doorhandles.

'Gestaltung der Reklame', dated June 1924, was the first of a short-lived series edited by Burchartz and published by Canis, *Flugblätter mit dem Buntquadrat* (Pamphlets of the colourful square), referring to the Constructivist red square that came to form part of the Werbebau signet. It itemized with great concision the principles behind Werbebau's activity:

Good advertising	
is straightforward [*sachlich*]	1
clear and concise	2
uses modern means	3
has a striking form	4
is inexpensive.	5 [58]

Tschichold visited Burchartz in Bochum soon after the publication of *Elementare Typographie*, and Burchartz continued to send Tschichold examples of his design work (including prospectuses for the steel manufacturer, Bochumer Verein, which were featured extensively in *Die neue Typographie*). Lissitzky, on similarly receiving one of Burchartz's commercial catalogues, wrote enthusiastically to Tschichold: 'Max is on a promising path. The movement that we started is bearing good fruit.'[59] Like several of his contemporaries, Burchartz also taught graphic design,

52. *ABC* reciprocated by publishing an abridged ver-sion of Tschichold's 'Die neue Gestaltung'. See Hollis, *Swiss graphic design*, p.56n.
53. Postcard Helma Schwitters to Tschichold, 6 February 1925.
54. Steinitz cited in Schwit-ters, 'Typographie kann unter

Umständen Kunst sein', p.135. *Die Scheuche* was probably issued too late for Tschichold to consider including in *Elemen-tare Typographie*. Steinitz wrote to him (6 November 1925; DNB Leipzig) regretting that it was not included and offering to send him a copy. He

lists it in *Die neue Typographie*. It was reissued as *Merz* 14/15.
55. Schwitters and Küppers both helped to mount an exhi-bition of Lissitzky's work that opened in January 1923 at the Kestner gallery, which led to it publishing the luxurious port-folio of his Proun lithographs.

56. Tschichold: 'The New Typography uses the effec-tiveness of the former "back-ground" quite deliberately, and considers the blank white spaces on the paper as formal elements just as much as the areas of black type.' *The New Typography*, p.72. See also the

report of Tschichold's Munich lecture in *Typographische Mitteilungen*, H.1, 1927 .
57. Letter Burchartz to Walter Dexel, 10 March 1923.
58. 'Gestaltung der Reklame', *Flugblätter mit dem Buntquad-rat*, no.1, June 1924. Repro-duced in Stürzebecher, 'Max ist

endlich auf dem richtigen Weg'.
59. Letter Lissitzky to Tschichold, 22 October 1925. Translated in Perloff & Reed, *Situating El Lissitzky*, p.248. On Burchartz's association with Bochümer Verein, see Jeremy Aynsley, *Graphic design in Ger-many 1890–1945*, pp.173–4.

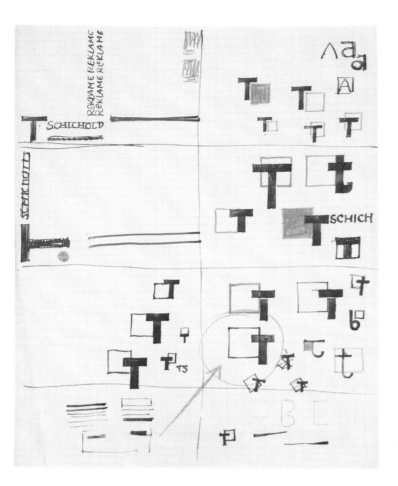

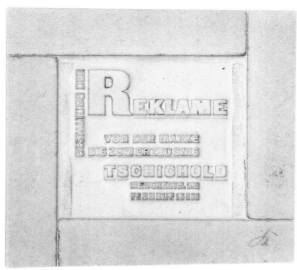

Flong of a business card (probably never printed). *c.*1925. 8.3 × 9.5 cm. Tschichold adopted the same term for advertising his services as Burchartz: 'Gestaltung der Reklame' (Advertising design). 'From brandmark to product' reads his slogan.

Sketches towards a personal symbol. *c.*1925. 17.2 × 14 cm. The variations on a square reveal the influence of Burchartz, who took it as a principal motif (see spread of *Elementare Typographie* illustrated on p.35 above. These sketches probably fed into Tschichold's postcard shown on that same spread).

Newspaper advertisement for UNS-Bücherstube, a left-oriented bookshop. *c.*1925. Shown at same scale as item below.

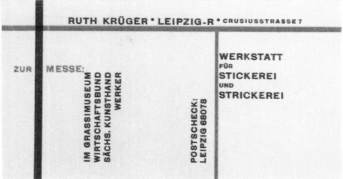

Business card for embroidery and knitting workshop. *c.*1925. 7.5 × 13.8 cm.

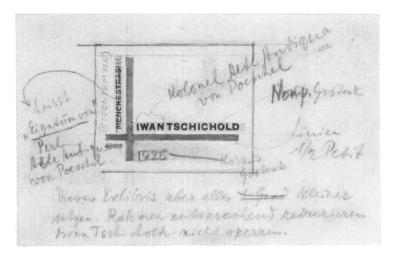
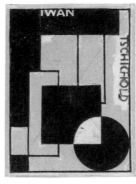

More sketches for Tschichold's new Construct-ivist identity. 1924/5 (75% of actual size). Such experiments resulted in the Ex Libris design that he reproduced on the last page of *Elementare Typographie* (below left).

Final page of *Elementare Typographie* within the October 1925 issue of *Typographische Mitteilungen*. Following it is the magazine's regular, literary supplement 'Das Schiff' (The ship), which reverted to the customary text typeface, Bauer Baskerville. It is strange that Tschichold chose a different text typeface for his section, given that Bauer Baskerville was in fact a more elegantly functional roman type than that used for his text, Dissertations-Antiqua.

Nina Chmelowa, whose letterhead is pictured on Tschichold's last page, was a dancer. Her partner was dancer & choreographer Lasar Galpern, for whom Tschichold designed an almost identical letterhead. He trained in Moscow and became ballet master at the Municipal Drama School in Leipzig (1926–32), in addition to being active in avant-garde dance performances in Germany during the Weimar Republic. (See the poster for his dance school opposite.)

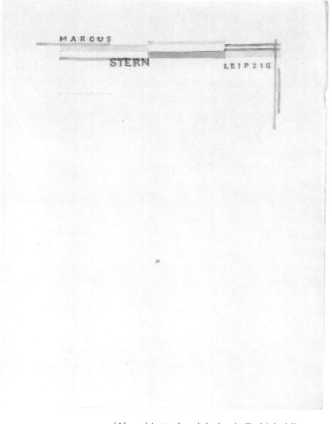

(Above) Letterhead design in Tschichold's
Constructivist style of 1924/5. 14.7 × 11.5 cm.

(Above right) Poster for the School of Dance
Culture in Leipzig led by dancer & choreographer
Lasar Galpern. c.1926. 45 × 30 cm.

(The copy of this poster shown here has had its
bottom margin trimmed off.)

taking up a position in October 1926 at the Kunstgewerbeschule in Essen.[60]

Another painter-turned-typographer active in teaching
was Johannes Molzahn, whose work in typography had
come to Tschichold's attention early enough for him to
feature an example in *Elementare Typographie*. Molzahn,
who also had some training as a photographer, taught
typography and graphic design at the Kunstgewerbe- &
Handwerkschule in Magdeburg from 1923, moving on to
the Breslau Kunstakademie in 1928. He had studied at the
Großherzogliche Kunstschule (Grand-ducal art school) in
Weimar that later became the Bauhaus, and was still living
there immediately after the First World War. He was one
of the first people that Walter Gropius contacted when setting up the Bauhaus in 1918, asking him to make a survey
of artistic work in the area, although Molzahn was never
officially attached to the Bauhaus faculty.[61] Tschichold went
on to feature Molzahn's archetypal and instructive invoice
form for his design activity in *Die neue Typographie*.

The teaching post vacated in Magdeburg by Molzahn was
filled by his friend Walter Dexel, who also taught art history
there. The multifaceted Dexel was exhibition director of the

Kunstverein gallery in Jena between 1916 and 1928. Many
notable modern artists exhibited their work there, including
Kurt Schwitters and Max Burchartz. Dexel showed some of
his own non-objective paintings at the Kunstverein's 1923
exhibition of Constructivism, along with Lissitzky and Willi
Baumeister. He had been in contact with Moholy-Nagy since
early 1922, before his Bauhaus appointment, and, given
the proximity of Jena to Weimar, Dexel exhibited work
by Moholy-Nagy and other painters on the Bauhaus staff,
notably Klee and Kandinsky. Yet he maintained a certain
distance and independence from the Bauhaus. Dexel trained
as an art historian in Munich and went on to write several
important books about modern design.[62]

On establishing contact with Dexel by sending him a copy
of *Elementare Typographie*, Tschichold evidently admitted
that his survey was incomplete, perhaps as a way of excusing

60. Burchartz was initially an
adjutant teacher, but he was
appointed professor of typography in April 1927. In a letter
to Tschichold of 9 December
1926, he wrote enthusiastically
of plans to turn the school

into a specialist college for
interior design and advertising
graphics.
   61. Presumably through
the connection with Gropius,
Molzahn designed publicity
from 1922 for the Fagus works

at Alfeld, housed in Gropius's
seminal steel & glass building.
   62. *Das Wohnhaus von heute*
(1928), co-written with his wife
Grete, and *Unbekanntes Hand-
werksgut* (1935), a history of
everyday design objects.

his not having included Dexel's work. Dexel's reply was informed by his concerns as a historian, as well as a certain chagrin:

> Dear Mr Tschichold
> many thanks for sending your booklet 'Elementare Typographie'. I do not miss myself in your compilation, rather the necessary overview of the material. Among the Germans are lacking precisely *those*, who first worked in the area of New Typography, and priority is quite an important point in such a compilation. So, e.g. Schlemmer, Baumeister, Röhl, my absence and many others. It is also a misjudgement of the course of history to include Moholy and leave out Van Doesburg and the whole Stijl group. Indeed Russians and Hungarians seem to me to be disproportionately represented. I am glad to hear that you would like to inform yourself more extensively in the future. As thanks for the booklet, which is very beautiful in itself, I am sending here a couple of typo. works, mostly of recent date, as my older stock is somewhat depleted.[63]

Tschichold met Dexel soon afterwards in Munich and they remained in friendly contact during the 1920s. Yet, in his books and articles about New Typography, Tschichold never featured Dexel's work to the extent that it perhaps deserved. Having designed pioneering illuminated traffic signs for Jena in 1925, Dexel was summoned in the following year to Frankfurt am Main, where he contributed in the same capacity to the programme of modernist urban development led by Ernst May and Adolf Meyer. In Frankfurt Dexel designed neon-lit architectural lettering for buildings, advertising pillars and even telephone boxes, applying an effective variation of Constructivist style. In addition to publicity material for the Jena Kunstverein, he also designed the jackets and covers for the Prometheus Books series on modern themes published by Hesse and Becker of Leipzig. These would seem to be precisely the kind of typography that Tschichold was keen to illustrate in his writings, but he never included them.[64]

Dexel organized one of the first exhibitions of New Typography at the Jena Kunstverein in May and June 1927 entitled 'Neue Reklame' (New advertising), in which Tschichold did not participate. Dexel's essay 'Was ist neue Typographie?' (What is New Typography?) was published in the catalogue of a further exhibition held at the Basel Gewerbemuseum between December 1927 and January 1928, in which Tschichold's work was shown.[65] Opposite the entrance to this exhibition, as an orientation panel, was placed a frame in which an image of the Petit Trianon was

shown alongside a book title-page of the eighteenth century, and a photograph of modern architecture from Stuttgart alongside a title-page in New Typography.[66]

To what extent Dexel's initial criticism of Tschichold's approach in *Elementare Typographie* made an impact on him is uncertain, but he certainly did broaden his scope in *Die neue Typographie* to include many more German and Dutch examples: by that time he could include the work of Piet Zwart, for example. A key figure mentioned by Dexel as one of the German pioneers of New Typography was Willi Baumeister, more than a decade older than Tschichold, who had been exhibiting his paintings in avant-garde circles since 1913 and was a founder member of the radical artists' group, Novembergruppe. Tschichold followed Dexel's lead and sent a copy of his publication to Baumeister, who had a studio in Stuttgart, asking him for information about his typographic work. Baumeister replied:

> I composed advertisements from a new standpoint already in *1920*, and since then I have also spoken publicly on the subject in Berlin and elsewhere. My main activity has become to force my way into periodicals and newspapers. Perhaps I still see a difference between myself and some of the other gentlemen designing in the new way [*neugestaltenden Herren*]. You will read about this in my little essay for the Anzeigen-Zeitschrift.[67]

The essay Baumeister refers to here was 'Neue Typographie', which was also published later in 1926 in the journal of the German Werkbund, *Die Form*; indeed Tschichold's *Elementare Typographie* started something of a ball rolling, and articles about new advertising design written by Burchartz and Molzahn were also published in *Die Form*.[68] For Baumeister: 'Typography consists above all in the division of a limited surface'; from this premise he drew a parallel with fine art but stressed the different principle behind typography, which stems from verbal content and a definite direction of reading.[69] Tschichold's correspondence with Baumeister resulted in some items of printed ephemera that he designed being featured in *Die neue Typographie*.

Berlin, Munich, and the little black book

Tschichold's final words in *Elementare Typographie* contained a request for readers to send him new material ('preferably two copies'), with a view to his including them in a projected exhibition and 'further essays and lectures'. His plans became more ambitious: ideas for the book that became *Die neue Typographie* probably began to develop in

63. Postcard Dexel to Tschichold, 4 December 1925, written on his printed 'Neue Reklame' postcard. Dexel's championing of the Dutch cause was natural, given that he had been in touch with Van Doesburg since the beginning of 1922, and got to know him during his sojourn in Weimar. Karl Peter Röhl was one of the first students at the Bauhaus, but was closely involved with Van Doesburg's rival course in Weimar. Dexel wrote an affectionate obituary for Van Doesburg in *Das Neue Frankfurt* (no.6, 1931).

64. Two jackets for Prometheus Books are illustrated in *Gefesselter Blick* (see p.103). See also Friedl, *Walter Dexel: neue Reklame*. In his 1931 article, 'New paths in poster work', Tschichold featured Dexel's now famous poster 'Fotografie der Gegenwart', which Dexel

sent to him along with other posters. (Letter Dexel to Tschichold, 21 January 1930.)

65. Lists of exhibitors are given in Fleischmann, *Bauhaus*, pp.346 & 352. The foreword to the Basel Gewerbemuseum exhibition catalogue, probably written by curator Georg Schmidt, is an unusually perceptive text.

66. Described in *Das Werk*, January 1928, p.26.

67. Letter Baumeister to Tschichold, 17 February 1926.

68. Burchartz, 'Neuzeitliche Werbung', and Molzahn, 'Ökonomie der Reklame-Mechane', both reprinted in Fleischmann, *Bauhaus*.

69. Like Schwitters, Baumeister also asserted: 'Space between lines of type and blocks of text has an essential significance.' Baumeister, 'Neue Typographie' in Fleischmann, *Bauhaus*, p.339.

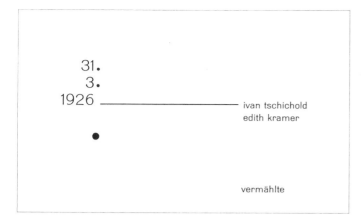

31.
3.
1926 ————————————————— ivan tschichold
                                        edith kramer

        ●

                                        vermählte

(Above) Marriage announcement card for the Tschicholds. 9.8 × 15.3 cm. It reads simply: 'ivan tschichold / edith kramer / married.'

(Right) Jan & Edith Tschichold, c.1930.

the first half of 1926, when Tschichold was living in Berlin. He moved at the beginning of that year from Leipzig to live in the Charlottenburg area of Germany's capital city, famed at this time for its hedonistic nightlife and avant-garde culture. Coincidentally the organization that would go on to publish *Die neue Typographie*, the Bildungsverband, also moved its central office from Leipzig to Berlin in early 1926, along with the affiliated Büchergilde Gutenberg. Tschichold maintained contact there with Bruno Dressler, editor of *Typographische Mitteilungen* and now director of the printing workshop at the Buchdruckerhaus in Berlin, a building designed by leading modernist architect Max Taut as the seat of the Verband der deutschen Buchdrucker. It is likely that Dressler and Tschichold discussed a possible book project, as Tschichold was already collecting material for 'a book about New Typography' in August of that year.[70]

Tschichold was to be joined in Berlin by his future wife and lifelong companion, Edith Kramer. She was due to take up a position as a trainee journalist there. Their decision to marry was hastened by the wish to cohabit in their Berlin lodgings, which the landlady would not allow otherwise. Indeed Tschichold's actual proposal of marriage seems to have been of such urgency that it was not made in person to Edith (still then in Leipzig) but instead by a combination of post, telegram and telephone. He only gave the invited witnesses to the wedding two days' notice of the ceremony.[71] Ivan and Edith were married on 31 March 1926.

Edith Tschichold remembered later:

> Berlin was wonderful with regard to contact with painters and other artists. But very expensive. Even the tickets for the 'Sturm' – those famous evenings that took place there, poetry readings linked to exhibitions and with dancing afterwards. They were so expensive as to be totally out of the question for us. We only managed to go once.[72]

According to Edith, publishers in Berlin were generally conservative, and it was difficult for her husband to find work there. She felt that, in the long run, his associations with the Bildungsverband hindered him in this respect: 'All of the printers, every publisher saw him as a man of the left. He was simply branded.' Indeed she believed that the accusation of being a communist remained attached to him in Germany for his whole life.

Yet Tschichold had less than half a year in which to sample life in the Berlin metropolis because he would soon move on again to take up a teaching position in Munich, confirming the opinion of the novelist & journalist Joseph Roth, who was based in Berlin between 1920 and 1925, that 'Berlin is a point of transit, where, given compelling reasons, one may end up staying longer'.[73] In Berlin Tschichold received a letter from Paul Renner, the principal of the Graphische Berufsschule (Graphic trade school) in Munich, suggesting initially that he take over a teaching position Renner had left vacant at the Frankfurt Kunstschule.[74] Renner, a skilled traditionalist typographer moving carefully towards modernism, would have seen Tschichold's issue of *Typographische Mitteilungen* and was partly spurred to contact Tschichold by accusations in a review of it that both men were 'Bolshevists'. The same writer, Hermann Hoffmann, who had accused Tschichold of taking

70. Letter Lissitzky to Tschichold, 26 August 1926. Lissitzky's interest in designing for the Büchergilde had been passed on to Dressler by Tschichold.
71. Doede, 'Beim Tee' in

Luidl, *J.T.*, p.16.
72. [Edith Tschichold], 'Interview mit Edith Tschichold in Berzona am 16.8.1979' p.183.
73. Roth, *The wandering Jews*, (New York: Norton, 2001) p.68.

74. Renner only took up his post in Munich at Easter 1926, although he had been discussing the position for some months before. See Burke, *Paul Renner*, p.56.

Standardized letterhead designed by Tschichold for the director of the Graphische Berufsschule in Munich. 1926. A4. The typed text explains the origins of the DIN standards.

Brochure for the Munich Meisterschule, c.1928. A4. Possibly designed by students under the supervision of Tschichold.

orders from Moscow, went on directly to wonder 'how far Renner is connected with all this', having already labelled his ideas for constructing letters from geometric parts (later realized in Futura) as 'Bolshevism'. In his published reply to these accusations, Renner pointed out coolly that if Hoffmann believed he or his 'esteemed colleague' Tschichold had answered the call of Moscow, he was mistaken.[75]

Renner obviously discovered some common ground with Tschichold, who knew of Renner's 1922 book *Typografie als Kunst*, and consequently Renner invited Tschichold instead to teach with him in Munich, where preparations were underway to found a new national school for training the future directors of printing firms.[76] Edith Tschichold recalled that her husband was already inclined to accept the offer of the Frankfurt post – 'Above all, because he needed a way of making a living' – but that the Munich school was more attractive because it was a specialist school for printing, not an art school.[77] Tschichold took up his post in Munich on 1 June 1926 and the new Meisterschule für Deutschlands Buchdrucker (Master school for Germany's

printers) opened there on 1 February 1927, alongside the existing Graphische Berufsschule.

Thomas Mann, an acquaintance of Renner, asserted that Munich was the 'artistic' antithesis to 'political-economic' Berlin.[78] Edith Tschichold reminisced that the charm of Munich lay in its people and in the city's architecture; politics did not matter to them. At the time the Tschicholds moved to Munich, it was a more conservative city than Berlin: after the terrible bloodshed that occurred on its streets during the overthrow of the short-lived, Soviet-style Räterepublik there in 1919, 'Bavaria turned in the following years into a bastion of the conservative Right and a magnet for right-wing extremists throughout Germany'.[79]

75. Renner's reply published in *Zeitschrift für Deutschlands Buchdrucker*, Nr 33, April 1926, pp.266–7.
76. The adolescent Tschichold would have seen examples of Renner's book design work for the publisher Georg Müller in 1914 at the Bugra exhibition, which awarded Renner its grand prize. Renner commented later that what endeared Tschichold to him more than anything in their initial correspondence was his beautiful handwriting.
77. [Edith Tschichold], 'Interview mit Edith Tschichold', p.183.
78. Mann, 'München als Kulturzentrum' (1926), *Politische Schriften und Reden*, vol.2 (Frankfurt: Fischer Bücherei, 1968), p.161.
79. Kershaw, *Hitler*, p.115.

Booklet for Munich's Meisterschule für Mode (fashion). *c.*1930. 20.4 × 13 cm. Probably designed by students under Tschichold's supervision in Munich.

Tourist brochure for Munich and South Bavaria. *c.*1930. 22.9 × 14 cm. Probably designed by students under Tschichold's supervision in Munich.

Some of the prominent figures in the Munich Soviet had been Russian-born communists,[80] a fact which stoked the fears exploited by the National Socialists, who were steadily building their power base from Munich during the 1920s. Into such a climate Renner felt that he could not 'present the inhabitants of Munich with an Ivan'.[81] Edith Tschichold recalled later: 'The "Ivan" disturbed the Munich school authorities, including Paul Renner, who were not at all well-disposed towards this typographical revolutionary, and they demanded time and again that he call himself by his "correct" name.' She added that the school authorities put pressure on him by refusing to accord him the title of professor, and, not wishing to return to his given forename, he opted instead for its Czech & Polish form, Jan, which he retained thenceforth.[82] A few days after he started work, Tschichold signed a letter to his friend Werner Doede: 'now jan instead of ivan, since munich! ivan is impossible here!' He found his new situation challenging but not disagreeable: 'the work here is satisfying when it comes to the goals, the path is naturally a struggle ... but munich is a beautiful city'.[83]

There was some confusion surrounding Tschichold's appointment at the Munich school. Renner evidently offered him the post of professor, having misunderstood the situation: Tschichold would only become a professor after a number of years. Renner later recalled the 'composure' with which Tschichold met this situation, although Tschichold never seems to have attained the title of professor during his seven years of teaching there, remaining a *Studienrat* (teacher). Apart from diminished status, this must have also entailed a lower salary, and perhaps contributed to a certain strain on the relationship with Renner, which was not a close one.

Tschichold was involved in teaching at both of the parallel Munich schools, which occupied the same building in the Pranckhstraße. Tschichold took over direction of teaching in typography at the Graphische Berufsschule, where the students (printing apprentices) spent two of their nine hours of study per week doing *Schriftschreiben* (formal writing as a way of learning about letterforms); in their fourth year this was replaced by workshop experience of the printing machinery. In Tschichold's first year at the Meisterschule in 1927/8 he taught *Schriftschreiben* for two hours per week in semesters one and two (there were three in all, spread over one and a half years). By 1930 (now with four semesters spread over two years of study) he taught type composition

Leaflet for American educational visit to Munich. 1931. A5. Designed by Hans Süß, one of Tschichold's students at the Graphische Berufsschule.

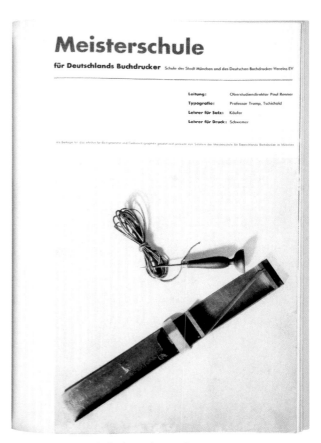

Periodical supplement featuring student work from the Meisterschule. c.1930. 32 × 23.2 cm. Listed teachers of typography: 'Professor Trump, Tschichold.'

80. Both Max Levien and Eugen Leviné, a veteran of the 1905 revolution, were Russian.
81. Renner, 'Über moderne Typographie' p.119.
82. Edith Tschichold · 'Johannes Tzschichhold · Iwan Tschichold · Jan Tschichold' in Luidl, J.T., p.31. Renner claimed later that Tschichold chose Jan 'as it was Polish, and he seemed to be as proud of his Polish origin as his great compatriot Nietzsche'. (Draft of 'Über moderne Typographie', 1948; Haushofer Archive.)
83. Letter Tschichold to Doede, 5 June 1926, in Luidl, J.T., p.19. When registering the simplified spelling of their surname with the Munich authorities, Edith Tschichold met with the ignorance of a 'complacent official', who suggested that her husband change the name for an altogether more Bavarian one, given that he would be a public official. She explained that his name was already well known in his field. Luidl, J.T., p.32.

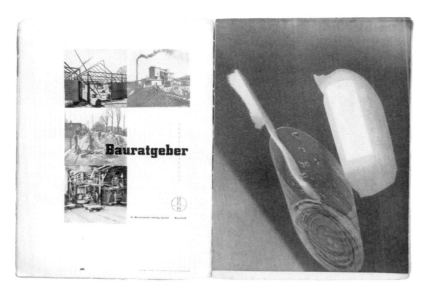

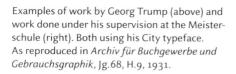

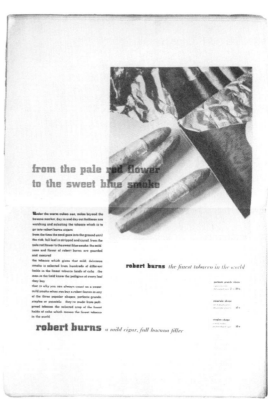

Examples of work by Georg Trump (above) and
work done under his supervision at the Meisterschule (right). Both using his City typeface.
As reproduced in *Archiv für Buchgewerbe und
Gebrauchsgraphik*, Jg.68, H.9, 1931.

(*Satz*) jointly with Josef Käufer, the technical tutor, for a
total of twenty-two hours per week in the first semester,
and seventeen in the second semester, in which he also
taught two hours per week of *Schriftschreiben*. The second
year of study at the Meisterschule was more occupied with
business theory for printing house management, printing
technology, and a small amount of advertising theory.[84]

Examples of work done at Munich's Graphische Berufsschule were shown in the major international printing
exhibition, Pressa, held at Cologne in 1928. A party from the
Munich schools that most probably included both Renner
and Tschichold visited Pressa, where examples of typography done at the Kunstgewerbeschule in Bielefeld were
also on display.[85] A successful graphic design workshop had
been built up at that school under the direction of Georg
Trump, and Renner, who was impressed by its work, invited
him to teach at the Meisterschule. Renner's action was
partly prompted by an expectation that Tschichold would
not remain in employment there much longer. After only
eighteen months of teaching in Munich, Tschichold told
Piet Zwart that he did not like living there.[86] It is likely that,
as an atheist, he felt uncomfortable in staunchly Catholic
Bavaria. He evidently made it known to Renner that he was

restless in his position. In a letter to Hans Baier (Munich's
municipal director of education and a supporter of Renner's plans at the Meisterschule) Renner commented that
Trump was one of the only young candidates with real
practical experience in composition and printing:

> That is particularly important because Tschichold so often
> shuts me out [*den Stuhl vor die Tür stellt*] and has very little
> affection for Munich. If he should once more offer his resig-
> nation, business at the Meisterschule would be endangered
> because I have no other man at the school who is thoroughly
> versed in typography.[87]

Trump took up his position at the Meisterschule in the
second half of 1929 and from 1930 he taught type composition and 'typographic sketching' (making accurate layouts)
in semester four. In contrast to Tschichold, Trump, having
previously led a department at the Bielefeld school, was
accorded the title of professor. Although Trump's work
probably came to Tschichold's attention too late for inclusion in *Die neue Typographie*, it was featured in his second,
shorter book, *Eine Stunde Druckgestaltung*. Trump was a
remarkably fine practitioner of New Typography, in addition
to being a prolific and innovative typeface designer. Tschichold implicitly approved of Trump's slab-serif typeface,

84. Curriculum details compiled from the prospectus supplement to *Archiv für Buchgewerbe und Gebrauchsgraphik*
(Jg.69, H.8, 1932) and from the
Meisterschule's anniversary
book, *Fünfundzwanzig Jahre*

*Meisterschule für Deutschlands
Buchdrucker München, 1927 /
1952*.
85. At Pressa the Bauhaus
had a separate exhibit entitled
'Elementare Buchtechnik'
(elemental book technique),

directed and designed by
Bayer. He was the only modernist on Pressa's organizing committee, which was mostly made
up of Tschichold's former mentors and teachers from Leipzig
& Dresden. See *Pressa: amtli-*

cher Katalog (Cologne, 1928),
and Aynsley, *Graphic design in
Germany 1890–1945*, pp.147–8.
86. Letter Tschichold to
Zwart, 26 January 1928. Later
that year he remarked that he
was 'currently compelled to

remain' in Bavaria. (Letter Tschichold to Kner, 25 July 1928;
Békés Archive.)
87. Letter Renner to Baier, 17
October 1928.

(Right) Lecture invitation card. 1927. A5. The explanatory paragraph ends: 'the lecture will be accompanied by over a hundred, mostly full-colour slides; a discussion will not take place.'

(Middle: left and centre) Front and inner spread of invitation card for Tschichold's lecture in Karlsruhe. 1928. Although it uses his ex libris, it is unlikely to have been designed by him. (Right) Invitation card (similary not designed by Tschichold) to the event in Zurich billed as 'For and against New Typography'. 1928. Both cards had holes punched for filing by Tschichold.

(Below) Spread from *Graphische Revue* (Jg.30, H.1, 1928) containing the text of Tschichold's lecture, 'Die neue Typographie', given in Vienna in December 1927. Shown on the right is one of his earliest, modernist posters, lettered entirely by hand in sanserif. (Tschichold dated it 1926 in *Die neue Typographie* but it was given the impossible date of 1930 in his *Leben und Werk*.)

jan tschichold:

lichtbildervortrag **die neue typographie**

am mittwoch, 11. mai 1927, abends 8 uhr, in der aula der graphischen berufsschule, pranckhstraße 2, am marsfeld, straßenbahnlinien: 3 (haltestelle hackerbrücke), 1, 4 und 11 (haltestelle pappenheimstraße) ● der vortrag wird von über hundert größtenteils mehrfarbigen lichtbildern begleitet, eine diskussion findet nicht statt

freier eintritt

veranstalter: bildungsverband der deutschen buchdrucker ortsgruppe münchen vorsitzender: j. lehnacker münchen fröttmaninger-straße 14 c

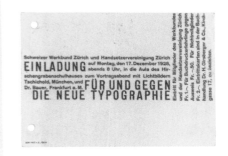

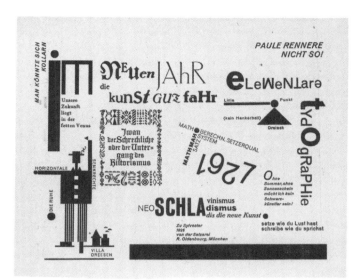

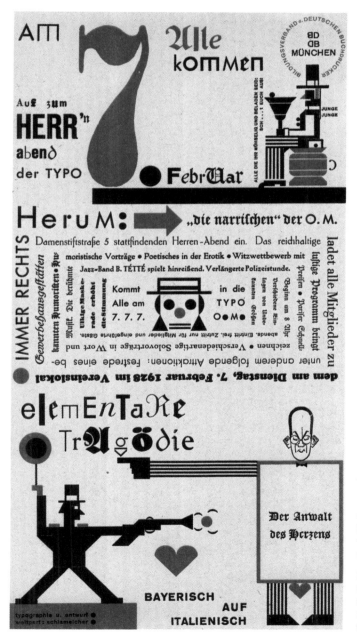

City, by using it in some of his design work of the 1930s. However, Trump did not initially stay long in Munich, leaving in 1931 to teach at the Berlin Kunstgewerbe- und Handwerkerschule, although he would return in 1934 – one year after Renner and Tschichold were dismissed – as director of the Meisterschule.[88]

Evidence of Tschichold's book taking shape during his first year of teaching is given by a public evening lecture with the same title, 'Die neue Typographie', that he held on 11 May 1927 at the Munich Graphische Berufsschule. It was organized by the local branch of the Bildungsverband, his publisher. Tschichold's invitation card for the event conforms to the spare, asymmetrical style of purely sanserif typography familiar from *Elementare Typographie*, and the description that it contains of the lecture gives a telling clue about his methods of teaching: 'the lecture will be accompanied by over a hundred, mostly full-colour slides; a discussion will not take place.' Such a dogmatic way of thinking about his subject was not peculiar to this period: he would prove equally dogmatic, with different recommendations, in later years. Yet this did not correlate with a reluctance to speak in public: Tschichold gave no fewer than nineteen lectures (mostly with the title 'Die neue Typographie') to typographical societies in various cities of Germany, Austria and Switzerland during 1927 and 1928. In one lecture he explained:

> I would like to say, by the way, that I definitely see the art in old typography; I only doubt that typography done in the previous manner can carry any weight in our time.

In a later talk he suggested a shift in terminology, proposing the term 'neue Drucksatzgestaltung' (new design with printing type) instead of 'neue Typographie', which he felt was a 'somewhat vague concept' to specialists and non-specialists alike. Here he also summarized the most important requirements for contemporary typography:

1. the disregard of the given, conventional prejudices,
2. the avoidance of personal expression,
3. a content-driven ordering of the visible forms
4. the total exploitation of all modern printing processes.[89]

Two pastiches of elemental typography designed by Weitpert & Schlameicher:

(Top) New year card 1926/7. Tschichold is named in the ornamented box as 'Ivan the Terrible' (prefiguring the film poster illustrated in the spread from *Graphische Revue* shown opposite).

(Bottom) Invitation card to Bildungsverband event. 1928. Tschichold is caricatured (and being shot) at bottom right. The gothic type in the box replacing his body reads 'The heart's advocate', while the heart itself has slipped netherwards.

88. Renner was reluctant to let Trump leave in 1931, and in fact kept his position open for him in case he should want to return from Berlin. It is likely that he did this with the expectation that Tschichold would leave, and Renner continued to actively entice Trump back to Munich into the early months of 1932. Despite difficulties at the Berlin school, Trump decided to stay there.

89. Lecture typescripts 'Elementare Typographie' and 'für die neue Drucksatzgestaltung' (DNB Leipzig).

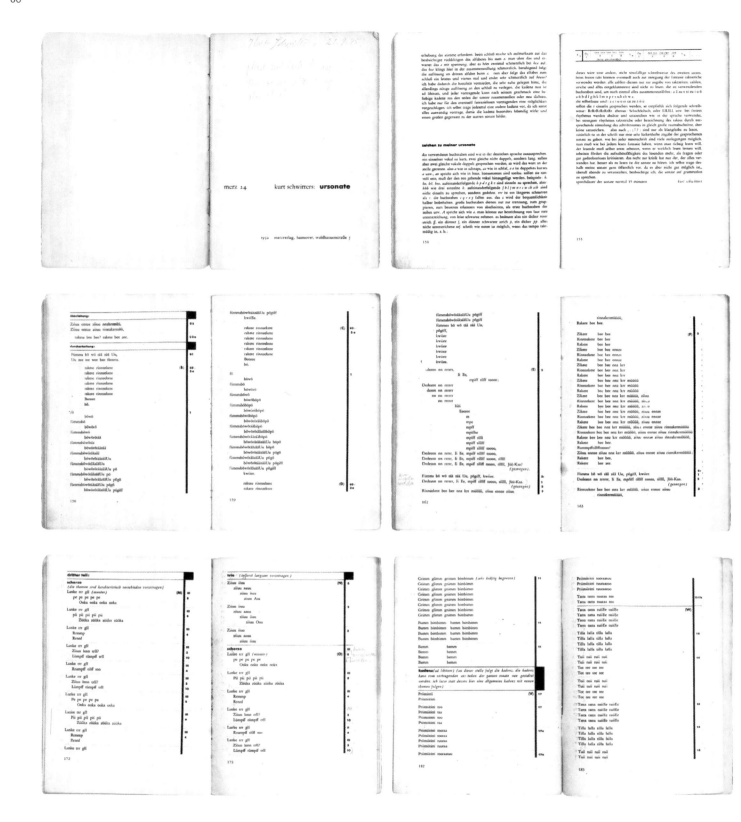

Spreads from Kurt Schwitters, *Ursonate*. Issued as *Merz* 24. 1932. 20.7 × 14.4 cm. Designed and typeset by Tschichold and his students at the Meisterschule. Typeset in Futura and Garamond; without capitals throughout. Pencil annotations by Schwitters.

The typography of this nonsense poetry 'sonata' approaches a kind of musical notation. The sanserif numbers on the right correspond to the recurring themes. Schwitters stated in his introduction (top right) that the usual performance time was 35 minutes.

A difference of opinion was deliberately programmed for an event organized in December 1928 by the Swiss Werkbund, at which Tschichold was invited to speak alongside printing historian Konrad Bauer. The evening in Zurich was billed as 'For and against New Typography', although Bauer was not entirely unsympathetic. Both went armed with slide illustrations.

There is ample evidence of Tschichold's dedication to teaching during his Munich years: in addition to his regular classes he was the principal lecturer for practical courses held for Munich members of the Bildungsverband during 1927. Renner and Josef Lehnacker led a course on 'The beautiful book', but Tschichold gave courses in formal writing, typographic sketching and 'New Typography'. The chronicler of events for the Munich division of the Bildungsverband reported in *Typographische Mitteilungen*:

> At the centre of all technical issues, and of those relating to the present day, stood New Typography, which was explained to us by Herr Tschichold, one of the leading representatives of this movement, in several informative lectures, sometimes with slide illustrations. If the seeds did not always fall on fruitful ground, the new ideas will nevertheless break through, as is already shown by the numerous pieces of work in the new manner.[90]

As this report hinted, Tschichold's ideas were not universally welcomed among the seventy participants in the courses. Indeed New Typography, and Tschichold in particular, were subjected to some inventive mockery in an invitation card for an evening of humorous speeches held in February 1928 by the Bildungsverband's Munich group (see p.59).

Teaching at both of the Munich schools while writing *Die neue Typographie* doubtless left Tschichold little time for much else. The difficulty of fitting practical design work into such a schedule is demonstrated by his involvement in an edition of the *Ursonate* by Kurt Schwitters. Lissitzky had already declined to design this and Tschichold promised Schwitters in 1926 that he would do it; however it was not finished until 1932, when it was released as the last issue of *Merz*. The delay was at least partly caused by the decision to have it typeset and produced as a student project at the Meisterschule. Yet, for a small booklet of forty pages, more than five years is a remarkably long time, and it is to the credit of Schwitters that he remained patient and did not let it affect their friendship.[91] Similarly, Tschichold apologized to Piet Zwart in June 1928 for a long delay in replying to his letters, explaining that the school kept him extremely busy, with little time left for his own commercial work: 'Of late

it was principally the work in finishing my book that has robbed me of the majority of my time.'[92]

A preview of *Die neue Typographie* was given in a short piece Tschichold wrote for *Die literarische Welt* (The literary world), a weekly paper from the progressive Berlin publisher Rowohlt that dealt with modern literature (among those who wrote for it were Walter Benjamin and Robert Musil). Tschichold's article, in the issue for 22 July 1927, was spurred by the Internationale Buchkunst-Ausstellung (International exhibition of book art) in Leipzig. He was among a few 'moderns' whose work was exhibited there, along with Renner, Bayer and 'Ladislaus' Moholy-Nagy, as he was listed in the catalogue, which also curiously described Tschichold as 'Teacher for binding design, title-pages and typographic designs [*Gestaltungen*].'[93] The exhibition was however dominated by traditional book design, with professors from the Leipzig academy (where Tschichold had trained) being prominent on the selection committee. Renner, who bridged the worlds of pre-First-World-War 'book art' and New Typography, had an article published in an earlier issue of *Die literarische Welt* that was mainly dedicated to the exhibition: it was even typeset in his Futura typeface, then on the verge of being released.

Despite being concerned with avant-garde literature, *Die literarische Welt* had a certain bibliophile aspect. In a review of the Leipzig exhibition, its editor Willy Haas (a Czech) had little positive to say about Soviet poster art and summarized Tschichold's work with a single, mysterious sentence: 'Good interim solutions shown by Tschichold.' Judging by his editorial foreword, it was with some scepticism that Haas allowed Tschichold to present his views, which were published along with short contributions by Georg Mendelssohn and Lissitzky. Although Tschichold had written his piece before the opening of the exhibition, Haas explained that he had not wanted to include the opinions of the 'strongly industrial and collectively disposed young radical book-technicians' in the previous coverage. 'Their opinions and principles', he declared, 'have nothing to do with today's book art.' Indeed Tschichold's essay must have contained some shockingly new ideas for readers of this literary weekly, given that he chose deliberately provocative illustrations, including a Futurist poem by Marinetti and a photomontage by Rodchenko. Tschichold complained that contemporary book design still followed in the footsteps of William Morris: 'Can it really be called culture', he asked, 'when the woman sitting in an automobile or an aeroplane is reading a book that could have been made in the time of Goethe?' (See a full translation in appendix B.)

The design work that Tschichold was able to do during his first few years in Munich consisted mainly of tasks other than book design, including commercial stationery and a series of film posters for the Phoebus-Palast, a grand cinema in Munich owned by the Phoebus film production company

90. The *Schriftführer* of the TGM, Neumeyer, cited in Typographische Gesellschaft München, *Hundert Jahre TGM*, p.72.

91. Schwitters to Tschichold: postcard 3 September 1926 and letter 3 December 1931.

92. Letter Tschichold to Zwart, 13 June 1928. He had reported to Zwart on 12 September 1927 that the book was already being typeset, so it must have been substantially written by that point.

93. *Internationale Buchkunst-*

Ausstellung, Leipzig 1927. Amtlicher Katalog, p.80. The explanation for this description is that, within the mainly traditionalist remit of this exhibition, Tschichold's 'book art' for Insel Verlag was considered his most important work.

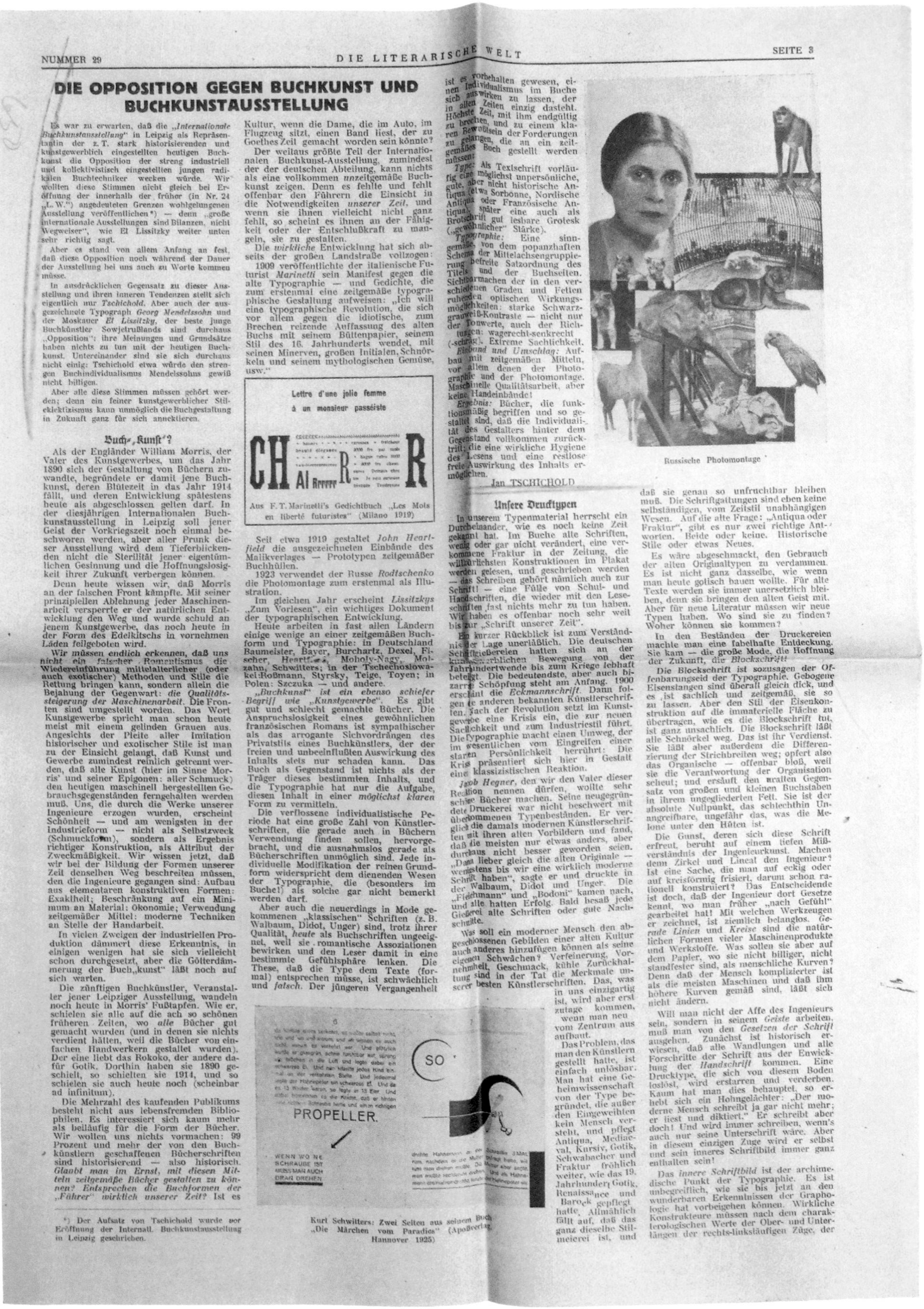

NUMMER 29 DIE LITERARISCHE WELT SEITE 3

DIE OPPOSITION GEGEN BUCHKUNST UND BUCHKUNSTAUSSTELLUNG

Es war zu erwarten, daß die *„Internationale Buchkunstausstellung"* in Leipzig als Repräsentantin der z. T. stark historisierenden und kunstgewerblich eingestellten heutigen Buchkunst die Opposition der streng industriell und kollektivistisch eingestellten jungen radikalen Buchtechniker wecken würde. Wir wollten diese Stimmen nicht gleich bei Eröffnung der innerhalb der früher (in Nr. 24 „L. W.") angedeuteten Grenzen wohlgelungenen Ausstellung veröffentlichen*) — denn „große internationale Ausstellungen sind Bilanzen, nicht Wegweiser", wie El Lissitzky weiter unten sehr richtig sagt.

Aber es stand von allem Anfang an fest, daß diese Opposition noch während der Dauer der Ausstellung bei uns auch zu Worte kommen müsse.

In ausdrücklichen Gegensatz zu dieser Ausstellung und ihren inneren Tendenzen stellt sich eigentlich nur *Tschichold*. Aber auch der ausgezeichnete Typograph *Georg Mendelssohn* und der Moskauer *El Lissitzky*, der beste junge Buchkünstler Sowjetrußlands sind durchaus „Opposition": ihre Meinungen und Grundsätze haben nichts zu tun mit der heutigen Buchkunst. Untereinander sind sie sich durchaus nicht einig: Tschichold etwa würde den strengen Buchindividualismus Mendelssohns gewiß nicht billigen.

Aber alle diese Stimmen müssen gehört werden; denn ein feiner kunstgewerblicher Stileklektizismus kann unmöglich die Buchgestaltung in Zukunft ganz für sich annektieren.

Buch-„Kunst"?

Als der Engländer William Morris, der Vater des Kunstgewerbes, um das Jahr 1890 sich der Gestaltung von Büchern zuwandte, begründete er damit jene Buchkunst, deren Blütezeit in das Jahr 1914 fällt, und deren Entwicklung spätestens heute als abgeschlossen gelten darf. In der diesjährigen Internationalen Buchkunstausstellung in Leipzig soll jener Geist der Vorkriegszeit noch einmal beschworen werden, aber aller Prunk dieser Ausstellung wird dem Tieferblickenden nicht die Sterilität jener eigentümlichen Gesinnung und die Hoffnungslosigkeit ihrer Zukunft verbergen können.

Denn heute wissen wir, daß Morris an der falschen Front kämpfte. Mit seiner prinzipiellen Ablehnung jeder Maschinenarbeit versperrte er der natürlichen Entwicklung den Weg und wurde schuld an jenem Kunstgewerbe, das noch heute in der Form des Edelkitschs in vornehmen Läden feilgeboten wird.

Wir müssen endlich erkennen, daß uns nicht ein falscher Romantismus die Wiedereinführung mittelalterlicher (oder auch exotischer) Methoden und Stile die Rettung bringen kann, sondern allein die Bejahung der Gegenwart: ***die Qualitätssteigerung der Maschinenarbeit.*** Die Fronten sind umgestellt worden. Das Wort Kunstgewerbe spricht man schon heute meist mit einem gelinden Grauen aus. Angesichts der Pleite aller Imitation historischer und exotischer Stile ist man zu der Einsicht gelangt, daß Kunst und Gewerbe zumindest reinlich getrennt werden, daß alle Kunst (hier im Sinne Morris' und seiner Epigonen: aller Schmuck) den heutigen maschinell hergestellten Gebrauchsgegenständen ferngehalten werden muß. Uns, die durch die Werke unserer Ingenieure erzogen wurden, erscheint Schönheit — und am wenigsten in der Industrieform — nicht als Selbstzweck (Schmuckform), sondern als Ergebnis richtiger Konstruktion, als Attribut der Zweckmäßigkeit. Wir wissen jetzt, daß wir bei der Bildung der Formen unserer Zeit denselben Weg beschreiten müssen, den die Ingenieure gegangen sind: Aufbau aus elementaren konstruktiven Formen: Exaktheit; Beschränkung auf ein Minimum an Material: Ökonomie; Verwendung zeitgemäßer Mittel: moderne Techniken an Stelle der Handarbeit.

In vielen Zweigen der industriellen Produktion dämmert diese Erkenntnis, in einigen wenigen hat sie sich vielleicht schon durchgesetzt, aber die Götterdämmerung der Buch„kunst" läßt noch auf sich warten.

Die zünftigen Buchkünstler, Veranstalter jener Leipziger Ausstellung, wandeln noch heute in Morris' Fußtapfen. Wie er, schielen sie alle auf die ach so schönen früheren Zeiten, wo *alle* Bücher gut gemacht wurden (und in denen sie nichts verdient hätten, weil die Bücher von einfachen Handwerkern gestaltet wurden). Der eine liebt das Rokoko, der andere dafür Gotik. Dorthin haben sie 1890 geschielt, so schielten sie 1914, und so schielen sie auch heute noch (scheinbar ad infinitum).

Die Mehrzahl des kaufenden Publikums besteht nicht aus lebensfremden Bibliophilen. Es interessiert sich kaum mehr als beiläufig für die Form der Bücher. Wir wollen uns nichts vormachen: 99 Prozent und mehr der von den Buchkünstlern geschaffenen Bücherschriften sind historisierend — also historisch. *Glaubt man im Ernst, mit diesen Mitteln zeitgemäße Bücher gestalten zu können? Entsprechen die Buchformen der „Führer" wirklich unserer Zeit?* Ist es Kultur, wenn die Dame, die im Auto, im Flugzeug sitzt, einen Band liest, der zu Goethes Zeit gemacht worden sein könnte?

Der weitaus größte Teil der Internationalen Buchkunst-Ausstellung, zumindest der der deutschen Abteilung, kann nichts als eine vollkommen *unzeitgemäße* Buchkunst zeigen. Denn es fehlte und fehlt offenbar den Führern die Einsicht in die Notwendigkeiten *unserer Zeit*, und wenn sie ihnen vielleicht nicht ganz fehlt, so scheint es ihnen an der Fähigkeit oder der Entschlußkraft zu mangeln, sie zu gestalten.

Die *wirkliche* Entwicklung hat sich abseits der großen Landstraße vollzogen:

1909 veröffentlichte der italienische Futurist *Marinetti* sein Manifest gegen die alte Typographie — und Gedichte, die zum erstenmal eine zeitgemäße typographische Gestaltung aufweisen: „Ich will eine typographische Revolution, die sich vor allem gegen die idiotische, zum Brechen reizende Auffassung des alten Buchs mit seinem Büttenpapier, seinem Stil des 16. Jahrhunderts wendet, mit seinen Minerven, großen Initialen, Schnörkeln und seinem mythologischen Gemüse, usw."

Lettre d'une jolie femme
à un monsieur passéiste

CH Al Rrrrrr R R

Aus F. T. Marinetti's Gedichtbuch „Les Mots en liberté futuristes" (Milano 1919)

Seit etwa 1919 gestaltet *John Heartfield* die ausgezeichneten Einbände des Malikverlages — Prototypen zeitgemäßer Buchhüllen.

1923 verwendet der Russe *Rodtschenko* die Photomontage zum erstenmal als Illustration.

Im gleichen Jahr erscheint *Lissitzkys* „Zum Vorlesen", ein wichtiges Dokument der typographischen Entwicklung.

Heute arbeiten in fast allen Ländern einige wenige an einer zeitgemäßen Buchform und Typographie: in Deutschland Baumeister, Bayer, Burchartz, Dexel, Fischer, Heartfield, Moholy-Nagy, Molzahn, Schwitters; in der Tschechoslowakei: Roßmann, Styrsky, Teige, Toyen; in Polen: Szczuka — und andere.

„Buchkunst" ist ein ebenso schiefer Begriff wie „Kunstgewerbe". Es gibt gut und schlecht gemachte Bücher. Die Anspruchslosigkeit eines gewöhnlichen französischen Romans ist sympathischer als das arrogante Sichvordrängen des Privatstils eines Buchkünstlers, der der freien und unbeeinflußten Auswirkung des Inhalts stets nur schaden kann. Das Buch als Gegenstand ist nichts als der Träger dieses bestimmten Inhalts, und die Typographie hat nur die Aufgabe, diesen Inhalt in einer *möglichst klaren* Form zu vermitteln.

Die verflossene individualistische Periode hat eine große Zahl von Künstlerschriften, die gerade auch in Büchern Verwendung finden sollen, hervorgebracht, und die ausnahmslos gerade als Bücherschriften unmöglich sind. Jede individuelle Modifikation der reinen Grundform widerspricht dem dienenden Wesen der Typographie, die (besonders im Buche!) als solche gar nicht bemerkt werden darf.

Aber auch die neuerdings in Mode gekommenen „klassischen" Schriften (z. B. Walbaum, Didot, Unger) sind, trotz ihrer Qualität, *heute* als Buchschriften ungeeignet, weil sie romantische Assoziationen bewirken und den Leser damit in eine bestimmte Gefühlsphäre lenken. Die These, daß die Type dem Texte (formal) entsprechen müsse, ist schwächlich und *falsch*. Der jüngeren Vergangenheit ist es vorbehalten gewesen, einen Individualismus im Buche sich auswirken zu lassen, der in allen Zeiten einzig dasteht. Höchste Zeit, mit ihm endgültig zu brechen, und zu einem klaren Bewußtsein der Forderungen zu gelangen, die an ein zeitgemäßes Buch gestellt werden müssen:

Type: Als Textschrift vorläufig eine möglichst unpersönliche, gute, aber nicht historische Antiqua (etwa Sorbonne, Nordische Antiqua oder Französische Antiqua), später eine auch als Brotschrift gut lesbare Grotesk („gewöhnlicher" Stärke).

Typographie: Eine sinngemäße, von dem popanzhaften Schema der Mittelachsengruppierung befreite Satzordnung des Titels und der Buchseiten. Sichtbarmachen der in den verschiedenen Graden und Fetten ruhenden optischen Wirkungsmöglichkeiten: starke Schwarzgrauweiß-Kontraste — nicht nur der Tonwerte, auch der Richtungen: wagerecht-senkrecht (-schräg). Extreme Sachlichkeit.

Einband und Umschlag: Aufbau mit zeitgemäßen Mitteln, vor allem denen der Photographie und der Photomontage. Maschinelle Qualitätsarbeit, aber keine Handeinbände!

Ergebnis: Bücher, die funktionsmäßig begriffen und so gestaltet sind, daß die Individualität des Gestalters hinter dem Gegenstand vollkommen zurücktritt; die eine wirkliche Hygiene des Lesens und eine restlose freie Auswirkung des Inhalts ermöglichen.

Jan TSCHICHOLD

*) Der Aufsatz von Tschichold wurde *vor* Eröffnung der Internatl. Buchkunstausstellung in Leipzig geschrieben.

Russische Photomontage

Kurt Schwitters: Zwei Seiten aus seinem Buch „Die Märchen vom Paradies" (Apossverlag, Hannover 1925)

Unsere Drucktypen

In unserem Typenmaterial herrscht ein Durcheinander, wie es noch keine Zeit gekannt hat. Im Buche alte Schriften, wenig oder gar nicht verändert, eine verkommene Fraktur in der Zeitung, die willkürlichsten Konstruktionen im Plakat werden gelesen, und geschrieben werden — das Schreiben gehört nämlich auch zur Schrift! — eine Fülle von Schul- und Handschriften, die wieder mit den Leseschriften fast nichts mehr zu tun haben. Wir haben es offenbar noch sehr weit bis zur „Schrift unserer Zeit".

Ein kurzer Rückblick ist zum Verständnis der Lage unerläßlich. Die deutschen Schriftgießereien hatten sich an der kunstgewerblichen Bewegung von der Jahrhundertwende bis zum Kriege lebhaft beteiligt. Die bedeutendste, aber auch bizarrste Schöpfung steht am Anfang. 1900 erscheint die *Eckmannschrift*. Dann folgen die anderen bekannten Künstlerschriften. Nach der Revolution setzt im Kunstgewerbe eine Krisis ein, die zur neuen Sachlichkeit und zum Industriestil führt. Die Typographie macht einen Umweg, der im wesentlichen vom Eingreifen einer starken Persönlichkeit herrührt: Die Krisis präsentiert sich hier in Gestalt einer klassizistischen Reaktion.

Jakob Hegner, den wir den Vater dieser Reaktion nennen dürfen, wollte sehr schöne Bücher machen. Seine neugegründete Druckerei war nicht beschwert mit überkommenen Typenbeständen. Er verglich die damals modernen Künstlerschriften mit ihren alten Vorbildern und fand, daß die meisten nur etwas anders, aber durchaus nicht besser geworden seien. „Dann lieber gleich die alten Originale — wenigstens bis wir eine wirklich moderne Schrift haben", sagte er und druckte in der Walbaum, Didot und Unger. Die „Fleischmann" und „Bodoni" kamen nach, und alle hatten Erfolg. Bald besaß jede Gießerei alte Schriften oder gute Nachschnitte.

Was soll ein moderner Mensch den abgeschlossenen Gebilden einer alten Kultur auch anderes hinzufügen können als seine eigenen Schwächen? Verfeinerung, Vornehmheit, Geschmack, kühle Zurückhaltung sind in der Tat die Merkmale unserer besten Künstlerschriften. Das, was in uns einzigartig ist, wird aber erst zutage kommen, wenn man neu vom Zentrum aus aufbaut.

Das Problem, das man den Künstlern gestellt hatte, ist einfach unlösbar. Man hat eine Geheimwissenschaft von der Type begründet, die außer den Eingeweihten kein Mensch versteht, und pflegt Antiqua, Mediaeval, Kursiv, Gotik, Schwabacher und Fraktur fröhlich weiter, wie das 19. Jahrhundert Gotik, Renaissance und Barock gepflegt hatte. Allmählich fällt auf, daß das ganz dieselbe Stilmeierei ist, und daß sie genau so unfruchtbar bleiben muß. Die Schriftgattungen sind eben keine selbständigen, vom Zeitstil unabhängigen Wesen. Auf die alte Frage: „Antiqua oder Fraktur", gibt es nur zwei richtige Antworten. Beide oder keine. Historische Stile oder etwas Neues.

Es wäre abgeschmackt, den Gebrauch der alten Originaltypen zu verdammen. Es ist nicht ganz dasselbe, wie wenn man heute gotisch bauen wollte. Für alte Texte werden sie immer unersetzlich bleiben, denn sie bringen den alten Geist mit. Aber für neue Literatur müssen wir neue Typen haben. Wo sind sie zu finden? Woher können sie kommen?

In den Beständen der Druckereien machte man eine fabelhafte Entdeckung. Sie kam — die große Mode, die Hoffnung der Zukunft, die *Blockschrift!*

Die Blockschrift ist sozusagen der Offenbarungseid der Typographie. Gebogene Eisenstangen sind überall gleich dick, und es ist sachlich und zeitgemäß, sie so zu lassen. Aber den Stil der Eisenkonstruktion auf die immaterielle Fläche zu übertragen, wie es die Blockschrift tut, ist ganz unsachlich. Die Blockschrift läßt alle Schnörkel weg. Das ist ihr Verdienst. Sie läßt aber außerdem die Differenzierung der Strichbreiten weg; opfert also das Organische — offenbar bloß, weil sie die Verantwortung der Organisation scheut; und ersäuft den uralten Gegensatz von großen und kleinen Buchstaben in ihrem ungegliederten Fett. Sie ist der absolute Nullpunkt, das schlechthin Unangreifbare, ungefähr das, was die Melone unter den Hüten ist.

Die Gunst, deren sich diese Schrift erfreut, beruht auf einem tiefen Mißverständnis der Ingenieurkunst. Machen denn Zirkel und Lineal den Ingenieur? Ist eine Sache, die man auf eckig oder auf kreisförmig frisiert, darum schon rationell konstruiert? Das Entscheidende ist doch, daß der Ingenieur dort Gesetze kennt, wo man früher „nach Gefühl" gearbeitet hat! Mit welchen Werkzeugen er zeichnet, ist ziemlich belanglos. *Gerade Linien* und *Kreise* sind die natürlichen Formen vieler Maschinenprodukte und Werkstoffe. Was sollen sie aber auf dem Papier, wo sie nicht billiger, nicht standfester sind, als menschliche Kurven? Denn daß der Mensch komplizierter ist als die meisten Maschinen und daß ihm höhere Kurven gemäß sind, läßt sich nicht ändern.

Will man nicht der Affe des Ingenieurs sein, sondern in seinem *Geiste* arbeiten, muß man von den *Gesetzen der Schrift* ausgehen. Zunächst ist historisch erwiesen, daß alle Wandlungen und alle Forschritte der Schrift aus der Enwicklung der *Handschrift* kommen. Eine Drucktype, die sich von diesem Boden loslöst, wird erstarren und verderben. Kaum hat man dies behauptet, so erhebt sich ein Hohngelächter: „Der moderne Mensch schreibt ja gar nicht mehr; er liest und diktiert." Er schreibt aber doch! Und wird immer schreiben, wenn's auch nur seine Unterschrift wäre. Aber in diesem einzigen Zuge wird er selbst und sein inneres Schriftbild immer ganz enthalten sein!

Das *innere Schriftbild* ist der archimedische Punkt der Typographie. Es ist unbegreiflich, wie sie bis jetzt an den wunderbaren Erkenntnissen der Graphologie hat vorbeigehen können. Wirkliche Konstrukteure müssen nach dem charakterologischen Werte der Ober- und Unterlängen der rechts-linksläufigen Züge, der

Tschichold's article 'Buch-"Kunst"?' (Book 'art'?) in *Die literarische Welt* (22 July 1927).

based in Berlin. These were low-budget posters produced for a single cinema and had to be designed and printed within two to four days. Tschichold designed around thirty posters for Phoebus-Palast during 1927. Almost half of them were purely typographic, using large wooden type; for combination with photographs, Tschichold mostly drew the lettering himself, and it was then either printed lithographically or by letterpress with a linocut. Considering the time limitations, he produced some remarkable results, of which he boasted in *Die neue Typographie* that they were 'the first practical attempt to make true film posters', illustrating no

less than seven of them in the book. He found it 'really astonishing' that film companies had not made more use of photography for posters, but also recognized the technical and economic limitations on printing large photographs at that time.[94] He was pushing against the limitations of the technology available to him. Among the films for which he designed posters were classics from the final years of the silent era such as Abel Gance's *Napoleon* and Buster Keaton's *The general*. Looking back from his old age, when he habitually overruled the young Tschichold, he admitted that they were still 'noteworthy'.[95]

The following pages show a sequence of Tschichold's posters for Phoebus-Palast. All date from 1927 and they are all around 120 × 84 cm in size. Those posters printed by letterpress were produced in two halves on separate sheets, which helps to explain why their design itself features a strong separation in the middle: for example, *Kiki* (p.64) and *Die drei Niemandskinder* (p.66).

Several of the posters feature prominent diagonal arrangements, which Tschichold felt to be appropriately dynamic for publicizing moving pictures. This he explained in a lecture of December 1927, in which he showed slides of some of the posters. He pointed out that 'these works must be done at an outrageous tempo. I often have only a few hours to do everything all together – design and execution.'

Two of the posters incorporate schematic representations of cinema projection – *Frau ohne Namen* (left) and *Laster der Menschheit* (p.65). Of the latter Tschichold explained: 'Here I had to draw the letters, as the printing office had no wood letters.' But it would have been difficult to achieve the same effect typographically.

(Lecture typescript 'Elementare Typographie'; DNB Leipzig.)

In Tschichold's *Leben und Werk* the poster on the left is shown with a paste-on addition in the area marked with a red line at the bottom (see below). It announces a short film accompanying the main feature. Presumably this is how the poster would originally have been seen.

94. *The New Typography*, pp.185–6.　　**95**. 'Jan Tschichold: praeceptor typographiae', p.20.

DAS EDLE BLUT
NACH ERNST VON WILDENBRUCH

PHOEBUS-PALAST

ANFANGSZEITEN: 4⁰⁰ 6¹⁵ 8³⁰
SONNTAGS: 1⁴⁵ 4⁰⁰ 6¹⁵ 8³⁰

PRINZ LOUIS FERDINAND

PHOEBUS-PALAST

ANFANGSZEITEN: 4 6¹⁵ 8³⁰
SONNTAGS: 1⁴⁵ 4 6¹⁵ 8³⁰
ENTWURF JAN TSCHICHOLD, PLANEGG B. MCH. ■ DRUCK: GEBR. GIPKENS A.G. MÜNCHEN

NORMA TALMADGE
in **KiKi**

PHOEBUS PALAST

ANFANGSZEITEN: 4 6¹⁵ 8³⁰
SONNTAGS: 1⁴⁵ 4 6¹⁵ 8³⁰

NACHT DER LIEBE
MIT VILMA BANKY U. RONALD COLMAN

PHOEBUS PALAST

ANFANG: 4⁰⁰ 6¹⁵ 8³⁰
SONNTAGS: 1¹⁵ 4⁰⁰ 6¹⁵ 8³⁰

TSCHICHOLD

LASTER DER MENSCHHEIT
MIT ASTA NIELSEN ALFRED ABEL WERNER KRAUSS
PHOEBUS-PALAST
ANFANG: 4, 6.15, 8.30 SONNTAGS: 1.45, 4, 6.15, 8.30

TSCHICHOLD

DIE LADY OHNE SCHLEIER

PHOEBUS
PALAST
ANFANGSZEITEN:
4⁰⁰ 6¹⁵ 8³⁰
SONNTAGS:
1⁴⁵ 4⁰⁰ 6¹⁵ 8³⁰
tschichold

BUSTER KEATON
IN: ›DER GENERAL‹

PHOEBUS
PALAST
ANFANGSZEITEN: 4⁰⁰ 6¹⁵ 8³⁰
SONNTAGS: 1⁴⁵ 4⁰⁰ 6¹⁵ 8³⁰

entwurf: tschichold

DIE 3 NIE
MANDS
KINDER

PHOEBUS-PALAST

ANFANG ● 4 6¹⁵ 8³⁰
SONNTAGS ● 1⁴⁵ 4 6¹⁵ 8³⁰

entwurf: tschichold, zürich

PIQUEDAME
MIT JENNY JUGO UND RUD. FORSTER
PHOEBUSPALAST
ANFANG: 4⁰⁰ 6¹⁵ 8³⁰ SONNTAGS: 1⁴⁵ 4⁰⁰ 6¹⁵ 8³⁰

ENTWURF: TSCHICHOLD

68

JAN TSCHICHOLD: Filmplakat 1927

194

Poster for *Die Hose* as reproduced in *Die neue Typographie*. Unfortunately, in this copy of the original edition, black and red have been printed with inaccurate register. The black type should be centred in the white box. The title of this film translates literally as 'Trousers' but German film historian Siegfried Kracauer gave his own translation as 'Royal scandal'. He called it 'one of the best films of the period'. It was a production of Phoebus Film AG, based on a pre-war theatre play.

(Opposite) When this poster for *Casanova* was later reproduced in Tschichold's *Leben und Werk*, his signature and the printer's credit line (F. Bruckmann AG, Munich) were deleted.

CASANOVA

MIT IWAN MOSJUKIN

PHOEBUS-PALAST
ANFANG 4.00 6.15 8.30
SONNTAGS 1.45 4.00 6.15 8.30

TSCHICHOLD

In his article 'New paths in poster work', Tschichold set
out his views on 'what the new typographic poster aims at':

> using existing type material; maintaining simpler outlines
> of positive and negative plane surfaces which promote com-
> prehension and 'legibility' in the fullest sense; consciously
> employing every possible kind of contrast and tone-variation
> to increase the effect (horizontal and vertical movement,
> large and small type, close and wide spacing, positive and
> negative, colour and monochrome etc., etc.).

If there was no good typeface available, he recommended:

> The letters can then de drawn in clear practical form and cut,
> in linoleum perhaps, not in rough expressionist style but with
> the sternest avoidance of all 'handwriting' effects.*

The Phoebus posters were represented in an exhibition
of New Typography held in early 1928 at the Dresden Kunst-
gewerbebibliothek (Arts & crafts library), where Wieynck
was among the directors. In a short review of the exhibition,
he judged Tschichold's posters to have been too complex
and not 'stimulating' enough for the majority of cinema-
goers; but he singled out for praise what he regarded as
Tschichold's best cinema poster, for *Laster der Menschheit*,
which 'by means of photomontage has attained in large
degree a spiritual dimension for its subject'.[96]

(Above) Cover of programme for the Phoebus-
Palast. 1927. 31.1 × 23.4 cm. Symbol not designed
by Tschichold.

(Above right) The *Violantha* poster was printed
on two sheets: of the copy shown here only the
bottom half survives; the top half was solid blue
with a strip of white on the left edge corresponding to the blue strip on the right edge of the
bottom half.

(Right) This poster for Danish director Carl
Dreyer's famous film about Joan of Arc is not
for the Phoebus-Palast, but instead seems to be
for a screening organized by UFA, the principal
German film company. c.1928. 60 × 84 cm.

* English translation by E.O.
Lorimer in *Commercial Art*
(June 1931), p.245.
   96. Wieynck, 'Neue Typographie', p.29.

NAPOLEON

PHOEBUS
PALAST

ANFANGSZEITEN:
| 4^{00} | 6^{15} | 8^{30} |

SONNTAGS:
| 1^{45} | 4^{00} | 6^{15} | 8 |

DRUCK: F. BRUCKMANN AG. MÜNCHEN

As well as some small posters for events at the Meister-schule – among them a lecture on 'New building' by Gropius – Tschichold designed a series of purely typographic posters for another local client during his Munich years, the Graph-isches Kabinett (Graphic cabinet). These included one for an exhibition of 'the Jan Tschichold collection' at the beginning of 1930 entitled 'posters of the avant-garde', reflecting the systematic way in which he was collecting contemporary work for historical purposes. The list of designers featured in the exhibition provides a roll-call of those he considered to be in the typographical vanguard, with all of whom he had already, or soon would, establish personal contact.

Between 1926 and 1930, apart from a few cover designs and other sundries for Insel Verlag in Leipzig, Tschichold designed few books that he had not also written; not even for the Büchergilde Gutenberg did he design another book until *Aus der Werkstatt der Natur* in 1931.[97] Some interesting titles in that book club's list, offering prime opportuni-ties for integrating type and photography, were instead designed by other modernists, including Georg Trump and Wilhelm Lesemann, who had been Trump's colleague at the Bielefeld Kunstgewerbeschule (see p.219 for illustra-tions).[98] Tschichold's principal concern while writing *Die neue Typographie* with designing 'non-literary' material was transformed into the programme of the book, which deals

(Top left) Poster for lottery on the occasion of an exhibition of Bavarian craft. 1927.

(Top right) This poster for a lecture by Gropius at the Munich Graphische Berufsschule dates from 1926, not 'c.1931' as was later stated in Tschichold's *Leben und Werk*. Lettered, not typeset. There is no evidence that either Tschichold or Renner were ever reciprocally invited to lecture at the Bauhaus. 43.5 × 68 cm.

(Above right) Two typographic exhibition posters for the Graphisches Kabinett, Munich. 1930. 'Posters of the avantgarde' 42 × 60 cm; 'Artists' self-portraits of our time' 60 × 84 cm.

97. On sending some of his work to Piet Zwart in February 1929, Tschichold commented that he had not done much due to lack of commissions. Post-card 3 February 1929.

98. Another Büchergilde book, with an interesting design by Heinrich Schulze, Gerhard Kutzebach and Adolf Pohl, was *Kohlenpott* (1931). See http://wiedler.ch/felix/books04.html.

Top section, spine, cover and title-page of *Die neue Typographie*. 1928. A5.

Many copies of the original edition have lost their silver blocking on the spine to some extent.

with the design of many kinds of printed items almost to the exclusion of books. The small section on book design at the end seems like something of an afterthought in which Tschichold proposed that New Typography could refresh illustrated books, especially with the use of photomontage, but admitted that for common books (novels and scientific literature) *Sachlichkeit* (objectivity) was not a new principle:

> it is not a question of making a really new kind of book (in a technical sense), because the old book form is perfectly suitable for such literature, and will remain so until a better form is discovered. There is absolutely no need for change, which would only be justified when a really new form is found. Also in connection with typographic form, only modifications in traditional book design are possible.[99]

Die neue Typographie, which was finally published in June 1928, cannot be deemed the first modern manual of typography, but it is the first practical guide to modern graphic design, with its sections on designing newspapers, magazines, posters and standardized commercial stationery.[100] Tschichold's own design for the book itself is iconic, though not entirely revolutionary: it is typeset throughout in sanserif, with page numbers in a bolder weight also used occasionally for emphasis, and printed on a coated paper in order to integrate text and images; yet some peculiar old-

fashioned features persist, such as the use of letterspacing for emphasis, a standard feature of typography with gothic type that traditionally lacked italic. As Gerd Fleischmann has pointed out, an inspired stroke was the frontispiece consisting of a totally black page, perhaps alluding to Malevich's famous painting of a black square.[101] The austere external appearance of the book was also eloquent: good-quality black cloth, with no jacket, nor marks on the cover, but with the author and title reversed out of a silver bar at the top of the spine. During the near seven decades in which this book remained unavailable in English, the great unread book of modern typography, it gained a status reminiscent of the mysterious black monolith in Stanley Kubrick's *2001: a space odyssey* – mute, yet somehow the fount of all knowledge.[102]

It is not the place here to give a full account of the content of *Die neue Typographie*, given that it is now available in an adequate English translation. The lengthy preliminary sections preceding the case studies provide the ideological programme of the book, getting all of 'The old typography 1440–1914' out of the way before prefacing several chapters on the history and principles of New Typography with a section on 'The new art', reflecting Tschichold's firm belief in the connections between his own profession and non-objective or concrete painting.

Although Tschichold's text is not overtly political, the pervasive underlying presence of reformist hope kindled by international communism can be clearly felt. Try supplanting 'communism' for 'the New Typography' in the following passage:

99. Slightly modified from the translation in *The New Typography*, p.224.

100. A rival contender for this honour would be *Layout in advertising* (also 1928) by W.A. Dwiggins, who is credited with first using the expression 'graphic design'. The book

called *Graphic design* by W.G. Raffé (1927) is essentially a product of an earlier era, dealing with what was known as 'commercial art'.

101. Fleischmann, '»Können Sie sich einen Flieger mit Vollbart vorstellen?«', p.35.

102. Also in Germany, to some degree, the book had fallen into obscurity, from which it was revived by Brinkmann & Bose's facsimile edition of 1987.

'Preferential offer' leaflet for *Die neue Typo-graphie*. 1928. A4. Showing through the front of the thin paper is the subscription form on the reverse (shown below).

The New Typography, after being violently attacked and often decisively condemned, has now established itself in Central Europe. Its manifestations confront modern man at every step. Even its most ardent opponents have eventually had to resign themselves to accepting it.[103]

Indeed it was specified in the book's statement of copyright that Tschichold reserved all rights, particularly 'those of translation into other languages, including Russian'. He was probably fearful that an unauthorized edition could easily be made in the Soviet Union without his consent, but this also implies that he had such a possibility in mind, and he certainly pursued plans for having a Russian translation published before any other.[104]

Tschichold followed the lead of others, such as Le Corbusier and the Constructivists, in eulogizing 'the engineer' as a modern hero, leading the way out of empty decoration to purposeful design. His book is a vital and fascinating document of heroic modernism's liberating passion for technology and new modes of life: 'Car Aeroplane Telephone Wireless Factory Neon Advertising New York!' exclaimed Tschichold in a breathless, comma-free list.[105] Indeed New Typography was only one manifestation of a fashion in Weimar Germany for all things 'New': there was New Architecture (Mies van der Rohe, Gropius, Erich Mendelsohn and many others), New Music (Schoenberg and Hindemith), New Photography (Albert Renger-Patzsch,

103. *The New Typography*, p.7.
104. Tschichold stated in 1931 that a Russian translation by M. Ilyin would be published, but it never was. Letter Tschichold to Rodchenko, 10 October 1931, in *Rodtschenko*, p.175. See also the illustrations on p.96 below.
105. *The New Typography*, p.11.

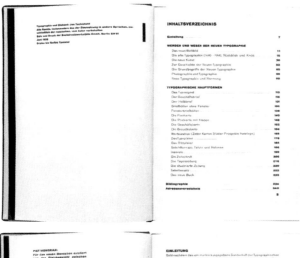

Contents page and spreads from the beginning of *Die neue Typographie*. 1928. A5.

Maschinenproduktion zu erkennen und zu gestalten, begnügte sich diese Zeit mit der ängstlichen Nachfolge einer übrigens nur eingebildeten „Tradition". Ihr stehen heute jene Werke gegenüber, die, unbelastet durch Vergangenheit, primäre Erscheinungen, das Antlitz unserer Zeit bestimmt haben: Auto Flugzeug Telephon Radio Warenhaus Lichtreklame New-York! Diese ohne Rücksicht auf ästhetische Vorurteile gestalteten Dinge sind von einem neuen Menschentyp geschaffen worden: **dem Ingenieur!**
Dieser Ingenieur ist der Gestalter unseres Zeitalters. Kennzeichen seiner Werke: Ökonomie, Präzision, Bildung aus reinen, konstruktiven Formen, die der Funktion des Gegenstands entsprechen. Nichts, das bezeichnender für unsere Zeit wäre, als diese Zeugen des Erfindergeistes der Ingenieure, seien es Einzelleistungen: Flugplatz, Fabrikhalle, Triebwagen der Untergrund; seien es Standardformen: Schreibmaschine, Glühbirne oder Motorrad. An

Detail of *Die neue Typographie*, p.11 (reduced to around 66%) showing use of extra bold to highlight the important figure of the engineer.

Moholy-Nagy), and of course *die neue Sachlichkeit* (replacing the old *Sachlichkeit* of the German Werkbund), a term which came to encompass much cultural activity of that period.[106] Tschichold and his publisher, the Bildungsverband, were conscious that *Die neue Typographie* could not be separated from the cultural context from which it emerged. In the prospectus for the book it was stated that its author sought

> to show the close connections of New Typography with the *total complex of life today* and to demonstrate that New Typography is an equally necessary expression of the new attitudes as New Architecture and everything else New that has dawned with our era.

In Tschichold's view, the 'too-rapid penetration' of new technology into all strata of society had created 'complete cultural chaos' that caused panic in the older generation, but would be clarified by the enthusiastic and unprejudiced attitude of his own, younger generation to such novelty. It is clear from *Die neue Typographie* that Tschichold had reflected a great deal on the nature of his modern era, and, as a result, he emerges as less of a technological determinist than some of his contemporary modernists: 'Electromechanization as an end in itself is nonsense: its true purpose, by satisfying basic needs through mass-produced objects of highest quality, is to awaken our creative powers.' In his view, geometric form did not emerge organically from mechanized production, rather: 'Modern engineering and standardized machine manufacture have of necessity led to the use of precise geometric forms.' Yet, his underlying functionalism was clear in the assertion that beauty was no longer 'an end in itself, an autocratic entity, but a result, an attribute of rightness and fitness in construction'. For Tschichold, 'purity of form' had a higher purpose – the ultimate goal was *'Unity of Life!'*[107]

In his introduction Tschichold warned:

> An examination of the intellectual foundations of New Typography is an urgent necessity for all those who wish to be creatively active in the field of printing. Mere imitation of outward appearance is only a new formalism, no better than the old.

He stressed the need to change the fact that 'Many still regard the New Typography as essentially a kind of technical-symbolical formalism, which is the exact opposite of what it is.' He was pre-empting here the judgement of later historians that, in the final assessment, modernist style in art and design was only expressive of modernity and not inherently derived from it.[108] He accepted that:

106. Willett argued that the standard English translation as 'the new objectivity' is misleading, and that *Sachlichkeit* instead implies 'a neutral, sober, matter-of-fact approach, thus coming to embrace functionalism, utility, absence of decorative frills' (*The new sobriety*, p.112). For *Sachlichkeit* as applied to design, John Heskett suggested 'practicality' (*Design in Germany 1870–1918*, p.111).

107. *The New Typography*, pp.12–13 (original emphasis in bold).

108. See Eric Hobsbawm, *The age of extremes: the short twentieth century 1914–1991* (London: Michael Joseph, 1994), p.515. Tschichold is also given honourable mention in this classic history of the twentieth century (p.185).

Schaffung selbständiger Zeichen für sch, ch, ng, die Abschaffung über-
flüssiger Buchstaben (z, q, c) und als Ziel die Regel „Schreibe, wie du sprichst"
mit ihrer Umkehrung „Sprich, wie du schreibst" Auf dieser Basis wäre eine
neue, sinngemäßere Rechtschreibung aufzurichten, denn ohne sie kommt
die Literatur nicht aus.

Selbstverständlich vollzieht sich eine solche Umwälzung in der Rechtschreibung und der Schrift nicht von heute auf morgen, aber ihre Zeit
kommt mit Sicherheit. Unbewußt oder bewußt schafft die kulturelle Entwicklung und jeder einzelne Mensch an ihr mit. Darum wird die Schrift der
Zukunft nicht von einem einzelnen, sondern nur von einem Kollektiv geschaffen werden können.

Es ist bezeichnend, daß eins der besten neueren Bücher über Sprache,
Schrift und Rechtschreibung nicht etwa von einem Künstler oder einem
Philologen, sondern von einem Ingenieur geschrieben worden ist: „Sprache
und Schrift" von Dr. W. Porstmann. Für jeden, der sich mit diesen Problemen
befaßt, ist es eine unumgängliche Voraussetzung.

Wenngleich die Neue Typographie die Beseitigung der Versalien für
wünschenswert hält, ist diese doch nicht unbedingte Forderung. Sie liegt

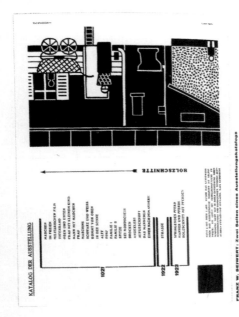

Jan TSCHICHOLD: Typographisches Konzertplakat. Schwarz und rot auf Silber.
84

aber, genau wie eine sinngemäßere Gestaltung der Rechtschreibung, auf der von uns
verfolgten Linie: einer unbeirrten Gestaltung
der Typographie gemäß den Bedingungen
und Forderungen unserer Zeit.

**Fehler,
denen man oft begegnet**

Viele haben im Anfang in der Neuen Typographie einen neuen Formalismus gesehen,
d. h., sie übernahmen aus den Ergebnissen
der neuen typographischen Gestaltung die
auffallendsten Formen — Kreise, Dreiecke,
Balken — also die geometrischen Formen,
um sie in der Art des früheren Ornaments
anzuwenden. Die „elementaren Schmuck-
formen", ein Widerspruch in sich selbst,
die dann einige Schriftgießereien unter verschiedenen Namen in den Handel brachten,
haben dieses Mißverständnis nur noch
weiter verbreitet. Solche geometrischen
Grundformen, auf die wir jede Form zurück-
führen möchten (daher die Kreisformen an-
stelle der Sterne in diesem Buche) müssen
aber, wenn man sie schon anwendet, funk-
tionelle Bedeutung haben: sie müssen also
die Worte oder Gruppen des Textes betonen
oder aus Gründen der harmonischen Ge-
samtform angebracht sein. Statt dessen
trifft man auch heute noch eine rein spiele-
rische, schein-konstruktive Formung, die
dem Wesen neuer Typographie durchaus
entgegengesetzt ist.

Die nebenstehende Zeitungsanzeige ist ein
charakteristisches Beispiel für einen Schein-
konstruktivismus, der noch immer weit verbreitet ist. Die Form hat sich hier nicht
natürlich ergeben, sondern bestand als Idee,
ehe sie gesetzt war. Das Inserat ist nicht
mehr Typographie, sondern Malerei mit
Buchstaben, es wendet guten typographi-

Ein Beispiel pseudomoderner Typographie.
Der Setzer ging von einer vorgefaßten äußerlichen Formidee aus und preßte die Wörter des Textes um. Die typographische „Form" muß aber organisch aus dem Wortlaut des Textes entwickelt werden.

85

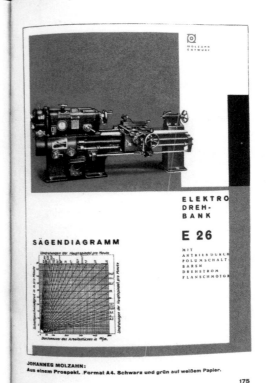

JOHANNES MOLZAHN:
Aus einem Prospekt. Format A4. Schwarz und grün auf weißem Papier.
175

FRANZ W. SEIWERT: Zwei Seiten eines Ausstellungskataloges
174

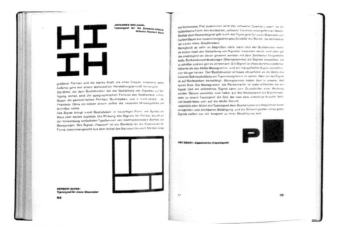

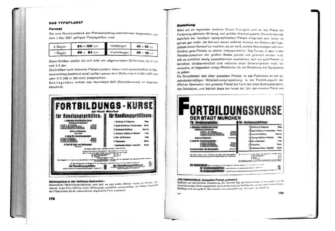

The 'form' of New Typography is also a *spiritual* expression of our world-view. Therefore it is necessary first of all to learn how to understand its principles, if one wishes to judge fairly the mode in which they are expressed, or oneself to design according to them.[109]

He was making a case for some tenets that were more fundamental than the obvious stylistic attributes of the new movement. Yet here, in Tschichold's own struggle to bind an outward style with the inner principles of New Typography, one can sense his awareness of a potential debasement of its true meaning, as he saw it. Nevertheless, some of his statements of general principle still blast us today with their common sense and enduring validity; for example:

Above all, a fresh and original intellectual approach is needed, avoiding all standard solutions. If we think clearly and approach each task with a fresh and determined mind, a good solution will usually result.[110]

A dark underside of the modernists' belief in technology and their obsession with unornamented form was an implicit Western bias and a chauvinism towards other cultures. Tschichold was already interested in the Far East and perceived similarities with European New Typography in some Japanese typography and graphic design.[111] Yet, with what seems today like outrageous arrogance, he lumped together Chinese and Japanese script along with Greek, Cyrillic and other 'exotics' as symbols of nationalism, which would inevitably be superseded by roman type as 'the international typeface of the future'.[112] His mention of Papuans among the 'exotics' betrays his allegiance with the writings of Viennese architect and design theorist, Adolf Loos, whose (in)famous views on the equivalence of ornament with crime are cited approvingly by Tschichold in *Die neue Typographie*. According to Loos, for a Papuan to tattoo his body was to be expected, because 'for us' he was amoral, like a child; but a 'modern' (i.e. Western) person who did the same was either a 'criminal or a degenerate'.

Loos's inclination to strip form down to its bare essentials made him an early advocate in the modern movement of *Kleinschreibung*. This practice became associated with an attempt to forcibly westernize the Turkic parts of the USSR when Anatole Lunacharsky, the Soviet Commissar for Enlightenment, expressed his desire in 1929 to adopt the roman alphabet, without capitals, instead of the 'half-greek'

Spreads from *Die neue Typographie*. 1928. A5. These show the marking of key sentences (sometimes already letterspaced) with black bars in the margin. In the bottom spread Tschichold gives a before and after demonstration.

(Opposite) Spreads showing a music poster by Tschichold and work by Franz W. Seiwert and Johannes Molzahn. Because Seiwert's exhibition catalogue is shown in its side, Gerd Arntz's illustration (which is similarly on its side in the original catalogue) ends up being upside down.

109. *Die neue Typographie* & *The New Typography*, pp.7–8.
110. Marked in the original with a thick bar in the margin. *The New Typography*, p.69.
111. 'Japanische Typographie, Flaggen und Zeichen' (1928), pp.38–9.
112. *The New Typography*, pp.74–5.

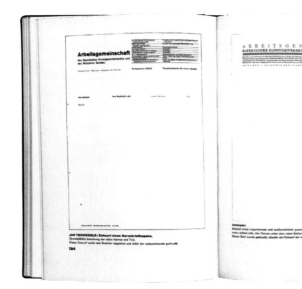

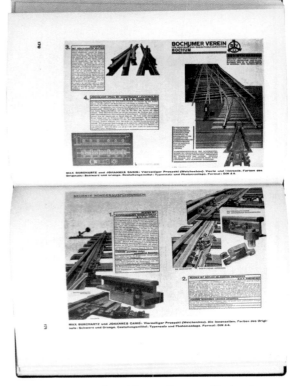

Spread from *Die neue Typographie* showing
design work by Max Burchartz & Johannes Canis
(Werbebau).

Tschichold's advocacy of standardization:
(above) an example by Zwart; (below) comparison of a standardized letterhead by Tschichold on
the left with an unstandardized one.

Cyrillic script.[113] However, Lunacharsky resigned that same year, and so the *Kleinschreibung* idea was forgotten, although Latin script was imposed for a short while on the Turkic languages of the USSR in place of the traditional Arabic script.[114]

Die neue Typographie is the clearest expression of Tschichold's double role as historian and theoretician of his subject. Undoubtedly he counted himself among the 'few clear heads, the avant-garde of all nations' that he identified as leading the way.[115] But it is mainly the historical aspect of his writing that differentiates him from others who wrote short theoretical texts. In comparison with his introduction to *Elementare Typographie*, he broadened the historical base of New Typography in his longer book to encompass Italian Futurism, including a lengthy quotation from Marinetti's book *Les Mots en liberté futuristes* (Words in Futurist free-dom; 1919) advocating the use of discordant type distinctions (italic, bold) to shake up the traditional harmony of the printed page (see also appendix B). It was to the 'non-specialist' in printing, Marinetti, that Tschichold credited the beginning of a 'change-over from ornamental to functional typography', thereby coining a version of the genesis of modern typography that has to a large extent become accepted wisdom. He followed this with a brief overview of Swiss and German Dada, and then returned to the influence of Constructivism, reprinting Lissitzky's 'Topography of typography'. He also gave more credit than he had previously to the early 'ornament-free typography' of Van Doesburg in the publications *De Stijl* and *Mecano*.[116]

113. Reported in *Typographische Mitteilungen*, Jg.26, H.8, 1929, p.186.
114. This inspired Kemal Ataturk to do the same in Turkey, where Latin script officially replaced Arabic within a very short period in 1928. Probably as a consequence of this, to avoid political solidarity of Turkic Soviet republics with Turkey, Latin script was then ousted in the mid-1930s by Cyrillic for literacy initiatives in the eastern USSR, reflecting the cultural dominance of Russia.
115. *The New Typography*, p.13.
116. Tschichold had however not seen *Mecano* himself, and mentioned it only on the strength of a communication with Van Doesburg. Letter Tschichold to Raoul Hausmann, 3 April 1930.

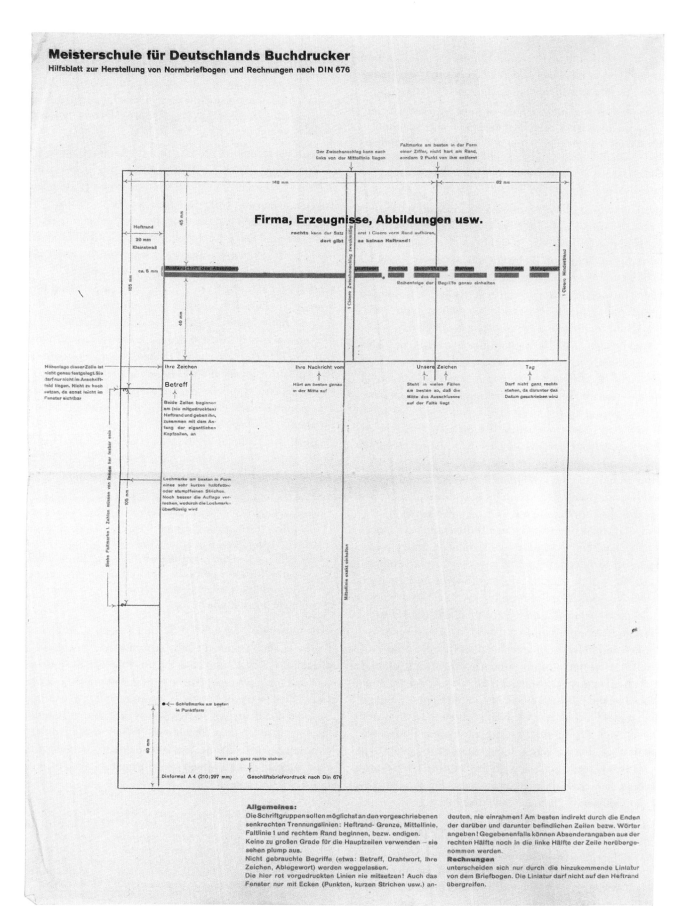

Sheet prepared at the Meisterschule for instruction on how to design a standardized letterhead, with special attention given to typographic detail.

A monochrome version of this was published in *Typografische Entwurfstechnik*.

Tschichold took into account the claims for priority made to him personally by Dexel and Baumeister in the careful listing of pioneers in *Die neue Typographie*:

> In the period after the war the creators of abstract painting and Constructivism worked out the rules for a contemporary style of typography in practical work. ... In Germany it was principally Willi Baumeister, Walter Dexel, Johannes Molzahn, Kurt Schwitters and a few others who by 1922 had made the New Typography a reality.[117]

He meticulously credited Baumeister and Dexel for their essays on the subject and went on to give a fuller list of those currently active in the field.[118] Of course, once *Elementare Typographie* had been published, it too, along with Tschichold himself, became part of the development he was documenting, and so, in matter-of-fact way, he lists himself and his earlier publication in the reference section at the end of the book, and includes a short paragraph on it in the main text. Here he also took the opportunity to get his own back for the malicious criticism that he had suffered in the pages of *Schweizer graphische Mitteilungen*, attacking his critics as 'a few dissenting bigots', who pretended to fall back on a 'moderate' point of view, which Tschichold claimed did not exist – a telling judgement from this period of extremes in Germany, in which for some, like Tschichold, progress lay inevitably and unarguably in a certain direction.[119]

Proportionally, Tschichold placed even less importance on the Bauhaus in his book than he had in his special issue of *Typographische Mitteilungen*. Only one example by Moholy-Nagy was illustrated – again the leaflet for Bauhaus books, this time in its original form; notably absent is his 'Dynamic of a metropolis', an example of filmic typography from his book in that series, *Malerei, Fotografie, Film* (1925). Two items by Joost Schmidt and five by Bayer were shown, including the latter's Bauhaus letterhead in the section on standardized stationery (one of the many DIN standards recommended in the book). Perhaps Tschichold felt that the institution itself had already done a good enough job of disseminating its work (the special Bauhaus issues of certain journals and the Bauhaus books are listed in his extensive bibliography).[120] Yet Bayer himself seemed to maintain an idea of New Typography as somehow equivalent with 'Bauhaus style', even after quitting his teaching post there in 1928. He was uncomfortable with the political overtones of Tschichold's account, as he expressed in a lengthy response to the publication of *Die neue Typographie*:

> i myself would like to say the following: if one considers the book from the aspect of the connection in which you have written it – i mean the commission from the bildungsverband – the structure and practical examples are certainly correct. if that was not so, i would consider it false to introduce this subject with a world-view. in this way the area appears more problematic than it is. we will certainly find that the narrowness and rigidity that is reflected in the book

> (i think we can calmly say this without doing ourselves any harm) will be worn down, *sachlichkeit* and utility will become a matter of course and we will design in a freely creative, but purpose-bound way, with symmetry or asymmetry, as is only right. without theses or rules, less problematically and more loosely.[121]

Bayer was aware of the fact that the new artistic designers of typography, like himself and Tschichold, were creating personae through their work and published statements. There is a sense in what he wrote here that *Die neue Typographie* somehow put the seal on a particular, puritanical approach that he began to feel was not flexible enough. In his new career as a graphic designer in Berlin, Bayer pragmatically adapted his considerable illustrative skills to the kind of magazine and advertising design work that he was doing there, which was quite different from the limited tasks of Bauhaus printing. He became 'art director' of both the German office of the international advertising agency, Dorland, and the German edition of *Vogue*. As a commentary on some new issues of *Vogue* that he sent to Tschichold, Bayer explained, a little apologetically: 'due to the many given conditions, i had to seek different solutions than if i had to do it as a genuine "elemental typographer".'[122]

Ironically, Tschichold's book was also criticized for not being political enough in *Die rote Fahne* (The Red Flag), the official journal of the German Communist Party:

> Tschichold totally fails, however, when it comes to ideology (his section 'The new world view'); instead he espouses a primitive technological romanticism, without addressing the real ideological – in other words *political* – questions of the present. Bound up with this is the exclusive treatment of typography in its function as a means of advertising, neglecting its problems and enormous possibilities as a means of political propaganda.[123]

This sentiment was echoed by an anonymous writer at the Bauhaus, then under the new, communist-leaning regime of Hannes Meyer, who took over as director from Gropius in April 1928. A vitriolic review in the Bauhaus journal also took issue, as Bayer had done, with the narrowly-defined approach, but suggested that it was ultimately shallow. Taking a cue from a comment of Tschichold's in which he equated a printed frame around an advertisement with 'the past, individualistic epoch', the unnamed Bauhaus reviewer launched a tirade:

117. *The New Typography*, p.58.
118. In deference to Dexel he lists Röhl and Schlemmer, although categorizing Schlemmer as a New Typographer was stretching the definition. His main point of qualification would have been his Bauhaus signet, which fulfils Tschichold's criteria in 'Elementare Typographie' for a 'Typo-signet' in that it can be set afresh from type-case material.
119. *The New Typography*, p.61.
120. Tschichold's historical view of the Bauhaus is shown in a footnote mentioning a work from its 'expressionist' period, Johannes Itten's *Utopia* (1922). This he classed as 'symbolist' typography, outside the scope of New Typography but nonetheless of 'contemporary significance'. (*The New Typography*, p.58.)
121. Letter Bayer to Tschichold, 26 November 1928.
122. Letter Bayer to Tschichold, 24 July 1929.
123. Review signed 'Dur.', *Die rote Fahne*, 16 December 1928.

if you want to get rid of individualism in the nature of advertising, then it is not enough to replace axial arrangement with asymmetry, fraktur with sanserif typefaces, drawings with photos, and ornament with a supposed functional geometry in design. to that end you must, for better or worse, throw out the baby with the bathwater and deny absolutely all capitalist advertising, root and branch. while private commerce remains in existence, then it is still better for it to remain recognizable as such by its appearance. you, mr tschichold, seem to be content with formal superficialities and speak already of a new philosophy just because you are able to fill a whole book with illustrations of tectonic-constructivistically designed printed examples. forgive us, but this endless series of schematically applied constructivisms is deadly boring ... to what end this excessive systematization, this cramped geometry, which moreover is not at all always *sachlich* and elemental, rather very often arbitrarily stylized, sometimes to the point of complete illegibility ...

but credit where it is due. tschichold's book is a solid, industrious piece of work. anthologizing, but serious. useful even for enlightened typographers, if they have a healthy feeling for creative freedom and the needs of the moment and do not let themselves be tied down too rigidly to tschichold's systematism.[124]

To someone with left-wing inclinations like Tschichold this, along with Bayer's criticism, may have struck home, and a partial response to both can be detected in some of his published statements from only a few years later.

Less political, but equally severe criticism came from Heinrich Wieynck, who returned to the theme of New Typography in no less than four articles in two years, as if he felt duty bound to explain, or at least address, the views of his former pupil. In a review of *Die neue Typographie* entitled 'Die Wandlungen des Johannes' (The changes of Johannes) he also attacked the 'tiringly similar' examples illustrated in the book, and asserted:

The secret of good typography does not lie in obeying a one-sided school of thought, instead it will always remain bound up with personal creative capacity. Whether old or new paths in typography are followed is absolutely beside the point, but there should be more behind the result than the frantic problems of a few fanatics who perceive *the* New only in the achievements of our time.

In conclusion Wieynck made a prophetic observation:

Tschichold's book has its value as an interesting document of its time; it is certainly a milestone in the entirely natural development of its author, which I do not consider yet to be at an end; indeed, perhaps the Johannes in him will someday return once again to a place of honour.[125]

Another of Tschichold's early teachers, Walter Tiemann, also finally came out in opposition to New Typography about

six months after *Die neue Typographie* was published. At a lecture given in February 1929, the director of the Leipzig academy criticized in particular the theories of Renner and Tschichold (teachers at a rival institution), which in his view had found favour with 'the uncritical masses'. Given the strength of the workers' movement in the printing trade, this term was incendiary, and Tiemann's comments met with indignant response in the pages of *Typographische Mitteilungen*. An anonymous respondent to Tiemann felt that printing apprentices had been implicated by his slur and suggested instead that the future belonged to those masses, who were 'inspired by collective working spirit and communal creative will'. Tschichold's honour was also defended:

You also polemicized against Tschichold's book, which was published by the Bildungsverband ('the uncritical masses'): nobody would begrudge you that prerogative in itself, but consequently we await your book, Herr Tiemann, then we can speak further.[126]

Objections from a traditionalist point of view also came from Imre Kner, although in a friendlier form. Kner took over a printing house in rural Hungary from his father and so grew up in the trade; he had also studied at a technical school in Leipzig and so wrote excellent German in his letters to Tschichold. From the beginning of their correspondence, Kner was sceptical about New Typography, although, having seen examples of Tschichold's early work in calligraphy and lettering, he already considered him a master craftsman and was intrigued to see what he could achieve in 'the new direction'. Reciprocally, Tschichold appreciated the eternally modern aspects in Kner's classical typography and valued his opinions. Even before seeing *Die neue Typographie*, Kner criticized Tschichold's work in elemental typography as 'individualistic' and 'completely untypographic', by which he meant that it did not ensue naturally from printing technique. This raised an issue that lay behind much of the criticism stemming from the printing trade of Tschichold's initial theories: the tension between printers and designers. As guardians of the black art, printers resented outsiders presuming to tell them their business. In Kner's view:

Forgive the observation, but I consider it impossible that you, dear Herr Tschichold, or somebody like you, can create a new typographic style! You are not enough of a printer for that! I, who have grown up in this profession, and can claim to have experienced all of its possibilities and made them my own, still continually discover problems and possibilities that I have not come across in the previous twenty years, and which could not be imagined by outsiders.

A technology cannot be stimulated [*befruchtet*] from outside to have its forms of expression renewed![127]

124. Anonymous review of *Die neue Typographie* in *Bauhaus*, Jg. 3, Nr 2, 1929.
125. Wieynck, 'Die Wandlungen des Johannes', p. 79. Tschichold evidently did not take kindly to Wieynck's criticism, dismissing him two years later in *Eine Stunde Druckgestaltung* as a proponent of a new historicism, a 'renewed Biedermeier'.
126. 'Bescheidenheit und Demut: die Raben und die unkritische Masse', *Typographische Mitteilungen*, Jg. 26, H. 4, 1929, p. 85. The anonymous writer was likely to have been Bruno Dressler, who addressed the matter in a lecture to the Berlin group of the Bildungsverband in March of that year. His criticism was based on two printed reports of Tiemann's lecture, but Tiemann denied having used the controversial phrase in a reply published in the next issue of the journal.
127. Letter Kner to Tschichold, 11 September 1927 (Békés Archive).

This was precisely what had happened in Tschichold's view: that outsiders had given impetus for renewal in design for print. Kner was not unsympathetic to the intentions of the modernists, but he considered them misguided: 'One cannot forcibly hasten the tempo of progress', he warned, because innovations made in such a way would not last. He realized that he and Tschichold represented two entirely different standpoints, admitting that 'tradition is too valuable to me', but their exchange of views here at the crucial time of Tschichold's first transformation is enlightening, not least in making Tschichold justify his commitment to modernity. In reply to further criticism from Kner on receiving a copy of *Die neue Typographie*, Tschichold explained:

> i doubt that it is possible to fully convince you about the new tendencies. i believe that the whole difference between you and me is a generational one. i grew up after the war and am therefore filled with a considerable scepticism of everything that was done before the war. the reason for our work, as must be the case with every new culture, is the negation of the old. this may lead to the odd false step, yet i consider the desire for renewal and for reconstruction as the most decisive factor. towards this goal we are strengthened by the young apprentices and trainees, the vast majority of whom are in favour of the new. ...
>
> what we want fundamentally is anything but a total disregard for structure, and not at all in a purely intellectual sense. in my opinion it is important for new typography to recognize the congruence in classical typography between content, technology and form, for it is now really the case that this form is completely hostile to the intellectual expression of our nature. the new spiritual tendencies will undoubtedly arrive at their own, similarly appropriate expression.[128]

Forming the avant-garde

A typographer with whose work Tschichold discovered great affinity when compiling *Die neue Typographie* was Piet Zwart, a Dutch designer gifted with great versatility. He worked as assistant to the architect H.P. Berlage between 1921 and 1927, wrote a column on architecture for a newspaper, designed glassware, furniture and clothing for mass production, in addition to teaching history of art and technical design at the Rotterdam academy between 1919 and 1933. Moreover, he became active as a typographer in 1921, having had no formal training, but learning quickly from printers with his natural talent for practical matters. In 1923, through a family connection of Berlage's, Zwart began to design publicity for the Nederlandse Kabelfabriek (Netherlands Cable Factory; NKF), a client that allowed him the freedom to develop strikingly innovative and modern

techniques appropriate to the industrial nature of its product. He designed purely typographic advertisements with playful contrasts of weight and scale, which temper the chaotic inclinations of Futurism and Dada with a Constructivist outlook. Indeed Zwart met Lissitzky when the Russian visited the Netherlands in May 1923, and received from him a copy of *For the voice*. Lissitzky also taught Zwart the photogram technique and, on a later visit, photomontage. Zwart soon began to use photograms in his previously purely typographic advertisements for NKF, including that which Tschichold illustrated in *Die neue Typographie*.

Tschichold had seen some of Zwart's work for NKF featured anonymously in the Dutch advertising magazine *De Reclame* (January 1927), and wrote to the company asking for some examples. He was referred to Zwart himself, and so he wrote to him in August of that year to request material, initiating an enduring exchange of each other's work by enclosing some of his own. Tschichold obviously had no doubt about their kinship, telling him: 'I work in an extremely similar spirit to yourself.'[129] Such an assertion was rare for Tschichold, who went on to say in his next letter, when thanking Zwart for the material he had sent: 'I like all of your work without exception; I am happy to have made your acquaintance.'[130] The common spirit in which they worked was mentioned more than once by Tschichold in his letters to Zwart, and he made it clear that he felt them to be members of a select elite. He was dismissive of others who were not among his chosen few, including Paul Renner (his boss) and Fritz Helmut Ehmcke, both of whom had progressed from the classical revival in book design before the First World War to a qualified acceptance of the 'new' style. Ehmcke, according to Tschichold, was 'falling to the rear of the modern movement' – in other words, he was in the rearguard, not the avant-garde.[131] Of Renner he commented, when requesting Zwart not to send copies of his work to him: 'Renner still doesn't know who you are. And he is someone who has changed sides [*ein überlaufer*].'[132]

Tschichold was keen to illustrate some of Zwart's work in *Die neue Typographie*, although there was little time available in which to get photo-etched printing blocks made for this purpose because, as he commented to Zwart, 'the book is already being typeset'.[133] Tschichold's close guarding of his collection of material is shown by him asking his new friend to send an old, spare copy of the original Dutch version of an advertisement for NKF's 'paper insulated cables', of which Tschichold already had an English version,

128. Letter Tschichold to Kner, 25 July 1928 (Békés Archive). Perhaps encouraged by their increasing differences, Tschichold exaggerated the age gap between himself and Kner by making the curious mistake (at this advanced stage in their correspondence) of addressing his letter to Izidor Kner, Imre's father and the founder of the Kner printing dynasty. Imre Kner explained (in a letter of 27 July 1928) that he was in fact only 38 (twelve years Tschichold's senior)

but, given that his 'intellectual development' occurred during the First World War, he conceded that he felt himself to have been formed by pre-war culture.
129. Letter Tschichold to Zwart, 15 August 1927.

130. Letter Tschichold to Zwart, 31 August 1927.
131. Letter Tschichold to Zwart, 15 August 1929. When reviewing 'Elementare Typographie' in 1925, Ehmcke had been very complementary about Tschichold, calling him

'one of our most gifted and skilful writing artists'. Cited in *Typographische Mitteilungen*, Jg.23, H.8, 1926, p.218.
132. Letter Tschichold to Zwart, 14 December 1927.
133. Postcard Tschichold to Zwart, 12 September 1927. In

a letter to Zwart of 26 January 1928 Tschichold expressed hope that the book would be published in about eight weeks, but it did not appear until the summer.

Pages from *Die neue Typographie* (left) and
Gefesselter Blick featuring Zwart's work.

because he feared that his own copy would get ruined at the
process engravers. He explained: 'as i consider this example
to be characteristic of your work, it is very important to me
to reproduce that specific one.'[134]

   As a typographer Zwart adopted the mantle of 'Typotect',
and his rigorously planned approach evidently appealed to
Tschichold, along with his willingness to use the DIN standard paper formats, which were adopted in the Netherlands
as national standards in 1925. Zwart also taught himself
photography after difficulty in getting the required results
for a remarkable A4-format brochure for NKF that employed
micro photographs of the firm's cables. Zwart had sent some
proof pages of this to Tschichold, who requested that he
send him the finished booklet in spring of 1928: 'i would be
really be most pleased if you could send me a copy of your
new catalogue for nkf. i greatly approve of what i have seen
of it so far, and would regret not being able to get to know
the whole thing.'[135] The catalogue arrived too late for it to be
included in *Die neue Typographie*, but Tschichold wrote to
Zwart congratulating him on the booklet, although he could
not resist a slight criticism worthy of a perfectionist:

> i find your catalogue for nkf really excellent. the only thing
> that I would, if pressed, find fault with are the black stripes
> on the outer margins, which I feel to be a little too formalistic.
> but that is the only thing; the beauty of the whole catalogue
> does not suffer from this in any way.[136]

Tschichold was evidently eager to meet Zwart, and had
mentioned early in his correspondence with him that, if

Zwart was by chance planning to visit the Werkbund's 'Die
Wohnung' exhibition in Stuttgart, then they could meet
there. Zwart contacted Tschichold from Stuttgart when
he did visit the exhibition, which was based around the
Weißenhofsiedlung model development of houses by leading modernist architects, including Le Corbusier, Gropius
and Peter Behrens. Tschichold had already seen the exhibition but sent an express letter from Munich to Zwart in
Stuttgart:

> i will now arrive on saturday (tomorrow) with the fast train
> at 16.30 hours in stuttgart, in order to meet you. immediately
> after i have found a room for myself, so around 1 hour later,
> i will come to your hotel to meet you. should this time not be
> convenient for you, please could you leave a note for me as to
> where and when we could meet in the evening.[137]

But after posting his letter Tschichold received a missive
from Zwart cancelling any plan they had to meet on that
occasion. He wrote back expressing hope that they could
meet one day, which they did the following year when
Tschichold visited Zwart in The Hague during a holiday to
the Dutch coast. On this occasion he sent a postcard asking
if Zwart or his wife could meet him when disembarking the
train: 'sign of identification at the station: paper ribbon in
buttonhole.'[138]

   Zwart wrote an essay entitled 'From the old to the new
typography' for a prospectus of the Trio printing house in
The Hague (it was never actually printed). His text borrowed
many specific points from Tschichold's writings, but with

134. In the end Tschichold
had to use his own copy for
Die neue Typographie, but the
Dutch version sent by Zwart
was used in Tschichold's
related article 'Fotografie

und Typografie' in *Die Form*.
Tschichold was equally careful
in not wanting to use his own
archival copies of Zwart's work
as 'exemplary material' in
his Munich teaching, instead

requesting further examples
specifically for the Graphische
Berufsschule (letter to Zwart,
30 November 1927).
   135. Letter Tschichold to
Zwart, [March/April] 1928.

136. Letter Tschichold to
Zwart, 13 June 1928. On receiving a copy of the English edition
of this publicity booklet in summer 1929 Tschichold suggested
writing about it in *Die Form*, but

nothing seems to have come of
this (letter Tschichold to Zwart,
15 August 1929). The brochure
in question is reproduced in
Broos & Hefting, *Dutch graphic
design*, p.86.

137. Letter Tschichold to
Zwart, 20 October 1927, copied
in the letter sent the following day.
   138. Undated postcard from
Tschichold to Zwart.

Poster for lectures given in Munich by Dziga Vertov. 1929. 54 × 79.4 cm.

one main difference. In asserting the advantage of asymmetric arrangement he stated:

> While the old typography was arranged symmetrically (the lines were lined up with respect to the page's central axis and this layout was maintained even at the expense of logic) the new typography sets the lines with ragged-edge aligning them up on the left and letting them end where they may, or by controlling line breaks to cause a certain tension in the text (that is what happens in advertising).[139]

Although the final phrase here reveals that Zwart was referring to advertising, which was almost exclusively his area in typography, there is a clear implication that New Typography should entail ranged-left or unjustified typesetting. This was, in reality, almost never the case when it came to substantial passages of continuous text; Tschichold never specified this mode of composition in any of the work that he designed during his 'modernist' period, not even in advertising matter. Ranged-left text is the logical result of a theory of asymmetry in typography, but it would have been quite controversial to demand it of a compositor in a printing house during the 1920s and 1930s. Yet its almost total absence from both Tschichold's theoretical writings and his practical work should not necessarily be explained on such pragmatic grounds, or characterized with hindsight as a mysterious failure; he simply did not take this extra step in pursuing the principle of asymmetry. The time was not yet ripe.[140] (See also the illustration on p.299 below.)

Tschichold and Zwart also shared a passion for cinema. Zwart organized the International Film Exhibition held in The Hague between April and May 1928, and Tschichold gladly sent him German material, including almost a complete collection of his own Phoebus cinema posters. Of this work he commented: 'as the phoebus company went bankrupt, i unfortunately have no more film posters to do. that is quite a loss for me, particularly from a material standpoint.'[141] (Phoebus Film AG was shut down after a high-profile corruption scandal involving misuse of funds that had been illegally amassed from the marine division of the Reichswehr for propaganda film production.) Tschichold felt that German film posters were almost unexceptionally poor, although he had seen some 'not bad' posters for Fritz Lang's now classic *Metropolis*, which had been released just two years earlier, and which Tschichold described as 'one of the worst films of all time'.[142] One might imagine that Lang's vision of a futuristic city, inspired by New York and resembling an ultra Le Corbusian utopia, would have appealed to Tschichold, but he seems to have shared the misgivings of contemporary German cultural critic, Siegfried Kracauer, who later described Lang as having 'a penchant for pompous ornamentation'.[143]

Tschichold lamented that the quality of German films had declined since the nationalist takeover of Germany's biggest film studio, UFA in Berlin, and told Zwart that he was on the preparatory committee of a 'Volksverband für Filmkunst' (Popular association for the art of film) in Munich,

139. Cited in Monguzzi, 'Piet Zwart: the typographical work 1923/1933', p.7 [unnumbered]. On Trio printers see Broos & Hefting, *Dutch graphic design*, pp.106–7.

140. See Kinross, 'Unjustified text and the zero hour' in *Unjustified texts*, pp.286–301. Tschichold finally pronounced on the matter in 1971, stating in no uncertain terms: 'Unjustified setting is simply hostile to reading.' ('Flöhe ins Ohr', p.364.)
141. Undated letter Tschichold to Zwart [March/April 1928].
142. Letter Tschichold to Zwart, 20 October 1927.

Tschichold recommended instead the documentary film by former painter and musician Walter Ruttmann, *Berlin: Symphonie einer Großstadt* (1927), which followed Dziga Vertov's example. (Ruttmann went on to assist Leni Riefenstahl in editing *Olympiad* [1936] and was fatally wounded while making a Nazi propaganda film in 1941.)

143. Kracauer, *From Caligari to Hitler*, p.149. He summarized Lang's approach as 'Virtuosity alienated from content posed as art.' (p.150)

Poster for film festival in Munich. 1928. 60 × 42 cm.

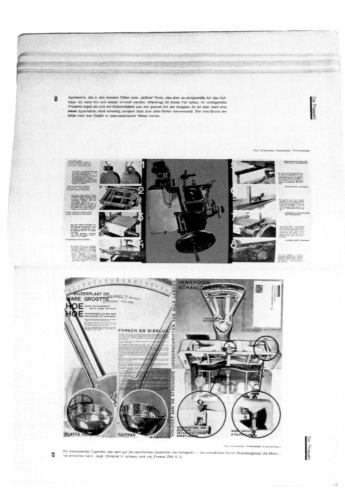

one of many springing up around the country to campaign for 'socially valuable' films.[144] He even had a standardized letterhead printed for himself in this capacity, although it is unclear whether the association progressed beyond a preparatory stage. In addition to his work for Phoebus, Tschichold designed some publicity for other film events in Munich, including posters for a municipal film festival and for lectures by Dziga Vertov in summer 1929. The innovator of Soviet cinema was in Germany principally to supervise the installation of Lissitzky's design for the USSR's section at the Film und Foto exhibition co-organized by Tschichold.

In one of his first letters to Zwart Tschichold enquired after the address of another New Typographer whose work had caught his eye, Paul Schuitema. Tschichold had also seen in *De Reclame* the publicity work designed by him for the firm of Berkel, manufacturers of meat and bread slicing machines (and powdered milk).[145] Schuitema was indeed a friend of Zwart, along with Gerard Kiljan, Zwart's colleague at the Rotterdam academy, and all three of them co-operated

Schuitema's work as shown in *Eine Stunde Druckgestaltung*. Tschichold's caption at the top reads: 'Symmetry, which in most cases is an "outward" form and so not driven by content, can be meaningful now and again. Yet such cases are rare. In the example presented here it resulted necessarily from the whole nature of the task. But it is a **new** symmetry: not doctrinaire, but total (harmonious from all sides). The red background in the middle heightens the realism of the object.'

144. Letter Tschichold to Zwart, 13 June 1928. UFA, which originated during the First World War from a government-directed merger of major film companies, was taken over at the end of 1927 by media tycoon, Alfred Hugenberg, one of Hitler's supporters.
145. Letter Tschichold to Zwart, 31 August 1927.

Postcard from Tschichold requesting a copy of
The next call. Dated 21 August 1926. A6.

H.N. Werkman, *The Next Call*, number 6. 1924.
27.2 × 21.5 cm.

in 1928 in a joint initiative to learn the techniques of photography, trading German manuals between each other. They all made striking typophoto designs for Dutch postage stamps around 1931. Some of Kiljan's stamps, concerning child mental welfare, had impressed Tschichold when arriving on mail from the Netherlands. He assumed they had been designed by Zwart, and asked him to send unfranked samples for reproducing in the magazine of the Munich schools, *Grafische Berufsschule*, to which Tschichold was a frequent contributor. Zwart sent him copies of his own and Kiljan's stamps, which were illustrated in a short feature in the magazine. Tschichold intended to re-use the printing blocks of the stamps in the planned second edition of *Die neue Typographie*.[146]

It was probably from either Zwart or Moholy-Nagy that Tschichold received the address of Piet Mondrian in Paris.[147] Tschichold illustrated one of Mondrian's paintings in *Die neue Typographie* and took its introductory quotation from him: 'We must never forget that we are now at a turning-point of civilization, at the end of everything old. This parting of the ways is absolute and final.' Tschichold had the Bildungsverband send a copy of the book to Mondrian, to which he responded gratefully. Then, on receiving a letter from Tschichold personally, he replied (in French):

> Dear Mr Tschichold
> it is curious, but I have just sent a letter to your publisher to gratefully acknowledge the receipt of your book, and asking them if they would be so kind as to tell you that I am touched by your appreciation of my ideas and of my work. I know how to read only a little German, and so I am writing to you in French.
> I never make criticism, instead I only appreciate all good efforts that are made for the new spirit. I believe that you have done good work.
> My distinguished salutations
> Piet Mondrian
> When you come eventually to Paris, I would like it if you visit me.[148]

The Tschicholds did subsequently get to know Mondrian. In early 1931 they acquired one of his paintings through participating in an act of collective kindness to the artist. Along with some other mutual acquaintances, including Hans Arp of the original Zurich Dadaists, Tschichold contributed a small amount of money to an emergency fund for Mondrian, who was in dire financial straits at that point. All that Mondrian could give in return to the group was one of his paintings, and when lots were drawn to see who would keep it, Tschichold won. He intended to reproduce the painting in the second edition of *Die neue Typographie* but it eventually appeared instead in the Dutch and Danish editions of *Typographische Gestaltung* (see p.143 and p.269).[149]

A Dutch figure whose work seems not to have interested Tschichold a great deal during these years was Hendrik Werkman, a provincial printer in Groningen, who made playful experiments with printing and typography. Tschichold mentioned Werkman as one of the Dutch representatives of the typographic avant-garde in *Die neue Typographie*, but he did not illustrate any of his work, nor did he include the periodical produced by Werkman, *The Next Call*, in his bibliography. We can assume that Tschichold saw this publication, since he wrote to request a sample copy of it in August 1926. Werkman sent *The Next Call* out free to avant-garde figures in many lands, including Kurt Schwitters. Perhaps Werkman's *druksels*, which were effectively paintings executed with techniques of the printing office, did not correspond to Tschichold's utilitarian ideas for what New

146. Letter Tschichold to Zwart, 16 February 1932.

147. Zwart had known Mondrian since the first decade of the twentieth century, and they remained good friends: see Zwart's report of a visit to Mondrian's Paris studio in 1926 in Monguzzi, 'Piet Zwart', p.4. Zwart never belonged to De Stijl and clashed publicly with Van Doesburg as early as 1919;

Mondrian also broke with Van Doesburg in 1925.

148. Letter Mondrian to Tschichold, 2 October 1928, and postcard from Mondrian to Bildungsverband, 30 September 1928.

149. Letter Mondrian to Tschichold, 17 February 1931. My thanks to Cornelia Tschichold for filling in the details of this story. Tschichold corresponded

with Arp from at least 1931 concerning an edition of Arp's poetry that Tschichold would design, which was eventually published in 1939 as *Muscheln und Schirme* (see illustration on p.285). A similar collection was published posthumously as *Der gestiefelte Stern* (Zurich: Arche, 1978) from corrected proofs among Tschichold's papers.

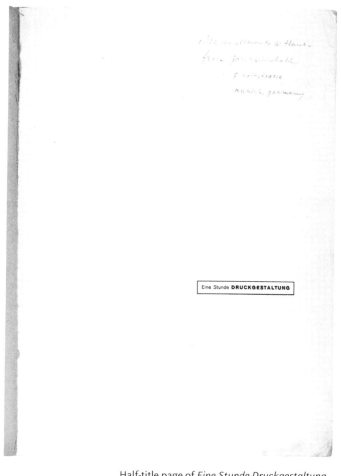

Half-title page of *Eine Stunde Druckgestaltung*.
1930. A4. This copy signed by Tschichold. Note
the attention to detail even in the apparently
simple boxed title (detail below at actual size):
the type is vertically centred on the x-height, not
the capital height.

Eine Stunde **DRUCKGESTALTUNG**

Typography should be at that time. After the Second World
War (during which Werkman was executed by the Nazis), his
work was incorporated into the canon of pioneering modern
typography by Willem Sandberg and Herbert Spencer.[150]

A further contribution by Tschichold to establishing the
canon of New Typography was his second book *Eine Stunde
Druckgestaltung* (1930), which was principally a collection in
A4 format of illustrated examples, and as such was subtitled
'Fundamental concepts of New Typography in pictorial
examples for compositors, advertising specialists, users of
printed material, and bibliophiles', reflecting the wide remit
that he set himself. The main title could be translated as
'A short lesson in designing for print'. The book was part
of a projected series of introductory texts, of which Adolf

Behne's *Eine Stunde Architektur* and Werner Graeff's *Eine
Stunde Auto* had already appeared. This was explained to
Tschichold by Willi Baumeister, who suggested writing
the book to him in November 1928, having first been asked
to do so himself by the publisher, Wedekind of Stuttgart.
Baumeister had been based there before being appointed
in April 1928 as director of the class in advertising graphics
and typography at the Frankfurt Kunstschule, bringing him
into the progressive design circle around the journal, *Das
neue Frankfurt* (The new Frankfurt), of which he took over
the design in 1930.[151] While in Stuttgart he had designed
publicity for the Werkbund's Weißenhofsiedlung exhibition, for which Graeff was the press and publicity officer.

Baumeister, who became a valued friend to Tschichold
and with whom he remained in contact until well after the
Second World War, conveyed the offer to him with the question: 'i received the enclosed offer and i'd like to enquire
if you want to publish a second book. i can imagine that
a short book of an introductory character would perhaps
make no competition with your first.'[152] To Tschichold, who
lacked commissions for design work to supplement his
teaching salary, this would certainly have been a welcome
suggestion from a financial standpoint. The short introduction that he wrote for the book has been rightly described by
Robin Kinross as his 'most compact and compelling statement of the principles of New Typography' (and for this reason it is included in full translation here as appendix C).[153]
Moreover it is a significant revision, or at least a refinement,
of some points in *Die neue Typographie*, softening the narrow dogma of that book, for which he had been criticized by
some of his colleagues. In this essay, 'Was ist und was will
die neue Typographie?' (What is New Typography and what
are its aims?), he once again re-asserted that 'abstract' painters were 'the founders' of New Typography, although he
clarified that the relationship between these two disciplines
was not 'formalistic, rather genetic': the difference being
that art is free of given purpose and typography bound to it.
He stressed that the 'nearest possible attainment of purpose
is the highest demand of New Typography' and to this end
a variety of means might be possible, including the use of
'historical typefaces' as a contrast to the favoured sanserif.
He corrected the interpretation that what he proposed was a
complete disregard of history, stating that New Typography
was 'less anti-historical than un-historical', and denied that
it led to a 'flattening of expression'.

150. Sandberg organized an
exhibition about Werkman at
the Stedelijk Museum, Amsterdam, in 1945, and Spencer
wrote an essay on his work
in *Typographica*, [old series]
no.10, 1955.
151. See Wingler, *Kunstschulreform*. Paul Renner had taught

typography at the same school
between 1925 and 1926.
152. Letter Baumeister
to Tschichold, 8 November
1928. In the introduction
to the exhibition catalogue
Neue Werbegraphik (Basel
Gewerbemuseum, 1930), which
Tschichold helped to compile,

the title of his forthcoming
book was mysteriously given
as 'Einfache Druckgestaltung',
whereas it was envisaged from
the beginning in the 'Eine
Stunde' series.
153. Kinross, Introduction to
The New Typography, p.xxxv.

JAN TSCHICHOLD:

EINE STUNDE DRUCKGESTALTUNG

Grundbegriffe der Neuen Typografie in Bildbeispielen für Drucksachenhersteller und -verbraucher

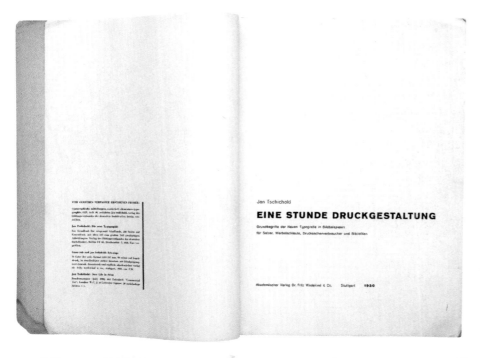

Title-page of *Eine Stunde Druckgestaltung*. 1930. A4. Among other titles by Tschichold listed opposite the title-page are *Elementare Typographie* ('out of print'), *Die neue Typographie* ('almost out of print') and the English translation of this book's introduction, 'New life in print' (see p.92).

Text spread from *Eine Stunde Druckgestaltung*, showing Tschichold's introductory essay 'Was ist und was will die neue Typografie?' (see appendix C for translation). Typefaces are Venus Grotesk and Ratio Latein, with bold used for emphasis in the text. The binding method (as with the earlier *Foto-Auge*; see p.109) involves wire stitches punched a little way in from the spine. This results in the book not being able to open very flat, and in some cases pages break open.

Details from *Eine Stunde Druckgestaltung* showing illustrations of stationery for the Süddeutsche Holzwirtschaftsbank, before and after Tschichold's redesign. Tschichold commented of the 'un-standardized' versions that the variety of typefaces and layouts created 'optical disorder'; whereas his own redesigned versions adhering to DIN Standards showed 'optical order and clarity through well-considered construction and utilization of contrasts in colour and form', and had the added benefit of usability with window envelopes.

This short introduction occupies a mere three pages of *Eine Stunde Druckgestaltung,* with the rest consisting of annotated pictorial examples. Tschichold's exposition here is more explicitly didactic than in his previous book: there are several 'before and after' demonstrations of the virtues of standardization, and some contrasting of (anonymous) 'bad' examples with 'good' ones, usually designed by Tschichold or one of his colleagues in New Typography. With a general audience in mind, the prescriptive advice to follow closely DIN standards in business (and personal) documentation occupies first place.

> The precondition of a contemporary design for print is the application of the Norm- or Din-formats according to DIN 476. The Din formats bring the user many advantages; they make work easier and less expensive for the printer, paper supplier and paper producer!

He proffered a full-page reproduction from DIN 476, which explained the derivation of DIN paper sizes by progressive halving of the dimensions, with the simple recommendation: 'Check for yourself the persuasive logic behind the principle of the standard formats'.[154]

A consistent principle underpins all of his examples: to get rid of clutter, decorative typefaces and needlessly complex structure. Tschichold moved on to cover more complex tasks of advertising, incorporating images, for which there was no simple recourse to standards. Indeed the book is almost exclusively focused on advertising and commercial printing; while it touches on magazines and newspapers, it does not treat book design at all. Tschichold defined the characteristics of appropriately modern imagery and determined the correct way of combining it with type through his chosen examples. Among these are several by Schuitema, but most space is accorded to advertising brochures by Johannes Canis, who no longer worked with Burchartz.

Tschichold's commentary on his illustrations confirms that, from his theoretical point of view, New Typography was a kind of closed system. With rhetorical deftness, details that diverge from his doctrine are dismissed as inconsequential or deemed to be expedient for the greater good in order to allow them into his canon.

The introduction to *Eine Stunde Druckgestaltung,* along with many of its illustrations, was published soon after in several periodicals around Europe, including the French magazine *Arts et Métiers Graphiques* and the English journal *Commercial Art.* Aside from spreading the word of New Typography, any author's fees would have been welcome in Tschichold's straitened circumstances. The English translation initiated a series of short articles by Tschichold in *Commercial Art,* some written specifically for it. He also seems to have acted as its German correspondent, collecting and sending printed material by himself and others that was featured in the related annual publication, *Modern Publicity.*[155]

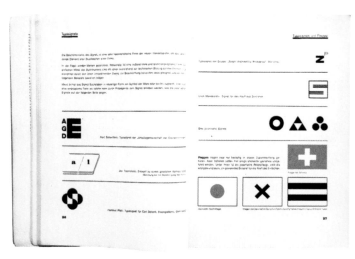

154. *Eine Stunde Druckgestaltung,* pp.10–11.
155. Letter from Walter Seifert, 22 March 1931, whose work was featured in *Modern Publicity* for that year through Tschichold's agency.

Spreads from *Eine Stunde Druckgestaltung:*

(Top) Book covers by Feuerstein, Krejcar, Sima & Teige, and by Werner Graeff; (middle) Posters by Arp & Cyliax, and Lissitzky; (below) Signets and symbols, including Japanese flags.

(Opposite) Brochures by Canis, including one for a 'Progress chair'. Page 43 contrasts a traditional book cover ('shockingly boring') with one by Schwitters using 'clean typographic means'.

Der Prospekt

Erste und letzte Seite eines kleinen Prospekts.
Vorbildliches Typofoto. Mit Foto und guter Typografie ist höchste Klarheit und Übersichtlichkeit erreicht werden. Nicht zum wenigsten ist diese auch eine Folge des ausgezeichnet abgefaßten Textes.

40

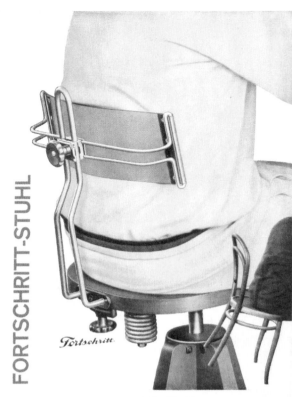

FORTSCHRITT-STUHL

Wiedergabe eines vorbildlichen Prospekts von Johannes Canis in wirklicher Größe

---

Der Prospekt-Umschlag

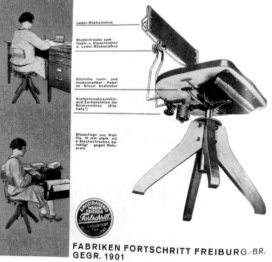

FABRIKEN FORTSCHRITT FREIBURG/BR.
GEGR. 1901

Rückseite des Prospekts von Seite 41 (Entwurf Canis)

Umschlag der Vorkriegszeit. Papier täuscht Leder vor, falsches Gold und häßliche Farbfolien sind Druckfarben. Komplizierte, unruhige Schrift, das Ganze von erschreckender Langweile.

Unten:
Schöne und geistreiche, mit sauberen buchdruckerischen Mitteln hergestellte Komposition, die das Notwendige klar heraustreten läßt.

Vorder- und Rückseite eines Umschlags. Entwurf Kurt Schwitters

kleines LINIATUREN MUSTERBUCH

EDLER & KRISCHE HANNOVER

43

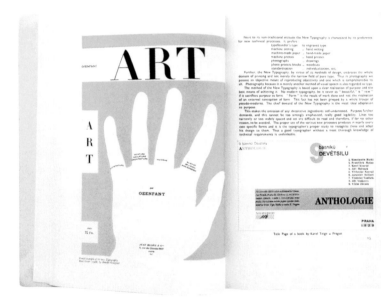

THIS number presents the first exposition in English of the new conceptions of typography and of the arrangement of the printed page, which has begun already to establish a twentieth-century style. To advertisers, advertising agents, printers and designers it is a matter of vital importance.

The advertising pages of all the magazines in the world, to say nothing of booklets (and of books themselves), already show innumerable applications of the new principle, sometimes superficially imitated with poor results. To make use of the emancipation of type and take full advantage of the way in which it is capable of combination with a drawn design or photograph, it is necessary to understand the PRINCIPLES behind it. These Herr Jan Tschichold, whose work, "Die Neue Typographie," has in itself established little short of a revolution in typography, here explains.

(This page) The issue of *Commercial Art* in which Tschichold's article 'New life in print' appeared. 1930. 29.2 × 20.5 cm. It is unlikely to have been designed by Tschichold, although the article was typeset in a sanserif (Gill Sans). Above is an editorial paragraph that was placed alone on the page preceding the article.

Illustrated in the first spread (above right) is the cover of the second and last issue of the short-lived British magazine, *Ray: art miscellany* (1927). It featured work by Moholy-Nagy and Ben Nicholson. (Illustrated opposite, on the left-hand page of Tschichold's article in *Arts et métiers graphiques*, is an example of photomontage by *Ray*'s editor, Sidney Hunt.)

(Above & overleaf) Spreads from the French translation of the introduction to *Eine Stunde Druckgestaltung*, published in *Arts et métiers graphiques* (no.19, September 1930). 31 × 24.6 cm. The poster (top right) was an unaccepted competition entry. Caption states: background silver, 'München' blue.

Tschichold received further criticism for defining New Typography too narrowly again in *Eine Stunde Druckgestaltung*. This time the objection came from Zwart, who was much more active in the field of advertising design for which Tschichold was now presuming to lay down laws. Tschichold replied to Zwart, good-naturedly:

> i am of the opinion, however, that what i teach is not doctrinaire, unless one calls the demand for an organic layout of type doctrinaire. i perhaps set too much value in 'logic', but that is not the same as 'formalistic'. you would not be wrong to think that i don't like the book much any more. it was a difficult project.[156]

Instead he seemed to be very optimistic about the second edition of *Die neue Typographie*, which he commented to Zwart would 'also appear soon' when sending him a copy of *Eine Stunde Druckgestaltung* in September 1930. In that book, *Die neue Typographie* was listed as 'almost out of print', and in his short book on 'Formal writing for compositors' (*Schriftschreiben für Setzer*, 1931) it was unequivocally declared 'out of print'. This marked quite a success – 5,000 copies sold in three years. He intended to enlarge the format to A4 for the second edition, presumably to better incorporate illustrations, of which there would be a greater number, including many of newer examples. Among the contemporaries whose work he wanted to feature was Josef Albers, then still in charge of the preliminary course at the Bauhaus, who late in 1932 sent Tschichold material for inclusion in his 'new big book'. 'I am astonished at your enthusiasm for publication', declared Albers.[157] Strangely Tschichold seems to have had little or no contact with Joost Schmidt, who taught the Bauhaus advertising class at that time, although their professional paths would overlap in early 1933 (see pp. 224–5).

Others from whom he solicited work for inclusion were Imre Reiner, a Hungarian who had studied under F.H. Ernst Schneidler at Stuttgart and was then working in Germany, and Xanti (Alexander) Schawinsky, a former Bauhaus student then active as a graphic designer in Berlin, where he shared lodgings with Herbert Bayer. The Swiss-born Schawinsky, from an orthodox Jewish background, had done an apprenticeship in architecture, and was also a painter. At the Bauhaus, as well as playing saxophone in the Bauhaus band, he was involved in the stage workshop and specialized in exhibition design. Before settling in Berlin in 1932, he had worked as a graphic designer for the municipal building office in Magdeburg, for which he designed

156. Letter Tschichold to Zwart, 16 February 1932.

157. Letter Albers to Tschichold, 28 December 1932.

QU'EST-CE QUE LA NOUVELLE TYPOGRAPHIE ET QUE VEUT-ELLE ?

surfaces non imprimées dont les possibilités d'action ont été également découvertes à nouveau par la « Nouvelle Typographie ». Les espaces blancs cessent d'être un fond passif et deviennent un élément actif. Parmi les couleurs proprement dites, on préfère le rouge. En sa qualité de couleur par excellence, il forme le plus vif contraste avec le noir normal. Les tons clairs du jaune et du bleu intéressent également en première ligne parce qu'ils sont aussi des couleurs franches. Il ne s'agit pas d'employer la couleur comme élément décoratif « embellissant », mais de tirer parti des qualités psychophysiques propres à chaque couleur pour amener une graduation ou un affaiblissement de l'effet.

L'image est fournie par la photographie. C'est celle-ci qui rend l'objet de la façon la plus objective. Il est ici sans importance de savoir si la photographie en tant que telle est un « art » ou non, mais sa combinaison avec le caractère et la surface peut être de l'art, car il s'agit ici uniquement d'une estimation, d'un équilibre des contrastes et des rapports de structure. Beaucoup de gens montrent de la méfiance vis-à-vis des gravures dessinées; les dessins d'autrefois constituent souvent des faux et ne vous convainquent plus. Leur caractère individualiste nous est désagréable. Si l'on veut donner en même temps plusieurs impressions d'images, juxtaposer différentes choses par contraste, on a recours au photomontage. On emploiera pour celui-ci les mêmes méthodes de composition que pour la typographie. Unie à cette dernière, l'image photographique collée devient une partie de l'ensemble et c'est dans cet ensemble qu'elle doit être évaluée exactement afin qu'il en résulte une forme harmonieuse. Cette fusion ainsi produite de la typographie et de la photographie (ou photomontage) donne la typophoto. Le photogramme, dont nous donnons aussi un spécimen, constitue également une possibilité photographique rare, mais pleine de charme. Le photogramme se fait sans appareil photographique, en posant simplement des objets plus ou moins transparents sur des couches sensibles (papier, film ou plaque.)

Les facilités extraordinaires d'adaptation de la « Nouvelle Typographie » à tous les

PIET ZWART : Annonce entièrement typographique.

buts imaginables en fait un phénomène essentiel de notre temps. Son point de vue fondamental fait qu'elle n'est pas une question de mode, mais se trouve appelée à former la base de tout travail typographique postérieur.

Karel Teige (Prague) a résumé comme suit les traits marquants de la « Nouvelle Typographie » :

La Typographie constructive, synonyme de « Nouvelle Typographie » suppose et comporte :

1º *La libération des traditions et des préjugés : élimination de tout archaïsme ou académisme ou aussi de toute visée décorative.* Ne pas respecter les règles académiques et traditionnelles ne reposant pas sur des raisons optiques, mais constituant simplement des formes pétrifiées (partage d'une ligne en moyenne et extrême raison, unité des caractères).

2º *Choix de caractères d'un dessin parfait, très lisibles et simples dans leur construction géométrique.* Bien comprendre l'esprit des types en question qui doivent répondre au caractère du texte. Mise en contraste des matériaux typographiques pour accentuer davantage le contenu.

3º *Compréhension parfaite du but à atteindre et accomplissement de la tâche donnée.* Discernement des buts particuliers. La réclame, qui doit être visible à distance, a des exigences tout autres qu'un livre scientifique ou une œuvre littéraire.

4º *Équilibre harmonieux de la surface donnée et de la disposition du texte d'après des lois optiques objectives : structure claire et organisation géométrique.*

5º Mise à profit de toutes les possibilités fournies par toutes les découvertes techniques du passé ou futures. *Union de l'image et de la composition par la typophoto.*

6º *Collaboration la plus étroite entre l'artiste graphique et les gens de métier de l'imprimerie,* de même qu'est nécessaire la collaboration de l'architecte traçant le plan, avec l'ingénieur de construction, ou du chef de l'entreprise avec l'exécutant. Il faut réaliser *aussi bien la spécialisation et la division du travail que le contact le plus intime.*

Nous n'avons rien à ajouter à ces stipulations, sauf que le partage de la ligne en moyenne et extrême raison ou autres mesures exactes sont souvent plus efficaces comme impression que des rapports fortuits et ne doivent par conséquent pas être éliminés en principe.

Prof. JAN TSCHICHOLD, Munich.

Les illustrations insérées dans cet article ont été réunies par l'auteur.

CI-CONTRE : I) KAREL TEIGE (Prague) : Page de titre. — II) G. KLUZIS (Moscou) : Couverture de livre. Photomontage. — III) EL LISSITSKY (Moscou) : Couverture de catalogue de l'exposition polygraphique à Moscou 1917. Typographie. — IV) KAREL TEIGE : Couverture de périodique. Typographie. — V) JOHANNES CANIS : Prospectus pour la ville de Hattingen (Ruhr) qui montre bien simultanément la situation et les caractéristiques de Hattingen. — VI) LADISLAV SUTNAR (Prague) : Couverture de périodique. — VII) LISSITSKY : Couverture de livre. Composition photographique. — VIII) GEORG TRUMP : Prospectus. — IX) PIET ZWART (La Haye) : Page de titre d'un catalogue de T. S. F. Photomontage.

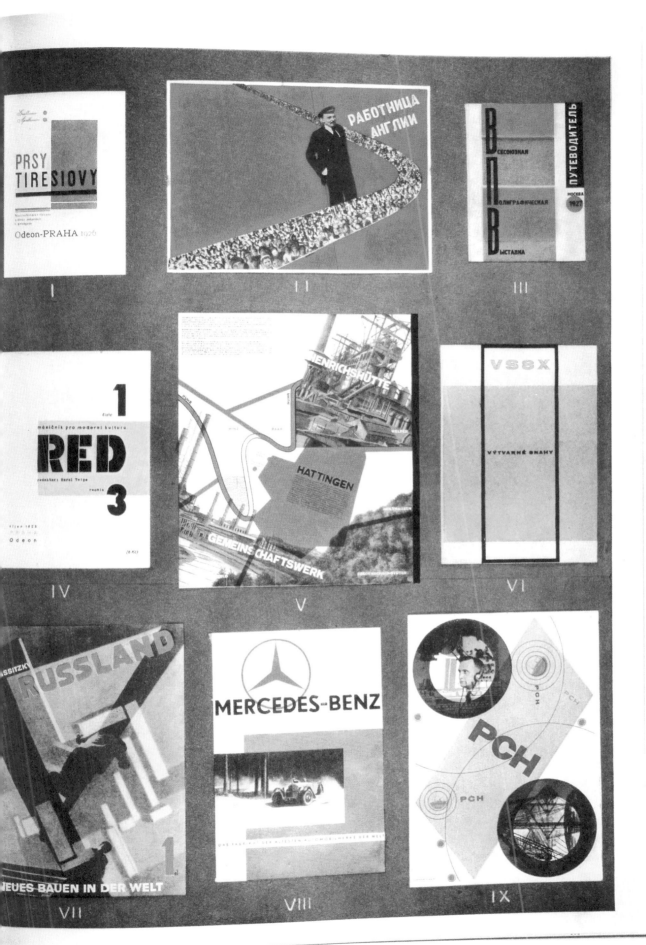

I

II

III

IV

V

VI

VII

VIII

IX

Sketch for binding of projected second edition of *Die neue Typographie*, slightly renamed as *Handbuch der neuen Typographie*.

Typeset title-page design and a paste-up implying that there was either a hope or possibility that the second edition would be

published in both Russian and German editions by the Soviet State publishing house.

a quite astonishing publicity brochure about its commercial harbour. This employed an ingenious combination of diagrams, photography within letterforms, and enormously extended fold-outs, and it appears that Tschichold intended it for reproduction in the second edition of *Die neue Typographie*.[158]

An advertisement in the Fototek monograph about Moholy-Nagy (1930; see p.111) announced that the revised edition of *Die neue Typographie* (a further 5,000 copies) would be published in early 1931 as *Handbuch der neuen Typographie* (Handbook of New Typography), with 200 mostly renewed illustrations. Josef Albers posted a leaflet for it at the Bauhaus at the beginning of 1932, in order to help solicit pre-publication orders. However, the book's progress faltered, partly due to Tschichold being busy with other things, but also due to circumstances beyond his control, as he explained to Zwart in February of that year:

> unfortunately it is still uncertain when this will appear. the manuscript is ready and can be typeset any day now. but conditions here are so bad that the publisher feels it cannot take on the risk. the russian translation of the second edition, which is firmly on order, will probably appear sooner than the german original.[159]

In the event, neither appeared. When the Bildungsverband became discouraged by Germany's worsening economic crisis, Tschichold sought another publisher, informing Imre Reiner that it would be Wedekind of Stuttgart, which had

published both *Eine Stunde Druckgestaltung* and the book on photography co-compiled by Tschichold, *Foto-Auge*.[160] At the same time he told Friedrich Vordemberge-Gildewart: 'the new edition or at any rate a totally new book will appear in the coming year.'[161] Among the subscribers to the new edition was Moholy-Nagy, then working in Berlin after leaving the Bauhaus in 1928 along with Gropius and Bayer.[162] Tschichold's next major book, *Typographische Gestaltung* (1935), would be published in Switzerland, and it was indeed something other than a second edition of *Die neue Typographie*.

158. A copy is now kept in the collection of material later sold by Tschichold to the Victoria & Albert Museum, London, and he retained several cut leaves from another copy, presumably for reproduction.

159. Letter Tschichold to Zwart, 16 February 1932.

160. Letter Tschichold to Reiner, 27 November 1932.

161. Letter Tschichold to Vordemberge, 28 November 1932.

162. Letter Moholy-Nagy to Tschichold, 20 September 1932.

(Opposite below and this page) Alternative designs for cover of the Werkbund periodical, *Die Form*. 1929–30. Layout sketches shown at 30% of actual size. These attempts may have originated with a competition held by the journal in 1928, but Tschichold seemed to pursue it as a kind of demonstration case. The version that he seemed to settle on is shown on the right as an illustration in *Eine Stunde Druckgestaltung*. A4. His caption states: 'Unused competition entry by the author. Not to be used without his permission, even with another title.'

The Ring of new advertising designers

A select band of designers that Tschichold considered to be 'like-minded people' – in other words those working in what he deemed the correct, new manner – united in late 1927 to form an association for raising awareness of their work. This group, called the Ring 'neue Werbegestalter' (Ring of new advertising designers), was initially referred to by Tschichold as consisting of 'radical, practical artists', betraying the fact that its principal purpose was to further the cause of the embryonic profession of graphic designer, most practitioners of which indeed came from an 'art' background.[163] As Kees Broos has observed:

> Meanwhile it became apparent that there was money to be earned in advertising and that was an attractive perspective for the fine artists, who were not employed at an academy or a graphics school and were having great trouble in selling their Dada and Constructivist paintings.[164]

In this sense the final denomination of the Ring as an association of designers, and not artists, was a significant shift.

Early discussions for the association took place in the second half of 1927 among a circle around Schwitters and Dexel, and it was presumably Schwitters, the Ring's prime mover, who then approached Tschichold. The founding members were: Baumeister, Burchartz, Dexel, Cesar Domela, Robert Michel, Schwitters, Trump, Tschichold, and Friedrich Vordemberge-Gildewart.[165] The latter was a close friend of Schwitters, and both had also been co-founders of 'Die Abstrakten Hannover' (Hanover abstract artists' group) along with Domela earlier in 1927. After training in carpentry and interior design, Vordemberge turned to painting and then, like many of his contemporaries in the lean inflation years, to typography. In 1924 he moved into a studio previously occupied by Lissitzky at the Kestner-Gesellschaft in Hanover. Lissitzky had left many samples of his graphic work there due to his haste in leaving for Switzerland, and Vordemberge found these inspiring. Vordemberge's work seems to have been unknown to Tschichold until after the publication of *Die neue Typographie*, in which he is not mentioned, although they later developed a regular correspondence, seemingly initiated by Vordemberge subscribing to the second edition of that book. He had a productive connection with the Kestner-Gesellschaft, for which he designed most of the publicity between 1928 and 1934. His professionally-minded approach to typography gives lie to the fact that artists were dilettantes in this respect; he himself later rejected the notion that painters, sculptors

or poets of the Weimar period only 'ploughed the typographic field on financial grounds', considering it to be quite natural to take typography as 'visual communication' and 'at first investigate it and then design it anew'.[166] Naturally, the degree to which those approaching typography from outside learned the conventions of the craft depended on the interest or willingness of each individual.

The membership fee of the Ring 'neue Werbegestalter' was 18 marks, and new members had to be nominated by an existing member, with a majority of the whole membership voting in their favour on the evidence of ten pieces of work that they were 'statutorily obliged' (as Schwitters put it) to send for circulation among existing members. It was Tschichold who first suggested to Piet Zwart in November 1927 that he become one of the first members of the Ring from outside Germany, claiming this to be his idea, and also suggesting Lajos Kassak, Karel Teige and Lissitzky. He described the purpose of the new organization as: 'representation of interests for exhibitions etc.'[167] The main activity of the Ring was indeed to organize touring exhibitions of its members' work, under the enthusiastic administration of Schwitters and his wife Helma. Two sets of material toured Germany and the Netherlands simultaneously, being exhibited in numerous cities during 1928 and 1929. The Ring also participated in larger exhibitions, such as the 'Neue Typographie' show of 1929 in Berlin, for which Schwitters invited guest exhibitors, Bayer, Moholy-Nagy, Teige, Van Doesburg and Molzahn, who all agreed but never became members.

A text entitled 'Leitsätze der typografischen Arbeit' by Moholy-Nagy was circulated at the Berlin show and at subsequent Ring exhibitions. Despite Moholy-Nagy not being a member, it was evidently felt that his text provided a good summary of the Ring's aims. It was indeed a pithy text, confirming Moholy-Nagy's importance in originally defining New Typography but also showing how his views had developed by interaction with Tschichold's:[168]

> The nature of typographical progress is not a formal but an organizational achievement! Current typography is no longer a work of mere type composition, it has become a work of print technology, in which the montage can be executed as a 'layout' outside the printing house with other means than typesetting. ...
> At first the principles of a painterly division of surfaces prevailed. Under the influence of Constructivist paintings, precise geometrical solutions came to the fore. Instead of the traditional stylistic trimmings arose the fashion for eye-catching devices. For many, the overgrowth of such features

163. Letter Tschichold to Zwart, 30 November 1927.
164. Broos in *Ring 'neue werbegestalter': Amsterdamer Ausstellung von 1931*, p.7.
165. Michel was principally an architect who, after an early association with the Bauhaus, became connected with the New Frankfurt around Ernst May. This latter connection may explain the election of Adolf Meyer, an architect then working in Frankfurt but not active in graphic design, as an honorary member of the Ring.

166. Lecture 'Zur Geschichte der Typographie' (1959, when Vordemberge-Gildewart was teaching at Ulm) in *Vordemberge-Gildewart*, p.93. He stated that his judgement applied particularly to Schwitters.

167. Letter Tschichold to Zwart, 30 November 1929.
168. The text partly derives from Moholy-Nagy's earlier essay 'Zeitgemäße Typographie' but his historical account of New Typography's development borrowed from Tschichold's. In the copy of the typescript sent to Tschichold, Moholy-Nagy prudently added a handwritten footnote reference to *Die neue Typographie*. Indeed Tschichold may have played some part in the Ring's adoption of the text. It was published (uncredited and slightly modified) in *Typographische Mitteilungen* (Jg.28, H.8, 1931, pp.214–5) and it is from this published version that the quotations above are taken.

obscured the true meaning of the new initiatives: typographic organization of the text. This should be achieved by the following means: clarity, concision and precision. As it happens, the thick rules, bold points and large squares disappeared from the work of most creative typographers as soon as they realized that a functional organization of a text can be executed without superficial eye-catching elements but instead, for example, with varying weights and sizes of type.

Moholy-Nagy stressed the importance of DIN standards and proposed that the same principle should be applied to developing a 'unified script'. Intriguingly, he identified a new role – the 'creator of typographic layout' – which contradicts the prominence Tschichold always gave to the type compositor in his writings:

> The massive dissemination of today's press – newspaper, illustrated periodical, magazine – has become the basis of a new development. The discovery of photography and the techniques of reproduction stemming from it force a fundamental revaluation in the planning of printing work. The place of the compositor has been taken by the 'monteur of the printing layout [*Druckmodell*]'. The page put together from photos, hand-lettering and typewritten matter, typesetting, colour etc. will be photographed, reproduced and a printing plate will then be made from the photographic plate. Printing can then be carried out by a technology determined by economic considerations.
>
> Undoubtedly, in the future not only ephemeral material and illustrated magazines will be produced in this way, but also books. This eventuality depends solely on future developments in the price of the 'printing plate', which seems likely to provide the solution by eliminating the expensive zincographic technology. This future-typography allows total design of the whole visual image. The practical restrictions in hand composition to the horizontal and vertical planes will thereby be lifted. The New Typographers – 'creators of typographic layouts' [*typographische Modellhersteller*] – will in future only be governed by the laws inherent in any given typographical task.

In prophesying the freedoms to be brought by a move away from lead type towards photographic origination and lithographic printing (all of which has come true), while tempering this with commercial pragmatism, Moholy-Nagy and the Ring struck just the right note in order to persuade potential clients that the 'new advertising designers' offered the best of both worlds. The prohibitive cost of producing photo-etched blocks for printing halftone photographs was evidently a big issue in the lean years after 1929, and must have been frustrating for designers (and clients) who were excited by the potential of photographic imagery in print production.

Among those who joined the Ring were the brother and sister team of Hans & Grete Leistikow, who were employed by the Frankfurt city authority and had designed the journal associated with its enlightened architectural programme, *Das neue Frankfurt*.[169] Paul Schuitema also joined, and

Tschichold's personal membership card for the Ring.

helped Zwart to organize the Ring's exhibition in Rotterdam in December 1928. Schwitters invited several more applicants, including Graeff, Richter and Heartfield, but none replied. Graeff was evidently included in the founding discussions but was then struck off, to his dismay, after failing to respond to correspondence. There was much discussion among the group as to whether links should be fostered with the Bauhaus, with some members expressing the desire to maintain a certain independence from that institution. Tschichold, along with Burchartz, was in favour of electing the head of the Bauhaus advertising department to the Ring so long as Hannes Meyer remained director of the school; at that time this was Joost Schmidt, but he never became a Ring member.[170] It is interesting that F.H. Ernst Schneidler was considered for membership, given that he was not really a New Typographer, rather an expert calligrapher and typeface designer who taught at the Kunstgewerbeschule in Stuttgart between 1920 and 1949. His nomination was enthusiastically approved by Tschichold and Trump, one of Schneidler's former pupils, but consternation among the Ring's ranks caused by Schwitters's peremptory election of Schneidler led to confusion, and he eventually declined membership.[171]

Schwitters, the Ring's president, dedicated himself almost exclusively to graphic design in the years between 1924 and 1933, producing some memorable civic information posters for the Hanover tram service and a whole system of documentation for the municipal authorities of Hanover and Karlsruhe. Here he exercised marked restraint for an old Dadaist, deploying the Futura typeface delicately balanced with geometric corporate symbols. Much of Schwitters's other typographic work possessed a boldness bordering

169. The Leistikows are listed in *Die neue Typographie*, but their impressive work was not ever illustrated in Tschichold's publications. Hans Leistikow travelled to the USSR with Ernst May in 1930 and stayed working there for seven years, during which he also befriended Lissitzky.　**170**. *Ring 'neue werbegestalter'*, p.114. See the summary of discussion in Kinross, 'The Bauhaus again', *Unjustified texts*, pp.256–8.　**171**. *Ring 'neue werbegestalter'*, pp.116–8.

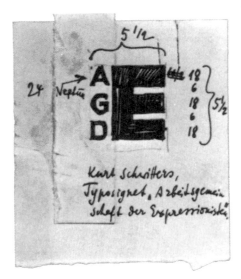

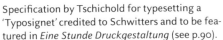

Specification by Tschichold for typesetting a 'Typosignet' credited to Schwitters and to be featured in *Eine Stunde Druckgestaltung* (see p.90).

One of the spreads dedicated to Schwitters in the Rasch brothers' book, *Gefesselter Blick* (1930).

on the effectively crude. Indeed this modest man prized the visual judgement that he saw in Tschichold's work. In congratulating Tschichold on the design of the *Ursonate* for *Merz*, Schwitters wrote:

> When I see your printed work and then look at my own, so mine seems clumsy, coarse. I will make an effort from now on to use lighter weights of type more often. I am always afraid that with light type the effect will be aesthetically weak, but I see that this is not necessarily the case.[172]

Schwitters perceived an important part of Tschichold's work to be his 'logical standardization'.[173] Schwitters aligned with the DIN paper sizes in designing municipal stationery, although he did not accept entirely the corresponding standard for placement of elements on the paper. When sending some examples of this work to Tschichold, he confessed : 'I do not really orientate myself so precisely according to Din.'[174]

The Ring's profile-raising activities undoubtedly brought some of its members new commissions, although perhaps not as many as some may have hoped; the shock waves of the Wall Street Crash in 1929, precipitating a worldwide economic crisis, would also have militated against this. Tschichold himself, after bemoaning his lack of commissions to Piet Zwart, commented that 'now however i am launching a big advertising campaign'.[175] This may have been publicity for women's swimwear from the firm of Lindauers, for which Tschichold designed at least one poster around this time. He featured it in *Eine Stunde Druckgestaltung* and it was shown in the Ring's Amsterdam exhibition of 1931. On reproducing it in *Arts et Métiers Graphiques* he added the comment in a caption: 'The brandmark Lindauers was

imposed by the client'. This implies simply that the mark was not of his own design, and leads to the interpretation that he was not comfortable in a situation where commercial imperatives might impede his own wish to create exemplary work. Lack of control would not have been appealing to him. He somewhat enviously congratulated Zwart on the sympathetic client that he had found in the NKF, and it is easy to imagine that Tschichold would ideally have wanted to design advertising for industrial products or machine parts of some kind, for which the machine-age pretensions of New Typography were stylistically appropriate. American historian Maud Lavin has described the world-view contained in advertising imagery created by the Ring as a 'masculinist avant-garde utopia for the masses'.[176] In Tschichold's Lindauer poster the swimsuit model's skin is indeed printed in a silvery blue tone, giving the impression of a flat metallic surface, but women's fashion somehow sits uncomfortably with the *sachlich* intentions of Tschichold's design. As a theorist concerned to practise what he preached, he was less flexible in this respect than Herbert Bayer, for example, who adapted his style quite successfully to the glamour industry.

The lack of forthcoming advertising work lends credence to Edith Tschichold's later assessment that her husband found it difficult to get design jobs due to his socialist connections. Evidence of his continuing favour in left-wing circles, which most likely presented work that was more to

172. Letter Schwitters to Tschichold, 3 December 1931.
173. Letter Schwitters to Zwart, 1 April 1931.

174. Letter Schwitters to Tschichold, 3 December 1931.
175. Letter Tschichold to Zwart, 3 February 1929.

176. Lavin, *Clean new world*, p.43.

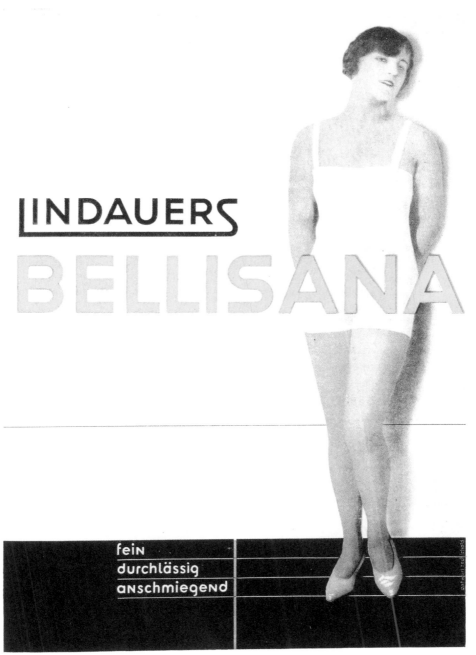

LINDAUERS BELLISANA

fein
durchlässig
anschmiegend

Showcard designed by Jan Tschichold (Munich)
(In the original, the figure is printed in silver)

Small poster for swimwear as reproduced in *Commercial Art. c.*1929. 40 × 29.6 cm. Original in black, blue (word 'Bellisana') and silver for the model's skin. The lettering at bottom left is a version of Tschichold's *Einheitsschrift* (see also pp.154–9 below).

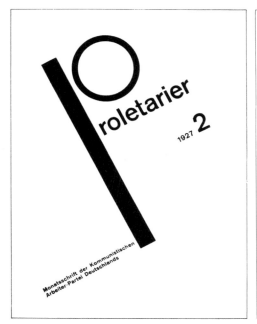
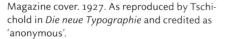

Magazine cover. 1927. As reproduced by Tschichold in *Die neue Typographie* and credited as 'anonymous'.

Magazine cover. 1928. 31 × 23.5 cm. Tschichold also designed the interior text typography.

Cover of exhibition catalogue, which Tschichold is credited with 'putting together'. 1930. A5. A definite precursor of 'Swiss typography'.

Tschichold's taste, is given by his design of the magazine *Sportpolitische Rundschau*, which commenced publication in 1928 and reflected the enthusiasm for workers' sporting organizations in Germany during the Weimar years. Additionally, in *Die neue Typographie*, he showed a very similar cover for *Proletarier*, the journal of the KAPD, a revolutionary splinter group of the German Communist Party; it is captioned as 'anonymous', but it is tempting to think that Tschichold may have had a hand in it. In any case, his decision to illustrate it in his book made his sympathy clear.[177]

Despite altering his personal letterhead to read 'jan tschichold nwg' (the German acronym for 'new advertising designer'), the Ring did not evidently bring Tschichold an enormous amount of work, and in the summer of 1929 he was in desperate need of money to cover the costs of sending his wife Edith for a recuperative treatment after illness. Instead of advertising work, Tschichold instead conceived the idea of designing a new display typeface as a way of making some money relatively quickly. He sold the drawings for the typeface, Transito, for 500 marks, and two later display typefaces in 1931 for a total of 1800 marks, with a small royalty thereafter.[178] The idea of designing a typeface would have appealed to Tschichold not only because his knowledge of letterforms would enable him to do it easily, but also as a task over which he could exercise greater control, although he was disappointed also in this respect at least with Transito, which was not produced to his satisfaction. (For more on these typefaces see pp.162–76.)

Tschichold personally represented the Ring by giving an inaugural speech at the Basel Gewerbemuseum in March 1930 for the exhibition of 'Neue Werbegraphik' (New advertising graphics), which featured work by the Ring's members. The exhibition was dominated by a selection of posters put together by Tschichold that mostly featured photomontage, and Tschichold's speech was entitled 'Das neue Plakat' (The new poster).[179] The Ring's exhibition programme stretched as far afield as Stockholm in 1931 but by this time the organization was petering out. Schwitters complained to Tschichold that 'I believe our Ring exists no longer, as nobody replies, nobody sends material', including Tschichold it seems.[180] Schwitters was still enthusiastically pursuing new projects, such as a publication of design by Ring members in collaboration with the Bauer typefoundry, which eventually came to nothing. Illustrations of work and a short mission statement by all of the Ring members had already been included in the book *Gefesselter Blick* (Captured glance), compiled by the brothers Heinz & Bodo Rasch in 1930. This provided a complement to Tschichold's own illustrated surveys of New Typography, providing alternative

177. In the following years Tschichold moved in cultural circles connected with the KAPD as designer for the Bücherkreis (see pp.204–17) and as contributor to *A bis Z* (journal of the 'Cologne progressive artists', co-edited by Party member Franz Seiwert).
178. Letter Tschichold to

Albers, 8 December 1931. The average monthly salary in 1930 for industrial and handcraft workers was 178 marks and for white collar workers it was 371 marks. (Statistics from Berghahn, *Modern Germany*, p.288.)
179. Published in the exhibition catalogue and also in

Offset: Buch und Werbekunst, Jg.7, H.7, 1930, pp.233–6. It was subsequently translated into English as 'New paths in poster work' (*Commercial Art*, vol.10, June 1931, pp.242–7) and into Czech (see illustration on p.125).
180. Letter Schwitters to Tschichold, 28 March 1931.

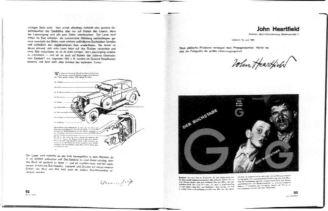

Cover and spreads from *Gefesselter Blick*. 1930 (facsimile edn). 26.5 × 21.5 cm. Illustrations of work by Baumeister, Dexel, Graeff, Heartfield, Rasch brothers (the book's editors) and Richter.

examples and in some ways a more diverse range of them; indeed *Gefesselter Blick* contained more illustrations (140) than *Die neue Typographie* (125). The half-width, red front paper of the book that shows through the adventurous, transparent plastic cover acknowledges the support (possibly financial) of the Ring in producing it and Schwitters is accorded special thanks inside. The publication arose from an exhibition at the Graphische Klub Stuttgart in February 1930, which also travelled to other cities and in which the Ring had participated along with the other designers featured in the book.

The Rasch brothers, both architects, had their own firm that manufactured furniture, specializing in chairs, and their typographic work grew initially from the needs of this business. Their introduction to the book displays a clear acquaintance with Tschichold's work, featuring his phonetic script design of 1930, and, perhaps not coincidentally, *Gefesselter Blick* is typeset in the same sanserif as *Die neue Typographie*. Additionally the typesetting in *Gefesselter Blick* is cleverly specified to a different measure for each of the three type-sizes used, so that an optimum line length of between sixty-five and seventy characters is maintained. Tschichold naturally addressed the same matter, for example in *Eine Stunde Druckgestaltung*, in which he stressed the importance of 'really good legibility' and advises against lines that are too short or too long; but the particular terms in which the Rasch brothers explain their decision on the verso of their book's title-page suggests some knowledge of recent scientific research into legibility, whereas it was Tschichold's unfailing visual judgement that was leading him to similar conclusions.[181]

In compiling their book, the Rasch brothers offered two to four pages to each contributor, and requested their age and background details for inclusion. Contributors' texts arose as answers to the question: 'What principles do you follow in the design of your typography, or, do you actually have principles in this respect?'[182] This resulted in a more pluralistic overview of contemporary work and working than Tschichold could provide in his own books. It is the field of advertising design that dominates *Gefesselter Blick*, and Tschichold's own disenchantment with this activity is perhaps shown by his somewhat perfunctory contribution of a single sentence, accompanied by only two pieces of his work. He does not address the specific nature of advertising, as many of the other contributors do, but his statement is a characteristically precise expression of his over-arching principle: 'i attempt in my advertising work to attain a maximum of fitness for purpose and a unity of the individual, constructional elements – to design.'

181. Some articles about legibility that were published in German scientific journals during the first two decades of the twentieth century are listed in Herbert Spencer's bibliography for *The visible word*.

182. Letter Heinz Rasch to Zwart, 29 January 1930.

Page dedicated to Tschichold in *Gefesselter Blick* (1930). His own brief statement of principle contrasts with the lengthy caption (probably written by the Rasch brothers) purporting to explain the visual functioning of his design. It reads: 'poster. black and red on yellow. a poster is perceived like an image, at least it is not "read" on the first glance. for this reason it is necessary to direct the eye forcefully. the fore-edge is determined by the strong, vertical bar. a visual target, and therefore the starting point for the text, is the steep "50". the area that first captures the eye stretches from here and the "M" of the name to the black bar. in a still further field of vision are the related details: time and place. hence a clear spatial division between eye-catching elements (in this case headline words) and related details. in order to absorb the details the eye must return a long way back.'

Such a rarefied aim reflects the peculiarity of Tschichold's position as both a leading practitioner and the principal (if not only) contemporary historian of New Typography. He could not achieve much critical distance from it, and could not perhaps be as honest about its limitations as he may have wished to be, for fear of jeopardizing his own chances of receiving much-needed commercial work. A dispassionate, contemporary analysis of modernist design in advertising was given by the art historian Gustav Hartlaub, who had coined the phrase *die neue Sachlichkeit* in 1923 and organized the seminal exhibition in 1925 of paintings under that title. He curated the exhibition 'Graphische Werbekunst' (Graphic advertising art) held at the Städtische Kunsthalle in Mannheim between August and September 1927, for which Tschichold designed the poster. In an article published the following year, entitled 'Kunst als Werbung' (Art as advertising), Hartlaub reflected on the modernity of New Typography in the field of publicity. He mentioned no designers in his text, although he showed some of Tschichold's cinema posters, and commented: 'It may be that the days of the modern cinema poster with its show-booth hideosity are numbered, that the public will soon demand more.' At a time when cinema was coming into its own (and television had only just been invented), he was convinced of advertising's impact as a mass medium:

The art of advertising is now, along with modern functional architecture, the only truly public art. It alone – as graphics, as printed duplication of type and image – reaches with its formal language even those nameless urban masses whose enthusiasm belongs no longer to the church, and not much to state authority, but instead to sport and fashion and to 'business' in general; that compact majority of football grounds, boxing matches and six-day races, that select cross-section of the mundane, in short that great, wide 'public', which is more at home everywhere other than in the galleries, exhibitions and theatres of high art. Advertising art is truly collective, a true art of the masses: really the only one that exists today. It shapes the visual habits among the nameless collective of the public.

He felt that the 'puritanically sober' style of new advertising corresponded to 'the will of a generation, which is averse to all romanticism, says a resolute yes to our standardized and "American"-oriented lifestyle and which is trying to "make the best" from it artistically and morally in terms of a future culture'. Hartlaub could see, however, that New Typography was not appropriate for all purposes:

In fact the modern, *sachlich*, Constructivist style is only suitable for certain advertising purposes: such as for tasks of machine industry, instrument making etc., generally for everything technical, and perhaps also for cinema publicity. However it is not at all appropriate for more old-fashioned kinds of goods, such as pipe-tobacco or cigars, or generally in cases where the consumer's conservative taste dictates archaic forms and where the frosty *Sachlichkeit* of the new style would only irritate the clientèle.[183]

183. Hartlaub, 'Kunst als Werbung', pp.173–5.

Poster designed by Tschichold for exhibition of 'Graphic advertising art: an international display of contemporary publicity' at the Mannheim Kunsthalle. 1927. 86 × 62.8 cm. All lettering drawn by Tschichold; printed by lithography.

Photography and photomontage

Sustained work by Tschichold on his book projects would not have been helped by difficulties in finding satisfactory accommodation in Munich: the Tschicholds moved from two different addresses before settling in the Voitstraße, located in the housing development named Borstei, around the time that their son, Peter, was born in early 1929. Situated on the road that leads north-west out of Munich to Dachau, Borstei was modern but not built in the functionalist style, which barely touched Munich in comparison with Berlin or Frankfurt. The Tschicholds' apartment there boasted central heating and hot running water (not standard in those days) and they furnished it in modern style with their Bauhaus furniture; a newspaper even came to interview them about it and to photograph the interior. One of their neighbours in Borstei was the art historian

Franz Roh, who became a friend and collaborator of Tschichold's. Roh had coined the term 'magic realism' (later applied to South American literature) in the title of his 1925 book about contemporary European painting, *Nach-Expressionismus, magischer Realismus*, and he was an adviser for the 'Neue Sachlichkeit' exhibition of that same year. Roh and Tschichold shared a strong interest in photography: Roh was active as an avant-garde photographer and photomonteur while Tschichold was passionate about it from a theoretical standpoint, considering it to have become an integral aspect of the modern age.

Both men were among a small group of friends in Munich that met every month to discuss matters of contemporary interest. Each member was a subscriber to relevant journals, and these were passed on to the other members, in a fixed sequence, every Friday. The group consisted of Jan & Edith

106

Georg Trump, exhibition poster for the showing of the Film und Foto exhibition in Munich, where it was retitled 'Das Lichtbild' (the photograph). 1930.

Page from Tschichold's article 'Fotografie und Typografie' in *Hand und Maschine* (Jg.1, Nr 11, February 1930). Shows a prospectus designed by him in 1927. In this article Tschichold asserted: 'the photograph has become such a distinguishing feature of our time that it can no longer be ignored.'

Tschichold, Roh, the photographer Eduard Wasow, Wilhelm Meyer (a neurologist), Hilde Horn (who had studied at the Bauhaus) and her husband Will, and two young teachers, Kurt Seelmann and Alfons Simons. Seelmann remembers Tschichold making unorthodox but incisive observations during one of the monthly meetings, when the subject of discussion was non-objective art.[184]

Tschichold also became acquainted in Munich with Hans Eckstein, a design journalist with connections to the Münchner Bund, the local group of the German Werkbund, which had been established in 1907 to foster German design culture. Along with Paul Renner, Eckstein was one of the few 'moderns' associated with the rather conservative Münchner Bund. He was also a supporter of the Neue Sammlung, a 'new collection' of contemporary artefacts established in 1925 at the Bayerischen Nationalmuseum, which was one of the few venues for exhibiting modern design in Munich. Eckstein was later to assist Tschichold in finding work in Switzerland when he had to leave Germany.

Renner was a leading member of the Werkbund, but neither Eckstein, Roh nor Tschichold were members. In summer 1927 Tschichold had asked Max Burchartz, who was already a Werkbund member, to be an advocate for his own application to join. Burchartz welcomed his decision, stating that '*all* those interested in new things should at least join the D.W.B.'[185] But either Tschichold changed his mind

or was not accepted into the Munich division. Nevertheless, he was chosen as one of the selection committee for the 1929 exhibition 'Film und Foto' (Fifo), initiated by Gustav Stotz of the Werkbund's Württemberg working group, who had overseen the two previous major Werkbund exhibitions, 'Form ohne Ornament' (Form without ornament; 1924) and 'Die Wohnung' (The dwelling; 1927). Joining Tschichold on the selection committee were two older men, Bernhard Pankok, an artist who had moved into applied art during the Jugendstil period, and Hans Hildebrandt, an art historian with modern interests who taught at the Stuttgart Technische Hochschule. Fifo was on show in Stuttgart between May and July 1929, and proved a great success, provoking much debate in the photographic press. It then went on an extensive tour to Zurich, Berlin, Danzig, Vienna, Munich, Tokyo and Osaka.

Victor Margolin has persuasively suggested that the emphasis in the selection of material for Fifo was depoliticized, ignoring left-wing applications of contemporary photography, such as the 'worker-photograph', in favour of an artistic approach.[186] This is not surprising given the variety of interests and inevitable compromises that must have arisen between the members of the selection committee, and in any case it accords with the Werkbund's aim of

184. Seelmann,'Erinnerung an Jan Tschichold' in Luidl, *J.T.*, p.24.   185. Letter Burchartz to Tschichold, 7 July 1927.   186. Margolin, *Visions of Utopia*, p.157.

Both sides of advertising leaflet (folded out) for
Foto-Auge. 1929. 13.5 × 10.2 cm.

staying out of politics. Tschichold's influence can undoubtedly be seen in the selection of 'typophoto' examples of graphic design, including some of his own and others from his 'special typographic class' at the Meisterschule. Extensive sections for the Netherlands and the USSR were organized respectively by his friends Zwart and Lissitzky. The exhibition was designed by F.H. Ernst Schneidler and it was accompanied by special film showings selected by Hans Richter, an avant-garde filmmaker with whom Tschichold shared an austere view of cinema.[187]

The content of the exhibition changed in its different venues: when shown at the Neue Sammlung in Munich between June and September 1930 it was given a new title, 'Das Lichtbild' (The photograph), and a local selection committee comprising Wolfgang Wersin (director of the Neue Sammlung), Renner, Roh and Wasow assembled additional sections with new material on scientific photography, photo-reportage, advertising, and abstract photography. Roh was in charge of a historical section. The poster for the Munich exhibition was designed by Georg Trump, and the stationery by Tschichold.

The original catalogue of Fifo did not contain many illustrations, which perhaps encouraged the publication of two larger books on the same theme: the first was *Es kommt der neue Fotograf* (Here comes the new photographer; 1929) by Werner Graeff, who had collaborated with Richter on abstract films, and *Foto-Auge/oeil et photo/photo-eye*, co-compiled by Tschichold and Roh. Tschichold later commented that the plan for their book arose during the train journey from Munich to Stuttgart taken by himself and Roh while the exhibition was being planned.[188] This tri-lingual edition contained an introduction by Roh, 'Mechanism and expression', and 76 images including photographs by Moholy-Nagy, photomontages by Heartfield, Hannah Höch

and Hans Leistikow, and many examples of photography used in advertising by Burchartz, Zwart and Tschichold himself. Also included were some film stills from Vertov's *Kino-eye*, which may have provided some inspiration for the book's title. The cover featured Lissitzky's now famous self-portrait montage, 'The constructor' (1924), of which the artist had sent a small, rather darkly reproduced print to Tschichold with a personal dedication. The *Foto-Auge* reproduction was made from the original print shown in the Fifo exhibition, and Tschichold preserved a half-tone proof from the printing block for the rest of his life, using it again in an essay on Lissitzky of 1970. There he had it carefully enlarged to its original size, which he was able to specify from the photogram element of Lissitzky's letterhead included in the composition.[189] Tschichold had also illustrated 'The constructor' in an article of 1931 dedicated to Lissitzky, in which he judged it as 'an important stage of development in photography, one of the most important photographic works of the last ten years'.[190]

Foto-Auge did not initially sell well. The international economic crisis of these years was setting in. Foreign investement in Germany had already halved since the previous year and the collapse of the American stock exchange led to a calling in of loans from the USA, causing a credit crisis within Germany. The publisher of *Foto-Auge*, Wedekind, paid Roh & Tschichold with copies of the book instead of money, but it was difficult for the authors to sell them. (Tschichold was simultaneously working with the same publisher on *Eine Stunde Druckgestaltung*, which, it might be assumed, did not make any profits either.) Nevertheless *Foto-Auge* was selected among the winners of the first annual competition for the 'fifty most beautiful books' in 1929, and Tschichold remained proud of its design. In the 1970s he was asked to write a short note about it for a bookseller's

187. To tie in with Fifo Hans Richter wrote a booklet that was a rallying call for the campaigning film societies, *Filmgegner von heute – Filmfreunde von morgen* (Film-opponents of today – film-friends of tomor-

row). He criticized commercial German and American cinema, including *Metropolis* (as Tschichold had done), for being over-designed. See Willett, *The new sobriety*, p.148. The last (double) issue in 1926 of the

journal *G* (edited by Richter) had been dedicated to film and Tschichold discussed with him its revival with an issue about typography, but this never came about. Letter Tschichold to Zwart, 31 August 1927.

188. 'Wie das Buch *Foto-Auge* (1929) entstand', p.413.
189. Letter Tschichold to Jan Leering, Director of Van Abbe Museum, Eindhoven. Tschichold described the original of 'The constructor' as a *Unikum*

('not a *Unikat* as some *Dummköpfe* say today') which he considered to be 'missing' at that point. It now seems to have been found in the Tretiakov Gallery, Moscow (see Tupitsyn, *El Lissitzky*, p.81).

190. 'The "Constructivist" El Lissitzky', pp. 149–50.

catalogue: 'My aim was to make a modest, unpretentious book, which should be beautiful but inexpensive. Above all without a hard binding.' As a way of adding bulk to the book, which consisted of a mere 84 pages, he had it bound in Chinese folds (pages of double paper thickness, folded & uncut at the fore-edge), with the paper coated only on the one side to be printed.[191]

Roh's introduction to *Foto-Auge* stressed, rather as Tschichold had done for typography, that the main impetus for new initiatives in photography came from 'outsiders', not professionals. Modern artists including Lissitzky, Moholy-Nagy and Rodchenko were excited by the possibilities for the medium offered by the newly available, lightweight 35 mm cameras, such as the Leica L1 first mass-produced in 1925.[192]

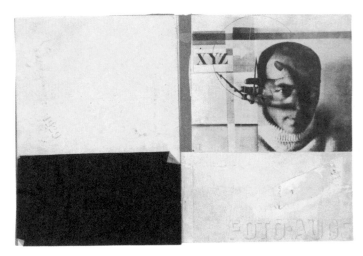

Sketch layout for the cover of *Foto-Auge*. 1929. 14.7 × 21 cm.

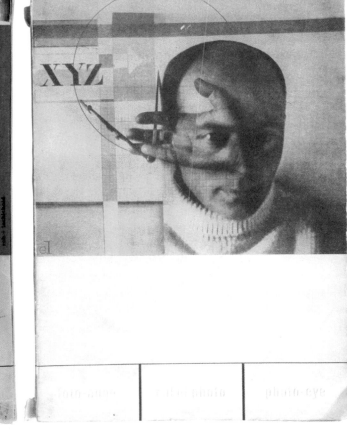

191. 'Wie das Buch *Foto-Auge* (1929) enstand', pp.413–5.
192. Moholy-Nagy's eyes were opened to the potential of photography by his first wife, the photographer Lucia Schultz.

Top section, back cover, spine and front cover of *Foto-Auge*. 1929. A4. Tschichold claimed to have invented a new kind of softback binding which allowed the flexible board covers (slightly bigger than the book block) to open fully. But it did not allow the pages of the book to open very well, as shown in the spreads opposite. The cover is made from two sandwiched pieces of card, which allowed the blind embossing on the front not to show through to the other side. It is also prone to flaking, as shown in the spine above and the cover detail from another copy (opposite below).

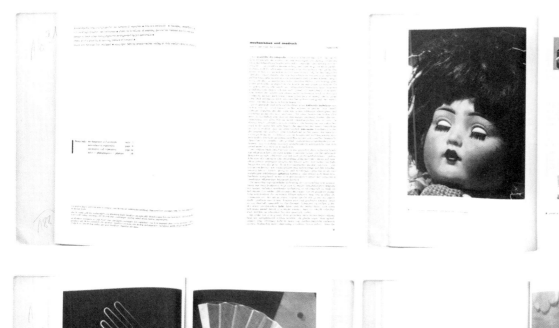

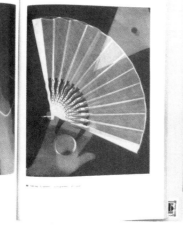

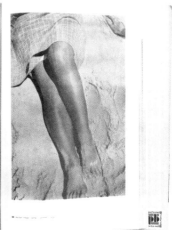

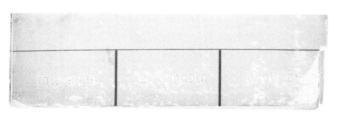

Spreads from *Foto-Auge*, showing work by Burchartz and Grosz & Heartfield; Walter Peterhans; a 'medical photo' and Grosz; Brett Weston and Bayer. (This copy belonged to the bookseller Paul Breman, whose label is visible on the inside back cover.)

Spreads from *Foto-Auge*, showing work by Höch and Benesch-Müller; Burchartz and Vertov.

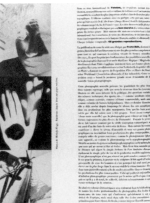
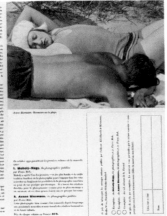
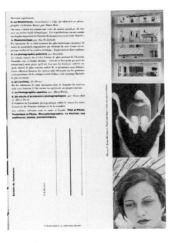

Front, centre spread and back of publicity leaflet (mainly in French) for the Fototek series. *c*.1930. 24.8 × 17.5 cm. The future titles announced are:

The monstrous; Photomontage; The police photograph; El Lissitzky; The sport photograph; A century of academic photographs.

Due presumably to its illustrations of Russian work and of photomontage by Heartfield, *Foto-Auge* was later included by the Nazis in the officially published list of 'harmful and undesirable literature', which meant that distributing or selling the book was forbidden.[193]

Roh and Tschichold's shared passion for 'New Photography' led to a further publishing venture, a projected series of photographic monographs, again with tri-lingual texts and designed by Tschichold. The series was christened 'Fototek: books of modern photography', and the list of envisioned titles reflected a catholic survey of modern photography, including studies of sport photographs and 'the concept of kitsch in photography'. Doubtless due partly to unfavourable economic circumstances, only the first two volumes in the series were published, monographs on Moholy-Nagy and Aenne Biermann (both 1930) with introductions by Roh. The fifth of the titles announced in

an initial prospectus for the series (after no.4 'The police photograph') was a study by Lissitzky of 'Photo and typophoto in the USSR'. This was advertised without Lissitzky's knowledge, despite his having visited Tschichold during 1930 when working on two exhibitions in Germany. Lissitzky was not annoyed about the announcement, but demurred and suggested instead to Tschichold that his German wife Sophie, who was frequently an equal collaborator in his work, could do it better. He was more than happy for Fototek to publish a book dedicated to his work alone.[194] Indeed for the list of future publications included in the *Aenne Biermann* monograph the title of the projected book was changed to the eponymous 'El Lissitzky. 60 photos and typophotos'.

193. *Liste des schädlichen und unerwünschten Schrifttums.* Published by the Reichsschrift-tumskammer, December 1938. *Foto-Auge* is listed alphabetically under R[oh].

194. Letter Lissitzky to Tschichold, 22 August 1930.

L. Moholy-Nagy

60 Fotos   herausgegeben von Franz Roh
60 photos   edited by Franz Roh
60 photographies   publiées par Franz Roh

Klinkhardt & Biermann Verlag - Publishers - Editeurs Berlin W 10

Band 1 der „Fototek" (Bücher der Neuen Fotografie). Alle Rechte vorbehalten.
Gesamteinrichtung des Buches: *Jan Tschichold*, München.
Herstellung der Druckstöcke und Druck: F. Bruckmann AG, München.

1st volume of "Fototek" (Books of modern photography).
Entire get-up by *Jan Tschichold*.
Clichés and print by F. Bruckmann AG, Munich.

1er volume de la «Fototek» (Bibliothèque de la photographie nouvelle). Tous droits réservés.
La disposition générale du livre est due à *Jan Tschichold*.
Clichés et texte de l'imprimerie F. Bruckmann AG, Munich.

Printed in Germany.
Copyright 1930 by Klinkhardt & Biermann, K.-G. a. A., Verlag, Berlin W 10.

Moholy-Nagy und die neue Fotografie   *Franz Roh*

Moholy-Nagy, ein seit Jahren in Deutschland lebender Ungar, spielt eine entscheidende Rolle in der Geschichte *neuester Fotografie*. Bekannt wurde er durch seine Tätigkeit am „Bauhaus", dem er bereits in Weimar, später in Dessau angehörte, von wo er wichtige Anregungen über Gestaltungsfragen der Zukunft ausgehen ließ, besonders durch die mit Gropius herausgegebenen „Bauhausbücher" (Verlag Albert Langen, München). Moholy rechnet als Maler zu den „Konstruktivisten", jener Gruppe, die den Abstraktionsdrang heutiger Malerei bis zum äußersten führt, also die Gegenstände der Außenwelt nicht mal mehr *fragmentarisch* einbezieht, wie dies Expressionismus und Kubismus noch wollten. Reines Pigment der Farbe unter Organisierung streng geometrischer Formenwelt soll hier allein sprechen. Die Malereien dieser Gruppe aber sind zugleich Signalscheiben für eine Umorganisierung auch ganz anderer Gebiete: Moholy versuchte die Bühnengestaltung in konstruktivistischer Form zu durchdringen (an der Berliner Staatsoper unter Klemperer, ferner mit Versuchen für Piscator), ebenso die Ausstellungsfragen neu zu beantworten (Zehlendorfer Wohnausstellung 1928, Pariser Werkbundausstellung 1930), ferner die Typografie umzustellen, schließlich in kunsterzieherische Probleme einzugreifen (in seinem Buche „Von Material zu Architektur" (Albert Langen, München 1929). Als Hauptmöglichkeit der „Malerei" der Zukunft schwebt Moholy räumliche Gestaltung mit farbigem, reflektorischem Licht vor (er stellte 1930 in Paris ein „Lichtrequisit", ein elektrisches Bewegungs- und Farbenspiel aus).

Schon diese Vielseitigkeit der Gestaltungsinteressen Moholys zeigt, daß der Purismus der abstrakten Malerei, der sich bei diesem neuen Typus Mensch häufig findet, nicht etwa Purismus im *Lebensganzen* bedeutet: der gesamte Umkreis des Menschlichen soll erhalten bleiben, gewisse Urbedürfnisse des Daseins werden nur auf andere Gebiete abgeschoben. So bleibt auch Hunger nach dem Ausdrucksgehalt der *gegenständlichen Außenwelt* durchaus bestehen, er wird nur aus Malerei und Grafik, wo er sich früher befriedigt hatte, ausgeschieden und dem Gebiete der Fotografie zugelenkt. Moholy glaubt, daß im Fotokasten diejenige Apparatur vorliege, die (manuell schwer zu überbieten) gerade für Sättigung jenes Gegenstandshungers geschaffen sei. Erfahrung und Gestaltung, welche sich gestern in oft unklarer Mischung befanden, werden heute betonter geschieden, auf ihre eigenen spezifischen Pole verwiesen und in sinnreiche Spannung zueinander gesetzt. Bezeichnend, wie heute einerseits die Formfragen als solche betont werden (die freiesten, rein gestalterischen Möglichkeiten etwa), auf der anderen Seite aber der Begriff der Reportage — auf vielen Gebieten — in neuer Schärfe auftaucht.

Fotografie *ist* nun zunächst Reportage. Aber zwischen Reportage und Gestaltung besteht letzten Endes doch nur ein gradweiser, kein absoluter Unterschied. Denn schon durch die Art, wie ich aus unab-

3

(This page and overleaf) Cover, title-page and spreads from the Fototek edition, *L. Moholy-Nagy: 60 photos*. 1930. 25 × 17.6 cm. Tschichold's design credit ('Gesamteinrichtung des Buches') was endearingly translated into English on the verso of the title-page as 'Entire get-up by Jan Tschichold'.

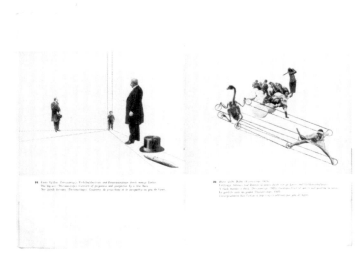

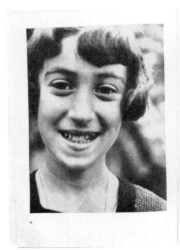

Tschichold himself was to compile the third volume in the series about 'Fotomontage', to be printed in two colours. With this in mind he also established contact with Alexander Rodchenko in Moscow at this time, having seemingly attempted to do so previously:

> i was extremely pleased that you wrote to me. i have often tried to get in touch with you, but i have not managed to do so until now. i have known your name for a long time from exhibitions etc; also i already possess several numbers of lef and the book 'pro eto' by mayakovsky with your photomontages, of which it is probably true to say that it was the first book illustrated with photomontage.[195]

Tschichold sent Rodchenko the first two Fototek volumes, and *Foto-Auge*, explaining that his omission from the latter was not deliberate, and that he had been featured in the Fifo exhibition. He asked for a large collection of Rodchenko's photographs in original prints so as to make a further monograph on his work. Rodchenko replied: 'I am full of admiration for your volume "Foto-Auge", and I can only regret that I did not make contact with you earlier and am therefore not included in it along with my foto-colleagues.'[196] Tschichold had also requested some of Rodchenko's photo-

montage posters for inclusion in his planned Fototek book, but Rodchenko explained that he was then concentrating on pure photography, whereas his wife, Varvara Stepanova, was more active in graphic design for Soviet purposes. The importance Tschichold placed on Soviet photomontage is demonstrated by his also seeking material for the book from Gustav Klucis, one of the earliest practitioners of the technique in the USSR and the designer of some iconic propaganda posters. Tschichold had written twice, in March and April 1930, to the Soviet State publishing house requesting copies of the postcard series that Klucis designed for the 1928 Spartakiade sporting event and for some of his posters. Tschichold wrote a short article about Klucis's posters, which was intended for publication in *Commercial Art* but never appeared. Here he explained: 'The bold and fully accomplished composition of Klucis's works elevates them above related works, and Klucis can be regarded as a classic of photomontage.'[197]

195. Letter Tschichold to Rodchenko, 10 October 1931, in *Rodtschenko*, p.175. Tschichold had indeed made a statement to this effect in *The New Typography*, p.224.
196. Letter Rodchenko to Tschichold, 28 October 1931.
197. 'Über die Fotoplakate von G. Kluzis'. One-page typescript (Getty).

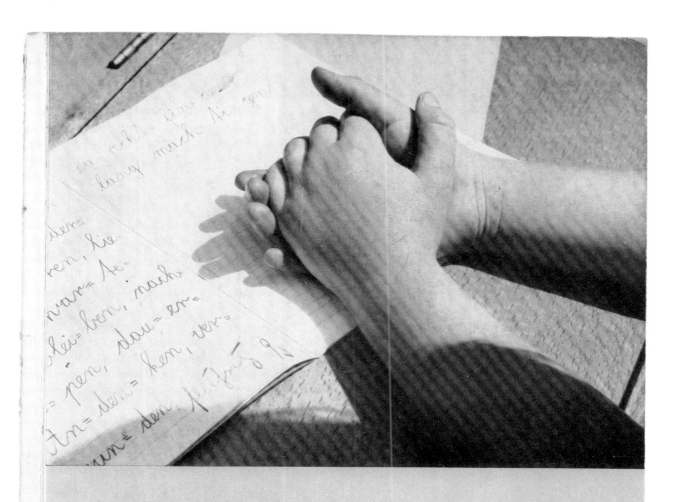

Aenne Biermann

60 Fotos   mit Einleitung von Franz Roh   »Der literarische Foto-Streit«
60 photos   with introduction by Franz Roh   "The literary dispute about photography"
60 photographies avec introduction par Franz Roh «La querelle au sujet de la photographie»

Fototek **2**   Klinkhardt & Biermann   Verlag - Publishers - Editeurs   Berlin W 10

Cover of Fototek 2, *Aenne Biermann: 60 photos.* 1930. 25 × 17.6 cm.

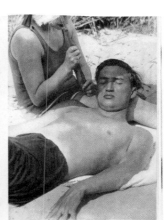

Spreads of Fototek 2, *Aenne Biermann: 60 photos*.
1930. 25 × 17.6 cm. Biermann died in 1933 aged
only 35.

Spine and photomontage cover by Tschichold for Dubreuil, *Arbeiter in USA*. (Leipzig: Bibliographisches Institut, 1930). 18.5 × 12.5 cm.

Jacket for Reiners, *Die wirkliche Wirtschaft* (Munich: Beck, 1931). 23.4 × 16.9 cm. The lack of finish in some of the lettering here is not characteristic of Tschichold, but the version of Gill Sans in the title (with an ft ligature) implicates him.

Although the Fototek volume on photomontage was never published, Tschichold's outline survives, showing that he intended to treat both the history and theory of the subject, and hoped to include texts by Moholy-Nagy and Roh. His stated aim was 'to prove that talk of the "out-datedness" of these graphics is empty chatter'. Some idea of his approach may perhaps be surmised from a short article written for *Commercial Art* entitled 'The composite photograph and its place in advertising' ('composite photograph' being a translation of photomontage). While admitting that it is contestable whether all photography can be considered art, he asserted: 'Photography can, however, become a real art in three forms: as a composite photograph, as a double-copy and as a photogram.' He distinguished primitive trick photography from modern photomontage:

> In the Stenger Collection, Berlin, there are composite-photographs dating from the very earliest days of photography, photo-caricatures, consisting of small bodies with enormous heads. This old type of composite-photography, however, is very different from the new. The former is really only a type of photographic fraud, having an appearance of reality. This false ambition is entirely wanting in modern composite-photography, which is really an invention of the dadaist movement. The circle of Raoul Hausmann, John Heartfield, Hannah Höch, and George Grosz were really the originators of composite photographs of the modern type. Their aim was to get at the forms of reality, using photographs instead of painted pictures.[198]

Tschichold's placing of Raoul Hausmann first among the innovators in photomontage was a deliberate compensation in response to claims that Hausmann made in correspondence with him. The Vienna-born Hausmann, an important figure in Berlin Dada and subsequently Constructivist circles, wrote a heated letter to Tschichold on 2 April 1930, asserting his primacy not only in the development of photomontage but of New Typography also. He accused Tschichold of leaving his name out of the account given of Dada in *Die neue Typographie*, and of giving too much prominence to Heartfield's role in the invention of photomontage. Hausmann explained that he had directed the typography of certain key Dada publications himself and also claimed to have made the first ever photomontage in 1920. He believed that Tschichold must have been influenced to consciously exclude him:

> That which can have been explained to you by a vindictive clique does not justify your distortion of the historical truth. I request that you answer me within the next eight days otherwise I will be forced to take other steps.

Hausmann's objection to Tschichold's historical version shows the dangers of writing contemporary history, especially when the historian has a stake in the movement under

198. 'The composite photograph and its place in advertising', pp.244–8. The content of this article overlaps slightly with 'Fotografie und Typografie' (1928).

Gute Fotomontage — sie vermittelt den Sinn auf eine drollige Weise —, aber schlechte Gesamttypografie, die weder optisch mit der Fotomontage zusammenhängt, noch im einzelnen gut ist. Die zu vielen Schriftarten und die Vermischung von Symmetrie und Asymmetrie ergeben einen Wirrwarr. Eine strenge Beschränkung in den Mitteln und das Streben, jedes Teilchen „interessant" zu machen, wäre im Vorteil für die Gesamtgestaltung gewesen. So aber bewirkt die allzu ornamentale (dabei selbst in diesem Sinne schlechte) Gruppierung mangelnde Übersichtlichkeit und Unruhe.

Paul Schuitema: Werbeblatt für Trockenmilch

Gute Fotomontage. Häufig ohne Verwirrung. Richtige psychologische Wirkung. Klarheit im Gesamtaufbau. Die Schrift ist ein untrennbarer Bestandteil des Ganzen.

Bild 1: Schlechte Reklamephotographie. Langweilige anormale Sicht (Kniebeuge!), wirkungslose Beleuchtung. (Mit dem häßlichen Klischeerändchen.)
(Photo Wasow-Tschichold)

stehen, wo er sie normalerweise vorfindet, und photographiert sie von oben. Das mag manchem zunächst seltsam vorkommen; in Wirklichkeit ist diese Art hier die einzig richtige. Oder er muß sein Service photographieren. Das ist es noch heute die Regel, daß dieses ohne sichtbare Tischplatte, ohne Speisen und Blumen usw., also „ganz ohne alles" und in Kniebeuge aufgenommen und dann ausgiebig retuschiert wird. Das Ergebnis ist an Langweiligkeit nicht zu überbieten. Ein guter Lichtbildner wird das Service auf einem vielleicht halb angerichteten Tisch, mit Gläsern und allem Tafelzubehör (nicht zuviel natürlich, damit das Service nicht etwa zurücktritt) aus dem Blickpunkt des Betrachters (also auch von oben) mit starker schattenbildender Beleuchtung aufnehmen und sein Bild nur dort, wo es absolut notwendig ist, vorsichtig retuschieren. Ergebnis: eine lebendige, die Wirklichkeit spiegelnde Photographie.

Es zeigt sich also, daß die Photographie ein hervorragendes Werbemittel sein kann, aber nicht sein muß. Photographie ist nicht gleich Photographie. Die kommende Ausstellung „Film und Foto" wird das Interesse an der guten Photographie wecken und heben und das Ergebnis der Arbeit der fortgeschrittenen Lichtbildner aller Länder vorführen. Es wird sich hier zeigen, daß es in Deutschland Reklame- und Sachphotographien gibt, deren Leistungen hinter denen etwa Amerikas und Frankreichs nicht zurückstehn, nur daß sie von den Industrie- und anderen Verbraucherkreisen kaum gekannt und ungenutzt sind. Niemand, der in der Photographie in seiner Werbung bedarf, sollte darum den Besuch der „Fifo" versäumen.

An den zwei obenstehenden Beispielen sei einer der möglichen Unterschiede zwischen schlechter und guter Werbephotographie gezeigt. Es ist eine Werbung für Grammophone schlechthin angenommen, die mit einem abgestimmten, an das Gefühl appellierenden Text als Inserat in einer Wochenschrift erscheint (etwa eine Gemeinschaftswerbung der Sprechmaschinenfabrikanten). Bild 1, eine sachliche, aber werbeunwirksame Photographie, zeigt das übliche Bild aus einer Ansicht, die man wie hat, auch wenn der Apparat auf dem Tisch steht. („Aber die Senkrechten sind ja wenigstens senkrecht", würde ihr Verteidiger sagen, was aber falsch ist, da man die faktisch Senkrechten eben nie senkrecht sieht.) Auch wenn man den ganzen Untergrund wegnehmen und den Apparat also frei auf Weiß erscheinen lassen würde, wäre selbst nach einer Retusche die Wirkung langweilig und trocken. Niemand braucht dabei Lust zu bekommen, sich einen solchen Apparat anzuschaffen. Wie anders wirkt Bild 2! Hier ist zwar der Teil für das Ganze gesetzt, aber durch eine wirksame Kontraste schaffende Beleuchtung, Aufsicht und tonmäßige Differenziertheit ist ein Bild entstanden, das Lustgefühle weckt und in Verbindung mit einem passenden Text, etwa „der Klang der Schallplatte" usw., geeignet ist, durch seine emotionale Kraft kaufanregend zu wirken. Besonders an der Wirkung beteiligt sind dabei der Bildausschnitt, der Wechsel von scharf und unscharf, die Weichheit der rückwärtigen Partien. Diese letzte mag unsachlich im Sinne der exakten Wiedergabe sein, ist aber sachlich durch die stärkere optisch-gefühlsmäßige Wirkung berechtigt.

Bild 2: Gutes Werbephoto. Der Teil fürs Ganze. Effektvolle Beleuchtung, differenzierte Schatten- und Lichtwirkung. (Ohne Klischeerändchen.)
(Photo Wasow-Tschichold)

Wohl ist die Photographie heute ein wichtiger, allerdings nicht offen bejahter Teil der Werbetypographie — zu häufig noch sieht man sie als Zeichnungsersatz an —, aber sie bedarf noch fast überall des hinzutretenden Wortes, des Schriftsatzes, der Typographie im engeren Sinne. Als „optisches Wort" ist das Photo oft besser als das geschriebene, weil es oft schneller und besser informiert als lange Aufsätze, aber mindestens muß der Firmenname hinzutreten, der das Ganze erst zur eigentlichen Werbe, verständlich und werbewirksam macht.

Die Verbindung von Photo- und Typographie, von Klischee und Drucksatz, unterscheidet sich wesentlich von der früheren Methode, Gegenstandswiedergabe und Schrift manuell herzustellen. Es wäre nun ein Irrtum, zu glauben, daß diese neue Art leichter und einfacher sei. Reklame kann heute nicht mehr wie früher überhaupt, gleichgültig wie, gemacht werden. Heute ist infolge des Konkurrenzkampfes und der Konkurrenzreklame die „blinde" Werbung geschäftlich untragbar. Die gute Reklame fordert heute mehr denn je neben einem wohlüberlegten Aufbau des Werbewerkes und der einzelnen Werbefeldzüge, guter Streuung usw. auch eine gute formale Durchführung der einzelnen Werbesachen. Gute formale Durchführung bedeutet Klarheit im Aufbau und harmonische Formgestaltung. Die Klarheit des Aufbaus ist unter allen Umständen an die erste Stelle zu setzen, da eine Reklame sehr wohl „schön" wirken, aber nicht zugleich auch „wirken", also zum Kauf antreiben muß. Es wäre falsch, sich mit einer leidlichen Klarheit zu begnügen, die auf alle optischen Wirkungen durch gute statt mittelmäßige Photos, gute und klare Schrift statt verzierter Schriftarten, Intensität der Farb- und Formkontraste und Harmonie des Ganzen verzichtet.

Neben dem Werbefachmann, der die Werbung organisiert und die Textgestaltung übernimmt oder überwacht, ist daher auch ein Werbgestalter zuzuziehen, der, werblich gebildet, die Formgestaltung übernimmt.

Grundsätzlich wäre zu bemerken, daß die Photoreklame das Ornament ausschließt. Das exakte

discussion, as Tschichold did. His interests lay in a rational consolidation of Dada and Futurist initiatives but he was undoubtedly trying to be accurate in his historical approach, as is clear from his explanation in reply to Hausmann. Tschichold often delayed replying to letters for a month or more, excusing himself for being very busy, but, naturally shaken by Hausmann's concluding threat, he wrote to him the very next day:

> dear mr hausmann
> i have had the intention to write to you for a while, but have not got around to it before now due to lack of time. then your letter reached me today, which left me somewhat stunned. i want to assure you in all honesty that i did not deliberately leave out your name from the passages that you cite. like you i am a friend of kurt schwitters and perhaps you could take this as a reason to ask him what experience he has of me. i would like to believe that it is you, and not me, who has been the victim of machinations [*Verhetzung*] by some interested party, although it is a mystery to me who they could have been. in my chronicle of new typography i proceeded with utmost scrupulousness, and consulted all of the sources that were available to me. in this i was every now and then obliged to rely on the possibly subjective reports of third parties. that i left your name out in my citations did not occur out of bad intent – i did not seek there to give a complete register of names. i cited merely the names that also appeared later in a wider public sense. as far as i am aware, you have perhaps not emerged publicly since those days.
> i believe that it leads to endless and useless squabbles if one seriously wants to discuss who invented photomontage. i would also no longer maintain today that heartfield invented it. several people, certainly with subjective reason, claim credit for this, and it is perhaps the most reasonable course to grant them all their subjective belief. i have taken note of your assertions with great interest and will make use of them at the next available opportunity.[199]

As a further proof of his 'absolute loyalty' Tschichold explained that he had wanted to write to Hausmann requesting examples of his typographic work 'for literary use at the next available opportunity'. Indeed their correspondence took place while Tschichold was preparing *Eine Stunde Druckgestaltung*, and he made sure to mention Hausmann along with the other Berlin Dadaists in that book's short historical summary. He also promised to help Hausmann publish an article about his work of the Dada years, and invited him to participate in a lecture evening, along with Arp and Schwitters, which he and Roh were planning in Munich. In correspondence with Tschichold, Arp also asserted his own (more modest) claim to a share in the credit for inventing 'montage' (although not specifically photomontage), sending him 'the original work of collage by masters arp and [max] ernst' from 1920, which he described as the 'adam and eve of all such works of collage'.[200]

Hausmann declared himself content with Tschichold's diplomatic reply, explaining that his aggressive tone was due to a 'planned campaign' against him by Hannah Höch, his former colleague, with whom he had also been romantically linked.[201] He agreed that, because he had withdrawn from public view 'for purely artistic reasons', Tschichold was not 'in a position to have seen things as they really were.'[202] But he took further offence when, on purchasing a copy of *Foto-Auge* (which featured photomontages by Höch and Heartfield & Grosz, but not Hausmann), he read the quotation of a letter from Georg Grosz in Roh's introductory essay, which stated that Grosz and Heartfield already made 'photo-pasting-montage-experiments' (*foto-klebe-montage-experimenten*) in 1915. Hausmann countered that Grosz and Höch had still been students at that time.

Tschichold's revision of his position on this matter, in order to distance himself from such claims, shows admirable historical circumspection, which had perhaps been influenced by impressions gained from other friends and colleagues of the intense rivalry surrounding the invention of photomontage.[203] His view anticipates later historians – for example Timothy O. Benson in his book *Raoul Hausmann and Dada*:

> A desire among the Dadaists for an 'official history' of 'photomontage' was foiled by innumerable disputes, inaccuracies, distortions and petty rivalries. Perhaps desiring recognition in an art world which has tended to construe the history of art as one of linear development within media categories, Grosz, Heartfield, Höch, and Hausmann have all made claims to the invention of 'photomontage'. Their conflicting anecdotal accounts have shifted attention from the primary artefacts.[204]

(Opposite above) American example illustrated in *Eine Stunde Druckgestaltung* and captioned by Tschichold: 'Good photomontage – it communicates the sense in a drastic way – but bad overall typography, which neither combines well visually with the photomontage nor is any good in itself. The surfeit of different type styles and the mixture of symmetry and asymmetry result in a confusion. A strict restriction of the means and of the tendency to make every little bit "interesting" would have been an advantage for the overall design.' In contrast, the example on the right by Schuitema is captioned: 'Good photomontage.

Accumulation without confusion. Correct psychological effect. Clarity in the overall structure. The type is an inseparable part of the whole.'

(Opposite below) Spread from Tschichold's article, 'Gute und schlechte Reklametypographie' (Good and bad advertising typography; 1929), with photographs credited to him & Eduard Wasow. Caption on the left: 'Bad advertising photograph. Boring, odd view (knees bent!), neutral lighting. (With ugly outline rule.)' On the right: 'Good advertising photo. A part represents the whole. Effective lighting, differentiated play of light and shadow. (Without outline rule.)'

199. Letter Tschichold to Hausmann, 3 April 1930. In a later letter of 28 April 1930 Tschichold concluded: 'your representation of historical events is of great value to me. please be assured that i will make the most objective use of your information.'
200. Letter Arp to Tschichold, 29 May 1931.
201. Höch later admitted that Hausmann 'influenced her indescribably'. Handwritten 'Lebensbild' of 1958 (Getty).
202. Letter Hausmann to Tschichold, 7 April 1930.
203. Tschichold confidently wrote in *Die neue Typographie* that Heartfield made the first photomontage book jackets. Tschichold does not seem to have had any contact with him at this time.
204. Benson, *Raoul Hausmann and Dada*, p.110.

Work by most of the pioneers was featured in the first major exhibition dedicated to photomontage shown at the Staatliche Kunstbibliothek, Berlin, during April and May 1931. This was curated by Tschichold's fellow Ring member Domela, and Tschichold may have had some input into the selection.[205] Hausmann re-emerged onto the public stage to give an inaugural lecture at the opening, perhaps partly as a result of his contact with Tschichold. The exhibition also contained a Soviet section – featuring Lissitzky, Rodchenko, Klucis and his partner Valentina Kulagina – and many pieces of 'typophoto' advertising, including an exhibition poster designed by Tschichold (below).

205. See a full list of exhibitors in Fleischmann, *Bauhaus*, p.353. Hausmann and Höch also exhibited as guests in the Ring's 1931 exhibition at Amsterdam.

raoul haußmann, fotomontage 1920

hannah höch, „liebe im busch"

Cover and spreads from exhibition catalogue, *Fotomontage*. 1931. 20.8 × 14.5 cm. Not designed by Tschichold, but featuring one of his posters (right). The exhibition's curator, Dutchman Cesar Domela (based in Germany), had been involved with the Novembergruppe, as well as being a member of De Stijl.

(Above left) Shows an excerpt from Hausmann's essay, where he defines photomontage as 'the artistic working of one or more photographs (with type or colour) into a unified composition'. By this definition Tschichold's poster fits within the category, although it does not strictly accord with our idea of photomontage today. Tschichold himself defined photomontage as 'images, which are either entirely put together from individual photos (foto-collage) or which use the photo as one component along with other pictorial elements (photo-drawing, *fotoplastik*).' ('Fotografie und Typografie' [1928] p.43.) Along with Hausmann's speech, the catalogue above contained a German translation of Gustav Klucis's essay 'Photomontage in the USSR', in which he staked his claim for the invention of political photomontage.

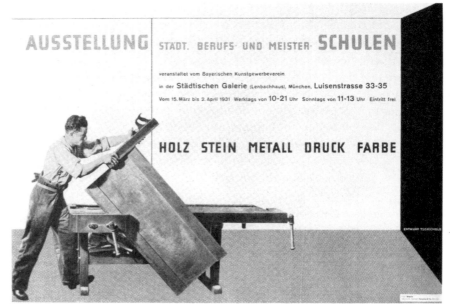

jan tschichold, plakat

Statistics in Vienna

Tschichold spent a short time in Vienna working with the
group producing pictorial statistics at the Gesellschafts- und
Wirtschaftsmuseum (Museum of society and economy).
The precise dates of his stay are unknown, but it was probably some time in the first half of 1929, when the major
publication *Gesellschaft und Wirtschaft* was in preparation
there. The museum, established in 1925, was developed out
of a museum of housing and urban development, reflecting the close involvement of its director, Otto Neurath, with
the housing movement in Vienna immediately after the
First World War. Neurath, who was not himself an artist
or designer, was the originator of the 'Vienna method' of
statistical representation, later known as Isotype.[206] He
sought to educate the public on the history and progress of
social welfare, not only in Vienna but internationally, and
saw the potential for international communication in statistics represented by means of pictures and not by numbers
alone. 'It is better to visualize quantity graphically than to
forget arithmetical exactitudes', was the museum's motto.
Tschichold was attracted to the institution largely on political grounds, describing it as an institute for 'popular education and enlightenment'. It soon acquired an international
reputation: Bertolt Brecht was among those who established
contact with Neurath.

The design of the museum's charts had already begun
to incorporate aspects of 'elemental' design before Tschichold arrived in Vienna, mainly due to the involvement
of German artist Gerd Arntz. In 1926 Neurath asked Arntz
to design repeatable picture units, having seen some of
his woodcut prints featuring schematized human figures.
Arntz moved to Vienna to work full-time at the museum
in September 1928, by which time it had already acquired
fonts of Paul Renner's Futura typeface, which became
the standard typeface used in Isotype (although Arntz
remembered that they had not yet been unpacked when
he arrived). Arntz acquired a copy of *Die neue Typographie*
soon after its publication, and so would have been well
aware of Tschichold's ideas. He was involved in a journal
called *A bis Z*, published by the Gruppe progressiver Künstler, Köln (Group of progressive artists, Cologne) between
1929 and 1933. It featured two articles by Tschichold and
was a well-designed piece of orthodox New Typography,
typeset entirely without capitals (following the example
of Roh and Tschichold's *Foto-Auge*). It may have been
partly through Arntz's agency that Tschichold was invited

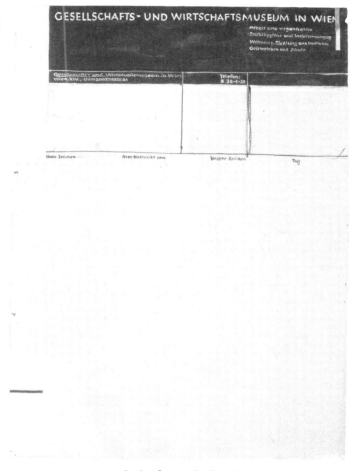

Design for standardized letterhead made by
Tschichold during his short stay at the Gesell-
schafts- und Wirtschaftsmuseum in Vienna.
1929. A4. Never printed.

to collaborate in Vienna, although the connection could
also have been made by the mutual friend of Neurath and
Tschichold, Franz Roh.[207] Neurath had met Roh in 1919
when the former came to Munich as a civil servant in the
Social Democrat government there, but left soon after in the
confusion during the short-lived Bavarian Soviet Republic.

It is not clear exactly what Tschichold did in Vienna,
although unproduced designs by him for a letterhead and
a sign-board survive. He is likely to have contributed something to *Gesellschaft und Wirtschaft*, for which he was full
of effusive praise: 'The task that confronts all science, that
is, to popularize itself, is here smilingly solved', he wrote in
an article (published in English) expounding the principles
of the Vienna method. As a champion of standardization,
Tschichold was attracted to the Vienna statistics by the
internal standards within each chart: a symbol's form and
value was fixed and it was repeated to convey quantity. This
was the best kind of *Sachlichkeit*. The graphic qualities created by Arntz's design also appealed to him:

206. Neurath has been
described as a social scientist
(Michael Twyman, *Graphic
Communication through Isotype*, p.7) and an encyclopedist
(Kinross, 'Blind eyes, innuendo
and the politics of design', *Visible Language*, 28, 1, 1995, p.76).

207. Lissitzky and his family
visited the Gesellschafts- und
Wirtschaftsmuseum around
the middle of 1928, where they
got to know Neurath. Edith
Tschichold had joined them
briefly on holiday in Austria
before their Vienna visit, and

it is feasible that these connections also paved the way for
Tschichold's stay. The Lissitzkys'
friendship with Neurath led to
the Vienna team visiting the
USSR to help set up an institute
for visual statistics. Lissitzky-
Küppers, *El Lissitzky*, p.86.

120

From our point of view the most important thing in the work of the museum is the systematic emphasis laid on essentials, and expressed in pictorial symbols universally intelligible, valid as international currency.

Irrelevancies of every kind, especially the merely decorative, are sternly excluded. Every item of the picture has sense and significance. A definite surface means a plane surface. Objects and figures are represented with severe simplicity. The representation of larger numbers by larger masses is avoided; they are indicated by a greater number of signs. The misleading tri-dimensional illusion produced by larger and smaller cubes is likewise avoided, for the most part only two-dimensional figures are employed.[208]

In the 'Vienna method' Tschichold perceived the same clarity, precision and international potential that he desired for New Typography.

The lynchpins of the Vienna team producing pictorial statistics were those who analysed complex data and then rendered it in draft, graphic form ready for final execution as a chart. This role – a prototype of the modern graphic designer, and certainly one that Tschichold would have appreciated – was named the 'transformer'. The principal transformer for *Gesellschaft und Wirtschaft*, and for most of the team's major projects, was Marie Reidemeister, who later married Neurath.

Tschichold toyed with the idea of taking up a full-time position at the museum in Vienna, but decided against it on financial grounds.[209]

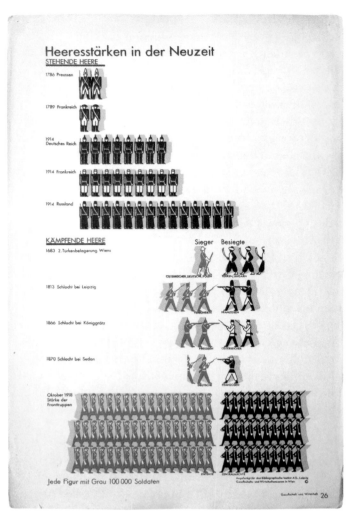

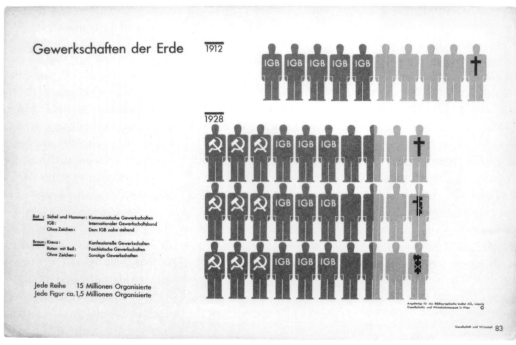

208. 'Statistics in pictures', p.114.

209. Letter Tschichold to Zwart, 15 August 1929. Nevertheless his appointment in Vienna was prematurely announced in *Typographische Mitteilungen*, Jg.26, H.9 (September 1929) p.225.

(Above) Marie Reidemeister & Gerd Arntz, sheets from *Gesellschaft und Wirtschaft* (Leipzig: Bibliographisches Institut, 1930). 31 × 46 cm.

(Opposite) Sheets from the Isotype 'Picture dictionary'. Designs by Gerd Arntz: (above) workers, including unemployed; (below) emigrant.

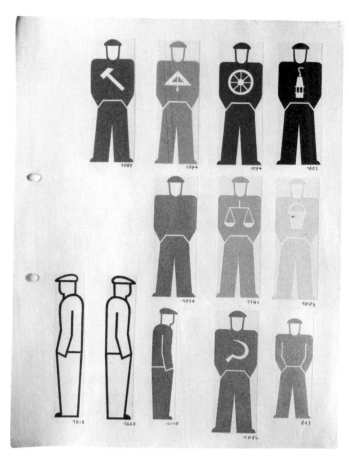

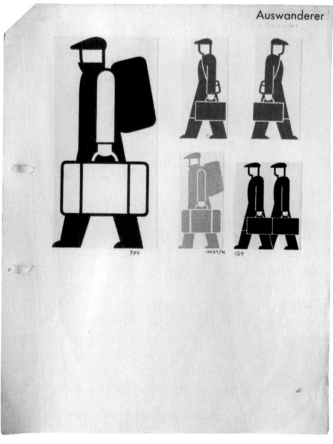

Auswanderer

Eastern European connections

As a corollary of his being 'ethnically a Slav' Tschichold later stated that he felt related to the Czechs, and had a particular affinity with Czech book art.[210] In an international survey of New Typography from 1930 he wrote: 'Outstanding achievements have also been made in Czechoslovakia, which has always had a strong feeling for typography.'[211] Already by the time of compiling *Elementare Typographie* he had seen the journal *Pásmo* (Zone; 1924–6), an organ of the principal Czech avant-garde group, Devětsil, and in the bibliography of *Die neue Typographie* he listed several Czech books written and designed by members of that group, including *Život II*, an anthology akin to *Ma*'s 'Book of new artists'. Devětsil had been founded in Prague in 1920 and espoused an optimistic search for a modern way of life appropriate for the new democratic republic of Czechoslovakia that emerged after the First World War. From among its membership of writers, painters, photographers and musicians, the art & architecture critic Karel Teige emerged as its leading theorist and the most important figure in modernist Czech typography.

Teige's cover for Devětsil's first eponymously published anthology (1922; overleaf), consisting merely of the group's name and a black disc, showed an initial affinity with contemporary Russian tendencies, albeit with a preference for circles instead of Malevich's and Lissitzky's squares. Indeed the first, short-lived Devětsil journal was called *Disk*. The particular character of Czech modernism soon manifested itself by tempering utilitarianism with a more playful and poetic element that Devětsil christened Poetism – a 'modern Epicureanism', or 'the art of wasting time', as Teige explained in its manifesto (1924). He expressed Devětsil's new direction as a combination of Constructivism and Poetism: 'Poetism is the crown of life; Constructivism is its basis.'[212]

The most characteristic manifestations of Poetism were the so-called picture poems, which represented a category of photomontage somewhat distinct from Dada or Constructivist versions. They were notably applied to book covers by the painter/typographers of Devětsil, Jindřich Štyrský and Toyen (Marie Čermínová).[213] Czech publishers were uncommonly open to avant-garde ideas in book design and Teige in particular became a prolific typographer in a delicate, Constructivist style. He designed many books for the Odeon publishing house, Devětsil's official publisher from 1925, including the delightful *Abeceda* (1926), in which photographs of a dancer emulating letter-shapes were used to counterpoint Vítěslav Nezval's poetry. In addition to editing the left-wing architectural journal *Stavba* since 1922, Teige

210. 'Jan Tschichold: praeceptor typographiae', p.12.
211. 'Die Entwicklung der neuen Typographie im In- und Auslande', p.83.

212. Teige, 'Poetism manifesto', translation given in E. Dluhosch & R. Švácha (ed.) *Karel Teige 1900–1951*, pp.67–9.

213. Tschichold planned to include work by Teige and Jaromír Krejcar in his abortive photomontage book project.

(Right) Karel Teige, jacket of first Devětsil publication. 1922. 23 × 16 cm.

(Far right) Karel Teige, Cover of journal *Red*. 1929. As shown in 'New life in print'. Original: 22.8 × 18.5 cm

Karel Teige, spreads from Nezval, *Abeceda*. 1926 (facsimile edn). 30 × 23.2 cm.

was editor and art director of the most important Devětsil journal, *Red*, which was published by Odeon between 1927 and 1931, when the group dissolved due to internal conflict. Teige's increasingly strong communist inclinations were reflected in the title and contents of *Red*, which also published the texts of lectures he gave in 1929 at the Bauhaus.

It is likely that Tschichold made contact with Teige after the publication of *Die neue Typographie* (although no record of their correspondence survives) and he may have met him on his first trip to Prague in early 1931.[214] Examples of photomontage by Teige were among the significant amount of Czech work shown in the Fifo exhibition co-curated by Tschichold, and he was keen that Teige should be invited to join the Ring 'neue Werbegestalter'; he never did, although he exhibited as a guest in some of its exhibitions.

Tschichold quoted with approval a numbered list of typographical principles from Teige's essay 'Moderní typo' (Modern typography; 1927) in *Eine Stunde Druckgestaltung*, an honour that he had only previously accorded to Marinetti and Lissitzky. Teige's text was published (simultaneously in both Czech and German) around the time that *Die neue Typographie* was being typeset, yet there were some remarkable similarities between the two: both authors rejected Art Nouveau/Jugendstil, with its decorative typefaces, and drew strong parallels between modern typography and non-objective art. On a particular point of uncanny agreement – suggesting that Tschichold may have become aware of

214. Tschichold published Teige's address in *Eine Stunde Druckgestaltung* (1930), which he is unlikely to have done without his permission. Among Teige's personal papers there is an undated manuscript, 'Jan Tschichold in Prague' (Museum of Decorative Arts, Prague).

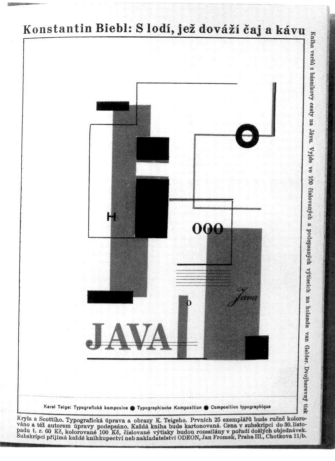

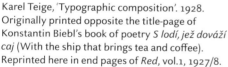

Karel Teige, 'Typographic composition'. 1928.
Originally printed opposite the title-page of
Konstantin Biebl's book of poetry *S lodí, jež dováží
caj* (With the ship that brings tea and coffee).
Reprinted here in end pages of *Red*, vol.1, 1927/8.

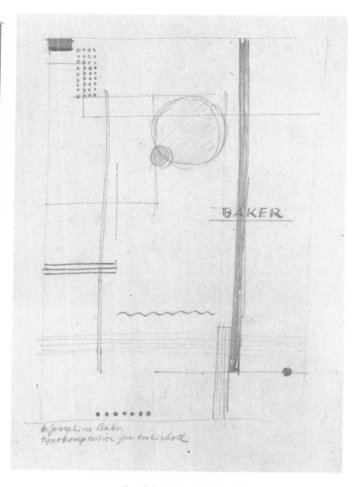

Sketch by Tschichold for a 'typo-composition'
called 'Josephine Baker', apparently inspired by
Teige's typographic compositions. *c.*1928.
57% of actual size.

Teige's article before *Die neue Typographie* was printed –
they both predicted that Arabic and Far Eastern scripts
would disappear in favour of the Latin script. It is clear that
Teige had a good knowledge of German developments in
New Typography, including Bauhaus theories and Tschichold's 'Elementare Typographie', when formulating his
approach to what he was content to call 'Constructivist
typography'.[215] (See appendix C.)

Another Devětsil member whose typographic work
attracted Tschichold was Zdeněk Rossmann. Tschichold,
Teige and Rossmann were about the same age and this was
younger than most of their contemporaries in New Typography. Rossmann had designed *Pásmo*, the journal of
Devětsil's Brno chapter, and its compendium *Fronta* (1927),
which Tschichold must have admired not only for its pioneering use of images bled off the edges of pages (see p.218)

but also for having its text set without any capitals. This was
an early incidence of *Kleinschreibung* applied to a whole
book, and probably resulted from Rossmann's knowledge
of Bauhaus typography. Indeed Rossmann went to study at
the Bauhaus for one year around 1929 after graduating from
technical university in Prague.

Enabled by the fact that, like all of Tschichold's Czech
colleagues, Rossmann was able to write to him in German,
the two men began an exchange of printed work in early
1930, which they maintained until 1935, when Tschichold
featured some of Rossmann's work in *Typographische
Gestaltung*. Rossmann became the editor of the 'monthly
journal of the new Slovakia', *Das neue Bratislava* (no doubt
modelled on its Frankfurt equivalent), and was appointed to
a teaching post in September 1931 at the Škola Uměleckých
Řemesel (Arts & crafts school) in Bratislava. At his invitation Tschichold taught there for a few days around the turn
of 1932/33. This was Tschichold's second trip to Czechoslovakia; he had visited Prague and Brno in January 1931. In
Prague he was met at the railway station by Ladislav Sutnar,

215. There is an offprint of
Teige's German text ('Moderne
Typographie') among Tschichold's papers (Getty), presumably sent to him by Teige, or at

Teige's behest. The periodical
Typografia, in which the essay
appeared, had also published
Czech translations of essays
by Moholy-Nagy and Bayer

from the Bauhaus issue of
Offset: Buch- und Werbekunst.
(*Typografia*, roč.34, číslo 3,
1927.)

124

Ladislav Sutnar, cover of *Žijeme*. 1931. 25.2 × 17.8 cm.

Ladislav Sutnar, cover for Czech edition of Shaw's *The apple cart*. 1932. 19.1 × 14.1 cm.

Zdeněk Rossmann, prospectus for Bratislava Arts & Crafts School. 1932. (From *Typographische Gestaltung*).

Ladislav Sutnar, cover and spread from *Žijeme*. 1931. 25.2 × 17.8 cm.

who was a leading Czech typographer and exhibition designer, having designed the Czech sections at the Pressa exhibition in Cologne (1928) and the Barcelona World Exhibition (1929). Sutnar, who had taught at the Státní Grafické Školy (State school of graphic arts) in Prague since 1923, was never a member of Devětsil; instead he became artistic director in 1929 of the publishing house Družstevní Práce (Co-operative work) and of the associated industrial design firm specializing in furniture and household objects, Krásná Jizba (Beautiful household).[216] Sutnar designed glass & chinaware for Krásná Jizba and co-wrote a book on modern

living, *Nejmenší dům* (Minimal housing; 1931). He applied an elegant version of New Typography to his designs for dustjackets and covers, often combining cut-out photographs in artful diagonal arrangements with sanserif type. Examples can be seen in his covers for Czech editions of Bernard Shaw, and in the journal published by Družstevní Práce, *Žijeme* (We live), which is also distinguished by its systematic and consistent text design that still looks fresh

216. There was no animosity between Sutnar and Devětsil. Indeed Teige gave a speech in early 1934 at the opening of a major exhibition of Sutnar's typographic work in Prague.

125

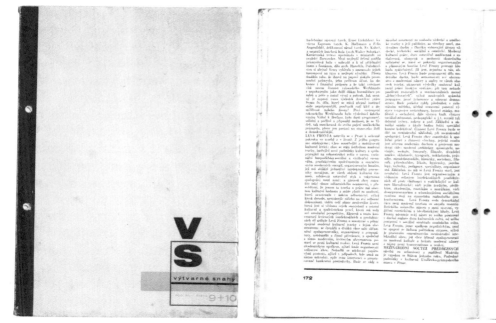

Ladislav Sutnar, cover and spread from *Výtvarné Snahy*. 1930. 25.4 × 18 cm.

Shows Tschichold's article 'Nový plakát' (The new poster).

today. Sutnar was the designer, as well as being among the editors, of another journal, *Výtvarné Snahy* (Decorative arts), which occasionally featured articles entirely set in sanserif, including a Czech translation of the speech given by Tschichold at the Basel Gewerbemuseum in 1930 about new poster design.[217]

Tschichold's early design work in 1924 for the Warsaw publisher Philobiblon seems not to have brought him at that time into contact with the already active avant-garde circles in Poland. Indeed, one principal figure in modernist Polish typography, Henryk Berlewi, escaped Tschichold's attention during the years that he dedicated to writing about New Typography. This is all the more perplexing because Berlewi came to typography via their mutual friend Lissitzky, whom Berlewi had met and befriended in 1921 at a lecture in Warsaw, where the Russian had stopped on route to Germany. Berlewi, who had trained as a painter in Belgium and Paris, was inspired by Lissitzky's advice to him, as a fellow Jew, to turn away from working in local Hebrew traditions towards Constructivism. Berlewi followed Lissitzky to Berlin a few months later, where he successfully exhibited his paintings in an abstract style that he called 'Mechano-faktura' (mechanical reproduction), borrowing terminology from the Constructivist manifesto. He had his

own manifesto published in the German journal *Der Sturm* in 1924, and in the same year, back in Warsaw, he founded an advertising agency (contemporary with Burchartz & Canis's Werbebau in Germany) called Reklama Mechano, along with the writers Aleksander Wat and Stanisław Brucz.[218] The advertisements they made are examples of Constructivist typography that are as impressive as contemporary work by Lissitzky, and more consistent in the use of typefaces (all sanserif) as opposed to drawn lettering. Berlewi left Poland in 1928 to settle in Paris, where he worked mainly as an artist, and so he slipped through the net of Tschichold's survey of New Typography.[219]

Berlewi's influence was strong, however, on a key periodical of the Polish avant-garde, *Blok* (1924–6), edited by Mieczysław Szczuka, Teresa Żarnower, Henryk Stażewski and Edmund Miller. Szczuka, who died in 1927 (aged only 29) after a mountaineering accident, was the Polish pioneer of photomontage and was the only Polish practitioner named by Tschichold in *Die neue Typographie*. Tschichold was not then aware of *Blok* but afterwards he acquired the first number of its successor publication, *Praesens*, which appeared in only two issues (1926 and 1930) and, like *Blok*, featured a list of contributors from the international avant-garde. Among these was Władysław Strzemiński, who initiated contact with Tschichold in January 1930. Strzemiński's German was extremely good: in his first letter to Tschichold he expressed his great approval of *Die neue Typographie*, having recently got hold of a copy. He asked for confirmation of Tschichold's address in order to send him examples of his own work.[220]

217. Tschichold, 'Nový plakát', *Výtvarné Snahy*, roč.11, číslo 9–10, 1929–30, pp.173–8.
218. Indeed there was a great similarity with Werbebau in the expressed objectives of Reklama mechano: 'purposefulness, rapidity, low-cost, ingenuity, simplicity and beauty'. See Gresty & Lewison (ed.), *Constructivism in Poland 1923 to 1936*, p.47. It is likely that Berlewi and Burchartz knew of each other's work through the connection with Lissitzky.
219. After leaving Germany, in a letter of 3 May 1934, Tschichold asked for Berlewi's address from Strzemiński, who had probably told Tschichold about him.
220. Letter Strzemiński to Tschichold, 27 January 1930.

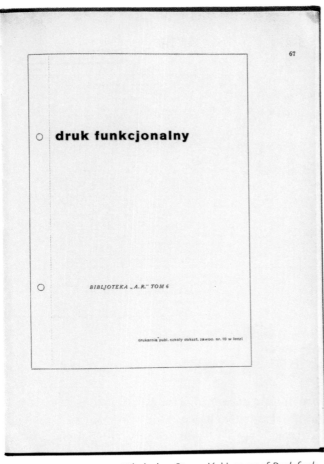

67

○ **druk funkcjonalny**

○   *BIBLJOTEKA „A.R." TOM 6*

drukarnia publ. szkoły dokszt. zawod. nr. 10 w Łodzi

Władysław Strzemiński, cover of *Druk funk-cjonalny* (1930), as illustrated by Tschichold in *Typographische Gestaltung*.

Strzemiński (1893–1952), along with his wife and partner in art, Katarzyna Kobro (1898–1951), embodied a direct link to Russian revolutionary art and design. He was born in Minsk, Belarus, a territory of historical dispute between Poland and Russia. After graduating from the St Petersburg engineering school, he served in the Russian army during the First World War and was wounded in 1916, resulting in the amputation of his right leg and left forearm. During his convalescence he met Moscow-born Kobro, who had volunteered to care for the war-wounded. After the war they both studied at the Free Studios in Moscow, and Strzemiński became active in the fine arts department of Narkompros. In 1919 he co-founded with Malevich branches of Unovis and of the Vitebsk artistic-technical institute (where Lissitzky was teaching) at nearby Smolensk, where both he and Kobro taught until it was dissolved in 1922.

This was the year that the Belarus Soviet Socialist Republic was formally established, after the treaty of Riga ended the Polish-Russian war over Belarus, which in 1918 had briefly enjoyed the status of an independent republic. Strzemiński and Kobro left the Soviet Union, somewhat disillusioned with the revolution, and settled in Poland.[221] Soon after his arrival, Strzemiński helped to organize the first Polish exhibition of 'new art' at Vilna, co-designing a catalogue that is a striking example of Suprematist–Constructivist typography. Strzemiński was obviously speaking from first-hand knowledge when he offered his opinion to Tschichold that Lissitzky's early typography was a 'mere continuation' of Malevich's printed work between 1918 and 1920. Tschichold replied to Strzemiński: 'as i will still be able to find good opportunities to write about the "history" of new typography, your information was very valuable to me.'[222]

Strzemiński and Kobro were contributors to *Blok* but became critical of its hardline Constructivist stance and split to join the group around the journal *Praesens*, which proclaimed itself a 'modernist quarterly' (a surprisingly early use of this term in the European avant-garde). By the time Strzemiński contacted Tschichold he had initiated his own '-ism', Unism, and co-founded another artistic group with Kobro and Stażewski called 'a.r.' Strzemiński told Tschichold that this acronym did not stand for anything, perhaps reflecting the confusion whereby Strzemiński interpreted it as *awangarda rzeczywista* (real avant-garde) and Stażewski as *artyści rewolucyjni* (revolutionary artists).[223] Under the aegis of 'a.r.' Strzemiński campaigned for the establishment of a permanent gallery of modern art in Łódź, which was realized between 1930 and 1932 with support from the socialist municipal authority. It was only the second such permanent collection in Europe after that in the Provinzialmuseum Hanover (designed by Lissitzky), and through its international connections the 'a.r.' group was able to persuade leading artists to donate works to it, including Schwitters, Van Doesburg and Picasso. An international exhibition of typography was also organized by 'a.r.' in Łódź, and Strzemiński asked Tschichold's advice on who to contact in other countries for acquiring material, commenting that 'Naturally only the "new" comes into consideration'.

Strzemiński directed the evening classes in typography at the Łódź city college and sent Tschichold examples of the work done there, as well as a booklet he had written, *Druk funkcjonalny* (Functional typography; 1930). Tschichold was impressed and offered his analysis of how Polish and German New Typography differed:

221. See Strzemiński's essay 'Notes on Russian art' (1922) in Benson (ed.), *Between worlds*, pp.272–80. He attacked the utilitarianism of Tatlin and instead praised Malevich, who he claimed as a Pole. For biographical information on

Kobro and Strzemiński see Monika Król, 'Collaboration and compromise: women artists in Polish-German avant-garde circles' in Benson (ed.), *Central European avant-gardes*, pp.339–56.

222. Letter Tschichold to Strzemiński, 6 April 1930, and from Strzemiński to Tschichold, 26 November 1930. It seems that Tschichold never established contact with Malevich, as he would have liked to, and was still on the trail of this influence

in the last few years of his life (in correspondence of 1971 with Jan Leering of the Van Abbe Museum, Eindhoven). The kind of work by Malevich that Strzemiński may have meant could be his *Suprematism: thirty-four drawings* (1920),

which was printed lithographically in the workshop at Vitebsk directed by Lissitzky.

223. Letter Strzemiński to Tschichold, 6 May 1930. See also Gresty & Lewison (ed.), *Constructivism in Poland*, p.10.

new typography in poland takes up the design methods of abstract painting in a particularly conspicuous way. the essential difference between the typography here and yours perhaps resides in the fact that we here exploit to a greater degree the specific, visual effects of available printing types in typography. your typography strikes us for the frequent occurrence in particular of the so-called cicero rule [heavy bar]. all this in no way signifies an adverse opinion. i am simply assuming that a characterization of your typography from our standpoint is of interest to you.[224]

Tschichold was possibly referring to a manifesto-like leaflet for the 'a.r.' group and to a 1930 edition of poetry by Julian Przyboś that Strzemiński designed, in which his colourful cover lettering becomes a purely formal composition.[225] Indeed, in a subsequent letter, Tschichold commented: 'In a painterly way your works are quite wonderful and perhaps the best to have been achieved in this direction. They are almost paintings.'[226]

Tschichold informed Strzemiński that he hoped soon to write something about Polish New Typography: 'I hope in fact to be able to establish a periodical for "typo foto grafik", which would dedicate itself exclusively to new design in these areas.'[227] Nothing came of this immediately, although the idea for such a periodical perhaps fed into plans for what became the Swiss magazine, *Typographische Monats-blätter* (see p.259). However, Tschichold resurrected the idea of writing about Polish modern typography late in his life, indicating an enduring affection for it; the only other modernist subject (apart from himself) that he wrote about in his later years was Lissitzky. He made layouts for an article called 'Polnische neue Typographie um 1930' (Polish New Typography around 1930) sometime in the 1960s, probably to be published in *Typographische Monatsblätter*.[228] It never appeared and no typescript of his article remains, but he also prepared a German translation of a text by Strzemiński for publication with a new commentary of his own. Tschichold's copious comments show his rejection of most of the ideas in Strzemiński's essay by that time, and he perhaps realized that the contrariness of his presentation was problematic, and did not pursue it.

By 1928 Tschichold was already aware of avant-garde tendencies in other East European countries, including Romania, where the former Dadaist Marcel Janco was among the founders of *Contimporanul* (Contemporaries, 1922–32, the first of several modernist journals to be published there), and Yugoslavia, where Ljubomir Micić edited the journal *Zenit* between 1921 and 1926. Based in Zagreb and then Belgrade, Micić cultivated international connections: as guest editors for the issue of *Zenit* published in September/October 1922, he invited Lissitzky & Ehrenburg, whom he had met in Berlin. From Ljubljana there also appeared a short-lived modernist periodical, *Tank* (1927–8), featuring occasional Constructivist typography.

Sketches by Tschichold for his projected magazine 'typo foto grafik'. 1930. Shown at 42% of actual size (lower sheet A4.)

224. Letter Tschichold to Strzemiński, 14 May 1930.
225. Reproduced in Becker & Hollis, *Avant-garde graphics*, p.81.
226. Letter Tschichold to Strzemiński, 3 May 1934.
227. Letter Tschichold to Strzemiński, 14 May 1930.
228. Tschichold pasted up a rough layout (without text) and marked it to be typeset 'all in Univers'. (Getty)

The international progress of New Typography

The importance of graphic design from Northern, Central and Eastern Europe in inter-war modernism of the twentieth century is now well recognized. In *Die neue Typographie* Tschichold had already acknowledged little-known figures active in Belgium and Denmark. In Scandinavia, where the connections with German printing culture were strong, his influence began to manifest itself in advertising and in the printing trade from 1929. But what of southern Europe: France, Spain and Italy? By following the logic of the universalist statements he made in *Die neue Typographie*, one can assume that, during his eight years of evangelizing for New Typography, Tschichold believed that it could (and probably should) conquer all of Europe, if not the world. He made some admiring comments about contemporary Japanese typography, and was apparently in touch with one of the first proponents of New Typography in the USA, Douglas C. McMurtrie. In his book *Modern typography and layout* (1929) McMurtrie acknowledges his debt to *Die neue Typographie* and to Tschichold personally for clarifying its principles to him. He considered modern typography 'a force that is bound to exert a revolutionary influence on all printing for many years to come'.[229] However, for the most part Tschichold limited his sights initially to Europe. In his short article of 1930, 'Die Entwicklung der neuen Typographie im In- und Auslande' (The development of New Typography at home and abroad), he implied that New Typography should not be adapted to new circumstances, but that the world should change according to it:

> The development of New Typography does not consist in modification of its principles, rather in growing understanding for the abstract expressive power of pure, typographic forms in its adherents. Outsiders see in this a progression, whereas in reality it is merely that the observations and works of its founders are being understood and becoming common knowledge [*allgemeines Bildungsgut*].[230]

He asserted that New Typography was making progress in those parts of the world that had previously 'stood in denial against it', including France and Britain, although his judgement here may partly have ensued from his having been able to publish articles on the subject in those countries. France, historically resistant to Germanic advances, never really embraced the rationalist side of New Typography. Emblematic of this is perhaps the long-running magazine, *Arts et Métiers Graphiques* (Graphic arts and trades; 1927–38), which applied a tasteful version of modernist style, but remained eclectic and pluralist in its content. Tschichold had naturally seen Le Corbusier's books and knew the related periodical, *L'Esprit Nouveau* (1920–5). He admired greatly the posters designed by A.M. Cassandre – already worthy of description as 'classic achievements' in his view [231] – and it is likely that he knew of the remarkable book by Paris printer Alfred Tolmer, *Mise en page:*

the theory and practice of layout (1931). This was co-published by The Studio (London publisher of *Commercial Art* and *Modern Publicity*) and William Rudge (New York).[232] Although a French text was included in Tolmer's book, it was principally in English – no doubt with one eye on American advertising and magazine design. It employed all manner of virtuoso printing techniques on a variety of papers in a *tour de force* of Art Deco style. Tschichold never mentioned the book, although he recognized that modern design in French printing became more noticeable after the exhibition that gave Art Deco its name, the 1925 Exposition des Arts Décoratifs in Paris, from which certain themes were explicitly picked up in *Mise en page.*[233]

Tschichold believed that France had no great need for the purifying influence of New Typography because the late neo-classical tradition in typesetting, which he admired to some degree, had endured there and still provided an effective set of norms for compositors, however old fashioned. In a short article of October 1931 entitled 'Neuere Typografie in Frankreich' (Recent typography in France), he loosened the *cordon sanitaire* that he had placed around New Typography to encompass some contemporary French examples that could even be described as decorative. In fact his sample was limited to type specimens from the Paris typefoundry of Deberny & Peignot, which was exceptional in its connections with modern trends in France: its director Charles Peignot was a member of the Paris group Union des Artistes Modernes. Peignot's principal collaborator was Maximilien Vox, who edited the typefoundry's in-house magazine, *Divertissements Typographiques*. Tschichold commented:

> The work of Maximilien Vox demonstrates the endeavour to use the familiar, traditional material in a new and humorous way. Clearly discernible, above all in the use of typewriter typefaces, is a certain ironic attitude, which absolves this kind of typography from the suspicion that it is historicist.

Humour did not generally enter into Tschichold's conception of New Typography and it is possible that his appreciation of the charm and irony in Vox's work encouraged his own admission of historical typefaces into the armoury of New Typography around this time, so long as they were used in a similarly self-conscious way (see p.176). A type specimen co-designed by Charles Peignot and Cassandre for the latter's typeface Bifur (1929) was singled out for Tschichold's highest praise.[234] In his view, it was 'one of the

229. McMurtrie, *Modern typography and layout* (Chicago: Eyncourt Press, 1929), p.18. Tschichold listed this book in his bibliography for *Eine Stunde Druckgestaltung*. Renner was also in contact with McMurtrie.

230. 'Die Entwicklung der neuen Typographie im In- und Auslande', p.82.

231. *Die neue Typographie*, p.190.

232. The volume of *Modern Publicity* for 1930 carried a full-page advert for *Mise en page*.

233. My thanks to Ann Pillar for sharing with me her (as yet) unpublished studies of this book and of other aspects of modern French typography.

234. The specimen is reproduced in Wlassikoff, *The story of graphic design in France*, pp.84–5. Peignot was also the director of *Arts et métiers graphiques*, which Tschichold singled out as providing 'superb' information on recent French trends.

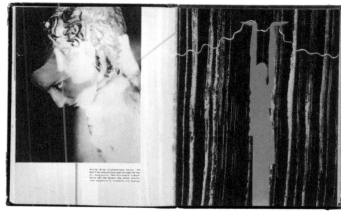
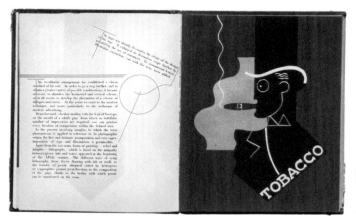

Cover and spreads from Alfred Tolmer, *Mise en page*. 1931. 27.5 × 21.5 cm. Tolmer, whose name appears on the cover of the book, was its printer but the layout of the book was done in collaboration with a team of artists.

In *Anatomy of printing* (London: Faber & Faber, 1970), John Lewis commented that 'this book rather than Tschichold's disciplined *Die neue Typographie* became the bible of advertising agencies in the 1930s' (p.215).

most beautiful of its kind', and he waxed lyrical about its sumptuous material qualities, concluding rhetorically: 'Can there be any higher praise than to be able to say of it that it awakens the appetite to purchase the type and use it in an equally luxurious manner.' He almost gives the impression of being enticed from the true path into thoughts of 'luxury' by the sensual nature of his chosen examples. Indeed the feeling that New Typography was even then perceived to be alien to 'Latin' culture was something he was clearly aware of. The examples that he praised confirmed to him

> the welcome participation of France in endeavours of which it was hitherto accepted that they were restricted to Central Europe and that they would be rejected further west as too 'nordique'.[235]

In his article of 1930 on 'The development of New Typography at home and abroad', Tschichold remarked: 'Only in the dictator states, Italy, Spain and Poland are there still no signs to be seen of a development, or at least they remain without echo.'[236] For him New Typography was clearly inseparable from left-wing conviction: he naturally would not have perceived Stalin's USSR as a dictator state in these years when it was still a source of inspiration and hope for

socialists in Europe. (Indeed several of Tschichold's contemporaries were leaving at precisely this time for extended working visits to the Soviet Union, including his friends Neurath, Reidemeister & Arntz from the Vienna Gesellschafts- und Wirtschaftsmuseum.)[237] His correspondence with Strzemiński would soon inform him that the military coup in Poland, which ousted its republican government in 1926, had not stopped the progress of the avant-garde there. He was right about Spain at this time, where the influence of New Typography was only really felt after the Second Republic replaced Primo de Rivera's dictatorship in 1931. In particular, a journal published from the Canary island of Tenerife (somewhat marginal even in the Spanish context), *Gaceta de Arte* (Art gazette), made a specific connection to Tschichold's ideas. Its editor and publisher Eduardo Westerdahl, who had travelled in Germany and could read German, knew Tschichold's books and even took the radical step of following for a while the example of *Foto-Auge* by excising

235. 'Neuere Typografie in Frankreich', (1931) pp.382–4.
236. 'Die Entwicklung der neuen Typographie im In- und Auslande', p.84.

237. Among others visiting the USSR then were Hannes Meyer, Mart Stam, and Frankfurt City architect Ernst May and his group. See, for example, Willett, *The new sobriety*, pp.213–21.

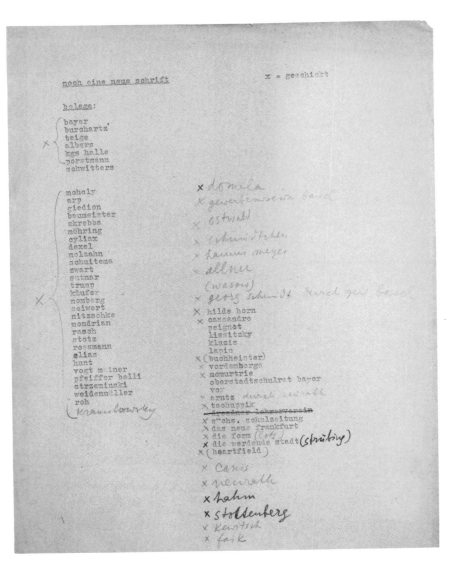

One of the lists customarily made by Tschichold of people to whom he would send copies of his new publications. This one is for 'noch eine neue schrift'. 1930. The handwritten addition of 'Schmidtchen', the common name for Joost Schmidt at the Bauhaus, implies that Tschichold was on familiar terms with him, although no correspondence between them has survived.

capital letters from the text of his journal. Westerdahl made contact with Tschichold soon after he had left Germany, and they discussed some possible collaborative projects, although these came to nothing (see also p.265 below). Westerdahl cultivated a more fruitful relationship with Willi Baumeister, about whom he published a monograph.[238]

Regarding Italy: Tschichold had fully recognized the importance for New Typography of Marinetti, who was one of the earliest supporters of the Italian Fascist Party, and later held an official position in Mussolini's government. In Italy, almost uniquely, modernist style adorned the public face of a right-wing regime. Yet Tschichold's refusal to see signs of influential development in Italy implies that he could not accept an alignment of the avant-garde with the political right. The Futurists' love afair with machines of war had been clear from the beginning in Marinetti's writings, and, not surprisingly, there is no evidence of Tschichold ever trying to contact him. In his historical version of New Typography's beginnings, Tschichold was content to detach the implications of Futurism for graphic design from other, more pernicious parts of its ideology. He may

have had some contact with one of Marinetti's followers, Fortunato Depero, who adapted Futurist typography to more commercial applications.[239] Depero's maniacally egotistical book, *Depero Futurista* (1927), showcases his own work between thick board covers bound with two metal bolts. It is a visual feast of inventive typographic display, a bravura achievement of letterpress composition, in which Depero was assisted by a sympathetic, small printing house in his home town of Rovereto. He claimed to pursue 'typographic architecture', but he interpreted this phrase somewhat superficially and what he proposed did not correspond to Tschichold's structural approach.

Tschichold's opening out of his definition of New Typography between 1930 and 1933 reflected a feeling voiced

238. See Patricia Córdoba, *La tipográfia moderna en España* (in press).

239. Tschichold evidently wrote a postcard to Depero on 10 November 1933, having been inspired by seeing a copy of *Depero Futurista* belonging to Schwitters (although he must have seen the book some while before writing, given that he had left Germany in summer 1933 and did not see Schwitters again until 1935). Tschichold requested a copy for himself, offering to send one of his own books in exchange, and purportedly explained how influential Depero's typography had been for him. Unfortunately this document has been lost from the Depero Museum in Rovereto. See Manuela Rattin & Matteo Ricci, *Questioni di carattere: la tipografia in italia dal 1861 agli anni settanta* (Rome: Stampa alternativa / Graffiti, 1997) p.46. Depero's work was also shown in *Gebrauchsgraphik* in April 1930.

by some of his German contemporaries that *die neue Sachlichkeit* had already become stale. As early as 1928 it had been pronounced dead in the pages of *Die literarische Welt*.[240] A suggestion that at least its first phase was over was made by Tschichold himself in a rather mysterious pronouncement of 1930:

> Perhaps we are approaching a time that is spiritually related to the Biedermeier period despite a totally different conception of form, a time of cosmopolitan humility and of modest, idealistic consolidation.[241]

This sentiment spurred the following comment in *Typographische Mitteilungen* at the beginning of 1931: 'Can we perceive, showing through here, the hope for a "Third Reich" also in typography?'[242] It is unlikely that any kinship with National Socialism on Tschichold's part was implied here, over two years before the Third Reich came into being (the term had been coined in 1922 by the conservative writer Moeller van den Bruck, who was a prophet of Nazism in some ways). Nevertheless, with hindsight, it seems like an ominous observation.

das werk 3

architektur   freie kunst   angewandte kunst   *verlag gebr. fretz ag, zürich*

das werk   achtzehnter jahrgang   heft 3   seite 98--128   zürich, im märz 1931

Cover designed by Tschichold for Swiss Werkbund journal, *Das Werk*. 1931. 21.2 × 29.2 cm.

240. Willett, *The new sobriety*, p.176.
241. 'Die Entwicklung der neuen Typographie im In- und Auslande', p.84.
242. Unsigned review of *Eine Stunde Druckgestaltung* and *Klimschs Jahrbuch* in *Typographische Mitteilungen*, Jg.28, H.1, 1931, p.32. In 1930 a book titled *Kommt 'das dritte Reich'?* had been published by Rowohlt, followed by the release of a leftist propaganda film, *Ins dritte Reich* (1931).

The eye of the storm: a survey in *Typographische Mitteilungen*, 1933

During the first three months of 1933, at the very time that fateful events were being played out on Germany's political stage, the journal of the Bildungsverband published numerous responses to a four-part questionnaire that it had circulated to leading designers, typefounders and educators. *Typographische Mitteilungen* had been a barometer for thinking in New Typography ever since it had set the agenda with Tschichold's *Elementare Typographie* in October 1925. With its socialist and educational bias, it was the principal forum for questions of modern typographic design and orthographic reform. Tschichold had resurfaced with two further articles in its pages, including his essay of the previous year, 'Wo stehen wir heute?' (Where do we stand today?), which to some extent anticipated the subject of the 1933 survey (see appendix D).

The survey posed these questions: whether 'objective [*sachlich*] typographic design' had reached a standstill, how typography would develop further, whether sanserif had lost its status as 'the type for modern typographic expression', and whether a greater employment of Fraktur was imminent. The last question makes clear the political background to the survey, with Fraktur already becoming a nationalist symbol in the 'current, widespread cultural reaction', as one respondent put it. (The questions specifically relating to type-style are dealt with on p.176 below.) The sense that New Typography had somehow atrophied perhaps found a parallel in the collapse of Weimar democracy, its final few years racked by constitutional and economic crises. Indeed, the editor of *Gebrauchsgraphik*, Hermann Karl Frenzel, took an intriguing historical view in his response, identifying *die neue Sachlichkeit* as a concomitant of the new form of state embodied by the Weimar Republic. The forty-five contributors to *Typographische Mitteilungen*'s survey included Albers, Bayer, Burchartz, Moholy-Nagy, Renner, and Trump. Tschichold's response, in which he was introduced as 'the well-known pioneer of New Typography', was not printed until the March issue, by which time Hitler was already Chancellor and the National Socialists were on the point of winning the decisive election that would bring forth his dictatorship. Tschichold's text was brief (in compliance with the wishes of the journal's editors) but to the point:

> the change in typographic style [*Stilwandel*], which is called 'new typography' and is referred to in the survey by the expression 'objective typographic design', cannot have reached a standstill if only for the simple reason that it has hardly got underway. we should not deceive ourselves that a penetration of the new ideas or indeed their practical realization can only be spoken about in terms of a minority of colleagues. the change in style should not be confused with a fashion, which disappears after a short while. we are not

at all concerned with the new for its own sake, rather with the right, the good. the struggle is not directed against everything old, but against all that is unusable and bad, and not least against the falsely new! a turning away from unpleasantly monumental to nothing-other-than meaningful, visual form would be desirable. the task of those dedicated to the new style is to make it more profound, and incidentally we want to ensure its dissemination. something new is not to be expected and is entirely superfluous, since the new has so far been absorbed by so few, though for this reason its fruits have been all the richer. the need for a pleasant change in a merely modish sense attests to superficiality and a lack of understanding for the meaning of the change in style. only the 'bad economic conditions' [schlechte konjunktur] are hampering the effects of the new.[243]

By his ironic reference to the prevailing conditions he may have meant more than just the economic situation.

It may surprise us today that Tschichold was content to describe New Typography as a 'change in style'; but, for him, style was not superficial – it had to be underpinned by deeper principles. Bayer, who was a leader in diversifying New Typography, addressed this matter in his contribution. He considered the superficial adoption of the new style in typography, which had erroneously been called 'Bauhaus-style', to indeed have reached a standstill: 'i am not speaking here of elemental typography, for this has its sense, and will retain its value – regardless of the formal enrichments and variations it experiences.' Nevertheless he repeated the complaint he had made personally to Tschichold, that 'i can only wish that typography be carried out and perceived with less ideology, and instead with rather more graphic sense'.[244]

Two thirds of the contributors to the survey denied that there was an impasse in New Typography. Among the few who perceived it to be at an end were Tschichold's former professors, Hugo Steiner-Prag and Walter Tiemann. In Tiemann's opinion: 'A tendency in taste derived from a fascination for rationalism and functionalism is already turning quite easily into a dogma and is beginning to caricature a principle.' Manifestations of 'taste' could, in his view, never be considered 'progressive', instead they were simply changes. He characterized the tendency to build such things quickly into a dogma as a particularly German trait.[245] Also doubtful about New Typography's future was H.K. Frenzel. He did consider it to have 'brought insights that future colleagues in our area will fall back on time and

again', but he felt that it had stiffened into a tiresome schema. 'The disappointment about this fact would not be so great,' he continued, 'if the advocates of "New Typography" had not behaved in such an arrogant and self-important manner.' He believed that in future 'imagination' would play a bigger role than 'reason'.[246] Indeed the rationalist ideology of New Typography would become a sacrifice to the unreason of the Third Reich. Once the Nazis came to power, progressive artists and designers were persecuted for propaganda purposes as opponents of völkisch (folkish) culture, as Tschichold was soon to experience personally.

A kind of postscript to the Typographische Mitteilungen survey was an 'open letter' written by one of Tschichold's former mentors, Carl Ernst Poeschel, and published by the journal Archiv für Buchgewerbe und Gebrauchsgraphik in April 1933 (by this time Tschichold was already being held in custody at the behest of the Nazis). It was printed as a small booklet (in Weiß-Fraktur) at Poeschel's Leipzig printing house and bound into the journal. Its title, 'Gegen Mechanisierung – für die Persönlichkeit' (Against mechanization – for personality), left no doubt as to Poeschel's standpoint. Although Tschichold is not mentioned by name, he is clearly implicated in Poeschel's reaction against 'mechanization mania and standardization madness':

What has become of German printing in the endeavour to regiment it with theoretical experiments and standardization?... Should it be called freedom when typographic unions, associations or schools dictate how typesetting is to be done and which typefaces are permissible.[247]

Here was a veiled reference to the Bildungsverband, and Poeschel went on to make an unmistakable reference to the Munich Meisterschule in particular. He directly addressed aspects of New Typography that were recognizable from Tschichold's writings: for example, he considered photography to be of limited use as a means of book illustration ('the camera has not yet been able to supersede the hand of the artist'). Indeed Tschichold is all but identified as the main culprit by his conspicuous absence from a list of 'young' typographers whose work Poeschel praised, including Bayer, Burchartz, Cyliax, Schneidler, and Trump. Neither did Poeschel name the tendency with which he associated standardization and restrictive rules, but it is likely that they smacked too much of socialism for his taste (he did refer disparagingly to 'class-consciousness').

243. Typographische Mitteilungen, Jg.30, H.3, March 1933, p.65; Schriften, 1, p.119. Contributions were set in Kleinschreibung, or not, according to the wishes of the authors. Tschichold's concern to have his views published in unadulterated form prompted him to apply a little economic blackmail. Typed above the

text that he submitted (marked with red pencil in the margin) were the words: 'i only agree to receive no fee for the publication of the following lines so long as they are reproduced unabridged, unchanged and in kleinschreibung.' (DNB Leipzig)
244. Typographische Mitteilungen, Jg.30, H.3, March 1933, pp.70–1

245. Typographische Mitteilungen, Jg.30, H.3, March 1933, p.72. At least part of Tiemann's contribution is taken from his essay of 1931, Kunst und Geschmack (Art and taste), printed at the Leipzig academy.
246. Typographische Mitteilungen, Jg.30, H.3, March 1933, p.70. Frenzel's view, as editor of Gebrauchsgraphik maga-

zine, may explain Tschichold's conspicuous absence as an author from its pages between 1925 and 1933. He did not even contribute a short note to the survey questionnaire on the current state of graphic design in January 1933, whereas his colleague Renner did. In May 1930 'elemental typography' was described in Gebrauchs-

graphik as 'the stale leftovers of art from the inflation period' (abgestandener Quark der Inflationskunst). Cited by Roland Jaeger in his essay about the magazine in Holstein (ed.), Blickfang, pp.296–7, where details are given of its suspicious stance towards the avant-garde (and towards Tschichold in particular).

247. Poeschel, 'Gegen Mechanisierung', p.7. Paul Renner (author of the book Mechanisierte Grafik) was perhaps also implicated by Poeschel in his title.

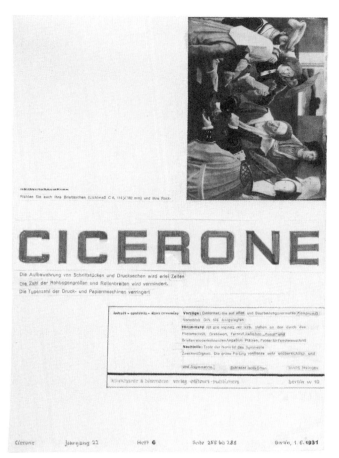

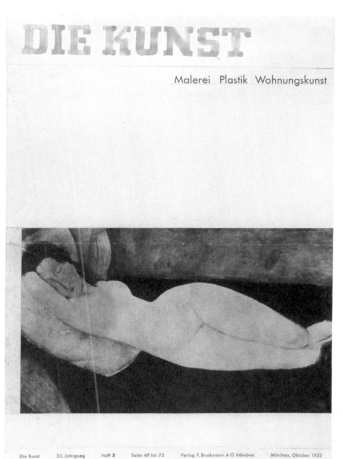

Magazine cover design. *c.*1931. Seemingly an
exercise, as *Der Cicerone* ceased publication at
the beginning of that year and was absorbed by
the journal *Pantheon*, published by Bruckmann.
Both sketches shown here at 39% of actual size.

Magazine cover design. 1932. Renner was first
approached to do this job but, due to his being
on holiday, he passed it on to Tschichold. The
publisher of *Die Kunst*, Hugo Bruckmann of
Munich, was a financial supporter of Hitler
and introduced him into Munich high society.

Poeschel's text is by no means a rant, and indeed some
commonalities with Tschichold's approach are evident:

> It is already in itself an error to talk of old, musty, classical,
> sickly-sweet typography as opposed to elemental, functional,
> objective, pure and clear typography. There is in reality only
> *one* difference, and that is between good and bad typography.
> It is immaterial whether it is constructed symmetrically or
> asymmetrically, or which typefaces it employs, if it correctly
> orientates itself only for the specific purpose at hand and if it
> transmits the concepts destined for the reader by the shortest
> route and in the most easily understandable form possible.[248]

He admitted that thanks were due to New Typography for
having performed a 'work of purification, which was absolutely necessary' (a caveat Tschichold would inherit after
his 're-conversion').[249] Where Poeschel differed with Tschichold was in his rejection of an impersonal and collective
vision: 'Is there a collective conscience? No! Conscience is
something absolutely personal.' He concluded: 'Let us put
an end to all schematization experiments and the hysterical
tyranny of standardization.'[250]

Although Poeschel did not partake of the empty nationalist rhetoric so typical of the Nazis, the sentiments in his
essay were favoured by the new political climate. As Julius
Rodenberg remarked in his introduction to the 'open letter',
Poeschel was leading a path away from 'the intellectual-
istic tendencies that have prevailed in recent years', with
their tiresome theories, towards an unspoken reliance on
strength of character. In Germany, the tide had definitely
turned against Tschichold.

248. Poeschel, 'Gegen
Mechanisierung', pp.9–10.
   249. See 'Glaube und Wirklichkeit', p.312. If Tschichold
recognized himself as a target
of Poeschel's protest he seemed
to hold no grudge, praising

Poeschel two years later in
Typographische Gestaltung,
p.11; *Asymmetric typography*,
p.19.
   250. Poeschel, 'Gegen
Mechanisierung', pp.10 & 22.

3   Seizure

'In Munich at the beginning of 1933 it was believed that things in Bavaria could not develop Hitler's way', reflected Tschichold late in life.[1] Yet Bavaria, particularly its rural parts, had served as the bedrock of support for National Socialism during the 1920s. The appeal of the Nazis in unexpected circles had also been increasing for several years: for example, already in November 1928 Hitler received a rapturous reception for a speech he gave at Munich University.[2] At a national level, the fall of the Social Democrat administration in March 1930, coupled with the ensuing parliamentary crisis, left the way open for the National Socialists to radically increase their vote in the national elections that followed in September. As a result they became the second largest party in parliament. Their powerful use of propaganda – at the centre of which was the carefully crafted visual identity of the movement – hypnotized millions, and the growing paramilitary violence of the Sturmabteilung (SA; Nazi stormtroopers) against left-wing parties galvanized the general anti-communist feeling in the country. Although the National Socialists lost votes in the election of November 1932 (the fifth of that year alone), Hitler was appointed Chancellor at the end of January 1933 as part of a compromise prompted by the reigning political chaos. As Tschichold later testified, the majority of Germans shared the suspicion of the short-sighted power-brokers who levered him into power that he would not last long. However, after the burning of the Reichstag, carried out by a lone protester but exploited by the Nazis as a communist plot, emergency legislation effectively turned the whole of Germany into a centralized police state. The National Socialists' victory in the March election sealed their hold on power.

Avant-garde art and design had not become pervasive during the Weimar Republic: they were always a minority affair, depending on sympathy from progressive patrons, galleries or local, public administrations. The fate of the Bauhaus clearly demonstrated the precariousness of modern initiatives: after being forced out of Weimar in 1925 by a right-wing takeover of its sponsor, the Thuringian state government, it came under threat again in 1931 when the Nazis gained control of the Dessau city parliament, which had funded its re-establishment there. The Dessau Bauhaus was closed at the end of September 1932 and the Nazis threatened to destroy Gropius's iconic building. From the middle of the 1920s New Architecture had provided ground for cultural conflict in Germany between modernist and folkish factions. Prominent in the latter was the architect Paul Schultze-Naumburg, who peddled racial theories of art and design. In 1930 he was appointed to an administrative position in Thuringia as part of the first Nazi foray into state government. His cultural ideas were then officially adopted by the Kampfbund für Deutsche Kultur (Militant League for German Culture), an organization formed in

the same year by Alfred Rosenberg, editor of the Nazi newspaper *Völkischer Beobachter*, after an inaugural meeting in Munich. Schultze-Naumburg made a lecture tour of six major German cities in 1931: at the Munich lecture, where he was joined by Rosenberg, a young artist from the audience who spoke up in dissent was beaten severely by stormtroopers. Tschichold's acquaintance Hans Eckstein organized a protest among Munich's cultural organizations about the incident, but the conservative Munich division of the German Werkbund refused to join.[3]

Tschichold had long been exploring the possibility of finding employment elsewhere than Munich. At the end of 1932 he informed Josef Albers (who had moved to Berlin after the dissolution of the Dessau Bauhaus) that from the beginning of April 1933 he too would be based in Berlin. He intended to take up a position leading the 'typographic department' at the Höhere graphische Fachschule (Higher graphic technical college), which had developed out of the Berlin Kunstgewerbe- und Handwerkerschule under the direction of his former Munich colleague, Georg Trump.[4] Around the turn of 1933 he finally tendered his resignation from the Meisterschule. However, after Hitler's appointment as Reich Chancellor in Berlin at the end of January, he changed his mind and decided that he wanted to stay in Munich. He informed Trump of his decision in a letter and turned to Renner for advice on how to maintain his job at the Meisterschule. Renner was somewhat annoyed at Tschichold's indecision, and warned him that he must personally enquire at Munich city council whether he could continue his employment at the school. His resignation had been officially accepted on 24 January 1933: the letter of acceptance (addressed 'Johannes Tzschichhold', no doubt to Tschichold's annoyance) stipulated that he would lose eligibility for his pension and any provision for his dependents. The matter was not settled before the Nazi election victory at the beginning of March, leaving Tschichold in a kind of professional limbo.

Tschichold was arrested in the middle of March 1933 and it was during the twenty-nine days of his subsequent imprisonment that his own resignation from 1 April onwards came into effect. He received final notice in prison that he had lost his job. Soon after he explained to Imre Reiner: 'I lost my Munich post and the Berlin job through a chain of ridiculous circumstances.'[5] Renner later remarked: 'It was his own tough luck for having placed himself between two stools at that moment.'[6]

1. 'Jan Tschichold: praeceptor typographiae', p.1.
2. Kershaw, *Hitler*, p.307.
3. See the report of the incident in Renner, *Kulturbolschewismus?*, p.9.
4. Letter Tschichold to Albers, 30 December 1932.

5. Letter Tschichold to Reiner, 23 May 1934.
6. Renner in a letter to Dr K. Salzmann, c.1944 (Haushofer Archive). Tschichold's appointment in Berlin was prematurely announced in *Typographische Mitteilungen* (Jg.30, H.3, March 1933, p.92), and this was then

corrected by a notice in the following issue (H.4, p.114), which stated that Tschichold had turned down the Berlin post and explained that the previous notice had been based on an announcement from the school itself.

Tschichold's arrest was not connected with the Reichsgesetz zur Wiederherstellung des Berufsbeamtentums (Professional civil service restoration act), under which Paul Renner was eventually dismissed from his position at the Meisterschule. That law was was only passed on 7 April 1933. Indeed, as Renner later commented, the Nazis had no evidence against Tschichold, who was never a member of the German Communist Party and, according to Renner, had only briefly been a subscribing member of the Social Democratic Party.[7] Tschichold's supposed communist tendencies were raised by the Nazis as evidence against Renner himself, due to his championing of Tschichold's initial appointment in Munich. An official Nazi report on Renner's case cited an article that had appeared three years earlier in the *Völkischer Beobachter,* in which Tschichold was defamed as being a bad influence on his pupils. Entitled 'Unverständliche Anstellungen' (Incomprehensible appointments), the piece in turn referred to the report by Albert Giesecke on Tschichold's lecture of December 1924 in Leipzig, at which he had allegedly described himself as a communist (the Nazi newspaper changed the epithet to 'Bolshevist'). 'Even in Leipzig, well accustomed to the reds,' proclaimed the anonymous Nazi journalist, 'the remarks of the Bolshevist had a repulsive and extremely unsettling effect.'[8] Considering that the lecture in question had been given almost ten years earlier, the Nazi watchdogs must have been fed this incriminating information, noted by Tschichold's opponents in the early years of the Nazi movement.

The printer of the *Völkischer Beobachter* in Munich, Adolf Müller, had been personally very close to Hitler for a long while.[9] Renner's later comment that it would have been impossible to present 'the inhabitants of Munich with an Ivan' in the 1920s indicates the degree of anti-Soviet feeling there at that time.[10] By having Russianized himself as Ivan, Tschichold inadvertently played into the Nazis' hands. Indeed he was mentioned in the reports of evidence compiled by the National Socialists against Renner as either 'Iwan Tschichold' or 'Johannes Tzschichhold', not Jan Tschichold. The antipathy towards him among conservative officials that had persisted since his appointment in Munich now hardened into the description of him as a 'bolshevistically disposed graphic designer' (as one Nazi report referred to him), thereby precluding any possibility of him regaining his teaching post. Unsurprisingly, the propagandist rant in the *Völkischer Beobachter* about Tschichold's employment at the Meisterschule twisted the evidence of his brief use of a Russian forename into the following gross inaccuracy:

> That such appointments are possible without precise checking of the person in this respect must be described as shameful. Shameful for the reason that we need no foreigners, especially no bolshevistic Russians as teachers for our German schools.

Although Tschichold never specifically criticized Nazi cultural policy in print, as Renner had done in his book

Kulturbolschewismus? (1932), his left-wing inclinations were clear from his writings, and from his connections with the Bildungsverband. He maintained a close connection with the Munich division of that organization, giving its principal lecture in 1932 and providing himself as the object of a question and answer session inaugurating its 'Typographic seminar' in February 1933. Moreover, from 1930 he was the principal designer for a socialist book club and publisher, the Bücherkreis (see pp.203–28).

As part of the immediate imposition of Nazi control on all regions of Germany at the beginning of the Third Reich, Hitler appointed Heinrich Himmler (later head of the SS) as commander of the Munich police and Reinhard Heydrich (later one of the architects of the Final Solution) as head of the Bavarian political police. Under this new regime 10,000 'communists and socialists' were arrested in March and April 1933 alone.[11] The arrest of Tschichold barely ten days after the National Socialists' election victory on 5 March reflects the degree of anti-'bolshevist' hysteria whipped up by Nazi propaganda during the preceding months. Tschichold was never in a strict sense politically active, despite his somewhat 'red' reputation, but even so-called 'cultural bolshevism' was in itself sufficient grounds for imprisonment. As John Willett explained, the Nazi attitude to culture was not rational: 'any innovatory ideas in the arts fell under the heading of Art- or Cultural-"Bolshevism", quite irrespective of the real cultural-political alignments suggested by such terms'.[12]

Tschichold's arrest was mainly due to the personal initiative of a Nazi stormtrooper who was a fellow inhabitant of the Borstei housing estate in Munich. The headquarters of both the SA and SS were located in Bavaria and many uniformed members of both had moved into the Tschicholds' neighbourhood. They felt that they had been closely observed – it probably did not help that, in accordance with the modern decor of their apartment, they eschewed curtains. Edith Tschichold believed that their cleaning lady had heard them express anti-Nazi sentiments and had informed on them. The particular SA officer who instigated the arrest evidently hated both Tschichold and their mutual neighbour, Franz Roh, who was also taken into custody at the same time. The stormtrooper acted without proper authority and he was later arrested himself and ejected from the Party.[13] (Undisciplined conduct in the SA had

7. Letter Renner to Salzmann, c.1944. Edith Tschichold commented later that Franz Roh was 'also' a Social Democrat, providing some confirmation that her husband had been a member of that party. [Edith Tschichold], 'Interview…', p.187.
8. 'Unverständliche Anstellungen', *Völkischer Beobachter (Münchener Beobachter,* Ausgabe 68), 22 March 1930.

9. It was Müller who met Hitler on his release from prison in 1923 to drive him home (Kershaw, *Hitler,* p.239). His name was also later used to lend weight to the Nazi ban on gothic type in 1941. The article about Tschichold appeared in the daily Munich supplement of the *Völkischer Beobachter,* the only such regional addition to the newspaper. (The *Völkischer*

Beobachter had in fact developed from the *Münchener Beobachter* in 1919, before the Nazis took it over in 1920.)
10. Burke, *Paul Renner,* p.177.
11. Kershaw, *Hitler,* pp.462–4.
12. Willet, *The new sobriety,* p.208.
13. Account by Renner in letter to Salzmann, c.1944.

always been a problem for the National Socialists and would remain so until the purge of 30 June 1934, known as the 'Night of the long knives'.)

During his Munich years, Tschichold often travelled in Germany to give lectures, and on the day that the storm-troopers came to arrest him he was away on such a trip to Stuttgart and Donaueschingen. On 11 March armed SA men came to the Tschichold's flat in Voitstraße. Edith Tschichold recalled the events later:

> When the SA came to search our house, Tschichold was on a lecture trip. On that Saturday evening there was a loud banging at the door. There stood six SA men in front of me, with drawn pistols. They asked for Tschichold. I replied that I did not know where he was. Then they rummaged through the whole flat and seized a table full of things, mostly books. They wrote all over these: 'Seized for the Kampfbund für Deutsche Kultur'. Then the SA men left, leaving only one of them to 'guard' me. He went frequently to the bathroom, closing the door behind him. I took this opportunity to lock myself in the room where the telephone was. I quickly phoned some friends to tell them to go immediately to the train station and warn Tschichold. They realized straight away what was wrong and hid Tschichold in their cellar after they had met him at the station. Between four and five in the morning all of the SA men came back and asked if Tschichold had returned in the meantime, to which I replied no. After that they all left, even my guard. I woke my son (who was three-and-a-half-years-old at the time), dressed him and fled through the back door to our friends in Schwabing. There I met Tschichold. We discussed what we should do. First of all we decided that we should leave Munich. We went to a guest-house in the country. On the radio there we heard many reports that the arrests had ended and we believed this. We therefore decided to return to our flat the next day. Tschichold first had to call on our friends. When I arrived at our flat, the front door was mysteriously ajar. The same SA men were there. They wanted to know where I had been. Then they said I was under arrest. Meanwhile they had seized more of our things, including a beautiful collection of Russian children's books. I remember now that Tschichold told me later that about three quarters of his pupils at the Meister-schule were in SA uniform when he arrived at class that day. This gave him a shock from which he never really recovered. I was taken to the police station in Ettstraße. I was then questioned by a man, about whom I immediately felt, this is no Nazi. The SA didn't appear much after that. This man questioned me and then I was able to sleep in a single cell. Tschichold returned to our friends' house after teaching. He only got strange voices answering the telephone at our flat in Voitstraße. The friendly policeman came to my cell and told me that the SA men who had arrested me were now looking for Tschichold, and if he fell into their hands, it would be terrible for him. The police, on the other hand, would handle him according to the law. It would therefore be better if I told him where Tschichold was. After some consideration, I then told him that Tschichold might be at his doctor's house. Tschichold drove straight to the prison in a taxi when he

was told that I had been arrested and would be released when he presented himself. We saw each other briefly in the police officer's room. Tschichold was arrested and I was released.[14]

The Tschicholds' apartment was occupied by the storm-troopers for four days in total: 'by happy accident I escaped a beating' he explained afterwards to Imre Reiner, adding that 'an elderly Jew close by in the neighbourhood had the soles of his feet whipped'.[15] He was transferred to Neudeck prison, just south of the river Isar in Munich city centre, and held in 'protective custody' (*Schutzhaft*), which meant that he was not formally accused of any crime.[16] He was not questioned once during his incarceration there and must have experienced terrible uncertainty about when – or whether – he would be released, as well as about the safety of his wife and young son. At Edith Tschichold's request Renner intervened on behalf of both Roh and Tschichold. Renner later believed that his action led directly to his own arrest, which took place on 4 April after harassment begin-ning on 25 March. The Tschicholds' friend Hilde Horn asked the well-known Munich book illustrator Emil Preetorius for help on their behalf, but without success. Accompanied by Tschichold's colleague at the Meisterschule, Hermann Virl, Edith also called on Fritz Ehmcke at the Munich Kunst-gewerbeschule, despite (or perhaps because of) the fact that Tschichold did not consider him part of the avant-garde. But Ehmcke felt his own position to be under threat and he was not able to help.[17] Edith Tschichold lamented later that there was nobody among their acquaintances who had suf-ficient influence with the Nazis to enable Tschichold's quick release, as was the case with both Roh and Renner. The Tschicholds had a tenuous connection to a Nazi via Oskar Schlemmer, but the person in question refused to help.

Some tolerance was shown by Tschichold's jailers, how-ever: having lost his teaching job, he was without income, and so Edith sought permission to take him material for executing a commission to design a book cover for Insel Verlag ('Indian ink and a pen, a drawing board and a T-square'), which she was allowed to do. Tschichold was released shortly before Easter, on 13 April, under a general amnesty. Edith recalled him expressing a wish to leave Germany as soon as possible thereafter, although their departure was not immediate. They had been planning to vacate their apartment in Borstei, even after their decision not to move to Berlin, because it was too small and cramped. They had found accommodation with larger rooms in a turn-of the-century building in Munich but Edith was forced

14. [Edith Tschichold], 'Interview…', pp.189–91. Her son Peter was just over four years old at that time, a little older than she recalled here.

15. Letter Tschichold to Reiner, 28 May 1934.

16. The decree for the Protection of the German People, under which political opponents could simply be imprisoned, had been passed on 4 February 1933. A notice in the Scandinavian journal *Grafisk revy* (Aarg. 4, Hefte 2, 1933, p.20) reported that Tschichold was being held in a 'concentration camp in Saxony', which was one of several errors contained in the piece.

17. Ehmcke had taught at the Munich Kunstgewerbeschule since 1913 and was pensioned at the age of 60 in 1938.

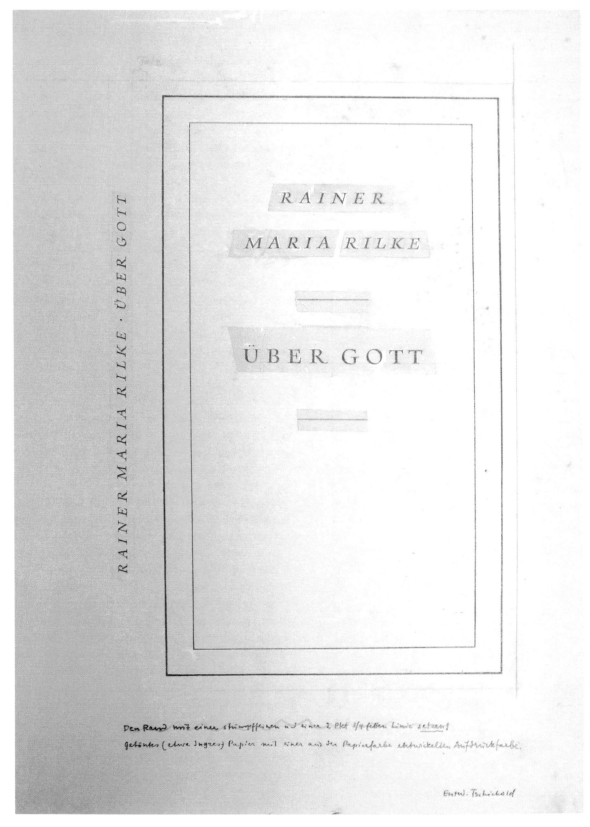

Jacket design for Insel Verlag. 1933. Possibly done by Tschichold while in prison. The instructions at the bottom read: 'Tinted (something like Ingres) paper with a colour of ink attuned to the colour of the paper.' (Directions for typesetting the outline rules are crossed out.)

to cancel the rental agreement when Tschichold was imprisoned and lost his job. After Tschichold's release they moved
temporarily into a two-room studio apartment in Munich's
Schubertstraße, south-west of the city centre, where they
stayed until leaving Germany in July.

Although Edith Tschichold still harboured some resent-
ment late in life towards Paul Renner for not having helped
her husband more at this time of crisis, Tschichold himself
was grateful for his intervention at the time, and felt that it
had helped to precipitate his release. He wrote to Renner on
17 April:

> Dear, esteemed Oberstudiendirektor
> last Thursday I was released from my four-week imprison-
> ment. I would like to thank you sincerely for your efforts,
> which contributed to shortening my incarceration.
> My wife and I are extraordinarily sorry that her visit to you
> brought unpleasant consequences. Since, against expecta-
> tions, my petition for the repeal of my requested, and already
> accepted, resignation was not granted, I have experienced
> great financial worries. I hope that I succeed in struggling
> through.
> I sincerely wish you and your family well and remain yours
> Jan Tschichold.[18]

Here there was perhaps a veiled plea for Renner to
help Tschichold further in some way. But meanwhile, on
11 April, Renner himself had been temporarily relieved of
his position at the Meisterschule pending an examination
under the 'professional civil service restoration act'.
Renner's complaint about his colleague's arrest confirmed
his link with Tschichold, which added weight to the investi-
gation that finally led to Renner's own dismissal. In its
judgement against Renner, the Bavarian State Ministry
asserted vaguely (and falsely) that Tschichold had been
arrested due to 'communistic activities'. Yet, as Tschichold
explained to his friend Vordemberge-Gildewart soon after
being released from prison (referring to himself and Edith):
'We have never been active politically, in particular we are
far removed from communist endeavours. My interests
move merely in an artistic direction.' He added: 'Naturally
I never expressed myself politically at the school. I am very
badly off right now.'[19]

Even if the state authorities had not found the opportunity to dismiss Tschichold from his post at the Meisterschule,
evidence against him could easily have been assembled.
Regardless of his protestation that he was not politically
active, his work as principal designer for the Bücherkreis at
a time when it was directed by Karl Schröder, a prominent
member of the KAPD, would have proven incriminating in

the eyes of the Nazis. It is also probable that extracts from
his writings, particularly *Elementare Typographie*, would
have been cited as proof of 'bolshevistic' tendencies, as was
done in the case of Renner.[20] It was clear to Tschichold that
his job at the Meisterschule was irrevocably lost, and he
immediately began to explore an alternative. On the day
after his release from prison he wrote asking about a possible teaching post to Mies van der Rohe, who had recently
re-established the Bauhaus on a privately funded basis in
Berlin. Yet, unknown to Tschichold, the Bauhaus had been
closed down by the National Socialists only three days
before, on 11 April. Mies was hoping to revive the school,
given that the political suspicion leading to its closure had
not been followed up, and his reply to Tschichold was delayed
until more than a month later. He informed Tschichold
tactfully that he could give no concrete answer to his request,
as it was not clear whether the school would continue. Yet,
on the same day, Mies wrote to Renner, whom he knew well
from their joint involvement in the committee of the
German Werkbund, informing him that he hoped to re-open
the Bauhaus in the coming weeks, and had only temporarily
given Tschichold a negative response. He continued:

> You know that Tschichold interested me as a teacher, but as
> I must be careful in the current situation, I would like to ask
> you to inform me confidentially about his character and the
> position that he currently occupies. I would be very grateful
> if this could be done quickly. I would also be obliged to you
> if you could tell me what Tschichold should receive as a
> minimum salary.[21]

This letter to Renner implied that there may have been previous discussions between Mies and Tschichold about the
teaching position in the Reklameklasse (advertising class),
which had been occupied by Joost Schmidt since Bayer left
in 1928. Mies rejected Schmidt's systematized teaching
programme and wanted instead to pursue a more pragmatic
approach.[22] Schmidt, whose role as designer for the Uhertype phototypesetting company was soon to be taken over
by Tschichold (although in a somewhat different capacity),
almost lost his Bauhaus position to him also. However, nothing came of Mies's plans for reviving the Bauhaus and the
school was definitively dissolved in August 1933.[23]

During the short period between Tschichold's release and
his emigration he was able to take some stock of events,
indeed literally so in the case of the material from his
typographic collection that had been confiscated by the
Kampfbund. In a letter to Vordemberge from his temporary
accommodation in Munich, he expressed his bitterness:

18. Letter Tschichold to
Renner, 17 April 1933, cited in
Luidl, 'München – Mekka der
schwarzen Kunst', p.205.
19. Letter Tschichold to Vordemberge, 23 May 1933. Edith

Tschichold recalled later that,
despite their friendships with
Lissitzky and Moholy-Nagy,
'politics rarely came up in our
circle'. ([Edith Tschichold],
'Interview...', p.186.)

20. Renner's case was more
complex given that he was
a more established figure in
Munich with some influential
connections.

21. Letter Mies to Renner,
16 May 1933, cited in Luidl,
'München – Mekka der
schwarzen Kunst', pp.205–6.
22. Brüning (ed.), *Das A und O
des Bauhauses*, p.217.

23. Curiously, as early as
October 1929, Piet Zwart had
been offered the post of teaching the Reklameklasse at the
Bauhaus, instead of Schmidt,
by its then director Hannes

Meyer. Despite a successful
teaching visit to the Bauhaus,
Zwart did not leave the Netherlands to take up the offer.
Meyer was forced to resign on
political grounds in July 1930.

A great deal of my rather large and valuable collection was confiscated, almost everything by Lissitzky and all Russian typography. As I possess a unique collection, particularly concerning the development of New Typography and New Art, these losses are painful to me. Hopefully I will get everything back. It is still unclear.

His concern over the seizure of this material shows the importance he placed on it as the primary source for his work as a chronicler of the modern movement; it was the fruit of years spent patiently establishing connections that enabled him to acquire it. He thanked Vordemberge for sending him new examples of his own printed work, and asked if he could keep them, so that they could then be 'incorporated into my aforementioned private museum and (let us hope) preserved for history'. The confiscated material was obviously not returned to him, but Vordemberge felt optimistic that things would improve:

> it is to be hoped that you can re-acquire your extensive and valuable collection, as the understanding of it will one day be as great as it is in italy, where mussolini and marinetti are absolutely avant-garde.
> that this misunderstanding caused you to give up your professional position is very regrettable. i hope also that here everything will be brought back to order, as the current state will undoubtedly need modern artists.[24]

With hindsight this seems like the naive hope of a non-political artist. It is significant that Vordemberge, who had not yet been victimized by the regime, continued to write to Tschichold in *Kleinschreibung*, whereas Tschichold, who had previously written to Vordemberge without capital letters (as to all of his most modern colleagues) now wrote to him with conventional German orthography – capital letters for all nouns. He was obviously wary of leaving any hostages to fortune. It would soon become apparent how unwelcome modern artists were in Hitler's Germany, where the propaganda campaign against their 'degenerate art' soon began to develop. In 1938, when violence against the Jews intensified, Vordemberge fled to the Netherlands with his Jewish wife.

The state of uncertainty in which Tschichold and his family found themselves did not prevent his continued thinking about projects, such as his much-vaunted, enlarged edition of *Die neue Typographie*. He planned to include in it typography by Vordemberge, although Tschichold criticized him for frequently making use of all-capital typesetting and for specifying lines that were too long in measure:

> I believe I will not hurt your feelings by writing these things, and that you, as a modern person, will not suffer from morbid self-consciousness or an inferiority complex, nor close your mind to the healthy criticism of a friend.[25]

Tschichold was now very pessimistic about the chances of having a second edition of *Die neue Typographie* published. The 250 subscriptions that had been received up to that point were not enough to justify production. He presumed that the Bildungsverband would be dissolved, thereby ending any chance that they would publish it, although they had been reluctant for some time. (Towards the end of 1932 he had been discussing the project instead with the firm of Wedekind, which had published *Foto-Auge* and *Eine Stunde Druckgestaltung*.) Tschichold was right to assume that the Bildungsverband would fall prey to the new regime: its seat in Berlin, the Buchdruckerhaus, was taken over by the Nazis on 2 May 1933 and swastika flags were hung outside. The Büchergilde Gutenberg was taken over in the same stroke and its left-wing literary director, Erich Knauf (who himself had written a reportage novel on the Kapp Putsch of 1920), was later executed. Bruno Dressler went into exile in Switzerland, like Tschichold, and very rapidly recommenced the book club's programme there, bringing out the first issue of its revived journal from Zurich the very next month.

The opportunity for Tschichold to find some way of making a living in Switzerland came through the kindness of Hans Eckstein, who reported on what had happened to him in the Swiss newspapers, *Neue Zürcher Zeitung* and Basel's *National Zeitung*, as well as in the Swiss Werkbund journal, *Das Werk*. Here, in his monthly 'Munich chronicle', Eckstein described the arrest of Roh and Tschichold (as well as the dismissal of G.F. Hartlaub from the Mannheim Kunsthalle) as evidence of an 'enforced conformity of the intellect'.[26] Due to Eckstein's intervention, an offer of work in Switzerland was soon received by Tschichold: he was invited to teach typography for two hours per week at the Basel Gewerbeschule by its director Hermann Kienzle. Tschichold had met Kienzle in his other capacity as director of the Basel Gewerbemuseum when they collaborated on the exhibition 'Neue Werbegraphik' there in 1930. Tschichold had put together the catalogue for that exhibition and Kienzle probably envisaged further work of this kind: he secured for Tschichold a half-day position as typographer at the Basel printer/publisher Benno Schwabe, which produced catalogues for the Gewerbemuseum. This offer of some guaranteed income, along with the hopes of long-term work for Uhertype in Zurich, persuaded the Tschicholds to emigrate to Switzerland, a decision they also took for the sake of their young son, Peter.[27] However, given that emigration from Germany had been officially banned when Hitler became Chancellor in January 1933, there remained the problem of getting a passport. Edith Tschichold takes up the story again:

24. Letters: Tschichold to Vordemberge, 23 May 1933; Vordemberge to Tschichold, 2 June 1933.

25. Letter Tschichold to Vordemberge, 23 May 1933.
26. *Das Werk*, Jg.20, H.4, April 1933, p.XLI.

27. 'Jan Tschichold: praeceptor typographiae', p.20.

Tschichold in his study at Voitstraße in the Borstei housing estate, Munich. Sometime between early 1931 and March 1933. Resting on the wardrobe is the Mondrian painting, *Composition 1930*, acquired from the artist.

Soon the first letters arrived from Basel, asking if Tschichold could go for a meeting. But we had problems getting a passport. So I went back to the nice policeman who had questioned me. But opposite him in his office sat an SA man. I apologized quickly for having gone into the wrong room, and closed the door again. The policeman came out shortly after. I said to him that Tschichold needed a passport in order to go to Basel. He advised me in a soft voice: tomorrow, go to this and that room, and ask for this and that man. Bring a passport photo with you. He really took care of a passport for us. It was unbelievable. Tschichold went immediately to Basel. He called me from there afterwards and said that I should pack everything and prepare to move. So we emigrated to Basel.

The family left Munich in the latter part of July. The safety of their belongings, which they left with a transportation firm, caused them some concern: particularly in the case of the Mondrian painting that they had acquired directly from the artist. This had provided some confusion during the search of their Voitstraße apartment, as Edith Tschichold explained:

The SA men believed that this picture had concealed the door to a safe in our Borstei flat: they requested that I open the safe. At first I didn't understand at all. Then I told them, that it was actually a picture and we had no safe.[28]

By 1 August 1933 they had managed to settle already in the Basel suburb of Riehen. In a postcard to Franz Roh, still in Munich, Tschichold wrote (now reverting again to small letters only):

finally we have managed to find a little peace. the calm that surrounds us suits us very well. everyone is so friendly and prepared to help, just like old friends. at the moment we are occupying a pretty room in a very well appointed house in the country, later we shall get two further rooms and then we will stay living here. we have a wonderful view over basel, a marvellous garden and our landlady is an intelligent and pleasant schoolteacher. in any case, we are glad to be so well out of it [*so fein heraus zu sein*]. ... the house is situated on a hill, north of the rhine, onto which we look, and about 200 metres south of the german border. before us lies the actual airport and the spiritual one (crematorium à la sans-souci). otherwise only trees and fields, the whole a permanent summer holiday.[29]

28. [Edith Tschichold], 'Interview...', p.191.

29. Postcard Tschichold to Roh, 4 August 1933.

144

Despite financial hardship during his first years in Switzerland, Tschichold evidently appreciated the surrounding peace and security that allowed him to concentrate on what mattered to him, his typographic work and writing. Yet the nerves of the avant-garde in Germany were severed by the National Socialists' accession to power, and the period of what has sometimes been called 'heroic modernism' in Europe was over. Undoubtedly its representatives in typography and graphic design intended initially to keep the flame alive, but the new political reality, and for some the new social circumstances of exile in which they found themselves, inevitably meant that things would never be the same again.

When Lissitzky heard from the Tschicholds in Switzerland he was relieved:

> Dear Tschicholds, we were most pleased to hear your news. We had heard something from Neurath a little while ago about the strains you suffered in 卐-Reich. We are glad first of all that you are safely out of the hell and secondly that you did not go over to the other side; it would have been very sad for me if Tschichold had submitted to the 卐. So, can we perhaps now establish a new Typo-International? [30]

In Germany itself, if one was out of favour with the National Socialists, it was almost impossible to continue making a living. The Reichskulturkammer Gesetz (Reich culture chamber law) of September 1933 enabled Goebbels's propaganda ministry to control and police activity in all areas of culture. *Gleichschaltung* (enforced conformity) with Nazi ideology in the fields of art and design was governed by the Reichskammer für Bildende Künste (Reich chamber for fine art) and, without ratification by this body, one was effectively barred from practising one's profession. Tschichold would certainly not have been accepted into the Fachgruppe Gebrauchsgraphik (Graphic design division) of the Reichskammer für Bildende Künste. [31]

Although Tschichold was one of the first who chose to emigrate, he was only one of many in his field to lose their positions of employment in Germany at this time. The list of those dismissed reads as a litany of those with whom Tschichold had fostered contact. The Breslau academy, where Johannes Molzahn taught, was closed due to political pressure already in April 1932, although Molzahn and his colleagues, the architects Adolf Rading and Hans Scharoun, carried on teaching there until they were dismissed in 1933. After a few years trying to make a living as a graphic designer in Berlin, Molzahn emigrated to the USA in 1937. His paintings were among those expropriated from German collections by the Nazis and included in the principal 'degenerate art' exhibition of that year, along with those of Herbert Bayer, Willi Baumeister, Max Burchartz, Walter Dexel, Moholy-Nagy and Kurt Schwitters. It was for his activity as a modern painter that Dexel was dismissed from his teaching post in Magdeburg in 1935. One of a series of

Constructivist portraits he made in the early 1930s was of Hitler, but his family advised him to destroy it when the dictator came to power, and so he tore it into pieces and threw it into the waters of the Berlin Wannsee.

The Nazis began to confiscate avant-garde paintings from galleries in 1935, but, while decrying them for propaganda purposes, they did not lose the opportunity to profit financially from the exercise by selling many of them to international customers conscious of their value. Some of the art dealers approved by the Nazis to mediate these sales were sympathetic to modern art and believed that selling the stolen paintings abroad was the best way to prevent them being burned. That fate befell five thousand paintings in 1939, destroyed in order to vacate warehouse space needed to store grain. [32]

After having his teaching contract at Berlin's Vereinigte Staatsschulen für Kunst (United state schools for art) terminated in August 1933, the former Bauhäusler Oskar Schlemmer enlisted Tschichold's help to ascertain whether some of his paintings that were left in Zurich could be secured somehow. Schlemmer had already begun to feel the effects of the emergent policy for shaming modern art in German museum collections and was understandably wary of leaving his work open to confiscation. [33] Tschichold selected one painting to remain in Switzerland but the others were returned to Germany in 1935, and some of Schlemmer's work was exhibited in 1937 as 'degenerate'. [34]

In late 1933 Kurt Schwitters was forced out of his role as artistic adviser to the city of Hanover because he was not accepted into the Bund Deutscher Gebrauchsgraphiker: this was due to his being 'a typographer and not a graphic designer', explained his wife Helma to Tschichold. [35] Having a certain income from property, Schwitters remained at first in Germany and was even able to travel frequently, visiting the Tschicholds in Basel in both December 1935 and March 1936. Shortly before this, two of his paintings had been confiscated by the Nazis for inclusion in the first touring exhibition of 'degenerate art' (1933–6), and it became increasingly dangerous for him to stay in Germany. He followed his son into exile in January 1937, and wrote to the Tschicholds from Norway several months later, reflecting on the ridiculous nature of National Socialist cultural oppression:

> It seems that I cannot go home. Between January and now the Gestapo called at my house three times and asked after me. I wrote from Oslo and requested that they give me some

30. Letter Lissitzky to Tschicholds, autumn 1933, in Lissitzky, *Proun und Wolkenbügel*, p.140. (Swastika presumably handwritten in original.)

31. The Bund Deutscher Gebrauchsgraphiker, which published the magazine *Gebrauchsgraphik*, was assimilated by this body. The antipathy between Tschichold and

this publication on at least one side (see p.132, n.246 above) further precluded any probability of his later being accepted into the Reichskammer.

32. Annegret Janda, 'The fight for modern art: the Berlin Nationalgalerie after 1933' in Barron (ed.), '*Degenerate art': the fate of the avant-garde in Nazi Germany*, pp.105–20.

33. Letters Schlemmer to Tschichold, November 1933 to June 1935.

34. Schlemmer had written a letter of protest to Goebbels as early as April 1933. Tut Schlemmer (ed.), *The letters and diaries of Oskar Schlemmer*, p.310.

35. Letter Helma Schwitters to Tschichold, 10 September 1933.

information about what they allegedly want to ask me by post, telephone or at the embassy, but no reply was forthcoming. So it seems clear that they don't want my testimony, instead they want me.

The reason for this was unclear to me for some time. But after the last speech by Hitler and the arrest of Dorner it seems clear to me that I have to answer for my art.[36] When I painted Merz-pictures, like the one shown in the degenerate exhibition, there was as yet no concept of National Socialism, perhaps it had not yet even entered into Hitler's head in 1919. But they will charge me with having worked against the national community [*Volksgemeinschaft*], and with thereby being a traitor to the Fatherland. However I only made an entirely unpolitical composition from found materials, and I still cannot believe today that such a thing can have any subversive effect at all.[37]

Just before this Schwitters had celebrated his fiftieth birthday 'in the ice and snow' and lamented: 'I was forgotten by all those interested in modern art.'[38]

Sibyl Moholy-Nagy (László's second wife) gave a colourful account of a kind of last supper for German modernism in Berlin that was attended by both Schwitters and Moholy-Nagy in early 1934. It was on the occasion of a visit by Marinetti, who had been appointed by Mussolini as his minister of cultural affairs. Sibyl described his lecture as 'a last gathering of German artists and intellectuals before the great diaspora'. Moholy-Nagy received a personal invitation from Marinetti to attend an official banquet dinner the night following his lecture but he did not want to go, feeling under threat from the new regime. Schwitters was staying with him at the time and he eventually persuaded Moholy-Nagy and Sibyl to accompany him. The dinner was also attended by many senior National Socialists, including Goebbels, Goering, Hess and Röhm. Schwitters got rather drunk and began to taunt the uniformed Nazi sitting next to him. Then Marinetti began to recite some of his cacophonic Futurist poetry, at which point Schwitters's innate Dada reflexes were activated and he stood up, jerking his body almost involuntarily to the sound of Marinetti's words. As a final touch, Marinetti tried the old parlour trick of pulling the tablecloth out from under the table settings, instead launching food into the laps of the Party faithful. It was a sign that the modernist honeymoon was over. Moholy-Nagy left the next day to the Netherlands, where he had been offered work at a printing firm. He only briefly returned to Germany before leaving it for good in May 1935.[39]

Willi Baumeister was relieved of his position at the Frankfurt Kunstschule soon after the National Socialists gained power in 1933, along with the school's director Fritz Wichert and the painter Max Beckmann. Baumeister remained in Germany and found it difficult to survive during the Third Reich. Others, such as Burchartz and Bayer, despite also being deemed 'degenerate artists', were able to prosper to some extent in the Nazi era: Burchartz was dismissed in 1933 from teaching at the Folkwangschule, Essen, but in 1934 he carried out a photographic documentary project on the German Reich navy, which was then published. Bayer, who had made clear to Tschichold his suspicion of attaching ideology to New Typography, proved the adaptability of modernist graphic design by executing several commissions for the Nazi Party, including the 'Deutschland' exhibition on the occasion of the 1936 Berlin Olympics and its accompanying catalogue. This was a prime example of inventive photomontage, somewhat akin to the Russian photographic propaganda of *USSR in Construction*. Modern designers found some favour with the more progressive contingent of the National Socialists led by propaganda minister Joseph Goebbels, who created the Reichskulturkammer to siphon power away from the staunchly conservative and folkish leader of the Kampfbund, Alfred Rosenberg. Nevertheless at least one of Bayer's design proposals was rejected by Goebbels as 'too modern'.[40] In 1937 Bayer began plans to leave Germany with his Jewish wife and daughter for America, where he became one of the principal figures in adapting European modernism to an American context.

The eventual successor in 1934 of Paul Renner as director of the Meisterschule in Munich was, at Renner's own suggestion, Georg Trump, whom Tschichold had intended to join teaching in Berlin one year earlier. Trump remained in this position until 1953. When it became known that Trump was to be appointed, Tschichold commented to Imre Reiner that he did 'not envy our friend Trump his having to bow to the Nazis, which he no doubt has to do like all the others'.[41]

Nazi purges were opportunist and not exclusively driven by ideology: it was not only modernists who were forced out of their jobs – traditionalist typographers lost their teaching positions also. Hugo Steiner-Prag, who had taught since 1907 at the Leipzig academy (where Tschichold had studied), was dismissed for being Jewish, briefly returning to his native Czechoslovakia before again fleeing from German occupation to the USA. Emil Rudolf Weiß, whose new Fraktur type had been used from 1909 in the tasteful series design for the Tempel classics printed at Poeschel & Trepte, was obliged to quit his post at the educational institute of the Berlin Kunstgewerbemuseum, where he had taught mural painting and life drawing since 1910. Nevertheless it was the modern movement that, for propaganda purposes, bore the brunt of Nazi powermongering. The German avant-garde was now suppressed and splintered.

36. Alexander Dorner was director of the Niedersächsisches Landesmuseum, Hanover.

37. Letter Schwitters to Edith Tschichold, 31 July 1937.

38. Letter Schwitters to Tschicholds, 3 July 1937.

39. Sibyl Moholy-Nagy, *Moholy-Nagy: experiment in totality*, pp.98–104. One should perhaps allow for the possible embellishment of the story by Sibyl, who was a former screenwriter.

40. See Burke, *Paul Renner*, pp.147–8.

41. Letter Tschichold to Reiner, 23 May 1934.

4 Script, type and book

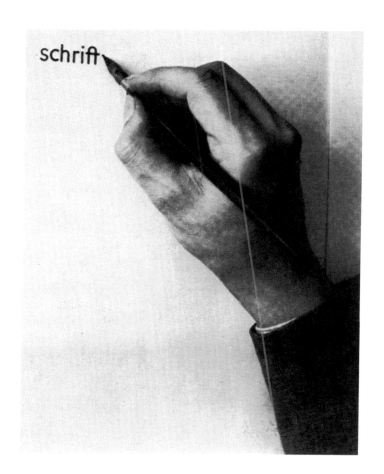

Sanserif and small letters

A preference for sanserif typefaces is evident from the earliest manifestations of New Typography, at least for use in larger sizes for titles and headings. The name of Devětsil was set in condensed sanserif capitals on the cover of its eponymous first publication (1922), and Moholy-Nagy introduced headings in sanserif type into Bauhaus typography in 1923.[1] For the first time, an ideological dimension was given to sanserif, a style of type developed by typefoundries during the nineteenth century mainly for advertising. It held an appeal for New Typographers equivalent to that of engineer-designed buildings for modernist architects. Tschichold did the most to establish sanserif type as a key element of New Typography: he went further than his contemporaries in advocating it as a typeface that should be used for lengthy texts. It was implicit in his advocacy that it should be used to typeset whole books, although he himself rarely achieved this outside of his own publications. Yet his views on this matter were always complex, and reflected from the beginning his acute sensitivity to the historical and stylistic qualities of typefaces.

Lissitzky only made oblique hints towards sanserif in his theoretical writing on typography, calling for 'lack of flourishes' in typefaces. This was a reference to the Fraktur types commonly used in Germany at that time, which possessed elaborate curlicues in their capitals (known in German as *Schnörkels*). A further hint towards sanserif is perhaps discernible in his idealistic requirement that letters be made up of basic geometric shapes, reflecting the reductionist obsession within modernism.[2] Moholy-Nagy, who was more visually attuned to the details of typography, recognized sanserif as a partial fulfilment of such demands, although the nineteenth-century sanserifs employed in early New Typography were not really geometric and only superficially appeared so. While he felt that there was still no adequate text typeface available without 'individual character', 'contortions' or 'flourishes', Moholy-Nagy accepted that there were typefaces for headings and emphasis in which the 'geometric and phonetic root-form' was visible, namely Venus Grotesque (a sanserif produced by Bauer) and Lapidar.[3] In his view these provided the required strength of contrast when mixed with normal 'grey text types' (presumably he meant roman) but tended to 'shimmer' when used extensively for text themselves. The typography that Moholy-Nagy was involved with at the Bauhaus, such as the series of Bauhaus books, almost always employed roman type for the principal text.

In 'Elementare Typographie' Tschichold echoed Moholy-Nagy's sentiments, listing sanserif type as 'the elemental letterform', alongside photography as the only acceptable, modern form of image. Then he went on to qualify his assertion:

> As long as there exists no thoroughly elemental form that is also legible in text setting, it is appropriate to prefer (against a sanserif) the least obtrusive form of Mediäval-Antiqua [old style roman] – one in which period or personal characteristics are least evident.[4]

He explained that unpretentious roman typefaces still had 'the advantage of better legibility over many sanserifs'. Indeed, for the main text of *Elementare Typographie*, Tschichold specified a roman type of this kind named Dissertations-Antiqua, with sanserif used on the cover, title-page, for (very large) page numbers, in lists, and for occasional displayed quotations. Sanserif played a similar, secondary role (although again in dominant type-sizes) in Tschichold's design for *Das Fahrten- und Abenteuerbuch* by Colin Ross (1925; see p.218); that book's principal text was typeset in Fridericus Antiqua (a German adaptation of a French roman type.) The first book designed by Tschichold to be fully typeset in sanserif was his own *Die neue Typographie*. Here he had more to say about the role of sanserif type, but, again, he was not unequivocal. In a sentence marked by a bold rule in the margin of the book, he stated:

> From among all the available typefaces, the so-called 'grotesque' or block-letter (the right description would be 'skeleton-script') is the only one in spiritual accordance with our time.

Yet, characteristic of the way in which the subtlety of his own text counteracted the effect of such highlighted phrases, he continued:

> There is no doubt that the sanserif types available today do not yet fulfil the demands of an entirely satisfactory typeface. The specific characteristics of this type have scarcely been worked out yet: the small letters especially are still too dependent on the humanist minuscule.[5]

Nevertheless, he considered new designs, such as Erbar and Kabel, to be too individualistic, preferring instead the 'anonymous, old grotesques'. Already, in response to *Elementare Typographie*, Konrad Bauer had criticized this preference for confusing 'plebeian dullness with objectivity'. While welcoming Tschichold's exposition as an earnest attempt to define a typographic style for the technological age, Bauer felt that the 'dictatorial restriction to sanserif type' not only limited New Typography's means of expression

1. An early, concerted use of sanserif in a version of Futurist typography is to be found in *Blast* (no.1, 1914), the periodical of the British Vorticists.
2. 'Typographische Tatsachen', *Gutenberg Festschrift*, 1925, p.152–4. In an article in

the same compilation Renner recognized this feature in the basic forms of Roman capitals.
3. 'Zeitgemäße Typographie', p.314. Lapidar (referring to an historical association of sanserif letters with stone inscriptions) was the name given to

some grotesques of the late nineteenth century. See Burke, *Paul Renner*, p.86, n.33 on terminology in sanserif type. The sanserif most commonly used in Bauhaus typography was the Breite fette Grotesk issued by Schelter & Giesecke.

4. From appendix A, p.311. Already perceptible here is the nucleus of Tschichold's later preference for Garamond. His former calligraphy teacher, Wieynck, closely prefigured Tschichold's later view when criticizing his proposal of

sanserif for text: 'The classic latin [roman] printing type in itself already does away with all merely decorative details.' (Wieynck, 'Neueste Wege der Typographie', p.380.)
5. *Die neue Typographie*, p.75. Tschichold could not have

equivocated more over the very question: 'Is it really inherent in the purpose of a typeface that it express spiritual matters?'. His answer to his own question was: 'Yes and no.' (p.79)

Detail (actual size) of the Aurora Grotesk as used to typeset the text of *Die neue Typographie* (p.76). In the middle of this passage Tschichold described what he considered to be ugly letters in the common Venus Grotesk type. Though it is quite hard to see, the word 'Akzidenzgrotesken' (split over the first and second lines) is letter-spaced for emphasis.

Vorläufig scheinen mir unter allen vorhandenen Groteskschriften die A k -z i d e n z g r o t e s k e n (zum Beispiel von Bauer & Co., Stuttgart) wegen ihrer verhältnismäßig sehr sachlichen und ruhigen Linienführung am geeignetsten. Schon weniger gut sind die Venus-Grotesk und ihre Kopien, wegen der schlechten Form der Versal-E und -F und des gemeinen t (häßliche schräge Abschnitte der Schäfte). In dritter Linie folgen — wenn nichts Besseres zur Hand ist — die „malerischen" Blockschriften (magere und fette „Block" usw.) mit ihren scheinbar angefressenen Rändern und runden Ecken. Die exakten, konstruktiven Formen der fetten Antiqua, der Aldine und der (alten) Egyptienne genießen, soweit Auszeichnungsschriften in Betracht kommen, den Vorrang vor den übrigen Antiquaschriften.

but its potential life-span.[6] Considering the qualifications made by Tschichold, Bauer's characterization of his advocacy of sanserif was too strong, although this criticism may have planted a seed which came to fruition in Tschichold's own later views. Towards the end of his life, he reflected:

> In 1925, in place of the host of almost exclusively ugly types, I demanded that only one kind of type should be used, sanserif [...], along with asymmetry as a principle of form (asymmetry being an imprecise word for non-centred setting). In that way I threw the baby out with the bathwater, yet the results were healing. The ugly typefaces and the stupid ornaments disappeared. It would have been correct to first seek out good cuts of type and help to popularize them. My thought process in those days – 'What is the best type? The simplest type. What is the simplest type? Sanserif. Therefore sanserif is the best type' – is a fallacy. The best typeface is the most legible one.[7]

In his statements of the 1920s it is clear that Tschichold already felt himself to be in a difficult position. The common jobbing grotesque, having been produced by anonymous nineteenth-century engineers, provided the aura of impersonality required by New Typography, but he was unwilling to admit that its visual qualities were entirely acceptable. He claimed to have used such a grotesque, Aurora, for composing the text of *Die neue Typographie* in order to demonstrate how legible it could be, but simultaneously offered a veiled apology for the typeface itself, explaining that his particular choice was limited by what the printer had available.[8] It is tempting to assume that the lack of elegance in the common grotesques offended the

sensibilities of Tschichold, who, after all, had become a master calligrapher at the age of nineteen, by then already schooled in the tradition of creating beautiful letterforms.[9]

He conceded that the Futura typeface represented 'a significant step forwards' in sanserif design – although perhaps a little grudgingly, given a certain tension between Tschichold and its designer, Paul Renner. The first three weights of Futura had been released in early 1928 but it is likely that the Buchdruckerwerkstätte in Berlin had not yet acquired it before printing *Die neue Typographie*.[10] Tschichold continued to favour the grotesque style of sanserif in his practical work, although he began to use Futura around 1930 in publicity and books that he designed for the Bücherkreis publisher. Futura was the text typeface in Tschichold's short instructional book, *Schriftschreiben für Setzer* (Formal writing for compositors; 1931), and he also featured it as the representative sanserif example in his book on how to draw layouts, *Typografische Entwurfstechnik* (1932), although he did not refer to it by name, but simply as a 'grotesque'.[11] Futura did manifest one of Tschichold's stated requirements for an ideal sanserif: the eradication of calligraphic features from the lower case. It was really the typeface that came closest to the ideal described by Tschichold and other modernist typographers, and the immediate success of Futura perhaps dissuaded Tschichold (before 1933) from pursuing a sanserif design of his own into production.

Tschichold did not expressly provide his own suggestion for exactly how sanserif should be 'worked out' to his satisfaction. He stated idealistically in *Die neue Typographie* that no single person could design the requisite typeface,

6. Bauer's comments cited in Friedl, 'Echo und Reaktionen auf das Sonderheft »elementare Typographie«', p.8.

7. 'Flöhe ins Ohr', pp.360–1. In the elision here Tschichold clarified in parenthesis that his preferred term ('since 1953') for sanserif was *Endstrichslose* (without terminal strokes) and not *Serifenlose Linear-Antiqua* (serifless lineal roman), referring to the term adopted in the

DIN 16518 typeface classification of 1964.

8. *Die neue Typographie*, p.78. Tschichold pointed out that sanserif types were seldom used to typeset the text of a whole book because they were not commonly available in the necessary quantity (of metal type) for such a purpose. This was due to their previously having been used mainly as display types. Such were the 'economic

considerations' he had mentioned in his first manifesto as favouring a retention of roman for lengthy texts. The few sanserifs available for mechanical composition at that time were restricted to the Monotype system, which had not fully infiltrated the German printing trade. The Aurora typeface used in *Die neue Typographie* had its origins in the grotesque of Wagner & Schmidt (Leip-

zig), which was adopted by several typefoundries under various names (see Bertheau, *Buchdruckschriften im 20. Jahrhundert*, p.110, and Wetzig, *Handuch der Schriftarten*, p.193). Tschichold maintained some affection for this typeface even during the later period in which he came to see sanserif as an aberration. In first place among the sanserif typefaces he selected in a special issue of

Schweizer Reklame (Nr 2, May 1951, p.16) to illustrate his proposed typeface classification system was Normal-Grotesk, which is equivalent to Aurora.

9. Wieynck criticized *Die neue Typographie* for being typeset in sanserif: 'This weak type – what is more, printed on coated paper – does not make reading the book a pleasant task, as Tschichold seems to think it does.' ('Die Wandlungen des Johannes', p.77.)

10. When asked specifically by British designer Ken Garland in 1960 why he had not used Futura in *Die neue Typographie*, Tschichold answered disingenuously that he never considered it suitable as a text typeface. (Conversation with Garland and Gerard Unger, 18 November 1993.)

11. Renner rejected the term 'grotesque' to describe Futura. (Burke, *Paul Renner*, p.95.)

instead it would be the work of a group, among whom he thought 'there must also no doubt be an engineer'.[12] The implication here was that sanserif type could have been standardized, rather as paper formats and printed stationery had been. Indeed a DIN Schrift was proposed in 1926 by the Normenausschuss für das Graphische Gewerbe (Standardization committee for the graphic trade) for standard use in internal documentation and on machine-nameplates at printing houses. It was a sanserif and shared a basis in geometric construction with letterforms designed around the same time at the Bauhaus. Certain pragmatic criteria determined the choice of style for the DIN Schrift, but it was also described by the standardization committee as being 'independent of fashion and simple', making clear the affinity with theories of New Typography. Indeed *Typographische Mitteilungen* interpreted the DIN proposal generically and recommended the use of any grotesque type for a printing job requiring DIN Schrift.[13] Any attempt at standardizing printing type itself met with strong opposition from Albert Giesecke (who was presumably linked with the Schelter & Giesecke typefoundry of Leipzig) in the pages of *Gebrauchsgraphik*:

> Type was never, is not, and will never be something that can be standardized. The formats of paper can be standardized, but not its qualities. Similarly, type-sizes have been standardized since the seventeenth century, but not type-forms themselves. Those of us, who are able to judge matters level-headedly, should be made sceptical of the fact that this movement is particularly encouraged by radical revolutionaries, by the bolshevistic typography of the Russian state, by the Dessau Bauhaus, by Kurt Schwitters with his *Systemschrift*, by Paul Renner and other *Radikalinskis*.[14]

No doubt Giesecke, who had been one of the earliest critics of Tschichold's Constructivist stance, counted him in the last category of this broad and distorting sweep of supposed radical tendencies.

In 1930 Tschichold published a sanserif alphabet design which could be interpreted as a suggestion for his ideal letterform, although he deliberately did not propose it as such, instead combining the presentation of his design with ideas for orthographic reform. It was a single-case alphabet (a mixture of capital and minuscule forms with a predominance of the latter) rendered as a strictly geometric sanserif, the elegance of which stems from its light weight. Tschichold himself gave the dates of 1926 to 1929 for the development of his script, thereby claiming to have been working on it since the year in which the most famous example of

a reformed script design, Herbert Bayer's 'universal alfabet', was published.[15] Bayer's alphabet, and the attempt along similar lines by his Bauhaus colleague Joost Schmidt, maintain strict geometrical construction in letters of a thicker weight than Tschichold's, and so they begin to seem more ungainly, exposing the problems of geometrical letter design best solved by Renner and the Bauer typefoundry in the Futura typeface. A small glimpse of how Tschichold's geometrical sanserif would have worked in a regular weight is given in his shop card for Lindauers (see p.101).

The inspiration for rationalizing the Latin script within New Typography was drawn from the book *Sprache und Schrift* (1920) by Walter Porstmann, who also helped to devise the DIN paper standards. As well as recommending that capital letters be dispensed with, he proposed a reform of orthography on phonetic principles. The Bauhaus adopted the first of these ideas in 1925 and in the same year Moholy-Nagy wrote: 'For example, we demand a *unified script* [*Einheitsschrift*], without minuscules and majuscules; only unified letters – not according to their size but their *form.*'[16] From this ensued Bayer's alphabet. Perhaps the earliest response to Porstmann's suggestions was an alphabet designed in 1924 by Max Burchartz, who had connections with the Weimar Bauhaus.

Cover of Walter Porstmann, *Sprache und Schrift*. 1920. 29.1 × 22.5 cm. (Not designed by Tschichold.) Even in a pubication advocating the exclusive use of small letters, the display typography is all in capitals (as it would be later in *Die neue Typographie*).

ain laut — ain zeichen
ain zeichen — ain laut

dieser Satz, dem es an einfachheit nicht fehlt, sei als leitstern für die schrift der stahlzeit aufgestellt . er ist eine selbstverständlichkeit . er bedarf keiner erläuterung; er harrt bloss der tat.

grosstaben

zählen wir einen deutschen text ab, so finden wir innerhalb hundert staben etwa fünf „grosse buchstaben". also um fünf prozent unseres schreibens belasten wir die gesamte schreibwirtschaft vom erlernen bis zur anwendung mit der doppelten menge von zeichen für die lautelemente: grosse und kleine staben . ain laut — tsvai zeichen . wegen fünf prozent der staben leisten wir uns hundert prozent vermehrung an stabenzeichen . — hier ist der erste hieb beim schmieden der neuen schrift anzusetzen . dieser zustand ist unwirtschaftlich und unhaltbar.

Text detail (85% of actual size) from book above, showing Porstmann's preferred manner of orthography without capitals. This section begins: 'one sound – one sign', using a reformed spelling.

12. *Die neue Typographie*, p.76. In some corrective notes made by Tschichold in 1967 for an English translation of this book he praised Adrian Frutiger's Univers as 'one of the best sanserifs', adding that it was 'what I dreamed of in 1928'.

(*The New Typography*, p.xii.)
13. 'Zur Normung der Schrift', *Typographische Mitteilungen*, Jg.23, H.12, 1926, p.346.
14. Giesecke, 'Rückblick auf das Schriftschaffens Deutschlands in den letzten 30 Jahren', p.22.
15. Tschichold used his

script for the credit line in his Phoebus poster for *Der General* (1927; p.66), lending support to the dates he gave for its design.
16. Moholy-Nagy, 'Zeitgemäße Typographie', p.314. Italic corresponds to letter-spacing in original.

It was probably Moholy-Nagy who made Tschichold aware of Porstmann's book, and in 'Elementare Typographie' he quoted a passage from it in favour of dropping capital letters (see appendix A; the same passage was also printed as an explanatory footnote on the Bauhaus letterhead designed by Bayer). Both Bayer and Tschichold designed personal letterheads for themselves with the printed footnote: 'ich schreibe alles klein, denn ich spare damit zeit' (i write everything small [lower case], in order to save time). Some authors also began to 'write small': Brecht adopted the practice for typing in 1925, although his works were published with conventional orthography.[17] Capital letters were retained in 'Elementare Typographie' and *Die neue Typographie*, despite Tschichold's advocating their elimination in both, but *Foto-Auge* was printed without them. That book was issued with an inserted loose leaf containing a kind of manifesto on the matter. Its argument (see opposite) had particular force in the context of the German language, which employs an initial capital for all nouns, not merely proper nouns as in English.

Yet *Foto-Auge* itself was neither typeset in sanserif (rather in the modern face roman, Ratio-Latein), nor did it employ the method for marking the beginning of sentences proposed in its manifesto insert (bolder full points); instead sentence beginnings were marked by the old-fashioned technique of using a larger space after the preceding full point. This technique was also subsequently rejected by Tschichold, who claimed to have made thorough trials of precisely how to compensate for a lack of capitals at the beginning of sentences. He rejected the further alternative of a full point placed higher than the baseline because it seemed to 'swim' in space (and was rarely available in type cases), arriving at the solution of using the same (changeable) wordspace applied to any given line of justified typesetting both before and after the full point – in other words, placing the full point mid-way between the two sentences in order to isolate it spatially to some degree.[18] (The problem was complicated by the necessity of contending with justified typesetting.) Independently of Tschichold the Bildungsverband arrived at the same solution in *Typographische Mitteilungen*, which presented some articles and reports without any capital letters when that was the author's wish.

In the article about his own geometric script design Tschichold clarified his position, stating that 'radical', exclusive use of small letters was a first step towards a more profound revision of the alphabet. He identified three groups interested in reforming the use of capitals in German: Germanists and school reformers, artists (specifically recognizing

jan tschichold

Letterhead. *c.*1926. A4. At bottom right is stated: 'i write everything small, in order to save time'. Original presumably printed in red.

Stefan George, whose poetry was typeset in a modified grotesque prefiguring Tschichold's suggestions by twenty-five years), and 'new designers, engineers (porstmann) and a few pedagogues, who are intent on the total elimination of double-case writing on grounds of fitness for purpose and economy'. Porstmann perceived script as a 'technical' rather than an 'artistic' problem, which Tschichold commended while implying that there was an aesthetic element that also needed consideration. The problem was initially 'more organizational than formal', reasoned Tschichold, declaring that 'a really new script is inconceivable without a better orthography. this has not hitherto been sufficiently heeded in new type designs.'

The title of Tschichold's article, 'Noch eine neue Schrift' (Another new script) suggested his wariness of joining the bandwagon of recent modernist script reformers. He surveyed the field, although, despite illustrating Bayer's universal alphabet, he passed no direct comment on it. He criticized Kurt Schwitters's 'Systemschrift' indirectly for taking capital letters as the basis for a single-case alphabet: 'For these, as the clarified script form of antiquity, can hardly be developed further, because they are simply and

17. Willett, *The new sobriety*, p.135.
18. Tschichold proposed this preferred solution in *Typografische Entwurfstechnik*,

p.22. He also explained his thoughts on this issue at some length in a letter to Willibald Hahn, 17 December 1932. Hahn worked on the committee for

simplified orthography of the regional association of Dresden teachers.

$$\mathfrak{A} + a + A + a$$

a

warum 4 alphabete, wenn sie alle gleich ausgesprochen werden (großes lateinisches, kleines lateinisches, großes deutsches, kleines deutsches)? warum 4
verschiedene klaviaturen einbauen, wenn jede genau dieselben töne hervorbringt?
welche verschwendung an energie, geduld, zeit, geld! welche verkomplizie-
rung in schreibmaschinen, schriftguß, setzerkästen, setzmaschinen, korrekturen
usw.! warum hauptwörter groß schreiben, wenn es in england, amerika, frankreich ohne das geht? warum satzanfänge zweimal signalisieren (punkt und großer
anfang), statt die punkte fetter zu nehmen? warum überhaupt groß schreiben,
wenn man nicht groß sprechen kann? warum die überlasteten kinder mit 4 alpha-
beten quälen, während für lebenswichtige stoffe in den schulen die zeit fehlt?

die kleine schrift ist „schwerer lesbar" nur, solange sie noch ungewohnt. „ästhe-
tischer" ist sie nur für die verflossene zeit, die in der architektur das auf und
ab von dächern und türmchen wollte.

unser vorschlag wäre puristisch? im gegenteil: wir sind für bereicherung aller
wirklichen lebensregungen. aber alle 4 klaviaturen drücken ja dieselben lebensregungen aus.

und das „deutsche lebensgefühl"? hatte unser eigenstes gut, die deutsche
musik etwa nötig, eine deutsche (und vierfache) notation hervorzubringen?

franz roh

Loose leaf inserted into *Foto-Auge*. 1929.
Actual size. It was signed by Roh alone, without
Tschichold, and indeed the formulation of the
argument here seems a little coarser than Tschichold's version of it elsewhere. The typographical
formula above adds the element of type-style to
the equation. The first paragraph states:

'why four alphabets if all of them are pronounced
the same (latin majuscule and minuscule, german
majuscule and minuscule)? why construct four
different keyboards when each one of them produces the same notes? what a waste of energy,
patience, time, and money! what a complication
in typewriters, typefounding, printer's cases,
composing machines, proof correcting, etc.

why write nouns with capital letters if this is not
necessary in england, america, and france? why
mark twice the beginning of a sentence (with full
point and capital letter) instead of making the full
point bolder? above all, why write big if it is not
possible to talk big? why torment overburdened
children with four alphabets when time is already
lacking in school for matters of vital importance.'

clearly designed.' Instead Tschichold persuasively argued that the existing, roman small letters should be taken as a starting point because their ascenders and descenders increased legibility. He also signalled some awareness of legibility research by demonstrating that the upper half of a line of type is more decipherable then the lower half (although he determined from this that the full point should be placed at x-height, an opinion he soon revised). Essential to his own script proposal was the modernist desire for visual purity and clarity:

> the complete elimination of all superfluous elements and the attempt to design absolutely characteristic letterforms, which are also unambiguous when taken out of context (compare my L, to which i restored a curve at the base, in order to exclude the danger of confusion with a 1 or also an old I [i]).

Compared with those of his contemporaries Tschichold's 'new script' was perhaps the best worked out in both visual and structural terms, yet he was clearly aware of the idealism behind it: 'the whole thing is not as utopian as it seems', he declared somewhat defensively. His concluding note was a strange mixture of modesty and territorialism:

> i make no claim to have designed something perfect. it seemed preferable to make this publication a contribution to clarifying the question of script and orthography than to leave it undefined or to leave others, who like me see the topicality of this problem and want to work towards its solution, to produce similar suggestions independently.

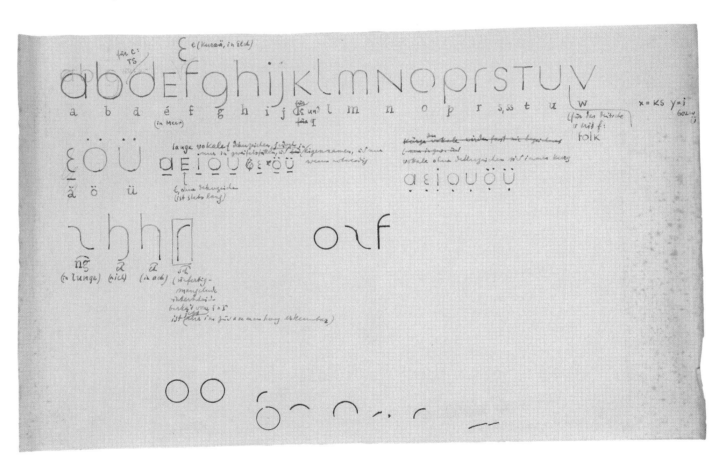

Tschichold's rough working out of his script reform. c.1929. Around 75% of actual size.

(Opposite) Finished execution of alphabet and explanation of its application to phonetic orthography based on Porstmann's suggestion. Around 50% of actual size. Prepared for reproduction in 'Noch eine neue Schrift' (1930). The full point is positioned on the x-height, following the findings of legibility research that the top half of a line of letters is more decisive for recognition. It was also made significantly thicker than stroke width.

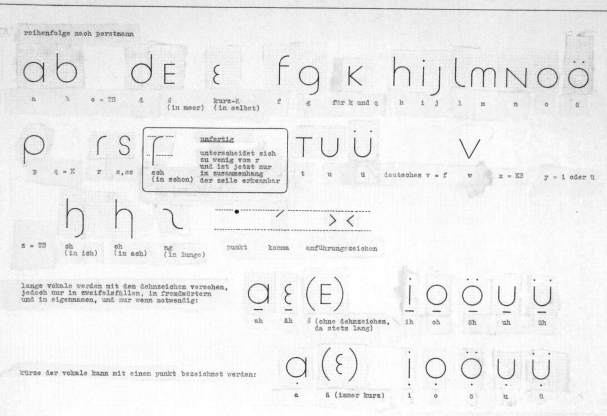

abcdɛfghijklmnopqrstuvwx
yz

jan tschichold 1926-29

reihenfolge nach porstmann

ab   dE   ɛ   fg k   hijlmNOÖ

| a | b | c = TS | d | ɛ (in meer) | kurz-ä (in selbst) | f | g für k und q | h | i | j | l | m | n | o | ö |

p   rs   r   TUÜ   V

unfertig
unterscheidet sich
zu wenig vom r
und ist jetzt nur
im zusammenhang
der zeile erkennbar

| p | q = K | r | s,ss | sch (in schon) | t | u | ü | deutsches v = f | w | x = KS | y = i oder ü |

ŋ h ʒ

| z = TS | ch (in ich) | ch (in ach) | ng (in lunge) | punkt | komma | anführungszeichen |

lange vokale werden mit dem dehnzeichen versehen,
jedoch nur in zweifelsfällen, in fremdwörtern
und in eigennamen, und nur wenn notwendig:

a ɛ (E)   i o ö u ü

| ah | äh | é (ohne dehnzeichen, da stets lang) | ih | oh | öh | uh | üh |

kürze der vokale kann mit einem punkt bezeichnet werden:

a (ɛ)   i o ö u ü

| a | ä (immer kurz) | i | o | ö | u | ü |

jan tschichold: versuch einer neuen schrift. 1926-29.

156

für den neuen menschen existiert
nur das gleichgewicht zwischen
natur und geist· zu jedem zeit-
punkt der vergangenheit waren
alle variationen des alten ›neu‹·
aber es war nicht ›das‹ neue· wir
dürfen nicht vergessen´ dass wir
an einer wende der kultur stehen´
am ende alles alten· die scheidung
vollzieht sich hier absolut und

für den noien menſen eksistirt nur
das glaihgeviht tsviſen natur unt
gaist· tsu jedem tsaitpunkt der
fergaꞑenhait varen ale variatsjo-
nen des alten ›noi‹· aber es var
niht ›das‹ noie· vir dürfen niht
fergesen´ das vir an ainer vende der
kultur ſtehen´ am ende ales alten·
di ꞅaiduꞑ foltsiꞇ sih hir absolut
unt entgültik· (mondriaꞑ) jan tschichold 1929

typografische mitteilungen, berlin
beilage zu heft **3**, märz 1930

noch eine neue schrift

beitrag zur frage der ökonomie der schrift

von **jan tschichold**

soweit versuche, eine neue schrift zu erfinden, aus dem bedürfnis hervorgehen, eine „schönere" form an die stelle einer „schlechteren" zu setzen, haben wir es nur mit artistischen, meist eklektischen bemühungen zu tun, die die wirkliche entwicklung kaum beeinflusst haben. wichtiger waren die experimente, die gültige schrift in der richtung auf eine klarere, unserer zeit angemessene form zu **verändern.**

bei dem versuch aber, eine bessere schrift zu erfinden, darf es sich nicht **allein** darum handeln, klarere staben zu erhalten. das wäre noch kein entscheidender fortschritt. im grunde ist das nur eine frage der typenauswahl.

auch ob man heute die oder jene bessere oder schlechtere grotesk verwendet, ist im prinzip dasselbe, selbst wenn künstler-groteskschriften zur debatte stehen. nur die im wesen **veränderte,** niemals die nur modifizierte form ist für die entwicklung von belang.

notwendig ist, zu erkennen, dass das problem einer neuen schrift eng mit dem einer neuen, gesünderen **rechtschreibung** verknüpft ist.

die radikale **„kleinschreibung"** wäre der erste schritt auf dem wege zu einer besserung. — **warum** man nur kleinstaben verwenden sollte, ist in meinem buch „die neue typografie" ausführlich dargelegt. hier in kürze das wesentliche:

1. die antiqua, unsere heutige schrift, besteht aus **zwei** alfabeten, die zeitlich und kulturell ungleichen ursprungs sind: den gross- und den kleinstaben. daher auch die disharmonie der form, die sich besonders deutlich im heutigen bild der deutschen sprache zeigt, da infolge der grossschreibung der substantive noch mehr grossstaben in die schrift gemischt werden als etwa im französischen oder englischen.

2. drei hauptgruppen wollen diesen zustand ändern:
    a) einige germanisten (dazu ein teil der schulreformer), die schon seit etwa 100 jahren für die **anpassung der deutschen rechtschreibung an die sonst übliche** eintreten: es sollen nur die satzanfänge und die eigennamen grossgeschrieben werden.
    b) künstler und einige dichter, die die reinliche **scheidung** der zwei alfabete aus gründen der **ästhetik** wollen: entweder nur „grosse" oder nur „kleine", auch nebeneinander, aber nicht durcheinander — etwa grossstaben für die überschriften, kleinstaben für den text, oder umgekehrt (von dichtern z. b. stefan george, ferner hauptsächlich französische künstler — anzeigen der „vogue" – ladenaufschriften in paris).
    c) neue gestalter, ingenieure (porstmann) und einige pädagogen, die auf die vollständige beseitigung der zweischriftigkeit aus gründen der **zweckmässigkeit** und **wirtschaftlichkeit** ausgehen. sie fordern die „nurkleinschrift", weil diese besser lesbar ist als die nurgrossschrift.
       von diesen hat **porstmann,** der erfinder der normformate und der normen für den geschäftsbrief, die postkarte usw. in seinem 1920 erschienenen buch „sprache und schrift" die technische seite des problems als erster durchdacht. schrift erscheint ihm mit recht nicht als ein „künstlerisches", sondern als technisches problem. sein buch ist die grundlage jeder weiterarbeit, **auch der formgebenden.**

die abbildungen zeigen bisherige versuche einiger gestalter, die heutigen stabenformen auf eine klarere, leichter erfassbare form zu bringen. albers, renner und der autor der schrift der kunstgewerbeschule halle sehen die weiterverwendung beider schriftarten vor. schwitters versucht, die grossstaben völlig umzuformen. diese aber, als die abgeklärte schriftform der antike, sind kaum weiterzubilden, weil sie einfach und eindeutig gestaltet sind.

(Opposite) Artwork of Tschichold's new script for his article, using both conventional and reformed orthography. Around 30% of actual size.

(Above) First page of Tschichold's article, subtitled 'contribution on the matter of economy in script', *Typographische Mitteilungen* (Jg.27, H.3, March 1930). 32 × 22.5 cm. Presumably designed by him, it was printed on a coated paper different to the journal's normal paper.

beispiel 1:
paul renner: futura-type

DURCH DIE SCHÖNHEIT WIRD DER
sinnliche Mensch zur Form und zum
Denken geleitet; durch die Schönheit
wird der geistige Mensch zur Materie
zurückgeführt und seiner Sinnenwelt

beispiel 2:
josef albers: schablonenschrift
aus der zeitschrift „offset- buch-
und werbekunst", 1926, heft 7

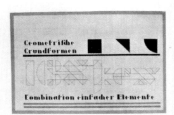

Geometrische
Grundformen

Kombination einfacher Elemente

beispiel 3:
plakat der kunstgewerbeschule halle
1926

beispiel 4:
max burchartz: geschäftsbrief
nach din 676, 1925, mit anwendung einer
neuen schrift von burchartz in der hauptzeile

werbe-bau

beispiel 5:
herbert bayer: alfabet
aus der zeitschrift „offset- buch-
und werbekunst", 1926, heft 7

abcdefghi
jklmnopqr
stuvwxyz

sturm blond

beispiel 6:
karel teige: prag: reformversuch
der schrift bayers
aus der zeitschrift „red", prag, 1929, heft 8

abcdefghi
jklmnopqr
stuvwxyz

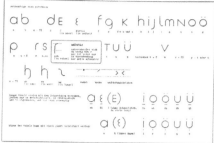

In late 1929 Tschichold did in fact submit designs for a sanserif typeface to the French typefoundry of Deberny & Peignot. His proposal was related to his geometric script design (Deberny & Peignot rejected his submission and Tschichold's article on 'another new script' was published a few months later). The drawings show that, in being developed conventionally for upper and lower case, the design inevitably grew to resemble Futura in some respects. Given the tension in his relationship with Renner, it could not have pleased Tschichold that Charles Peignot informed him in reply to his submission that Deberny & Peignot had just purchased the rights from Bauer to produce Futura in France. This they did, renaming the typeface Europe, and so, as Peignot explained, their acceptance of Tschichold's 'series' (implying that it was a typeface family), 'however interesting it might be', would entail a duplication of work on their part concerning sanserif type.

(Opposite and above) Spreads from 'Noch eine neue Schrift'. 1930.

(Left) Advertisement for Futura used as a basis by Tschichold for making sketches towards his own geometric sanserif typeface. He has worked over and altered the letterforms in the names of the three weight variants of Futura on the right.

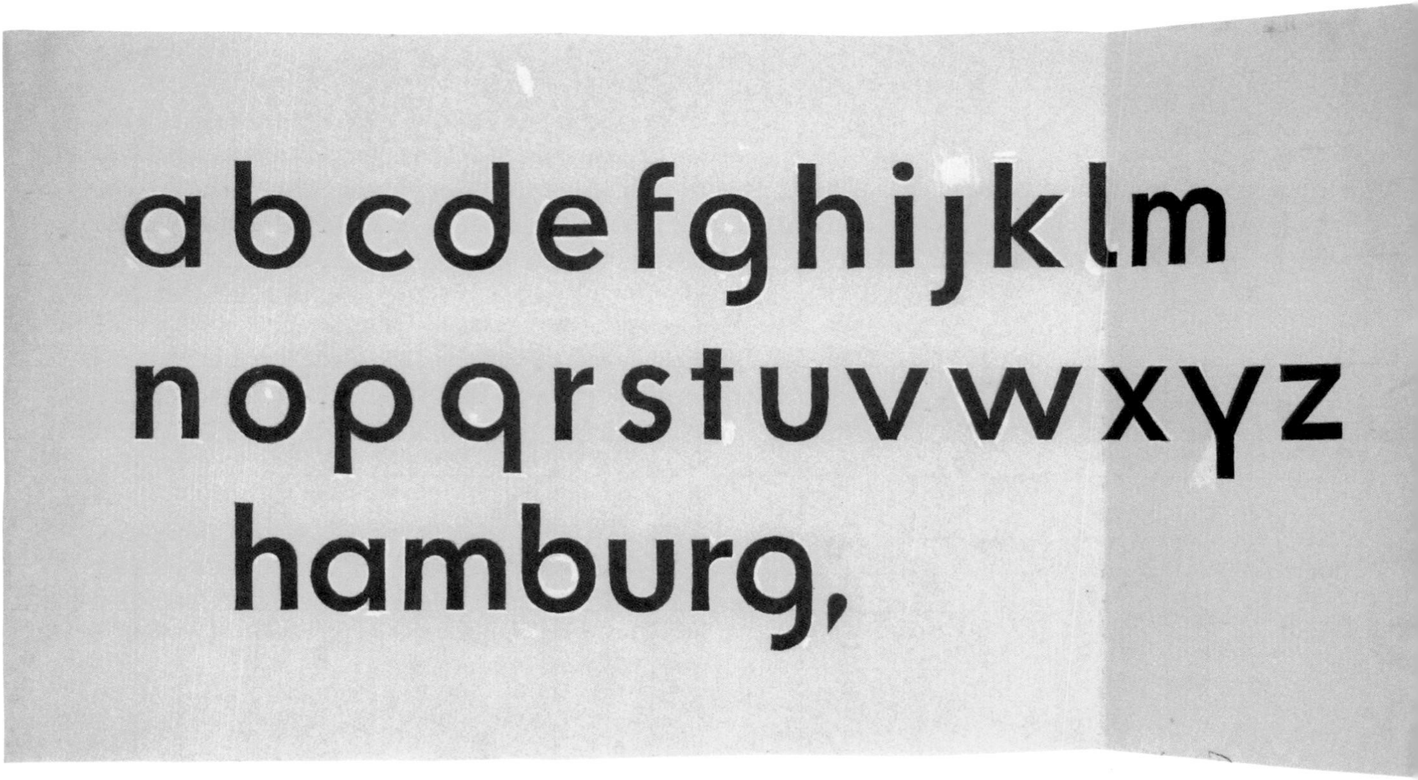

160

ABCDEFGHIJK
LMNOPQRSTU
VWXYZ!.

stärken: h h **h h**

zart buchschrift halbf. fett

abcdefghijklm
nopqrstuvwxyz
hamburg,

Drawings for geometric sanserif submitted
to Deberny & Peignot. c.1929. Around half of
actual size.

Drawings for bold capitals related to the design
opposite. *c*.1929. Around half of actual size.

It is understandable that Tschichold would not want to
offer his sanserif as direct competition to Futura in the
German type market, in which Renner's typeface was
proving a great success; he had also perhaps been attracted
to Deberny & Peignot by their release of A.M Cassandre's
typeface Bifur in 1929. Tschichold appreciated in this a
different kind of attempt to analyse the essentials of letters,
albeit capitals:

> Cassandre has attempted in 'Bifur' to make the distinguishing
> characteristics of the individual letters darker in comparison
> to the more lightly rendered, less important parts. A danger-
> ous undertaking, even if it stems from a proper consider-
> ation. Precisely because the resultant form is so witty and
> surprising, 'Bifur' can only be used signet-like in individual
> words as display lines. Indeed that is how it is intended. But
> even so the legibility is not great; because the form is extrava-
> gant and one cannot always recognize the letters clearly
> at first sight. The fascinating effect of such lines of type is,
> however, undeniable. It would be good if the German type-
> foundries adopted something of the courage of this French
> typefoundry to produce more essential types than the usual,
> mostly inferior repetition of old and new typefaces.[19]

The last sentence here gives another hint towards the
reason why Tschichold did not submit his sanserif design
of the late 1920s to a German typefoundry. Perhaps he
cared too much about that design to let it get lost in what
he called the 'hypertrophy of matrix production' in German
typefounding. Yet, before the publication in 1931 of this
severe comment on the German type market, there had
been two display typefaces produced by German typefoundries following designs by Tschichold, and another by a
Dutch firm. His bitterness towards the German type trade

may well have reflected some bad experiences during the
production of these typefaces, which he undertook mainly
because of having to earn some money in the depression
years after 1929. He rarely, if ever, used them in his own
typography and did not mention them in his autobiographical account of his career.

In a published response to Tschichold's disparagement
of trends in German typefounding Konrad Bauer pointed
out that, in identifying a 'hypertrophy' of type production,
Tschichold 'seems to forget that he has already sold three
new typefaces'. Bauer, who had been a relatively sympathetic early critic of Tschichold, was dismayed by his denial
of German typefounding's positive reputation, listing
several typefaces that had enjoyed international success
during the previous thirty years. Among these were several produced by the Bauer foundry, with which Konrad
Bauer was connected, including Futura.[20] That typeface, he
pointed out, was used to typeset the very journal in which
this discussion was published (*Die Form*) and had also been
issued by 'the most important French typefoundry', which
surely must have rankled with Tschichold. Bauer concluded:
'These facts are known to Tschichold. It is uncertain why he
withholds them and inverts the circumstances for the sake
of a rousing phrase.'[21]

Yet, earlier that same year, Bauer had identified precisely
the same problem with German typefounding in the bibliophile yearbook, *Imprimatur*:

> Part of the production in new types each year is of poor qual-
> ity, confusing and detrimental, because it is impossible that
> three to four dozen good, and in some respect necessary type-
> faces can be designed and cut in the space of twelve months.
> It is apparent that many new releases are prepared in too
> much haste and are simply 'thrown onto the market'.[22]

The subtext of Bauer's analysis was an attempt to isolate
the worthy products in the glut, such as Futura, and so he
could not tolerate Tschichold's blanket dismissal of German
typefounding.[23] Tschichold's overstated position was borne
of frustration with his own experiences in the saturated
type market.

19. 'Neuere Typografie in Frankreich', p.382. An illustrated explanation of the reasoning behind Bifur was given by Vox in no.19 of *Arts et métiers graphiques* (September 1930), the same issue which featured Tschichold's article 'Qu'est-ce que la nouvelle typographie et que veut elle?'

20. Konrad Bauer was not related to the family that gave its name to the typefoundry, which had in any case passed by this time into ownership of the Hartmann family.

21. Bauer, 'Deutsche Typografie', *Die Form*, Jg.7, H.2, 1932, p.70.

22. Bauer cited in *Typographische Mitteilungen*, Jg.28, H.7, 1931, p.182.

23. Renner had perhaps been the first to observe the confusing proliferation of new typefaces in *Mechanisierte Grafik* (1931), as a kind of prelude to offering his Futura as the solution.

Typeface designs 1929–31

The first typeface design sold by Tschichold for commercial production was Transito. His drawings were purchased by the 'Amsterdam' (formerly Tetterode) typefoundry in 1929 but the typeface was not produced until two years later. It occupies the category of stencil letterform (*Schablonenschrift*) that became fashionable within New Typography. The fact that stencils require letters to have internal breaks (so that the stencil does not fall apart) creates potential for constructing letters from discrete geometric parts, which appealed to the modernist sense for rationalization. The status of stencil letters as a kind of industrial vernacular, associated with engineering, would also have endeared them to modernist typographers.[24] Such letterforms had been favourites of the avant-garde since Cubism, and vaguely geometric, disjointed letters were featured in some of the earliest examples of New Typography produced for the *De Stijl* and *Ma* journals. Perhaps the first attempt at consciously constructing an alphabet of such letterforms was by Josef Albers at the Bauhaus. Although it was published first in 1926, Albers himself gave the date of 1923 for his design and believed it to be 'the first, modern stencil-script', as he described it to Tschichold. Between 1931 and 1932 Albers corresponded with Tschichold about their shared interest in this area, and Tschichold reassured him: 'as far as i know, you are the first to have made a modern stencil script. at any rate, earlier attempts are unknown to me.'[25]

Of course, none of the modernist essays in so-called stencil letters were actually produced commercially for stencils – Albers came closest by having his applied to letter stamps for marking paper, cardboard and wood.[26] There were in fact some real stencil letters produced in Germany during the first decades of the twentieth century that approach what the modernists set out to achieve (see above right). The adaptation of modernist stencil designs for metal type confirmed the entry of the trend into the mainstream of fashionable style. Before Transito Tschichold had not specifically expressed any great enthusiasm for stencil letters in his writings, or drawn versions of them in his practical work, but he probably perceived the commercial possibilities in designing a typeface along these lines. Indeed he seems to have made two separate designs for a stencil type: another was developed to the stage of a trial casting in 48 point size by the Stempel typefoundry but for some reason was never released. It is a shame that it never saw the light of day, as it is rather beautiful and more original than Transito.[27]

German stencil made by firm of A. Neumann. Uncertain date in first third of twentieth century. 11 × 21.5 cm.

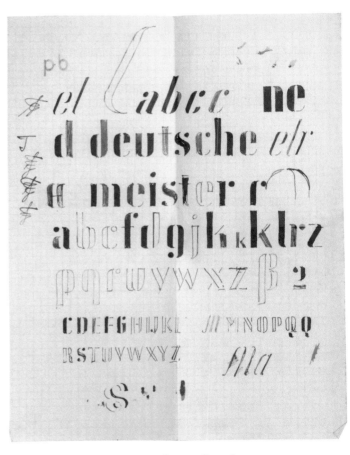

Sketch for stencil typeface. c.1929.

Metal type from the trial casting in 48 point of Tschichold's stencil typeface for Stempel. Just under 200% of actual size.

(Opposite) Tschichold's original drawings for capitals of the Stempel stencil typeface. c.1929. 32% of actual size.

24. A suggestion made by Eric Kindel in his thorough study 'Recollecting stencil letters', p.97. Kindel identifies genuine stencil letters used on propaganda posters made by Soviet ROSTA artists (1919–22) as some of the first consciously modernist occurrences.

25. Letters from Albers to Tschichold, 6 January 1932, and from Tschichold to Albers, 21 January 1932.

26. Letter Albers to Tschichold, 6 December 1931.

27. Copies of drawings for this typeface and a packet of the 48 pt trial casting were discovered by Hans Reichardt in the Stempel Archive, now in the Haus für Industriekultur, Darmstadt. I am grateful to Hans Reichardt for sharing this information with me and providing illustrations. The type has been digitized by Klaus Sutter.

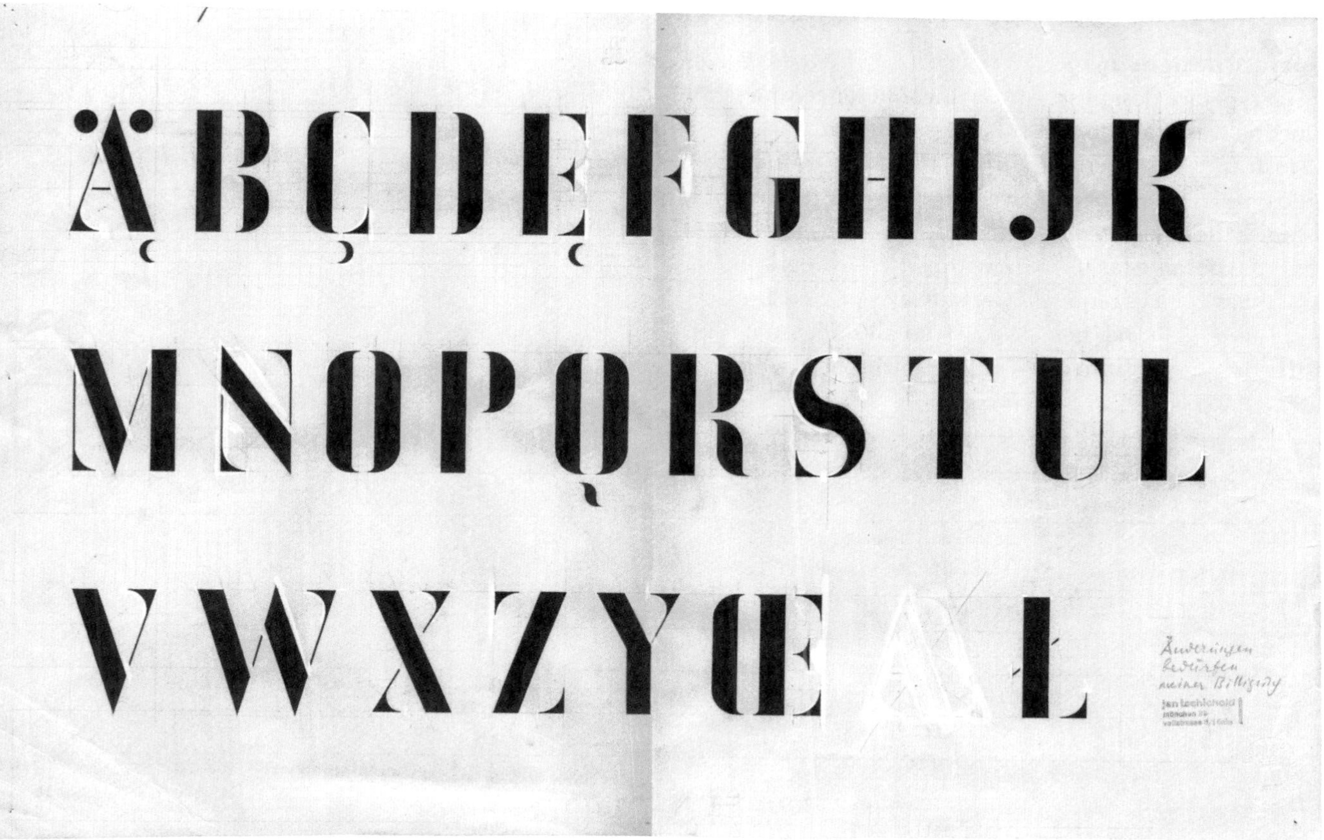

ǍBÇDĘFGHIJK

MNOPQRSTUL

VWXZYŒÆĿ

ÖÜŻÉ`ˆGŘÆ :·!?/

œæ;-.–[]()134»«*

2567890₤

& §$

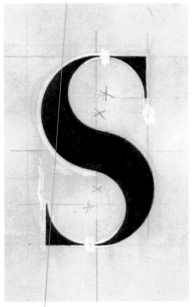

Actual-size detail from sheet of drawings
shown on previous page.

Publikation der Rundschau

Neuzeitliche Bucheinbände

Aus der Werkstatt der Natur

Kultur und Leben in Persien

Handelsblatt für Düsseldorf

Boxkämpfe in der Festhalle

Proof of trial casting in 48 pt of the Stempel
stencil type. 43% of actual size.

The drawings for the lower case of Tschichold's
stencil typeface for Stempel have only survived
in this copy, several generations removed from
the original. c.1929.

0 7 8 8 9 . , : ; ! ? ' † * »

« [( ) „ H A B C C k î j l s

n o ó ò ô ö p q r t u ú ù

û ü v w x y z ß § & 1 0 è

& 1 2 3 4 5 6 œ æ Æ Œ

É Ë b í o e i a d h ù m á

à â ä c ç è é ê ë f g h Ç

D E F G I J K Ł Ł L M N O

P Q R S S T U V W X Y Z

Ä Ö Ü Ü É Ê Ë

A recent proof taken from the trial casting of the
Stempel stencil type in 48 point (actual size).

Tschichold was disappointed with Transito as it was produced, and, if one compares his drawings with the rather crude final type, it is easy to see why. The proportions and details of his letters have been altered and over-rationalized to the detriment of the final typeface. Tschichold expressed his annoyance about the matter to Piet Zwart:

> your criticism of my typeface transito is quite justified. i am now long past having any illusions about it. in summer of 1929 i was in pressing need of money, at any cost, as my wife had to go to the mountains for recovery. and so i made this type, in the hope of selling it quickly for a pretty lump sum. this backfired on me in germany, since the 'futura-black', which is similar to my type, came out. (i had not seen this beforehand.) the berthold typefoundry advised me to offer the typeface to the tetterode foundry (amsterdam), with which they had a friendly connection and which then acquired it in sketch form. several letters were unfortunately changed, but i did not bother myself any further with the thing. i only did the new type specimen.[28]

Tschichold sent a copy of this specimen to Albers, who replied at some length (referring here to 1925 as the date for his own first stencil script, which he subsequently explained to Tschichold had originated in 1923):

> your 'transito' is naturally of particular interest to me. it reminds me of my first stencil script from '25, & i believe that is due to the proportions and the heavier verticals (which are therefore more conspicuous) alongside the smaller append-ages. in this way the legibility is also reduced, as in mine of '25, in comparison to which, however, your many roundings are a great advantage.

Albers was referring, for example, to the rounded right-hand element in Transito's lowercase e, which accords more with traditional letter shape than Albers's original e with its awkward equilateral triangle in this position (see p.158). He recognized that the more distinctive wordshapes formed by lowercase letters were helpful in such scripts 'because the numerous vertical spaces within the letters do not readily foster unity'. Evidently Moholy-Nagy had originally criti-cized Albers's alphabet on several points, but 'these days he makes heavy use of the subsequent futura-black', com-mented Albers wryly. Tschichold was ambiguous about the value of his own type, but unequivocal in his view of Futura Black, the stencil-like addition to Renner's typeface family:

> as you do, i like the small letters of my transito much more than the capitals. these are probably always conceptually rigid. i had to sell this type as a sketch, since the typefoundry did not want to pay out a further 200 marks for a finished drawing. that is why in many ways it is incomplete. anyhow it is still much better than the idiotic futura black. i can't under-stand why moholy tends to use it so much lately. typefaces other than ~~futura or~~ grotesque only really make sense when one is dealing with pure typography – if photos must be added, then grotesque should be sufficient.[29]

(Top) Sketches for Transito. c.1929. Around half of actual size; (middle and below) drawings for Transito. 1929. Around one third of actual size.

The crossing out in Tschichold's original letter (repro-duced here) betrays that he did think of Futura, at least in its principal variants, as some kind of ideal modern typeface, but that he did not like to be seen to think so.

28. Letter Tschichold to Zwart, 16 February 1932.

29. Letters: Albers to Tschichold, 6 December 1931;

Tschichold to Albers, 8 Decem-ber 1931.

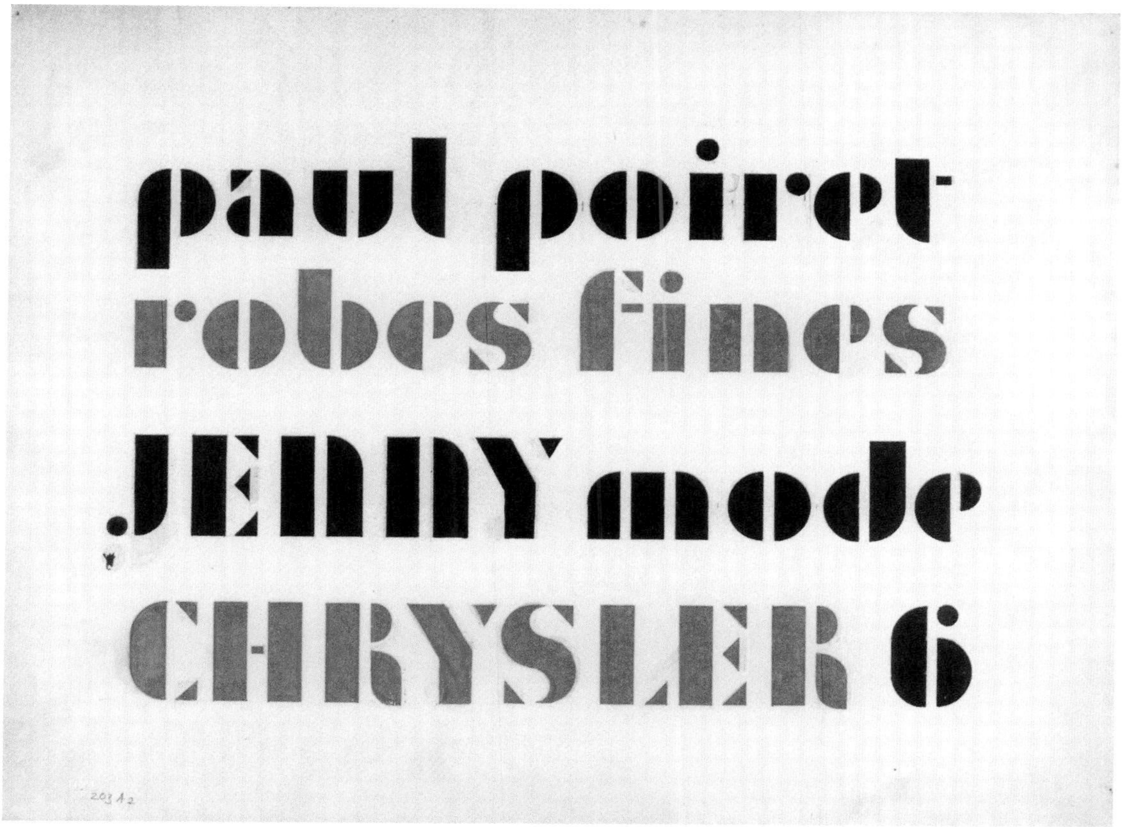

paul poiret·

robes fines

JENNY mode

CHRYSLER 6

frankfurter

illustrierte

heute neu!

Further drawings by Tschichold used as models
by the 'Amsterdam' typefoundry. These are
signed on the back: 'Jan Tschichold 1929'.

A B C a b c d e f g
D E F h i j k l m n
G H I o p q r s t u
J K L v w x y z ! ?
M N O
P Q R
S T U
V W X . , ; : ' -)
Y Z &
1 2 3 4 5 6 7 8 9 0

Ontwerp van letter en proef door Jan Tschichold

N. V. Lettergieterij „Amsterdam" voorheen N. Tetterode, Amsterdam, Bilderdijkstraat 157-165

Corps 84/72 No. 2560	PLETPERS	Minimum 18 Kg. 4 A, 7 a	De Binder
Corps 72/60 No. 2559	NOIR ROUGE	Minimum 15 Kg. 4 A, 10 a	bleu et gris
Corps 60 No. 2558	LETTERBORD	Minimum 13 Kg. 5 A, 10 a	Letters en wit
Corps 48 No. 2557	EFTERGIVENHED	Minimum 11 Kg. 5 A, 13 a	Danmarks musik
Corps 36 No. 2556	BULLETIN DES HALLES	Minimum 10 Kg. 7 A, 17 a	Fonderie de Caractères
Corps 28 No. 2555	HANDBUCH DER ERDKUNDE	Minimum 8 Kg. 9 A, 22 a	Schriftschreiben für Setzer
Corps 24 No. 2554	UNOBTRUSIVE CHARACTERISTIC	Minimum 7 Kg. 12 A, 27 a	Remunerative method introduced

Transito Moderne letter voor slagregels Ontworpen door Jan Tschichold   N. V. Lettergieterij „Amsterdam" voorheen N. Tetterode Amsterdam (West)

a strikingly new
type face
something quite
different
which will please
your customer:

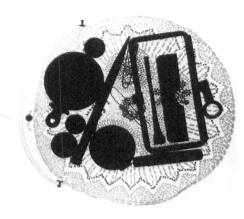

Showroom en Magazijn · Spui 7, Amsterdam · Telefoon No. 33511

bardin & cie

TRANSITO

intertype

For the first time a cross section of up-to-date development in photography is given in Franz Roh's and Jan Tschichold's book

PHOTO-EYE

76 photos of the period. Size 210 × 297 mm. in two-coloured stiff brochure with imprint 76 pages. China in black stitching one-side print. English and German text. In boards RM 2.50

The main styles are considered: the reality-photo the photo without camera, photomounting, photo and painting, photo-typography.

A material as actual, novel and comprehensive as will scarcely be met with again. Only what may be considered an expression of the new age has been taken. The book contains work by Atget, Baumeister, Bayer, Burchartz, Max Ernst, Feininger, Finsler, Gross, Heartfield, Florence Henri, Lissitzky, Man Ray, Moholy-Nagy, Priester[?], Petschow, Renger-Patzsch, Schuitema, Stone, Tabard, Vordemberge, Weston, Zwart and many others.

Not only should it be in the hands of everyone who photographs and wishes to measure his own capability with masterly achievements, and thereby to improve but in the hand of all concerned with seeing, such as artists, lay-out-men architects, historians of the arts, lovers of nature and connoisseurs.

Akademischer Verlag Dr. Fritz Wedekind & Co. Stuttgart, Kanzweinstrasse 58

de betere zetmachine, zoowel voor boek- als courant- en handelswerk. De eenvoudigste uitvoering

(type A, éénmagazijnmachine) kan te allen tijde uitgebouwd worden tot bijvoorbeeld bovenstaande

machine (type C·3sm, 3 groote en 3 zijmagazijnen) en vormt dan een complete zetterij op zichzelf.

N.V. Lettergieterij „Amsterdam" voorheen N. Tetterode

Transito type specimen designed by Tschichold.
1931. A4. (Opposite) back/front; other side.
(Above) Specimen fully folded out.

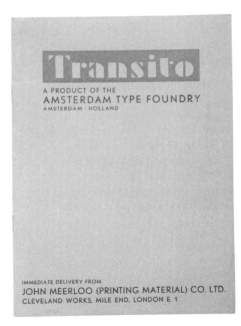

Cover and spreads from English type specimen
for Transito (not designed by Tschichold).
c.1931. 27 × 19.7 cm.

Detail of 48 & 30 point type sizes from
specimen above. Actual size.

Grand Exteriors
FRENCH EDITION
Historic Marine Invention
ELECTRIC POWER HOUSE 5

It seems that Tschichold alerted Albers to some geometric type units from the Otto Weisert typefoundry (Stuttgart) that were clearly an unauthorized adaptation of Albers's second iteration of his stencil-like design, the 'Combination script', published in the Bauhaus journal at the beginning of 1931. Here Albers took his theory much further, advocating the design as a kind of deconstructed typeface, with which letters could be assembled in a variety of ways from a limited number of geometric type units. This very system was realized in the type units from Otto Weisert, with some results that were similar to Albers's proposals. Albers asked Tschichold if he might provide an expert testimony for an ensuing lawsuit, which he did in a letter, also recommending that Albers ask Burchartz ('he has fortunately not needed to make any typefaces, and is therefore unsuspicious, reputable, a professor etc.'). Albers's 'Combination script' went on to be produced, with his authorization, as units of glass for making letters in signs. Tschichold asked for a specimen to be sent to his brother Werner, who was going to take over their father's sign-making business in Leipzig.

The spate of new stencil typefaces around 1930, dominated by the success of Futura Black, must have persuaded the Berthold typefoundry, which had declined Tschichold's design, to reconsider this category of type. Albers was discussing with Berthold the adaptation of his own design during the correspondence with Tschichold. In reply to Albers's request for some advice on what to demand as a fee, Tschichold informed him:

> either one sells type designs for a flat fee, so for a one-off payment – i sold my transito like this for 500 marks as a sketch – or one arranges a sum for the drawing and a royalty, which is greater or smaller depending on the kind of type (display or text type), mostly 2% to 5%. on this basis, for an italic type i received 800 marks and 5%, and for another display type i received 1000 marks and 2%. i believe that you would do best to take a one-off payment, and i suspect that you could be very satisfied with 4–600 marks, given the bad situation of the berthold foundry.[30]

The italic type referred to here was Saskia, produced in 1931 by the Schelter & Giesecke foundry of Leipzig. In its own way it could also be termed a stencil typeface, given that its letters are characterized by disjunctions between their different strokes. It is a true sanserif italic, rather a rarity in those days, produced in one delicate weight but in a range of sizes beginning at 10 point. When well printed, as it was in its sumptuous type specimen, the breaks in the letters survived even at smaller sizes and did not prove so disturbing. Given that the basic idea of the typeface was this relatively intrusive novelty, it was resolved in the best way possible.

30. Letter Tschichold to Albers, 16 February 1932.

Sketch for Saskia. c.1931. Half actual size.

Saskia in 10, 28 & 48 point sizes as shown in the type specimen (see overleaf). Actual size.

einer Gasterei, an der der Rektor, Johann Erhard Kapp, Professor der Eloquenz, verschiedene Professoren der Universität und die meisten Buchhändler der Stadt Leipzig teilnahmen. Kein Redner war nach seiner Stellung, nach seinen Ideen und Plänen in der wissenschaftlichen und gesellschaftlichen Welt mehr berufen, eine solche Aufgabe zu erfüllen, als Gottsched.

na per baciare le chiome bionde; ma sorridevo allorquando sentivo dirmi che il fuoco del ca-

Die Entwicklungsgeschichte

SASKIA

S · A · S · K · I · A

Raucht
Nestor Lord
Zigarette

Cover, title-page and spreads of type specimen for Saskia, designed and printed in-house at the Schelter & Giesecke typefoundry. 1932. 30 × 21.2 cm. Tschichold was paid 75 marks for overseeing the design (his credit was 'Artistic consultant'). On seeing the finished object he commented: 'although i am not completely satisfied with everything in the saskia specimen, the booklet does make a very nice impression.' (Letter Tschichold to Schelter & Giesecke, 27 October 1932; DNB Leipzig.) 'Saskia' was the name of Rembrandt's wife, hence the portraits on the cover and title-page.

Tschichold was not entirely happy either with the realization of the typeface. He regretted that the typefoundry had adhered to the *Normallinie* (standard line) of the German type industry, which determined vertical proportions and specifically the position of the baseline on the metal type body, so that typefaces mixed on the same line would share this baseline. The standard line was biased in proportion towards gothic type, resulting in short descenders, which was Tschichold's principal objection in the case of Saskia. He wondered afterwards whether the baseline could not be placed one point higher, given that other types would rarely be mixed with Saskia on the same line.

Although it was not a bestseller, Schelter & Giesecke were happy with the initial sales of the typeface.

On the left here are two images of the same spread: the first showing the cover of a tipped-in booklet on the right-hand page; the second showing it open.

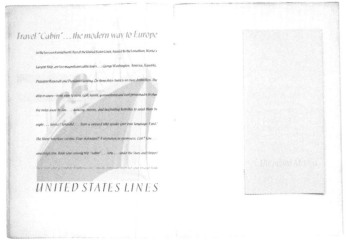

Two views of the same spread from the Saskia type specimen. 1932. The tipped-in leaflet on the right hand-page is shown first closed, and then folded out.

When fully extended and held flat (as it is not here) the left hand edge of the leaflet aligns precisely with the edge of the opposing page of the specimen.

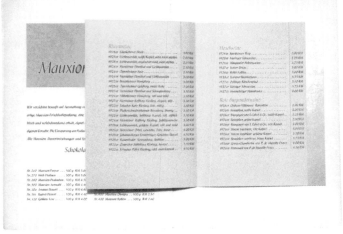

Again, two views of the same spread, with tipped-in leaflet shown first closed, and then folded out.

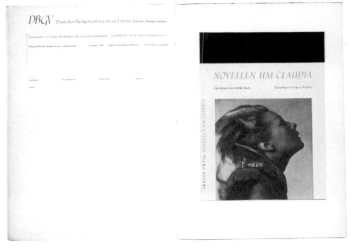

Two more spreads from the Saskia type specimen, showing tipped-in leaflets (unopened) on different papers.

The most lucrative of Tschichold's three early typefaces, assuming that his royalties never amounted to much, was Zeus, produced by Schriftguß AG of Dresden (formerly Brüder Butter typefoundry). It was another single-variant display type, which Max Caflisch accurately described as a 'cross between fat-face roman and so-called calligraphic sanserif [*Federgrotesk*]'.[31] Again, the novelty value of such a hybrid character accords with Tschichold's intention to make some quick money by entering into the rapacious market for new typefaces in Germany. Zeus is an elegant and inventive twist within typographic tradition, which could have found an effective, if limited, place in New Typography. Yet none of Tschichold's three typefaces (all produced in 1931) were likely to have become popular in the renewed enthusiasm for gothic type that began a mere two years later in the Third Reich's period of 'national uplift'.

Tschichold's experiences in designing his trio of display types provoked a temporary disdain for the activity. Presumably this was due in large part to the faulty real-ization of Transito, although he developed a principled argument against designing new typefaces, which he explained to Albers:

> personally i am sick and tired of making typefaces. essentially, in my opinion, it is not a task of typography. i have done two others apart from transito, but only to earn money, and at that time i really had to do it. i find new typefaces fundamentally and absolutely superfluous. in the best cases, new typefaces have a momentary effect, and that is really quite minimal. what we make should be lasting, but: primum vivere …
>
> the production of new types is only a 'necessity' within capitalism. where advertising is transformed into scientific communication (in socialism) the typeface nonsense is pointless.[32]

Type specimen folder for Zeus. 1931.
26.2 × 20 cm. Not designed by Tschichold.

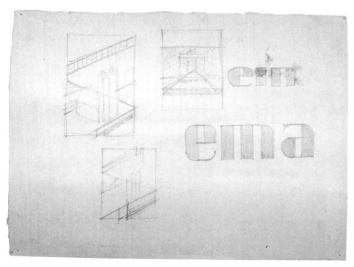

Sketch for Zeus (alongside thumbnail for poster shown on p.93). c.1930.

Zeus used on cover of *Typographische Mitteil-ungen* (1932). 32.5 × 23.1 cm. Probably designed by Tschichold.

31. Caflisch, *Die Schriften von Renner, Tschichold und Trump*, p.28.

32. Letter Tschichold to Albers, 8 December 1931.

Die Scholle

von Vicente Blasco Ibañez, ins Deutsche übertragen von Elisabeth und Otto Albrecht van Bebber, enthält nicht weniger als 21 große Illustrationen nach Zeichnungen des spanischen Künstlers José Benlliure. Das reich illustrierte Werk wird zum **Vorzugspreis von 1,60 Mark** an die Mitglieder der Büchergilde Gutenberg abgegeben. Jedes Mitglied

Detail of advertisement for the Büchergilde Gutenberg from *Typographische Mitteilungen* (1932). Probably not designed by Tschichold.

Geschlecht und Liebe

Zeus used on the cover of a Büchergilde Gutenberg edition (1932). Not designed by Tschichold.

The second part of this argument showed perhaps that Tschichold had taken to heart the critical Bauhaus review of *Die neue Typographie*, which had made a very similar suggestion (see p.81). The idea resurfaced in Tschichold's important essay of 1932, 'Wo stehen wir heute?', in which he further developed his theory of New Typography (see appendix D). He elaborated his own suggestion made two years earlier in *Eine Stunde Druckgestaltung* that, while sanserif was still the most modern type style, historical typefaces could provide useful variation when used alongside it, mainly for headings. Indeed from 1930 Tschichold's own practice of New Typography began to loosen up, with typefaces other than sanserif, including fat-face, slab-serif and script types, featuring on some book covers and book jackets that he designed (see pp.205–14). This was also reflected in the occasional use of such typefaces for display purposes in student work supervised by Tschichold at the Munich schools. In 1932 he stated categorically: 'For us today *one* typeface for all purposes is, in the long run, too *boring*.' He now believed that 'structure' (*Aufbau*) was a more decisive factor in typography than choice of typeface.[33] This confirms a viewpoint that was implicit in his theories from the beginning: namely that sanserif type was not absolutely essential for 'elemental' typography.

In some ways Tschichold may also have been attempting to clarify the seemingly contradictory position that Konrad Bauer had highlighted in his published reply to Tschichold earlier that year. Bauer had already remarked that the appearance of Saskia, and moreover the fact that it was designed by Tschichold, signalled the beginnings of a middle way that would develop between the extremes of historicism and modernism.[34] Tschichold referred obliquely to Bauer's comments: 'Also the Zeus and Saskia types are not "more modern" than sanserif; they merely offer the possibility of a variation. A programmatic meaning does not benefit them in any way.'[35]

When responding in early 1933 to the questions specifically pertaining to letterform style in *Typographische Mitteilungen*'s survey, Tschichold reasserted that 'sanserif will remain the most valid stylistic expression of the period

in type for a long time to come'; yet, on the matter of gothic type, he allowed that 'the use of very small doses in new typography is justified, when fraktur is used as a contrasting typeface'. On historical types in general he continued: 'to leave unexploited all earlier typefaces is so absurd that one surely does not need to take a position against it. new effects can also be achieved with old typefaces through contrast (the most important artistic means of new typography).'[36] Although he had conceded from the beginning, in 1925, that elemental typography would 'necessarily also change continually' (see appendix A), he probably did not have in mind the re-inclusion of 'historicist' elements, and so he felt obliged, seven years on, to dialectically justify his allowance of historical typefaces into New Typography's repertoire: they could only be admitted so long as they served a greater aim – the creation of 'contrast'.

Tschichold himself sought a commission to design a new gothic typeface for display purposes during the three months between his being freed from prison and his emigration to Switzerland. In May 1933 he proposed several ideas to the Schelter & Giesecke typefoundry for 'gotische Schriften', by which he meant typefaces in the most rationalized and severe category of broken scripts (Textura), which could be used mainly in combination with Fraktur text types. Given that he had lost his teaching post and was without income or secure future prospects, his suggestions were naturally a pragmatic attempt to exploit the resurgent preference for gothic type fostered by the Nazis. He remarked neutrally to the typefoundry: 'It is probable that Fraktur typefaces will be more frequently requested by customers in the next few years.'[37] His proposals, which were in any case not taken up, were more historically based than the brutalist school of new gothic types that emerged during

33. 'Wo stehen wir heute?', pp.102–5. Tschichold further elaborated his strategies for 'Type mixtures' in an article of that name first published in German in 1935.

34. Bauer in *Klimschs Jahrbuch* (Jg.24, 1931), p.18.

35. 'Wo stehen wir heute?', p.104.

36. *Typographische Mitteilungen*, Jg.30, H.3, March 1933, p.65; *Schriften*, 1, p.120. He concluded: 'every astute person will object to a use of fraktur meant in any other way.' (Incidentally, here he implied

that contrast was more important than, for example, asymmetry.)

37. Letter Tschichold to Schelter & Giesecke, 10 May 1933 (DNB Leipzig). Tschichold was so concerned to phrase his suggestion correctly that he made three drafts of the letter.

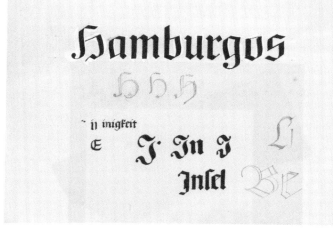

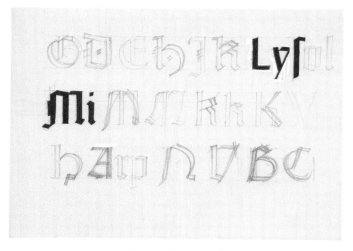

Sketches for new gothic typefaces submitted to
Schelter & Giesecke. 1933.

the Third Reich. Four years later, from the perspective of his
Swiss exile, he attacked that style of typeface – examples of
which were Element, National, and Tannenberg – as coarse
travesties of a worthy historical type-style:

> After the rupture [*Umbruch*] it was attempted in Germany to
> give typography a new face with certain, new Textura types
> robbed of any finer form. Unfortunately these typefaces are
> devoid of the slightest feeling for good draftsmanship and of
> any knowledge of historical precedent. They will not stand
> the test of time. Their traditionless form, empty of invention,
> is concealed by a bluff of clumsy strength.[38]

He maintained here the view that an exclusive use of gothic
type was 'an uncontemporary, reactionary exaggeration and
is at least unthinkable in other countries where German
is spoken' (namely Switzerland). Yet, as a calligrapher and
historian, he could appreciate the qualities of good Fraktur
types and defended them from the aesthetic and ideological
abuse they were suffering under Nazi rule:

> Unfortunately the equation Fraktur = German = Third Reich,
> which is in every respect incorrect, will only hasten the
> decline of this beautiful historical type-style in the countries
> outside of Germany.

(The Nazis later realized that gothic type was a hindrance
to communication with foreign subjects of their expanding
empire, and banned it in favour of roman in 1941.)
   During his last few years in Germany, Tschichold had
already begun to appreciate again the graphic qualities of
classic types from the past. As his friend Werner Doede later
remarked, this may well have ensued from his responsibilities as a teacher in Munich:

> Perhaps his teaching activity there stimulated him to broaden
> the basis of what he was offering, perhaps the magnificent,
> inborn gift for calligraphy demanded satisfaction and gave
> rise subliminally to an initially almost imperceptible tension
> with the exclusive reform programme of the revolutionary
> typographer: in any case Tschichold began to investigate the
> history of script and printing in an autodidactic (and self-
> critical) manner. A practical consequence of this was that he
> began to collect early type specimens and writing manuals.[39]

In Doede's view, 'The self-certainty of the reformer had not
hardened Tschichold.' He must have realized that teaching
at the Munich schools could not be exclusively ordered
around the stylistic preferences of New Typography if it was
to realistically serve the students in their working lives. His
historical studies led to a very useful summary of 'the most
important historical typefaces' for the Munich schools'
journal, *Grafische Berufsschule* (plus, more obscurely, a short
piece on 'pre-gothic book illumination'). That he felt a new
approach could only develop from an appreciation of
history was made clear in the two instructional manuals
exemplifying his teaching of this period.

38. 'Die Entwicklung der
neuen Typographie in den
mitteleuropäischen Ländern',
p.126. From this judgement he
excepted modern gothic types
by Trump, Weiß and Koch.

39. Doede, 'Beim Tee' in
Luidl, *J.T.*, p.20. This passage is
also later taken into Doede's
contribution to *Beiheft Die neue
Typographie*.

Two books on writing and drawing letters

Schriftschreiben für Setzer (Formal writing for compositors; 1931) and *Typografische Entwurfstechnik* (The technics of typographic layout; 1932) make clear the consummate craft skill that lay beneath Tschichold's theorizing. The first is a concise and precisely written calligraphic primer and shows that, despite his eschewing the technique in his own works of New Typography, Tschichold never lost his feeling and appreciation for historical scripts. He saw calligraphy as an important educational tool:

> Formal writing [*Schriftschreiben*] is not an end in itself for the printer, nonetheless it is a necessary supplement to his specialist knowledge. Since all earlier forms of script more or less clearly show the form-defining influence of broad-nib pens, it enables him to better understand the historical categories of script, to distinguish between good and bad typefaces, and to more easily prepare layout sketches.[40]

This was the principle behind the prominent place occupied by such writing practice in the curricula of the Graphische Berufsschule and Meisterschule in Munich. Tschichold felt that, in *Schriftschreiben für Setzer,* he treated the subject 'in a contemporary form, free from ballast'.[41]

After an informative summary of historical development in script, Tschichold began with an exercise for writing roman capitals & small letters in sanserif form with a mono-line pen. He recommended this as the best place to start and also the most important of the scripts to be learned, partly because it could be used as a substitute for others. Of the roman capitals he stated: 'Their forms live in us as a model', and offered his 'Block-script' version as the 'skeleton form of the ancient Roman script.'[42] He employed such sanserif writing for the smaller text elements on early posters from his avant-garde period. His approach to making these letters was different to the strictly geometric and modular script construction taught at the Bauhaus. In a typically precise and succinct sentence, he summarized: 'Rhythm and legibility derive not from similarity and identical width of letters, rather from characteristic form and regulated difference.'[43] Although Tschichold recommended writing his exercises on squared paper, the grid was only taken as a guideline on the vertical axis; the widths of letters were not rigidly defined by modules of the grid, nor were the stroke thicknesses of the letters, which were instead derived from the flow of the writing tool. Indeed he explained:

The essential forms of the skeletal small letters are the same as in the capitals: circle, triangle, square. Yet all three basic forms should not have their full width; otherwise the script will run too wide. So proportionally 'narrow' circles and generally narrow forms should be constructed.[44]

In contrast, the script teaching by Joost Schmidt that formed an obligatory part of the Bauhaus preliminary course was at first restricted to constructing capital letters geometrically, and then took Bayer's universal alphabet as its basis. In Schmidt's teaching letters were drawn with compass and ruler within the confines of a grid, compared to the organic definition of Tschichold's written letters. The only purely grid-bound script proposed by Tschichold was a model for quickly making letters by cutting out and adding to photographic prints for producing artwork. This was published in no fewer than eight journals. Perhaps its most interesting appearance was in the *Börsenblatt für den Deutschen Buchhandel,* where it breaks into a page typeset in Fraktur (see overleaf).

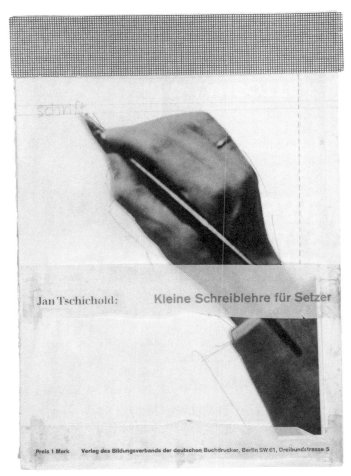

Jan Tschichold: Kleine Schreiblehre für Setzer

Preis 1 Mark   Verlag des Bildungsverbands der deutschen Buchdrucker, Berlin SW 61, Dreibundstrasse 5

40. *Schriftschreiben für Setzer*, p.1.

41. *Typografische Gestaltung*, p.7. Renner also wrote an article justifying the teaching of formal writing: see Burke, *Paul Renner*, p.209.

42. This had also been Edward Johnston's view. On receiving copies of Tschichold's two instructional books, Lissitzky congratulated him: 'all in all your books will have the same importance for our movement as larisch and jonston [sic] for the last one, and more besides.' Letter Lissitzky to Tschichold, 29 September 1932. Translated in Perloff & Reed, *Situating El Lissitzky*, p.256.

43. *Schriftschreiben für Setzer*, p.6.

44. *Schriftschreiben für Setzer*, p.8.

Rough layout for cover of the book that became *Schriftschreiben für Setzer. c.*1931. A4. Shows that it was initially intended for publication by the Bildungsverband. Disagreement over Tschichold's historical approach may have resulted in it being issued by another publisher (Klimsch). The Bildungsverband did publish its own manual, *Elementare Schriftunterweisung* (1931) by Wilhelm Lesemann and H. Wehmeier, which concentrated on geometric construction of letterforms. A rather curt review of *Schriftschreiben für Setzer* in *Typographische Mitteilungen* (Jg.28 H.12, 1931) pointed out sharply that Tschichold's book did not address 'constructive script design'.

ABCDEFGHIJKK?
LMNOPQRRSTUV
WXYYZ DORNIER
123456789 Rudi

Jan Tschichold: Neue konstruierbare Blockschrift. Grossstaben.

abcdefghijkklm
nöpqrstuvwxy
yzß .,:!()
blumen manoli

Jan Tschichold: Neue konstruierbare Blockschrift. Kleinstaben.

Artwork of Tschichold's 'new, constructible block-script'. *c.*1930.

(A digital version of this script is used for chapter headings in the present book.)

180

Wir erwähnen noch die bibliographischen Nachschlagewerke über alte Bücher und Kunstpublikationen. Jeder Buchhändler, der in antiquarischen Büchern spezialisiert ist, kann sich über sie leicht informieren.

Schließlich besitzt jeder Buchhändler allgemeine Nachschlagewerke in seinem Geschäft. An erster Stelle sollte er die großen Enzyklopädien von Larousse benutzen, die universellen Ruf haben, und die mit den Biographien der Schriftsteller auch ihre Werke aufführen. Auch den „Manuel bibliographique de la Littérature française« von G. Lanson kann man zu Rate ziehen, doch gibt es leider die Verleger nicht mit an.

Man kann diese kurze Übersicht einer Fachbibliothek des Buchhändlers nicht beenden, ohne auf die Publikationen hinzuweisen,

die er lesen muß, um sich über seinen Beruf zu unterrichten. Es ist sehr bedauerlich, daß die Bibliographie de la France keine redaktionellen Seiten bringt, ähnlich den wichtigen und reichhaltigen des Börsenblattes. Das »Bulletin de la Maison du Livre Français« und das »Bulletin des Libraires« bringen Vereins-Mitteilungen, die zu lesen eines jeden Buchhändlers Pflicht ist. Das letztere ist nur den Mitgliedern des französischen Sortimenter-Vereins zugänglich und kann nicht abonniert werden. Für seine Allgemeinbildung wäre es erwünscht, daß der Buchhändler sich mehr für Publikationen interessiere wie: „Les Nouvelles Littéraires« und »La Quinzaine critique«, die ihm die Augen über die Geistesbewegungen der Gegenwart öffnen.

(Übersetzt von Fritz Franke, Leipzig.)

Jan Tschichold: Leicht und schnell konstruierbare Schrift für Aufschriften aller Art, Schilder, Entwürfe, Ausstellungen, Ladendekorationen, Fotomontagen usw., ohne Vorkenntnisse von jedermann herstellbar.

Man zeichnet auf farbiges Papier oder Karton ein Netz aus Quadraten und trägt darauf die Buchstaben nach der Vorlage ein. (Man benützt zweckmäßig die Rückseite des Papiers und zeichnet die Buchstaben spiegelverkehrt. Damit spart man die Beseitigung der Hilfslinien.) Dann ausschneiden und rhythmisch montieren (z. B. auf das Foto aufkleben).

(Gleichmaß der Wörter entsteht nicht durch gleiche lineare Distanz der Buchstaben: in dem Worte SIRIUS z. B. müßten SI und US dichter zusammenstehen. Auch erlaubte die Netzeinteilung keine rhythmische Ordnung der ABC-Folgen.)

Kleinbuchstaben sind besser zu lesen und schneller herzustellen, daher den Großbuchstaben vorzuziehen.

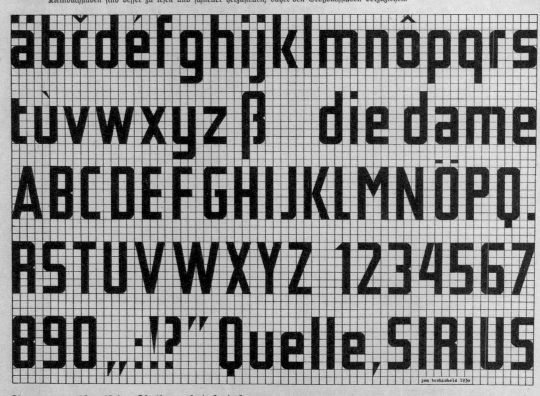

Neue amerikanische Antiquariatskataloge.
Von Ludwig Schütz (Chicago).

Soweit zu übersehen ist, zeigt das Gesamtbild der stattlichen Reihe von amerikanischen Antiquariatskatalogen, die vom Herbst 1929 bis zum Frühjahr 1930 erschienen sind, wenig Unterschied von dem der letzten Jahre. Es bleibt vorwiegend die Tendenz, Auswahl- und Sammelverzeichnisse zu bringen und sich darin etwas einseitig auf die übliche Auswahl von Americana Erstausgaben, Englische Literatur, Seltene Werke, Pressendrucke usw. festzulegen. Die Produktion der Kataloge ist steigend, manche neue Namen von Antiquaren tauchen auf, während die Qualität der Verzeichnisse — von

den New Yorker Auktionen abgesehen — im allgemeinen wieder auf gutes Durchschnittsangebot herauskommt. Es sei deshalb heute davon Abstand genommen, über die gemischten Kataloge der bekannten und rührigen New Yorker und Provinzantiquare (wie Dauber & Pine, C. H. Wells, C. Dressel North, Argosy Bookstore, Cadmus Bookshop, sowie Libbie-Boston, Ruebush-Dayton, Dawson-Los Angeles usw. usw.) zu berichten, sondern es sollen einige bedeutendere Spezialkataloge erwähnt werden, die ihrer persönlichen Note in Inhalt und Einteilung wegen von besonderem Interesse erscheinen: The French Book Store-New York bringt einen reichhaltigen Katalog ausschließlich französischer Bücher aller schöngeistigen Ge-

Tschichold's 'quick and easy' method for constructing letters. 1930. The explanation reads: 'for inscriptions of all kinds, signs, drawings, exhibitions, shop decoration, photomontages etc; can be made by everyone, no previous experience necessary. / Draw on coloured paper a grid of squares and map the letters onto it following the model. (Use the rear side of the paper and draw the letters back to front, to save having to get rid of the construction lines.) Then cut out and assemble rhythmically (for example, stick onto a photo). / (Regularity of the words does not stem from using the same space between all letters: in the word SIRIUS, for example, the SI and US should be closer together. Also the grid prevented rhythmical placement of the alphabet itself.) / Small letters are better to read and quicker to make, and are therefore preferable to capitals.'

In *Schriftschreiben für Setzer* Tschichold moved on to the broad-pen scripts, including Latin minuscule (without serifs) and roman, and several gothic hands. He placed the gothic scripts last in a recommended order of contemporary relevance (although they do not appear last in the book), but dedicated as much respect and attention to his explanations of how to achieve them as to any other. He also included the article he had written for *Grafische Berufsschule* about the best available 'historical' types, both roman and gothic. Here he commented that, among roman types, 'One of the purest forms is the roman of the French punchcutter Garamond, dating from around 1540.'[45] This would become a refrain throughout the rest of Tschichold's career, culminating in the design of his own dignified version of Garamond, Sabon (released in 1967).

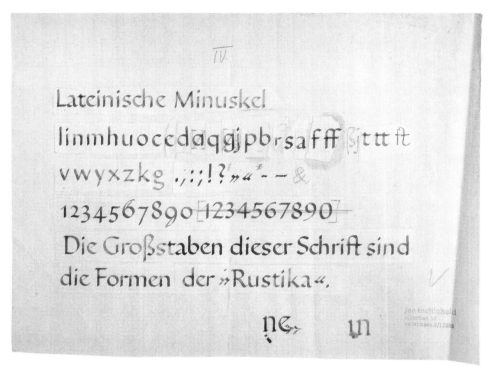

Preliminary sketches for *Schriftschreiben für Setzer*. c.1931. Around half of actual size.

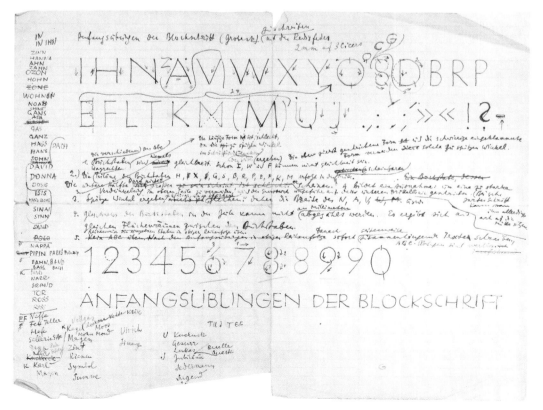

45. *Schriftschreiben für Setzer*, p.27. In the original article, Tschichold also mentioned and showed an example of another of his later favourites, the type known as Janson.

Cover and pages from *Schriftschreiben für Setzer*. 1931. A5.

(Overleaf) Spreads from the same book.

Unterlängen gelten als Nebenlinien, sie sollen nicht gesondert gezogen, sondern frei bestimmt werden. (Dies ist wichtig für alles spätere Skizzieren! Die meisten Irrtümer über die Länge von Zeilen entstehen aus falschen Zeilenlinien. Man nimmt beim Skizzieren bestimmter Grade, wenn es sich nicht um reine Versalzeilen handelt, immer die Höhe des kleinen a ab; die

Größe der Ober- und Unterlängen ist ohne Einfluß auf die Breite der Schrift.)

Die **Buchstabenabstände** müssen gleichmäßig gebildet werden. Parallelen dürfen nicht zu eng stehen: so soll der Raum zwischen i und n im Worte »in« nur wenig kleiner sein als der Abstand zwischen beiden Senkrechten des n. Sonst rückt

iltvwyxzköädqgb pc
esnmhrfßjüttffft.,:;!?-
»Gemeine« 12345678
90 fotomechanisch cm

alte Regel, daß z. B. i-n nicht wesentlich enger stehen dürfen als die beiden Senkrechten im n, ist auch hier zu beachten. Alle Antiqua, auch diese Schrift, muß ziemlich offen dastehen. Die Zeilen sollen in dieser Schrift niemals ganz dicht zusammenrücken, sondern immer »durchschossen«, die Wortabstände aber enger sein als die Zeilenabstände.

Wenn wir die Kleinstaben (in verschiedenen Größen) beherrschen, nehmen wir die Großstaben aus unserer »Rustika« hinzu. Diese werden, wie in unserer Skelettschrift, ein wenig kleiner als die Oberlängen der Gemeinen geschrieben, da sie sonst zu groß wirken und stören. — Die einfache Kursiv von Seite 31 kann gleich nach dieser Schrift geschrieben werden.

linmhüöcedqpbrsäfffßjttt
ftvwyxzkg.,:;!?»«-&
1234567890 minuskel 800
Die Großstaben bilden die
Formen der Rustika · Konrad

184

18 Schwabacher (6)

Die sogenannte Schwabacher-Druckschrift ist aus der gotischen Verkehrsschrift abgeleitet, die schneller als die feierliche Textur geschrieben wurde und daher, im Gegensatz zum Gitter der Textur, einen Wechsel runder und gerader Striche zeigt. Die meisten Rundungen der Karlingischen Minuskel sind geblieben; sie bilden jedoch keine reinen Kreise, sondern werden oben und unten zugespitzt geschrieben. Der gotische Stil zeigt sich weiterhin in den gebrochenen aber einfachern Formen g, f, m, n, r, u und den Großstaben, die im Wesen denen der Textur gleichen, doch ein wenig flüssiger sind. Die Rundungen vieler Gemeinen und die einfachern Versalien machen die Schrift besser lesbar als die Textur und geben der Schrift eine große Lebendigkeit (siehe auch die Übersicht auf Seite 22).

Wir üben zunächst mit der Rundschriftfeder 2 (To 62) und mit Tinte die Gemeinen (das n auf 1¹/₂ Kästchen oder 3 Nonpareille), wozu wir mit Bleistift eine Hilfslinie in der Mitte zwischen zwei Linien des Heftes ziehen. Die Oberlängen wie b und die Versalien sollen dann etwas über zwei Kästchen

(etwas über 2 Cicero) hoch sein, ebenso die Unterlängen. Zunächst schreiben wir die Kleinstaben, einzeln, dann zusammenhängenden Text nur aus solchen; dann folgen Einzelübungen der Großen, schließlich zusammenhängende Texte mit Kleinen und Großen. Die Ziffern werden genau wie in der lateinischen Minuskel (Seite 13) gebildet. Der Zwischenraum zwischen den Zeilen darf nur gering sein. Die Schwabacher muß dicht zusammenstehende Buchstaben mit geringem Wort- und geringem Zeilenabstand zeigen. Die späteren Übungen schreibt man mit schmäleren Federn in kleineren Größen.

Wer Zeit und Lust hat, kann nach den Übungen der Vorschrift die gotischen Verkehrsschriften der Seite 20, später die »Bâtarde« (am Fuße der Seite 20) nachschreiben. Ähnlich der deutschen gotischen Verkehrsschrift ist diese französische Schrift, wie der Name sagt, eine Mischform aus Textur und Karlingischer Minuskel, wie die Schwabacher. Sie gehört der gleichen Zeit an. Wir zeigen eine ihr nachgebildete Type, zu der bemerkt sei, daß die Formen H und L, wenn nicht falsch, doch mißverstanden, und V, W und Y neugebildete Formen sind. Wer die Type nachschreibt, verwende lieber ら, ℒ, 𝒱, 𝔴, 𝔜.

20 Punkt Alte Schwabacher. Schriftgießerei Genzsch & Heyse, Hamburg.

In einem schönen, fernen Reiche, von dem die Sage
ABCDEFGHIJKLMNOPQRSTUVWXYZ
abcdefghijklmnopqrstuvwxyzäáöüfffiflssistßtz& .,-:!?

24 Antiqua (8)

Die Antiqua, eine Mischung der Kapitalformen mit der Karlingischen Minuskel, versieht die Minuskelformen mit gleichen oder ähnlichen Schraffen wie die Versalien, um den stilistischen Zwiespalt zwischen Versalien und »Gemeinen« zu mindern. Die Antiqua ist eine Erfindung der Renaissance und wird von den Schreibern gegen Ende des 15. Jahrhunderts aus der wieder aufgenommenen Karlingischen Minuskel entwickelt. Sie bildet die Vorlage für die ersten reinen Antiquatypen, für die Mediävalantiqua (siehe das geschichtliche Beispiel Seite 26).

Die Grundformen der Versalien sind die unserer »Rustika« (Seite 11), die der Gemeinen jene der »Lateinischen Minuskel« (Seite 13) Zunächst nehmen wir eine Rundschriftfeder 2¹/₂ (=To 62¹/₂) und schreiben damit die n-Größe auf 2 Kästchen (2 Cicero). Die Oberlängen sind 1¹/₂ Kästchen (3 Nonpareille) höher, die Unterlängen fast ebensoviel länger. Später kann man mit schmäleren Federn kleiner schreiben. Immer aber soll die Antiqua zart, der Raum zwischen den Zeilen groß bleiben. Wir können gleich mit Tinte schreiben. Die Schraffen etwa des I sind straff waagerecht und kurz zu halten. Der schräge Ansatz, wie er etwa beim i oben und beim h oben erscheint wird mit einem schrägen Abstrich nach links begonnen. Dann schreibt man, ohne abzusetzen, einen schrägen hohlen Bogen nach rechts, setzt jetzt ab und schreibt von oben her den Senkrechten. Vergleiche das Beispiel nebenan. Die Antiqua setzt große Sorgfalt beim Schreiben voraus. Sie soll exakt, aber nicht gezwungen, sondern flüssig wirken. Alle Bogen (bei n, m, h, u, c, d, a, g, p, r, s, f, ff, ß, j, U, C, G, S, J) müssen,

sehr flach geschrieben werden; hohe Bogen würden optische Flecken ergeben und den Lauf der Zeile stören.

Die Abstriche bei u, d und a sind kleine, die des l und t dagegen große Bogen.

Die Versalien müssen wie in allen Schriften ein wenig kleiner geschrieben werden als die Oberlängen der Gemeinen. Die Ziffern gleichen denen der lateinischen Minuskel von Seite 13; nur die 1 erhält unten eine Schraffe.

Durch leichte Schrägstellung und Engerführung läßt sich aus unserer Antiqua unschwer eine passende Kursiv entwickeln. Das Wort »und« der letzten Zeile der gegenüberstehenden Vorschrift zeigt ein Beispiel. Man übe aber vorher die einfache Kursiv von Seite 31.

Das historische Beispiel auf Seite 26 gibt eine schön geschriebene Buchseite wieder aus der Zeit, als man die karlingische Minuskel zu neuem Leben erweckte. Sie zeigt besonders edle Verhältnisse des Zeilenzwischenraums und der Ränder.

So schreibt man den Kopf oben bei i und h:

Die Schwabacher-Type, um 1470 entstanden, ist noch den gotischen Schriftarten zuzurechnen, doch bereitet sie die Formen der Fraktur vor. Die Alte Schwabacher entspricht ziemlich genau den frühen Schwabachertypen, dagegen ist die Gewöhnliche Schwabacher eine blasse, verballhornte Form aus dem Ende des 19. Jahrhunderts, in der alle ursprünglichen Eigenheiten vermieden sind. Sie sollte in guten Drucksachen nicht vorkommen.

19

abcddefghijklmnoopqrſstuvwxy

33·ſſffſt.,:; ſtßtzflſi·!?´&() 1470

ABCDEFGHJKLMNOPQ

RSTUV WXYZ3

Die Schwabacher gehört zu den

gotiſchen Schriftarten; ſie blieb aber

länger im Gebrauch als die Textur.

25

inmhulocdqeapbrsgfffſttt.

vwxyjzkß.,:;-!? 1500

ILHEFTUOQCGDSJJPB

RKVWAXZYNM

Antiqua besteht

aus Versalien *und* Gemeinen

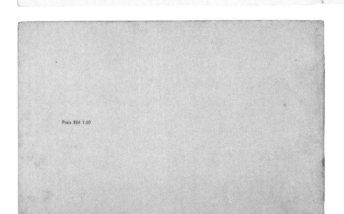

Spreads and back cover from *Schriftschreiben für Setzer*. 1931. A5.

Der moderne Mensch hat tägl
ich eine Unmenge von Gedr
ucktem aufzunehmen, das,
bestellt oder umsonst, ihm in
s Haus geliefert wird und ihm
außerhause in den Plakaten,
Schaufenstern, der Wanders
chrift usw. entgegentritt. Die
neue Zeit unterscheidet sich

man verwerfe das wort vaterland, und
viele stille und edle taten des menschen-
freundes fallen weg, viele steine, die er
trug, weil das wort vaterland darauf-
stand, schüttelt er ab, er tritt auf die la-
sten die er vorher mit patriotischem stolz
auf sich nahm. man verwerfe das wort

52e

FREIBERGER.

Exercises in formal writing carried out by
Tschichold's students in Munich. Around a third
of actual size.

In einem schönen fernen Reiche, von welchem die Sage
ABCDEFGHIJKLMNOPQRSTUVWXYZ
abcdefghijklmnopqrstuvwxyzßäöü!?&1234567890

In einem schönen fernen Reiche, von welchem die Sage lebt, daß
ABCDEFGHIJKLMNOPQRSTUVWXYZ AJKNTV
abcdefghijklmnopqrstuvwxyzßäöü!?&1234567890

In einem schönen fernen Reiche, von welchem die Sage lebt
ABCDEFGHIJKLMNOPQRSTUVWXYZ
abcdefghijklmnopqrstuvwxyzßäöü!?&1234567890

In einem schönen fernen Reiche, von welchem die Sage lebt
ABCDEFGHIJKLMNOPQRSTUVWXYZ
abcdefghijklmnopqrstuvwxyzßäöü!?&1234567890

In einem schönen, fernen Reiche, von welchem die Sage
ABCDEFGHIJKLMNOPQRSTUVWXYZ 1234567890
abcdefghijklmnopqrstuvwxyzchckfffiflßäöü.,-?!*+!§&()

In einem schönen fernen Reiche, von welchem die Sagen
ABCDEFGHIJKLMNOPQRSTUVWXYZÄÖU+!§&*
abcdefghijklmnopqrstuvwxyz ckfffiflß äöü 1234567890

In einem schönen, fernen Reiche, von welchem die
ABCDEFGHIJKLMNOPQRSTUVWXYZ 1234567890
abcdefghijklmnopqrstuvwxyzfffifläöü (.,:;!?'-«) abcd

38

In einem schönen, fernen Reiche, von welchem die
ABCDEFGHIJKLMNOPQRSTUVWXYZ (.,;;!?'-)
abcdefghijklmnopqrstuvw.xyzfffifläöü 1234567890

Tschichold

Unterscheidungsmerkmale der wichtigsten Schriftarten

Gotisch: Alle Rundungen in den Gemeinen gebrochen.

adovs

Mediäval: Schräge Ansätze, bzw. schräger vermittelter Druck bei

lijmnrep

Schwabacher: Link- und rechtseitige Rundung bei

adovs

Französische Antiqua: Nur rechtwinklige Ansätze; Druck in den Bogen senkrecht, kaum vermittelt.

lijmnrep

Fraktur: Halb rund, halb gebrochen.

adovs

Tschichold

Ordnung in der Setzerei

Mitunter ist es nötig, über scheinbar Selbstverständliches zu sprechen, weil merkwürdigerweise gerade das Alltägliche zuerst in Gefahr gerät, vergessen zu werden.

Die Setzerei ist kein Geschäftsunternehmen, hinter dem die konkreten Begriffe Gewinn und Verlust stehen. Als wichtiger Teil des Betriebes aber beeinflußt sie die Bilanz günstig oder ungünstig, kann im übertragenen Sinne rentabel sein oder nicht. Daß sie es nicht ist, hört man leider nur allzuoft, und der Eingeweihte weiß, daß diese Klage vielfach berechtigt ist. Es gibt mancherlei Ursachen hierfür, die außerhalb der Setzerei liegen. Es gibt aber auch eine Menge Dinge innerhalb der Setzerei, deren Nichtbeachtung ihre Produktivität ungünstig beeinflußt. Kein gewissenhafter Betriebsleiter wird sich, vielleicht im glücklichen Besitz ständiger Massenauflagen, mit der Erkenntnis zufrieden geben, daß die Setzerei unrentabel arbeitet, sondern im Gegenteil energisch darauf hinarbeiten, das zu ändern.

Das Erstrebenswerte bei der Setzerei wie beim Gesamtbetrieb ist: Qualität und Wirtschaftlichkeit. Bekanntlich läßt sich sehr leicht das eine auf Kosten des anderen erzielen, also Qualität auf Kosten der Wirtschaftlichkeit und umgekehrt. Daß diese Methode bequem, aber verderblich ist, braucht kaum betont zu werden. Man muß also auch bei mangelnder Rentabilität das gute Niveau seiner Leistungen zu behaupten versuchen und die Abhilfe in anderen Dingen suchen.

Das Wichtigste ist in jedem Falle die richtige Disposition. Wo schlecht disponiert wird, wo die auszugebende Arbeit ständig falsch gewertet wird, wo die Möglichkeiten der Setzmaschine nicht erkannt oder überschätzt werden, wo Personalstand und Bestand an Aufträgen dauernd sich im Mißverhältnis befinden, so daß entweder mit teuren Überstunden gearbeitet wird oder lange Wochen mit unproduktiver Arbeit gefüllt werden, ist ein befriedigender Abschluß nicht zu erwarten. Immerhin sind Mißstände in der Disposition leicht erkennbar und deshalb nicht übermäßig zu fürchten, weil sie sich ziemlich unmittelbar auswirken.

Schwieriger ist es schon, die unproduktiven Stunden herauszufinden und von dieser Seite aus das Problem „Wirtschaftlichkeit" in Angriff zu nehmen. Zur Erfassung der wirklich unproduk-

39

Spread from Tschichold's article 'Die wichtigsten
geschichtlichen Druckschriften' (Most important
historical typefaces) in the journal of the Munich
schools, *Grafische Berufsschule* (Heft 3/4, 1930/1).
A4.

Din A 4 = 210 × 297

Jan Tschichold: **Typografische Entwurfstechnik**

Din A 5 = 148 × 210

Din A 6 = 105 × 148

Din A 7 = 74 × 105

Din A 8 = 52 × 74

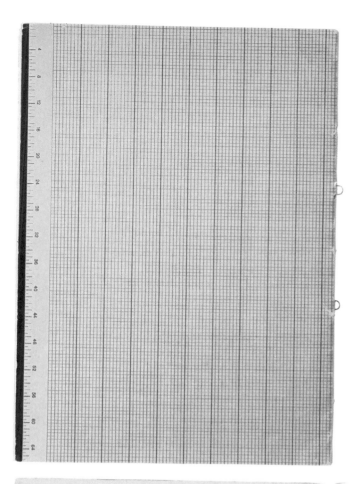

The Garamond type as recut by the Stempel typefoundry (the best version then available) was used as the representative roman typeface for illustrating how to sketch layouts in *Typografische Entwurfstechnik*, the companion piece to *Schriftschreiben für Setzer*. This book documents the now almost lost art of rendering type by hand as a way of planning, in Tschichold's words, the 'typographic structure of typesetting before its technical execution'; furthermore he directed his text towards the 'technique and possibilities of mechanical typesetting', for which a preparatory sketch was vital. Again, sanserif is taken as the first example (Futura in four weights) followed by Garamond, Bodoni and Walbaum Fraktur (but strangely no slab-serif type), all typeset alongside reproductions of Tschichold's careful, but not obsessively perfect sketched versions. His practical recommendations included the endearingly pedantic: 'All pencils must always be perfectly sharpened. With blunt pencils one cannot sketch. Sharp points are produced with fine sandpaper or with a pencil file.'[46]

46. *Typografische Entwurfstechnik*, p.3.

(Opposite and this page) Cover, back cover and introductory spread from *Typografische Entwurfstechnik*. 1932. A4.

(Overleaf) Spread from *Typografische Entwurfstechnik*.

6

4/6 Punkte
Unsere Kultur von den frühesten Zeiten bis in die Gegenwart
WISSENSCHAFT IM DIENSTE DES SEEVERKEHRS

5/6 Punkte
Die Harmonie und Charakteristik der Druckfarben
JAHRESBERICHT DER REEDEREIEN

6 Punkte
Internationale Sport- und Spiel-Ausstellung
ERFINDUNGEN DER ELEKTROTECHNIK

8 Punkte
Rheinischer Verkehrsverein Bingen
DIE WANDLUNG DER STILE

9 Punkte
Statistik der deutschen Industrie
BAYERISCHE MOTOREN

12 Punkte (10 Punkte nebenan)
Führer durch den Spessart

14 Punkte
Lichtreklame in Mainz

16 Punkte
Neuere Musikwerke

24 Punkte (20 Punkte nebenan)
Gewerbebank

28 Punkte
Naturkunde

36 Punkte
Hamburg

48 Punkte
Botanik

60 Punkte
Dachs

72/60 Punkte
Form

84/72 Punkte
Köln

20 Punkte

Werkstätte für moderne Dekoration
Überseedienst Hamburg-New York
BREMEN . COLUMBUS . EUROPA

10 Punkte
Die Reform der geltenden amtlichen Rechtschreibung wird immer dringlicher von weiten Volkskreisen gefordert. Mit wenigen Ausnahmen ist jeder von der Notwendigkeit einer durchgreifenden
UMFRAGE ÜBER DIE REFORM DER RECHTSCHREIBUNG

Werkstätte für moderne Dekoration
Überseedienst Hamburg-New York
BREMEN . COLUMBUS . EUROPA

Die Reform der geltenden amtlichen Rechtschreibung, wird imme dringlicher von weiten Volkskreisen gefordert. Mit wenigen Ausnahmen ist jeder von der Notwendigkeit einer durchgreifenden
UMFRAGE ÜBER DIE REFORM DER RECHTSCHREIBUNG

Figurenverzeichnis (10 Punkte)
abcdefghijklmnopqrstuvwxyzäöüchckfffifflß &.,-:;·!?('«»§†*
ABCDEFGHIJKLMNOPQRSTUVWXYZÄÖÜ 1234567890

Den 20-Punkt-Grad der **halbfetten Grotesk** können wir nicht mehr wie die magere Grotesk aus einfachen Strichen zusammensetzen. Wir müssen jeden Zug aus etwa 2 Strichen «aufbauen», die wir neben-, fast übereinander setzen. Wir wollen bemüht sein, mit möglichst wenig Strichen auszukommen. Wenn wir die Vorlage nachskizziert und einige andere Wörter dargestellt haben, wollen wir einmal versuchen, den 20-Punkt-Grad ohne Linien zu skizzieren. Wenn eine Zeile beendet ist, ziehen wir **aus freier Hand** die beiden Hauptlinien darüber. Dem Anfänger fällt es natürlich schwerer, gleich die richtige Größe des «Bildes» zu treffen, selbst wenn er wie hier eine gedruckte Zeile der gemeinten Größe vor sich hat. Aber man muß dahin kommen. Vor allem aber muß man sich hüten, die Schrift so offen darzustellen, daß man sie in der Ausführung sperren müßte.
Den 10-Punkt-Grad der halbfetten Grotesk kann man entweder mit ziemlich festen, **einfachen** Strichen und dem Bleistift Nr. 2 skizzieren oder aber mit dem härtern Stift Nr. 3 **aufbauen**. Wir verfahren sonst wie bisher.

Bei der **dreiviertelfetten Grotesk** verfahren wir ähnlich wie beim 20-Punkt-Grad der halbfetten. Nur genügen hier in den größern Graden nicht mehr zwei Striche für jeden Zug, sondern wir müssen (mit dem Bleistift

Dreiviertelfette Futura . Bauersche Gießerei, Frankfurt am Main   **7**

20 Punkte

Schillers Briefwechsel mit Goethe
Dramaturgie des Schauspiels
BUCHGEWERBEHAUS LEIPZIG

12 Punkte

Ein großer Teil der Befürworter der Kleinschrift, Einschrift oder Fließschrift (wie das Kind heißen soll, spielt jetzt keine Rolle; nennen wir es Kleinschrift) geht mit DIE KLEINSCHRIFT ALS WIRTSCHAFTLICHER FAKTOR

Schillers Briefwechsel mit Goethe
Dramaturgie des Schauspiels
BUCHGEWERBEHAUS LEIPZIG

Ein großer Teil der Befürworter der Kleinschrift, Einschrift oder Fließschrift (wie das Kind heißen soll, spielt jetzt keine Rolle; nennen wir es Kleinschrift) geht mit DIE KLEINSCHRIFT ALS WIRTSCHAFTLICHER FAKTOR

Figurenverzeichnis (12 Punkte)

abcdefghijklmnopqrstuvwxyzäöüchck ff fi fl ß &.,-:;·!?('«»
ABCDEFGHIJKLMNOPQRSTUVWXYZ 1234567890 §†*

6 Punkte

**Kleine philosophische Schriften in 3 Bänden
AUS DER SÄCHSISCHEN SCHWEIZ**

8 Punkte

**Atelier für moderne Raumkunst
ELEKTRIZITÄTSWERK**

9 Punkte

**Gesellschaft für Meteorologie
UNIVERSITÄT FRANKFURT**

10 Punkte

**Deutsches Museum München
MARTINSWAND**

14 Punkte (12 Punkte nebenan)

**Handel und Gewerbe
LABORATORIUM**

16 Punkte

**Akademie in Berlin
MALEREI**

24 Punkte (20 Punkte nebenan)

Setzmaschine

28 Punkte

Monument

36 Punkte

Fahrplan

48 Punkte

Dichter

60 Punkte

Kunst

72/60 Punkte

Seite

84/72 Punkte

Bad

Nr. 2 oder Nr. 1) je etwa drei Striche machen. Man kommt natürlich manchmal mit zweien aus, hin und wieder braucht man aber auch vier.

Der 12-Punkt-Grad verlangt als kleiner Grad wieder einen härtern Stift: Nr. 3. Wir probieren nun immer öfter, ohne vorgezogene Linien zu skizzieren. Erst die Grade, mit denen wir durch die Übungen schon bekannt geworden sind, dann auch andere, kleine und große.

Die **großen Grade** aller Fetten kann man selbstverständlich nicht in einfachen Strichen skizzieren, auch nicht mit den sogenannten Zimmermannsstiften. Diese ergeben ein viel zu rohes, dazu ganz unrichtiges Bild. Ebenso unzweckmäßig ist es, große Grade der Grotesk mit einer Breit- oder gar einer Redisfeder darzustellen. Es ist sehr umständlich, und ein annähernd richtiges Schriftbild kann auf diese Weise nicht zustande kommen. Man muß sie alle (ausgenommen die magern Grade bis 36 Punkt) mit dem weichsten Bleistift, Nr. 1, aufbauen. Doppelte und dreifache Striche genügen hier nicht mehr. Wir setzen für jeden Buchstabenteil soviel normale Striche dicht zusammen, bis die richtige Fette erreicht ist. Bei den großen Graden ist es auch richtiger, das Maß des gemeinen a oder n abzunehmen und die beiden Hilfslinien zu ziehen, damit unsere Skizze den wirklichen Lauf der Schrift möglichst genau trifft.

192

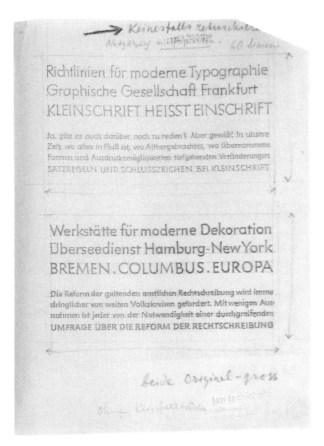

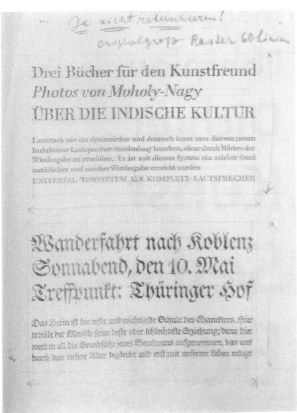

Tschichold's original sketches on tracing paper for *Typografische Entwurfstechnik. c.*1932. Shown at just over half of actual size.

Each one is marked: 'Do *not* retouch!'; there are also instructions to reproduce at same size with a half-tone screen of 60 lines per cm.

Spread (pages 8–9)

8

4 Punkte
Literarische Gesellschaft Ludwigshafen
SUCHGEWERBE IN NORDAMERIKA

8 Punkte
Gewerbebank in Königsberg
NORDDEUTSCHLAND

10 Punkte
Ausstellung in Düsseldorf
GEBRAUCHSGRAPHIK

14 Punkte (12 Punkte nebenan)
Frankfurt am Main
BUCHHANDEL

16 Punkte
Schreibmaschine
TANZSCHULEN

24 Punkte (20 Punkte nebenan)
Oberitalien

28 Punkte
Anatomie

36 Punkte
Moldau

48 Punkte
Blüten

60 Punkte
Harz

72/60 Punkte
Lied

84/72 Punkte
Zoll

20 Punkte
Zeitschrift für Maschinenbau
Reklame im Wandel der Zeit
DEUTSCHE TEXTILINDUSTRIE

12 Punkte
Zu den reizvollsten, jedoch auch schwierigsten Aufgaben gehören die Innenaufnahmen. Wie oft schon kam der Wanderer auf einer Fahrt NEUE STRÖMUNGEN IN DER PHOTOGRAPHIE

Zeitschrift für Maschinenbau
Reklame im Wandel der Zeit
DEUTSCHE TEXTILINDUSTRIE

Zu den reizvollsten, jedoch auch schwierigsten Aufgaben gehören die Innenaufnahmen. Wie oft schon kam der Wanderer auf einer Fahrt NEUE STRÖMUNGEN IN DER PHOTOGRAPHIE

Figurenverzeichnis (12 Punkte)
abcdefghijklmnopqrstuvwxyzäöüchckfffiflß
ABCDEFGHIJKLMNOPQRSTUVWXYZ ÄÖÜ &!?
1234567890 .,-:;!('«»§†'

Ganz fette Schriften, wie diese, skizziert man nur mit den weichsten Stiften, also mit Nr. 2 oder Nr. 1. Die härteren ergeben ein graues Bild und damit eine falsche Wirkung. Hier brauchen wir bei jedem Buchstaben verhältnismäßig Striche, sonst aber setzen wir jeden Zug wie bisher zusammen. Keinesfalls darf man etwa ins Konturieren verfallen, also in den größeren Graden zuerst den Umriß der Buchstaben angeben und diesen nachher ausfüllen. Das ergibt immer eine falsche, weil unverstandene Form. Wer einmal Schrift geschrieben hat, wird wohl gar nicht erst darauf kommen. Wir üben die fette Grotesk in gleicher Weise wie die dreiviertelfette.

Vor allem soll die Skizze deutlich zeigen, ob halbfette oder fette oder magere Schrift gemeint ist. Darum wollen wir jetzt einmal versuchen, einen neuen Text in einem oder zwei beliebigen Graden in gemischter Schrift zu skizzieren, also etwa 8 Punkt mager mit halbfetter, 16 Punkt dreiviertelfett mit fetter (wenn möglich aus der Vorstellung heraus, ohne Musterbeispiel). Man soll dann unbedingt erkennen können, welcher Grad und welche Fette gemeint sind.

9

Regeln für die Gestaltung des Akzidenzsatzes

(Randnotiz: Wertabstufung der Teile)

Man liest das Manuskript sorgfältig und überlegt, aus welcher Entfernung die Zeilen gelesen werden sollen. Dann bestimmt man, unter Berücksichtigung des Formats, die Schriftgrößen. Plakate verlangen andere Grade als Zeitungsanzeigen, diese andere als das Buch. Die Grade müssen genau nach der verhältnismäßigen Wichtigkeit des Textinhaltes gewählt werden. Jedoch sollen in der Regel nicht mehr als höchstens vier Grade verwandt werden. Zwei Grade wirken meist langweilig und schaffen keine wirkliche optische Ordnung. Drei Grade sind als Normalzahl der verwendeten Schriftformen anzusehen. Kursiven vorhandener Grade zählen dabei nicht besonders. Man kann die Wertunterschiede sowohl durch genügend abweichende Größen (ältere Satzweise), wie durch abweichende Fetten deutlich machen. Abweichende Fette ist deutlicher und daher moderner. Fortlaufenden Text aus zarter oder gewöhnlicher Grotesk zeichnet man am besten durch fettere Grotesk aus. Man beschränke sich dabei möglichst auf eine abweichende Fette. Antiqua zeichnet man mit Kursiv oder halbfetter Antiqua (in manchen Fällen mit beiden zugleich) aus. Sperrung als Auszeichnung lateinischer Schriften ist eigentlich nur angängig, falls keine geeignete fettere Grotesk oder, bei Antiqua, keine passende Kursiv oder halbfette Antiqua da ist. Dagegen ist es üblich, Fraktur zunächst durch Sperrung auszuzeichnen.

(Randnotiz: Die Grundregel über die Satzweise)

Als Norm auch der wichtigsten Zeilen ist der ungesperrte Satz aus Groß- und Kleinbuchstaben anzusehen. Er ist am besten lesbar und läßt sich am schnellsten einwandfrei herstellen. In den kleinern Graden der Antiqua ist ein · Ausgleichen · zu eng stehender Figuren selten nötig (ll, lf und ähnliche Fälle mit langen Parallelen). Dagegen fordern die größern Grade nicht weniger Schriften ein gewisses Ausgleichen. Es ist zwar nicht so dringlich wie bei Versalzeilen, aber wünschenswert und notwendig bei teuren Arbeiten, wie Briefbogen, Buchtiteln, feinen Prospekten und dergleichen. Hier ist als Regel anzusehen, daß etwa n-i nicht dichter zusammenstehend erscheinen dürfen, als die beiden Striche des n:

nicht ausgeglichen

ausgeglichen

Im nicht ausgeglichenen Wort fallen die Öffnungen in n, c, g heraus, während sie im ausgeglichenen unauffällig geworden, neutralisiert sind. Versalzeilen sollte man nur in ganz besonderen Ausnahmefällen verwenden. Sie müssen sorgfältig · ausgeglichen · gesetzt werden. Bei den Graden bis zu 8 Punkt kann man darüber hinweggehen, falls es sich nicht um einzeln stehende Zeilen (wie auf Privatbriefen, Besuchskarten und dergleichen) handelt. Aber besser vermeidet man Versalzeilen aus so kleinen Graden ganz. Ebenso unschön wie unausgeglichene Versalzeilen sind auseinandergezogene Versalzeilen. Sie sind vor allem schwer lesbar, da man sie buchstabieren muß.

(Randnotiz: Versalie?)

Die drei Ausnahmefälle, in denen man auch Versalien verwenden **kann** (nicht muß), sind diese:

1. Sehr kurze Wörter (mit weniger als 5 Staben), besonders solche mit lauter verschiedenen oder gar verschiedenformigen Zeichen.

2. Kurze Wörter mit schiefem oder sonst ungünstigem Umriß, in denen etwa ein Versal einem Buchstaben mit Unterlänge am Schluß gegenübersteht, wie Hang oder Wiese. (3. Fall auf der nächsten Seite!)

Spread (pages 12–13)

12

Der Blick muß von einer Gruppe zur anderen geführt werden. Das soll nicht mit Linien bewirkt werden, sondern die Stellung der Gruppen muß so sein, daß der Blick **zwangsläufig** von der einen zu andern gleitet. Ein bloßes Untereinander genügt nicht immer:

In dem ersten der obigen Schemen, in welchen Linien für Zeilen gesetzt sind, liegt Zeile 1 wohl über Zeile 2. Der Blick soll natürlich von Zeile 1 zu den Zeilen 2, 3 und 4 gleiten. Er ist es aber nicht, sondern fängt bei 2 an und geht dann zu 3 und 4. Die Zeile 1 wird · geschnitten ·, übersehen. Man kann nun den Blick entweder durch eine deutliche Höherstellung von 1 zuerst auf 1, dann auf 2 lenken (Schema II), oder man legt, wenn es der Sinn des Textes erlaubt, eine Linie zwischen 1 und 2, die · oben · und · unten · herstellt, dann liest man erst das Obenstehende, dann das Darunterliegende. Oder man rückt 1 weiter nach links (Schema IV). Es gibt auch noch andere Wege. Der Blick gleitet lieber von links nach rechts als umgekehrt. Die Gegenbewegung (von links oben nach rechts unten) empfindet man deutlicher als Zwang; man kann sie aus diesem Grunde unter Umständen vorziehen.

(Randnotiz: Aufbauelemente)

Den Gruppen verwandt sind die Aufbauelemente. Dieser Sammelbegriff faßt die Schrift- und die Fettigkeitsgrade, die Gruppen als Zusammenhänge, Fotos und andere Bilder, Linien und Farbgruppen zusammen. Von diesen Elementen gilt das gleiche wie von Schriftgraden und den Gruppen: man soll im allgemeinen nicht mehr als drei bis vier anwenden. Sonst wird der Aufbau leicht unklar. Verfeinerungen soll sich nur der Geübte erlauben.

(Randnotiz: Bildsatz?)

Schriftzeilen aus sogenanntem Bildsatz sind kein Wirkungsmittel des Setzers. In äußerst seltenen Ausnahmefällen können sie wohl an Stelle richtiger Schrift verwendet werden, etwa wenn es an einem passenden Grade mangelt. Wer sie verwendet, sollte sich über alle Extravaganzen der Form meiden. Jedenfalls sollte man es nicht probieren, ohne sich mit den Gestaltungsfragen der Schrift eingehend beschäftigt zu haben.

Fortsetzung der Skizzierübungen

Man unterscheidet zwei Hauptarten der Antiqua: die ältere oder Mediäval-Antiqua — mit schrägen Ansätzen bei i, l, j, n, m und einer im allgemeinen weichern Linienführung — und die jüngere oder französische Antiqua — mit durchweg waagrechten Schraffen und geometrisierter Form. Die nächste Seite zeigt die ältere Antiqua in einer ihrer reinsten Formen, der Garamond-Antiqua. Von der Grotesk unterscheidet sich die Antiqua durch den Wechsel stärkerer und schwächerer Striche und die Schraffen. Beides muß auch in der Skizze einigermaßen zum Ausdruck kommen. Weniger wichtig ist es, daß auch die besonderen Eigenschaften

13

Der große Irrtum *unserer Zeit* beruht nun darauf, daß viele meinen GOLDSCHMIEDEKUNST

Ergreifender noch als diese mehr passiv erlittenen Schicksale sind die Kämpfe derjenigen, die *mit aller Kraft versehen,* sich allen Widerständen zum Trotz durchzusetzen. Da ist der Sohn eines stellungslosen Ingenieurs, der als Aushilfsschreiber NEUE FRANZÖSISCHE KUNST IN LONDON

Der große Irrtum *unserer Zeit* beruht nun darauf, daß viele meinen GOLDSCHMIEDEKUNST

Ergreifender noch als diese mehr passiv erlittenen Schicksale sind die Kämpfe derjenigen, die *mit aller Kraft versehen,* sich allen Widerständen zum Trotz durchzusetzen. Da ist der Sohn eines stellungslosen Ingenieurs, der als Aushilfsschreiber NEUE FRANZÖSISCHE KUNST IN LONDON

Figurenverzeichnis der 36 Punkte
abcdefghijklmnopqrstuvwxyzäöüchckfffiflfflffiffl&
ABCDEFGHIJKLMNOPQQRSTUVWXYZÄÖUÆŒ
abcdefghijklmnopqrstuvwxyzäöüchckfffiflfflffiffl&
ABCDEFGHIJKLMNOPQRSTUVWXYZÄÖÜ Œ QU
ABCDEFGHIJKLMNPQRTÆŒ ....!?()'"'-»
1234567890 · 1234567890 · 1234567890 · 1234567890

AUSZUG AUS DER RAABE-FESTSCHRIFT

SÜDTEXTA-VERLAG FRANKFURT M

SCHICKSAL EINER OBERPRIMA

GYMNASTIK-UNTERRICHT

Die Bilanz der Werftindustrie für das vergangene Jahr zeigt

Auf einer Hebrideninsel westlich Schottlands

Der *bedeutende* Faktor ist die Beleuchtung

Kurzstreckenlauf

Domrestaurant

Inkunabel

Einkauf

Nadel

Herd

der Mediäval klar erscheinen. In den kleinern Graden ist dies ohnehin schwer zu erreichen. Selbstverständlich ist es besser, wenn größere skizzierte Grade schon zeigen, daß eine Mediäval gemeint ist.
Wir setzen also (oder mit dem Stift Nr. 2) die Buchstaben aus einzelnen Strichen, ähnlich wie die halbfette Grotesk, zusammen, wobei wir darauf achten, daß die Striche senkrecht betont sind. Es kommt nicht darauf an, daß jeder Buchstabe seine sämtlichen Schraffen erhält. Andeutungen genügen. Neu ist hier die Kursive, eine schräge, enge, aus der Handschrift abgeleitete Type, die als Auszeichnung verwendet wird.

Spreads from *Typografische Entwurfstechnik*. 1932. A4.

Spread from *Typografische Entwurfstechnik*. 1932. A4. Tschichold did not ignore Fraktur type in his treatment of type sketching. In the text here he asserts: 'A compositor who sets text in Fraktur should be in a position to sketch it fairly correctly. It is advisable to study the forms of Fraktur until one is familiar with them. Yet most people who use Fraktur today understand as good as nothing about its form. (Can you for example draw a Fraktur-V from memory?)'

Typografische Entwurfstechnik also contained some sections reprinted from *Grafische Berufsschule* about basic rules for jobbing typography – again book design is excluded as if outside the scope of New Typography or not in need of revised ground rules. Tschichold sought to supersede older practical handbooks that 'only know the method of axial symmetry, which is outmoded'. Yet he stressed that his principles were informed by the past:

> Our rules are the result of many years' educational work at the Meisterschule für Deutschlands Buchdrucker. It was not the author's intention to erect merely *new* rules. Not all are new; many are indeed so old as to have been almost forgotten. What is crucial is their usefulness.[47]

Tschichold recognized the continuing validity of these two practical manuals even after he had renounced New Typography. They formed the kernel of his later book, *Schriftkunde, Schreibübungen und Skizzieren für Setzer*, which went into two editions (1942 & 1951). *Schriftschreiben für Setzer* of 1931 was taken almost verbatim into the later book – indeed it would have been difficult to improve on its lucid exposition – and amplified slightly, with more illustra-tions and newly calligraphed models to fit into the smaller, upright format.[48] On the other hand, only the central idea of typographic sketching remained from *Typografische Entwurfstechnik*, so as not to inherit its earlier bias towards New Typography.[49] In the later book, Tschichold put into practice his treatment of gothic typefaces by using the Nürnberger Schwabacher of the Haas typefoundry on the title-page and for section headings. This might seem a bold step in the middle of the Second World War, especially as it would have been unthinkable for him to have actually used gothic type in the design of one of his own books ten years earlier. In *Typografische Entwurfstechnik* he had considered Fraktur as 'obsolete', without wishing to 'disparage its beauty'.[50] Tschichold never accepted the official Nazi co-option of gothic type as a national German symbol, and

47. *Typografische Entwurf-stechnik*, p.1. Emphasis in bold in original.

48. The revised script models used in 1942 first surfaced in 1940–1 in the journal *Schweizer Reklame und Schweizer graph-ische Mitteilungen*, reprinted in *Schriften*, 1, pp.228–41.

49. An article on the history of numerals was added as a chapter in *Schriftkunde...* and the 1951 edition incorporated several more articles that had been published in Swiss print-ing periodicals during the inter-vening years.

50. Ruari McLean's translation in *How to draw layouts*, p.ix.

Title-page and pages from *Schriftkunde, Schreib-übungen und Skizzieren für Setzer*. 1942. 22 × 13.4 cm. The revised model for writing sanserif has the embedded message: 'not the basic form'.

In the spread from the 'sketching' section, the sanserif chosen by Tschichold as a model was neither Futura nor Gill Sans but Berthold's Akzidenz Grotesk, which would go on to be the key

typeface in Swiss typography. In the 1951 edition of this book, the representative sanserif is Gill Sans, by then Tschichold's firm favourite.

he may have felt encouraged to use it for display purposes in 1942 by its having been released from the chains of Nazi ideology in the previous year, when roman type was instead declared the 'standard' type-style of the Third Reich.

A significant addition to Tschichold's revised publication of his instructional texts in 1942 was a new passage denigrating sanserif typefaces of the grotesque variety, reflecting how far his opinion had shifted in a relatively short time:

> We begin our exercises with grotesque, a typeface which is held to be the best by the layperson, as it appears to them to be the 'simplest'. Because it is in reality only an inadequately developed, exaggerated late form and does not belong to the true phases of development, it is not mentioned at all in our historical overview. It occurs occasionally from 1816 and appears for the first time in an English type specimen in 1832. That it was already then considered as a bizarre variant follows from the name 'grotesque', which was soon attached to it. Only in our time has it been more frequently employed, also as a text type. Actually it is only a display type; lengthy text setting in grotesque tires the eye; for grotesque lacks both the terminal strokes (serifs) of roman and also the gentle variation of thick and thin strokes, which better characterize letters and wordshapes than is possible with the almost monotonously consistent stroke thickness of grotesque.[51]

He was already lamenting a trend that he had helped to create: a greater everyday use of sanserif. This is made clear if we contrast the following passage, written seven years earlier, from *Typographische Gestaltung*, Tschichold's mature modernist manual:

> We desire simplicity and therefore require simple and clear typefaces. Closest to the new stylistic tendencies is the Grotesk- or Steinschrift (French antique, English sanserif), which is mostly called Block-script by non-experts.

He continued with an account of sanserif type's first appearances in English type specimens, based on an account by A.F. Johnson:

> Thorowgood called it 'Grotesque', Figgins 'Sans Surryphs'. The one name probably implies that the new type looked peculiar, and the other means 'without serifs' (sans sérifs). Today grotesque no longer appears peculiar to us, instead it seems natural. Yet it would no doubt prove difficult to introduce a new and better generic name for it.
>
> So, although it is not actually new, grotesque is, thanks to its simplicity and clarity, the obvious type for most printed matter today and for a long time to come. In the years 1925 to 1930 it was used in such great quantities that many developed an aversion to it and since then it has been maintained again and again that it has passed 'out of fashion'. However, New Typography is no fashion, rather it is the natural expression of a far greater timespan than is encompassed by a fashion.

Tschichold still maintained here (in 1935) that 'sanserif remains *the* typeface of the present day' due to its possibilities for creating contrast through a variety of weights. Yet he tentatively clarified his argument:

> For our present sensibilities the old grotesques have become a little old-fashioned; they seem common and are visually uninspiring. The proportions of the letters in them are less refined than in the best new grotesques, such as Gill Sans and Futura. Very often these new types will lend a job the final degree of distinction.[52]

Concerning 'book types' he added: 'Only the old grotesques are tiring, as their letterforms are insufficiently differentiated.'[53]

51. *Schriftkunde...* (1942) pp.65–6.

52. *Typographische Gestaltung*, pp.25–6.

53. *Typographische Gestaltung*, pp.28 & 104.

It is tempting to suggest that it was an inkling of this judgement that prevented Tschichold from ever commending fully the common grotesques available in the early years of modernist typography. A possible source for the reservations about the form of grotesque that were always implicit in his writings on New Typography is suggested by his assertion in *Die neue Typographie*: 'Grotesque is the logical progression along the path taken by Didot.'[54] Here he expressed an idea that has been developed by later letterform theorists and historians, that the sanserifs of the grotesque category share certain constructional principles with modern face types in the tradition of Didot and Bodoni. In a review of 'European script over two thousand years', published in his early Swiss years of mature New Typography, Tschichold declared:

> Roman typography experienced at that time (1800) a pinnacle never again reached thereafter. It disposes of almost all ornament and achieves a true greatness of form. The splendid, noble inevitability of that typography should invite us not to take as models any previous eras of printing, which were in fact left behind by Didot and Bodoni.[55]

While Tschichold came to prefer the modern face ('neo-classical' [*klassizistische*] in German) among roman types for his own typography during his modernist period – most notably having *Typographische Gestaltung* set in Bodoni – he never unequivocally recommended such typefaces at the expense of the classical, old face roman. In 'Elementare Typographie' he had described 'Mediäval-Antiqua' (a nineteenth-century style somewhere between the two) as preferable to most sanserifs. Several revivals of Garamond types were made in the first half of the 1920s (notably the Stempel version) and so, by the time of writing *Die neue Typographie*, he could recommend 'a classical roman – say Garamond' as a typeface suitable for books.[56] By 1935 Tschichold was developing a great appreciation of Gill Sans, which had not grown out of the modern face tradition of Didot and Bodoni but was instead the first, widely available sanserif typeface to be consciously formed on the principles of old face roman types like Garamond. Already in 1932 Tschichold used Gill Sans in at least one small printed announcement for an art gallery, and the sanserif typeface that he himself designed between 1933 and 1935 for Uhertype bears a very close resemblance to Gill Sans (see pp.230–44). By 1942, when he had settled into the role of traditionalist book designer,

Tschichold was openly advocating a return to old face roman type, giving a considered assessment of what was wrong with intervening developments, including implicitly the modernist preference for seemingly geometrical sanserifs:

> The editions of Bodoni and Didot, which show the 'neo-classical' roman in pure form, are, considered as books, works of art of the highest order. Their letters however introduce an erroneous development, at the end of which stands the current disorientation in script matters, connected with an overestimation of geometrically constructed and – in a two-fold sense – inorganic forms. It has been forgotten that script, like all practical activity, derives its justification only from an absolute achievement of service. This means for script not ease of production and not clumsy obviousness of letter construction, but rather legibility. Identical formation of individual, unrelated elements in geometrically constructed letterforms decreases in a dangerous way the individuality and clarity of the letters and thereby the legibility of the whole, which results from their distinctive differences.[57]

In a typescript for one of his lectures (probably dating from the early 1940s) Tschichold summarized: 'Geometry is a good servant, but a bad master.'[58]

The reasoning behind Tschichold's demand for a return from the 'degenerate neo-classical types of Bodoni, Didot and their emaciated successors to the better legible, classical letters of the fifteenth and sixteenth centuries' marks him as an eventual follower of William Morris in this respect.[59] In *Typographische Gestaltung* he had criticized Morris's 'aesthetic Renaissance' as a backward step, yet less than a decade later Tschichold's arguments specifically echoed the views of that 'great Englishman', as he called him (although Morris's stylistic preference really lay further back in the medieval period).[60] More particularly, Tschichold can be seen to have been deeply influenced by the calligraphic revivalism of Edward Johnston, from whose manual he first learned to write formal scripts. Tschichold's own calligraphic primer, *Schriftschreiben für Setzer*, showed the influence of both Johnston and Rudolf von Larisch, but in its text – written during his period of New Typography – he reasserted the Johnstonian primacy of writing with a broad pen as the basis for western script, and so already began to undermine the legitimacy of roman typefaces in the modern face tradition, and by extension the grotesque style of sanserif.*

54. *Die neue Typographie*, p.21.
55. 'Europäische Schriften aus zweitausend Jahren', p.167.
56. He clarified this meaning of Mediäval in *Schriftkunde...* (1951), p.101, and declared it an incorrect epithet for Garamond.
57. *Schriftkunde...* (1942), p.28. This paragraph originated in slightly different form in 'Schreiben und Drücken', an

article of 1940 (*Schriften*, 1, pp.267–8) and was refined further in the second edition of *Schriftkunde...* (1951), pp.28–9. Again, Tschichold's view was anticipated by his mentor Wieynck, who wrote in 1931: 'The most legible type is not the one with the simplest and most similar letters, rather it is the one in which the letterforms

are clearly differentiated from each other and are strongly & vividly articulated.' ('Leitsätze zum Problem zeitgemäßer Druckschriftgestaltung', p.70.
58. Undated typescript (DNB Leipzig).
59. *Schriftkunde...* (1942), p.29.
60. *Typographische Gestaltung*, p.10; *Asymmetric typography*, p.16. The later English

edition omitted Tschichold's original assertion in 1935 that Karl Faulmann's views on typographical progress in his *Illustrirte Geschichte der Buchdruckerkunst* (1882) were much fresher than Morris's. Tschichold's steady progress towards an advocacy of old face roman type also runs broadly parallel to the same inclination

in Stanley Morison, who was feeling his way towards the idea from 1922.
* In *The stroke* (London: Hyphen Press, 2005), Gerrit Noordzij's theories of letterform construction take account of the formative influence exerted by calligraphy with a pointed pen that produces a thicker line under pressure,

as opposed to the broad pen, which Tschichold asserted 'should not write thicker than it is' (*Schriftschreiben für Setzer*, p.10). Noordzij's concept of 'translation' for the variation in stroke thickness created by the broad pen was perhaps anticipated by Tschichold when he wrote of its 'vertebral traces', as opposed to a linear trace.

Book design 1925–33

Tschichold's design for Colin Ross's *Das Fahrten- und Abenteuerbuch* (1925) did not lead to regular work for its publisher, the Büchergilde Gutenberg. This is surprising when one considers his link with the initiator of the Büchergilde, Bruno Dressler, and with the associated Bildungsverband. During his first three years in Munich (1926–8), Tschichold did some work for another publisher, the Volksverband für Bücherfreunde (Popular association for friends of the book), which was in fact the first book club to have been formed during the Weimar Republic, and went on to become the largest in Germany. The Volksverband was not a socialist society and its books were traditional in appearance. Tschichold's involvement was confined to the conventional task of a 'book artist': he designed only the book spine, using gothic lettering and decorative lines – precisely the kind of style he criticized at that very time in his essay 'Buch-"Kunst"?', published in *Die Literarische Welt* (see appendix B).

While Tschichold hardly designed any more books (apart from his own) in a modernist vein before 1930, he continued to occasionally design bindings and title-pages for books published by Insel Verlag (based in Leipzig), which had been one of his earliest clients. Moreover, these books show that he kept his hand in with the traditionalist style of his early years while simultaneously preaching the gospel of New Typography in his writings. Much of Insel Verlag's output, dominated by fiction and poetry, was typeset in Fraktur. For the bindings of these editions Tschichold appropriately applied his skills as a calligrapher, which remained almost entirely hidden in his practical work as a New Typographer. In particular he developed a kind of series style for the novels of Albrecht Schaeffer, varying the colour of cloth on the binding but maintaining a consistent decorative pattern and style of lettering on the spine and cover.

Design for title-page of Insel Verlag edition. 1925.
Around half of actual size.

Insel Verlag catalogue cover. 1926. 18.4 × 11.3 cm.

Spine designed by Tschichold for Tolstoy,
Die Kreutzersonate (Volksverband für
Bücherfreunde/Wegweiser Verlag, [1927]).
19.5 × 13.2 cm.

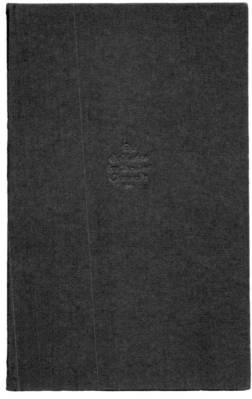

Binding design for Albrecht Schaeffer, *Die Geschichte der Brüder Chamade* (Insel Verlag, 1928). 18.6 × 11.7 cm.

Book jacket (spine and front). 1926. 17.5 × 10.5 cm. Lettering by Tschichold. First of many volumes of Goethe's works published by Insel Verlag.

Detail (enlarged to 200%) of Tschichold's calligraphic lettering on the cover of the book above. Shows an image quality in foil blocking on cloth that is rarely achievable today.

Experiment by Tschichold in making a photogram for the cover of the publication pictured opposite. The bleached-out, open book is not very effective and it is understandable that it was not used.

Spine and cover for *Insel Almanach*. 1929.
18.2 × 12.2 cm. The signet is the original
one designed for the publishing house by
Peter Behrens in 1899.

Tschichold did not design the interior of
the catalogue but he drew the calendar
symbols on the pages below.

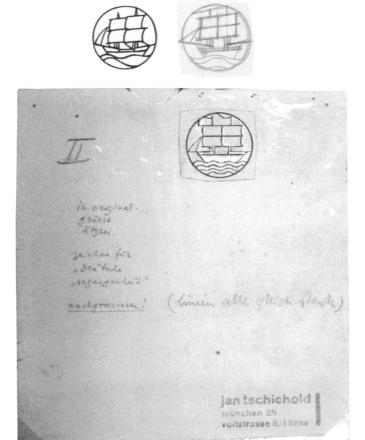

Versions of the Insel-Verlag signet designed by
Tschichold. c.1930.

Layout for *Die Delphine* (Insel Verlag, 1930).
Lettering by Tschichold; drawing by Felix
Timmermans.

Sketches for Insel Verlag's autumn 1931 catalogue
and the final printed version (18.3 × 11.7 cm).

Binding design for Marcus Lauesen, *Und nun warten wir auf das Schiff* (Insel Verlag, 1932). 20.4 × 13.4 cm.

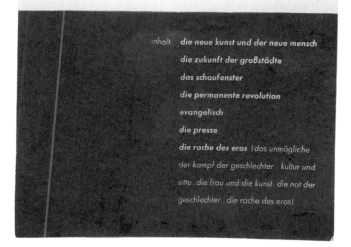

Design for Insel Verlag book jacket. 1932. 23 × 16 cm.

Among the selection of the 'fifty most beautiful books' for 1932 was an Insel edition of poetry by Hans Carossa, for which Tschichold designed the binding. Tschichold's involvement is not credited inside the book, nor is it in other Insel editions shown here, implying that he considered this journeyman work in comparison with his avant-garde projects.[61] Another book for which Tschichold designed the binding was judged as one of the fifty best in 1931: *Neuzeitlicher Verkehrsbau* by H. Gescheit & K.O. Wittmann, a large-format edition about modern traffic planning, dominated by photographs and typeset in Futura. As such it was safely within the realm of New Typography and Tschichold's involvement was credited in the book.

61. Some of the Insel books for which he designed bindings are identified in the catalogue *Jan Tschichold: typographer and type designer 1902–1974*, and by signed, original artwork.

Binding of Insel edition of Hans Carossa's poetry, designed by Tschichold and judged one of the fifty most beautiful books in Germany for 1932. 19.3 × 12.3 cm.

Design for jacket, spine (faded) and cover for
Nitti, *Flucht* (Müller & Kiepenheuer, 1930).
19 × 13 cm. The book's publisher grew out of
the Gustav Kiepenheuer Verlag, which had also

employed other modernists to design jackets,
including Moholy-Nagy and Georg Salter. It is
probable that a book such as this drew the attention of the Bücherkreis to Tschichold's work.

Cover and spread from Gescheit & Wittmann,
Neuzeitlicher Verkehrsbau (Müller & Kiepenheuer, 1931). A4. Tschichold was credited only
with the jacket and binding design of this book.

Indeed the interior pages seem to lack the
refinement he brought to such material (compare
illustrations on pp.109–14).

Designs for covers (including spine) of prospective series of titles on modern design. Never published. *c.*1930. 19.6 × 14 cm.

Whether it was due to a lack of appropriate commissions or to a personal disinclination (most probably a combination of both), Tschichold had developed a distaste for advertising work by the early 1930s, which is surely the subtext to his anti-capitalist sentiments expressed in 'Wo stehen wir heute?'. He was no doubt glad to develop a strong relationship from 1930 with another socialist book club, the Bücherkreis, for which he became the sole designer until he left Germany. Despite his published opinion that New Typography had little to offer book design, his association with this publisher perhaps marks his affinity – already here in his last years in Germany – for this more traditional branch of typography, which would come to dominate the latter part of his career. During approximately two-and-a-half years he designed around twenty-five books for the Bücherkreis, in which he was able to test the applicability

of a modern style to literature and to put into practice his demand in *Eine Stunde Druckgestaltung* for 'cheap books, not private-press editions; active literature, not passive leather-bindings'.[62]

Such an aim fitted well with the aims of the Bücherkreis, which had been founded in 1924 by an educational committee set up by the Social Democratic Party. As with the Büchergilde, a monthly fee of 1 mark earned its members four books per year, plus the eponymous monthly magazine of the Bücherkreis (quarterly from 1930). From 1929 members were offered a choice of books in any given quarter and the economic crisis that began in that year did not seem to hinder the growth in membership of the workers' book clubs. By the end of 1930 the Bücherkreis had supplied

62. *Eine Stunde Druckgestaltung*, p.7;
Schriften, 1, p.90; appendix C, p.315.

more than a million volumes to its international membership. The political orientation of the Bücherkreis became distinctly more radical in 1929 when Karl Schröder took over as its director. Schröder had been a founding member of the German Communist Party in 1918, and was one of the leaders in its hardline offshoot, the KAPD. He himself wrote one of the Bücherkreis's most acclaimed titles of 1929, *Jan Beek*, 'a study of the revolution'. The Büchergilde also moved further to the left under the new direction of Erich Knauf in 1929, which was in general a year of sharpening political allegiances in the arts. The magazines *Die neue Bücherschau* and *Die Linkskurve* began publication in that year, both of them concerned with workers' literature.

The intentions for the Bücherkreis under Schröder were clearly expressed in the yearbook of the Social Democrats for 1929:

1. Educational work within the working class through literature.
2. Contemporary literature should be given space: in other words, literature that in some way serves the current socialist struggle.
3. If possible, socialist writers from Germany and the International should be given a voice to influence the working class, to encourage new talent, to gain new readers, and thereby assist the entire socialist book trade in establishing a wider basis and a potentially stronger position.
4. Production should be systematically built up so that a clear picture of socialist cultural efforts in Germany and the International emerges.[63]

Tschichold was undoubtedly in sympathy with these ideals at this time, and his design work for the Bücherkreis gave its editions a consistently serious aspect that was appropriate to its programme. The first of its titles that he designed was *Das Buch vom Bauen*, by Albert Sigrist (a pseudonym for Alexander Schwab, also a member of the KAPD). Schwab wrote regularly for the Werkbund journal *Die Form*, and his book's subject of modern architecture may well have occasioned Tschichold's being asked to design it. He is credited only with the binding but the cool mixture of grotesque and modern face roman type on the title-pages also indicates his influence. Thenceforth Tschichold took over the design of binding, interior typography and dust jackets for all Bücherkreis editions. Apart from two further, photographically illustrated volumes in the same larger format (24 × 17 cm) as *Das Buch vom Bauen*, these were mainly books of text only, with cloth bindings, mostly in a format appropriate for novels (19 × 13 cm). In accordance with his reservations about revolutionizing the typography of such books, there is nothing extraordinary about their text design, with Tschichold generally sticking to good roman typefaces and occasionally using sanserif for headings and page numbers. The only elements of the text typography that can be considered asymmetric are the ranged-left headings; title-pages and bindings offered more

scope for dynamic arrangement. Yet Tschichold's designs for Bücherkreis bindings were discreet and muted. As the lasting cover of a book he considered the binding to be quite distinct from a dustjacket, the purpose of which resembled that of a poster.[64] In his typography for bindings he was always inclined to communicate in a softer tone than some of his contemporary New Typographers (take *Die neue Typographie* itself, for example).

A short article by Tschichold – 'Einiges über Buchgestaltung' (Some notes on book design) – can be read partly as a reflection on his design work for the Bücherkreis, several illustrations of which accompanied his text in *Klimschs Jahrbuch* (1932). Tschichold stated that the same secondary, display type that may feature on the title-page should also be used on the binding. This he considered to be a relatively new suggestion, and it was by such strategies for the integrity of each individual book that he managed to create a coherent impression for the Bücherkreis output between 1930 and 1933, although each of the books was given an individual graphic treatment. Uncharacteristically, Tschichold's article verges on the humorous in describing how too many hands can spoil a book. He invents a list of characters in a chaotic scenario, each of whom is designated by a letter of the alphabet (A the compositor; B the artist; Miss C, engaged to 'make the book more beautiful'; D a 'type artist'; and E 'a specialist in bindings of a rococo style'):

> Even when the individual work by A, B, C, D and E respectively is faultless, the result is bound to be terrible due to the lack of any unifying supervision. The book has long ceased to be a unity, nor even a conglomeration; it is a rubbish heap. The publisher now needs a colourful illustrated dustjacket (fortunately an infrequent occurrence here) so he turns to the famous draftsman F, the master of 'vivacious female forms'. Eventually, then, six people have 'collaborated' on the book, merely because the manager of the publishing house, a businessman, with all his efforts to achieve the best, does not know how to use the personnel correctly, that is – in unison. (This ironic account is not freely invented, but is rather one of many such true occurrences!)[65]

One might imagine that he may have had this kind of experience with Insel Verlag, for which he often designed only bindings, with the text being taken care of by compositors and printers, and an illustrator sometimes employed to design a dustjacket.[66] Instead Tschichold proposed that

> *the choice of typeface, the leading, the placement of the type area, the indication of chapters, the prelims, the binding design and when possible also the design of the dustjacket must be entrusted to one hand*, if a *unity* is to be produced.[67]

63. *Jahrbuch der Sozialdemo-kratie für 1929* (Kraus reprint, 1976) p.243. The writer is not credited but the text is contained in a section subtitled 'Report of the Party Committee'.

64. 'Einiges über Buchgestaltung', pp.116–7.
65. 'Einiges über Buchgestaltung', p.114.
66. As with Marcus Lauesen's *Und nun warten wir auf das*

Schiff (1932), for which the Norwegian Olaf Gulbransson designed the jacket.
67. 'Einiges über Buchgestaltung', p.115. Italic in original.

ALBERT SIGRIST:

DAS BUCH VOM BAUEN

Tschichold's first book for the Bücherkreis. 1930. Actual size. He was only credited with the cover.

Books designed by Tschichold for the Bücherkreis. All in format 19 × 13 cm. 1930–2.

208

UNION DER SOZIALISTISCHEN SOWJETREPUBLIKEN

TUWA

CHINA

Otto Mänchen-Helfen

REISE INS ASIATISCHE TUWA

Mit 28 Photobildern

Otto Mänchen-Helfen

Reise ins asiatische Tuwa

Mit 28 Photobildern

1931 Verlag Der Bücherkreis GmbH Berlin SW68

Die neue Schrift

Cover (actual size), title-page and spreads from Mänchen-Helfen, *Reise ins asiatische Tuwa*. 1931. Photographs were printed by gravure, separately from the letterpress text. The image above right shows a literacy initiative using Latin script for the native Tuvin language, which had hitherto not been written.

Junge Frau im Prunkkleid

210

Blick von der Brückenfähre in Marseille auf die Stadt

Grisar: **Mit Kamera und Schreibmaschine**

durch Europa

Frau mit Kindern in Marseille

Mit Kamera und Schreibmaschine
durch Europa

Bilder und Berichte von Erich Grisar

Verlag Der Bücherkreis GmbH, Berlin SW 61   1932

Cover (actual size), title-page, spreads and back
cover from Grisar, *Mit Kamera und Schreibmaschine durch Europa*. 1932. 24 × 17.5 cm.
Photographs printed separately from text by
gravure.

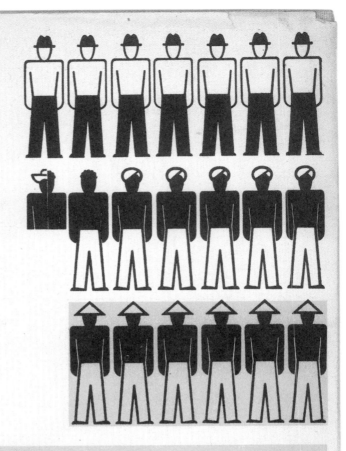

Völkergruppen der Erde
Jede ganze Figur 100 Millionen Menschen
Schätzung für 1930

Weiße

Indianer
Mestizen
Neger
Mulatten
Orientalen
Inder
Malaien

Mongolen

Drittel der Menschheit

Ein Ostasienbuch von O. Mänchen-Helfen

Ostasien erwacht und versucht, die Ketten und Fesseln der imperialistischen Groß-mächte von sich abzustreifen. Krieg und Bürgerkrieg, Revolution und Konterrevo-lution, Bauernaufstände und Barrikadenkämpfe des streikenden Arbeitervolkes sind die äusserlich sichtbaren Anzeichen dieses grandiosen Freiheitsringens. 600 Millionen Arbeiter und Bauern sind auf dem Marsch! Den tiefern Sinn dieser Vorgänge deutet uns dieses Ostasienbuch. Die Entscheidungen, die am Stillen Ozean fallen, sind auch Entscheidungen über unser eignes zukünftiges Geschick!

Preis in Leinen gebunden 4.30 Reichsmark

Jacket for Mänchen-Helfen, *Drittel der Menschheit*. 1932. Actual size.

The image is taken from an Isotype chart using symbols designed by Gerd Arntz.

Books designed by Tschichold for the Bücherkreis
in format 22.5 × 15 cm. 1931–3.

Müller: Novemberrevolution

Vorwärts:

Das ist ein handfestes Buch von einem geschrieben, der weiß, was er will, von einem, der seinen Weg sieht und ihn auch im Dunkeln nicht verliert. Eine Fülle von Material ist in der Schrift verarbeitet, man erfährt manche wichtige Einzelheit daraus zum ersten Male. Das Wesen des Mannes spiegelt sich in seiner Schrift. Kein himmelstürmender Eroberer, wohl aber ein zuverlässiger und treuer Verwalter und Mehrer übernommenen Gutes. Er hält Distanz zu den Menschen und Dingen, und darum ist sein Urteil über sie weder von Haß noch von Liebe getrübt. Nur selten spricht er in seinem Buche von sich selbst. Ich bedaure es, daß er an einer Stelle das private Vorleben eines Politikers erwähnt. Aber dazu trieb ihn der Wille zur Genauigkeit, der ihn an einer anderen Stelle noch zu der Erzählung veranlaßt hat, daß er kurz vor Ausbruch der Revolution ohne sein kleines Gepäck eine Reise nach Kiel nicht antreten mochte. Vielleicht hätten wir anderen es ebenso gemacht; aber trotz aller Liebe zur Wahrheit hätten wir wahrscheinlich solche Menschlichkeit der Nachwelt unterschlagen.

Vossische Zeitung:

Müller-Franken, der diese Erinnerungen verfaßt hat, ehe durch die Wahl vom 20. Mai an die Spitze der Reichsregierung gebracht wurde, sagt selbst, daß er keine Geschichte der deutschen Revolution habe schreiben, sondern nur das Material für den künftigen Geschichtsschreiber habe zusammentragen wollen. Dieses Material ist nicht lückenlos, kann es auch nicht sein, weil Müller-Franken nur erzählt und mit Dokumenten belegt,

was er, der schon damals in den ersten Reihen der sozialdemokratischen Partei stand, selbst erlebt hat.

Münchener Neueste Nachrichten:

Die Anzeige des Buches eines aktiven Reichskanzlers gehört noch nicht zu den alltäglichen Dingen in Deutschland. Wir vermuten auch, daß der Reichskanzler Hermann Müller sein Buch („Die Novemberrevolution, Erinnerungen", Verlag: Der Bücherkreis G. m. b. H., Berlin) wohl vor seinem letzten Amtsantritt geschrieben hat. Aber immerhin, als Reichskanzler läßt er es in die Welt gehen. Das Buch schildert die Ereignisse vom Ausbruch der Revolution bis zum Zusammentritt der Nationalversammlung, soweit der Verfasser ihnen persönlich nahestand. Die eigentliche Revolution hat er nicht in Berlin erlebt, da er, was bislen nicht mehr erinnerlich sein wird, kurz vorher zur Unterstützung Noskes nach Kiel entsandt worden war. Er kehrte bald darauf zurück und spielte dann, zunächst als Mitglied des Berliner Vollzugsrats, später des von ersten Parteikomitees, eingesetzten, lediglich aus Mehrheitssozialisten bestehenden Zentralrates eine Rolle.

Berliner Tageblatt:

Müllers Werk ist ein zuverlässiger, aktenmäßig belegter Bericht über die Vorgänge der beiden ersten Revolutionsmonate.

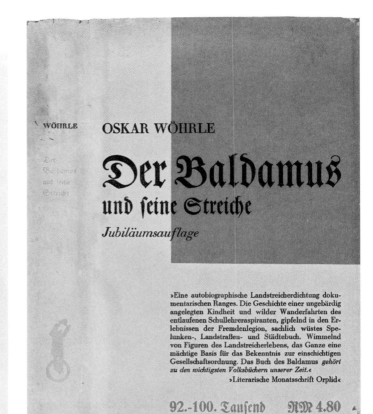

Broido: Wetterleuchten der Revolution

Eva Broido

Wetterleuchten der Revolution

Eva Broido sitzt zurzeit in sowjetrussischem Kerker. Sie ist eine alte Menschewikin, bahnte sich unter schwersten Entbehrungen den Weg zum akademischen Beruf und wurde Sozialistin. Sie leistete mehrjährige illegale Agitationsarbeit im zaristischen Rußland und hat zwei berühmte Episoden in der revolutionären Geschichte Rußlands miterlebt: die Protestaktion der „Romanowzy" in Jakutsk und die armenisch-tartarische Metzelei in Baku … Ihr heroisches Leben weiß sie schlicht aber packend zu erzählen … meisterhaft die Kapitel über Baku

Memoiren einer russischen Sozialistin

2. Auflage (11.–16. Tausend)

Preis in Leinen 4.30 RM

Thomas Morus	16.	Jahrhundert
Bellamy	19.	Jahrhundert
Illing	20.	Jahrhundert

Illing
uto-
polis

Werner Illing

utopolis

Phantastischer Zukunftsroman

„Ein Zukunftsgemälde einer freien Gemeinschaft Utopien mit der Hauptstadt Utopolis. Von erfinderischer Phantasie mit allen technisch-mechanischen Fortschrittsmöglichkeiten ausgestattet • In vielem ist das Buch Gegenwartssatire am Stoff einer imaginär erschauten Zukunft. Illing hat Phantasie, einen einfachen, bildhaft genauen, unprätentiösen Stil und als Bestes eine gute, tatwillige Gesinnung."   Die Literatur.

In Ganzleinen gebunden 4.30 RM

Jackets (spine & front) designed by Tschichold for reprinted editions of books first published before his involvement with the Bücherkreis. 1931. 19 × 13 cm and (above right) 22.5 × 15 cm.

Tschichold's theory about using historical typefaces in addition to sanserif, which he developed around the time of his Bücherkreis work, was given limited reign on the Bücherkreis dustjackets, which are dominated by sanserif, with slab-serif (notably Trump's City) and occasionally a bold modern face making an appearance. Intriguingly, Tschichold used none of the display typefaces he designed (Transito, Saskia or Zeus) on any of the Bücherkreis books.[68] Instead gothic type is used for display in books for which it was appropriate – for example, a biographical novel about Jan Hus and a biography of Karl & Jenny Marx. Tschichold is not credited with the design of these two books, although they otherwise bear his mark. This may have been a strategic omission. He used gothic type effectively on the jacket for a reprint in 1931 of Hermann Müller-Franken's memoir of the 1918 November Revolution. Here newspaper reviews of the book form a background in Fraktur that is overprinted with the author and title in bold condensed grotesque, symbolizing the new cancelling out the old.

Dustjackets were only added to copies of Bücherkreis books that were sold in shops (not those sent to members) in order to satisfy the need for window display. Despite much individual variation, Tschichold developed a theme for the jackets whereby what would today be called the blurb, a short paragraph summarizing the book's content, was featured on the front cover, whereas it would commonly be printed inside the front flap or on the back. This not only gave Tschichold more elements for his composition, given that purely typographic jackets were undoubtedly a necessity due to the cost of photographic reproduction, but also served to emphasize the subjects of the books, which were a prime consideration for the Bücherkreis.

Covers and spread from issues of *Der Bücherkreis* magazine (June 1928 & March 1930) before Tschichold was employed by the book club as designer. 21.5 × 14.6 cm.

Covers and spread from *Der Bücherkreis* magazine (1931–2) during Tschichold's tenure as designer. A5. Although he is not credited, the change seems to indicate his hand (especially the boxed sanserif type).

68. Zeus was used in a Büchergilde Gutenberg book not designed by Tschichold (see p.176).

216

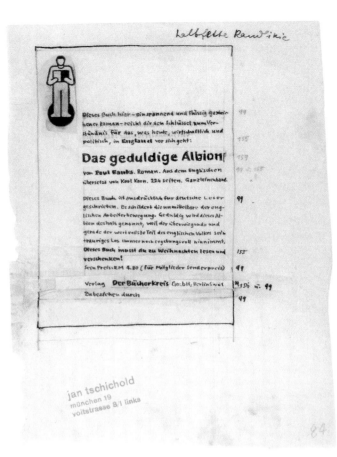

For the Bücherkreis, in addition to its books, Tschichold also redesigned its stationery, advertising and its symbol. This he changed from an angular figure almost hiding behind a book (like a shadow from an Expressionist film of the early 1920s) to a schematized figure openly reading in front profile, rendered in the style of his friend Gerd Arntz's Isotype symbols.

(Top) Sketch for the new symbol *in situ* as a postmark. 1931.

(Below) Publicity leaflet. 1932. A5.

Layout and printed result for book advertisement. 1932.

Catalogue list cover. Autumn 1932. 19.5 × 12.8 cm.

Bücherkreis circular explaining the benefits of Tschichold's involvement as typographer. 1932. A4.

In the early years of the Bücherkreis and Büchergilde, complaints were heard from the Bücherkreis about the ostentatious nature of the Büchergilde's books. Unlike the Büchergilde, the Bücherkreis had made no initial declaration of intent for high quality in the design and production of its books but eventually it realized the potential importance of such matters. This is reflected in a statement circulated to the 'distributors, advertisers and friends' of the Bücherkreis in 1932:

In previous years there were frequent complaints about the design of our books. In the last two years we have tried to address these grievances and to remedy the deficiencies. We enlisted one of the best-known modern book designers, namely Jan Tschichold of Munich, and assigned him the entire typographic design of our publications.

We have satisfaction in reporting today that the complaints about design have all but ceased.[69]

The circular goes on to cite book reviews that specifically praised Tschichold's design work.

The two travelogue books that Tschichold designed for the book club had laminated card covers featuring photographic illustrations. The photographic illustrations inside the books were not integrated on the same pages as the text, as Tschichold had demonstrated in the design of *Die neue Typographie*, due to their being printed by a different technique (gravure) to the type (letterpress), a decision presumably taken to achieve the richest reproduction of the images. Nevertheless the photographs were bled off the edge of

69. For a fuller translation of this circular see Schneider, 'Worker's literature meets the New Typography', p.11.

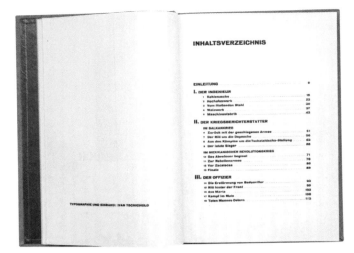

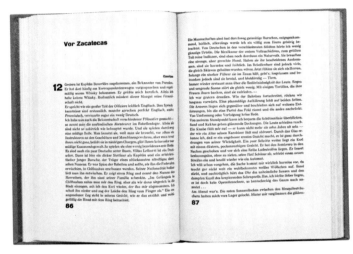

Contents list and spreads from Ross, *Das Fahrten-und Abenteuerbuch* (Büchergilde Gutenberg, 1925). 24 × 17 cm.

(See pp.45–6 for cover and title-page)

the pages, which was a relative novelty at this time. Indeed Tschichold was interested in establishing when this practice had begun, and was intrigued by Josef Albers's assertion that he had designed a publication in 1925 in which images bled off the edge of the page in this way. Tschichold asked him to send a copy of it:

> what you wrote to me about layouts without margins interests me particularly, as i am at the same time a writer of history. ... until now i was not able to say who consciously started this. the first work that is known to me was a little prospectus for the *fronta* yearbook (brno), which zdenek rossmann made around 1924.[70]

However, the author of one of the Bücherkreis books in which Tschichold employed this technique had some reservations about it and remarked that, at those pages where photographs bled off, readers' fingers would become inky from holding the book.[71]

70. Letter Tschichold to Albers, 8 December 1931.

71. Melis, *Die Buchgemeinschaften in der Weimarer Republik*, p.215.

For two books published by the Büchergilde Gutenberg – *Giganten der Landstraße* and *Sport und Arbeitersport* – Georg Trump and Wilhelm Lesemann fully integrated text and photographs in their respective designs. Even though Tschichold's first book for the Büchergilde, *Das Fahrten- und Abenteuerbuch*, was printed by the same single technique (letterpress) as those books, he had not taken the opportunity to combine photographs and type on the same page; only in his second and last book for the Büchergilde, *Aus der Werkstatt der Natur* (1930) did he fully integrate text, drawn illustrations and photographs into a sumptuous whole (see overleaf).

In his last few months in Germany Tschichold began writing an extended essay on 'Der Satz des Buches' (The composition of the book), which would become one of the first that he had published in *Typographische Monatsblätter* after moving to Switzerland. The opening assertion of his text – 'All typographic education begins and ends with the book' – reflects the dominant place that book typography had begun to occupy in his work. He justified his own

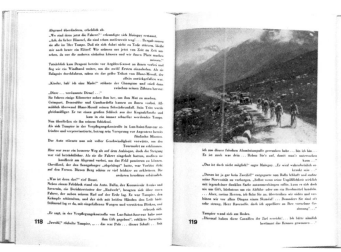

Georg Trump, cover and spread from *Giganten der Landstraße* (Büchergilde Gutenberg, 1928). 24 × 17 cm.

previous neglect of book design in theories of New Typography by stating that 'the form of the book as an object of use was settled long ago'. In his view, the relatively recent proliferation of advertising matter was 'more problematic' in design terms and was therefore 'more suitable as the object of typographical dispute'.[72] Tschichold nevertheless maintained a qualified hope at this point for a limited entry of contemporary style into books: 'Even our common, everyday book [*Gebrauchsbuch*] will soon show a new style, which will be distinct from previous book styles.' He set down in detail the possibilities for minor, modern modifications to the traditional book form; but, considering his view that the 'typography of the modern book is essentially the same as that of the old', his essay also contains the basic principles of detailed text typography that would continue to underpin all of his future writings on the subject, making quite clear the consistencies in his thinking that run across his supposed (re)conversion to traditionalism.

Wilhelm Lesemann, cover and spreads from *Sport und Arbeitersport* (Büchergilde Gutenberg, 1931). 24 × 17 cm.

72. 'Der Satz des Buches', p.121.

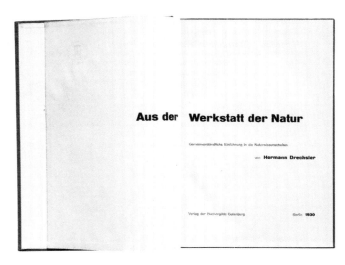
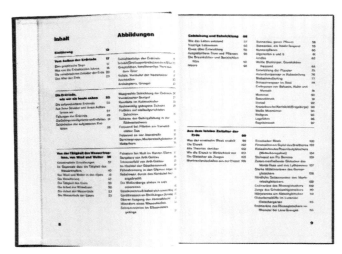
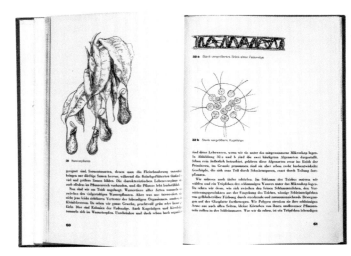

Cover, title-pages and spreads from Drechsler,
Aus der Werkstatt der Natur (Büchergilde
Gutenberg, 1930). 23.8 × 16.7 cm.

Gletscherstroms am Ende von 50 Meter, so hat er bei seinem Vorrücken in zwei Jahren eine halbe Million Kubikmeter Eis vorgeschoben. Würde der Gletscher einige hundert Jahre so vorrücken, dann wäre er bald wieder bis zum Genfer See, dessen Becken er ehedem ausgehöhlt hat, vorgedrungen.

Ein schönes Bild bietet die Zunge des Grindelwaldgletschers (Abbildung 56), der weit herab in die bewaldete und bewohnte Zone vordringt. Seine kolossalen, wunderbar blaugrünen Eismassen sind bis oberhalb Grindelwald in etwa 1000 Meter über NN vorgeschoben. Die alten Seitenmoränen sind dicht mit Nadelwald bestanden. Nicht weit vom Gletscherbruch entfernt stehen starke, fruchttragende Birnbäume. So dicht wie hier platzen die Gegensätze — blühende

53 Starke Mittelmoränen des Gornergletschers (Kanton Wallis)

108

54 Nördliche Seitenmoräne des Morteratschgletschers

55 Gletscherzunge und Endmoräne des Rhonegletschers

Sonnenbrand oder auf der schattigen Winterseite, das Weidenröschen kommt vortrefflich fort und blüht den ganzen Sommer über.

Einen prächtigen Herbststrauß bringen die abgeblühten Kreuzkrautarten hervor, die auf trockenen Halden, Eisenbahndämmen, Schuttabladeplätzen und dergleichen in mitunter ungeheuren Mengen wachsen. Auf sie trifft zu, was bei Disteln und Weidenröschen gesagt ist. Auch dieses Kraut dringt immer weiter vor, und alle menschliche Mühe, es zu verdrängen, wird vergebens sein.

Neben dieser Art der Samenverbreitung finden wir bei unseren Spaziergängen im Herbst auch noch andere Beweise dafür, wie sich eine Art, und sei sie auch ein ganz gemeiner Schädling aus dem Reich der niederen Pilze, behaupten kann. Wenn wir durch den herbstlichen Wald schreiten, fallen uns viele Blätter des Ahorns auf (Abbildung 76), die über und über wie von Teertropfen überzogen erscheinen. Mitunter ist es schwer, ein Blatt ohne solche Teertropfen zu finden, so ungeheuer zahlreich ist jener Pilz, der diese Mißbildung hervorruft. Es ist der Ahornschorf, der auf Millionen von Ahornblättern schmarotzt, mit dem fallenden Laub zur Erde fällt und im nächsten Jahr mit derselben Regelmäßigkeit wiedererscheint. Dieser Schmarotzer hat eine förmliche Lebensgemeinschaft mit dem Ahornbaum geschlossen, so daß wir uns ein Ahornblatt kaum ohne ihn denken können.

Eine ungleich schönere Mißbildung sind die Galläpfel, die auf Buchen, Weiden und vor allen Dingen auf Eichen vorkommen. Der Eichgallapfel (Abbildung 77)

76 Ahornschorf

77 Eichgalläpfel

wird hervorgerufen durch den Stich der Eichgallwespe, die das Blatt anstichst, um ein Ei in den Stichkanal zu legen. Wenn man einen der prachtvoll gelb bis karminroten »Äpfel« anschneidet, findet man die Larve der Gallwespe darin. Die Larve überwintert in ihrem eigenartigen Gehäuse bis zum Frühjahr, um dann auszukriechen und sich von neuem fortzupflanzen. Es darf als wunderbares Spiel der Natur betrachtet werden, daß der Zellaufbaustoff des Eichenblattes, durch den Stich der winzigen Gallwespe geätzt, eine so eigenartige Mißbildung hervorbringt.

Eine Glanzleistung des Herbstes ist die *Herbstzeitlose* (Abbildung 78). Man muß lange bei ihr verweilen, um die ganze Eigenart dieser Pflanze zu erkennen. Sie ist ein Muster von Anpassung. Ihre niedrige Blüte erscheint im Herbst, wenn die Wiesen zum letzten Male geschnitten sind. In höherem Gras kann sie wegen der Beschaffenheit ihres Blütenstengels nicht aufkommen. In ihrer schön hellila gefärbten Blüte sehen wir sechs Staubgefäße und drei gekrümmte Griffel, aber keinen Fruchtknoten wie bei anderen Pflanzen. Der Fruchtknoten sitzt tief in der Erde in einem Seitenstengel der Knolle, und von hier aus gehen die Stempel oder Griffel durch die ganze auch von hier aus wachsende

141

Typefaces for phototypesetting 1933–6

At the same time that Tschichold was writing his long article about book design, he also began a job designing new typefaces for the pioneering phototypesetting system called Uhertype. The first experiments in the application of photography to setting type date from around the turn of the twentieth century, and the sense of expectation that a successful resolution of the problem was imminent by the 1920s is reflected in the optimistic predictions by Moholy-Nagy and Lissitzky that photographic technology would soon carry typography free from its lead foundations. Early experimenters in phototypesetting were able to master the problems of spacing and justifying type along a line, but greater difficulties were presented by the requirements of correcting texts once exposed on a photographic substrate and of then making them up into pages. Making corrections in metal type composition was facilitated by the persistence of the modular nature of type into mechanical typesetting systems – traditional, single letter sorts on Monotype, and individual lines cast as single slugs on Linotype and Inter-type – but the removal of the letter image from its physical body presented wholly new challenges.

The breakthrough in this latter respect was made in 1930 by the Hungarian inventor Edmund Uher, who separated the procedure into two stages: exposing individual lines of typeset characters onto narrow strips of photographic film, and then combining them at a later stage into a text and page layout by a further photographic exposure. At the second stage the type image could also be increased or decreased in size photographically, a possibility which constituted the principal difference with traditional type-setting, in which type-size was physically locked into an immutable piece of metal. Uher also produced a separate device for outputting display lines in large type sizes (16 to 84 point), which was misleadingly dubbed the 'handset-ting' machine (and was roughly equivalent to a Monotype supercaster).[73] The Uhertype 'Metteurmaschine' (makeup machine) could paginate texts with inserted running heads and even combine type with images output as half-tones, anticipating the capabilities of today's digital imagesetters. It also had the capacity to set type not only horizontally but at angles, thereby fulfilling a desire shared by many New Typographers, which had until then required makeshift measures when using metal type. It was surely Lissitzky's habit of breaking the traditional rectilinear confines of let-terpress typography that Tschichold had in mind when he suggested to Uhertype that there would be strong interest from the USSR in its invention, and indeed he sent a pro-spectus for the Uher device to Lissitzky in autumn 1933.[74]

The freedom in layout brought by the Uhertype was rec-ognized by the editor of the *Penrose Annual*, R.B. Fishenden, when he saw the system on trial at a British printing house:

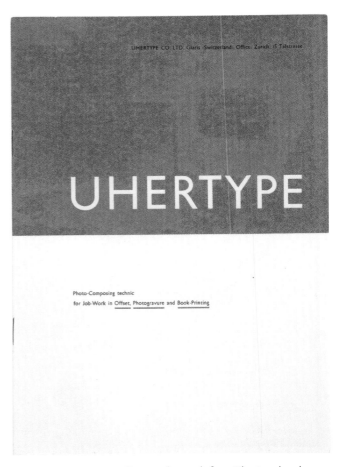

Cover and spreads from Uhertype brochure. 1933. A4. Designed by Tschichold and typeset in his Uhertype sanserif.

In display composition any part of the work can be set at unusual angles, letters or lines can be overlaid with line or suitable tints, backgrounds introduced, or line designs with ease and with greater speed than would be possible with similar complicated work if set in type. In fact many of the effects produced would be quite impracticable if an attempt were made to set them typographically.[75]

In 1927 Edmund Uher had entered into an agreement with MAN AG, the German manufacturer of printing presses, to develop his fledgeling machine into a prototype for commercial production. Uher principally envisaged that his invention would feed into lithographic and gravure printing, and so he was content to be in partnership with MAN (which provided a sizeable financial investment) due to its experience with printing machinery. Although Uher was based in Budapest and MAN in Augsburg, the business concern of Uhertype was set up in March 1929 with a base

73. For an overview of the Uhertype process see: Bretag, 'Das Problem der Lichtsatz-maschine – hat Uher das Problem gelöst?'; Münch, 'The origins of modern filmsetting'.

74. Letters: Uhertype to Tschichold, 9 September 1933; Tschichold to Uhertype, 14 September 1933. All corres-pondence cited concerning the Uhertype project is taken from the MAN Archive.

75. Fishenden, 'Uhertype at Waterlows'. Unpublished type-script, 1934 (St Bride).

The film holder is provided with an equal sized sighting disc on which a transparent paper can be stretched. They are both rigidly connected together and can be shifted at will. The image to be projected appears on the sighting disc, or on the film, in exactly the same position and size. Regulation is then effected to suit the dimensions to be worked to. The film holder is then opened and the film exposed.

Besides the raking of ordinary and complicated images, the making-up machine is suitable for all classes of photo-mechanical work. It is suitable also for adding, repeating and copying work; it is also provided with a device for the setting-up of tables; it is, further, a reproducing apparatus for the enlargement and reduction of images, and it is also fitted for the making of screens from Dia halftones. It yields work in any size and position: isolated lines, and series of lines, mitred closed-in lined frames, hatched lines,

halftones, parallel and crossed lines, screens, circles, ovals, ornaments single and intricate, closed ornamental frames, hatched and lined letters, letters placed one over the other, negative type, monograms, and many other kinds of work. The possible combinations are unlimited.

Quite a number of type and other work are now available. The Uhertype Co. is in a position to supply rapidly any miscellaneous new type and further fundamental elements.

➡ The machines can be seen in operation in Zurich.

It consists of a photographic reproduction camera, which carries on a glass disc, measuring 27×33 cm (lo 5/8×13 in.), the characters being dealt with at the time, and projects them for setting-up in any suitable size on a 35 mm (l 3/8 in.) film strip.

By this means it is possible to shift the letters over the height of one letter, also to insert underlinings and to arrange several lines one above the other.

The type images thus obtained are further dealt with by photo-mounting, or in the making-up machine. The operation of the hand photo-composing machine is very simple and requires no particular special training. The compositor is given simply the manuscript, with the indication of the kind of type to be used, its size, and the length of the pull.

The MAKING-UP MACHINE enables the carrying out without a break of even the most complicated artistic job-work, with a perfection hitherto unattainable. On the making-up machine, and after the pulls have been passed, the most complicated kinds of job-work are executed purely mechanically with the matter obtained in the photo-composing machine. This machine consists of the object-support, on which are placed the image carrier, film lines and transparent photographic images for reproduction, together with the making-up film holder and carriage.

Making-up machine

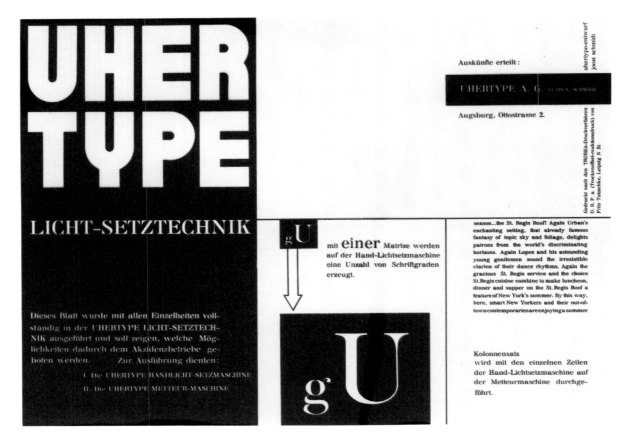

Joost Schmidt, leaflet for Uhertype (positive film output). 1932. A4. The text typeface is Deberny & Peignot's Romain No.16, specially adapted for phototypesetting. This typeface had previously been adapted for mechanical composition on both Linotype (as No.16) and Monotype (as Fridericus Antiqua, a name under which it had already become popular in Germany).

in Zurich, the other investment partner in the enterprise being a Swiss banking firm. By 1932 a second, greatly improved prototype of the Uher typesetting machine had been constructed and was installed at the Zurich printing house of Fretz, where all three major printing processes (letterpress, stone & offset lithography, and gravure) were in operation.

For the first attempts at printed publicity for the new technique of 'Lichtsatz' (literally, typesetting with light) Uhertype approached an institution famous for its positive attitude to new technology, the Bauhaus. Moholy-Nagy, principal evangelist for the properties of light, had left the Bauhaus by this time, and so Joost Schmidt, as head of the advertising department, was commissioned in autumn 1932 to design leaflets and an exhibition display for the new machine. Schmidt's geometric namestyle for Uhertype featured on this material struck an appropriately futuristic note, although the typeface used for the text, which was naturally typeset on the Uher machine, was not designed by Schmidt and was not any kind of modernist letterform.[76] It was a French roman, already popular in Germany, which had originated in the nineteenth century at Deberny &

Peignot and was adapted by that typefoundry specifically for Uhertype.[77]

In 1928 Moholy-Nagy had suggested that the advent of phototypesetting should provide a kind of 'year zero' for the form of typefaces. He believed that it was necessary 'to create a type-form functionally suited to the process':

> The problem of printing technology consists in the matching of composition and printing methods to the spiritual and technical discoveries of our time and not in improving the form of yesterday's type-form.[78]

Yet, like all technological innovations in formatting text, from Gutenberg onwards, the Uhertype would be measured by the standards and conventions of the previous technology; it would not have served the financial interests of its inventor and investors to restrict the machine's potential by offering typefaces that accorded only with the formal preferences of a few visionary modernists. The Uhertype had to prove that it could set type in the same fashion and just as

76. It is possible that some initial trials were made of Schmidt's letters as a typeface – see the photograph at top right of p.223 above.

77. Co-incidentally Tschichold had mentioned this very typeface in *The New Typography* (p.76) as one of the best, contemporary romans. He called it Französische Antiqua (it was renamed Fridericus Antiqua by the Genzsch & Heyse typefoundry in 1923).

78. Moholy-Nagy, 'Elementare Buchtechnik', pp.61–2.

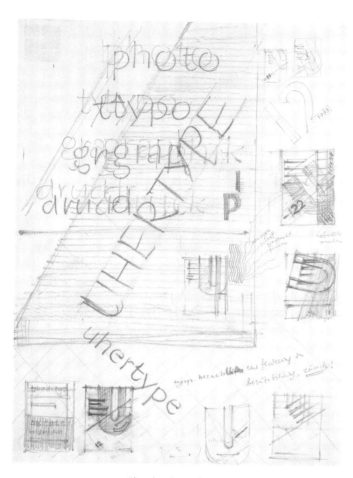

Sketches by Tschichold for Uhertype publicity, including a projected cover of *Typographische Monatsblätter*. 1933. A4.

well as metal typesetting machines before it could go on to prove its own particular advantages.

Joost Schmidt lost his job at the Bauhaus when the Nazis closed it down. He was certainly keen to continue work for Uhertype, even moving to the southernmost part of Germany, near to the Swiss border, in order to be near the source of his commission. But, cruelly, the Nazis froze his bank account and seized the funds that were paid into it from Uhertype, reflecting the pervasive nature of the cultural discrimination that characterized the Third Reich from its very beginning. Tschichold and Schmidt never seemed to have had any substantial contact and the latter's work for Uhertype was barely mentioned by Tschichold or Uhertype during their subsequent association.

It was Tschichold's former student colleague, Walter Cyliax, who acted as the agent for him receiving the commission to design new typefaces for the Uhertype. Fretz, where Cyliax was art director between 1924 and 1936, not only housed the prototype Uher machines but also seemed to be engaged as creative advisers to Uhertype. Having suggested to Tschichold the idea of designing typefaces for the new system on a previous visit to Munich, Cyliax wrote to him on 11 May

1933 explaining requirements for six typefaces (roman and italic in 'mediäval' character, sanserif and Egyptian in light and bold versions) and asked him to make an estimate of his fee. He added that it was obviously necessary 'to exploit the special possibilities and characteristics of the photosetting machine' and advised him to contact either Uher himself or the MAN works at Augsburg in this regard.[79] Given his status as an unemployable 'cultural bolshevik' in Nazi Germany, Tschichold impressed on Cyliax the importance of this commission for him: 'With this my existence will be secured for the coming months, and you can imagine that everything relies on me getting this job.' He expressed a preference for progressive payments over several months, with an agreement to finish the six typefaces in six months. He asked for 800 German marks for each typeface (with a discount of 15 per cent if all six were commissioned at once), although he pointed out that his quoted fee was 'already well below normal'. (In fact he had accepted much less for his typeface designs in 1929.) 'As it happens,' he commented to Cyliax, 'the whole thing excites me very much, as there are many new problems to solve here.'[80]

It seems that Cyliax advocated Tschichold strongly for the job, for which he could easily have been presented as the ideal candidate: an enthusiast for new technology, yet possessing a thorough grounding in calligraphy and typography. It may partly have been Tschichold's decision to begin by designing the sanserif from among the list of requested type-styles, but in general his approach to designing the Uher typefaces was conservative: understandably, he did not want to risk endangering such a substantial commission by forcing revolutionary ideas on his clients. He wrote to Uhertype expressing his enthusiasm, but also indicating one of his priorities: 'I am excited by your discovery and would be very pleased if a lasting business relationship can be built up between us.'[81] In his precarious and uncertain situation at this time, with a wife and young son to support, he saw a welcome opportunity to secure some lasting work that usefully stemmed from outside Germany. No doubt the Uhertype management, as advised by the people at Fretz, perceived some commercial advantage in producing original typefaces unique to its machine, and the prospect of having its own dedicated designer may have appealed more than continuing to rely on producers of metal type, whose market they intended to usurp. It is clear from Tschichold's dealings with Uhertype that he wanted to become the sole provider, at least in the short term, of typefaces for the new system. His connection with the Zurich-based company seems not to have been a determining factor in his being given authorization to settle in Switzerland, but prospects of a long-term collaboration are likely to have influ-

79. Cyliax addressed Tschichold as 'Hans', having known him since he was called Johannes.

80. Letter Tschichold to Cyliax, 12 May 1933.
81. Letter Tschichold to Uhertype, 17 May 1933.

enced his decision to go there. The degree to which Tschichold relied on his income from the Uhertype project during his first years in Switzerland is evidenced by his frequent begging letters for advance or at least prompt payment. With some understatement he explained his financial instability after the upheaval of leaving Germany in July 1933: 'At the moment I have no financial support, as the summer, with its unusual circumstances for me, has cost me an extraordinary amount of money.'[82]

When Tschichold learned that the number of characters he would have to draw for each typeface was at least 125, with additional accented variants, he informed Uhertype of a twenty per cent increase in his fee. The ensuing pay negotiations, which continued for the duration of the work, were complicated by Tschichold's determination to receive what he deemed fair. He also demanded a royalty on copies of the typeface to be sold, which turned out to be a futile request, given that the Uher machine was never produced commercially and so none of Tschichold's typefaces were ever purchased by customers. Uhertype was understandably reluctant to meet Tschichold's financial demands, given the massive financial outlay that had to be made in support of Uher's continuing experiments, which did not progress as had been hoped. The total payment that Tschichold eventually received for his work on the Uher typefaces was a mere trifle compared to the one million Swiss francs that MAN had already spent on the whole project by 1933.

Nevertheless an agreement was reached and Tschichold began work on six typefaces in June 1933, while still living in Munich. His first monthly advance was paid to him in Germany, which means that he was subject to fewer official sanctions at that point than Joost Schmidt, although the National Socialists might well have caught up with Tschichold in this respect if he had stayed in Munich (he only received two advance payments in Germany before emigrating to Switzerland). Due to the proximity of Munich to the MAN industrial works in Augsburg, Tschichold was able to meet engineers involved in the Uher project at this early stage in order to inform himself of the system's characteristics. Letters had to be allocated widths (including the space either side of them) according to fixed unit values, in order for the machine to handle the matter of escapement (regulating the placement of letters in sequence during photographic exposure onto film). The MAN engineers seem to have been a little unclear about the reason for this initially, referring to it principally as a requirement for automatically justifying type (distributing extra space in a line between the words so as to give a straight right-hand edge). A similar requirement underpinned the production of typefaces for the Monotype mechanical typesetter. Additionally Tschichold's drawings had to be of specific dimensions and be transferred onto pre-supplied zinc plates for delivery to Uhertype. The reason for this remains unclear, but these plates then provided masters

for making the small-scale photographic images of letters on a glass cylinder to be held within the Uhertype for exposure onto film.[83] In a typical adoption of terminology from the previous technology, the engineers referred to these as 'matrices'; ever the stickler for accuracy, Tschichold responded: 'I suggest the introduction of another name for this. They are not actually matrices.'[84]

Tschichold engaged a lithographer in Munich to make the transfer of his drawings to the zinc plates, on which he also marked the unitary width of each letter including its side-bearings. He was informed that characters could occupy one of twelve width variations resulting from dividing the square of a nominal type size on the Uhertype into twelve equal units. In practice these units equated to 12 mm increments on Tschichold's drawings. This was a relatively coarse unit system, which entailed significant restrictions on the subtlety of width variation in the letters. In this matter Tschichold's advice was pointed and persuasive, showing that he understood the nature of typeface design for industrial application. He asked if some intermediate widths could be introduced:

> This question is really of fundamental importance, as it decisively influences the artistic and rhythmic quality of the typeface. It is conceivable that this difficulty did not arise in the drawing of a roman by Deberny-Peignot. But that is no counter-evidence, for the production of a perfect rhythm in roman is significantly easier than in sanserif. In roman one always has the possibility of balancing faults in the precise rhythm by shortening or lengthening of the serifs (the thin horizontal endstrokes). In sanserif this possibility is wholly absent. (Think of typewriter typefaces as an extreme case of forcible balancing by rigorous lengthening and shortening of the serifs.)
>
> I would like most pressingly to advise that at least the interim widths of 42, 66 and 78 mm be introduced. We find ourselves here in a historical moment of the Uhertype: either we restrict the range of widths to too few, then the quality of the type suffers as much as in the Linotype, for which the typefaces are catastrophically uneven in spacing, in my opinion (due to too few available widths), or we refine the width divisions so as to open the way for such perfect types as those on the Monotype. It seems to me absolutely necessary to follow the latter path, and I ask you for the quickest possible decision on the matter.[85]

As a result of this the MAN engineers agreed to an effective spacing system of sixteen units (equating to 10 mm increments on the drawings), which Tschichold admitted was a significant improvement, permitting standards of quality equivalent to handset metal type. He did not at any point question the rationale offered to him for the unit system (the need for the Uhertype to justify text); as we have seen,

82. Letter Tschichold to Uhertype, 16 December 1933.
83. In a contemporary report, it was stated simply that a 'special machine' was used to make

the glass cylinder. See Albert, 'Zum Problem der photomechanischen Setztechnik'. The 'hand-setting' version of the machine operated with the images held

in a flat 'matrix' plate
84. Letter Tschichold to Uhertype, 6 June 1933.
85. Letter Tschichold to Uhertype, 6 June 1933.

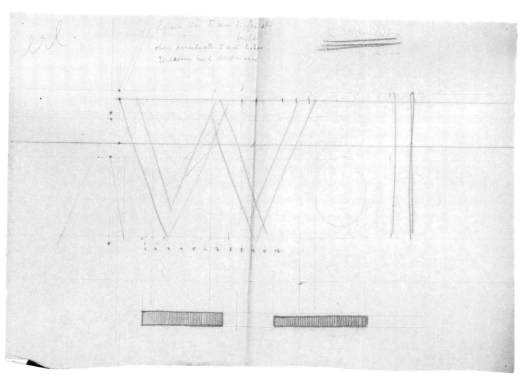

Sketch illustrating the proportions initially dictated by Uhertype for typeface drawings. It specifies twelve possible character widths, a system which was revised on Tschichold's advice.

Sketches and specimens sent by Tschichold to Uhertype for prospective typefaces. Some of these date from his previous burst of activity in type design, c.1929. A photographically reduced proof of his unproduced stencil typeface for Stempel is included here (left), showing a fine weight with an italic.

Early drawing for regular weight of the Uhertype
sanserif. 1933. This relates to his earlier attempts
at a geometric sanserif.

he never advocated unjustified (or ranged-left) typesetting
as part of his asymmetrical approach to typography.

It was partly due to the initial necessity of addressing
such technical complexities that Tschichold took longer to
deliver his typefaces than was hoped by his clients, and they
threatened to impose a penalty clause in the original agreement which would reduce his fee. Herr Mast of Uhertype
informed him in December 1933:

> we really need your typefaces for our practical work and you
> can well appreciate what a significant misfortune we suffer
> in the development of our phototypesetting technology in
> not yet having any usable typefaces at all at our disposal.

In a sense, then, Tschichold's typefaces were experimental
fodder for the Uher machine. Herr Mast added that

> we believed that with your collaboration we had won a per-
> sonality who would serve us with great understanding and
> full dedication and diligence in the rapid development of
> photosetting technology.

Tschichold replied to this on the same day:

> I regret very much that the delivery of the typefaces has
> been delayed. The reasons consist partly in the particular
> difficulties offered by production of Uhertype faces, which
> far surpass those of normal typefaces and which I could only
> dimly perceive when taking on the commission. Furthermore
> my moving to Switzerland and the circumstance that my
> removal van, containing a large quantity of important refer-
> ence material, was only allowed entry here eight weeks after
> my own entry has significantly contributed to this delay.
> I have however been tackling the job with doubled energy
> immediately after the granting of a work permit and am in

the position of being able to deliver at least four more types
by end of the year. ...

> I have often pointed out that the extent of this work
> far exceeds the amount that I expected, having based my
> estimate on the work for a normal typeface. Without exag-
> geration I can say that the job would not be too highly paid
> at double the fee. I do accept that I will be compensated in
> some degree for this considerable amount of extra work by a
> royalty payment, which still requires arrangement. But that
> depends on the success of the Uhertype and that will be deter-
> mined by factors over which I have little influence. I hope, in
> the light of these circumstances, that you will refrain from
> demanding the conventional penalty from me, especially
> because I drew attention to the fact on acceptance of the brief
> that a punctual execution was not entirely assured. ...

> You yourself can certainly confirm that I have gone about
> the drawing of the first sanserif with all conceivable care, and
> that the result, already in the first attempt, was as good as per-
> fect, probably coming as a pleasant surprise to all interested
> parties.[86]

Indeed most of the basic technical hurdles had to be overcome with the first version of the sanserif that was drawn;
thenceforth, once the norms were established, the other
typefaces followed in quick succession.

Uhertype itself also caused significant delays in the
progress of producing the typefaces. Both versions of the
prototype machine housed at Fretz were out of commission
for this purpose for a period of around five months in 1934,
during which they were on extended loan to the printers
Waterlow & Sons at Dunstable in England. Edmund Uher

86. Letter Tschichold to Uhertype, 6 December 1933.

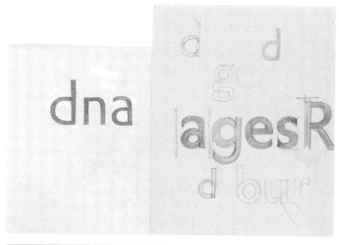

Sketches for development of the Uhertype sanserif, along with other ideas. The sketch on lined notepaper marks a change from a Futura-like capital R to one inspired by Gill Sans.

(Letterhead on the paper used for this sketch also designed by Tschichold.)

had taken out British patents in 1930 and MAN wanted to test the machine's potential *in situ*. Like Fretz, Waterlow & Sons printed by gravure and lithography, producing many posters for the London Underground. In fact the firm purchased the Uher 'handsetting' machine in 1936 for 22,000 marks and some limited work was typeset with it (see pp. 245–6).[87]

The extremely short time-schedule set by Fretz and Uhertype for delivery of Tschichold's drawings, with the first type due after only one month, perhaps led him to forego any great originality in his designs and to take inspiration instead from some good existing typefaces. The 'Uhertype Standard Grotesque' that he designed was not really a grotesque, instead it was very closely modelled on the humanist sanserif designed by Eric Gill for the British Monotype Corporation (1927–8). Indeed Tschichold's typeface is identical in many important details and the resemblance cannot be accidental; he would have been well aware of Gill Sans

from at least 1930, when his article 'New life in print' for *Commercial Art* was typeset in it. Yet Tschichold never mentioned Gill Sans in relation to his Uhertype sanserif, either while designing it, or subsequently. Neither did Cyliax or Max Fretz, who were charged with approving the 'artistic formation' of Tschichold's proposals and who accepted the sanserif as 'very good' towards the end of June 1933.[88] Such a close imitation by Tschichold of Gill Sans betrays the fact that by this point, just before leaving Germany, he had already developed a strong preference for a sanserif based on the proportions of classical roman letters instead of the common grotesque types he had used previously in his own typography. This was made clear when Tschichold showed a specimen of his Uhertype sanserif in an educational collection of 'good letterforms' published in 1942:

This grotesque, unlike most grotesques of the present day, does not fall back on the exaggerated simplicity of the decayed forms of roman and grotesque from the beginning of the nineteenth century; instead it displays in the capitals as well as in the small letters the original, fully developed form and width proportions of the classical, Renaissance roman.[89]

87. Münch, 'The origins of modern filmsetting', p. 36.

88. Letter Cyliax to Tschichold, 23 June 1933.

89. *Gute Schriftformen*, part 3: 'Inschriften und Aufschriften', pp. 13–17.

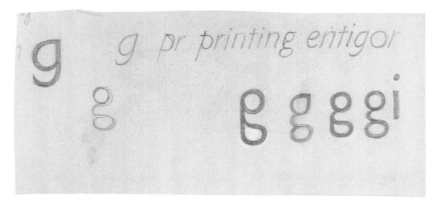

More sketches for the Uhertype sanserif, in particular for the small g (a character that can be the most challenging but also the most enjoyable for a typeface designer). Around half of actual size.

(Right) This sketch shows the clear influence of Gill Sans, especially in the numerals and in the bold letters, which are very similar to Gill Sans Extra Bold (1931).

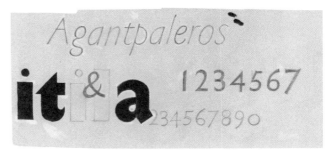

On several occasions in later years he expressed his admiration for Gill Sans and it is clear that he had recognized the same virtue in it:

> The common grotesque typefaces ... suffer from being derived from the common [modern face] roman and from having inherited its fatuous proportions. Gill Sans was the first to develop this category of type anew on the basis of the classical roman and give it the correct proportions. It is incomparably better than all these nineteenth-century grotesque forms with their tortured curves and the tendency to make all letters the same width, which has for a long time been recognized as incorrect. Gill Sans also has a matching italic, which is very necessary but is lacking in most sanserifs, and a precisely harmonious bold weight.[90]

Tschichold also provided a proper, cursive italic for the light weight of his Uhertype sanserif.

No negotiations of the rights to Gill Sans were made between Uhertype and Monotype, although there was some contact between the two companies regarding the possibility of Monotype supplying drawings of two of its typefaces for use on the Uher machine.[91] If the Uhertype had gone into production and proven a success, and if Tschichold's typefaces had thereby become more widely known, it is conceivable that Monotype could have sought some legal redress on the matter.

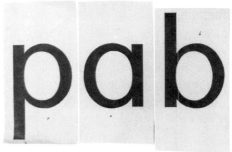

90. 'Was bei der Anschaffung neuer Schriften zu bedenken ist' (1951), p.9.

91. One of the proposed typefaces was Plantin but Tschichold instead suggested Baskerville, which he considered to be 'essentially more elegant'. Letter Tschichold to Uhertype, 9 January 1934.

Two sequences of drawings showing Tschichold progressing from static, oval-based letters to more dynamic shapes.

Selection of character drawings for regular,
bold and light weights of the Uhertype sanserif.
1933–6. 25% of actual size. The top line shows
both capital and small capital R. The second line
includes original and revised versions of the small
g. The drawings for small b and q are not simply
rotated versions of each other – there are subtle
differences in the way that curves meet the stem.

(Right) Spread from Uhertype specimen. 1935.
31.2 × 23 cm. Shows the light italic of the sanserif
and larger sizes of the regular weight.

Gill Sans made its first appearance
printing industry in 1928 in the pr
the *Federation of Master Printers'*
This was the titling, Series 231, whi
commissioned by The Monotype (
Limited from Eric Gill, and was based
bet used by Gill on the facia of a B
shop. Lower-case letters soon follo
lated bolds, titlings and other va
added from time to time until the
contained some twenty-four series.

11 point Gill Sans from a Monotype specimen.
Actual size.

(Below) Text from the first Uhertype brochure
(1933) typeset in the 'Uhertype Standard Grotesque'. It shows the first iteration of the design,
which is marked by the characteristic small g
without an ear at top right.

(Opposite below) The second version used in the
text of the booklet *Typesetting methods old and
new* (1938), produced at Waterlow & Sons. After
seeing proofs of the first version, Tschichold evidently realized that the small g definitely needed
the upper terminal. The text here explains the
method of justification of text on the Uhertype.

(Opposite above) Drawings for a third version of
the sanserif small g, which never reached production. Here Tschichold has closed the gap in the
lower bowl.

MAGERE GROTESK KURSIV

12 Punkt Durchschuss 2 Punkt

abcdefghijklmnopqrsßtuvwxyzäöü., --:;!?'„·(|+×»—|£$%
ABCDEFGHIJKLMNOPQRSTUVWXYZAÖÜ1234567890
In der Metteurmaschine werden die Zeilenvorlagen auf dem lichtempfindlichen Film mit den gewünschten Zeilenabständen untereinander
photographiert. Durch Verdrehung eines Einstellrades kann das Originalbild beliebig von dreieinhalbfacher Vergrößerung bis zweieinhalbfacher
Verkleinerung vergrößert bzw. verkleinert werden, wobei durch die auto-

12 Punkt Durchschuss 6 Punkt

matische Scharfeinstellung das projizierte Bild bei jeder Einstellung automatisch auf höchste Schärfe eingestellt bleibt. Somit kann also von
dem Zeilenprodukt, welches in der Schriftgröße an und für sich starr
ist, durch dieses Umbruchverfahren das Umbrechen in feste Kolonnen
IN DER METTEURMASCHINE WERDEN DIE ZEILENVORLAGEN

14 Punkt Durchschuss 2 Punkt

abcdefghijklmnopqrsßtuvwxyzäöü., --:;!?'„·(|+×»—|£$%
ABCDEFGHIJKLMNOPQRSTUVWXYZAÖÜ1234567890
In der Metteurmaschine werden die Zeilenvorlagen auf dem
lichtempfindlichen Film mit den gewünschten Zeilenabständen
untereinander photographiert. Durch Verdrehung eines Einstellrades kann das Originalbild beliebig von dreieinhalbfacher Ver-

14 Punkt Durchschuss 6 Punkt

größerung bis zweieinhalbfacher Verkleinerung vergrößert bzw.
verkleinert werden, wobei durch die automatische Scharfeinstellung das projizierte Bild bei jeder Einstellung automatisch
IN DER METTEURMASCHINE WERDEN DIE ZEILENVOR-

16 Punkt Durchschuss 2 Punkt

abcdefghijklmnopqrsßtuvwxyzäöü., --:;!?'„·(|+×»—|£
ABCDEFGHIJKLMNOPQRSTUVWXYZAÖÜ1234567
In der Metteurmaschine werden die Zeilenvorlagen
auf dem lichtempfindlichen Film mit den gewünschten Zeilenabständen untereinander photographiert.

16 Punkt Durchschuss 6 Punkt

Durch Verdrehung eines Einstellrades kann das Originalbild beliebig von dreieinhalbfacher Vergrößerung
bis zweieinhalbfacher Verkleinerung vergrößert bzw.
IN DER METTEURMASCHINE WERDEN DIE ZE-

In erster Linie wird die Herstellung des Schriftsatzes für OFFSET-
und TIEFDRUCK durch das Uhertype-Verfahren vereinfacht und
zeitlich verkürzt. Da diese Verfahren sich mit der fortschreiten-
den Entwicklung der Photochemie mehr und mehr ausbreiten, besteht schon seit langem das Bedürfnis nach einer Setzmaschine, die
Filme statt Metallzeilen erzeugt. Die seit drei Jahrzehnten ange-
strebte Erfindung des photomechanischen Setzverfahrens ist durch
die UHERTYPE-Lichtsetztechnik einwandfrei gelöst.

HALBFETTE GROTESK

abcdefghijklmnopqrsßtuvwxyz äöü
ABCDEFGHIJKLMNOPQRSTUVWXYZÄ
&.,-–:;!?'„"‹‹+×»—/£$%‰ 1234567890

20 Punkt Durchschuss 4 Punkt

UM DAS AUSSCHLIESZEN DER ZEI-
LEN AUF GLEICHE LÄNGE BEWIRKEN

abcdefghijklmnopqrsßtuvwxyz äöü
ABCDEFGHIJKLMNOPQRSTUVW
XYZÄÖÜ 1234567890

24 Punkt Durchschuss 4 Punkt

UM DAS AUSSCHLIESZEN DER

abcdefghijklmnopqrsßtuvwxyz ä
ABCDEFGHIJKLMNOPQRST
UVWXYZÄÖÜ 1234567890

28 Punkt Durchschuss 4 Punkt

UM DAS AUSSCHLIESZEN

abcdefghijklmnopqrsßtuv
wxyz äöü 1234567890
ABCDEFGHIJKLMNOP
QRSTUVWXYZÄÖÜ

36 Punkt Durchschuss 4 Punkt

word and uncovering the second. We see the second word in the window move a little to the left. The movement is effected by an ingenious device which forms the essential part of the machine. Of this justifying device outwardly little is visible except the crank which the operator turned at the start. It measures the blank space at the end of the un-justified line, mechanically divides it by the number of word intervals and causes the image of every word following the first to move to the left an even fraction of the blank space before it is projected. The second word is projected. The third word is uncovered and projected and so on word by word until the line now spaced to the proper length, is completed. The depression of a lever on the left hand side of the machine brings a new line into position for justifying and rotates the film in holder (3) the required distance, and we are ready to go on.

STANDARD GROTESQUE

20 point.

Turning over the leaves of a printed b
TURNING OVER THE LEAVES OF A

36 point.

Turning over the leav
TURNING OVER THE

Specimens of the Uhertype sanserif:

(Above) Second version of the regular weight shown in type specimen produced at Waterlow & Sons. 1938. 84% of actual size.

(Right) Bold weight in Uhertype specimen. 1935. 31.2 × 23 cm.

DREIVIERTELFETTE GROTESK

48 Punkt Kompress

ABCDEFGHIJKL
MNOPQRSTUVW
XYZÄÖÜ123456

60 Punkt Kompress

ABCDEFGHIJ
KLMNOPQRS

72 Punkt Kompress

ABCDEFG
HIJKLMNO

84 Punkt Kompress

ABCDEF
GHIJKLM

The second new typeface family designed by Tschichold for Uhertype was the requested Egyptian, which became known as Ramses. Again it bore strong similarities to an existing typeface – City, designed by his former Munich colleague Georg Trump – although the first, rough drawings for Tschichold's Egyptian are dated 1929, implying that any influence may in fact have run in the reverse direction. In any case, as the specimens of Ramses typeset on the Uhertype show, it took on more characteristics of City in its final form. As such it is a modernized and geometric essay in the Egyptian tradition, more deserving of the description slab-serif. Given the inordinately short time in which Tschichold had to design his typefaces, it seems natural for him to have revived earlier designs of his own, and he even sent to Fretz some small samples of the unreleased stencil typeface that he had designed in 1929 for Stempel, obviously in the hope of persuading them to commission more and different typefaces from him.

Georg Trump, cover and page of type specimen for his typeface City. 1930.

Initial rough drawings for slab-serif typeface that became Uhertype Ramses. 1929. 30% of actual size.

Further drawing for slab-serif typeface. c.1929. Tschichold has worked over the middle line, experimentally filling in the open junctions between stems and curves and thereby approximating a feature of the City typeface's regular weight.

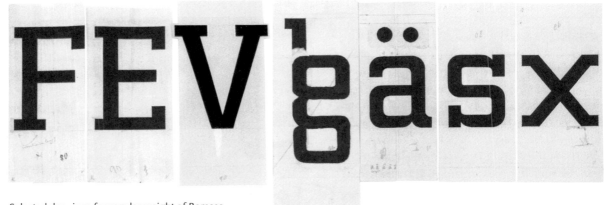

Selected drawings for regular weight of Ramses.
1933. 25% of actual size. Shows a rejected version
of small g. The drawing of V is made with ink of a
remarkably deep black.

Ramses regular in Uhertype specimen. 1935.
31.2 × 23 cm.

RAMSES HALBFETT

abcdefghijklmnopqrsßtuvwxyz äöü
ABCDEFGHIJKLMNOPQRSTUVWXYZÄÖ
Et.,-–:;!?'„''((+×« — /£$º/o 1234567890

BEI AUSFÜHRUNG DER AKZIDENZAR-
BEIT WERDEN DIE IN DIESEM SATZ-

2o Punkt Durchschuss 4 Punkt

abcdefghijklmnopqrsßtuvwxyz äö
ABCDEFGHIJKLMNOPQRSTUVW
XYZÄÖÜ 1234567890

BEI AUSFÜHRUNG DER AKZIDE

24 Punkt Durchschuss 4 Punkt

abcdefghijklmnopqrsßtuvwx
ABCDEFGHIJKLMNOPQRST
UVWXYZÄÖÜ 1234567890

BEI AUSFÜHRUNG DER AK

28 Punkt Durchschuss 4 Punkt

abcdefghijklmnopqrsß
tuvwxyz äöü 123456789
ABCDEFGHIJKLMNOP
QRSTUVWXYZÄÖÜ

36 Punkt Durchschuss 4 Punkt

Selected drawings for bold weight of Ramses.
1933/4.

RAMSES FETT

48 Punkt Kompress

ABCDEFGHIJKL
MNOPQRSTUVW
XYZÄÖÜ1234567

60 Punkt Kompress

ABCDEFGHIJ
KLMNOPQRS

72 Punkt Kompress

ABCDEFGH
IJKLMNOP

84 Punkt Kompress

ABCDEFG
HIJKLMN

Ramses bold in Uhertype specimen. 1935.
31.2 × 23 cm.

Diagram of character sets for typefaces on the Uhertype. From *Typesetting methods old and new* (1938).

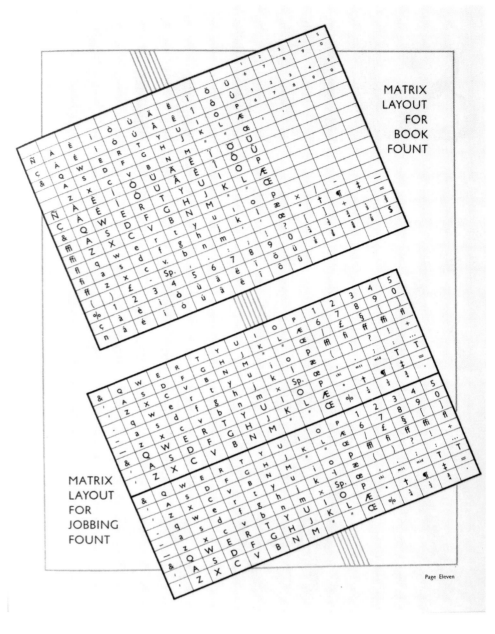

One problem that dogged the progress of designing the Uhertype faces was that there was no routine way of obtaining typeset proofs for Tschichold and others to assess. This was due to the constant revision and modification of the Uher machine itself, which meant that putting it into regular operation was problematic. In addition the whole process of transferring the type drawings onto glass cylinders for housing in the machine was largely untested and suffered mechanical setbacks. Methods of checking the quality of spacing between letters was still being worked out more than two years after Tschichold submitted his first designs. On occasion he also strategically delayed making revisions to his typefaces – which entailed laborious redrawing by hand (without extra payment) and transfer anew to the zinc plates – because he sensed that ongoing constructional changes to the machine could possibly render such work redundant.

There were a series of piecemeal demands from Uhertype for him to design new characters that they discovered a need for, which was the kind of work that would usually fall to in-house technical staff at a typefoundry but which in this case could only be taken on by Tschichold; he was fiercely protective of his control over the artistic side of the project and did not allow Uhertype to distribute any part of the work to a third party. A minor dispute arose over the issue of providing mathematical fraction characters for the typefaces. Uhertype demanded that Tschichold draw a fresh set of matching fractions for each of his fonts. He disagreed and used his scholarly credentials to support his objection, citing two 'fundamental' English-language reference works (Legros and Grant's *Typographical printing surfaces* [1916] and D.B. Updike's *Printing types* [1922]) as evidence that fractions were not traditionally integral to individual typefaces. A cursory look at some of the typefaces for hot-metal

Selection from Tschichold's redrawing of the
Deberny & Peignot 'French roman'. Regular, bold
and italic. 1934. 25% of actual size.

typesetting possessed by Fretz would show, he explained,
that fractions of a single, standard design were used with a
variety of metal typefaces. With such a fundamental shift
in technology as the Uhertype represented, it was difficult
to establish such norms, and this all contributed to delays in
the project. The frequent demand for Tschichold to expand
the character set led him to change his pricing system from
a per-font to a per-character basis, which naturally dis-
pleased Uhertype and MAN, considering the spiralling costs
they had to bear for mechanical development. Tschichold
was warned that he should bear in mind that Uhertype had

received much lower estimates for type design work from
other parties, to which he replied:

> I have very little reason to fear competitive offers, when I
> may be allowed to point out to you that your previous experi-
> ences, on the one hand with the biggest French typefoundry
> and on the other with a graphic designer [graphiker], do not
> exactly provide encouragement to make further experiments
> with less qualified draftspeople. A beautiful script in itself
> is far from a guarantee that it will look right when typeset.
> There would be nothing to object to in the drawing of the
> types that I refer to. When typeset however, they looked

Drawing for display typeface. 1935. Around half of actual size. It is unclear whether this was an idea for submission to Uhertype but it dates from the period of Tschichold's intensive work for that company.

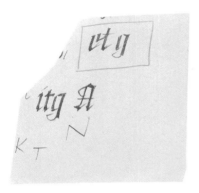

Sketches for a gothic italic (unusual) and roman typefaces intended for Uhertype. Around half of actual size.

catastrophic, as we know. I can only repeat that my prices are precisely calculated, and that it is inconceivable that you can be offered a product even remotely approaching the same quality for a lower price. There may be plenty of type designers who will assert that they can do the same, without however being qualified for the job. As it happens I have a reputation at stake, which I am not prepared to gamble.[92]

In the end, to placate Uhertype ('without recognizing an obligation') Tschichold agreed to design a single set of fractions for his sanserif, which could then be used with any of the typefaces.

Just as Tschichold would begin his association with printers and publishers during his exile by setting down composition rules, he drafted some short guidelines for micro-typography to be applied in making specimens of the Uher typefaces. In a document dated 8 September 1933, and marked at the top 'Keep safely!', Tschichold listed precise rules for, among other things, spacing out capitals

(perhaps his most enduring theme), the length of dashes and hyphens, and spatial compensations in problematic character combinations. In the regular weight of the Uhertype sanserif Tschichold even went so far as to design two variants for capital T with different lengths of crossbar (one intended for all capital setting, one for combination with small letters) – such was his concern for a harmonious rhythm. Tschichold's *bête noire* – spacing out small letters – also came up with regard to typesetting on the Uhertype. On seeing an occurrence of it in proofs of the sanserif he declared: 'I would like to express at this opportunity an absolute ban on spacing out the sanserif. The type cannot endure it.' At least he sought assurance that it would not be done again in literature produced by Uhertype, in order to set an example for future users.[93]

In accordance with his published statements about mixing 'historical' types with sanserif to provide variety in New Typography, Tschichold proposed an expanded 'type programme' to Uhertype at the beginning of 1935. This incorporated four weights of a roman 'in Didot style', a 'French roundhand' script, a Fraktur in two weights and a 'Gotisch' [Textura].[94] The first two of these type-styles were becoming firm favourites of his at this very time (both are used on the title-page of *Typographische Gestaltung*) but the

92. Letter Tschichold to Uhertype, 11 February 1935. His judgement of the roman type originally drawn at Deberny & Peignot was too harsh: from the text in the Uhertype leaflets designed by Joost Schmidt it can be seen to work quite well, both in terms of form and spacing. The 'graphiker' Tschichold referred to was probably not Schmidt but whoever it was that had drawn some rather inelegant grotesque types prior to Tschichold's work for Uhertype.
93. Letter Tschichold to Uhertype, 9 January 1934.
94. Letters Tschichold to Uhertype, 21 January 1935 and 2 February 1935.

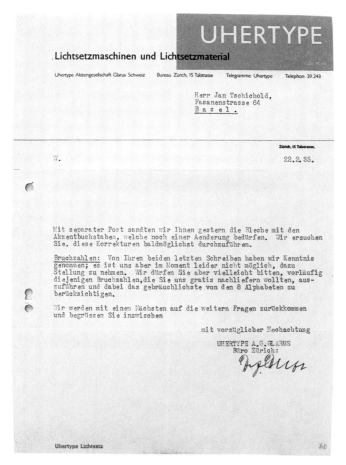

Letterhead designed by Tschichold for
Uhertype. 1934. A4.

two styles of gothic type were suggested in the interests of
capitalizing on the propagation of gothic type by the Nazis
in Germany. Whatever Tschichold's personal feelings may
have been about Nazi policy in this regard – having made
it clear in the *Typographische Mitteilungen* survey of early
1933 that he was not in favour of a broad re-adoption of
gothic – he realized the commercial necessity for Uhertype
to address the situation. He also saw it as an opportunity
to create much-needed work for himself. One year into his
association with Uhertype, he informed the company:

> Incidentally I would be pleased to be honoured with a
> commission for more typefaces. After the pressing need for
> roman types has first been covered, it would be advisable to
> produce a Fraktur and a modern Textura, which at present
> in Germany are the obligatory stock of a printing house.[95]

Tschichold reminded Uhertype regularly of his proposal:
'By the way, I would be glad, given serious interest from you,
to prepare sketches for Textura types, which are decidedly
better than the rough types that have recently come into
fashion in Germany.'[96] His suggestions were never taken up,

but he made some rough sketches of an italic for a proposed
gothic typeface – an unusual experiment (see opposite).

A crisis over which the design and production of the
Uhertype faces began to falter concerned the issue of optical
scale. Early communications by Uhertype with Tschichold
made clear its intention of maintaining the element of
optical compensation, which was customary in metal type,
for very small and for large type-sizes. Although such
distinctions could have fallen away with the transition to
type production by pantographic methods for machine
casting, producers of typefaces for mechanical typesetting
had rightly adopted the traditional adjustments made to
letterforms in order to increase the legibility of type below
average text sizes of 9 to 12 point and to refine character in
larger sizes. Letters designed for optimum performance at 9
to 12 point would generally lose visual strength when typeset at 6 point, for example, if the very same master image is
used. The obvious temptation inherent in phototypesetting
systems is to do precisely that: this technology marks the
transition to typefaces that are, in theory, infinitely 'scalable'
according to the wishes of the person operating the typesetting device. This is also the situation with today's digital
typography, and the issue of optical scale still remains
largely unaddressed.

Press reports about the Uher machine published around
the time that the prototypes were announced reflected its
developers' consciousness of the matter. Writing in *Deutscher
Drucker* in January 1933, Wilhelm Bretag mentioned that
the Uhertype's makers envisaged restrictions on the photographic enlargement and reduction in size of typefaces so
as to avoid distortion of the letters.[97] In the initial agreement
between Tschichold and Uhertype it was specified that his
typefaces should be provided for the following size groupings: 6–12, 14–26, and 28–60 point. Given the limited time
available and the burden of executing all drawings himself,
Tschichold only submitted a single design for each typeface,
which by default seems to have been intended for average
text sizes. It is likely that he did not wish to undertake
adjusted redrawing of his alphabets in two further versions
while the lack of adequate text proofs from the Uher
machine prevented him from properly assessing the initial
version. Again, such work, which would have been carried
out by in-house teams of draftspeople at Monotype, for
example, fell to Tschichold alone. On seeing typeset proofs
of the Uhertype sanserif in May 1936 (three years into the
project) he remarked positively that any previous rhythmical problems in the typeface were now solved, but added
that sizes of 9 point and below, reduced photographically
from the single master, should have a small amount of space
added between the letters to improve performance. However, after six months of very little activity, a letter from
Uhertype in early 1937 informed Tschichold that it would
like to re-establish its relationship with him in order to

---

95. Letter Tschichold to Uhertype, 20 July 1934.

96. Letter Tschichold to Uhertype, 2 October 1935.

97. *Deutscher Drucker*, Jg.39,
H.4, January 1933, pp.126–8.

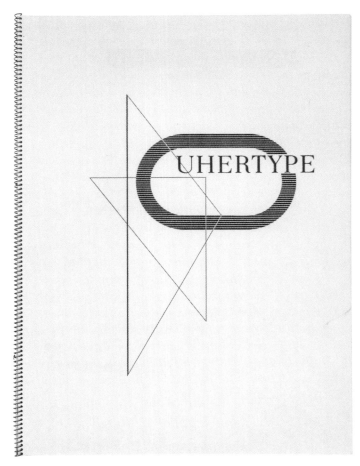

(Above and opposite) Cover and pages from Uhertype specimen. 1935. It is unclear whether Tschichold contributed to its design; the illustrative examples were designed by Imre Reiner. 31.2 × 23 cm.

correct the following problem: 'It has been demonstrated that the types that you designed for Uhertype AG are highly restricted in use because their production departed from the incorrect presumption about the unlimited possibilities for increasing and decreasing in size.' Mysteriously, the solution that Uhertype suggested for this was to prepare artwork for the typefaces as white on black images, instead of black on white.[98] Tschichold agreed to make another tedious round of drawings on this basis, rejecting the idea that it could simply be done photographically with the comment: 'I fear that even the best photography is not sufficiently precise and sharp.'[99] This reflects a doubt that must have affected his view of the project as a whole; indeed he claimed at an early stage to be taking pre-emptive measures in his drawings for the inevitable rounding of sharp corners in his letters that arose with photographic reproduction.

By this time the Uhertype initiative had almost lost momentum due to more serious problems with the machine itself, which proved insurmountable. Dissatisfied at the slow progress compared with its spiralling costs, MAN withdrew

its funding in 1938 and Uhertype AG was liquidated in 1940. The Second World War precluded any recommencement of the Uhertype project, although it was discovered later that one of the Uhertype prototype 'handsetting' machines was in fine working order and being actively used for cartographic applications until 1969.[100] Undoubtedly the Uhertype established a useful precedent for the further development of phototypesetting after the war. Perhaps it was not entirely by coincidence that Deberny & Peignot, which had provided the first typeface for Uhertype, was also involved in making some of the first typefaces for the Lumitype Photon (first of the second generation of electro-photomechanical typesetters). Among these was Adrian Frutiger's Univers (1957), perhaps the only one of the later generation of new 'grotesques' of which Tschichold to some degree approved.

98. Letter Uhertype to Tschichold, 3 January 1938 [erroneously dated 1937].

99. Letter Tschichold to Uhertype, 4 January 1938.

100. Münch, 'The origins of modern filmsetting', p.34.

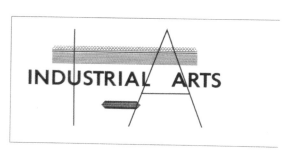

244

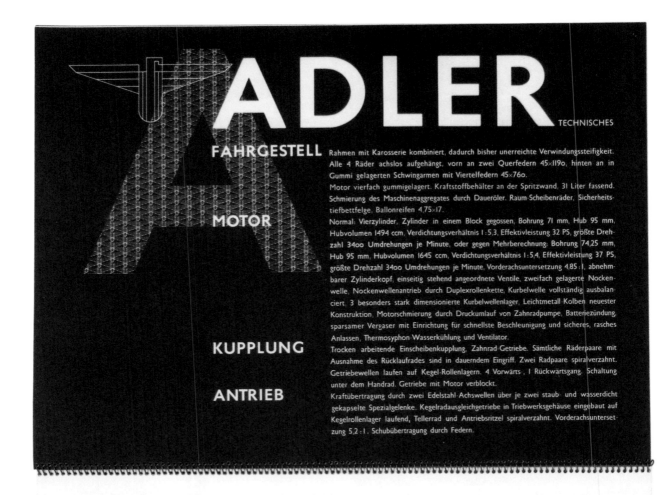

Imre Reiner, pages from Uhertype specimen.
1935. 31.2 × 23 cm. Tschichold's typefaces in use:
all three weights of the sanserif and numerals of
the redrawn roman.

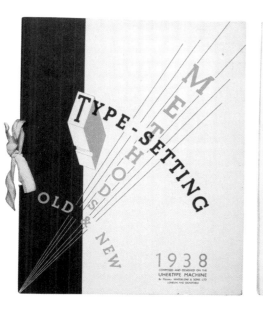

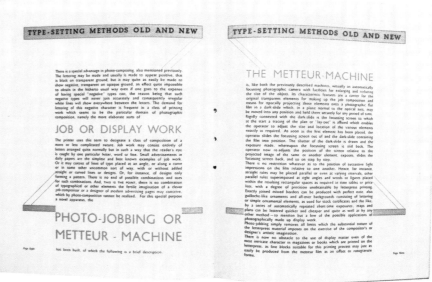

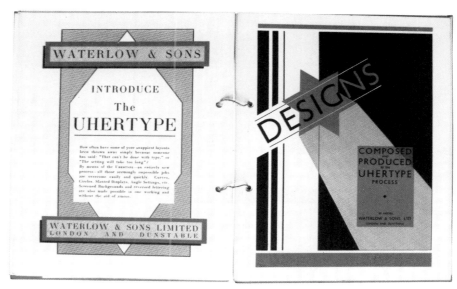

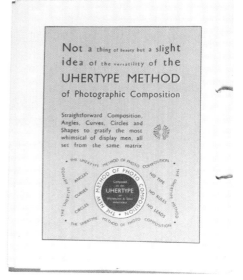

(Top row) Cover and pages from booklet produced by Waterlow & Sons. 1938. All items on this page measure 25.4 × 20.3 cm.

(Middle and bottom rows) Examples produced by Waterlow & Sons with Uhertype, demonstrating its versatility (diagonal and curved lines of type).

Tschichold's typefaces are used but he designed none of these items. Some pages show a decorative interpretation of New Typography.

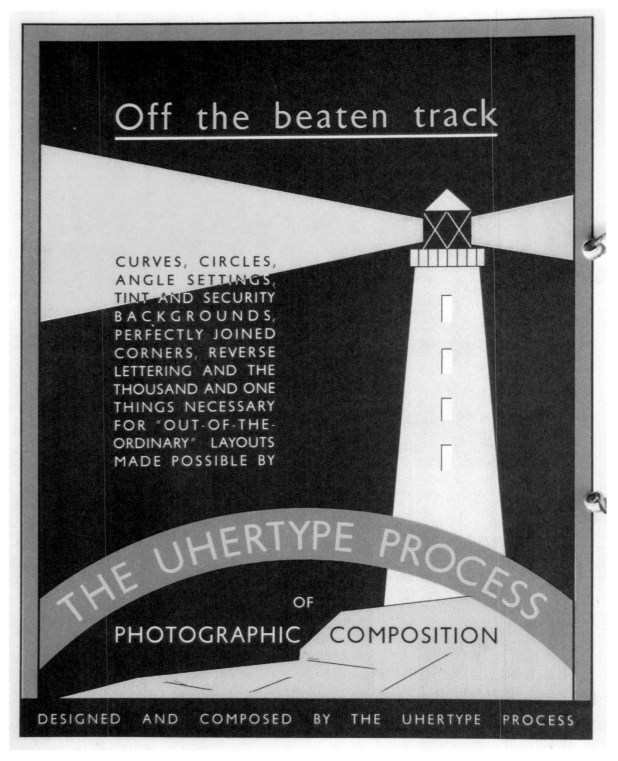

Example of typesetting with Uhertype sanserif, produced by Waterlow & Sons as a mock poster. 1938. 25.4 × 20.3 cm. Not designed by Tschichold.

Showing of modern face roman from specimen of Uhertype faces produced by Waterlow & Sons. 1938. This typeface is a mystery: it seems unlikely that it is the roman in 'Didot style' proposed by Tschichold, because he never received the commission to draw it. It would also have been surprising for him to have drawn it so thin that it could not function properly at text sizes.

32 point.

Turning over the leaves
TURNING OVER THE L

5 Exile

Page from *Typographische Gestaltung* (1935) showing catalogue cover designed by Max Bill.

Sketch and cover of leaflet for a kindergarten. c.1933. A6. Tschichold's landlady was a teacher at this nursery school.

Despite having visited Switzerland on several occasions prior to 1933 and making some strong personal connections there, Tschichold had not really explored Swiss manifestations of New Typography in his writings before emigrating there in that year. This is perhaps surprising given Switzerland's proximity to his base in Munich, but probably explicable for the same reason: in at least partially sharing a language with Germany, which enabled interchange of trade literature, Swiss typographic culture may not have seemed to offer anything fresh or exciting to Tschichold at that time. Undoubtedly he also remembered the virulent attacks from the conservative Swiss trade press on *Elementare Typographie* in 1925.

Yet, the ideas of New Typography had taken firm root among a minority in Switzerland, both in printing trade education and graphic design practice. The innovative publicity designed by Ch. Vohdin for the Zurich department store, Brann, caught Tschichold's attention and he wrote a short feature about it in 1931 for the British magazine *Commercial Art*. The piece's title – 'Advertising the German store' (probably not decided by Tschichold) – signals the conflation of German and northern Swiss culture.

The Rasch brothers' compendium of New Typography, *Gefesselter Blick* (1930), had featured the Swiss designers Otto Baumberger (who had also been featured in *Elementare Typographie*) and Max Bill, whose contribution to the book would certainly have been sympathetic to Tschichold. Bill had briefly studied at the Bauhaus, but returned to Zurich in late 1928 where he became a key figure in Swiss New Typography. While still in Germany Tschichold had expressed interest to Bill in his abstract paintings, being one of the first to do so, for which Bill later expressed his thanks.[1] Bill was on friendly, although respectfully distant, terms with the Tschicholds during the 1930s and he gladly loaned them one of his paintings. A prospectus that he designed to advertise washing machines was illustrated by Tschichold in *Typographische Gestaltung*.[2] Their relationship would turn sour soon after the Second World War with their public dispute about the meaning of modern typography (see pp.293–5 below).

During his first years of exile Tschichold also became aware of work by Swiss graphic designer Herbert Matter. He had worked between 1929 and 1932 in Paris with Le Corbusier and Cassandre, and for Deberny & Peignot's publicity department. Thereafter he worked in Zurich until emigrating in 1935 to the USA, where he remained, becoming professor of photography at Yale University. Matter's work was always marked by an inventive use of photography: an outstanding example was the brochure he

designed in 1934 for the Fretz printing firm, which Tschichold illustrated in a later article (see p.287). Fretz printed some of Matter's iconic photomontage advertisements for the Swiss Tourist industry. An example of these was illustrated by Tschichold in an essay he wrote for a catalogue of the exhibition 'Planvolles Werben' (purposeful advertising), held at the Basel Gewerbemuseum in April and May 1934. Matter's advertisement for his home-town ski & spa resort of Engelberg belonged to what Tschichold described as 'an excellent series of publicity items with photos, varied in nature but nevertheless belonging together'. Tschichold also illustrated publicity for an exhibition on office matters by Theo Ballmer of Basel, whose work he had noticed already in 1927, when he had mentioned it to Piet Zwart. After studying at the Bauhaus (1928–9) Ballmer returned to Switzerland and was a colleague of Tschichold's at the Basel Gewerbeschule, where he taught photography and graphic design.

Although Tschichold's work for Benno Schwabe was turning him toward book design, he designed a few pieces of 'typophoto' advertising during his first years in Switzerland. He was on the selection committee for the Gewerbemuseum's exhibition dedicated to advertising, no doubt partly due to his friendships with the Museum's director Hermann Kienzle and with its modern-minded curator Georg Schmidt. In his essay for the catalogue, 'Die Gestaltung der Werbemittel' (The design of advertising matter), Tschichold again advocated variety not uniformity in typography as necessary for competitive advertising, although here his advice was more pragmatic and unaccompanied by biting socialist rhetoric, as it had been in earlier manifestations:

> Old types can also be used to modern effect. The less well-known a typeface is, the more suited it is (in principle) for advertising, because it serves to characterize and remind. It should not however belong to a period that is held in low esteem at present, such as the years between 1880 and 1908. The sensitive person will make the association: old-fashioned typeface – old-fashioned business.

Characteristically, Tschichold was aware of the potential for vulgarity in what he suggested, adding:

> Although New Typography rejects the ornamental formalism of the old typography, its use requires no less artistic tact in order to protect it from unfortunately not infrequent *faux pas*.[3]

Tschichold's standardizing impulse was still strong, however, and he placed equal emphasis on the usefulness of standards for format and layout in advertising and commercial stationery, for which there were Swiss norms equivalent to the DIN. The design of the catalogue for 'Planvolles Werben' bears Tschichold's mark: its cover repeats the graphic reference to standard formats from that of his book *Typographische Entwurfstechnik*. He seems to have set some standards around this time for the printed output of both the Basel Gewerbemuseum and Gewerbeschule.

1. Letter Bill to Tschichold, 31 March 1938.

2. Bill also sent Tschichold a copy of his famous 'Negerkunst' poster in September 1935, too late for inclusion in *Typographische Gestaltung*.

3. 'Die Gestaltung der Werbemittel', *Planvolles Werben*, pp.17–27.

Cover and pages showing Tschichold's article in the exhibition catalogue, *Planvolles Werben* (Basel Gewerbemuseum, 1934). A5. Although the cover eschews capital letters, his text does not. The middle left spread illustrates an advertisement designed by Herbert Matter. The middle right spread compares a 'common, unstandardized and undesigned' letterhead with an 'unstandardized "modern"' one – Tschichold deemed the second worse than the first. The bottom right spread shows first an example of 'earlier [symmetrical] typography', which 'does not inspire reading'; even the 'good historical typeface [Garamond] does not in itself bring forth good typography'. The contrasting example (with gothic type) features typefaces that 'in themselves have a more historic effect, however the whole is significantly more modern'.

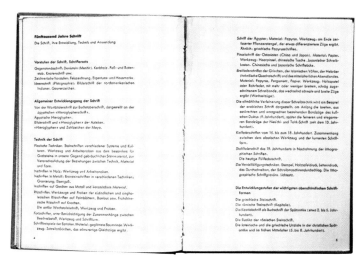

First and third page of an invitation for exhibition at the Basel Gewerbemuseum. A6; shown together on one page of *Typographische Gestaltung* (1935).

Spread from Tschichold's catalogue for the Basel Gewerbemuseum's exhibition 'Fünftausend Jahre Schrift' (Five thousand years of script). 1936. A5. Reproduced as whole pages in *Typografische vormgeving* (1938; Dutch edition of *Typographische Gestaltung*). The somewhat perverse placement of the type area – symmetrically but unconventionally towards the outer edges of the spread – was a feature suggested by Tschichold in his article 'Der Satz des Buches', as one of the ways that books also could be made to look modern.

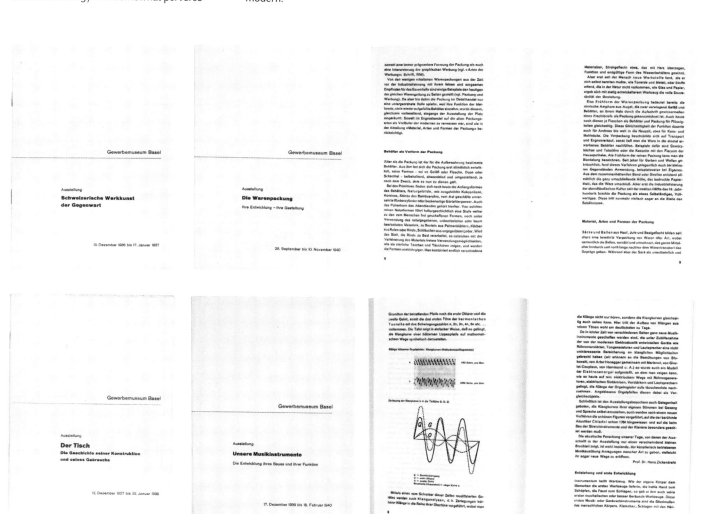

Cover and spreads from Basel Gewerbemuseum exhibition catalogues following the style set by Tschichold. 1937–40. A5.

252

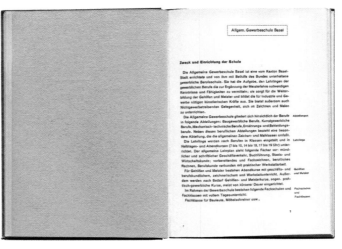

Cover and pages of an annual report for the Basel
Gewerbemuseum and Gewerbeschule as reproduced in *Typographische Gestaltung* (1935). A5.

Table of figures about student numbers at the
Basel Gewerbeschule from an annual report
reproduced in *Typographische Gestaltung* (1935).
A5.

Information poster for student induction
at the Basel Gewerbeschule, shown in *Typografische vormgeving* (1938). Much reduced
to A5.

(Opposite) Reports in *Typographische Monatsblätter* of courses in typographic drawing given
by Tschichold for local groups of the Swiss
Bildungsverband: (above) in Luzern, winter
1933/4 and (below) in Basel, January 1935.

The right-hand page in the Basel report charts
the development of designing a simple invitation card, with Tschichold's comments on each
variation:

1. The first line is overemphatic. Type justified in
a block at the top should be avoided. The lower
part is weak and unsure in its placing.

2. Type in the original too big.

3. 'Der neue Montag' too big. 'Goldene Berge' too
small. Upper two groups too far to the left;
above right too empty.

4. The three lines at the bottom must have less
leading to bind them together more strongly.
The lower and right-hand margins must be
wider.

5. The word 'bringt' does not need a line to itself.

6. Visually correct and content-driven choice of
type-sizes; breaking of lines appropriate to
meaning, and clearly & harmoniously divided
grouping.

Der Winterkurs 1933 34 des Typographischen Klubs Luzern

Wie in den vergangenen Jahren, veranstaltete die Luzerner Ortsgruppe des Bildungsverbandes der Schweizerischen Buchdrucker auch im letzten Winter einen Fachkurs an der Gewerbeschule Luzern, der diesmal von Kollege Jan Tschichold in Basel, früherem Fachlehrer in München, geleitet wurde. Er hatte einerseits die Ausbildung im werkgerechten Skizzieren, andererseits die fachliche Fortbildung im Aufbau von Drucksachen aller Art zum Ziele. Als Lehrmittel wurde das Buch des Kursleiters «Typographische Entwurfstechnik» von allen Teilnehmern benutzt. Da das richtige Skizzieren von Drucksachen keineswegs allgemein gebräuchlich ist, ihm heute dagegen eine ganz besondere Bedeutung zukommt, begann die Kursarbeit mit dem Üben der Darstellung einfacher Buchdrucktypen mit dem Bierstift. Mit diesem Werkzeug wurden fast alle Aufgaben bewältigt, ausgenommen diejenigen, deren Wirkung der ausgeführten Arbeit ganz besonders nahegeführt werden sollte. Die unvermeidlich etwas monotonen «Fingerübungen» (Darstellen bestimmter, größerer und kleinerer Typen zum Zweck einer hochgradig genauen Wiedergabe, welche allein die Grundlage einer genau ausführbaren Satzskizze ist) wurden von den Teilnehmern mit Geduld überwunden. Ohne sie wäre es nicht möglich gewesen, dem Kurse weiter zu folgen und einwandfreie Arbeiten zu erzeugen. Zwischen den Übungen gab der Kursleiter methodische Erläuterungen der modernen Satzweise, die durch einen relativ freien Zeilenfall, Vermeidung alles Sperrens, sehr geringe Anwendung von Versalienzeilen,

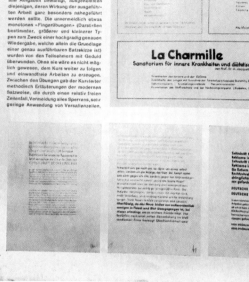

Leichtigkeit und Asymmetrie gekennzeichnet wird. Die von ihm entwickelten Satzregeln lassen sich sowohl im Handsatz wie im Maschinensatz anwenden. Durch ihren Gebrauch wird Zeit gespart, die nunmehr einem überlegten Aufbau und besserer Gliederung zugute kommt. — Fast alle Arbeiten wurden ausführlich durchgesprochen und in der Regel eine neue Fassung hergestellt. Textänderungen waren streng verboten. Nacheinander wurden Anzeigen, Geschäftspapiere verschiedener Art, Prospekte, Kleinplakate und schließlich ein Zeitschriftenumschlag als Themen behandelt. Der Umschlag für eine Fachzeitschrift für uns selbst stellt sicher eine der schwersten Aufgaben für einen Setzer dar. Auch hier kommt es darauf an, mit einfachen Mitteln, die dem Setzkasten entnommen sein sollten, eine Wirkung zu erreichen, die den Betrachter gefangen nimmt und in ihm das Gefühl der Klarheit und Ordnung, aber auch das des Erfindungsreichtums und der Harmonie hinterläßt. Einfacher Tonplattenschnitt und Rasterflächen durften als Hilfsmittel herangezogen werden, doch mußte auf jeden Fall als Schrift eine Buchdrucktype verwendet werden. Bildsatz war nicht gestattet. Wir glauben, daß der größte Teil der gefertigten Arbeiten auch vor gestrengten Augen bestehen kann. Die abgebildeten, stark verkleinerten Arbeiten stellen natürlich nur einen sehr kleinen Teil der Gesamtarbeit dar. Links unten sehen wir Übungsblätter; darüber Anzeigenskizzen von verschiedenen Händen, davon die untere aus Tusche ausgeführt. Unter den Umschlägen auf dieser Seite befinden sich sowohl manuelle Entwürfe wie aus gesetzten Zeilen und buntem Papier montierte. Auf die wichtige Farbe mußte hier leider verzichtet werden.

1 Kleine Zeile und Ziffer rot, das übrige schwarz. Weißer Grund.
2 Roter Grund mit weißem Ausschnitt und weißer Ziffer. Übrige Schrift schwarz.
3 Grauer Grund. Hauptzeile, Linie und «inhalt des Heftes» rot, das übrige grünblau.
4 Große Schrift und Linie schwarz, das übrige rot. Weißer Grund.
5 Schwarzer Druck auf weißem Papier. Unten Raster.
6 Senkrechte Gruppe rot, das übrige schwarz. Weißes Papier, unten Raster.

Skizzierkurs Basel Winter 1934–35   (Kursleiter Jan Tschichold)

Die hier gezeigten Beispiele sind aus einer Anzahl von Skizzierarbeiten für diesen Zweck ausgewählt worden. Die beiden ersten Skizzen sprechen für sich. Übersichtlichkeit und Klarheit, einwandfreie Satzstellung zu den Bildern kennzeichnen diese als hervorragende Qualitätsarbeiten. (Bitte die Angaben unter den jeweiligen Skizzen beachten.) Bei der Serie der Einladungskarte « Der neue Montag » gerät man in Versuchung, das Ganze als Spielerei zu betrachten, aber ein Vergleich ergibt die Folgerichtigkeit in der Lernmethode des Kursleiters. Die Skizze 6 wird unschwer als beste von jedem Setzer zu erkennen sein. In der Praxis sollten natürlich höchstens zwei Skizzen angefertigt werden müssen.

Beste Schulung bleibt immer noch die Gegenüberstellung von Beispielen in alter und neuer Fassung. Die Geschäftskarte der Basler Eisenmöbelfabrik in Sissach weist bei ihrer alten Ausführung und der Größe der Karte geradezu ein Kunterbunt von Schriften und Schriftgraden auf gegenüber der einfachen, realistischen Satzgliederung in der neuen Ausführung. Auch die Inserate « Fortuny-Stoffe » und « Glenk-Worch » (Normalgröße des Satzspiegels 53 × 49 Cicero) erfahren durch ihre Neugestaltung eine frappierende Belebung.

Man begegnet, besonders bei älteren Kollegen, häufig Äußerungen: die neue Satzweise ist zu nüchtern, zu schmucklos, und über kurz oder lang werde der Schmuck und Zierat seinen Einzug wieder halten. Die neue Satzart ist zwar nicht ganz schmucklos, das Linienmaterial wurde doch beibehalten und wird bei zweckmäßiger Anwendung gute Helferdienste leisten. Zur Bereicherung einer Arbeit trägt natürlich eine Photo bei entsprechendem Sujet viel bei; auch ein Schnitt in Blei oder Linol, sofern sie einwandfrei ausgearbeitet sind.

Wenn auch bereits Unkenrufe im Ausland hörbar sind, wie : Der Zierat kommt wieder! so ist vorläufig wenig davon zu halten. Neues wurde sozusagen nichts geschaffen in letzter Zeit, auch ist anzunehmen, daß in den Druckereien noch genug alter Schmuck und Zierat vorhanden ist, der gar oft nicht rentiert. Ob unter solchen Umständen Lust zu Neuanschaffungen in Schmuck besteht, der heute doch zu einem kurzlebigen Modeartikel würde, ist sehr fraglich. Die neue Typographie ist ein Zeitkind, mit andern aufgewachsen (Architektur, Malerei, Bildhauerei usw.); hoffen wir, daß es recht lange bei uns bleibt.

Über die Anwendungsmöglichkeit der neuen Typographie in der Praxis macht man nicht immer die besten Erfahrungen. Reklame «berater», Akquisiteure und auch bald jeder

Zoologischer Garten Basel

Alles für den Sport bei Metroux

Gesetztes Plakat, Format A4. Bildgröße gegeben. Schrift rot, Bild und Linie schwarz.

Gesetztes Plakat, Format A4. Bildgröße gegeben. Schrift blau. Wiedergabe der beiden Bilder nach Photos aus dem «Deutschen Lichtbild 1935»

Entwicklung des Satzes einer einfachen Einladungskarte, in halber fässiger Größe nach den Skizzen gesetzt

1 Die erste Zeile drängt sich vor. Der Blocksatz oben soll vermieden werden. Unterster Teil schwach und in der Stellung unsicher.

2 Schrift im Original zu groß.

3 «Der neue Montag» zu groß, «Goldene Berge» zu klein. Obere zwei Gruppen zu weit links; oben rechts ist leer.

4 Die drei unteren Zeilen durch weniger Durchschuß stärker gebunden, der untere und der rechte Rand breiter gemacht werden.

5 «bringt» braucht nicht auf einer eigenen Zeile zu stehen.

6 Sinngemäße, optisch richtig wirkende Gradwahl; sinngemäßer Bruch der Zeilen und klar gegliederte, harmonische Gruppierung.

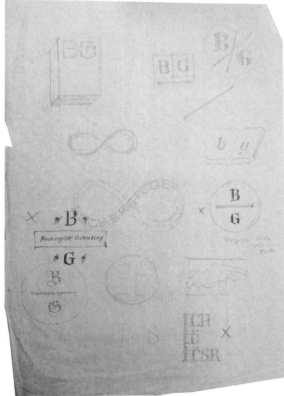

Tschichold was among the first wave of around two thousand emigrants to Switzerland from Nazi Germany. The Swiss government forbade foreigners from engaging in any kind of profitable occupation, although the Basel canton may have been more tolerant than others in this respect. Tschichold was allowed to work within the restricted positions that he occupied at Benno Schwabe and the Gewerbeschule, but he was forbidden to undertake any further salaried work outside of these. In addition to his teaching at the Gewerbeschule, he conducted several short courses in typographic design for the Swiss Bildungsverband, reports of which were published in the trade press. Meanwhile, the work for Uhertype that he had begun in Munich continued.

Tschichold entered a competition to design a new signet for the Büchergilde Gutenberg, then based in Zurich under the direction of its initiator Bruno Dressler. It is a little surprising that Tschichold undertook no book design work for the Büchergilde in Switzerland, although it should be remembered that he only designed two of its books before 1933. This book club, with its roots in German socialism, was regarded with suspicion by other Swiss publishers and it seems likely that Tschichold's employer, Benno Schwabe, which is descended from the oldest printing & publishing house in Basel (founded 1488), would have been reluctant to allow its in-house typographer to design books also for the Büchergilde. Schwabe's mixed list of literary, artistic, medical and municipal titles demanded of Tschichold a versatility of style, which he handled with his characteristic sureness of touch concerning typography and materials.

(Above) Sketches by Tschichold for competition to design a signet for the Büchergilde Gutenberg in its new home of Zurich. 1934. A4. In the top image there is an interesting sketch for a semi-gothic typeface, perhaps with Uhertype in mind.

(Right) Showing of competition entries in *Typographische Monatsblätter* (Jg.3, H.3, 1935). The version finally entered by Tschichold is illustrated bottom right. The jury's comments were: 'Despite the precision in idea and execution, it lacks a certain effect. The middle line demands

more contrast between the thick and thin strokes of the type.' It seems unfair to have judged it in such detail, as Tschichold's entry is so evidently a sketch intended to be typeset, whereas others are finished, lettered artwork.

255

(Above) Binding design, c.1934/5. 21.6 × 13.8 cm. Curious example of centred typography with sanserif. Tschichold gave a justification for occasionally doing this in his 1935 article on centred composition (see pp.270–1).

(Right) Cover, title-page and spread from a listing of good children's books put together by the Swiss teachers' union. 1934. 21.6 × 13.8 cm. Surprising and effective mixture of Unger Fraktur on the cover and title-page with a robust roman for the clear typography of the listing.

Cover of medical journal. 1934. A4.

Cover of book catalogue. 1936. 24 × 17 cm.

256

Jacket, cover and pages from Uehli, *Die Mosaiken von Ravenna* (Benno Schwabe, 1934; 2nd edn, 1939, shown here). 28 × 19.5 cm. Textured card for cover. Very traditional design, with text (typeset in Poliphilus) on off-white uncoated paper and a section of plates (printed only on right-hand pages) on coated paper.

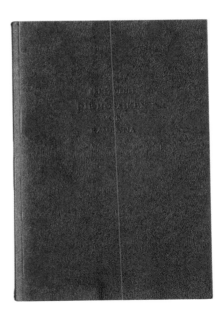

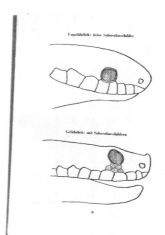

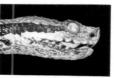
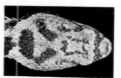

Jacket, cover and spreads from Hediger, *Die Schlangen Mitteleuropas* (Benno Schwabe, 1937). 24 × 17 cm. The delightful dustjacket features Tschichold's calligraphy with long and sweeping extenders appropriate to the subject of the snakes of Central Europe. The red box (with white frame) is repeated as a label stuck onto the soft, blue card cover in the same position. Text typeset in Bodoni.

Jacket, cover and spreads from Graber (ed.), *Der junge Delacroix* (Benno Schwabe, 1938). 24 × 17.8 cm. Contains letters, diaries and other documents. Typeset in Bodoni. Images printed on coated paper (of almost the same colour as the uncoated text paper) bound in at intervals around the text sections. This design was used for a series of books containing biographical material from the lives of nineteenth-century painters.

Having had connections with Switzerland before arriving there, Tschichold was not a typical refugee and he was more fortunate in his professional situation than some immigrants who were entirely forbidden to work there. This was initially the case for Imre Reiner, the Hungarian-born typographer and illustrator previously based in Stuttgart, who re-established contact with Tschichold in May 1934. Reiner was living in some isolation in Lugano, but learned of Tschichold's fate from Paul Renner, who had travelled to Switzerland around the same time as Tschichold to reform the typographic style of the Swiss railway and tourist board, working in Bern and Zurich respectively.[4] With bitter humour, Reiner referred to the 'grisly tales' he had heard about Tschichold's treatment at the hands of the Nazis: 'So you're a cultural bolshevik, but you're much better off not being a Jewish pig as well, like me.'[5] He described the situation under Hitler in Germany as 'these terrible, inhumane, unbelievable, beastly depths'.[6]

Tschichold explained to Reiner that his situation was much better than it had been during his final months in Germany, describing his work in Basel as 'artistic director' at Benno Schwabe and 'course director' at the Gewerbeschule.[7] There must have been some wishful thinking here on Tschichold's part: his position at the publishing house was part-time, and he only ever taught for two hours per week at the Gewerbeschule, much less than most of his colleagues there.[8] Indeed he complained to Heinz Allner, with whom he had worked briefly in Vienna in the late 1920s, that he had practically nothing worthwhile to do in terms of work, and had to survive on 400 Swiss francs per month. In excusing himself for not having written for so long to Allner, he explained: 'You must realize that I have it pretty bad at the moment, and that I'm only struggling through with difficulty. Even to afford the postage for a letter hits me hard.'[9] He may have been exaggerating slightly as an excuse for lateness in correspondence, but the Tschicholds' financial situation only really improved in 1941 with his appointment as typographer to the publisher Birkhäuser. In the meantime he was able to pick up occasional, satisfying design jobs, mostly for small publishers or art galleries.

Tschichold recollected much later (and somewhat inaccurately): 'Only writing was not forbidden to the emigrant Tschichold.'[10] Whether he would have received any fees for writing articles in Swiss printing periodicals is uncertain, but he certainly wasted no time in consolidating a relationship with the Zurich journal, *Typographische Monatsblätter* (Typographic monthly), published from the beginning of

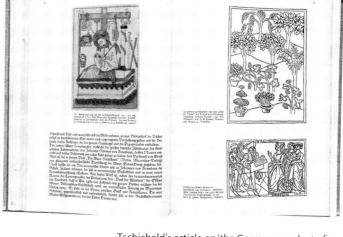

Tschichold's article on 'the German woodcut of the fifteenth century' in *Typographische Monatsblätter* (March 1935). 30 × 22.5 cm. Evidence of his developing historical interests at this time. It is set in gothic type and (perhaps deliberately) lacks an author's credit. (He claimed it when compiling a bibliography of his writings in 1972.)

1933 by the Schweizerischer Typographenbund (Swiss typographers' association) of Bern. His connection with the journal was made before his emigration to Switzerland in July of that year, given that his first article for it was published in the previous month. Indeed it seems that he made some contribution to the conception of *Typographische Monatsblätter*: in early 1929 Kurt Schwitters reported in one of his circulars to the Ring members that 'Tschichold is in contact with two people in Switzerland who wish to found a new periodical.'[11] One of these contacts must have been Walter Cyliax, art director at Fretz printers in Zurich. Cyliax was co-founder and production manager of *Typographische Monatsblätter*, which was printed at Fretz. The periodical's initial subtitle was 'typo photo graphik druck' – almost the same as the title of a prospective journal that Tschichold mentioned to Strzemiński in 1930. Tschichold had four articles published by *Typographische Monatsblätter* in 1933 alone. Among the shorter of his first pieces were two dealing with the style of handwriting taught to schoolchildren. He advocated the script developed by Paul Hulliger, one of Tschichold's first acquaintances in Basel, who helped him and his family to get settled there initially.[12]

During 1935, several issues of *Typographische Monatsblätter* led with substantial articles by Tschichold, including the well-illustrated essay, 'Die gegendstandslose Malerei und ihre Beziehungen zur Typographie der Gegenwart'

4. Renner's work in Switzerland may also have stemmed from Hans Eckstein's reports in the Swiss press. He stayed for one year but seems not to have had contact with Tschichold during this time. See Burke, *Paul Renner*, pp.140–3.

5. Letter Reiner to Tschichold, 26 May 1934.
6. 'dieser schrecklichen, unmenschlichen, unglaubwürdiger, bestialischer Tiefstand'. Letter Reiner to Tschichold, 27 July 1934.

7. Letter Tschichold to Reiner, 23 May 1934.
8. A teaching timetable of 1942 confirms this. Thanks to Juan Jesús Arrausi for bringing this document to my attention. Tschichold did not wish to be remembered by his teaching

in Basel, neglecting to mention it in his autobiographical text of 1972, in which he asserted that he had only held one teaching post, for eight years in Munich. No doubt he did not want to be associated with the Swiss Typography that became

synonymous with the Basel school after he stopped teaching there.
9. Letter Tschichold to Allner, 19 October 1934.
10. 'Jan Tschichold: praeceptor typographiae', p.24.

11. Ring NWG Mitteilungen no.25, 28 February 1929. Cited in *Ring 'neue Werbegestalter'*, p.124.
12. The first address in Basel given by Tschichold was 'bei [care of] Hulliger'.

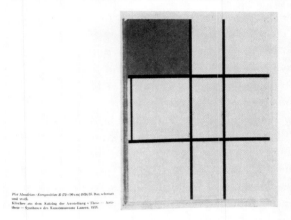

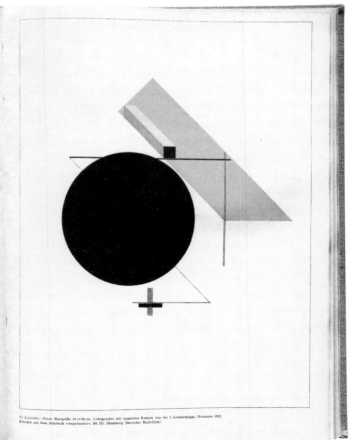

(Non-objective art and its connections with typography of the present). His proposition here (repeated in his book *Typographische Gestaltung* of the same year) can be seen as a significant foundation stone of later Swiss Typography. He proved his point about the relationship of New Typography to 'concrete' art being in the working method, and not in superficial resemblance, with his design of the now famous poster for the exhibition of 'Konstruktivisten' (1937; overleaf). No doubt it must have helped that the subject for this rarefied piece of typography was modern art itself.

Pages from Tschichold's article on the relationship of New Typography to non-objective art in *Typographische Monatsblätter* (Jg.3, H.6, June 1935). 30 × 22.5 cm. In the caption for the schoolbook (below left, presumably designed by Tschichold) he pointed out the 'similarity in kind of gradation and distribution of form-values' with those in Lissitzky's Proun (below right).

(Opposite) Further spreads from the article, with illustrations of work by Albers, Vordemberge, Nicholson, Hepworth, Hans Erni and Jean Hélion. (Opposite, below right) Tschichold likens the 'total effect' of the painting by Hélion (who was a direct link between the concrete art of Van Doesburg and that of Bill) to that of his own catalogue cover for 'These, Antithese, Synthese', the original of which was printed on grey card (dotted line marks fold).

184

Josef Albers: Segmente.
Holzschnitt. 1926.
Aus der Zeitschrift «Il Milione», Bolle-
tino della Galleria del Milione, Milano,
Via Brera 21.

185

Ben Nicholson: Geschnittes Relief in Holz. 1936.

naturalistischer Illusionen stehen, sondern nur sich selbst darstellen. Seit etwa
1910 hat die neue Kunst einen langen,
aber äußerst wichtigen Weg von der
Gegenständlichkeit zur Abstraktion zu-
rückgelegt, den man in kunstgeschicht-
lichen Werken verfolgen mag. Wir sprechen hier nur vom jetzigen Stand dieser
Kunst, die zuerst etwa 1920 allgemein
bekannt wurde und seitdem einen be-
deutenden Einfluß auf Architektur, Typographie und Mode und indirekt auf
viele andere Schaffensgebiete ausgeübt
hat. Sie ist unverändert aktuell und nicht
im mindesten «passé», wie uns manche
glauben machen möchten, die noch nicht
aus dem 19. Jahrhundert herausgetreten
sind oder dorthin zurückkehren möchten.

Ein Bild wie das auf Seite 185 von
Lissitzky zeigt nichts als reine Formen,
die nur sich selbst darstellen. Sie stehen
nicht für eine Menschenfigur, die Sonne
oder sonst etwas, sondern bedeuten nichts
außer sich selbst. Durch die Kunst des
Malers werden aber die Elemente des
Bildes so gestaltet und zueinander in
spannungsvolle Beziehung gesetzt, daß
ein lebendiges Werk entsteht, dessen Wirkung zwar nicht schnell ausgelöst wird,
dafür aber um so nachhaltiger ist. Der
Betrachter soll das Bild längere Zeit auf
sich wirken lassen und sich mit ihm
auseinandersetzen. So ist das neue Bild
also weit weniger als ein gegenständli-
ches, ein Gemälmittel, sondern sozusagen ein Instrument der seelischen Beeinflussung, ein Sinnbild der Harmonie.
Und wenn ein solches Bild von einem
wirklichen Künstler gemalt ist, so wird
die Beeinflussung immer größer, je länger es vor ihm hängt. Das gilt insbesondere von den Bildern Mondrians (Seite
181), so wenig der Laie es zuerst glauben mag. Die elementare und doch sub-
tile Kraft der Verhältnisse dieser Flächen zueinander sind einem dauernden
Aufruf zu Harmonie und Ausgleich der
Spannungen zu vergleichen. Obwohl
oder weil Mondrian nur Weiß, Schwarz
und die drei Grundfarben benützt, sind

Barbara Hepworth: Sculptur. Aus der Zeitschrift «Axis, a quarterly review of contemporary abstract
painting and sculpture» (Editor Myfanwy Evans, 40, Jermyn Street, London, W. 1).

lichkeit nur sehr wenig zu schaffen. Einem guten Maler ist
daher der Gegenstand ziemlich unwichtig; ihn zu malen, ist
ihm vielmehr bloß ein Anlaß, schöne Farb- und Formverhält-
nisse zu bilden.

Die Gegenständlichkeit unserer Umwelt getreu, «wie wir
sie sehen», abzubilden, dazu braucht es heute nicht mehr
notwendig den Maler. Der Photograph kann eine solche Aufgabe besser und schneller lösen. Will man auch die Farbe,

so kann man ein Farbenphoto machen. Ist aber ein Farbenphoto nach einem Sonnenuntergang Kunst? Nein.

Eine Anzahl von Malern, eben die Abstrakten, sind der Auffassung, man solle die Abbildung der Gegenständlichkeit dem
Photographen überlassen. Denn seit die Photographie erfun-
den, sei die Aufgabe der Malerei, sich ausschließlich ihrer
legitimen Mittel, der Farben und Formen auf der Fläche, zu
bedienen. Diese sollen nicht mehr nachbildend im Dienste

Anzeige, verkleinert. Der Vergleich mit dem benachbarten Bilde zeigt deutlich
die Verwandtschaft von neuer Malerei und neuer Typographie.

kunstsalon wolfsberg zürich 2
bedornstrasse 109

wandschmuck fürs schweizerhaus

Farbensberg-Güldenart: Komposition.
Aus der Zeitschrift «Campo Grafico», Via Rugabella 9, Milano.

186

Hans Erni: Komposition. 1934.

187

Jean Hélion: Peinture. 1934. (81 × 65 cm.)
Collection Winifred Nicholson.

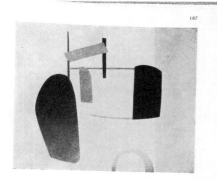

die Bilder des jetzt Dreiundsechzigjährigen von einer unerhörten
gebändigten Kraft und Jugend erfüllt.

Von ganz anderer Art als etwa Lissitzky und Mondrian scheinen
auf den ersten Blick Hans Erni, Jean Hélion und Barbara Hepworth. Doch auch diese ungegenständlichen Formen vermitteln dem
Aufnahmebereiten dauernd Kraft und intensive Anregung.

Alle abstrakten Bilder, insbesondere die «ganz einfachen»,
zeigen malerische oder graphische Elemente, die sowohl selbst
klar gestaltet sind, als auch klare Verhältnisse zueinander bilden.
Die sogenannten Konstruktivisten, zu denen Lissitzky und in ge-

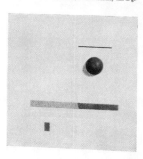

Neueste **Pappenschere**

Oben: Skizze für einen Prospekt. Von H. Jundt im Skizzenkurs Berufsschule ... (Lehrer: Jan Tschichold). Dem Konstruktivismus ver-
das nebenstehende Bild ganz unbekannt; trotzdem zeigen beide Abbildungen eine starke Ähnlichkeit im Rhythmus und in der Verteilung.

Links: Vordemberge-Gildewart: Komposition.
Aus der Zeitschrift «Campo Grafico», Via Rugabella 9, Milano.

Durschlag eines Kataloges, verkleinert. Man vergleiche die Gesamtwirkung und
die Verhältnisse mit dem obenstehenden Bild von Jean Hélion.

kunstmuseum luzern   28. februar bis 21. märz 1935

these
antithese
synthese

arp
braque
calder
chirico
dipada
erni
ernst
fernandez
glasmertt
gonzalez
gris
hélion
kandinsky
klee
léger
miró
mondrian
nicholson
ozefan
oxenfant
picasso
taeuber

wissem Sinne auch Vordemberge gehört, benutzen strenge geometrische Formen, von denen die Schritt zur Typographie nicht
weit ist. Ihre Werke sind Sinnbilder vollendeter Ordnung aus
einfachen, doch oft stark kontrastierenden Elementen. Da die
neue Typographie sich keine andere Aufgabe stellt, als solche
Ordnungen herzustellen, können viele Werke abstrakter Maler
und Bildhauer dem Typographen als Modellgestaltungen wesentliche Anregungen geben und ihm die optische Formwelt
der Gegenwart vermitteln. Sie sind die schönsten Lehrmittel optischer Ordnungen. Aber man darf auch hier nicht
an ein wörtliches Abschreiben denken, sondern nur im Geiste
jener Gestaltungen arbeiten. Aus dem Werke Mondrians etwa
auf die Notwendigkeit einer Blocksatztypographie zu schlie-
ßen, wäre ein böses Mißverständnis. Wir müssen im Rahmen
unserer Technik und des Zwecks unserer Arbeit bleiben, wenn
wir nicht bloßen Formalismus treiben wollen.

Schade, daß wir die farbigen Originale nicht zeigen können.
Versäume niemand, die seltenen Gelegenheiten wahrzuneh-
men, neue Malerei zu sehen. Die Reduktion der Farben-
wirkung auf die Grauskala ist gerade bei diesen Werken ein
sehr großer Verlust. Mögen recht viele durch diese Zeilen
zu der neuen Erlebniswelt geführt werden, welche die abstrakte Kunst geschaffen hat und der wir als Zeitgenossen
verbunden sind.   J. Tschichold

● vom 16. januar bis 14. februar 1937

kunsthalle basel

konstruktivisten

van doesburg
domela
eggeling
gabo
kandinsky
lissitzky
moholy-nagy
mondrian
pevsner
taeuber
vantongerloo
vordemberge
u. a.

Poster for exhibition of 'Constructivists'. Printed at Benno Schwabe. 1937. 90.5 × 63.5 cm.

František Kalivoda, cover and pages from *Telehor*, no. 1/2. 1936. The title-page is preceded here by a kind of half-title introducing the magazine as 'the international review of new vision'.

Tschichold felt duty bound to bring out a new book on typography during his first years in Switzerland to replace the long-promised second edition of *Die neue Typographie*. He now explained to Imre Reiner, some of whose work he had intended to include in it, that this would never appear. Instead he was finalizing an agreement with Benno Schwabe to publish a new book on typography, which would become *Typographische Gestaltung*.[13] Despite Tschichold's advisory position there, the proprietor of Benno Schwabe was sceptical of modern trends and imposed the A5 format on Tschichold's planned book, whereas the material he had previously collected from Reiner and others was intended for an A4 edition.[14] It was agreed that the book would be published if 200 pre-publication orders could be solicited. The prospectus issued for this purpose explained (with a little exaggeration):

> It should be remembered that Tschichold's book 'Die neue Typographie' (1928), which appeared in an edition of 5000, was already sold out after one year and since then has been absolutely unobtainable. The new edition under the title *'Handbuch der neuen Typographie' will not appear in the foreseeable future.* Consequently, the book 'Typographische Gestaltung' (which is in no way a reprint but instead a completely new work) will be a welcome new publication for many. [Italic in original.]

Some copies of this leaflet were issued with the line 'To date we have received almost 1000 subscriptions for the work!' overprinted diagonally across the back in a typewriter-style typeface, as if added by hand. This was perhaps a cunning marketing ploy, but if it approaches the truth then it must be taken as a mark of Tschichold's already growing international renown at this point. In any case, the target must have been reached and the book was produced in summer 1935. Significant interest seems to have come from Czechoslovakia, where František Kalivoda organized for the book's prospectus to be distributed by the Deutsche graphische Bildungsvereinigung in der Tschechoslowakischen Republik (German association for graphic education in the Czechoslovak Republic), based in Prague. This may have encouraged Tschichold to include in the book several illustrations of work by the Czechs Sutnar and Rossmann.

Tschichold also looked towards Eastern Europe for future job prospects, given his natural affinity in that direction and the difficulty of his professional situation in his first years in Switzerland. It was probably via Rossman that Tschichold established contact with Kalivoda, who trained as an architect but whose interests spread to cinema and typography. He designed several magazines, and in 1936 founded his own, *Telehor*, of which he was both editor and designer. Despite grand plans, including a regular review feature to be directed by Tschichold, there only appeared one issue of the publication, dedicated to the work of Moholy-Nagy, which coincided with a travelling exhibition of his work organized by Kalivoda in Czechoslovakia. This sole issue is an impressively restrained piece of New Typography, set

13. Tschichold initially had discussions with the Bildungsverband Schweizerischer Buchdrucker (the Swiss equivalent of *Die neue Typographie*'s German publisher) about publishing *Typographische Gestaltung*. Letter Tschichold to Strzemiński, 28 May 1934.
14. Tschichold explained that he would therefore require different material from him, although in the end no work by Reiner was included in *Typographische Gestaltung*, a fact which he met with kindly tolerance. Letter Reiner to Tschichold, 5 January 1938.

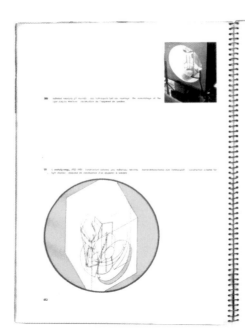
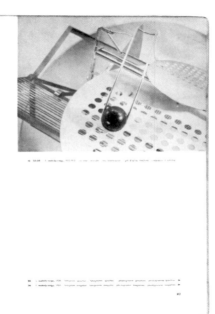

More pages from *Telehor*. This first and only
issue was dedicated to the work of Moholy-Nagy.

Advertisement for *Typographische Gestaltung*
in *Telehor*.

throughout in lower-case Futura, although the lavishness of
the production (four-colour photographs; texts printed in
Czech, English, French and German) may have contributed
to a lack of funds for its continuation.

Soon after moving to Basel, Tschichold had contacted
Ladislav Sutnar in Prague to ask whether a teaching
appointment or a position as designer was possible for him
there, confirming that he had not yet decided to settle in
Switzerland. Despite being director of the Státní Grafické
Školy (State school of graphic arts) in Prague, Sutnar could
offer Tschichold no firm prospects in his reply: 'Firstly,
concerning a teaching post at state-run schools, local state
citizenship and mastery of the language in which classes are
given will be strictly required.'[15] Even then, he warned that
a teacher's salary was not enough to live on, and advised
Tschichold that his chances of finding design work were
probably better in the 'small towns' of Switzerland than in
Prague, where there was much competition.

Although Tschichold made no similar overtures to friends
in his ancestral homeland, Poland, he did maintain contact
with Strzemiński, and the high value Tschichold placed on
his work is evident from their correspondence. Tschichold
was always sure of his own views, and did not generally
seek advice from colleagues on aspects of his writing, yet
he paid Strzemiński the compliment of requesting his view
on the title for the book that finally became *Typographische
Gestaltung*. His respect for Strzemiński's theoretical views
stemmed from having read some of the Polish designer's
writings, of which Tschichold had personally commissioned

German translations with a view to writing about Polish
New Typography. Firstly, in commenting on examples sent
by Strzemiński of work done in his typography classes,
Tschichold uncharacteristically allowed room for another
approach than his own:

> You follow quite a different direction than I do, in which you
> distribute the typographic form-values on the surface accord-
> ing to a predominantly painterly standpoint. You also restrict
> yourself to an *expansive* surface distribution. At any rate,
> among your works there are hardly any in which at least one
> of the groupings has a well-defined edge. Such designs one
> could perhaps describe as expansive, whereas another kind,
> in which lines and groupings move on a relatively neutral
> ground, could perhaps be described as compressive. As the
> latter is bound up with fewer technical difficulties, you will
> find it more often in my work. In my opinion the two kinds
> are equally justified. Personally, in my work, I proceed more
> from the requirements of technology outwards and derive
> the design laws from there.[16]

While the influence of abstract painting on typography
was for Tschichold a distinctive and positive virtue of New
Typography, he admitted that his own approach stemmed
more from an attachment to the craft of printing. On the
matter of the naming his new book, Tschichold went on to
ask Strzemiński: 'The title will be something like "Typography as form" or "Typography as design" [*Typografie
als Gestaltung*]. Which do you find better, by the way?'[17]
Strzemiński replied:

> It seems to me that the title depends on the slant [*Tendenz*] of
> the book. If it is oriented towards organization and fitness for
> purpose, it must be 'Typography as design'. If however it will
> be a 'survey' of contemporary typography, then 'Typography

15. Letter Sutnar to Tschichold, undated [c.1934].

16. Letter Tschichold to
Strzemiński, 3 May 1934.

17. Letter Tschichold to
Strzemiński, 28 May 1934.

Invitation card for Tschichold's lectures in Copenhagen, 1935, and a photograph of him in action there. He spoke in German, accompanied by a translator, to an audience of between four and five hundred people. The lectures were hosted by the Typografernes Fagtekniske Samvirke (Typographic technical co-operative) and supported by the Dansk Typograf-Forbund (Danish compositors' association).

as form' would be better, due to the *over* artistic tendencies of some printed work.[18]

Tschichold also expressed interest in having a short section designed for the new book by Strzemiński, featuring his students' work (corrected by him) and printed at the art school where he taught. Strzemiński considered this to be difficult because paper was neither as good or as cheap in Poland as it was in Switzerland. (In the end there was just one example of his work included in *Typographische Gestaltung*, the cover for *Druk funkcjonalny*; see p.126 above.) Tschichold even suggested including a Polish-language resumé of his book in a supplementary booklet of summaries in three other languages: French, English and Czech. The first two of these might be expected in a Swiss publication, but the Slavic languages again reflect Tschichold's interests and affinities. He felt that the inclusion of a Polish text would combat the widespread but erroneous impression that Poland had no culture worthy of note.

Tschichold also expressed great admiration for Strzemiński's paintings and proposed that an exhibition be suggested at the Basel Kunstverein, which had recently shown work by Mondrian and Arp. He exclaimed that: 'Switzerland is the country in which the most pictures are purchased. More than in America and above all the most modern!' Despite his precarious financial situation he himself was keen to acquire some of Strzemiński's work, asking him if he had made any lithographic prints and whether he could send some for reimbursement of costs. 'I'd be very

keen to buy one or two, even if my circumstances are also not so rosy at present.'[19]

During his first two years in Switzerland, Tschichold established links with like-minded people in several countries that had not previously figured much in his international picture of New Typography. In 1934 he was contacted by Eduardo Westerdahl, editor of the Spanish-language journal of modernism, *Gaceta de Arte*. Westerdahl asked Tschichold to design a cover and write and article for his journal, which Tschichold agreed to do. Soon after the publication of *Typographische Gestaltung* Tschichold in turn suggested making a Spanish edition of it, but none of these ideas were realized due to Westerdahl's failing finances.[20]

Already in the final stages of producing *Typographische Gestaltung*, Tschichold began to achieve more international recognition. In August 1935, around the time that the book appeared, he and Edith travelled to Denmark at the invitation of the Dansk Typograf-Forbund (Danish compositors' association). They had to take a circuitous route via France and Ostend in order to avoid falling into Nazi hands. Given that it was not so easy to make international money transfers in those days, Tschichold was unable to take the fee for his series of three lectures in Denmark out of the country and so instead spent it on goods before returning home. *Typographische Gestaltung* itself included a note that it would be published simultaneously in a Danish edition, although this did not appear until 1937. A Swedish edition was also published in that year, probably motivated by a lecture visit that Tschichold also made to Stockholm. In 1938 a Dutch translation was published by Franz Duwaer, for whom Vordemberge worked extensively in his exile. So began the international reputation of this book in northern Europe (it has still not been translated into a non-Germanic language).

18. Letter Strzemiński to Tschichold, undated (c.June 1934).

19. Letter Tschichold to Strzemiński, 3 May 1934.

20. Letters: Tschichold to Westerdahl, 7 April 1936;

Westerdahl to Tschichold, 19 April 1936 (Westerdahl Archive). Tschichold demanded no fee for writing an article, and requested 100 Swiss francs for the rights to translate *Typographische Gestaltung*.

He promised to write a review in the forthcoming Telehor magazine of *Gaceta de arte*'s monograph on Baumeister, from whom it is likely that Westerdahl initially received Tschichold's address.

Jacket, cover, title-page, contents, foreword and spread from *Typographische Gestaltung* (1935). A5. The title-page is a quintessential example of the 'type mixtures' advocated by Tschichold at this time. Main text typeset in Bodoni.

The epigraph from Goethe here reads:
'There is no past to which one may look back longingly,
there is only an eternal new that is formed out of the
    extended elements of the past,
and the pure longing must be continually productive,
    creating a new better thing.'

Example of the way that different papers are bound into the book and used for whole page illustrations.

Spreads from *Typographische Gestaltung* (1935). A5. Some illustrated examples seem to have been made especially for the book, or at least redesigned for it. For example, the leaflet illustrated on cream paper, middle left, of which alternative versions exist (see also p.269).

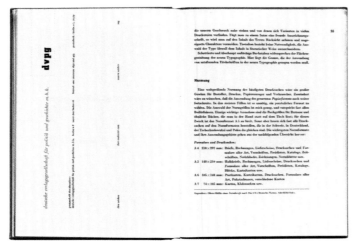

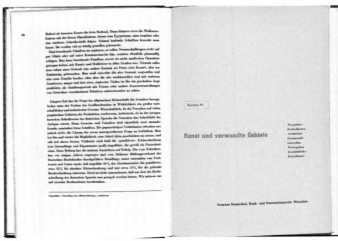

More spreads from *Typographische Gestaltung*. The photomontage with a rose, credited to Walter Cyliax, is an example of how material was tailored for showing in Tschichold's book: the original printed item used sanserif type and not a bold roman. Indeed the single line of type was reset in other languages for the translated editions of this book.

The final spread shows advertisements (apparently designed by Tschichold) included at the back of *Typographische Gestaltung*.

Keen to maintain neutrality, the Swiss government prohibited any political activity among refugees from Germany, and Tschichold would undoubtedly have wanted to steer clear of politics so as not to endanger his position in Switzerland. This may partly explain why *Typographische Gestaltung* has no political undertones, unlike *Die neue Typographie* with its rhetoric borrowed from Utopian socialism. Additionally, Tschichold would not have wanted to risk alienating his already reluctant publisher (and principal employer). The book deals more with the details of text typography (such as micro-spacing and punctuation), reflecting Tschichold's increasing occupation with book design, a subject hardly touched on in *Die neue Typographie*. A large proportion of the illustrations in *Typographische Gestaltung* were either Tschichold's own work or that of his students from the Meisterschule. Indeed a prefatory note explains that the book in some way embodies that school's teaching; despite his having been unsettled in Munich, he was evidently proud of the educational work he had done there.

The book is given a special quality by its materials: a variety of papers are bound into the volume at intervals, onto which full-page examples of work are printed and thus marked out from the main text in this way. This makes *Typographische Gestaltung* a pleasingly unconventional book, more so than *Die neue Typographie*, which followed the strict doctrine of integrating pictures and text on its glossy art paper.

Tschichold reaffirmed his belief that asymmetric design best suited modern needs, criticizing the 'old typography' of arrangement on a central axis as 'ornamental' and contradictory of 'fitness for purpose'. However, he did allow that 'fairness demands an assessment of the *advantages* of centred typography'. Principally, he explained, the central axis is such a strong binding element that it tolerates much variety in type size and line length, making the work of the

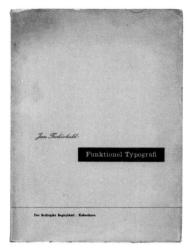
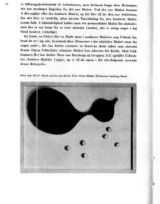
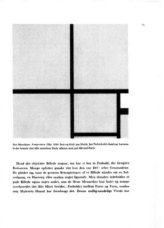

Cover and spread from *Funktionel typografi* (1937; Danish edition of *Typographische Gestaltung*). A5. Designed by Tschichold.

The Mondrian painting owned by him is captioned: 'The reader is asked to paint the little unscreened area with yellow water-colour.'

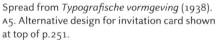

Spread from *Typografische vormgeving* (1938). A5. Alternative design for invitation card shown at top of p.251.

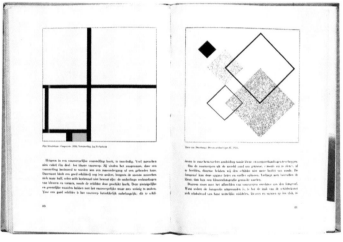

Spread from *Typografische vormgeving* (1938). A5. Again shows Tschichold's Mondrian painting, but this time in colour and rotated 90 degrees!

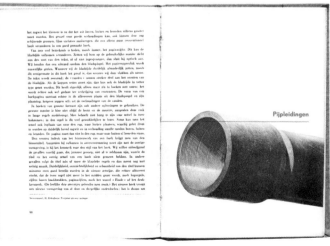

Spread from *Typografische vormgeving* (1938). A5. Right-hand pages shows a catalogue title-page designed by Hermann Eidenbenz.

Page from circular for medical conference: (left) as shown in *Typographische Gestaltung*; (right) in *Typografische vormgeving*, now in English. A5.

type compositor easier in some ways.[21] In the same year that *Typographische Gestaltung* was published Tschichold also wrote an article for *Typographische Monatsblätter* entitled 'Vom richtigen Satz auf Mittelachse' (Correct composition on a central axis). The tone of this short piece is grudging, as if to say 'if it must be done, then it should be done correctly' – nothing pained Tschichold more than bad typography, of any kind. In respecting appropriateness of form for content he felt there was 'no excuse for clothing every theme in modern dress'. With dizzying dialectic, he asserted of centred typography: 'It is an art, or can be an art. (But it is not the art of the present day!)'[22] Yet it was a sign that the old typography was still very much alive and demanding his attention in the activities that now occupied him in Switzerland.

An intriguing tension between the old and the new was making itself apparent in Tschichold's writing on typography, and this perhaps contributed to *Typographische Gestaltung* also immediately gaining notice in the United Kingdom, helping to consolidate the beginnings of Tschichold's long-lasting connection with that country.

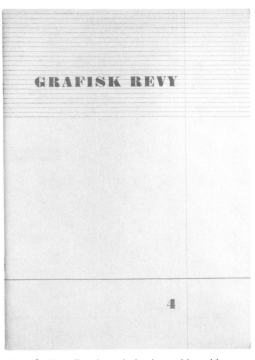

21. *Typographische Gestaltung*, pp.12, 14, & 23 (italic in original); *Asymmetric typography* pp.20–1 & 24.

22. Translation given in McLean, *Jan Tschichold: typographer*, pp.127–8.

Cover for Scandinavian printing journal (roughly equivalent to *Typographische Mitteilungen*). 1936. 33 × 23.6 cm.

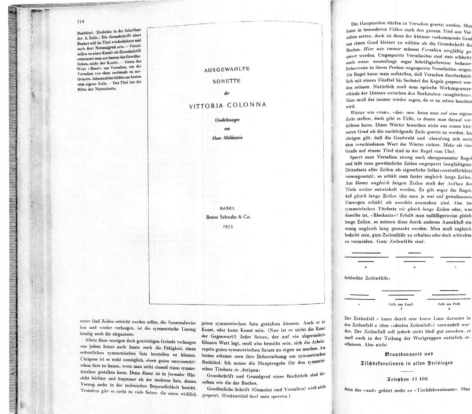

Spread from Tschichold's article on 'correct composition on a central axis', *Typographische Monatsblätter* (Jg.3, H.4, April 1935). 30 × 22.5 cm.

His caption for the title-page of a Benno Schwabe edition (left) recommends using a book's text type in the same type-size for the title-page also.

Further spread from article shown on previous page. Caption to the example on the right reads: 'Title-page of a book. In sanserif, as the book has no real base type, instead being set in many different typefaces (*Stehsatz*). Centred because almost all typography within is centred, apart from the advertisements. In one weight so as to give precedence to something calm as a dominant feature over the busy nature of the main text. Four sizes. The example shows that, even without equal lengths of line, a good form is achievable by breaking the lines according to sense and shape.'

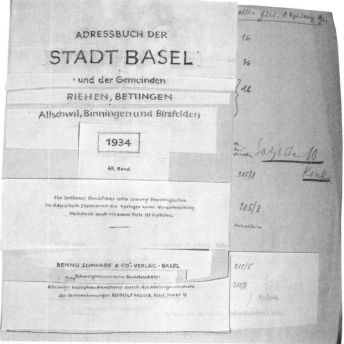

Tschichold's layouts and specification for the 1934 edition of the publication illustrated in the article shown above. Having the different elements on separate pieces of paper presumably allowed him to move them and to assess their best position before sticking them down.

British connections

In 1966, addressing the British Royal Society of Arts on the occasion of his being awarded the honorary distinction of Royal Designer for Industry, Tschichold confessed that he owed a great deal to 'English civilization'. In addition to the influence of Johnston and Gill on him as a letter designer, he declared that *The Fleuron*, a publication that exemplified more than any other the British renaissance of classical typography, exerted 'a deep and lasting influence' on him.[23] Admittedly these statements belong to Tschichold the mature traditionalist, but there is evidence that he cultivated a certain Anglophilia in his reading matter soon after moving to Switzerland, where English maintains its status as a lingua franca.[24] He is likely to have encountered the *Fleuron* at the latest in his early Swiss years, given that the last of its numbers had been published in 1930.

Tschichold had of course written articles for the British periodical *Commercial Art* in the early 1930s, but that connection fizzled out when the publication was transformed in 1932 into *Commercial Art and Industry*. Now, from Switzerland, Tschichold began to make more personal connections in England. Around the beginning of March 1935 he had been visited in Basel by the painter Ben Nicholson and the sculptor Barbara Hepworth, both of whose work was then being shown in an exhibition at the Luzern Kunstmuseum called 'These, Antithese, Synthese' (Thesis, antithesis, synthesis), for which Tschichold designed a catalogue (see p.261 for illustration). Among the litany of notable artists featured in the exhibition (including Braque, De Chirico, Kandinsky, Klee and Picasso) were Mondrian and Arp, either of whom may have introduced Tschichold to Hepworth and Nicholson.[25] Tschichold admired their work and he began to correspond immediately with Nicholson. Having been discouraged by Sutnar about work prospects in Prague, Tschichold now asked Nicholson about the possibility of finding long-term work in England. The British Isles may have seemed to him, as they did to other refugees from the Third Reich, to be one step further and more safely away from the Nazis. Tschichold sent some copies of the prospectus for *Typographische Gestaltung* to Nicholson and enquired about job prospects in London. Nicholson drummed up some interest in Tschichold's forthcoming

book from, among others, the American poster artist resident in London, Edward McKnight Kauffer:

> I saw Kauffer this evening & told him of your book and he will subscribe himself and also for a friend. [Holbrook] Jackson, & [John] Piper also will each subscribe – I told him it is best to do so through Zwemmer, the bookshop here. In talking to Kauffer I mentioned that you would like some lay-out jobs to do in England. – & he said he admires enormously your work & may even be able to find someone to offer you a real encouragement in London. He will be writing to you soon.[26]

Kauffer had worked at the London advertising agency of William Crawford for around three years from 1927, and had visited its Berlin office during that time. Kauffer and his colleague at Crawford's, Ashley Havinden, were among very few commercial artists working in a modern style at that time in Britain. Havinden had been directly inspired by German publications that he came across in a London bookshop, including some of Tschichold's manuals.[27]

Tschichold asked Nicholson to pass on a request to the art critic Herbert Read for review copies of Read's books *Art now* and *Art and industry*. Nicholson did so and in reply said of Read that 'he, too, says he admires your work very much indeed'.[28] Like Nicholson & Hepworth, Read lived in one of a row of artists' studio houses called the Mall, in the then bohemian district of Hampstead in London. Indeed there was a thriving community of modernist artists in this area: Henry Moore lived around the corner (Tschichold contacted him also before his first visit to London), and when Mondrian came to live briefly in London in 1938, he resided in the immediate vicinity. Read later described this as a 'nest of gentle artists' who were 'living and working together in Hampstead, as closely and intimately as the artists of Florence and Siena had lived and worked in the Quattrocento'.[29] They formed the nucleus of a group called the 'Unit', established in June 1933. Read edited its publication, *Unit one* (1934), subtitled 'the modern movement in English architecture, painting and sculpture'.[30] This community was soon to be expanded by the arrival of several eminent artists and architects exiled from Nazi Germany.

Tschichold thanked Nicholson for 'representing my interests' in London, and pursued his enquiry about work there:

> Above all I would be eager to know whether it will be possible for Mr McKnight Kauffer to discover for me a suitable position. I would most prefer one in which I had to work around 35 hours per week, but which would be allowed me without the pressing worries for living that I have here. Otherwise a teaching position would also be possible. This I tell you only for information, for I would be delighted to be able to work in England anyhow.[31]

Tschichold may also have been optimistic about being able to work in English. He could already read the language, and began to write letters in an intelligible version of it to Nicholson just over a month into their correspondence.[32]

23. Berthold Wolpe, 'A tribute to Jan Tschichold', *Jan Tschichold: typographer and type designer 1902–1974*, pp.17–18.

24. In his article of February 1935: 'Schriftmischungen' (p.170), Tschichold refers to A.F. Johnson's book *Type designs*, published in the previous year. (See illustrations of the English translation of this article on p.278) He later commented that his extensive, specialist library was principally in English ('Jan

Tschichold: praeceptor typographiae', p.29).

25. Nicholson visited Mondrian, Picasso, Braque and Arp in Paris in 1934.

26. Letter Nicholson to Tschichold, 14 March 1935.

27. Kinross, 'Emigré graphic designers in Britain', p.38.

28. The second of these had been designed by Herbert Bayer from Berlin in 1934, and so Read was well aware of New Typography. See Kinross, 'Her-

bert Read's *Art and Industry*: a history', pp.39–43.

29. Read, 'British Art 1930–40', p.5.

30. Still keenly collecting modernist material, Tschichold asked in his first letter to Nicholson if this publication was continuing and enquired as to how to acquire it. Letter Tschichold to Nicholson, 8 March 1935.

31. Letter Tschichold to Nicholson, 16 March 1935.

Through Kauffer a connection was made on Tschichold's behalf with the firm of Lund Humphries, which had a printing works in Bradford and a publishing office in London. An interest in modern art and design was cultivated by Eric Gregory, the director of the London office, and when it moved in 1932 to new premises at Bedford Square (in Bloomsbury, then a centre of the book publishing trade), Lund Humphries also set up its own design studio there, for which Kauffer was a kind of unofficial art director.

In May 1935 Tschichold travelled to London, probably in order to pursue the possibility of working with Lund Humphries. No substantial appointment ensued from this initiative, as he had hoped; instead what resulted was the idea of exhibiting Tschichold's work at Bedford Square, preparations for which probably occupied a further two-week visit he made to London in September. Lund Humphries had begun to host small exhibitions in December 1933: these were not principally intended to show its own work but instead included exhibits by progressive artists and designers of the time, mostly from outside Britain. Exhibitions had already been dedicated to Kauffer, Hans Schleger[33] and Man Ray, and Tschichold's exhibition was immediately preceded in the summer of 1935 by a showing of specimens from the German Klingspor typefoundry, in particular the typefaces of Rudolf Koch – quite a contrast to Tschichold's New Typography. (Tschichold had emulated Koch briefly in his early calligraphic work, but had since lost his taste for Koch's mainly gothic oeuvre.) Tschichold took advantage of his London trips to visit Nicholson and Hepworth, and to meet other members of the Hampstead community.[34] Evidently he also met Stanley Morison, who he came to esteem over the ensuing years, at the Monotype Office in London.[35] He was impressed by the quality of the station nameplates on the London Underground and was not surprised to learn that Edward Johnston had designed the lettering for them.[36] On his way home from his first London visit he stopped in Paris where he met Arp, Mondrian and Jean Hélion.

By coincidence, Tschichold returned from his first trip to London just a few days before his old friend Moholy-Nagy arrived there with the intention of staying. After spending much of 1934 working in Amsterdam, he had visited London in February 1935, where, as he explained to Tschichold, 'we were greeted in a most pleasant way and where

we spend a lot of time together with Gropius, among other friends'.[37] Moholy-Nagy may well have been encouraged to try his luck in England by Gropius, who had arrived there in October 1934 following an exhibition of his work and a lecture visit during the preceding summer. Moholy-Nagy wrote to Tschichold on 2 April 1935:

> we are moving to london (but don't tell anyone about this).... i hear from our many friends – scattered throughout the world – by turns happy and sad, but one can perhaps best discuss that in person. you wrote that you will come to london, jan, perhaps that will really happen soon.[38]

Between them Gropius and Moholy-Nagy were hatching a plan to revive the Bauhaus. This was given added impetus by the arrival in London, also in 1935, of Marcel Breuer, their former Bauhaus colleague and Moholy-Nagy's compatriot.[39] So there was a veritable Bauhaus enclave in the city for a couple of years; moreover, for a few months in the summer of 1935, all three of these emigrés lived in the same apartment building in Hampstead, one of the first examples of Bauhaus-influenced architecture in Britain. The Lawn Road Flats (now known as the Isokon building, newly restored in 2005) was financed by the entrepreneurs Jack & Molly Pritchard and designed by the Canadian architect Wells Coates, who was a member of the Unit group.[40] The Pritchards had set up a company called Isokon in 1931, which was intended to provide housing and furniture in a modern style. Pritchard was instrumental in making connections for Gropius with architects of the MARS group (the British branch of the international architecture organization, CIAM) and appointed him as Isokon's 'Controller of design'. The company produced furniture designed by both Gropius and Breuer, including Breuer's long, recliner chair.

During his two years in London, Moholy-Nagy designed brochures for Isokon products as well as publicity for the MARS group. After a shaky start, he began to receive a great number of commissions for work from various clients, including Imperial Airways and London Transport. He also executed photographic projects for several books and magazines and had his paintings exhibited at the London Gallery.

In December 1935 Moholy-Nagy wrote excitedly to Tschichold about his diversifying activity: 'what is most astonishing, all without having once to discuss it beforehand .... It happens by "word of mouth". come and see everything

32. In his first letter to Nicholson of 8 March 1935, Tschichold explained: 'You are welcome to write your reply in English, as I can read it fairly well.' On 27 April 1935 Nicholson thanked Tschichold for a 'very fine *English* letter'. Tschichold himself said he only learned English later during his working stay at Penguin Books (1947–9). Ruari McLean remembered that Tschichold's spoken English

was still not perfect at that stage, a fact that he sometimes exploited.

33. Schleger (also known as Zéro) was a German emigré who had worked in the Berlin office of Crawford's from 1929 and was helped by Kauffer after arriving in London in 1932. See Kinross, 'Emigré graphic designers in Britain', p.45.

34. Both Nicholson and Read sent Tschichold letters of invita-

tion for visa purposes, and Nicholson & Hepworth invited him to stay with them, although it is unclear whether he did so.

35. McLean, *Jan Tschichold: typographer*, p.63. McLean also mentioned that Tschichold met Havinden and Kauffer on his first trip to London, but a letter from Kauffer to Tschichold of 7 November 1935 (DNB Leipzig) implies that they had not yet met, despite Kauffer's active

involvement in Tschichold's exhibition.

36. 'Alfred Fairbank', p.301.

37. Letter Moholy-Nagy to Tschichold, 20 February 1935. Moholy-Nagy had already visited London in both 1933 and 1934.

38. Letter Moholy-Nagy to Tschichold, 7 May 1935.

39. There was some talk of Gropius becoming director of the Royal College of Art but

he would have been ineligible under the Aliens Restriction Act. Senter, 'Moholy-Nagy: the transitional years', p.88.

40. Gropius and his wife Ise stayed in one of the large studio apartments until March 1937, when they resettled for good in the USA. Moholy-Nagy & Breuer each stayed in very small apartments designed for 'minimum existence' [*Existenzminimum*] after the model of modernist

housing in Frankfurt and Berlin. They may well have found the accommodation too small – in particular Moholy-Nagy, whose second wife, Sibyl, and young daughter followed him after settling affairs in Berlin – as both of them moved out after a short time, although Moholy-Nagy and his family stayed in Hampstead for the rest of their time in England. See Alastair Grieve, *Isokon*, pp.23–4.

for yourself.'[41] By this point he had managed to find work in film-making, a field in which he had experimented extensively during his last years in Germany. A footnote in the bottom margin of a letter he sent to Tschichold on headed notepaper from London Films elucidated: 'I am working now here in London Film Studio and am doing "special effects" for the new h.g. wells film "things to come".' The studio in question – the largest film stage in Europe – was at Shepperton Studios, owned by the director of London Films, Alexander Korda, a self-styled movie mogul who had built up a film empire in a remarkably short time since arriving in London in late 1931. Korda, a Hungarian, employed many Central-European exiles in his company – including fellow Hungarians, composer Miklós Rózsa and screenwriter Emeric Pressburger – and so it seems natural that Moholy-Nagy was also brought into his fold. Moholy-Nagy's experimental film, *Light-play black-white-grey*, persuaded the head of special effects on *Things to come* to commission a sequence from him.[42] The famously workaholic Moholy-Nagy tore himself away from the film studio to visit the exhibition of Tschichold's work at Lund Humphries's London office in Bedford Square, which was on display from late November to mid-December 1935:

> warmest congratulations on your exhibition. i stole an after-noon away from the film work in order to see it. it is delight-fully done, with love and understanding, and the people who have organized it have done you a particularly good turn. there one hears, from the conversations that they hold with the visitors, that you are here an undisputed authority on typography, and i am sending you for example an issue of 'shelf appeal', in which they write that you also did the bau-haus books with me. in other words they apparently cannot imagine that anything new developed on the continent with-out your collaboration. naturally i didn't make any objection to this because it seems nicer to me to watch your reputation augment, in case you want to come here. the english only prize experts, only people who achieve something particular in their field, and that is also then a useful thing with the home office for the provision of a work permit.[43]

Moholy-Nagy's appreciation of his cherished friend's achievements was tinged here with a little envy; after all, it was he who had coined the phrase 'New Typography' before Tschichold adopted it. Also it seems that Kauffer had proposed Moholy-Nagy as the subject for one of the first Lund Humphries exhibitions (two years earlier), but discussions broke down and it never took place, to Moholy-Nagy's dissatisfaction.[44] In a letter to Gropius, Moholy-Nagy

stated clearly that he felt Tschichold owed him a debt, but he did not want to ruin his valued friendship with him over the matter. He remarked: 'tschichold is an excellent book typographer with classical ambitions in the best sense, and i do typography too because i want to prepare a unity of all graphic techniques in the future'.[45] This observation not only reveals the difference between the polymath Moholy-Nagy and the specialist typographer Tschichold, it also shows that Moholy-Nagy perceived the renascent classicism in Tschichold's mature, modernist work. His judgement was no doubt largely based on seeing *Typographische Gestaltung*, a copy of which he had received a month earlier, and for which his praise was unqualified:

> your book is the most beautiful that has been achieved in modern typography. it is a classic. i am exceedingly pleased that the decency, honesty, foresight and intelligence, the considered work in detail of new typography has been able to manifest itself in a textbook of such singular beauty and naturalness [*selbstverständlichkeit*]. i cannot find the least fault with the book. on the contrary: 'my congratulation!' [sic][46]

Kauffer, who supervised the exhibition of Tschichold's work at Lund Humphries, also praised *Typographische Gestaltung* on receiving a copy from the author: 'It is like all the rest of your work, a delightful and interesting design in thought and appearance.'[47] The exhibition was no doubt scheduled so that the book would already be in print, thereby adding to Tschichold's reputation as an authority. In the introduction to a booklet printed for the exhibition, entitled 'Typographical work of Jan Tschichold', the hosts showed a characteristically British wariness of any kind of dogma:

> Although we have gladly given an opportunity to Mr Tschichold to hold this exhibition, we do not therefore imply that we dogmatically abide by his principles of typography. We simply are anxious to let his work, which we believe to be of outstanding merit, speak for itself.

British reception of New Typography had been warming up before Tschichold's exhibition. An understanding, yet critical, examination of the ideas behind New Typography was made by the printing historian Harry Carter, based principally on a reading of *Die neue Typographie*. In a short article for the British periodical *Design for To-day*, he assessed the limitations of 'a theoretical belief in functionalism':

> The wholesome effect of the slogan Fitness for Purpose on printers in their chief capacity as rational technicians has sometimes led to its abuse in the belief that there is

41. Letter Moholy-Nagy to Tschichold, 17 December 1935. Meanwhile Moholy-Nagy's erstwhile colleague from Berlin, the photographer and fellow Hungarian Gyorgy Kepes, had joined him in London and later followed him to the USA. Kepes, who was an invaluable assistant to Moholy-Nagy, had previously sent Tschichold samples of his work and asked if he could include some in a future publication. Undated letter from Kepes (in Berlin) to Tschichold.

42. In the end, only 90 seconds of Moholy-Nagy's work on *Things to come* remained in the film. The job of designing the film's futuristic sets had first been offered to Fernand Léger, who was vetoed by Wells, and then Le Corbusier, who declined. Finally the designer Vincent Korda (Alexander's brother) designed them, inspired by *Towards a new architecture*. Moholy-Nagy had known Vincent Korda since 1930. See Terence Senter, 'Moholy-Nagy', p.88 and 'Moholy-Nagy's English photography', p.663.

43. Letter Moholy-Nagy to Tschichold, 17 December 1935.

44. See Senter, 'Moholy-Nagy', p.86, and 'Moholy-Nagy in England', pp.9–11. Kauffer seemed to get on well with most people and the break-down in communication may have arisen due to Moholy-Nagy's irascible personality.

45. Letter Moholy-Nagy to Gropius, 16 December 1935 (appendix to Senter, 'Moholy-Nagy in England').

46. Letter Moholy-Nagy to Tschichold, 3 November 1935.

47. Letter Kauffer to Tschichold, 7 November 1935 (DNB Leipzig).

LUND, HUMPHRIES & CO. LTD.
12 Bedford Square, W.C.1

Typographical Work of Jan Tschichold

From 27th November until 14th December 1935
Open Daily 10-6, Saturdays 10-1

PREFACE

Mr. Jan Tschichold's comments on typography have been translated from his German manuscript; rather inadequately in places because of the difficulty of giving the exact equivalent in English of ideas that are essentially technical and specialised. Moreover, we feel that not even the most perfect translation would be quite understandable without reference to the actual specimens of his work. It is for this reason that you are advised to refer back to Mr. Tschichold's comments after ending a visit to this Exhibition. Although we have gladly given an opportunity to Mr. Tschichold to hold this Exhibition, we do not therefore imply that we dogmatically abide by his principles of typography. We simply are anxious to let his work, which we believe to be of outstanding merit, speak for itself.

LUND, HUMPHRIES AND CO. LTD.

These are the fundamental ideas of my typography:

To-day the production and use of printed matter have increased enormously, yet anyone who publishes anything, whether an announcement, a prospectus, or a book, expects that it shall be read. Not only the buyer, but still more the reader of printing, unconsciously demands that it should be printed clearly and in an orderly fashion. For he is not at all willing to read everything. At best he does not read what is uncomfortable, and he prefers printing which looks orderly. He is pleased when something is set suitably and clearly, because his effort to understand what is printed is less than would otherwise be the case. Therefore the important parts must be brought out clearly; the unimportant must fall into the background. The resulting contrasts of black and white are not possible within the confines of the old laws of typography. These laws demand an appearance of more or less even grey: hence bold and extra bold types which primarily make possible a clear arrangement appear ugly in a traditional setting. Also, the sentence must be concentrated centrally, which is not always the best form, and does not always give an appearance which is easily understandable. Moreover, it has a tendency to make for a sameness in treating subjects which by their nature and purpose are different, and which therefore demand a difference in layout and treatment.

I attempt, therefore, to cultivate an asymmetrical form of make-up and setting, and believe this form is capable of improving present-day typography considerably. An asymmetrical style gives scope for greater variety and is better suited to the practical and aesthetic requirements of modern mankind.

This present age of speed demands that the technique of typography comes into line with it. We can only afford to spend a fraction of the time over a letterheading or other jobbing work which was spent on this subject in the 'nineties'. We therefore need new rules to work to, simpler than the old, which none the less result in an efficient layout. The number of these rules must be reduced and the new ones must offer, in spite of their simplicity, possibilities comparable with the old. These rules must harmonise exactly with the technique of machine composition, which to-day is gaining in importance in the setting of jobbing work. The old hand-setting and the modern machine work must be used in co-operation, for any variation of typographical technique between the two would only make for discord. Primarily, the rules must allow for machine setting throughout all jobbing work. I do not, however, belong to those who advocate machine setting unconditionally; I am convinced that really 'finished' hand-set work can never be entirely displaced by machine setting, because the finest 'shades' of typographical layout are so far unobtainable in machine setting. Modern methods of production are, however, bound up with machine setting, and to deny this technique of setting would be to oppose modern ideas.

Layout for me becomes a matter of logical page construction suited to the individual problem rather than the opportunist's realisation of any preconceived ideas on the subject. The problem is, therefore, to obtain a clearly organised layout by technical methods which shall be proof against criticism. These methods are created by the practical limitations of the subject—such factors as the length and meaning of the copy and the purpose in view—but, realising these limitations, we must make our decisions as to the final nature of the job, from both visual and aesthetic points of view. Not only should a typographical job be practical and easy to produce, it also should be a thing of beauty. As a plastic form, therefore, typography comes into line with present-day graphic art and painting. Five decades of interest in the layout of printed matter have raised considerably the general level of typography. Contemporary feeling demands that we enrich typography as a means of expression, and also fit it to the visual sensibilities of modern requirements by orderly layout combined with the emphasis of contrast. By freeing printed work from useless ornament, we make all its elements effective in a new way, and the mutual visual relationship of these elements, which previously we seldom noticed, has an important influence on the general appearance. The visual effect of these elements differs in every job and gives to each an individuality resulting from the purpose and intention of the task undertaken. This effect replaces that adventitious interest obtained by ornaments and similar frills.

JAN TSCHICHOLD

Translated from the German

PERSONAL DATA

Born 2nd April, 1902, in Leipzig.

1920-1926	Assistant Lecturer at the Staatliche Akademie für Graphische Künste und Buchgewerbe at Leipzig.
1927-1933	Lecturer in Typography at the Meisterschule für Deutschlands Buchdrucker in Munich.
1932	Called to Berlin as Lecturer in the Typographical Department of the Höhere Graphische Fachschule der Stadt Berlin.
April 1933	Dismissed from Munich.
	Since 1933 in Basle (Switzerland).

The following books by Jan Tschichold have appeared:—

Elementare Typographie. Leipzig 1925. Out of print.
Die neue Typographie. Leipzig 1928. Out of print.
Foto-Auge (Photo-eye). Stuttgart 1929. 4.50 marks. (in conjunction with Franz Roh.)
Eine Stunde Druckgestaltung. Stuttgart 1930. 3 marks.
Schriftschreiben für Setzer. Frankfurt-am-Main 1931. 1 mark.
Typographische Entwurfstechnik. Stuttgart 1932. 1.50 marks.
Typographische Gestaltung. Basle 1935. 8 francs.
Funktionell Typografi. Kopenhagen 1935. 3 crowns.

Further numerous articles have appeared, mostly in German, but also in English (Commercial Art), French, Czechoslovakian, Jugoslavian, Hungarian, Polish, Danish and Swedish periodicals.

LUND HUMPHRIES, LONDON

All pages of the booklet issued to accompany exhibition of Tschichold's work at Lund Humphries, London. 1935. 21.2 × 14 cm. Not designed by him. Typeset in Gill Sans.

The following, anonymous notice of the exhibition appeared in Shelf Appeal (December 1935, p.17), a magazine which described itself as 'concerned with the marketing, packaging, presentation and distribution of branded products':
'At 32, Jan Tschichold, Typographer, of whose work Lund Humphries held an exhibition in December, stands with Lissitsky as the founder of that "modern" typography which is just beginning to wear at the edges. Tschichold's predilection for masses of sans body type, his assymetrically [sic] set headings, his skilful blending of type and photograph seem a little too stark and mechanistic beside the slightly more decorative treatment now creeping into advertising and book work generally. It is, however, a pity that no translation of Tschichold's books on type, shown at Bedford Square, are available in English.'

necessarily beauty in an efficient thing or that a thing is an object of applied art because it is skilfully related to its practical function. The German modernists have embraced this fallacy in an extreme degree.

Carter went on to commend *Die neue Typographie* as a 'very valuable book, because it reconsiders the artistic nature of printing in a logically acceptable and consistent manner'. But he considered Tschichold to have chosen the wrong audience in his insistence on communicating with compositors and printing technicians:

> Indeed it is not to the printer that the reformist typographer should address himself in our time, for the printer has ceased to be a designer. Books are designed by publishers and practically all other printed work comes within the province of the publicity expert.[48]

It was perhaps the case that a conscious responsibility for 'design' had established itself outside printing houses to greater degree in Britain and the USA than in Germany, but Carter also pinpoints here the feeling that Tschichold, despite always referring to 'the compositor' in his writings, seemed to be reaching towards an ideal reader who was a typographic designer – or at least he wanted to re-educate the type compositor to fulfil that role.

One of the earliest British voices in favour of continental modernism was Bertram Evans, who wrote enthusiastically about it from an evidently first-hand knowledge of the German sources in the *Penrose Annual* for 1933. This annual compendium of essays on printing art and technology, published by Lund Humphries, contained several articles over the next few years (reaching a peak around the time of Tschichold's exhibition) that seriously addressed 'functionalist' typography, in most cases with some sympathy. Even Beatrice Warde, the publicity manager at Monotype and evangelist of a reborn classicism, had some positive things to say about it.

Evans went on to feature an article by Tschichold in the magazine that he edited, *Industrial Arts*. Entitled 'Abstract painting and the New Typography', it was an amended translation of the article that had appeared one year previously in German. According to Tschichold's English text: 'All abstract pictures, particularly the quite simple ones, show elements of painting or graphic art which are at once clearly defined in form and in plain relation to one another. From this to typography is no great step.'[49] Tschichold, introduced by Evans as 'prominent among the discoverers of New Typography', was credited with the layout of the article, which was typeset in Gill Sans. Evans's short-lived periodical,

which ran to only four issues, went on to feature articles by Bayer, Moholy-Nagy and Schawinsky.

Tschichold certainly began to get noticed in Britain, mainly by young typographers who felt oppressed by the doctrine of conservative book typography as defined by Stanley Morison. One such was Robert Harling, editor of the journal *Typography*, which featured an eclectic mixture of modernist leanings with Victorian revivalism. He undoubtedly saw Tschichold's exhibition at Lund Humphries, for it had been he who organized the preceding Klingspor exhibition.[50] Harling wrote what Tschichold himself considered to be the first article ever written specifically about him: it appeared in the issue for January 1936 of the London journal, *Printing* (see opposite). Harling also reviewed *Typographische Gestaltung* in *Typography*; here his light-hearted appreciation of the book contained the kind of equivocation which nevertheless may have begun to exercise some influence on Tschichold. Harling recommended counteracting the seriousness of Tschichold's book with a look at the productions of Francis Meynell's Nonesuch Press, concluding that 'It is so reassuring to find once again that there are two sides to any question: your truth and my truth, as Nietzsche so aptly puts it'.[51] Harling went on to include an English translation of Tschichold's 1935 article on 'type mixtures' in the third issue of *Typography* (1937), with slightly different illustrations from the original. This article was Tschichold's attempt to show a more playful side to the style of New Typography, and as such fitted the profile of the journal. Yet in the same issue, friendly criticism of Tschichold was made by Howard Wadman in his article 'Left wing layout', a title which recalled an aspect of Tschichold's approach that he himself had recently played down. Wadman praised Tschichold's 'clinical typography' as excellent for 'functional uses' but was suspicious of its elitism:

> Perhaps the just criticism of clinical typography at its best is that, like Democracy, men are not good enough for it. Tschichold, like Le Corbusier, makes no concession to our waywardness. A book to him is a machine for reading in. He has a touching faith that we are pure and rational, and while you and I may enjoy the discipline of responding to his principles, it's all my eye and Betty Martin to the common man.[52]

(Opposite) Article about Tschichold by Robert Harling in the London journal *Printing*. 1936. 30.4 × 23 cm. Worth reading.

48. Carter, 'Printing for our time', pp.60–2.

49. 'Abstract painting and the New Typography', p.158. In *Typographische Gestaltung* Tschichold argued that Theo van Doesburg's term 'concrete art' was more accurate than 'abstract' or 'non-objective'. Later, in *Asymmetric typography*, it was explained that 'concrete' was not appropriate in English. On this terminological issue see also 'Über El Lissitzky' (1932), p.106.

50. James Moran, 'Lund Humphries' exhibitions: a retrospect', p.88.

51. *Typography*, no.2, p.22. Tschichold wrote to Harling on 12 March 1972: 'When preparing a large special issue of *Typographische Monatsblätter* (St. Gall) devoted to my work, to celebrate my 70th anniversary at 2 April, 1972, I was forced to compile a Bibliography of all my articles and books. / In the section "Articles about J.T." an article of yours of 1936 is the very first. / I have never forgotten your far-sighted appreciation: You were among the very first to recognize my work, as tiny as it was in that time. Long ago!' Harling recalled meeting Tschichold in the 1940s: 'I found him a rather sad, introspective, gloomy fellow, overloaded by the manifold tragedies of the world, of which he had had his share. He looked, I thought, rather like a superannuated professor of physics looking for a mislaid formula.' (Letter to the author, 5 February 1993.)

52. Wadman, 'Left wing layout', pp.27–8.

What is this "Functional" Typography?

The Work of Jan Tschichold

By ROBERT HARLING

IN 1960 copies of *Die Neue Typographie* or *Funktionel Typografi* will appear at Sothebys or Hodgsons, and bidding will suddenly become brisk, perhaps very brisk, for by that time Tschichold will be accepted.

Time will once more have triumphed over tempers.

The recent exhibition at Lund, Humphries in Bedford Square shows us how the work of Tschichold is far ahead of even the most advanced of the modern school (if there is any school worthy of the term) in England.

Yet it is not so much a distance of technique as a distance of mind.

Logical Solutions

The logical solution to a problem is the rarest thing we are offered. To the problems of living in towns or sailing the seas we evolve such solutions as 20th century London or " Queen Mary." And gentlemen, I ask you !

When we see, therefore, a man solving a problem in a logical manner the processes of thought involved may seem at first a little strange to us. We are not accustomed to the logical *selective* mind at work. And when that mind begins to deal with something we had always accepted—pleasant age-old patterns of pages and margins—we are apt to be,

Specimen of Tschichold's typographical design

first, suspicious, then antagonistic and/or interested. It probably depends on your glands.

But it doesn't really matter whether you give prize or prejudice to Tschichold. He is already here, for keeps. Already he is the greatest contemporary figure in typography. Certainly his is the dominant voice in Continental typography, and that dominance is likely to increase, for his voice is deadly serious, quiet, insidious and *logical*.

What then is there about Tschichold's work which makes it too definitely a *new* voice ?

Chiefly it is the fact that it is a machine-made voice. Everything in Tschichold's technique, apart from its classical purity, is derived from the machine. I have dealt elsewhere with this background to Tschichold's work. Here I am more concerned with that which we see.

Austerity—and why

Our first thoughts on seeing these typographical exercises is that they are austere. Then we see that they are only austere because everything has been considered. The logical disposition of the type on the page may at first seem cold, but it certainly does not distract ; the shedding of unnecessary things does not offend.

Then we examine the types that Tschichold uses and we find that he is not eternally preoccupied with the sansserif as so many self-styled modernists are. He uses Futura, Gill, Erbar, but only when it would be difficult for the designer to use a serif letter. On suitable occasions you will find him using Baskerville, Bembo, Weiss, Bodoni, Walbaum.

If he has a typographical preoccupation I would say that it is rather with the Bodoni and Walbaum types ; types which we designate, somewhat loosely, as " modern."

There is, of course, no desecration in the traditional sense in Tschichold's work. There is perhaps a symbol or a house mark in what we know as the Germanic manner, but apart from this there is nothing. There are type rules certainly, but no typographer calls a 1-point rule a decoration ; yet one of the most interesting features of Tschichold's work is his supreme ability to introduce a 1-point rule into a page and give it the classical, inflexible beauty of a Grecian column.

He uses the 1-point rule, too, for

" boxes " in the most daring fashion. Other typographers have tried such a use but it just looked dull or didn't come off ; Tschichold does it amazingly well. It is all a question of balance ; a " box " in a Tschichold page has a definite part to play and the single rule looks anything but dull.

But types and rules are not the most important things about Tschichold's work. We come back once again to the intangible something behind the actuality before us. We call it a quality of mind, or an outlook, or some such thing. And it is that. Whatever we call it we cannot escape that simple explanation : the man is *different*.

Page Construction

" Layout for me," says Tschichold, " becomes a matter of logical page construction suited to the individual problem rather than the opportunist's realisation of any preconceived ideas on the subject."

But this, says the designer with an *ego* to be expressed, means that every job is alike. We shall have a book jacket looking like an engineering catalogue. To which Tschichold replies :

" By freeing printed work from useless ornament, we make all its elements effective in a new way, and the mutual visual relationship of these elements, which previously we seldom noticed, has an important influence on the general appearance. The visual effect of these elements differs in every job and gives to each an individuality resulting from the purpose and intention of the task undertaken."

Compositors Must "Modernise"

MR. DOUGLAS C. McMURTRIE, Director of Typography, Ludlow Typograph Company, speaking recently to Chicago printers, urged the importance of fitness to purpose in the planning of printing, of putting a " tone of voice " into typography, of greater vitality on noncentred layouts, and a new and higher regard than ever before for ease of reading.

He recommended closer spacing than is usual in machine composition, but warned against setting lines so tight that spaces between words were not clearly recognisable.

He favoured introduction of a normal word space only following periods at the end of sentences.

Robert Harling, covers for *Typography*, nos. 2 & 3. 1937. 27.9 × 23.3 cm. No. 2 shows a definite influence of Tschichold.

Tschichold's article 'Type mixtures', *Typography* no. 3.

The language barrier naturally prevented *Typographische Gestaltung* from being widely appreciated in Britain (a modified English translation was only published over thirty years later), although its own artefactual qualities spoke eloquently enough. Tschichold had previously acknowledged that the best contemporary, classical typography was being done in England under the aegis of Morison; in *Typographische Gestaltung* he wrote with further appreciation of the 'current English style, which under the influence of Stanley Morison strives for a rebirth of classical typography and in this sense provides by far the best examples of ornamental typography'. But he continued: 'The success of this attempt in book typography is however no proof that it is contemporary and generally valid.' At the end of the book he makes positive what is negatively implied here, that 'England is no bad example' for 'contemporary book design'.[53]

The short statement by Tschichold in the leaflet that accompanied his exhibition at Lund Humphries is a translation, in slightly abbreviated form, of the section from *Typographische Gestaltung* called 'The meaning and aims of the new or functional typography'. Retitled as 'These are the fundamental ideas of my typography', and with an added personal justification of his 'asymmetric' approach (important in the British context), these few paragraphs of Tschichold's mature, modernist views proffered some kind of possible meeting ground with British traditionalism. In particular he conceded here that trends in modern printing before the New Typography had been positive, signifying a softening of his position: 'Five decades of interest in the layout of printed matter have raised considerably the general level of typography.'[54] Also, after stressing the functional imperatives of typography, he concluded wisely with a line taken directly from his book: 'Not only should a typographical job be practical and easy to produce, it also should be a thing of beauty.'[55]

It is likely that the Lund Humphries exhibition was intended partly to engender commissions of design work specifically for Tschichold. A small amount of work did follow, including a redesign for the letterhead of Lund Humphries itself, typeset in Gill Sans, with the typography conspicuously credited to Tschichold.[56] A larger commission was the design of the volume for 1938 of the *Penrose Annual*. Tschichold's design is representative of his transitional period here between New Typography and classicism: despite asymmetric headings in Gill Sans, the text is set in

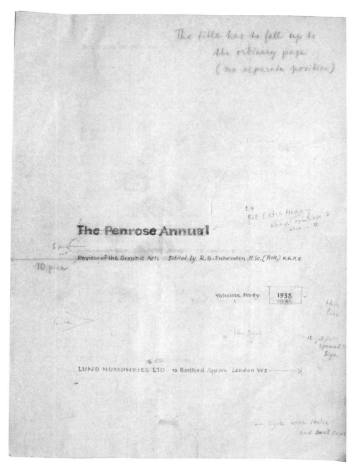

Tschichold's layout and specification for the title-page of *The Penrose Annual*. 1938.

justified, evenly grey columns of the Van Dijck typeface recently revived by Monotype.

The shift in Tschichold's interest away from New Typography at this time is demonstrated by his giving or selling to museum collections a great deal of the material he had collected over the years. Although he had habitually requested two copies of printed items for his collection, this step signified that he no longer planned to include such material as illustrations in his future publications. Tschichold's material contributed to building the collection of modern commercial typography at the Victoria & Albert Museum, London, which was initiated by the museum's librarian, Philip James. In a short note in *Typography* James explained that the aim was to 'exhibit contemporary specimens from time to time so that the trend of typographic

53. *Typographische Gestaltung*, pp.14 & 112; *Asymmetric typography* pp.21 & 93.

54. The original German sentence in *Typographische Gestaltung* is more grudging: 'Fünf Jahrzente neuer Bemühungen um die Gestalt des Schriftsatzes haben das Niveau der Typographie mind-
estens im großen und ganzen beträchtlich gehoben ...', which could be literally translated as (with my italics stressing the differences): 'Five decades of new efforts in the design of printed matter have *at least* considerably raised the level of typography, *by and large* ...'. The prefatory note to the
exhibition booklet (probably by Eric Gregory, director of the London office) mentioned the difficulty of translating Tschichold's text.

55. *Typographical work of Jan Tschichold*, p.4 [unnumbered].

56. Tschichold gives a date of 1938 for this letterhead in *Leben und Werk*; McLean dates
it 1935, and says that it was in use from 1936 to 1948. It seems likely that it was done sometime in 1936, towards the end of which Tschichold asked Moholy-Nagy's advice on how much to charge for such work, and received the reply 'with lund humphries, i would suggest the rates: for advertising 7 guineas; for letterhead 5 guineas; nothing less!'. (Letter Moholy-Nagy to Tschichold, 13 November 1936.) Moran mentions an exhibition at the Lund Humphries London office in June 1936, which 'showed specimens of the work which they had carried out for their clients in past years, designed
in collaboration with "such experts" as McKnight Kauffer, Man Ray, Zero, Jan Tschichold, Francis Bruguière and others' ('Lund Humphries' exhibitions: a retrospect', p.91) My thanks to Graham Twemlow for information about McKnight Kauffer and exhibitions at Lund Humphries .

design, both in this country and abroad, could be estimated by students of industrial art'.[57] The first small exhibition of material from the collection was shown at the V&A in late 1936. Soon afterwards Tschichold sold some material (including several items by Klucis) to the Museum of Modern Art, New York. His decision may partly have been influenced by financial considerations but it is also a sign that he was beginning to divest himself of connections to modernism.[58]

Robin Kinross has suggested 'that the contact with Britain played a part in Tschichold's move to a traditional manner'.[59] It is difficult say whether it was a cause or an effect of Tschichold's transition that he was invited in 1937 to read a paper at the Double Crown Club, the exclusive dining club of the British typographical establishment. It is unlikely that Morison would have initiated the invitation; it is more probable that Oliver Simon, who originally conceived of the club, had something to do with it, given that he was of partially German extraction and knew the language. The title of Tschichold's talk – 'A new approach to typography' (presumably delivered in English) – shows that he maintained his modernist stance in the decorous surroundings of the Club's sixty-first dinner gathering at the Café Royal, London, on 29 April. He had received the invitation early in the year and informed Moholy-Nagy, who advised him: 'really here "dinners" are generally in dress suit. could you perhaps ask the organizers if you could do it differently? or perhaps my dress coat will fit tschichold.'[60] What the eventual dress code was is unclear, but Moholy-Nagy was also present in the meeting, at which Tschichold showed illustrations of his own work to accompany his talk. 'According to the report', wrote James Moran, 'the discussion was marked by superfluities rather than essence, but was enlivened by contributions from Herbert Read and L. Moholy-Nagy, who were guests of the club. The discussion was finally terminated by a tired president (Walter Lewis) anxious to catch his train.'[61] Tschichold was undoubtedly gratified by the respect accorded him in the well-mannered milieu of the English gentlemen's typographic club, especially compared to his treatment as a 'cultural bolshevist' only four years earlier in Germany.[62]

Tschichold spent at least two weeks in England on this occasion, and Moholy-Nagy wrote to Edith Tschichold that he was 'looking after him'. His stay happened to coincide

with a visit to London by Herbert Bayer, whose work was being exhibited at the London Gallery. '... he arrived here from obergurgl like a bronzed demi-god', Moholy-Nagy wrote to Edith, 'and [regaled] us with fine and most festive reminiscences of the old bauhaus'.[63]

After briefly returning to Berlin, Bayer visited the USA, where he attended a more serious Bauhaus reunion. Gropius had already left London to take up his new teaching position at Harvard in March 1937, and summoned Breuer to join him. Bayer and Breuer travelled together in July, attending a meeting at Gropius's house in Providence, Rhode Island, to discuss the Bauhaus exhibition projected to take place the following year at New York's Museum of Modern Art. Bayer was commissioned to design the exhibition and collect material for it on his return to Germany. After settling his affairs there, he emigrated to the USA, where he would remain as a successful graphic designer for the rest of his life.

Moholy-Nagy was also present at the Rhode Island meeting, at which his proposed statutes for the New Bauhaus in Chicago were reviewed. Not long after Tschichold's speech at the Double Crown Club, Moholy-Nagy left London for good. In early June he received the invitation from Chicago to direct a new design school, having been recommended for the post by Gropius. Moholy-Nagy had begun to hanker after some teaching activity and soon realized that it would be impossible for him to break into the British educational system. He wrote to Tschichold at the end of the same month:

> dear tschicholds
> since jan left, things have been full speed ahead here. principally we have been showered with telegrams from america with the result that i am going over there in order to get an impression for myself of what is suggested.
> first i will visit gropius, who writes very contentedly of things over there, the conditions, the people, the air and skies. i hope that i can also report something similar to you in a few weeks.[64]

Again it seems that Moholy-Nagy hoped to keep Tschichold informed in case any prospects opened up for him in the USA. But none did, and Tschichold may have been discouraged from actively pursuing the possibility of moving to England at this point by the departure of the other emigrés who had settled there briefly – especially Moholy-Nagy, who

57. Philip James, 'Modern commercial typography', p.32. Curiously, he singled out both Tschichold and Max Bill (who would later disagree profoundly with each other) as 'Constructivists'.

58. The few items Tschichold sold in 1937 to MOMA were supplemented in 1950 by what seems to have been the major-

ity of his collection of New Typography, purchased as a lot with funds provided by architect Philip Johnson. The 'Jan Tschichold collection' at MOMA now exceeds 800 items.

59. *Modern typography*, p.127.

60. Letter Moholy-Nagy to Tschichold, 25 February 1937.

61. Moran, *The Double Crown*

Club, pp.42–3. Berthold Wolpe, who had also emigrated from Germany to Britain in 1935 (staying there for the rest of his life) was already then a member of the club, no doubt due to his working in a traditional style, which had led Morison to commission his Albertus typeface for Monotype. Wolpe designed the Double Crown

Club menu for the dinner at which one of Tschichold's early mentors, Carl Ernst Poeschel, had talked (one year before Tschichold did), and one imagines that Wolpe may also have had something to do with Tschichold's invitation.

62. By peculiar coincidence, Stanley Morison had been accused of 'bolshevism' when

presenting the new Gill Sans typeface in 1928 at a printers' conference in Blackpool, as if a whiff of continental air had blown into the proceedings. Tschichold later drew a parallel between himself and Morison in that both had been imprisoned for their beliefs (Morison as a conscientious objector in the First World War). 'Jan

Tschichold: praeceptor typographiae', p.1.

63. Letter Moholy-Nagy to Edith Tschichold, 16 April 1937. Obergurgl is an Austrian resort for which Bayer had designed a publicity leaflet when working at the Berlin Dorland agency.

64. Letter Moholy-Nagy to Tschicholds, 27 June 1937.

was his good friend. By 24 March 1938 Moholy-Nagy was writing to Tschichold in English on headed notepaper of 'the new bauhaus: american school of design' in Chicago (from England he had written in German, without capital letters):

> The long distance certainly does not help the intensification of correspondence, although I feel that you in Europe have to have a most intensive contact with us who are fortunate enough to be on a little bit safer continent.

There was perhaps a note of smugness here, although this may be an unfair deduction from Moholy-Nagy's imperfect English. In any case, he must indeed have felt lucky to be out of Europe, where the Nazis were soon to overrun Czechoslovakia and Austria as a prelude to their invasion of Poland. Switzerland had a history of vehemently defending its democracy but the National Socialists had been gaining strength there, holding conspicuous rallies and marches. Tschichold would certainly have sensed the threat of encroaching Nazi militarism from such a close proximity. (Another German refugee in Switzerland, Thomas Mann, fled at this time to the USA.) Moreover, by 1938 he had spent five years already in Switzerland and may well have felt that it was worth staying to build on that investment in waiting time for Swiss citizenship, which then, as now, could only be awarded after ten years.[65] Moholy-Nagy kindly told him that he 'would like very much to help if you have certain wishes here in America', but it soon became apparent, as his wife Sibyl explained to Edith Tschichold, that it would be wiser to wait a few years for the New Bauhaus to prove itself to the board of 'ten hard-boiled american businessmen' before insisting on inviting guest teachers from Europe.[66]

Since their first meeting, Ben Nicholson and Tschichold had maintained a regular correspondence based on a mutual respect for each other's work. Tschichold was so enthused by Nicholson's Constructivist, wooden reliefs that he asked permission to reproduce one in the article he wrote about the relationship of modern art to typography. Spurred by this Nicholson asked Tschichold if he would consider writing a short piece on his work for the English periodical, *Axis*:

> in the no.2 Axis they are to do two articles on Kandinsky's work & two articles on my work. I wonder if you would be interested to write one of the articles on my work? I do not expect this would interest you but I must ask you as I should particularly like to have your severe point of view in connection with my 'reliefs'.[67]

Despite being busy with *Typographische Gestaltung* at this point, in March 1935, Tschichold wrote the article, 'On Ben Nicholson's reliefs', for which he was paid a nominal fee of

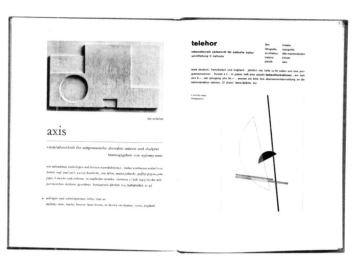

Advertisement for *Axis* in *Typographische Gestaltung*, showing one of Ben Nicholson's reliefs.

£1. The editor of *Axis*, Myfanwy Evans (whose husband was the artist John Piper), translated the article from German, and Herbert Read approved the translation before it was printed. Tschichold commented in his piece:

> I am certainly not a historian of art ... and I am very unwilling to write about art. I prefer to look at it. However, being an infinitely polite person, I cannot refuse the request of the editor of *Axis*, especially as it concerns the work of my friend Ben Nicholson.[68]

Tschichold's professed reluctance to write about modern art had not previously been evident: both *Die neue Typographie* and *Typographische Gestaltung* contained specific sections on the subject. He had nothing of great consequence to say in *Axis* about Nicholson's work, but Nicholson was delighted with the result nonetheless:

> The simple way in which you write is very sympathetic to me, & I like very much several of the points you made – particularly the difference between abstract art and Klee – & Rembrandt and Picasso – & also of course it is very important for the English public to have it said that as one's work becomes simpler it will become better. I think it was very nice of you to take the trouble to write it for me.[69]

Tschichold also wanted to reproduce one of Nicholson's wooden reliefs in *Typographische Gestaltung*, but in the end it did not appear as an illustration to the text but in an advertisement for *Axis* at the back of the book. Reciprocally, an advertisement for Tschichold's book was published in *Axis*, in which it was claimed that he, as a teacher in Munich, 'has had a decisive influence on the formation of the new style of typography, and has purified it from a few of its early mistakes'.

Herbert Read commented later that the Constructivist element in the London community of modern artists and designers was strengthened by the presence of Moholy-Nagy

65. There is a curious phrase in a letter from Renner to Tschichold of 20 April 1948, in which Renner wishes him success in a 'further transplantation across the great water', implying that

Tschichold was thinking of emigrating to the USA. This seems unlikely, given that he was by then a Swiss citizen.
66. Sybil Moholy-Nagy to Edith Tschichold, 11 May 1938.

67. Letter Nicholson to Tschichold, 21 February 1935.
68. 'On Ben Nicholson's reliefs', p.16.
69. Letter Nicholson to Tschichold, 27 April 1935.

Cover and spread from *Circle* (London: Faber &
Faber, 1937). 25.8 × 20 cm. Shows Tschichold's
article 'New Typography'.

and of Naum Gabo, the Russian sculptor who arrived in
England via Berlin and Paris. Indeed the mantle of Constructivism was adopted for an ambitious multi-disciplinary
publication in 1937 co-edited by Nicholson, Gabo, and the
architect Leslie Martin. The book (intended to be the first
in a series, but it was also the last) was entitled *Circle: international survey of constructive art*. The list of contributors
was impressive, including Mondrian, Read, Le Corbusier,
Hepworth, Moore, Breuer, Richard Neutra, and Siegfried
Giedion. Nicholson asked Tschichold to write something
for the project, which resulted in a new essay, simply titled
'New Typography'. The book contained several sections on
architecture, art, and sculpture, but Tschichold's essay was
lumped uneasily into a section on 'Art and life' with other
contributions by Gropius, Moholy-Nagy, Lewis Mumford,
and Léonide Massine (veteran of Diaghilev's Ballets Russes)
on 'Choreography'. Despite the editorially avant-garde
nature of the publication, Tschichold's text showed his
inclination by 1937 to find some common ground between
New Typography and what he called 'New Traditionalism',
a fitting term apparently of his own coinage, by which he
meant to describe the products of the British typographical
renaissance in the 1920s and 1930s.[70] Given that his text is
short, it is worth quoting here at length:

> The new typography aims at a clear presentation of typo-
> graphical images by immaculate technique and by the use
> of forms which correspond to the new feeling for space.
> Every deviation from tradition is by no means New Typo-
> graphy in our sense of the word. We demand also that the
> resultant form should be beautiful – thus it would be wrong
> to designate the New Typography as anti-aesthetic. But we
> consider the use of ornament and rules in the manner of

earlier styles as disturbing and contrary to the contemporary
spirit. The form should arise clearly and unequivocally out
of the requirements of the text and pictures only, and according to the functions of the printed matter. New Traditionalism in typography demands exactly the same. Yet in spite of
the great austerity and purity of its manner as well as other
qualities its products are characterized by a certain sterility
because these works proceed from an earlier feeling of space.
Even this can exercise a certain charm on the man of today,
but it corresponds to the charm that emanates from an *old*
work of art. It seems to us that the attempt to create from the
contemporary feeling of space is more worth while.

In the technical sense the New Typography cannot claim
any essential progress. Fundamentally, types are set today
as they were 500 years ago. Machine-setting only imitates
hand-setting and is hardly in a condition to create anything
formally better or even a legitimate form of its own. The
potentialities of the modern setting-technique (speaking
purely technically) must anyway be regarded as perfect. Our
efforts, too, at employing as simple a technique as possible in
planning the layout coincides with the methods of the early
printers and therefore need not be especially emphasized.
The real value of the New Typography consists in its efforts
towards purification and towards simplicity and clarity of
means. From this comes the partiality for beautiful sans such
as the Futura and the Gill Sans.

We seek to achieve clarity by contrasts. Contrasts as such
are not necessarily beautiful. There are beautiful and ugly
ones; thus every insertion of bolder types is not good New
Typography. In general the casual compositor uses everywhere too large and too heavy type; a considerable reduction
of sizes of type even makes the reading of the type more
agreeable.

70. Tschichold's article was
written in early 1937, before his
talk at the Double Crown Club
in April. Presumably he wrote it
in German and it was translated
into (slightly stilted) English.

The formal problem of the New Typography is *the creation of an asymmetrical balance from contrasting elements*, the proportions naturally chosen according to the sense. In books too a contrasting form which nevertheless preserves the unity of the whole in all the multiplicity, should be aimed at.

The diffusion of good New Typography is not proceeding everywhere at the same pace – it shares this fate with the other efforts of visual culture. In any case considerable time will elapse before the new potentialities are exhausted. Only new needs which for the time being are still unknown can engender new forms.[71]

His statements here make it clear that by this time he had developed a good appreciation of the ideas behind British New Traditionalism, almost certainly based on a reading of Stanley Morison's catechism 'First principles of typography' (published in the last issue of *The Fleuron*, 1930) with its famous definition of typography as 'the efficient means to an essentially utilitarian and only accidentally aesthetic end'.[72] Indeed there are some distinct similarities between the introductory statements in Morison's text and those made by Tschichold in his manifesto of 1925 'Elementare Typographie', and to some extent in *Die neue Typographie*. The difference is that Tschichold's emphasis was on fresh thinking and acting modern, whereas Morison was concerned with avoiding bad manners.

In fact, in his piece for *Circle,* Tschichold strayed further from a strictly utilitarian code than Morison did by stressing that beauty was an important outcome; Morison's principles, based as they were almost exclusively on book typography, assumed that beauty would take care of itself through the use of classic roman typefaces. Of course Tschichold had always allowed that New Typography could be done with seriffed type; it was centred layout that was still the obstacle for him here, although he does not say so explicitly. Yet Tschichold's assertion that New Traditionalism essentially demands 'exactly the same' thing as New Typography allows for the interpretation that both approaches contained the right idea, but that New Typography was simply more contemporary in style. This interpretation is supported by a table of comparison between the two that Tschichold included in his article, which is reproduced above.

Additionally, his opinion that typography had not fundamentally changed since Gutenberg's day re-confirms that he was less utopian than his friends Lissitzky and Moholy-

TABLE

NEW TRADITIONALISM	NEW TYPOGRAPHY
Common to both	
Disappearance of ornament	
Attention to careful setting	
Attempt at good proportional relations	
Differences	
Use of harmonious types only, where possible the same	Contrasts by the use of various types
The same thickness of type, bolder type prohibited	Contrasts by the use of bolder type
Related sizes of type	Frequent contrasts by the use of widely differentiated types
Organization from a middle point (symmetry)	Organization without a middle-point (asymmetry)
Tendency towards concentration of all groups	Tendency towards arrangement in isolated groups
Predominant tendency towards a pleasing appearance	Predominant tendency towards lucidity and functionalism
Preference for woodcuts and drawings	Preference for photographs
Tendency towards hand-setting	Tendency towards machine-setting

Tschichold's table from *Circle* comparing New Typography and New Traditionalism

Nagy.[73] Tschichold's conservatism here is a little unexpected given that he had been actively involved in designing typefaces for the new technology of phototypesetting, which was distinctly futuristic in breaking free from typography's leaden shackles into the realm of light and photography. Perhaps his first-hand experience made him realize the limitations of that technology, at least in its pioneering stage.

One consummate, late example of Tschichold's practice in the idiom of New Typography shows him fully exploiting the possibilities of letterpress printing technology. This is the poster and booklet for the Basel Gewerbemuseum's exhibition 'Der Berufsphotograph' (The professional photographer; 1938). Combined with a striking negative photograph, Tschichold employed the rainbow printing technique: several colours are added in a single impression, due to the ink roller being charged in a rainbow formation. The result here is the transition between the three primary colours on the bold sanserif of the exhibition title, with the yellow and red also highlighting elements on extreme left and right. This large format poster, which Richard Hollis has described as being of 'extreme economy and precision', was also perhaps Tschichold's last major piece of work in *Kleinschreibung*.[74] Indeed Tschichold later described it to Ladislav Sutnar as 'my last poster'.[75]

71. A review of *Circle* in *Typography* (no.4, autumn 1937, p.18), signed by Gordon Bromley, criticized the theory in Tschichold's essay as 'now being almost as well worn as William Morris's'.

72. Morison's text began life only one year after *Die neue*

Typographie as the definition of typography in the *Encyclopedia Britannica* for 1929. In his postscript to the final issue of *The Fleuron* Morison signals his dismissive awareness of modernism: 'The apostles of the "machine age" will be wise to address their disciples in a

standard old face – they can flourish their concrete banner in sans-serif on title-pages and perhaps in a running headline.' (cited in Barker, *Stanley Morison*, p.281.) Disregarding the disdain, this was a sentiment not so dissimilar from Tschichold's own view in the early

1930s, when working for the Bücherkreis.

73. Tschichold's prioritizing the quality of hand-setting over machine-setting again marks his view as somewhat less contemporary than Morison's, whose principal aim at Monotype was to bring the quality

of the past into machine production. Indeed manual type composition lasted longer in Germany than in Britain; *Die neue Typographie*, for example, was composed by hand.

74. Hollis, *Graphic design: a concise history*, p.80. Hollis gives a detailed analysis of

the poster's graphic structure here and also in *Swiss graphic design*, p.77.

75. Letter Tschichold to Sutnar, 14 April 1946. Tschichold designed some posters (in classical style) for the Basel Musik-Akademie during the 1960s. See *Leben und Werk*, pp.166–7.

284

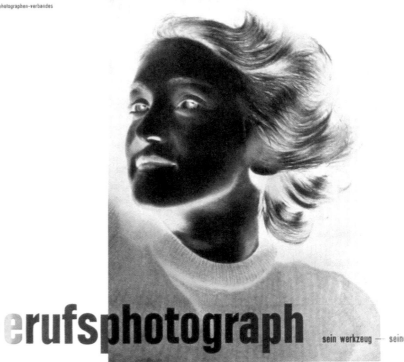

Exhibition poster for Basel Gewerbemuseum,
1938. 63.5 × 90.5 cm.

Cover and pages from catalogue of same exhibition. A5. Text area again placed towards fore-edge.

(Right) An advertisement at the back of the catalogue, apparently designed by Tschichold.

Cover and spreads of catalogue for exhibition of 'new art in Switzerland'. 1938. First exhibition organized by the 'Allianz' group of Swiss artists. The cover design set a style followed by designers of subsequent catalogues for Allianz exhibitions after the Second World War, including those designed by Max Bill and Richard Paul Lohse. The relief pictured in the lower spread is by Sophie Taeuber.

New Year's greeting card. 1938. A6.

Title-page spread and text spread from Arp, *Muscheln und Schirme* (privately published by the author, 1939). 22.5 × 15.4 cm.

Drawings by Sophie Taeuber; designed by Tschichold; printed in Czechoslovakia.

From avant-garde to rearguard

Tschichold persisted for a short while longer with an asymmetric approach in designing some small items of ephemeral printing and occasional books on modern art. But it was at this time, by his own later account (written in the third person), that he became a devotee of centred book typography:

> Since around 1938 Tschichold had dedicated himself entirely to book typography, which had become his principal and favourite area. He left behind the asymmetric layout-method [*Anordnungsweise*] of advertising typography and from then onwards arranged almost everything, really everything, on a central axis. He had recognized that an admittedly purified, yet traditional layout is the most reasonable and best course for many tasks. This only apparent change in his views brought him the enmity of those who could or would not follow him on this path, because they never, so to speak, had to critically address the typography of the book.[76]

His reorientation derived partly, no doubt, from his concern with text typography in designing books for Benno Schwabe. The date he gave later for his 'apparent change' is borne out by his writings of these very years. His two-part article entitled 'Von schlechter und guter Typographie' (Of good and bad typography), published in a Swiss printing journal in 1937 and 1938, shows an acceptance of both old and New Typography. It takes the form of an annotated list of rules for compositors, which could be equally applied to both traditional or modern typography – the overriding principle is the achievement of maximum effect with minimum means. Although his explanations favour asymmetric typography in detail, he states that 'Asymmetric setting is not better than symmetric; it is different'. He argued that both were valid in appropriate circumstances: 'In general it can be said that symmetrical setting is to be preferred in books (although one can also set books very beautifully in an asymmetric way), while asymmetric setting prevails in jobbing work and especially in advertisements.' It seemed invidious to him at this point to set them in opposition: 'The quality of the typesetting itself is a higher category. Like all summary judgements, the primitive opinion "New Typography–good, old–bad" and vice versa is erroneous.' In conclusion he stated that his rules were 'the sum of experiences of several generations and countries, and nobody who uses them will lose face.'[77] Here is the first incidence of his summoning tradition as the support for the correctness of his typography that would become characteristic of his later writings. Yet, intriguingly, an edited version of the very same text was published in another Swiss journal two years later under the title 'Proportionen in unsymmetrischer Typographie' (Proportions in asymmetric typography). The different concluding paragraph here makes clear the shift of

emphasis: 'From these disciplined methods arise forms, the purity of which is an appropriate expression of our spiritual objective: the suiting of typography to the visual sensibility of the present day.'[78] The opposition set up in each article was thus different: in the first it was 'good versus bad' in the second 'centred versus asymmetric'. The difference in stance can perhaps partly be explained by the identity of the respective journals in which these articles appeared: the first, *Schweizer Reklame und Schweizer graphische Mitteilungen*, was at this time more of a traditional printing journal, whereas the second was *Typographische Monatsblätter*, launched only in 1933 and firmly oriented from the beginning towards the modern.

Here Tschichold was at a turning point from which he could see clearly the virtues of both New Typography and New Traditionalism. His last essay as a contemporary historian of New Typography dates from around this point: its title – 'Die Entwicklung der neuen Typographie in den mitteleuropäischen Ländern' (The development of New Typography in Central-European countries) – made it clear that Tschichold's view was now centred outside Germany. While, strictly speaking, he maintained political neutrality, his dislike of what was happening under Hitler shone through:

> The last few years have not only brought a further refinement of New Typography but also its wider dissemination across the borders of those countries that originally took part in its creation. Indeed, it seems that its new friends are disposed to carry forward an inheritance, which today in Germany is being renounced in word and type. In fact New Typography continues to be applied there in practice, yet hardly developed further. For nothing new has emerged to replace it anywhere, including the Third Reich. There the best examples are nothing more than New Typography with the aid of Fraktur and Textura (inaccurately called *gotisch*) types; the rest are, in the best cases, traditionally correct, and a considerable remaining portion is, as everywhere, bad or misunderstood typography.

Tschichold considered the nationalistic propagation of gothic type by the Nazis as negative for both that category of type and for New Typography:

> While 'New' Typography of the Third Reich represents merely an unexportable deviation from the original, the seeds sown twelve years ago have borne valuable fruit in the democratic lands of Central Europe. This consists in an increasing refinement of feeling for relationships in size and contrast, a more relaxed sensitivity to the connections between unprinted and printed areas, and the use of the best historical types along with good, contemporary sanserif types. Photomontage, which is closely bound up with New Typography, has brought forth much beautiful work in recent years; the development of photomontage accentuated by, or even produced in colour deserves special mention.

In this last respect, Tschichold singled out for special praise the work of Herbert Matter, who he described as 'one of the

76. 'Jan Tschichold: praeceptor typographiae', p.24.

77. 'Von schlechter und guter Typographie', pp.212–3 & 218.

78. 'Proportionen in unsymmetrischer Typographie', p.250.

Spreads from Tschichold's article on 'the development of New Typography in Central-European countries'. [1937/8]. The top spread includes an illustration of the prospectus for Fretz printers designed by Matter (the original was printed in red and black).

best Swiss graphic designers' and whose photomontage work 'belongs among the most beautiful examples that have been achieved in this new form of graphic design'.

Tschichold's mention of the 'seeds sown' in 1925 (when *Elementare Typographie* was published) shows that he did not underestimate his own role in New Typography's development. His definition of *Mitteleuropa* in this article was rather idiosyncratic in encompassing parts of Scandinavia, where he perceived positive developments, mainly ensuing from his visits to lecture in Denmark and Sweden and from the publication of translated editions of *Typographische Gestaltung* in both countries. Yet his conclusion to this article reveals his view of the suprapersonal potential in New Typography for having a good moral effect:

> [The examples shown] demonstrate in the clearest manner, wherein lies the true goal of New Typography: in the clear, unprejudiced solution of the task; neat, technically simple manner of composition; easily comprehensible layout; the use of clear and beautiful typefaces, and a harmonious, imaginative design using contrasting elements, which does not lack grace. Their endeavour to avoid falseness and inappropriate pathos in each case is at the same time a confession of brotherly modesty, humanity and civilized behaviour.[79]

The implication that he considered these qualities to be lacking in Nazi Germany was unmistakable. This essay reads like an elegy for New Typography, a setting to rest of Tschichold's active engagement with it.

A mere two years later, Tschichold expressed sentiments in person that confirm his shift towards classicism. The Scottish typographer Ruari McLean sought him out in Switzerland almost immediately after beginning work in 1939 at Lund Humphries's Bradford Works, where he had found some of Tschichold's publications and been greatly inspired by them. During McLean's visit Tschichold told him that he no longer personally had any interest in his own book, *Typographische Gestaltung*, which had been published only four years previously.[80]

During the Second World War Tschichold increasingly took refuge in research and writing, concentrating on historical studies that would result in several volumes on Chinese wood-block printing and the first of his major surveys of great letterforms of the past, *Geschichte der Schrift in Bildern* (published in 1941). His employment at Benno Schwabe seems to have ceased around 1940, presumably due to financial pressures of the war years. Tschichold later described his situation at that time as being 'constantly under threat of his work permit and leave to remain not

Lettering atwork for Benno Schwabe edition, along with printed reproduction. 1942. Around 25% of actual size.

being extended'.[81] But he had good and somewhat influential friends now in Basel, including Hermann Loeb, a fellow German emigré and proprietor of the Holbein publishing house, which published the majority of Tschichold's books in the 1940s and 1950s. Tschichold began to design editions for Holbein, which specialized in art, and in 1941 he was summoned by the thriving Basel publishing firm of Birkhäuser to supervise its planned new series of classic literature, in addition to other collections. This activity in designing books for conservative publishers during the war in neutral Switzerland, combined with his recent historical research, led him to consolidate his leanings towards classical typography. In general he spurned ornament, in line with the austerity he appreciated in many products of the British New Traditionalism; his stripped-down classicism demonstrated the same sensitivity to scale and placement of type as his work in New Typography had done. He also judiciously redeployed his skills as a letterer and calligrapher on some jackets and title-pages. Tschichold now made extensive use of the range of classic book types revived by the Monotype Corporation, which had an active office in Switzerland.[82] Following his suggestion, an annual competition for the best-designed Swiss books was established.

79. 'Die Entwicklung der neuen Typographie in den mitteleuropäischen Ländern', pp.125–31. This article was prepared for publication in a journal (perhaps *Schweizer Reklame und Schweizer graphische Mitteilungen* or *Typographische Monatsblätter*) in 1937 or 1938, and was actually printed but not included in either of these journals. Some of Tschichold's comments in this article, especially those concerning gothic type (see p.177), would probably not have survived the pre-censorship that was instituted in Switzerland from 1940. A federal ban prohibited any published criticism of the Third Reich. See Peter Oprecht's essay in Hochuli, *Book design in Switzerland*, p.50.

80. McLean, *True to type*, pp.33–4. However, in a speech given in 1959 to the Type Directors Club of New York, Tschichold said that *Typographische Gestaltung* was 'still a useful book'. ('Quousque Tandem ...', p.157.)

81. 'Jan Tschichold: praeceptor typographiae', p.24.

82. In his office at Birkhäuser hung the Monotype poster of Beatrice Warde's text: 'This is a printing office ...'. In 1951 Tschichold declared: 'Hardly anyone else alive has exerted a greater influence on the typeforms of our printing than Morison.' ('Klassifizierung der von uns gebrauchten Buchdruckschriften', p.7.)

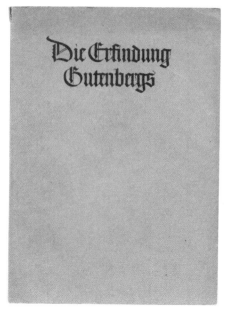

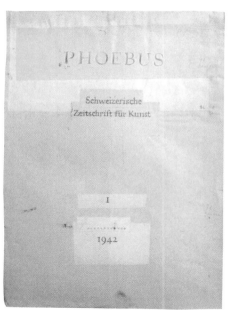

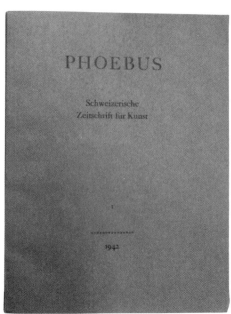

Calligraphy for exhibition catalogue cover
(Basel Gewerbemuseum, 1940). 23 × 16 cm.

Layout and printed result of journal cover design.
1942.

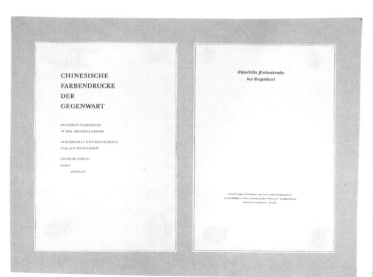

Tschichold's position at Birkhäuser must have counted
in his favour when he was awarded Swiss citizenship in
1943 – 'a very rare occurrence in those war years', he later
remarked.[83] As a Swiss citizen, he was called up for military
service during the Second World War: when in later years
he was asked the common question 'What were you in the
army?', his reply was 'A figure of fun'.[84] Now in a position of
some financial security, the Tschicholds were able to buy a
piece of land at Berzona in Ticino and have a small house
built there in 1944, to which they would later retire.

Alternatives for title-pages, showing symmetric
and asymmetric variants for each title. *c.*1944.
The glue used for pasting down has stained the
paper. It is possible that these were exercises
done by students of Tschichold at the Basel
Gewerbeschule; in any case it shows that he still
entertained the two approaches at this point. The
centred title-page for *Faust* here is very similar to
that finally printed in the edition shown overleaf.

83. 'Jan Tschichold: praeceptor typographiae', p.25.
Tschichold gave a date here of
1942, but that would have been
before the minimum waiting
period of ten years had elapsed.

It is likely that he began the
lengthy application process in
1942. One of the testimonials
needed for Tschichold's citizenship application was given by
Paul Sacher, the majority share-

holder of Tschichold's later
employer Hoffmann La Roche
and a famous Swiss conductor.
84. Conversation with Cornelia Tschichold, 10 July 2005.

Tschichold in 1949.

Spread from Birkhäuser edition of *Faust*. 1944.
19.5 × 12.3 cm. Typeset in Monotype Poliphilus.

Just as the war was ending in Europe Tschichold was contacted with a proposal for publishing his 1932 book *Typographische Entwurfstechnik* in English translation. This overture came from British typographer Anthony Froshaug, who had initiated his own imprint: Isomorph. Froshaug might be seen as a figure of the second generation of European modernism in design – he would go on to teach briefly in the 1950s at the school that consciously took on the mantle of the Bauhaus, the Hochschule für Gestaltung Ulm. He was not uncomplicatedly British (his father was Norwegian) and he was able to decipher Tschichold's books to some extent in the original German (he also had a copy of *Die neue Typographie*). He received Tschichold's address in Basel from Lund Humphries, for which Froshaug had done odd jobs, and wrote to him on 1 May 1945. As a result of their correspondence Tschichold sent Froshaug copies of several of his other publications, including *Typographische Gestaltung*, in which Froshaug recognized many of his own beliefs and principles. Given that Tschichold was reluctant to allow *Typographische Entwurfstechnik* to be translated in its original form, attention switched to *Typographische Gestaltung* as the first projected Isomorph edition of Tschichold, with a proposed title of 'Organic typography'.[85] Tschichold knew that Ruari McLean was interested in translating his books and so he suggested that Froshaug approach McLean with a view to aligning their interests.

Froshaug was primarily excited by the pre-war Tschichold of New Typography, and his attempt at publishing translations of the early books foundered partly on the obstacles encountered with Tschichold the reborn classicist. Tschichold advised that *Typographische Entwurfstechnik* be altered in translation by taking into account his subsequent, less

radical book *Schriftkunde, Schreibübungen und Skizzieren* (1942), which he had sent to Froshaug. Froshaug now appreciated that there had been a change in Tschichold's views:

> I have found it most interesting to see the development of your views through these books: but still cannot understand the reason for the apparent change round about 1940. While obviously symmetrical/asymmetrical are two different things, over here people do not seem to have absorbed the lessons of asymmetrical setting yet, and I personally favour it for that reason.[86]

Although it was not suggested that the new translations be produced in DIN formats, which were as yet unknown in the British printing trade, Tschichold objected to any renewal of his own previous enthusiasm for DIN standard paper sizes, which had been a motif in *Typographische Entwurfstechnik*. He wrote to Froshaug in his still imperfect English (with a little Latin thrown in for good measure): 'Once I have been a propagator for the DIN sizes, but I am it no longer. ... Now I look at the DIN sizes quasi as an invention of the devil and as a sin against the spirit.' He declared himself 'an admirer of the conservative, medieval paper sizes of the English people which are a model of my whole book production of to-day'.[87] It was an error of his, he explained to Froshaug, to have believed in a 'revolution of

85. There had been previous interest in making an English translation of *Typographische Gestaltung*, understandably given that its publication had coincided with Tschichold's first real exposure in Britain. Typographer Ellic Howe, who

used his German skills during the Second World War to create British 'black propaganda', annotated a copy with this aim (now in the St Bride Library).
86. Letter Froshaug to Tschichold, 17 September 1945, in Kinross, *Anthony Froshaug:*

documents of a life, p.50
87. Letter Tschichold to Froshaug, 19 February 1946, reproduced photographically in Kinross, *Anthony Froshaug: documents of a life*, p.53

book typography'.[88] The projected Isomorph editions never appeared, although McLean's translation *of Typographische Gestaltung* formed the basis for *Asymmetric typography* (1967). When Froshaug tried to revive the project in 1948 Tschichold discouraged it.

Renewed contact after the Second World War between Tschichold and his contemporaries in the modern movement illuminates the harsh realities of oppression or the difficulties of exile that many of them had to suffer. Willi Baumeister, who had remained in Germany throughout the war, wrote to Tschichold in December 1945:

> let this first opportunity bring you and your wife greetings. we are in the best of spirits, because the disaster is over. we are living again in our repaired apartment. furniture is almost all gone; things of value and art and books still here. whenever possible i painted, under restrictions then i drew, under further restriction i wrote. about art.[89]

The Nazi regime placed restrictions on many 'degenerate' painters: some, like Emil Nolde, were forbidden to paint at all. Baumeister was forbidden to exhibit his artwork in 1941, which left him without income, given that he had also been dismissed from his teaching job. He took refuge at this time as a tester in the paint factory run by Kurt Herberts in Wuppertal, along with Oskar Schlemmer and Heinz Rasch. After the war Baumeister became professor of painting at the Stuttgart Kunstakademie. The degree to which members of the relatively close-knit circle of modernist artists and designers in Weimar Germany were 'scattered to the winds' (as Schlemmer put it)[90] is reflected by Baumeister's comment to Tschichold on the occasion of Schwitters's death that he had lost touch with him completely since 1933. Schlemmer himself appended a one word postscript to a letter written to Tschichold in 1937, asking simply: 'Schwitters?'

Schlemmer died in 1943. In 1941 Lissitzky finally succumbed to the tuberculosis that had plagued him since 1923, although it is unlikely that news of his death spread beyond the USSR until after the war. Tschichold had planned to compile a monograph on Lissitzky in 1935, but lost touch with him around that time, when the show trials and purges began under Stalin's rule. Lissitzky was deeply involved at that point in designing propaganda for the second five year plan, published in *USSR in Construction*.[91] When, in 1936, Tschichold organized the foreign section for the third of the 'Grafa' printing trade exhibitions in Basel, he included no Russian work. Even if it had not been possible for him to acquire copies of *USSR in Construction* directly from Lissitzky, he could surely have procured them from somewhere, as this magazine was intended as propaganda for the world outside the Soviet Union, designed partly to mask its descent into famine and political violence with photographs of industrial prowess and racial harmony. To exhibit such material in politically conservative Switzerland at that time could have been a provocation that Tschichold was not inclined to risk. The Communist Party of Switzerland was outlawed in 1938.

America proved fruitful ground for European emigrés, especially those who had previously been associated with the Bauhaus. In addition to teaching at Harvard, Gropius and Breuer both founded successful architectural practices. Mies van der Rohe followed a similar path in Chicago. Albers, too, had written to Tschichold towards the end of October 1933, saying: 'I am also leaving soon: to North America'. To his postcard he attached a sticker with his new address at Black Mountain College, North Carolina, where he taught until becoming director of the design department at Yale in 1950. On his invitation, Xanti Schawinsky went to teach at Black Mountain College in 1936, after having spent three busy years in Italy as a designer. Moholy-Nagy died in 1946, aged only 51, after exhausting personal efforts to build up a school of design in Chicago. Johannes Molzahn taught with him there briefly after emigrating under difficult circumstances in 1937 and teaching initially at the University of Washington's School of Art, Seattle.[92] Tschichold seems to have lost contact with Bayer after his move to the USA.

Ladislav Sutnar effectively had little choice in his emigration to the USA: he was sent in April 1939 by the Czechoslovak ministry of education to set up the Czech exhibit at the New York World's Fair. At precisely this time the Nazis occupied most of Czechoslovakia, forcing Sutnar to remain in America. In 1940 he wrote to Tschichold asking him to send any printed material from his collection that had been designed by Sutnar, presumably in order to be able to show examples of his work to prospective clients. Tschichold sent the material without a covering letter but replied to Sutnar just after the war had ended, over five years later:

> My dear Sutnar
> this is indeed a late reply to your letter of 5.III.1940. At that time I immediately sent off to you what I could still find of your things in two or three packets, I believe, and I hope that you received everything.
>
> The date of this posting occurred shortly before the time that blind fear gripped us also and we believed that our last hour had come. We all join with you in happiness that the terrible reign of Nazidom has been brought to an end thanks to the victory of the allied powers.
>
> This letter should first of all serve as a short sign of life. Hopefully it reaches you. Please answer soon.
>
> You will probably also be thinking of returning to Europe and your country. Hopefully you find all your loved ones healthy.

88. Letter Tschichold to Froshaug, 13 January 1946, in Kinross, *Anthony Froshaug: documents of a life*, p.51

89. Letter Baumeister to Tschichold, 2 December 1945.

90. Schlemmer, *The letters and diaries of Oskar Schlemmer*, p.312.

91. Lissitzky informed Tschichold about this work in a letter of autumn 1933 (Lissitzky, *Proun und Wolkenbügel*, p.140), in response to Tschichold asking him to send a copy of a certain Soviet publication he had designed.

92. Molzahn then settled as a painter in New York, where he also taught (1947–52) at the New School of Social Research (founded in 1933 as the University of Exile). In 1959 he returned to Germany.

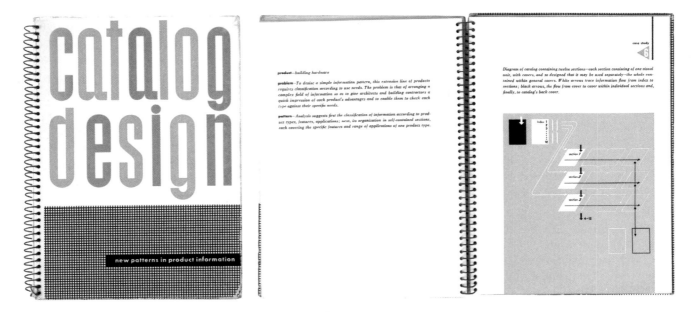

Ladislav Sutnar, cover and spread from *Catalog design* (New York: Sweet's Catalog Service, 1944). 20.8 × 14.8 cm.

Despite the great mental strain that the past has placed on us, I have still managed to produce various things, which I will inform you about, once I receive word from you.

For now all best wishes for your future
your old and true
Jan Tschichold [93]

Sutnar replied three months later (in English):

I am sorry to be so slow in answering your letter from June ... but I wanted to send with the letter a few new samples of my work. However, the post office still will not accept printed matter for Switzerland. – I hope it will be be better soon with the mail situation as I would like to have you see a few of the little booklets I had published, as well as a book on 'Catalog Design'.

Certainly I was glad to hear from you again, first from the human angle that you survived the horrible nightmare of the war and you are well ... and second that you were able to continue your work. I would be happy to hear more details about it.

Going back to the packages you sent with the posters ... In 1940 I received everything in good order and the samples helped me quite a lot. I understand when you didn't answer my letter at that time that you didn't wish to correspond for some reason, and I understand even better now.

It will interest you I'm sure, that last year the Museum of Modern Art in New York opened a very prominent exhibition '15th Anniversary of the Museum's Activities' and they asked me to contribute something for the modern poster division ... and so yours and mine dominated the exhibition. I am only sorry that I didn't have all of the best samples.

I hope to hear from you soon again and I will answer without delay

Your sincere friend
Ladislav Sutnar [94]

To a further letter, acknowledging receipt of some books from Tschichold, Sutnar appended a postscript: 'Don't be ashamed to answer in German, I am writing in English because I simply forgot the German to such an extent that I can't write properly.' Tschichold excused his late reply by saying that 'the end of the war and new contacts to the whole world have suddenly brought us a great deal of work'. Between them they lamented the fate of colleagues during the war, in particular two artists associated with the Isotype group: Sutnar had told Tschichold that his fellow Czech August Tschinkel 'disappeared someplace in the war', and Tschichold wondered what had happened to Gerd Arntz, who 'stayed in Holland when the Germans came and was conscripted'. (Arntz survived and went on to work for the Nederlandse Stichting voor Statistiek [Dutch foundation of statistics].) Tschichold enquired after the welfare of Sutnar's family: 'Were you able to bring them in time to New York? Are you thinking of staying there?' In fact Sutnar only managed to bring his family to the USA at that very time, in 1946. Of his own situation Tschichold wrote: 'I feel quite at home here, after having overcome the bitter early years and become a Swiss citizen (a highly rare exception!)'

Regarding the showing of his posters at MOMA, Tschichold explained to Sutnar: 'I myself no longer work in the field of advertising. My entire activity has turned towards the book. Not only do I continue to design books, I am also an editor and author.' Although there was clearly an enduringly warm friendship evident in their correspondence, there was a sense that the two men were now professionally at cross purposes. Sutnar formed a productive partnership

93. Letter Tschichold to Sutnar, 8 June 1945.

94. Letter Sutnar to Tschichold, 8 September 1945.

in New York with the Danish architect Knud Lönberg-Holm, with whom he collaborated on a series of publications about 'information design' for Sweet's Catalog Service. In a way these books are a direct continuation – in an American commercial context – of Tschichold's didactic writings from the 1920s and 1930s about the importance of clarity in presenting content. Of Sutnar & Lönberg-Holm's book *Catalog design* (1944), designed by the former in his own distinctive, modern style, Tschichold commented curtly: 'It shows all your qualities.' In return Sutnar responded to Tschichold's book on Chinese colour prints: 'Certainly you don't see from this book that the war was around the world.'[95]

Less fortunate than Sutnar was Strzemiński, who remained in Poland. He contacted Tschichold in the spring of 1939 and recounted a gruesome experience:

> Because I wrote several articles against Hitler's art and culture policies, my new-born daughter (three weeks old) was, with inhuman cruelty, poisoned by Hitler-sympathizers (sisters in the clinic). That was in 1936.
>
> Her illness was very severe and lasted more than two years. Now she is almost healthy. ...
>
> My hands shake and I do not know whether I will remain an artist. These severe strains and experiences made it impossible for me to send a letter.[96]

Five months later Poland was invaded by the Nazis. It seemed that these events, coupled with the war years, did damage Strzemiński, resulting in an acrimonious split with his wife, the artist Katarzyna Kobro, and a prolonged dispute between them after the war.[97]

It seemed to Tschichold that the Third Reich and Second World War had changed many things for ever. This view formed a principal theme in his published response of 1946 to Max Bill's accusation that he had betrayed the cause of modern typography. Tschichold's wise essay, with a title worthy of Goethe – 'Glaube und Wirklichkeit' (Belief and reality) – is a key text in understanding his shift from modern to traditional mode. Tschichold's argument is complex and perhaps self-contradictory: while he maintained that the 'creators of New Typography and related initiatives were, like myself, most vehement enemies of Nazism', he asserted that:

> *Its intolerant attitude conforms most particularly to the German bent for the absolute, and its military will to order and claim to sole domination reflect those fearful components of the German character that unleashed Hitler's rule and the Second World War.*
>
> This became clear to me only much later, in democratic Switzerland.[98]

Of those New Typographers who stayed in Germany, Tschichold named Burchartz and Dexel as having 'swung towards' Nazism, referring to them as 'Prof M.B., Essen, and Dr W.D., Jena'. Tschichold must have been greatly disappointed by Burchartz having worked on a documentary project with the German military (published in 1933) but he was ill-informed about Walter Dexel, whose teaching at the Staatliche Hochschule für Kunsterziehung (State college for art education), Berlin, between 1936 and 1942 often brought him into conflict with the authorities. After that he took a job at the Braunschwieg city museum, forming a collection of craft and industrial design there.[99]

Tschichold elaborated on the convoluted relationship of modernism to Nazism, as he saw it:

> For we considered ourselves pioneers of 'progress' and wanted nothing to do with such obviously reactionary things as Hitler planned. When the Hitler 'culture' called us 'cultural Bolsheviks' and called the works of like-minded painters 'degenerate', it was using the same obfuscating, falsifying methods here as everywhere else. The Third Reich was second to none in accelerating technical 'progress' in its war preparations while hypocritically concealing it behind propaganda for medieval forms of society and expression. And since deception was its basis, it could not bear the genuine modernists who, although political opponents, were nevertheless unwittingly not so very far from the delusion of 'order' that ruled the Third Reich. The role of leader that fell to me as the only specialist of the group was itself a 'Führer' role, signifying, as it did, an intellectual guardianship of 'followers' typical of dictator states.

Tschichold's observation about the Nazi ambivalence to modernity in practical terms was astute (whereas his final point here about himself was surely an exaggeration). New technology was in some ways an inspiration for New Typography but Tschichold no longer believed in technological progress as a force for good. He described Bill as having fallen prey to the same 'naïve worship of so-called technological progress' that Tschichold himself had 'between 1924 and about 1935'. From such precise dating it is clear that he was taking a historical view of his own development, as well as that of New Typography:

> The New or functional Typography is well suited for publicizing industrial products (it has the same origin), and it fulfils that purpose now as well as then.[100]

When first asked to account for the views that sparked this debate by Rudolf Hostettler (who went on to publish it as editor of *Schweizer graphische Mitteilungen*), Tschichold admitted that 'asymmetric typography is by no means

95. Letters: Sutnar to Tschichold, 22 December 1945; Tschichold to Sutnar, 14 April 1946.

96. Letter Strzemiński to Tschichold, 28 April 1939.

97. See Król, 'Collaboration and compromise: women artists in Polish-German avant-garde circles' in Benson (ed.), *Central European avant-gardes*.

98. Italic in original. Selecting quotations from Tschichold's text does no service to its argument; it deserves to be read as a whole. The translation here is modified (with help from Robin Kinross) from that given by McLean in *Jan Tschichold: typographer*, which was republished as part of a compendium of the whole debate in English in *Typography papers*, 4 (2000). An attractively alliterative alternative for the translation of the essay's title is given in Tschichold, *The form of the book* (p.xv): 'Faith and fact'.

99. Friedl, *Walter Dexel: neue Reklame*, p.7.

100. 'Belief and reality', *Typography papers*, 4, p.74. In an essay of 1952, which he gave the same title as Bill's initial article ('Über Typographie'), Tschichold asserted that New Typography, if it had not been strangled by the Nazis in 1933, would soon have reached a natural end (p.21).

obsolete and in the field of advertising is a great step forward'. He explained to Hostettler: 'In my lecture I was, I admit, thinking primarily of book typography'.[101]

The lecture in question was given by Tschichold in Zurich at the end of 1945 to the Zurich members of the Verband schweizerischer Graphiker (Association of Swiss graphic designers). Tschichold was not a member of this organization – a sign of his defining himself as a book typographer and not a graphic designer – but all of the principal figures working in a style that became broadly defined as 'Swiss Typography' were.[102] The association's Zurich group had the most members (105).[103] Many of them were both concrete artists and graphic designers, applying the same mathematical schemes of construction to both fields, and thereby fulfilling the desired relationship between modern art and New Typography that Tschichold had proposed on several occasions up to 1935. Indeed, in his article initiating the published debate of 1946, 'Über Typografie' (On typography), Bill made a conscious connection with Tschichold's first principles of 'elemental typography' as still being valid.

Bill did not name Tschichold in his essay, instead referring to 'one of the well-known typographical theorists'. When preparing his reply to Bill, Tschichold spent a little energy in confirming that it was actually him who was under attack, although there can have been little doubt. He sent a copy of Bill's article to Imre Reiner, asking him if Bill could possibly have been referring to him. Reiner replied:

> I marvel at your talent for struggle [Kampfismus] and also that of Mr Bill. I am convinced that Mr Bill cannot mean me, as he does not know me at all. I in fact have no theory and am an entirely principle-free [standpunktslose] coward, who has no other ideal than that of 'peace of mind', which I strive for even when the path leads to loneliness.[104]

Nevertheless Tschichold co-opted Reiner's name to keep him company as a traditionalist book typographer in 'Glaube und Wirklichkeit' while accurately reporting that Reiner 'would probably protest' against such a title (of theorist) for himself. Tschichold clarified: 'I am not, by the way, one of the "well-known typographical theorists", but, to the best of my knowledge, the only one in German-speaking Europe.' Here he disregarded the legitimate claim to such a title that could have been made by Paul Renner, who had been writing seriously about typography since 1908. Renner politely disregarded this in his own later contribution to the Bill/Tschichold debate. In an early draft of his article Renner explained the reasons why he had invited Tschichold to teach in Munich:

Tschichold's inner split [Zweispalt] already interested me in him. I knew that he carried on working anonymously for Insel Verlag and calligraphed very simple and beautiful bindings. I never perceived in this a lack of character but instead an inner range [Spannweite] that is perhaps necessary in our time, without which the artist has no possibility for development. For the new style must first be discovered. The path to it is however a dialectical movement; so long as thesis and antithesis are separated in two people there will only be squabbling and quarrelling, only when they collide with each other in an individual mind is the result a spark that lights up new syntheses.[105]

Kurt Schwitters, too, had been tolerant and understanding of Tschichold's purported betrayal of New Typography. In a letter to Nelly van Doesburg he wrote (in faulty English): 'Tschichold has worked so long time and so many times modern typography, that he is weak and would do it now without feeling. Therefore he does good to work for a time in old style.'[106] But Tschichold could hardly be called a reactionary; as Renner pointed out, he had always explored the validity of both traditional and modern approaches, to book design at least. In his writings on New Typography, Tschichold was never fully convinced of its applicability to books. The special nature of his case was that he was a high-profile theorist, who even while making calligraphic bindings for Insel Verlag, was preaching a largely one-sided, modernist approach, which he later recanted in favour of an equally dogmatic, traditionalist approach. Hence the accusations of betrayal: apostasy is rarely considered an endearing trait.

Tschichold was unrepentant about his views. One month after his response to Bill was published, he had an article published in Typographische Monatsblätter in which he contrasted the particular demands of 'Graphik und Buchkunst' (Graphic design and book art). This essay might be assumed to contain the crux of his initial lecture. 'Book typography must not advertise', he stated categorically and with a clear implication about which of the two activities he considered superior. (Perhaps as a further provocation, the title of the essay was typeset in a gothic typeface.)

Although Bill's initial criticism of Tschichold's post-war position was not overtly political, there is a sense in which his characterization of Tschichold's views as an escape into historicism was meant as a reproach for denying contemporary social responsibilities. Tschichold's experiences at the hands of the Nazis had disabused him of any previously held notion about a political dimension in typographic design, whereas – from within the context of Swiss neutrality in an embattled Europe – designers such as Bill, Ballmer, Richard Paul Lohse and Max Huber had re-affirmed the connection of modernist typography to left-wing beliefs.

Tschichold justified the critical stance that he developed towards New Typography after the Second World War in a long (and considered) letter to Paul Renner. He began here by referring to the title of his reply to Bill ('Belief and reality'):

101. Letter Tschichold to Hostettler, 31 January 1946, translated in McLean, *Jan Tschichold: typographer*, pp.153–4. Hostettler had evidently suggested that Tschichold's argument concerning Nazism was paradoxical.

102. Tschichold did design a cover for a publication (date uncertain) of the local Basel group of the VSG (formed in 1938).

103. On the VSG see Hollis, *Swiss graphic design*, pp.159–60.

104. Letter Reiner to Tschichold, 29 May 1946.

105. 'Über moderne Typographie' (draft; Haushofer Archive).

106. McLean, *Jan Tschichold: typographer*, p.71.

Concerning 'belief'. Such a thing is naturally the prerequisite for a style. We have no common belief (perhaps not even the Communists do) and therefore we have no style. 'Belief' and 'trust in our time' cannot be lumped together. I venture to maintain that good can only come from a minority in our time, those who can meet it with sufficient critical faculty – the true partisans of the intellect, of whom there are few. The fool may want to have 'trust'; I mistrust, precisely because I do not want the future to appear in the form that the fools believe they can give it. This opinion has nothing to do with 'splendid isolation' or extreme individualism, quite the opposite: not 'personal' truths, rather, in so far as it is at all possible, generally valid, actual truths uninfluenced by mass judgements; the responsible decisions of men who understand what they are saying – that is what we need. What kind of style can be matched with this! A total absence of style is truer and fundamentally more humane than a 'position' that one cannot believe in, because no critical stance lies behind it. A 'critical' stance seems to me to be the truly modern way; I leave the believers to their priests. Self deception is also a (very pleasant) way of living. But: Nemo alterius sit qui suus esse potest (Paracelsus).[107]

At Penguin Books. 1948.

His distrust of any kind of mass movement was now clear.

Tschichold readdressed the implications of his dispute with Bill in an essay of 1948, 'Wirken sich gesellschaftliche und politische Umstände in der Typographie aus?' (Do social and political circumstances have an effect on typography?):

> Many people believe that not only fashions, which pass themselves off as the style of the present, but also political conditions can express themselves in typography. Let us compare typography in such very different state structures as Germany, Russia, Italy and the USA during the highly politicized period between 1933 and 1945: we can scarcely discover a real echo of political conceptions in the typography of these countries, apart from a detrimental influence from many of these political structures on formal quality in general. ...
>
> Any work of typography has to be governed by the demands of greatest readability and meaningful construction in a craft sense, which are founded on long experience and are entirely independent of political conceptions. That is why there can be no really 'new' typography, nor a socialist, fascist or capitalist one, but only good or bad composition.

In an addendum to this essay written two years later, Tschichold explained that it was published in order to close the debate initiated by Bill, although he claimed to have had 'no particular persons' in mind when writing it: his text was more of a 'confession', only loosely related to the original

contributions. He considered it 'a gentle warning' to a new generation of radicals who, in his view, had not learned from the discussions of the 1920s. 'I was equally radical in those days as the curent New Typographers', he admitted, but he considered the 'purification' effected by his New Typography to have laid the ground for a freer creativity, based on individual, critical judgement.[108]

By the time of writing his 'confession', Tschichold's appreciation of traditionalist British typography had come full circle in that he was working in Harmondsworth, a suburban outpost of London, for Penguin Books. Perhaps his views were now influenced by 'a British scene' that was 'sceptical of radical systems' (in Willem Ovink's words).[109] On the suggestion of the Germanophile Oliver Simon, Penguin's director Allen Lane had invited Tschichold to England in order to revise the typography of its publications, which consisted mostly of cheap, mass-market paperbacks. Simon had been inspired to suggest this by Tschichold's recent work on the Birkhäuser classics, given that much of Penguin's output was also classic literature, with Shakespeare being a particular point of confluence.[110] It is a sign of Tschichold's inclinations towards Britain that he should consider removing himself and his wife from Switzerland, where they were now comfortably endowed with citizenship, to stay for a period that was intended to be a little longer than the two-and-a-half years that they finally spent in England. No doubt the fact that Tschichold was able to secure the highest salary of any Penguin employee encouraged them to go.[111] When Tschichold left for England, Max Bill wrote to Paul Rand: 'Tschichold is leaving Switzerland and so we will be rid of the evil that we invited in the first place.'[112]

107. Letter Tschichold to Renner, 4 March 1948. The Latin proverb translates as: 'Let no man belong to another that can belong to himself'.
108. 'Wirken sich gesellschaftliche und politische Umstände in der Typographie aus?' (& 'Zusatz'), pp.23–5.
109. Ovink, 'The influence of

Jan Tschichold', p.41.
110. Undoubtedly Tschichold would have been pleased with Simon's part in his Penguin appointment. During the discussions with Froshaug he had suggested that, if an English edition of his Eine Stunde Druckgestaltung was to be published, it should have the same

format as Simon's Introduction to typography, which had only recently appeared in 1945.
111. Baines, Penguin by design: a cover story, p.50.
112. Rand, 'Typography: style is not substance' in Barnes (ed.), Jan Tschichold, p.48.

After a reconnaissance visit in November 1946, Tschichold took up his position in March 1947.[113] This brought him into closer geographical proximity to his old friend Kurt Schwitters, who was by then living in the north of England. When German troops invaded Norway in April 1940, Schwitters made an arduous escape with his son and daughter-in-law via Scotland. After a year-and-a-half spent in internment camps, he settled in London. His wife Helma had remained in Germany, dutifully taking care of her husband's mother, and they were only reunited twice, briefly, before she died in 1944 of cancer. In June 1945 Schwitters moved to Ambleside in the Lake District with his new companion, Edith Thomas. Having mainly earned his living in exile by painting traditional landscapes and portraits, he would eventually begin work on a new Merz sculpture in a barn, assisted by a bursary from New York's Museum of Modern Art.

The Tschicholds had remained in contact with Schwitters, with Edith in particular acting as an intermediary between him and his family left in Germany (it was she who informed him of his wife's death). Tschichold had initiated for him a one-man show attached to an exhibition of Der Sturm at the Bern Kunstmuseum in February 1945. When the Tschicholds came to England they took the opportunity to bring with them many of Schwitters's books from his personal library, which had been left in Germany. Schwitters travelled to London in March 1947, just as the Tschicholds were arriving, for two Merz evenings held at the London Gallery, but he suffered an asthma attack and spent two weeks recuperating on the Kent coast. Edith and the Tschicholds' son Peter visited the ailing and bed-ridden Schwitters in summer 1947, and Jan planned to do so at Christmas of that year, but it is unclear whether the two men met again in person before Schwitters died on 8 January 1948, one day after being granted British citizenship.

Only rarely did asymmetric layout or sanserif letterforms resurface in Tschichold's Penguin work. He used sanserif letters, written with his own fingertip dipped in ink, to convey a primitive impression on the cover of the Puffin picture book, *Early man*. An echo of New Typography is evident in one of the final books he designed for Penguin, *The artist at work*, a fascinating illustrated edition arranged in three columns and typeset throughout in Gill Sans.[114]

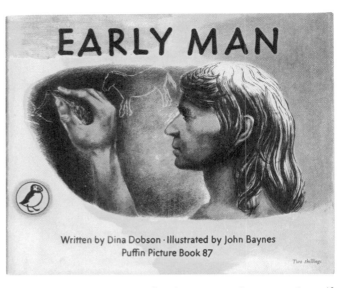

Cover of *Early man*. 1950. 18 × 22.2 cm. Sanserif lettering for title done by Tschichold with his fingertip. The smaller lettering at the bottom is effectively the sanserif model from *Schrift-schreiben für Setzer* (see p.183 above).

Jacket and cover for *The artist at work*. 18.7 × 23.5 cm. Although it was published in December 1951, negotiations with the authors began in 1942. The chaotic typescript (based on exhibition material) was provided in June 1947, hence Tschichold's involvement in designing it. Author's rewrites and technical problems delayed production until after Tschichold's departure from Penguin, and so his successor, Hans Schmoller, took care of some issues of detail in design. The cover is an asymmetric variation on the Penguin Modern Painters series design.

113. For details of Tschichold's work at Penguin see McLean, *Jan Tschichold: typographer* and *Jan Tschichold: a life in typography*. The editor of the King Penguin series was another exile from Hitler's Germany, Nikolaus Pevsner (coincidentally born, like Tschichold, in Leipzig in 1902).

114. See the reminiscence of Tschichold at Penguin by his Danish assistant there, Eric Ellegaard Frederiksen, 'In correspondence with Colin Banks'.

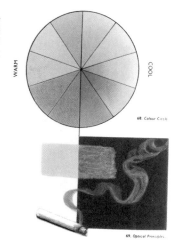

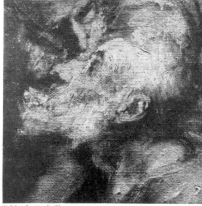

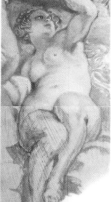

Spreads from *The artist at work*. Lynton Lamb commented of Tschichold's design for this book: 'there is again a break from "classical" typography, owing to the particular material with which he had to deal; so that on this, no less than in any other really well-designed book, the style is functional in fact rather than manner'. (Lamb, 'Penguin books – style and mass production', p.41.)

Despite the classicism of his typography for Penguin, Tschichold was upholding his earlier principle, expressed in *Die neue Typographie*, of making 'cheap, popular editions, not expensive luxury books for snobs'.[115] In an essay written towards the end of his life, Tschichold maintained this view (referring initially here to books of the German private presses):

> I was never able to buy any of these, but I do not regret this a great deal. For I have always found that the object of true book culture is the normal book for everyman, for scholars and libraries. Of course I have a few selected costly editions among my books: however I take them out only rarely and think 'next Sunday, when the others have gone to church' – and then I find something better to do. ...
>
> I can be proud of the millions of Penguin books for the typography of which I was responsible. Next to them the few luxurious books I have made play no role. We need no grandiose books for rich people, rather well-made normal books.[116]

Tschichold's former colleague Paul Renner considered his work in England to be 'eminently modern' and hoped, in vain, that the conservative surroundings there would once again turn him into a revolutionary. Tschichold explained to Renner that, while the British were conservative, they were not 'conservative through and through', as was thought in Germany. He recognized that some young people in England felt oppressed by their conservative environment, as he did himself as a young man at the Leipzig academy. Their response, he lamented, was to 'revolt through an only half-baked "New Typography" whereby they unfortunately follow in my early footsteps (here they call this "functionalistic typography" and – no doubt unintentionally – with good reason, for it is *not a truly functional manner of typography*)'.[117]

When, on 19 September 1949, the British government devalued the pound as a last-ditch measure to improve the post-war economy, the Tschicholds decided to return to Switzerland.[118] In an account of his work at Penguin for *Typographische Monatsblätter* he portrayed himself as the principled crusader from the Continent, struggling for typographic excellence with the ill-educated British type compositors.[119] A signal that he earned the respect of the British typographic establishment was his election as an honorary member of the Double Crown Club in 1949. In the same year

Tschichold had an essay published in the *Penrose Annual*, 'Clay in a potter's hand', in which he displayed his full tradititionalist colours in a rather authoritarian manner:

> Good taste, like perfect typography, is suprapersonal. ... What some may extol as personal style are in fact small and trivial peculiarities, which may even be damaging but which masquerade as innovations: such as, for instance, the use of only a single typeface, whether a sanserif or strange type-forms of the nineteenth century, the preference for particular type-mixtures or the application of seemingly courageous maxims, such as using a single type-size for an entire work, no matter how complex, and many more. Personal typography is defective typography. Only beginners and fools will demand it.[120]

His references to the exclusive use of sanserif and to restricting typography to a single type-size were clear criticisms of the grotesque-dominated style that was hardening into so-called 'Swiss Typography' at that time. A principal exponent of this style was, of course, Max Bill, and the previous dispute between Bill and Tschichold was touched on by Herbert Read in a contribution to the same volume of the *Penrose Annual*. Read, who had admired Tschichold's pre-war work (shown by his sensitive summary of its principles), seemed implicitly to support Bill's side of the argument in his essay entitled 'The crisis in bookcraft':

> The danger of all art based on theory is that it may degenerate into a sterile academicism. This has happened to certain types of abstract painting, and it was happening to similar types of bookcraft. It is inevitable that the name of Jan Tschichold should come into this discussion, for it is his change of front, which, more than any other personal factor, has been responsible for the present disarray of forces. Tschichold, before the war, was the foremost protagonist of *functional* typography. He led the revolt against *ornamental* typography, particularly against the age-long tradition of symmetry – the rigid formula of the middle-axis. Henceforth the form should be given by the function. Questions of type arrangement were not to be settled by *a priori* rules, but by the specific purpose of the printed words. A law of relative emphasis was substituted for a convention of symmetry. The architectural analogy still held good, but the style changed from Classical to Functional. ...
>
> The year 1948 finds us in a state of considerable confusion. Jan Tschichold has found his 'Mittelachse', but numerous disciples reproduce his functional principle as a meaningless formula – (a little cursive, a splash of Rockwell, heavy Bodoni numerals and a lot of white space). ...
>
> Perhaps only in Switzerland and the United States has there been any progressive development of the modern style.[121]

Read described new books designed by Bill and Paul Rand to support his final assertion here, commending their fresh, asymmetrical approach.

Given that Tschichold had stated during the dispute with Bill that New Typography remained suitable for advertising, one could assume that, if he ever did such work again,

115. *Die neue Typographie*, p.233.
116. 'Flöhe ins Ohr', pp.360 & 365.
117. Letter Tschichold to Renner, 4 March 1948. The italicized phrase here was originally written in English and underlined.
118. The pound was devalued by 30 per cent, from US$4.03 to US$2.80. Tschichold asked for a rise in salary but was refused.

119. Translated in McLean, *Jan Tschichold: typographer* as 'My reform of Penguin books'.
120. Newly translated from the original German, 'Ton in des Töpfers Hand', p.27, taking into account previously published translations.
121. Read, 'The crisis in bookcraft', p.14. A title-page for the *Penrose Annual* of 1949 designed by Tschichold, in classical-symmetrical mode,

was not actually used as such, as might be assumed from its reproduction in McLean's two books on Tschichold. It was in fact included as an illustration to Read's article (alongside his earlier, asymmetric design for 1938's volume), and was presumably prepared especially for that purpose to Tschichold's design.

he may have executed it in a modernist style. When he became typographer for the pharmaceutical company Hoffmann-La Roche of Basel in 1955, some of the leaflets and other ephemera that he designed were steadfastly bookish (mostly in serifed type) and symmetrical in style; yet others showed that the spark of New Typography was still alive in Tschichold. In designing 'throwaway' material, such as packet labels, he remained true to his early principles, which accorded such material as much importance as conventional 'literature'. He also maintained the fresh approach integral to his theory of New Typography by experimenting with new materials and techniques (printing on transparent plastic) and, in a house magazine for the company, he now fulfilled his dreams of 1925 by extensively using photographic illustrations, which had in the meantime become more commonly affordable. His use of photographs in the *Roche-Zeitung* was not dissimilar from that common in Swiss Typography of the same era – the principal difference was that Tschichold combined them with seriffed typefaces, in a number of different sizes (see illustrations overleaf).

It was mainly a disagreement about type-style that led Tschichold to become a dissenter from Swiss Typography in his writings during the late 1950s and early 1960s. A further published exchange of opposing views on the matter occurred between 1957 and 1959, this time involving responses from Karl Gerstner and Emil Ruder to Tschichold.[122] Tschichold now stood in absolute opposition to some of his own earlier views (in seeming contradiction of his work for Hoffmann-La Roche, unless he meant to restrict his terms of reference exclusively to 'literary' books): he characterized asymmetry in the double-page unit of a book as 'a sickness' and described the grotesque style of sanserif as 'a true monstrosity'. What most typography lacked at that time, in his view, was 'grace'.[123] Tschichold's opposition to Swiss Typography did not preclude amicable relations with some of its practitioners. Of Karl Gerstner (approximately half Tschichold's age), who derived inspiration from New Typography of the 1920s and 1930s, Tschichold commented: 'I have the greatest respect for Herr Gerstner and his ideas on typographic design, even though I do not share them.'[124]

This brochure cover is one of the few occasions when Tschichold specified unjustified text. 1960. A4.

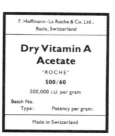 

Packet labels designed by Tschichold for Hoffmann-La Roche. 1960s. 8.5 × 7.3 cm.

Bookmark, printed on a semi-translucent blue plastic. 1960. 21 × 6.9 cm.

122. See Kinross, *Modern typography*, pp.151–3; Hollis, *Swiss graphic design*, pp.222–3; Arrausi, 'La tipografía integral versus Tschichold'.

123. 'Zur Typographie der Gegenwart' (1957), pp.258 & 261–2.

124. From Ken Garland's reminiscence of meeting Tschichold in 1960, in Barnes (ed.) *Jan Tschichold*, p.19. He had been introduced to him by Gerstner, who said exactly the same about Tschichold.

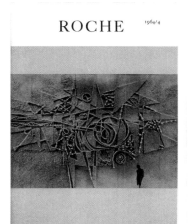

Cover, title-page and spread from three issues of
the Roche house magazine, *Roche-Zeitung*. 1964
& 1966. 27.6 × 19.7. The second colour is changed
on each issue. Tschichold's design for this publication remained unaltered until 1970.

Epilogue

G.K. Schauer suggested intriguingly that Tschichold's unending search for perfection in typography could be explained by a condition of 'tragic homelessness' (*Heimatlosigkeit*). He was a German of Slav origin, forced to leave the country of his birth; affiliated with Anglo-Saxon culture, but never at home in it.[1] Perhaps Schauer was effectively describing a widespread modern condition, marked by dislocation and varying degrees of alienation. Was Tschichold more affected by it than his contemporaries? The geopolitical shifts in Central Europe between the last quarter of the eighteenth century and the middle of the twentieth century made it not uncommon to have ancestral links traversing national borders. Nowhere more so did this apply than to the area of northern Central Europe that was home to Tschichold's paternal ancestors and was subject to long-running power struggles between Poland, Austria, Prussia and Russia (and eventually Nazi Germany and the Soviet Union). Take Malevich, Lissitzky and Strzemiński, all born in the Belarus lands that were a matter of dispute between Russia and Poland (Malevich is by turns referred to as belonging to both nationalities): they all found a sense of belonging in the Utopian project of the USSR, as did the Lithuanian Varvara Stepanova and the Latvians Gustav Klucis and Sergei Eisenstein.

Some of Tschichold's contemporaries were forced to settle in a more foreign environment than he was, including the core of the Dessau Bauhaus – Moholy-Nagy, Gropius, Albers, Bayer and Breuer – all ending up in a culture where they had to master a new language. Although any affection or allegiance that Tschichold had for Germany was effectively shattered by his treatment at the hands of the Nazis, he remained in a German-speaking culture and indeed embraced the Swiss way of life, mastering the Swiss dialect of German and even choosing to speak it at home with his wife. In a short curriculum vitae sent to Mehmet Agha in 1954 on being informed that he would receive the Gold Medal of the American Institute of Graphic Arts, Tschichold summarized his national identity as 'Born German, became Swiss'. Despite lengthy negotiations in the early 1950s concerning an invitation for him to return to the Munich Meisterschule as its director, he eventually declined because it was demanded of him that he relinquish Swiss citizenship.

The typographer Kurt Weidemann (who came to know Tschichold late in his life) questioned Schauer's thesis of Tschichold's 'homelessness', describing him instead as a 'cosmopolitan' rather than a 'countryman'.[2] The large-scale migration in Europe from countryside to city that peaked around 1900 severed the roots of traditional societies, while technological developments of the kind celebrated by the young Tschichold began to make the everyday aspects of urban life more internationally homogeneous. Rather as Hermann Simon in Edgar Reitz's epic film saga of the German twentieth century, *Heimat*, found his 'second home' in music, Tschichold found his in typography.

Nevertheless he considered himself to have been an outsider in his chosen field.[3] This explains why he repeated what he deemed to be the details of good composition over and over again in articles for trade journals; he recognized the creative autonomy of the type compositor but wanted to educate him. It was a strategy conditioned by the division of labour inherent in the printing trade prior to the electronic era: Tschichold was articulating good craft practice. While helping to establish typography as a modern discipline in this way, he always retained a strong personal attachment to craft – a potentially valuable thing for one's own sense of identity. In what was probably his last published utterance – a short contribution to papers for the 1973 ATypI conference – he asserted: 'This is a profession which no one can exercise on the sidelines. It calls for a lifelong dedication.'[4]

Returning to Schauer's thesis, one might wonder what indeed was 'tragic' about Tschichold's existence. He certainly believed that his work had made a difference; he prospered and left his mark. Perhaps the appraisal of Tschichold by Dutch printing scholar Willem Ovink is finally more persuasive: he considered Tschichold's shift from a modernist to a classicist position as a change from optimism to pessimism. An attitude of 'everything will be better in future' was replaced by 'everything was better in the past'.[5] It is easy to imagine that the traumatic events of 1933 and the subsequent hard years of adaptation could have affected his outlook in this way. Some credence is lent to this interpretation by Tschichold himself, writing in 1965:

> Nowadays we are all sceptics; we take technology for granted or view it with distrust. There is nothing astonishing in our ability to ring up New York at a moment's notice, and even a successful orbit of the moon stirs the excitement of far fewer people than have to pay for it. Our grandparents' Utopia has become our everyday life. Forty years ago, and above all in Russia after the 1917 revolution, attitudes were very different.[6]

As someone whose life and thinking were so strongly affected by the Third Reich, Tschichold had good reason to become sceptical of 'progress'. In 'Glaube und Wirklichkeit' (1946) he rightly remarked on the Nazis' seemingly paradoxical obsession with technological modernization. Yet his perception (stated in that same essay) of a similarly malevolent will-to-order in both New Typography and the Third Reich is more controversial. On a philosophical level his argument bears some similarity with a theme from Theodor Adorno & Max Horkheimer's *Dialectic of Enlightenment* – the inherent potential in rationalism for irrationality. But there is a kind of short-circuit in the logic of Tschichold's version, sparked by his employing the emotionally charged

1. 'Jan Tschichold: Anmerkungen zu einer tragischen Existenz'. p.A422–3.
2. Weidemann, 'Anmerkungen...', p.A115.

3. Letter Tschichold to Froshaug, 14 March 1946. Cited in Kinross, *Anthony Froshaug: documents of a life*, p.55.
4. 'Tschichold', p.62.

5. Ovink, 'Jan Tschichold 1902–74: Versuch zu einer Bilanz seines Schaffens', p.206.
6. 'El Lissitzky (1890–1941)', p.389.

term 'Führer' to describe his role in New Typography, as if alluding to Hitler in this way provided irrefutable support for his argument. The connotations of this word had been twisted by Hitler's dictatorship; in essence it means simply 'leader', a title that Tschichold had originally accredited to Lissitzky in terms of New Typography (naturally he did not tar the Russian with the same brush as himself in 1946).

Tschichold consistently maintained his thesis of a kindred spirit behind both New Typography and Nazism. In a speech given in 1959 to the Type Directors Club of New York, he explained:

> I detected most shocking parallels between the teachings of *Die neue Typographie* and National Socialism and fascism. Obvious similarities consist in the ruthless restriction of typefaces, a parallel to Goebbels' infamous *Gleichschaltung*, and the more or less militaristic arrangement of lines. Because I did not want to be guilty of spreading the very ideas which had compelled me to leave Germany I thought over again what a typographer should do.[7]

His proposal of sanserif as the only truly modern typeface could never have been described as 'ruthless' and one wonders what he meant by 'the more or less militaristic arrangement of lines' in New Typography. His advocacy of a creative, non-prescribed asymmetry for most tasks was much less strict than an unthinking obedience to axial symmetry.

Tschichold also described the uniformity of standardized paper sizes as a 'Nazi-minded (anti-humanistic) error'.[8] In remarking on Tschichold's 'reconversion' to Franz Roh, Paul Renner lamented: 'At the moment, in all the anti-Nazi fuss, everything that was propagated in the last decade is being blackened as "Nazism". For example, the standardization of letterheads and business documents etc., things which have nothing to do with Nazism.'[9] Later, in a review of *Asymmetric typography*, Froshaug commented of Tschichold:

> I doubt if he was ever able to separate in his mind the accuracy of dealing with text and meaning which was (and is) the heart of 'the new typography' from the accuracy of dealing with human beings which was (and is?) the soul and belly of Auschwitz and Houston, Texas. He confuses the one with the other: objects and humans.[10]

In specific terms there was very little similarity between Tschichold's rhetorical methods as chief ideologue of the New Typography and those of National Socialism; indeed he was much more intolerant and less reasonable in some of his writings after his conversion back to classicism. Witness his statement from late in his career that those typographers who do not specify indention for paragraphs in lengthy text 'don't know how to read and don't read' – hammering the point home by stating that '*Composition without indents is a typographical deadly sin.*'[11] He was never quite so dismissive of the old typography when trumpeting the New in the 1920s. A more reasoned assessment of where his youthful error lay – instead of accusing himself of fulfilling

the 'German bent for the absolute' – was given in his essay of 1970, 'Flöhe ins Ohr'. Concerning his total rejection of centred layout in favour of asymmetry, he reflected: 'I should not have damned the general defects lock, stock and barrel, but instead have detected the faults analytically and remedied them.'[12] Yet generally, in the second half of his career, he over-simplified his own earlier approach and the whole movement of New Typography in order to set it aside.

No doubt Tschichold was sincere in his abhorrence of Nazi Germany and the full horror of its deeds that came to light at the end of the war, less than a year before he first expounded the reasons for his rejection of New Typography. But it also served rhetorically as an effective way of dismissing the old Tschichold, for he felt embarrassed about having been wrong (as he now saw it), and there was no more effective way to do this than to associate his younger self with the odious regime of the Third Reich. It was really a bizarre act of extreme self censure, to associate one's own previous methods with those of the Nazis, and shows that Tschichold almost did intend to imply that he was not the same person that wrote those early books. Indeed he remarked to Anthony Froshaug that he 'would not like people to be confused by a book of a very different old Tschichold'.[13] He justified his denial of New Typography by describing it as only fit for advertising, a field of activity he came to deem less worthy than book design. If one does not share that view (or even if one does) then there is much still in the writings of Ivan and the early Jan Tschichold that is of value. Ovink remarked:

> However radical, immoderate and even occasionally indefensible his theories were – then and later – Tschichold was always moderate, reasonable, practical, and deeply satisfying in his actual work.[14]

His certainty of visual judgement, and his thorough knowledge of type and its history, also underpinned his writings, which, even if they inspire strong disagreement, deserve to be taken seriously. Those who differ greatly with Tschichold's views often find him useful as opposition.

It is the uniting of opposing views within Tschichold himself that makes him so intriguing and adds an extra dimension to whatever he wrote or designed. As Renner so wisely pointed out in correspondence with Tschichold, his trajectory can be taken as an example of dialectic: 'This is how I see your development from Johannes to Ivan to Jan. That was thesis, antithesis and synthesis.'[15] Renner elaborated on this in his own published commentary on the Bill-Tschichold dispute:

7. 'Quousque Tandem ...', p.157.
8. Letter Tschichold to Froshaug 19 February 1946, in Kinross, *Anthony Froshaug: documents of a life*, p.53.
9. Letter Renner to Roh, undated [1947].

10. *Anthony Froshaug: typography & texts*, p.191.
11. 'Gute Typographie in Gefahr' (1962), p.281. Italic in original.
12. 'Flöhe ins Ohr', p.361.
13. Letter Tschichold to Froshaug, 24 May 1948, in Kinross,

Anthony Froshaug: documents of a life, p.61.
14. Ovink, 'The influence of Jan Tschichold', p.40.
15. Letter Renner to Tschichold, 15 September 1947.

Seeming to go from one extreme to another, he was honestly seeking that 'mean', of which it is unjustly said that it suits undecided characters and the mediocre, whilst in antiquity it was prized as 'golden'. The 'middle' is, in any case, more energized than the one-sided extreme; it is the fruitful eye-of-the-storm in dialectical opposition; and this is best served by he who feels the conflict in his own being.[16]

Tschichold's mature, classical typography was such a synthesis, informed by New Typography. It was a 'purified' traditionalism, as he described it himself.[17] Schauer, always an insightful observer of Tschichold's work, commented:

Tschichold always brings tension into his activities, of which he, the advocate of rational harmony, is probably only half-conscious. He shows the present and past in constant dialogue.[18]

An eventual rapprochement between Tschichold and Germany occurred in 1964, following his participation in the two hundredth anniversary of the Leipzig academy where he had studied as a young man. Subsequently he liaised with the Verlag der Kunst in Dresden concerning publication of the monograph about him that finally appeared after his death. Leipzig and Dresden were at that time in Communist East Germany, and Tschichold no doubt appreciated the conservative values of typographic culture there. It was probably the preparation for his *Leben und Werk* (Life and work) that encouraged him to look back at his early years and consider himself from a historical viewpoint. There had already been an exhibition of his work at Stuttgart in 1963, which showed material mostly dating from his period of New Typography – 'before he turned from Saulus into Paulus, so to speak', as Kurt Weidemann phrased it in the catalogue. Tschichold added some sentences of his own to this essay (referring to himself in the third person):

He would never take his work of that time as a model for the present, but he acknowledges the role he played in the typography of the day. He even finds many of these old designs still beautiful in their own way, and concedes the charm of youthful *naïveté* to the rest.[19]

Yet his historical revaluation of himself during his last decade, as well as his research for an essay about Lissitzky, perhaps inspired a late flourish of asymmetry in his work. The cover for the issue of *Typographische Monatsblätter* in honour of his seventieth birthday mixes the centred placement of his name with asymmetrically disposed elements around it. This issue also contained an example of commercial stationery designed for the Rentsch printing house, which features a geometric revision of the firm's signet and

(Top) Cover of *Typographische Monatsblätter* (April 1972) commemorating Tschichold's seventieth birthday. 29.8 × 23 cm. (Bottom) Folder cover for Rentsch printers. 1969. A4.

16. Renner, 'Über moderne Typografie', p.119; 'On modern typography', p.88.
17. 'Jan Tschichold: praeceptor typographiae', p.24.
18. Schauer in Day (ed.), *Book typography 1815–1965*, p.132.

In his essay here on German book design, Schauer seriously undervalued Tschichold's role in New Typography, not even mentioning *Die neue Typographie* (whereas Willy Rotzler did in his essay on Switzerland).

This perhaps reflects how that book had fallen into obscurity in Germany by the 1960s.
19. As it appeared in the published English translation: Weidemann, 'Designer's profile: Jan Tschichold', p.25.

306

is typeset in sanserif. Despite the dismissive things he wrote about sanserif in his later years, Tschichold seems never to have lost interest in this category of letterform: the first designs he made for his classic serif typeface Sabon also included a sanserif version, which was never produced. Here he tried to incorporate elements of old-face roman type into sanserif, in a different way than Eric Gill had done, and his sketches show that he anticipated some of the features that surfaced in sanserif types of the 1990s (and later).

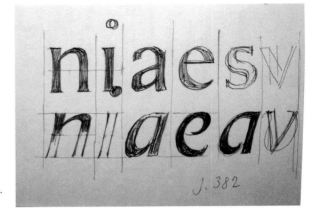

Sketch for Sabon sanserif. c.1960.

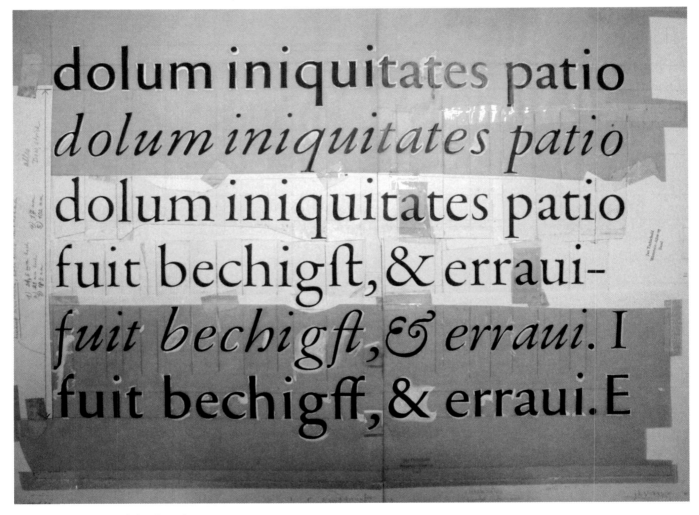

Drawings for Sabon: serifed, italic and sanserif versions. 1960.

Proofs made from Tschichold's early drawings for Sabon and Sabon sanserif. c.1960.

A quick brown fox jumps over the lazy dog. &

A quick brown fox jumps over the lazy dog, &

The National Socialists' intervention in culture, and particularly in graphic design, was an extreme case, but it reinforces the point that graphic design cannot avoid taking a social position. A consistent theme of social responsibility in typography ran through the whole of Tschichold's career: the duty of effecting clear communication. In his last major article, published the year before his death, he reflected on what he had come to see as the potential pitfall of his early, functionalist approach to this aim:

> The appeal to the allegedly necessary expression of one's own time is purely rhetorical and empty of meaning. The mirroring of its own time is in no way the task of typography and is false as an intention: for whatever we do is only possible here and now, and is a mirror of our time whether we like it or not.
>
> Clear order is a beautiful thing and is a requirement of every work of art, also of the modest work of art that is typography. But an order that makes itself conspicuous and becomes an end in itself stands in contradiction to the task of typography.

In the second half of his life Tschichold renounced the aim of making typography express the style of the modern era, but retained the notion that it must serve the given content:

> Nobody should forget that typography is the least free of all the arts. None other serves to such a degree. It cannot free itself without losing its purpose. It is more strongly bound than any other art to meaningful conventions and the more typographers heed these the better their work will be.[19]

Tschichold looking at examples of printed work from the Bauhaus at an exhibition. 1960s.

19. 'Typographie ist eine Kunst für sich', pp.282 & 284.

Appendices

Appendix A   **Elemental typography** 1925

Translated by Robin Kinross from 'Elementare Typographie', *Sonderheft elementare Typographie* [*Typographische Mitteilungen*, Jg.22, H.10, October 1925], pp.198–200.

1. The New Typography is oriented towards purpose.
2. The purpose of any piece of typography is communication (the means of which it displays). The communication must appear in the briefest, simplest, most urgent form.
3. In order to make typography serviceable to social ends, it requires the *inner organization* of its materials (the ordering of content) and their *outer organization* (the means of typography configured in relation to one another).
4. *Inner organization* is the limitation to the elemental means of typography: letters, numbers, signs, rules – from the typecase and the composing machine.

   In the present, visually-attuned world, the exact image – photography – also belongs to the elemental means of typography.

   The elemental letterform is the sanserif, in all variations: light, **medium**, **bold**, and from condensed to expanded.

   Letterforms that belong to particular style-categories or which bear definite national characteristics (Textura, Fraktur, Church Slavonic) are not elementally designed, and to some extent limit the possibilities of being understood internationally. Mediäval-Antiqua [old style roman] is the most usual form of typeface for the majority of people. For the setting of continuous text, it still – without being elementally designed – has the advantage of better legibility over many sanserifs.

   As long as there exists no thoroughly elemental form that is also legible in text setting, it is appropriate to prefer (against a sanserif) the least obtrusive form of Mediäval-Antiqua – one in which period or personal characteristics are least evident.

   An extraordinary economy could be achieved through the exclusive use of small letters – the elimination of all capital letters; a form of writing and setting that is recommended as a new script by all innovators in the field. See the book *Sprache und Schrift* by Dr Portsmann (Beuth-Verlag, Berlin SW19, Beuthstraße 8. Price: 5.25 marks). our script loses nothing through writing in small letters only – but becomes, rather, more legible, easier to learn, essentially more economical. for one sound, for example 'a', why two signs: A and a? one sound, one sign. why two alfabets for one word, why double the quantity of signs, when a half achieves the same?

   Through the use of strongly differentiated sizes and forms, and without consideration for previous aesthetic attitudes, the logical arrangement of printed text is made visually perceptible.

   The unprinted areas of the paper are as much a means of design as are the visually appearing forms.
5. *Outer organization* is the forming of the strongest contrast (simultaneity) through the use of differentiated shapes, sizes, weights (which must correspond to the value of their content) and the creation of the relation between the positive (coloured) formal values and the (white) negative values of the unprinted paper.
6. Elemental typographic design is the creation of the logical and visual relation between the letters, words, and text, which are given by the job in hand.
7. In order to increase the sense of urgency of new typography, vertical and diagonal lines can also be employed as a means of inner organization.
8. Elemental designing excludes the use of any *ornament* (also 'swelled' and other ornamental rules). The use of rules and inherently elemental forms (squares, circles, triangles) must be convincingly grounded in the total construction.

   The *decorative-artistic-fanciful* use of essentially elemental forms is not in keeping with elemental designing.
9. Ordering of elements in new typography should in future be based on the standardized (DIN) paper formats of the Normenausschuss der Deutschen Industrie (NDI), which alone make possible a comprehensive organization for all typographic design. (See: Dr Portsmann, *Die Dinformate und ihre Einführung in die Praxis*, Selbstverlag Dinorm, Berlin NW7, Sommerstraße 4a. 3.00 marks.)

   In particular the DIN format A4 (210:297 mm) should be the basis of all business and other letterheadings. The business letterheading has itself also been standardized: DIN 676, 'Geschäftsbrief', obtainable direct from Beuth-Verlag, Berlin SW19, Beuthstraße 8; 0.40 mark. The DIN standard 'Papierformate' is number 476. The DIN formats have only recently been introduced into practice. In this special issue there is only one job that is consciously based on a DIN format.
10. Elemental designing is, in typography as in other fields, not absolute or conclusive. Elements change through discoveries that create new means of typographic designing – photography, for example – therefore the concept of elemental designing will necessarily also change continually.

Appendix B   **Book 'art'?** 1927

> Translated from 'Buch-"Kunst"?', *Die Literarische
> Welt*, Jg.39, Nr 29, July 1927, p.3. (For original
> text see illustration p.62.)

Around 1890, when the Englishman William Morris, father of
the Arts & Crafts movement, turned his attention to the design
of books he established the 'book art', which had its heyday
in the year of 1914 and which must be regarded today (at the
latest) as being at the end of its development. In this year's
International Exhibition of Book art in Leipzig that pre-war
spirit is once again conjured up, but all the splendour of this
exhibition will not hide from perceptive observers the sterility
of this curious ethos nor the hopelessness of its future.

For we know today that Morris was fighting on the wrong
front. With his principled rejection of any machine work he
blocked the road of natural development and became culp-
able for the kind of arts & crafts, which posh shops offer for
sale in the form of kitsch.

We must finally recognize that a false romanticism in
reintroducing medieval (or even exotic) methods and styles
cannot save us; only an affirmation of the present can do that
– *the improvement of quality in machine work*. The fronts
have been transposed. The phrase 'arts & crafts' is now mostly
uttered with mild horror. Faced with the poverty of all imita-
tions of historic and exotic styles, one attains the insight that
art and craft should at least be cleanly separated, that all
art (all decoration, in the sense of Morris and his imitators)
should be kept far away from objects of use currently produced by machines. To those of us who have been brought up
on the work of our engineers, beauty appears not as an end
in itself (ornament), rather as a result of right construction,
as an attribute of suitability for purpose (at least in industrial
forms). We know now that, in making the forms of our time,
we must tread the path already marked out by the engineers:
construction from elemental forms; precision; restriction to a
minimum of material; economy; use of contemporary means;
modern technology instead of handwork.

In many branches of industrial production this realization
is dawning, in a few it has perhaps already set in, but the
twilight of book art is a long time coming.

The professional book artists, organizers of the Leipzig
exhibition, follow today in Morris's footsteps. Like him, they
hark back to the oh-so wonderful, earlier times when *all* books
were well made (and in which they would not have been able
to make a living because all books were designed by simple
craftsmen). This one loves Rococo, the other prefers gothic.
To these they harked back from 1890, then from 1914, and
still they hark back (apparently *ad infinitum*).

The majority of the purchasing public does not consist
of reclusive bibliophiles. It has hardly more than a passing

interest in the form of books. Let us not fool ourselves:
ninety-nine per cent of the typefaces created by the book
artists are historicist – in another word, historical. *Do they
seriously believe that contemporary books can be made by
these means? Do the forms of book made by the 'leaders'
really correspond to our age?* Can it really be called culture
when the woman sitting in an automobile or an aeroplane is
reading a book that could have been made in the time of Goethe?

By far the largest part of the International Exhibition of
Book art, at least of the German section, can only show a
completely *un*contemporary book art. For the leaders lacked,
and obviously still lack, the insight into the necessities of *our
time*, and if they do not lack them entirely, they do seem to
lack the ability or determination to give them form.

True development has been carried out off the beaten track
of the main road:

In 1909 the Italian Futurist *Marinetti* published his manifesto
against the old typography – and poems, which for the first
time display a contemporary typographic design: 'I initiate a
typographical revolution aimed at the bestial, nauseating idea
of the book of passéist and D'Annunzian verse, on seventeenth-
century handmade paper bordered with helmets, Minervas,
Apollos, elaborate red initials, vegetables, mythological missal
ribbons, etc.'[1]

From around 1919 *John Heartfield* has designed the excellent
bindings of the Malik Verlag – prototypes of contemporary
book covers.

In 1923 the Russian *Rodchenko* employed photomontage
for the first time as book illustration.

In the same year *Lissitzky's* 'For the voice' appeared, an
important document of typographic development.

Today, in almost all countries, there are a few people working on a contemporary typography and form for the book:
in Germany Baumeister, Bayer, Burchartz, Dexel, Fischer,
Heartfield, Moholy-Nagy, Molzahn, Schwitters; in Czechoslovakia: Rossmann, Styrsky, Teige, Toyen; in Poland: Sczuka
– and many more.

1. Translator's note: Marinetti's words here were first published in 'Destruction of syntax–Imagi-nation without strings–Words-in-freedom', *Lacerba* (Florence, 15 June 1913), not in 'The found-ing and manifesto of Futurism', *Le Figaro* (Paris, February 20, 1909), as might be interpreted from Tschichold's commentary. A more extensive passage from the same text was cited in *Die neue Typographie*, where Tschi-chold gives it the reference of *Les mots en liberté futuristes* (Milan, 1919), a collected edi-tion of Marinetti's writings in French. But, while this book is correctly dated in Tschichold's bibliography, it is given the erroneous date of 1909 in his text (*Die neue Typographie*, p.54; it is silently corrected in the English and Spanish translations). This is perhaps the source of the same, incor-rect date being given for a cita-tion from Marinetti's text in Herbert Spencer's *Pioneers of modern typography*. Tschichold's translation was not very faithful to the original, and so the excerpt given here is from the English translation by R.W. Flint, reprinted in Bierut et al (ed.) *Looking Closer 3*, p.10. [CB]

'Book art' is just as oblique a concept as *'applied art'*. There are well-made and there are badly-made books. The unpretentiousness of a common, French novel is more sympathetic than the arrogant pushiness of a book artist's private style, which can only ever hinder the free and uninfluenced functioning of the content. The book as an object is nothing more than the carrier of a certain content and typography has the sole task of communicating that content in the *clearest possible* form.

The bygone, individualistic period brought forth a great number of artist-typefaces, which even find employment in books, yet are without exception impossible for use as book-types. Every individual modification of the pure, basic form contradicts the nature of typography as a servant, which in itself should not be noticed at all (especially not in books!)

But also the 'neo-classical' types (e.g. Walbaum, Didot, Unger), which have recently come back into fashion, are, despite their quality, unsuitable as book types *today* because they effect romantic associations and thereby guide the reader into a specific sphere of feeling. The thesis that a typeface must (formally) correspond to a text is puny and *false*. The recent past stands alone in history for allowing individualism to have an effect on books. It is high time that we make a definitive break with it and attain a clear consciousness of the demands that must be placed on a contemporary book:

Type: as a text typeface, for the meantime, an impersonal, good but not historical roman (like Sorbonne, Nordische Antiqua or Französische Antiqua), in future also a legible sanserif (of 'regular' weight).

Typography: A content-driven ordering of the type on the title-page and text pages, free from the schematic bugbear of centred typesetting. Exploitation of the possibilities for optical effect in different type-sizes and weights: strong black-white contrasts – not only in the tonal values but also in directional alignment: horizontal-vertical-(diagonal). Extreme objectivity.

Binding and jacket: construction with contemporary means, above all with photography and photomontage. Mechanical production of quality, but no handmade bindings!

Result: Books that are functionally conceived and so designed that the individualism of the designer retreats completely behind the object, and which enable a true hygiene of reading and a totally free functioning of the content.

Appendix C   **What is New Typography and what are its aims?** 1930

Translated by Robin Kinross from 'Was ist und was will die neue Typografie?', introduction to *Eine Stunde Druckgestaltung*. An abridged English translation was first published as 'New life in print' (1930). The essay was translated into several languages: [Danish] 'Vad är och vad vill "Den nya Typografien"?', *Nordisk Boktryckare-konst*, Aarg. 31, Hefte 8, August 1930; [French] 'Qu'est-ce que la nouvelle typographie et que veut elle?', *Arts et métiers graphiques*, no.19, September 1930, pp.46–52; [Hungarian] 'Miből állás mit akar az új tipográfia', *Magyar Grafika*, 1930, pp.203–5; [Polish] 'Nowe drukarstwo', *Europa*, no.9[6], 1930, pp.272–5; [Serbo-Croat] 'Nova tipografija', *Grafička Revija*, God.9, Broj 2, 1931, pp.33–7.

The endeavours of some young designers, principally from Germany, the Soviet Union, the Netherlands, Czechoslovakia, and also Switzerland and Hungary, are being gathered under the single term of 'New Typography'. The beginnings of these endeavours in Germany reach back to the war period. One can see the existence of New Typography as the outcome of the **personal** work of its originators; it seems to me more correct however to consider them more as exponents of movements of the time and of actual necessity (which does not in any way mean that the creative achievements and the local innovations of the initiators should be devalued).

The movement would never have experienced the spread that it now has, uncontested, in Central Europe, if it had not matched present-day practical necessities. It meets these in such an exceptional way because the programme of New Typography demands first of all the unprejudiced adjustment of typography to whatever is the task at hand.

It is necessary to describe briefly the state of typographic development before the war. After the stylistic confusion of the 1880s, the Arts & Crafts movement followed, emanating from England (Morris, 1892); at least in the domain of typography it was predominantly historicist in orientation (imitation of incunables).

Later (around 1900) 'Jugendstil' attempted, without lasting success, to free design work of all historical models. With a misconceived copying of natural forms (Eckmann), finally even with a renewed Biedermeier (Wieynck), Jugendstil ended up as a new historicism. Historical models were discovered yet again and imitated, albeit with better understanding (German book art, 1911–1914–1920). This more intensive study gave rise to a new adoration of historical form and resulted of course in a limitation of creative freedom, which ended in paralysis. The most important achievement of these years was – against expectations – the rediscovery of old typefaces (Walbaum, Unger, Didot, Bodoni, Garamond, and so on), which have for some time already have been rightly preferred to their 'forerunners', in reality their imitators.

Let us look at the principles that were followed in the pre-war typography. The majestic historical model knew only one scheme of composition: the central axis and axial arrangement, whose clearest case was the title-page. Every kind of typography used this scheme, no matter what the nature of the job was – whether newspapers or brochures, letterheadings or advertisements. It was only after the war that a dark secret was revealed: that different tasks with quite different practical requirements could be resolved creatively.

The natural reaction to the stiffness of pre-war typography was New Typography, which brought a loosening of design methods to the task.

For any typographic work one can discern two parts of the job: recognition and fulfilment of **practical** demands – and the **visual** design, which is a matter of **aesthetics**. (It is useless to want to avoid this term.)

In this typography is quite different from architecture. In very many cases the visual form of a new house can be – and, by the best architects, is – derived completely from the practical demands on it; but in typography, apart from a few exceptions, an aesthetic dimension of the design process is clearly evident. This circumstance puts typography nearer to the domain of 'free' spatial design (painting and graphic art) than to that of architecture. In typographic and free graphics or painting it is always a matter of spatial design. One can understand from this why it is that these new painters – the 'abstractionists' – had to be the discoverers of New Typography. It would be too much of a detour here to add an account of the new painting: one only has to look at the exhibitions of abstract painting to see the obvious connections between this painting and New Typography. This connection is not, as some think – those who have not understood abstract painting either – a formalistic one; rather it is a genetic one. Abstract paintings are '**purpose-free**', designed relations of pure colours and forms, without literary admixtures. Typography means visual (or **aesthetic**) order of **given** elements (= practical demands, type, image, colours, etc.) in a space. The difference between painting and typography is just that in painting the elements are left to free choice and the resulting picture serves no practical purpose. The typographer can do no better than take up an intensive study of spatial design, as one finds it in abstract painting.

The speed of modern communication also compels the most exact calculation of the amount of text, for greater economy of design. Typography had to find forms that were simpler and clearer than centred title-page designs, and at the same time to design these in a way that was visually more stimulating and more varied. In France Guillaume Apolinaire with his *Calligrammes*, in Italy Marinetti with *Les mots en liberté futuristes* (1919), in Germany the Dadaists all gave impulse to the new development of typography. Dadaism is still regarded by many, who haven't taken the trouble to look into its motivation, as pure madness; only a later age will properly value the pioneer work of the circle of Hausmann, Heartfield, Grosz, Hülsenbeck, and others. In any event, the

pamphlets and writings of the Dadaists (which date from the war years) are the earliest documents of New Typography in Germany. Around 1922, the movement widened as some abstract painters made typographic experiments. The special number of *Typographische Mitteilungen, Elementare Typographie* (printed in an edition of 28,000 copies), edited by the author in 1925, contributed to the further effect in which these endeavours, brought together for the first time, were made known to the broad mass of compositors. At first the aims of New Typography were strongly attacked from almost all sides, but now, apart from a few ill-tempered people, no-one thinks of disputing the New. New Typography has prevailed.

If one wants to differentiate New Typography from what went before, it appears that the main characteristic is a negative: it is not historicizing. The blame for this negative description is its rival, which was exactly historically oriented. In fact New Typography is not so much anti-historical as un-historical, because it knows no formalistic limitations. The liberation from historical handcuffs brings complete freedom in the choice of means. To enrich typographic design, one can, for example, use all historical and ahistorical types, all kinds of spatial organization, all directions of line. The goal is only design: purposefulness and creative ordering of the visual elements. So limits, such as the demand for unity of type, admissable and forbidden mixtures of types, are not drawn. It is also wrong to propose some tranquility of appearance as the single aim of design – there is also designed **unrest**.

As well as its ahistorical focus, New Typography is characterized by its preference for new technical processes. **Thus:**

type	not drawn letters
machine composition	not hand-setting
photography	not drawing
process blocks	not woodcuts
machine-made paper	not hand-made paper
powered presses	not handpresses
etc.	

and also:

standardization	not individualization
cheap books	not private-press editions
active literature	not passive leather-bindings

Through its design methods New Typography encompasses the whole sphere of printing, not just the more narrow domain of typesetting. So for example with photography we have an objective process of graphic reproduction that is open to anyone. Photography is, along with type, another means of visual language.

The working method of New Typography rests on the clear identification of purpose and the best way of fulfilling it. However beautiful a piece of modern typography may be, it is not 'new' if it sacrifices the purpose of its form for this. Form is a **consequence** of the work and not the realization of some

external formal **conception**. This necessary truth goes unrecognized by a whole crowd of quasi-modernists. The nearest possible attainment of purpose is the highest demand of New Typography. Thus the shedding of all decorative additions becomes self-evident. And – this cannot be stressed enough – really good legibility is also part of purpose. Lines of text that are too short or lines that are long and too little leaded are hard to read and thus to be avoided from the outset. The correct application of various new printing processes almost always produces specific forms, which it should be one of the typographer's tasks to recognize and design with. Good typography is not conceivable without a thorough knowledge of technical conditions.

The number of printed things that concern any individual, and of which he will receive an often considerable part, demands the application of **standardized formats**.

Of the basic repertoire of **types**, the grotesque (sanserif) is closest to New Typography, because it is simply designed and has good legibility. The use of other legible and also historical types – **in a new sense** – is quite possible if the letterform has been **evaluated** against that of other types present, i.e. if the visual tensions between them have been designed. So this is not to demand that **everything** be set in grotesque, even if grotesque may be the most appropriate choice for a large number of printed items. Many applications are available in the different variants of this letterform (light, semibold, bold, thin, wide, narrow, spaced, etc.), and in juxtaposition this can result in rich and differentiated contrast. Another kind of contrast comes from using roman types together (Egyptienne, Walbaum, Garamond, italics, etc.), and there can be no objection to making use of this specific effect. (Another very particular and effective letterform is typewriter type.)

Typographic design is the best ordering and correct choice of type sizes, according to their place within the logical structure of the text (this can be heightened or played down). The conscious use of movement (through type, and occasionally a thick or thin rule or aggregation of rules), the visually judged contrast of small and large, thin and thick, narrow and expanded types; grey and coloured areas, inclined and horizontal, limited and open groups, and so on, are further means of design. They represent the 'aesthetic' aspect of typographic design. Within definite boundaries, drawn up by practical purpose and logical structure, one can often take very different routes, so that from there on the visual sense of the typographer is decisive. This becomes apparent when several designers are given the same job: as many different solutions follow, each probably with almost the same advantages. Essentially the same means thus encounter an extraordinary number of possibilities of application. These examples also show that modern means do not, as is often thought, entail a flattening of expression – on the contrary, the results are essentially more differentiated and above all more original than the typography of the pre-war years.

Colour is another part of the repertoire, like typeface. In a sense, colour should be seen alongside the unprinted space – the discovery of which is to be counted among the achievements of the young forces in typography. White space is to be regarded as an active element, not a passive background. Red is to be preferred among available colours; it is **the** colour in making the greatest contrast to normal black. The clear tones of yellow and blue take their place in the front rank, just because they are clear and simple. Colours are not to be used as decorative, 'beautifying' extras, rather one uses the characteristic psycho-physical properties of each colour as means to enhance, or diminish, an effect.

The **image** is produced by photography. The object is in this way reproduced at its most objective. Whether photography may or may not be an 'art' is not of importance here; its connection with type and space **can** be art, because here the criteria are merely those of structural contrast and visual relationships. Many people regard drawn images with distrust; the often false drawings of earlier times are no longer convincing and their individualistic manner is no longer attractive. The wish to present several images simultaneously, juxtaposing and contrasting different things, led to the origination of **photomontage**. Just the same general methods of design apply here as for typography; in conjunction with typography, the aggregate of photographs becomes part of the whole; so it has also to be correctly judged in this connection, to result in a harmonious design. The designed juxtaposition of typography and photography (or photomontage) is termed **typophoto**. A rare, but very rich possibility in photography is the photogram. A photogram is made without a camera, simply by placing an object – somewhat transparent or not – on a light-sensitive surface (paper, film or plate).

The extraordinary adaptability of New Typography to any conceivable purpose makes it an essential phenomenon of our time. It is not a matter of fashion; rather it can be used as the foundation of all future work in typography.

Karel Teige (Prague) has summarized the main features of New Typography:

Constructivist typography* means and requires:

1. **The liberation from tradition and prejudice: overcoming of archaism and academicism and elimination of any decorativism.** Disrespect for academic and traditional rules that cannot be supported on visual grounds, but which are merely rigid forms (Golden Section, unity of type).

2. **Selection of types of completely clear legibility and geometrically simple design,** understanding for the spirit of types and the use of them in accordance with the nature of the text: contrast in the typographic material for the purpose of greater emphasis of content.

3. **Complete fulfilment of the purpose of the job.** Differentiation of special needs. Posters, which need to be readable from a distance, pose demands that are different from those of a scientific book, which are different again from poetry.

4. **Harmonic balancing of the surface and of the type-area, according to visually objective principles; comprehensible structure and geometric organization.**

5. Exploitation of all possibilities that are offered by past and future technical discoveries; **union of image and type through typophoto.**

6. **The closest collaboration of the graphic designer with the people in the printing house** is to be desired, just as between an architect and the builders, and between the employer and those carrying out the job; this requires equally **specialization and division of work and the closest contact**.

We have nothing to add to this statement, apart from saying that the Golden Section, like other definite ratios of measurement, is often more memorable than arbitrary relationships, and so should not be completely ruled out.

---

* A term for New Typography.
[Note in original text.]

Appendix D   **Where do we stand today?** 1932

Translated from 'Wo stehen wir heute?',
Typographische Mitteilungen, Jg.29, H.2,
February 1932, pp.24–5.

After the appearance of the special issue *Elementare Typo-graphie* (1925) and the book *Die neue Typographie* (1928), the theory of New Typography has had to confront reality. This theory incorporates demands concerning type and structure.

a) Type. Originally *sanserif* was declared to be the *sole* type-face of the present day. By now it has been established that it is not possible to manage with sanserif alone. Without doubt it is the *typical* typeface of our time. It is definitely not a mere example of fashion, rather the clearest expression of our intentions. Neither will it become unmodern by the persistent claims of interested parties that it has become so. One could assert, with considerable justification, that the *time* is not ripe for sanserif. It is extremely unlikely that it will be superseded by a 'more modern' typeface. Similarly, a transformation in the form of sanserif is not foreseeable in the short term. Even the new sanserifs are not essentially New in comparison with the old. Sanserif is the type of the present, just as gothic was the type of the late Middle Ages, or as New Building is the architecture of our time.

(It is incidentally not very important which sanserif one favours. Among the new ones, there are many with an unmodern appearance; but the older ones are also not fault-less. One should not take the individual form too seriously in terms of its effect within the whole structure, which repre-sents the real task of the compositor. A bad compositor will hardly use a good sanserif, while a good compositor can produce outstanding work even with bad sanserif types.)

The amount of printed matter spilling over us is, however, too great to be composed in one typeface. The purely tech-nical factors, which for the meantime prevent an implemen-tation of sanserif as the unique typeface, will be overcome in a few years. But it will not happen in the near future. For us today *one* typeface for all purposes is, in the long run, too *boring*. A section of classified advertisements, for example, set in one typeface (albeit in different weights and also in a range of sizes) is not 'attractive' because not varied enough; it will hardly be read, or not be read at all. A very gifted typographer can probably design the advertisement section with sanserif alone in an ingenious way; yet the effort required is dispro-portionate to the difficulty of the task. Apart from the *struc-ture* itself, the *parts* can be designed in a varied way. Today, *photography*, as form rich in content, offers great possibilities for effect. But there is not always a suitable photograph avail-able; production is often too laborious and reproduction often too expensive. Also *colour* can naturally determine a different appearance for a document. Nevertheless, the principal means

for the compositor is *type*: variety in type-styles! If used too often, even the most beautiful typeface tires both reader and compositor. Boredom in advertising is an evident failing. An example is offered by the shop fascias in Frankfurt am Main, which have all been painted in sanserif, although admittedly in different colours and sizes. The result is deadly boring. This fact must be faced, even when one admires the new building activity in Frankfurt, as I do. Naturally we should use typefaces that we like; for this reason there is always a search, before designing, for the 'most beautiful' typefaces. Every period of time favours different cuts. Today we prefer types, which ten years or more ago were rarely allowed to stray into the type-case, yet are not essentially different from those of a hundred years ago. If Egyptian and Fat Face reappear now, then that does not mean that these are more modern than sanserif! These old typefaces have a neutral and impersonal effect on us, just as sanserif does; by using them one accentuates the New in the structure (individual structure from neutral forms). They have a stronger effect when they are used only as display types with sanserif used as the text type. In this way their historical odour is also removed from them. They are a variation; they enhance the sanserif and the sanserif also underlines the peculiar character of the old type-faces.* Even the types Zeus and Saskia are not 'more modern' than sanserif; they merely offer the possibility of a variation. A programmatic meaning does not benefit them in any way. (By the way, I cannot discern a *fashion* for cursive types.)

Doubtless the necessity for changing typefaces is partly a result of capitalism. The cessation of capitalist advertising would, as the example of the Soviet Union shows, transform all advertising into (scientific) communication, and communi-cations can very well be set without exception in sanserif. The vying of one with another for prominence ceases, and the theatrical showing off of capitalist advertising would become senseless. Since the communicative document demands above all clarity in type-form and structure, the neutral san-serif is also customary for this purpose, both as a text type and a display type (apart from in books, where one cannot use it without something else) – for example, in the editorial sec-tions of newspapers, scientific and enlightenment literature, textbooks, and children's books. In books it will only usually be used for display and headings; but even in this it determines the outward image of the structure. Additionally, advertising for *manifestly modern things* and books & newspapers which

* See the advertising section of the Fototek volumes designed by the author (Verlag Klinkhardt & Biermann, Berlin W10), in par-ticular volume 1 (Moholy-Nagy). [Note in original text.]

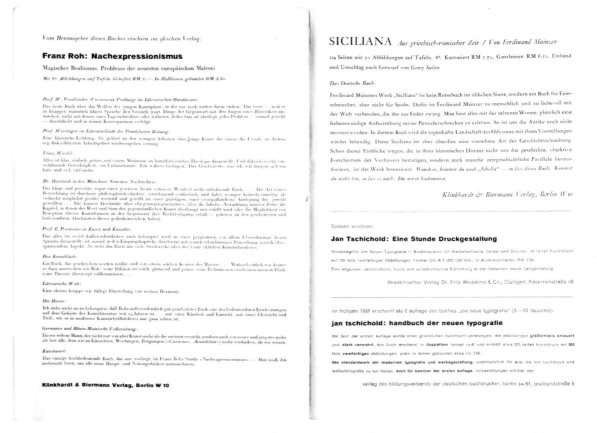

Advertisement pages referred to in Tschichold's
footnote on the previous page, from Fototek 1,
L. Moholy-Nagy. 1930. 25 × 17.6 cm.

(Illustration not included in original German
article.)

herald the New – these things can *only* be designed in *sanserif*.
It is impossible to set headings in books about New Architects
(Gropius, Mies van der Rohe, Karl Schneider) in an Egyptian.
Here sanserif alone is suitable. (The text typeface can natur-
ally also be a roman.)

The historical purpose of propaganda for sanserif as the
absolute type-style was to accord it due recognition, in order
for it to then be relieved of this role. It cleared the air, for one
simply had to learn to see again. Working with its elemental
forms moulded the sense for new typographic structure.
Sanserif is now, as before, the practice typeface of the begin-
ner and the *sole typeface of everything New*. It is sacred and
profane at the same time; it is the best typeface for a state
constitution (if only one could set everything in it!) just as it is
for a package label.

b) Structure. Nevertheless, type-form is not the point of
typography, rather its purpose is to be read. This entails
structure, which defines the total, typographic appearance
more than typeface.* And here is *the indisputable dividend
of the last ten years' development in the fundamentally new,
simpler structure of typographic design*. This transformation
is of a fundamental nature: one need only compare the trade
journals of 1923 to 1925 with *Typographische Mitteilungen* of
today to refresh one's memory.

Ornament, which was previously the compositor's principal
means for effect, has completely disappeared. I believe that it
will not return for some time. Instead of ornament, to which
the compositor can add little even in the best cases, there
has arisen a very refined balancing of type-sizes and surface
relationships – in other words, creative work itself. That is a
benefit that can hardly be overestimated.

The new construction in typographic design displays
contrasts in form, whereas the previous typography employed
forms of a *similar* nature. The old typography (taking into
account only the best of it) tended towards *resolution* of form
– New Typography takes *connections* as its starting point.
A new, vital feeling for the black/white values of forms and
for spatial design has developed. We always have the whole
surface in sight, whereas previously the first step was to
subtract a margin. The manifold possibilities of *asymmetrical
structure* have replaced simplistic, *axial symmetry*.

All the signs demonstrate that a completely radical change
has taken place in typography. The task of the present day
consists in tilling all fields of typography, without exception,
in the spirit of the New.

* The design of a typeface has
no really decisive importance
for the total appearance of a
printed document.

(*Die neue Typographie*, pp.78–9)
[This is not a direct quotation,
and the page numbers originally given, 178–9, do not deal

with this matter. So, assuming
that they were given in error,
the relevant page numbers
have been substituted . – CB]

Bibliographies
and sources

Select bibliography of Tschichold's writings

Only titles cited or referred to in the text are included here. The fullest bibliography so far published appears in the second volume of Tschichold's collected writings: *Schriften*, 2, pp.443–59 (see entry below). Details of inclusion in the *Schriften* are given where possible. Original sources are given for articles not included in the *Schriften*.
+ Marks items that have not previously appeared in any bibliography of Tschichold's writings.

As editor (and featured author)
Elementare Typographie (*Sonderheft*), *Typographische Mitteilungen*, Jg.22, H.10, October 1925, pp.191–214. Facsimile reprint – Mainz: Hermann Schmidt, 1986

Books (in chronological order)
Die neue Typographie: ein Handbuch für zeitgemäss Schaffende. Berlin: Bildungsverband der Deutschen Buchdrucker, 1928. (Reprint – Berlin: Brinkmann & Bose, 1987)

Foto-Auge / oeil et photo / photo-eye. Stuttgart: Wedekind, 1929

Eine Stunde Druckgestaltung: Grundbegriffe der neuen Typografie in Bildbeispielen für Setzer, Werbefachleute, Drucksachenverbraucher und Bibliofilen. Stuttgart: Wedekind, 1930

Schriftschreiben für Setzer. Frankfurt a.M.: Klimsch, 1931

Typografische Entwurfstechnik. Stuttgart: Wedekind, 1932. Facsimile reprint included in English translation (by Ruari McLean), *How to draw layouts*. Edinburgh: Merchiston, 1991

Typographische Gestaltung. Basel: Benno Schwabe, 1935

Gute Schriftformen. Basel: Lehrmittelverlag des Erziehungsdepartments, 1941–6

Schriftkunde, Schreibübungen und Skizzieren für Setzer. Basel: Holbein, 1942. 2nd edn – *Schriftkunde, Schreibübungen und Skizzieren*. Berlin: Druckhaus Tempelhof, 1951

Asymmetric typography. Translated by Ruari McLean from *Typographische Gestaltung* [1935]. Toronto: Cooper & Beatty / London: Faber & Faber, 1967

Leben und Werk des Typographen Jan Tschichold. 1st edn – Dresden: VEB Verlag der Kunst, 1977; 2nd edn – Munich: Saur, 1988

Schriften 1925–1974. 2 vols. Berlin: Brinkmann & Bose, 1991/2

The form of the book: essays on the morality of good design. Edited by Robert Bringhurst. London: Lund Humphries, 1991. Translated by Hajo Hadeler from *Ausgewählte Aufsätze über Fragen der Gestalt des Buches und der Typographie* (Basel: Birkhäuser, 1975)

The New Typography: a handbook for modern designers. Translated by Ruari McLean from *Die neue Typographie* [1928]. Berkeley: University of California Press, 1995

Articles (in alphabetical order)
'Abstract painting and the New Typography', *Industrial Arts*, vol.1, no.2, summer 1936, pp.157–64

'Advertising the German store', *Commercial Art*, vol.10, April 1931, pp.168–70

'Alfred Fairbank' [1946], *Schriften*, 1, pp.301–3

+ 'The ampersand: its origin and development', *British Printer*, January 1958, pp.56–62

+ 'Buch-"Kunst"?', *Die literarische Welt*, Jg.39, Nr 29, 22 July 1927, p.3

'Clay in the potter's hand', *Penrose Annual*, vol.43, 1949, pp.21–2

'The composite photograph and its place in advertising', *Commercial Art*, vol.9, December 1930, pp.237–48

'The "Constructivist" El Lissitzky', *Commercial Art*, vol.11, October 1931, pp.149–50

'Display that has dynamic force: exhibition stands designed by El Lissitzky', *Commercial Art*, vol.10, January 1931, pp.21–6

'Einige zweckmäßige Regeln für den Akzidenzsatz in neuer Typographie', *Grafische Berufsschule*, Jg.1930/1, H.3/4, pp.42–3; + [Danish translation] 'Regler för framställning av modärn accidenssats', *Grafisk Revy*, Aarg.4, Hefte 2, 1933, pp.29–32

'Einiges über Buchgestaltung' [1932], *Schriften*, 1, pp.113–7

+ 'El Lissitzky (1890–1941)', in Lissitzky-Küppers, *El Lissitzky: life, letters, texts*, pp.388–90; [in original German, with illustrations] *Typographische Monatsblätter*, Jg.89, H.12, 1970, pp.1–24

'Elementare Typographie', *Elementare Typographie* [1925], pp.198–200

'Die Entwicklung der neuen Typographie im In- und Auslande' [1930], *Schriften*, 1, pp.82–4

+ 'Die Entwicklung der neuen Typographie in den mitteleuropäischen Ländern' [1937/8, printed but not published] pp.125–32

+ 'Entwicklungslinie der neuen Malerei', *Volksfreund Recklinghausen* [newspaper], 29 October 1925. (Reprint, with new introductory paragraphs, of 'Die neue Gestaltung'.)

'Europäische Schriften aus zweitausend Jahren' [1934], *Schriften*, 1, pp.139–68

'Flöhe ins Ohr' [1970], *Schriften*, 2, pp.357–66

'Fotografie und Typografie' [1928], *Schriften*, 1, pp.41–51; + *Hand und Maschine*, Jg.1, Nr 11, February 1930

+ 'Für die allgemeine "Kleinschrift"', *Dichtung und Wahrheit*, *Sächsische Volksblatt*, 8 October 1929

'Gebrochene Schrift als Auszeichnung zur Antiqua' [1939], *Schriften*, 1, pp.221–6

'Die gegendstandslose Malerei und ihre Beziehungen zur Typographie der Gegenwart', *Typographische Monatsblätter*, Jg.3, H.6, June 1935, pp.181–7

+ 'Die Gestaltung der Werbemittel', *Planvolles Werben: vom Briefkopf bis zum Werbefilm* (Basel Gewerbemuseum exhibition catalogue, 1934), pp.17–27

'Glaube und Wirklichkeit' [1946], *Schriften*, 1, pp.310–28; translated as 'Belief and reality' in McLean, *Jan Tschichold: typographer*, pp.131–9, and in *Typography Papers*, 4, 2000, pp.71–86; + [Swedish translation] 'Jan Tschichold och den nya typografien', *Svensk Typograf-Tidning*, Aarg.61, 1948, pp.67–72

'Graphik und Buchkunst' [1946], *Schriften*, 1, pp.298–300

'Gute Typographie in Gefahr' [1962], *Schriften*, 2, pp.269–87

+ 'Gute und schlechte Reklametypographie', *Württemburgische Industrie*, Jg.10, Nr 16, 1929, pp.213–6

'Jan Tschichold: praeceptor typographiae' [1972], *Leben und Werk des Typographen Jan Tschichold*, pp.11–29

'Japanische Typographie, Flaggen und Zeichen' [1928], *Schriften*, 1, pp.38–9

'Klassifizierung der von uns gebrauchten Buchdruckschriften', *Schweizer Reklame*, no.2, 1951, pp.4–7

+ 'Konkrete Malerei', *A bis Z*, Folge 3, Nr 28, November 1932, p.109

+ 'Lichtbild und Druckgestaltung', *Monatsschrift für Photographie und Kinematographie*, Jg.25, Nr 4, April 1929, pp.127–9

+ 'Das neue Bildplakat', *Süddeutsche Graphischer Anzeiger*, Jg.5, Nr 8, August 1930, pp.2–3

'Neue Formen der statistischen Darstellung', *Grafische Berufsschule*, Jg.1931/2, H.3, pp.26–8. First appeared anonymously in + *Klimschs Druckerei-Anzeiger*, Jg.58, Nr 58, 1931, pp.935–7; reprinted in *Typographische Monatsblätter*, Jg.4, H.2, February 1936, pp.37–9. Published in English as 'Statistics in pictures'

'Die neue Gestaltung', *Elementare Typographie* [1925], pp.193–5

'Das neue Plakat', *Neue Werbegraphik* (Basel Gewerbemuseum, exhibition catalogue, 1930); *Offset: Buch und Werbekunst*, Jhg.7, H.7, 1930, pp.233–6. Published in English as 'New paths in poster work'

+ 'Die neue Typographie', *Kulturschau*, H.4, [spring] 1925, pp.9–11

+ 'Die neue Typographie' [text of 1927 lecture], *Graphische Revue*, Jg.30, H.1, 1928, pp.1–5

+ 'Neuere Typografie in Frankreich', *Die Form*, Jg.6, H.10, 1931, pp.382–4

'New life in print', *Commercial Art*, vol.9, July 1930, pp.2–20

'New paths in poster work' [1931], *Schriften*, 1, pp.95–100

'New Typography', *Circle: international survey of constructive art*. London: Faber & Faber, 1937, pp.249–55; *Schriften*, 1, pp.219–20

'Noch eine neue Schrift: Beitrag zur Frage der Ökonomie der Schrift' [1930], *Schriften*, 1, pp.74–81

+ 'Normung und typographische Gestaltung der Zeitschriften', *Zeitschrift für Deutschlands Buchdrucker und verwandte Gewerbe*, Nr 17, February 1928, p.134

'On Ben Nicholson's reliefs', *Axis*, no.2, 1935, pp.16–18

'Proportionen in unsymmetrischer Typographie' [1940], *Schriften*, 1, pp.245–50

+ 'Proportionerne i den ny typografi', *Grafisk Revy*, Aarg.6, Hefte 4, 1936, pp.5–16

'A quick and easy method of lettering for composite photographs', *Commercial Art*, vol.9, 1930, p.249. Also published in German as 'Leicht und schnell konstruierbare Schrift' in: + *Offset: Buch- und Werbekunst*, Jg.7, H.7, 1930, p.239; + *Börsenblatt für den Deutschen Buchhandel*, Nr 183, 9 August 1930; + *Papier-Zeitung*, Nr 53, 1930, p.1576; + *Neue Dekoration*, Jg.1, Nr 5, 1930; + *Das neue Bild* [precise reference unknown]; *Die Form*, Jg.8, H.2, 1933, p.57; *Schriften*, 1, p.85

'Quousque Tandem ...' [1959], in McLean, *Jan Tschichold: typographer*, pp.155–8; *Schriften*, 2, pp.314–18

'Der Satz des Buches' [1933], *Schriften*, 1, pp.121–38

+ 'Schriften für Photomontagen', *Klimschs Druckerei-Anzeiger*, Jg.58, Nr 15, 1931, pp.231 & 233. (Amplified version of 'A quick and easy method of lettering for composite photographs'.)

'Schriftmischungen' [1935], *Schriften*, 1, pp.169–77

'Statistics in pictures: a new method of presenting facts', *Commercial Art*, vol.11, September 1931, pp.113–17

'Ton in des Töpfers Hand' [1949], *Schriften*, 2, pp.26–9

+ 'Tschichold' in Baudin & Dreyfus (ed.), *Dossier A–Z 73* (Andenne: Rémy Magermans, 1973) p.62

'Type mixtures', *Typography*, no.3, summer 1937, pp.2–7

+ 'Typographie ist eine Kunst für sich', *Typographische Monatsblätter*, Jg.92, No.4, April 1973, pp.281–4

+ 'Das Typosignet', *Schweizer Graphische Mitteilungen*, Jg.46, H.1, 1928, p.9; *Klimschs Druckerei-Anzeiger*, Jg.55, Nr 8, 1928, p.162

'Über El Lissitzky' [1932], *Schriften*, 1, pp.106–12

'Über Typographie', *Typographische Monatsblätter*, Jg.71, H.1, 1952, pp.21–3

+ 'Vom Anzeigenumbruch und vom Satz kleiner Anzeigen', *Bundesblatt* (Monatliche Mitteilungen des Bundes der Meisterschüler), Jg.4, Nr 10, May 1932, pp.1–5 [unnumbered]

'Vom deutschen Holzschnitt des fünfzehnten Jahrhunderts' [uncredited], *Typographische Monatsblätter*, Jg.3, H.3, 1935, pp.69–73

'Vom richtigen Satz auf Mittelachse' [1935], *Schriften*, 1, pp.178–85; translated as 'The design of centred typography' in McLean, *Jan Tschichold: typographer*, pp.126–31

'Von schlechter und guter Typographie' [1937/8], *Schriften*, 1, pp.207–18

'Vorgotische Buchmalereien', *Grafische Berufsschule*, Jg.1931/2, H.3, pp.25–6

'Was bei der Anschaffung neuer Schriften zu bedenken ist', *Schweizer Reklame*, Nr 2, May 1951, pp.8–21

+ 'Wege ins Neuland der Typographie' [accompaniment to supplement of composition work from Meisterschule], *Deutscher Drucker*, Jg.38, H.10, July 1932, pp.432–4

+ 'Das wichtigste über die Herstellung typographischer Skizzen', *Scherls Informationen*, Nr 90–3, February–May 1933, pp.6–9. (Serialized extracts from *Typografische Entwurfstechnik*.)

'Die wichtigsten geschichtlichen Druckschriften', *Grafische Berufsschule*, Jg.1930/1, H.3/4, pp.35–9

'Wie das Buch *Foto-Auge* (1929) entstand' [1974], *Schriften*, 2, pp.413–5

'Wirken sich gesellschaftliche und politische Umstände in der Typographie aus?' [1948/50], *Schriften*, 2, pp.20–5; + [Swedish translation] 'Typografi och politik', *Svensk Typograf-Tidning*, Aarg.61, 1948, p.433

'Wo stehen wir heute?' [1932], *Schriften*, 1, pp.102–5

'Zeitgemäße Briefmarken' [1931], *Schriften*, 1, p.101

'Zur Typographie der Gegenwart' [1957], *Schriften*, 2, pp.255–65

General bibliography

Includes titles cited or referred to in the text
and others found to be generally useful during
research for this book.

Ades, Dawn, *Photomontage*. London: Thames &
Hudson, 1986

Albert, Karl, 'Zum Problem der photomechanischen Setztechnik: die Uhertype Lichtsetz-
maschine', *Deutscher Drucker*, Jg.37, H.3,
December 1930

Andel, Jaroslav, *Avant-garde page design 1900–
1950*. New York: Delan Greenidge, 2002

Arrausi, Juan Jesús, 'La tipografía integral versus
Tschichold', *Tipográfica*, 67 (no.3, 2005),
pp.16–23

*The art of the avant-garde in Czechoslovakia
1918–1938*. Valencia: IVAM Centre Julio
González, 1993

Aynsley, Jeremy, 'Art Deco graphic design and
typography' in Benton, Charlotte & Tim, and
Ghislaine Wood (ed.), *Art Deco 1910–39*.
London: V&A, 2005

–. 'Gebrauchsgraphik as an early graphic design
journal, 1924–1938', *Journal of Design History*,
vol.5, no.1, 1992, pp.53–72

–. *Graphic design in Germany 1890–1945*.
London: Thames & Hudson, 2000

Baines, Phil, *Penguin by design: a cover story,
1935–2005*. London: Allen Lane, 2005

Barnes, Paul (ed.), *Jan Tschichold: reflections and
reappraisals*. New York: Typoscope, 1995

Barker, Nicolas, *Stanley Morison*. London:
Macmillan, 1972.

Barron, Stephanie (ed.), *'Degenerate art': the
fate of the avant-garde in Nazi Germany*. Los
Angeles County Museum of Art / New York:
Abrams, 1991

Bartram, Alan, *Bauhaus, modernism and the illustrated book*. London: British Library, 2004

Becker, Lutz & Richard Hollis, *Avant-garde
graphics 1918–1934*. London: Hayward
Gallery, 2004

Benson, Timothy O. (ed.), *Between worlds: a
sourcebook of Central European avant-gardes,
1910–1930*. Cambridge, Mass.: MIT Press,
2002

–. *Central European avant-gardes: exchange
and transformation 1910–1930*. Los Angeles
County Museum of Art, 2002

Benton, Tim & Charlotte, and Dennis Sharp
(ed.), *Form and function: a source book for the
history of architecture and design 1890–1939*.
London: Crosby Lockwood Staples, 1975

Berghahn, V. R., *Modern Germany: society,
economy and politics in the twentieth century*.
2nd edn. Cambridge: Cambridge University
Press, 1987

Bertheau, Philipp, Eva Hanebutt-Benz & Hans Rei-
chardt, *Buchdruckschriften im 20. Jahrhundert:
Atlas zur Geschichte der Schrift*. Darmstadt:
Technische Hochschule Darmstadt, 1995

Bierut, Michael, Jessica Helfand, Steven Heller &
Rick Poynor, *Looking Closer 3: classic writings
on graphic design*. New York: Allworth Press,
1999

Bill, Max, 'Über Typografie', *Schweizer Graphische Mitteilungen*, Jg.65, H.5, 1946, pp.193–
200; translated as 'On typography' in
Typography Papers, 4, 2000, pp.62–70

Bojko, Szymon, *New graphic design in revolutionary Russia*. London : Lund Humphries, 1972

Bretag, Wilhelm, 'Das Problem der Lichtsatz-
maschine – hat Uher das Problem gelöst?',
Deutscher Drucker, Jg.39, H.3, December 1932,
pp.81–3

Broos, Kees, & Paul Hefting, *Dutch graphic
design*. London: Phaidon, 1993

Brüning, Ute (ed.), *Das A und O des Bauhauses*.
Berlin: Bauhaus-Archiv; Edition Leipzig, 1995

Bühnemann, Michael & Thomas Friedrich,
'Zur Geschichte der Buchgemeinschaften der
Arbeiterbewegung in der Weimarer Republik'
in *Wem gehört die Welt: Kunst und Gesellschaft in der Weimarer Republik*. Berlin:
Neue Gesellschaft für Bildende Kunst, 1977,
pp.363–97

[Bugra] *Internationale Ausstellung für Buchgewerbe und Graphik Leipzig 1914*. Amtlicher
Katalog

Burke, Christopher, 'The authorship of Futura',
Baseline, no.23, 1997, pp.33–40

–. *Paul Renner: the art of typography*. London:
Hyphen Press, 1998

Burke, Christopher & Patricia Córdoba, 'Technics
and aesthetics: Czech modernism of the 1920s
and 30s', *Baseline*, no.28, 1999, pp.33–40

Caflisch, Max, *Die Schriften von Renner,
Tschichold und Trump*. Munich: Typographische Gesellschaft München, 1991

Carter, Harry, 'Printing for our time', *Design for
To-day*, vol.1, no.2, 1933, pp.60–2

–. 'Sanserif types', *Curwen Miscellany*. London:
Curwen Press, 1931

Cohen, Arthur A., *Herbert Bayer: the complete
work*. Cambridge, Mass.: MIT Press, 1984

Day, Kenneth (ed.), *Book typography 1815–1965:
in Europe and the United States of America*.
London: Ernest Benn, 1966

Dluhosch, Eric & Rostislav Švácha (ed.) *Karel
Teige 1900–1951: l'enfant terrible of the Czech
modernist avant-garde*. Cambridge, Mass.:
MIT Press, 1999

Doede, Werner, 'Jan Tschichold', *Beiheft die neue
Typographie* (accompanying booklet to 1987
facsimile edition of *Die neue Typographie*),
pp.5–32

Ehmcke, F.H., *Schrift: ihre Gestaltung und
Entwicklung in neuerer Zeit*. Hanover: Günther
Wagner, 1925

Ehrlich, Frederic, *The new typography and
modern layouts*. London: Chapman & Hall,
1934

Ellegaard Frederiksen, Erik, 'In correspondence
with Colin Banks' [on Tschichold at Penguin].
Information Design Journal, vol.1, no.3, 1980,
pp.149–52

Evans, Bertram, 'A note on modern typography'
in John C. Tarr, *Printing to-day*. Oxford: Oxford
University Press, 1945

–. *Modern typography on the continent*. London:
Royal Society of Arts; Cantor Lectures, 1938

–. 'Typography in England, 1933: frustration or
function', *Penrose's Annual*, vol.36, 1934, p.59

Fleischmann, Gerd (ed.), *Bauhaus: Drucksachen,
Typografie, Reklame*. Düsseldorf: Marzona,
1984

–. '»Können Sie sich einen Flieger mit Vollbart
vorstellen?«', *Beiheft Die neue Typographie*,
pp.33–46

Friedl, Friedrich, 'Echo und Reaktionen auf das
Sonderheft »elementare Typographie«' in the
reprint (Mainz: Hermann Schmidt, 1986)

–. *Walter Dexel: neue Reklame* (Düsseldorf:
Marzona 1987)

Friedl, Friedrich, Nicolaus Ott & Bernard Stein
(ed.), *Typography: when/who/how*. Cologne:
Könemann, 1998

Giesecke, Albert, 'Ein Verfechter des Konstruktivismus', *Offset: Buch- und Werbekunst*, Jg.2,
H.11, 1925, pp.735–9

–. 'Rückblick auf das Schriftschaffens Deutschlands in den letzten 30 Jahren', *Gebrauchsgraphik*, Jg.5, H.7, 1928, pp.19–25

Gray, Camilla, *The Russian experiment in art*.
London: Thames & Hudson, 1971

Gresty, Hilary & Jeremy Lewison (ed.), *Constructivism in Poland 1923 to 1936*. Cambridge:
Kettle's Yard, n.d

Grieve, Alastair, *Isokon*. London: Isokon Plus,
2004

Hack, Bertold, 'Jan Tschichold: zu Person und
Werk', *Börsenblatt für den Deutschen Buchhandel* (Frankfurter Ausgabe), Nr 46, 8 June
1979, pp.B100–5

Harling, Robert, 'What is this "functional" typography?: the work of Jan Tschichold', *Printing*,
[London] vol.4, no.38, January 1936, p.4

Harrison, Charles & Paul Wood (ed.) *Art in theory
1900–2000*. 2nd edn. Oxford: Blackwell, 2003

Hartlaub, Gustav, 'Kunst als Werbung', *Das Kunst-
blatt*, Jg.22, June 1928, pp.170–6

Heller, *Merz to Emigre and beyond: avant-garde magazine design of the twentieth century*. London & New York: Phaidon, 2003

Heskett, John, *Design in Germany 1870–1918*. London: Trefoil, 1986

Hochuli, Jost, *Book design in Switzerland*. Zurich: Pro Helvetia, 1993

Hollis, Richard, *Graphic design: a concise history*. London: Thames & Hudson, 1994

–. *Swiss graphic design*. London: Laurence King, 2006

Holstein, Jürgen (ed.) *Blickfang: Bucheinbände und Schutzumschläge Berliner Verlage 1919–1933*. Berlin: Holstein, 2005

Idea, no.321 (vol.55, issue 2): 'Works of Jan Tschichold 1902–74'. Tokyo: Seibundo Shinkosha, 2007

Jackman, Jarrell C. & Carla M. Borden (ed.), *The muses flee Hitler: cultural transfer and adaptation*. Washington DC: Smithsonian Institution, 1983

James, Philip, 'Modern commercial typography', *Typography*, no.1, November 1936, p.32

Kapr, Albert (ed.), *Traditionen Leipziger Buchkunst*. Leipzig: Fachbuchverlag, [1989]

Kershaw, Ian, *Hitler 1889–1936: hubris*. London: Penguin Books, 2001

Kindel, Eric, 'Recollecting stencil letters', *Typography Papers*, 5, 2003, pp.65–101

Kinross, *Anthony Froshaug: typography & texts / documents of a life*. London: Hyphen Press, 2000

–. 'Emigré graphic designers in Britain: around the Second World War and afterwards', *Journal of Design History*, vol.3, no.1, 1990, pp.35–57

–. 'Herbert Read's Art and Industry: a history', *Journal of Design History*, vol.1, no.1, 1988, pp.35–50

–. *Modern typography: an essay in critical history*. 2nd edn – London: Hyphen Press, 2004

–. Introduction to Tschichold, *The new typography* (Berkeley: University of California Press, 1995)

–. *Unjustified texts: perspectives on typography*. London: Hyphen Press, 2002

Kostelanetz, Richard (ed.), *Moholy-Nagy*. London: Allen Lane, 1971

Kracauer, Siegfried, *From Caligari to Hitler*. London: Dobson, 1947

Lamb, Lynton, 'Penguin books – style and mass production', *Penrose Annual*, vol.46, 1952, pp.39–42

Lavin, Maud, *Clean new world: culture, politics and graphic design*. Cambridge, Mass./London: MIT Press, 2001

Le Coultre, Martijn F. & Alston W. Purvis, *Jan Tschichold: posters of the avant-garde*. Basel: Birkhäuser, 2007

Lissitzky, El, *Proun und Wolkenbügel: Schriften und Dokumente*. Dresden: VEB Verlag der Kunst, 1977

Lissitzky, El & Hans Arp, *Die Kunstismen / Les ismes de l'art / The isms of art*. Zurich, Munich & Leipzig: Eugen Rentsch, 1925. (Reprint – Baden: Lars Müller, 1990)

Lissitzky-Küppers, Sophie, *El Lissitzky: life, letters, texts*. London: Thames & Hudson, 1968

Lodder, Christina, *Russian constructivism*. London: Yale University Press, 1983

Luidl, Philipp, 'München – Mekka der schwarzen Kunst' in Christoph Stölzl (ed.), *Die Zwanziger Jahre in München*. Munich: Schriften des Stadtmuseums 8, 1979, pp.195–209

–. (ed.), *J.T.: Johannes Tzschichhold / Iwan Tschichold / Jan Tschichold*. Munich: Typographische Gesellschaft München, 1976

Lupton, Ellen & Elaine Lustig Cohen, *Letters from the avant garde: modern graphic design*. New York: Princeton Architectural Press, 1996

Margolin, Victor, *The struggle for Utopia: Rodchenko, Lissitzy, Moholy-Nagy 1917–46*. Chicago & London: Chicago University Press, 1997

McLean, Ruari, *Jan Tschichold: a life in typography*. London: Lund Humphries, 1997

–. *Jan Tschichold: typographer*. London: Lund Humphries, 1975

–. *True to type*. New Castle, Del.: Oak Knoll Press & Werner Shaw, 2000

[Meisterschule] *Fünfundzwanzig Jahre Meisterschule für Deutschlands Buchdrucker München 1927/1952*. Munich, 1952

Melis, Urban van, *Die Buchgemeinschaften in der Weimarer Republik: mit einer Fallstudie über die sozialdemokratische Arbeiterbuchgemeinschaft Der Bücherkreis*. Stuttgart: Hiersemann, 2002

Moholy-Nagy, László, 'Elementare Buchtechnik', *Pressa: amtlicher Katalog*, Cologne, 1928, pp.60–4

–. 'Zeitgemäße Typographie – Ziele, Praxis, Kritik', *Gutenberg Festschrift*, 1925, pp.307–17 (Republished in Fleischmann, *Bauhaus*)

Moholy-Nagy, Sibyl, *Moholy-Nagy: experiment in totality*. New York: Harper & Bros, 1950

Monguzzi, Bruno, 'Piet Zwart: the typographical work 1923/1933', *Rassegna*, no.30, 1987

Moran, *The Double Crown Club: a history of fifty years*. Westerham: Westerham Press, 1974

–. 'Lund Humphries' exhibitions: a retrospect', *British Printer*, June 1963, pp.88–92

Münch, Roger, 'The origins of modern filmsetting', *Journal of the Printing Historical Society*, new series no.3, 2001, pp.21–39

Neumann, Eckhard, *Functional graphic design in the 1920s*. New York: Reinhold, 1967

Nisbet, Peter (ed.), *El Lissitzky, 1890–1941*. Cambridge, Mass.: Harvard University Art Museums, 1987

Nonne-Schmidt, Helene & Heinz Loew, *Joost Schmidt: Lehre und Arbeit am Bauhaus 1919–32*. Düsseldorf: Marzona, 1984

Nündel, Ernst, *Schwitters*. Hamburg: Rowohlt, 1981

Ovink, G.W, 'Jan Tschichold 1902–74: Versuch zu einer Bilanz seines Schaffens', *Quaerendo*, vol.8, no.3, 1978, pp.187–220

–. 'The influence of Jan Tschichold', *Typos*, 2, n.d, pp.37–45 [abridged translation of the previous article]

Perloff, Nancy & Brian Reed (ed.), *Situating El Lissitzky: Vitebsk, Berlin, Moscow*. Los Angeles: Getty, 2003

Poeschel, Carl Ernst, 'Gegen Mechanisierung – für die Persönlichkeit: ein offener Brief', bound insert to *Archiv für Buchgewerbe und Gebrauchsgraphik*, Jg.70, H.4, April 1933

Pool, Albert-Jan, 'FF DIN, history of a contemporary typeface' in Jan Middendorp & Erik Spiekermann (ed.), *Made with FontFont: type for independent minds* (Amsterdam: BIS, 2006) pp.66–73

Pujol, Josep M., 'Jan Tschichold y la tipografía moderna', introduction to Tschichold, *La nueva tipografía* (Valencia: Campgràfic, 2003)

Purvis, Alston W., *H.N. Werkman*. London: Laurence King, 2004

Railing, Patricia (ed.) *Voices of revolution*, companion volume to the facsimile/translation of *For the voice*. London: The British Library & Artists Bookworks, 2000

Rasch, Heinz & Bodo, *Gefesselter Blick: 25 kürze Monografien und Beiträge über neuer Werbegestaltung*. Stuttgart: Zaugg, 1930. (Reprint – Baden: Lars Müller, 1996)

Read, Herbert, 'British Art 1930–40', introduction to *Art in Britain 1930–40 centred around Axis, Circle, Unit One*. London: Marlborough Fine Art, 1965

–. 'The crisis in bookcraft', *Penrose Annual*, vol.43, 1949, pp.13–18

Renner, Paul, *Kulturbolschewismus?* Zurich, Eugen Rentsch, 1932

–. 'Über moderne Typografie', *Schweizer Graphische Mitteilungen*, Jhg.67, H.3, March 1948, pp.119–20; translated as 'On modern typography' in *Typography Papers*, 4, 2000, pp.87–90

Ring 'neue werbegestalter': die Amsterdamer Ausstellung 1931. Wiesbaden: Landesmuseum, 1990

[Rodchenko, Alexander], *Rodtschenko: Aufsätze, autobiographische Notizen, Briefe, Erinnerungen*. Dresden: Verlag der Kunst, 1993

Rothschild, Deborah, Ellen Lupton & Darra Goldstein, *Graphic design in the mechanical age: selections from the Merrill C. Berman Collection*. New Haven & London: Yale University Press, 1998

Schauer, Georg Kurt, 'Die Herkunft von Linearschriften', *Börsenblatt für den Deutschen Buchhandel* (Frankfurter Ausgabe), Nr 22a, 19 March 1959, pp.294–8

–. 'Jan Tschichold: Anmerkungen zu einer tragischen Existenz', *Börsenblatt für den Deutschen Buchhandel* (Frankfurter Ausgabe), Nr 95, 28 November 1978, pp.A421–3

–. 'Meister und Mittler: zum 70. Geburtstag von Jan Tschichold', *Philobiblon*, Jg.16, H.2, 1972, pp.79–91

–. 'Wer war Jan Tschichold', *Börsenblatt für den Deutschen Buchhandel* (Frankfurter Ausgabe), Nr 43, 29 May 1979, pp.A189–90

Schleger, Pat, *Zéro: Hans Schleger – a life of design*. Aldershot: Lund Humphries, 2001

Schlemmer, Tut (ed.), *The letters and diaries of Oskar Schlemmer*. Evanston: Northwestern University Press, 1990

Schmidt-Künsemüller, Friedrich Adolf, *William Morris und die neuere Buchkunst*. Wiesbaden: Otto Harrassowitz, 1955

Schmoller, Hans. *Two titans: Mardersteig & Tschichold, a study in contrasts*. New York: Typophiles, 1990

Schneider, Kirsten, 'Worker's literature meets the New Typography', *Baseline*, no.37, 2002, pp.5–12

Schuitema, Paul, 'New typographical design in 1930', *Neue Grafik / New Graphic Design / Graphisme Actuel*, no.11, December 1961, pp.16–19

Schütte, Wolfgang U., *Die Wölfe: auf den Spuren eines leipziger Verlages der 'goldenen' zwanziger Jahre*. Leipzig: Connewitzer Verlagsbuchhandlung, 1999

[Schwitters, Kurt] *'Typographie kann unter Umständen Kunst sein'. Kurt Schwitters: Typographie und Werbegestaltung*. Wiesbaden: Landesmuseum, 1990

–. *Wir spielen, bis uns der Tod abholt: Briefe aus fünf Jahrzehnten*. Frankfurt a.M.: Ullstein, 1974

Senter, Terence, *Moholy-Nagy in England*. Unpublished PhD thesis: University of Nottingham, 1975

–. 'Moholy-Nagy: the transitional years', in Achim Borchardt-Hume (ed.), *Albers and Moholy-Nagy: from the Bauhaus to the new world*. London: Tate, 2006. pp.85–91

–. 'Moholy-Nagy's English photography', *Burlington Magazine*, vol.73, no.944, November 1981, pp.659–70

Sichowsky, Richard von, & Hermann Tiemann (ed.), *Typographie und Bibliophilie*. Hamburg: Maximilian-Gesellschaft, 1971

Spencer, Herbert, *Pioneers of modern typography*. London: Lund Humphries, 1969

–. *The visible word*. 2nd edn – London: Royal College of Art, 1969

Stiff, Paul, 'Tschichold's stamp: specification and the modernization of typographic work', *Printing Historical Society Bulletin*, no.38, winter 1994, pp.18–24

Stürzebecher, Jörg (ed.), *'Max ist endlich auf dem richtigen Weg'. Max Burchartz 1887–1961: Kunst, Typografie, Fotografie, Architektur und Produktgestaltung, Texte und Kunstlehre*. Frankfurt a.M.: Deutscher Werkbund / Baden: Lars Müller, 1993

Teige, 'Moderní typo' & 'Moderne Typographie', *Typografia*, roč.34, číslo 7–9, 1927, pp.189–207

[Tschichold, Edith], 'Interview mit Edith Tschichold in Berzona am 16.8.1979', *Die Zwanziger Jahre des Deutschen Werkbunds*. Berlin: Deutscher Werkbund und Werkbund-Archiv, 1982

Twyman, Michael, *Graphic Communication through Isotype*. 2nd edn – Reading: Department of Typography & Graphic Communication, 1981

Tupitsyn, Margarita, *El Lissitzky: beyond the abstract cabinet*. New Haven & London: Yale University Press, 1999

Typographische Gesellschaft München, *Hundert Jahre Typographie; Hundert Jahre Typographische Gesellschaft München: eine Chronik*. Munich: TGM, 1990

[Vordemberge-Gildewart, Friedrich], *Vordemberge-Gildewart: Typographie und Werbegestaltung*. Wiesbaden: Landesmuseum, 1990

Wadman, Howard, 'Left wing layout', *Typography*, no.3, summer 1937, pp.25–33

Weidemann, Kurt, 'Designer's profile: Jan Tschichold', *British Printer*, vol.11, no.4, 1963, pp.24–9

–. 'Jan Tschichold: Anmerkungen zu einer tragischen Interpretation', *Börsenblatt für den Deutschen Buchhandel* (Frankfurter Ausgabe), Nr 26, 30 March 1979, pp.A114–5

Wetzig, Emil (ed.), *Handbuch der Schriftarten*. Leipzig: Seemann Verlag, 1925

Whitford, Frank, *Bauhaus*. London: Thames & Hudson, 1984

Wieynck, 'Die Wandlungen des Johannes', *Gebrauchsgraphik*, Jg.5, H.12, 1928, pp.77–9

–. 'Leitsätze zum Problem zeitgemäßer Druckschriftgestaltung', *Gebrauchsgraphik*, Jg.8, H.2, 1931, pp.70–1

–. 'Neue Typographie', *Gebrauchsgraphik*, Jg.5, H.7, 1928, pp.28–9

–. 'Neueste Wege der Typographie', *Archiv für Buchgewerbe und Gebrauchsgraphik*, Band 63, H.6, 1926, pp.373–82

Wilkes, Walter, 'Twentieth-century fine printing in Germany', *Fine Print*, vol.12, no.2, April 1986, pp.87–99

Willberg, Hans Peter, *Schrift im Bauhaus / Die Futura von Paul Renner*. Neu Isenburg: Wolfgang Tiessen, 1969

Willett, John, *The new sobriety 1917–1933: art and politics in the Weimar period*. London: Thames & Hudson, 1978

–. *The Weimar years: a culture cut short*. London, Thames & Hudson, 1984

Wingler, Hans M. (ed.), *Kunstschulreform 1900–1933*. Berlin: Gebr. Mann Verlag, 1977

Wlassikoff, Michel, *The story of graphic design in France*. Corte Madera: Gingko Press, 2005

Website

http://wiedler.ch/felix/bookslist.html

Archive sources

Békés Archive

Békés Megyei Levéltár, 5700 Gyula, Petőfi tér 2, Hungary.
County archive containing correspondence from Tschichold to printer Imre Kner.

DNB Leipzig / DBSM

Deutsche Nationalbibliothek in Leipzig / Deutsches Buch- und Schriftmuseum.
Deutscher Platz 1, D-04103 Leipzig, Germany.
Holds the 'Arbeitsmaterial Jan Tschichold', a collection of his working materials. The museum also holds some of his designs for Insel Verlag, among examples by other designers.

Getty

Getty Research Institute, 1200 Getty Center Drive, Suite 1100, Los Angeles, CA 90049-1688.
The 'Jan & Edith Tschichold papers' are among the special collections. Contains mostly correspondence. The collections also hold papers of Walter Dexel, El Lissitzky, Franz Roh, Ladislav Sutnar, Piet Zwart and other contemporaries in European modernism.

Haushofer Archive

Family archive containing papers of Paul Renner.

MAN

Historisches Archiv und Museum, MAN Aktiengesellschaft, Heinrich-von-Buz-Straße 28, D-86153 Augsburg.
Correspondence and samples relating to Tschichold's typeface designs for Uhertype.

Roche

The Roche Historical Collection and Archive, Bau 21/ 098, Grenzacherstraße 124 CH-4070 Basel.
Comprehensive collection of Tschichold's design work for Hoffmann-La Roche.

St Bride

St Bride Library, Bride Lane, Fleet Street London EC4Y 8EE.
Holds some documents and type specimens relating to Uhertype among the papers of R.B. Fishenden.

Tate

Hyman Kreitman Research Centre, Tate Library and Archive, Tate Britain, Millbank, London SW1P 4RG.
Small amount of correspondence from Tschichold to Ben Nicholson.

Westerdahl Archive

Archivo Westerdahl, Santa Cruz de Tenerife
Papers of Eduardo Westerdahl principally relating to his magazine *Gaceta de arte*. Contains a few letters from Tschichold.

Picture sources

Apart from those listed below, illustrations are taken from private collections. Thanks to Robin Kinross, Paul Barnes, Felix Wiedler, Norbert Löderbusch, Ann Pillar, Michael Twyman, Ole Lund, Hans Reichardt, and Hans Dieter Reichert for lending material or providing images.

18		DNB Leipzig / DBSM
22–5		DNB Leipzig / DBSM
26	top left, bottom right	DNB Leipzig / DBSM
26	top right	*Typographische Monatsblätter*, April 1972
28–31		DNB Leipzig / DBSM
39		DNB Leipzig / DBSM
40		Luidl, *J.T.*
49		DNB Leipzig / DBSM
50	top row	DNB Leipzig / DBSM
51	top left	DNB Leipzig / DBSM
	top right	Merrill C. Berman Collection
53	top left	Luidl, *J.T.*
	top right	Nündel, *Schwitters*
54–6		DNB Leipzig / DBSM
58	middle & bottom	DNB Leipzig / DBSM
59	top	DNB Leipzig / DBSM
	bottom	Luidl, *J.T.*
62		DNB Leipzig / DBSM
63		Basler Plakatsammlung
64	top left	Basler Plakatsammlung
	top right	Merrill C. Berman Collection
	bottom (both)	Basler Plakatsammlung
65		Basler Plakatsammlung
66	top left	DNB Leipzig / DBSM
	top right, bottom left	Basler Plakatsammlung
	bottom right	Merrill C. Berman Collection
67		Merrill C. Berman Collection
69		*Gebrauchsgraphik*, Jg.5, 1928
70	middle left	Digital image © 2007 The Museum of Modern Art / Scala, Florence
	middle right	Merrill C. Berman Collection
	bottom	Merrill C. Berman Collection
71		Basler Plakatsammlung
72	top left	Basler Plakatsammlung
	right column	Tschichold, *Leben und Werk*
74		DNB Leipzig / DBSM
79		DNB Leipzig / DBSM

84		Merrill C. Berman Collection
85	top	Merrill C. Berman Collection
86	left & centre	Stichting H.N. Werkman, Groninger Museum
	right	Klingspor-Museum, Offenbach a.M.
96–9		DNB Leipzig / DBSM
100	top left	Nündel, *Schwitters*
102	centre	Tschichold, *Leben und Werk*
102	right	DNB Leipzig / DBSM
105		Merrill C. Berman Collection
108	top right	DNB Leipzig / DBSM
110	middle row	DNB Leipzig / DBSM
115	bottom	DNB Leipzig / DBSM
116	bottom	DNB Leipzig / DBSM
119–21		Otto and Marie Neurath Isotype Collection, Department of Typography & Graphic Communication, © University of Reading
122	top centre	*Baseline*, no.28, 1999
123	top left	*Baseline*, no.28, 1999
	top right	DNB Leipzig / DBSM
127		DNB Leipzig / DBSM
130–1		DNB Leipzig / DBSM
133		DNB Leipzig / DBSM
140		DNB Leipzig / DBSM
143		Tschichold family / *Idea*, no.321 (vol.55, issue 2)
152		Typographische Gesellschaft München, *Hundert Jahre Typographie*
154–6		DNB Leipzig / DBSM
159	bottom left	DNB Leipzig / DBSM
160–1		DNB Leipzig / DBSM
162	middle	DNB Leipzig / DBSM
163		Klingspor-Museum, Offenbach a.M.
164	top left	Klingspor-Museum, Offenbach a.M.
	top right	DNB Leipzig / DBSM
166		DNB Leipzig / DBSM
167		Tetterode Archive, Amsterdam University Library
168–9		DNB Leipzig / DBSM
171	middle	DNB Leipzig / DBSM
175		DNB Leipzig / DBSM
177–81		DNB Leipzig / DBSM
187	top: left & right	DNB Leipzig / DBSM
192		DNB Leipzig / DBSM
197	left & centre	DNB Leipzig / DBSM
198	top right, bottom right	DNB Leipzig / DBSM
200		DNB Leipzig / DBSM
201	top right	DNB Leipzig / DBSM
202	top left	DNB Leipzig / DBSM
203		DNB Leipzig / DBSM
214	all except top right	DNB Leipzig / DBSM
216–7		DNB Leipzig / DBSM
222–5		DNB Leipzig / DBSM
227	top	DNB Leipzig / DBSM
	bottom group	MAN
228		DNB Leipzig / DBSM
229	top left, right	DNB Leipzig / DBSM
	middle: left & centre	MAN
230–1		DNB Leipzig / DBSM
232–3	centre & top right	DNB Leipzig / DBSM
233	bottom	St Bride
234	top	St Bride
234	bottom	DNB Leipzig / DBSM
235	middle: left & right	MAN
	bottom	DNB Leipzig / DBSM
236–7		DNB Leipzig / DBSM
238		St Bride
239		DNB Leipzig / DBSM
240	top	DNB Leipzig / DBSM
	middle row	MAN
241		MAN
242–4		DNB Leipzig / DBSM
245–6		St Bride
248	bottom: left &right	DNB Leipzig / DBSM
251	middle & bottom rows	DNB Leipzig / DBSM
253	top	DNB Leipzig / DBSM
254	left: top & bottom	DNB Leipzig / DBSM
255		DNB Leipzig / DBSM
262		Merrill C. Berman Collection
265		DNB Leipzig / DBSM
270	top right	DNB Leipzig / DBSM
271	bottom	DNB Leipzig / DBSM
279		DNB Leipzig / DBSM
284	top	Basler Plakatsammlung
287–9		DNB Leipzig / DBSM
299–300		Roche
306		DNB Leipzig / DBSM

Sources and explanations of chapter portraits

Prologue	c.1918	Tschichold family / DNB Leipzig / DBSM
1	1920	Photo: Käthe Havemeister / Luidl, *J.T.*
2	c.1925	Tschichold family / DNB Leipzig / DBSM
3	1928	Photo: Eduard Wasow Tschichold family
4	c.1931	Posed for planned use on the cover of the book that became *Schrift-schreiben für Setzer* / Luidl, *J.T.*
5	Copenhagen 1935	DNB Leipzig / DBSM
Epilogue	1970s	Tschichold family

Principal photography by the author. Photography of items from Merrill C. Berman Collection by Jim Frank. Photography p.306 by Fred Smeijers.

Index

Page references in *italic* are to
captions to the illustrations.

Also by Christopher Burke
Paul Renner: the art of typography

Paul Renner is the first extended study of this designer.
Starting as a 'book artist', Renner (1878–1956) became a
prominent member of the Deutscher Werkbund. In the
1920s he began work on his enduring typeface, Futura.
Moving to Munich, he ran the printing school that included
Jan Tschichold among its teachers. In the crisis of 1933 he
was detained and then dismissed from his post. Living
through the Nazi years in inner emigration, Renner emerged
as a voice of reason in postwar debates. Christopher Burke
presents a wealth of unpublished material, writing with an
eye to present concerns.

*Typography would be a healthier profession if all its major
figures were honoured by a study as meticulous and
thoughtful as Burke's book.*
　　Robert Bringhurst, *Bulletin of the Printing Historical
　　　　Society* [London]
*One reads this biography of Renner as if it were a novel by
his friend Thomas Mann.*
　　Andrés Trapiello, *La Vanguardia* [Barcelona]

paperback, 224 pages, approx. 130 colour and black & white pictures
ISBN 978-0907259–12-1